Marketing Technical Ideas and Products Successfully!

Marketing Technical Ideas and Products Successfully!

Edited by

Lois K. Moore

**Technical Writer and Editor
Applied Physics Laboratory
The Johns Hopkins University**

Daniel L. Plung

**Publications Manager
Westinghouse Idaho Nuclear Co., Inc.**

A volume in the IEEE PRESS Selected Reprint
Series, prepared under the sponsorship of the
IEEE Professional Communication Society.

**IEEE
PRESS**

The Institute of Electrical and Electronics Engineers, Inc., New York

IEEE Order Number: PC01792

Library of Congress Cataloging in Publication Data

Marketing technical ideas and products successfully!

(IEEE Press selected reprint series)
"Prepared under the sponsorship of the IEEE
Professional Communication Society."
Bibliography: p.
Includes indexes.
1. Industrial marketing—Addresses, essays, lectures.
I. Moore, Lois K. II. Plung, Daniel L. III. IEEE
Professional Communication Society.
HF5415.M32374   1984   658.8   84-22414
ISBN 0-87942-185-1

Contents

Preface

THERE is probably no other facet of business more critical to an organization's achievement and success than marketing. Prosperous firms exist by selling ideas, products, and services, but these are only profitable when adequately marketed.

Marketing of technical products requires specialized customer liaison and personalized consultations because of the complexities of the engineering work involved. Consequently, engineers and scientists who originate and participate in technical projects must be available and qualified to respond to customer needs through all phases of product development, including the selling and servicing of the product.

Before a technical project can even begin, the engineer or scientist has to assure management and/or sponsors that the research work is worthwhile. They must be "sold" on the idea, and be convinced that the product is saleable and will be profitable to the organization.

In today's competitive technical environment, the marketing function can no longer be left solely to the marketing group of an organization. It must be a shared responsibility. Engineers and scientists must be willing to assume their roles in the process.

In *Marketing Management: Analysis, Planning and Control,* Dr. Philip Kotler defines marketing as "a social process by which individuals and groups obtain what they need and want through creating and exchanging products and values with others." This agrees exactly in principle with two other definitions offered by the American Marketing Association (*Marketing Definitions,* 1960): "The aggregate of forces or conditions within which buyers and sellers make decisions that result in the transfer of goods and services"; and "The aggregate demand of the potential buyers of a commodity or service."

In other words, marketing is the essence of proper presentation of any idea or product that has been adequately researched, developed, and tested. Ideas and products can be superior, but still fail because their producers do not know how—or have competent advice—to present them properly.

We can no longer assume that by building a better "mousetrap," customers, clients, or sponsors will automatically hear about it, find their way to our doors, and knock them down to get it. Today's busy, sophisticated buyers must be persuaded.

Consequently, this anthology has been published to inform the reader how to effectively accomplish this. Hundreds of American, Canadian, and European magazines and journals were reviewed before final article selections were made. Grouped by subject matter, they will lead you through a logical progression from understanding the problems to resolving them. Topics range from the new marketing responsibilities of the engineer and scientist and analyzing the market posture for technical ideas and products to writing better industrial catalogs and measuring program effectiveness.

Both seasoned marketing "pros" and novices wishing to enhance their careers will find this book useful. It is a synopsis of proven techniques and procedures on planning, developing, and completing successful marketing programs.

For convenience, *Marketing Technical Ideas and Products Successfully!* is organized into five parts: I. Industrial Marketing: An Overview; II. The Marketing Program, containing sections on Premarket Planning, Entering the Market, and Cost Factors; III. Marketing Methods; IV. Producing Marketable Copy, containing sections on Writing to Sell and Design and Layout Techniques; and V. Measuring Program Effectiveness.

The explicit "contents" pages make all references readily identifiable and subjects instantly accessible. A brief description of every paper is given on the divider page between each part or section, and a useful margin index is included to help you quickly locate the desired subject matter.

We hope that this logical organization of the book will simplify your use of it as a quick reference, will direct you efficiently to the topic, subject, or type of guidance you need immediately, and—most of all—that the information will assist you in marketing your technical ideas and products *successfully*.

Lois K. Moore
Daniel L. Plung
Editors

Part I
Industrial Marketing: An Overview

"New Marketing Roles and Needs of the Engineer and Scientist," by C.P. Stanford, explains why it is necessary for the technical person to be involved in the marketing function throughout all phases of product development.

"Growth of Industrial Advertising—from 1916 to the Present," by C. Swan, is a history of the industry up to 1976.

"Psycho-Marketing," by M. Paskowski, describes studies made in behavioral research concerning what part emotions play in industrial buying decisions.

"Harnessing Engineers and Scientists to the Sales Effort," by R.P. Andelson, presents a philosophy and technique for motivating and preparing the engineer and scientist to act effectively in a marketing capacity.

"Analyzing the Market Posture for a Technical Product or Idea," by J.A. Ledingham, focuses on planning an effective marketing strategy.

"The Marketing Concept Can Aid, Not Erode, Business Efficiency," by A. Parasuraman, cites examples of some firms which have successfully applied a proven marketing concept.

"Marketing in the 1980s—Back to Basics," by K.K. Cox, raises some important questions marketing professionals should address in planning for the 1980's and assesses their impact in the marketplace.

1

New Marketing Roles and Needs of the Engineer and Scientist

Clare P. Stanford*

The salesman gave way to the sales engineer who must now give way, in the sale of advanced technology products, to the marketing man who promotes and coordinates direct contact between the customer and the scientist and engineer. This direct contact is essential to obtaining the contract, to interpreting the customer's requirements, and to profitable performance within the contract.

INTRODUCTION

The system relationships and technical complexity involved in designing and producing many of the high-technology products of today are forcing a reappraisal of the role and needs of the engineer and scientist—particularly in his relationship to marketing and customer relations. To marketing personnel, the scientist or engineer is traditionally viewed as introverted, eggheaded and non-production-oriented. Similarly, the scientist "knows" that the salesman, or marketing specialist, is gregarious, irresponsible, and will promise anything to get a customer's signature on a contract.

As with most folklore there is just enough truth to these statements to indicate the existence of a problem. The "typical" engineer or scientist does feel more at home in the analysis and solution of sometimes abstract, but definable problems, than in the less easily measured field of customer relations.

THE TECHNICAL-MARKETING CONFLICT

It is assumed the "typical" slaesman, or marketing man, finds more satisfaction in meeting with people and persuading them to accept his cause than in attacking an abstract design or an analytical problem.

These differences, which are the result of training and of personalities, are emphasized in most corporations by organization and by a traditional "king-of-the-hill" attitude, in which a man in one department dare not present a useful idea for application to a second department, and formal memoranda with numerous carbon copies are the rule. This situation is always serious, but it can perhaps be lived with when one is selling a "standard" customer product. Living with these responsibility definitions and the attendant stilted communications will result in a lack of customer awareness and responsiveness on the part of the new product development personnel, and in misdirected research activities. These faults in a new product development group cause decreased sales and increased costs. Industry is full of organizations which survive in spite of this

---

*Vice President, Research and Engineering of Calumet & Hecla, Inc.

Reprinted with permission from *Proc. World Congress,* 1966, pp. S 37–S 42, J.S. Wright and J.L. Goldstucker, Eds. Published by the American Marketing Association.

compartmentalization and isolation of the technology and of the marketing efforts, and the resultant inefficiencies. When a corporation attempts to produce and sell at a profit a product which can be characterized as involving advanced technology, this compartmentalism, which is a detriment to standard products, becomes an absolute killer.

From the customer's viewpoint

A look at the situation from the viewpoint of the customer who needs a high-technology product may be of value. The customer has the need for, and is responsible for the performance of a complex product, one that brushes the forefront of several technologies. The performance to be demanded of the product with respect to environment and interrelationship with other associated products can be most constricting. In seeking outside assistance in the design and construction of the product, the customer can, and does, write out complete product specifications in his proposal request, attempting to spell out the system relationships. There is reason for concern, however, as to whether all information has been presented in a manner which is clear to the companies who may respond. In fact, the customer may have concern as to whether the bidder has read the proposal request carefully in order to understand fully the various implications of the specifications. If personnel of the responding companies have read it carefully, the customer can still be apprehensive regarding their ability to translate the specifications into engineered details, recognizing the various interrelated systems demands and the complexity of the technology involved. Finally, if the companies responding to the proposal request have the technical capability required, the customer desires assurance that this manpower is available and will be assigned to this program.

The customer is certain that many companies will want the contract and may be glibly prepared to affirm their competence and preparedness. The customer, however, cannot afford to make an incorrect decision. His profits depend upon having a performing product delivered on time. There will be no time for switching to another supplier if lack of performance is detected. If the customer has some farm background, he may recall that if you ask a farmer whether his eggs are fresh, he is going to say "yes", even if he had recently removed most of them, nearly ready to hatch, from under brooding hens. So the customer wants, in fact he must have, direct assurance that the company obtaining the contract is capable of performing with the personnel available and is not claiming a competence which does not exist.

Proper action by the selling firm.

Successful response to a proposal for a high-technology product becomes a problem of understanding the customer's needs and personality, and then of selling to the customer the corporation's ability and determination to respond promptly, at a price and, most importantly, with a product which will meet the customer's specialized needs.

The time is long past when most companies would send a salesman without technical training to attempt to obtain the contract for a complex product by high pressure or entertainment techniques. In recognition of the fact that the sales representative will be selling to procurement men with technical training, and frequently to an engineer, the salesman of old is frequently replaced by a salesman with technical training. This new breed of salesmen can thus understand, at least in a general way, the customer's problem and the general approach which should be followed in responding. If the product is not too complex in design or application, he may represent all the technical talent required to meet the customer's needs. This sales engineer cannot, however, by up-to-date on the latest technical matters and cannot exhibit the company's best technical talent, which is available for application to the program. In complex, advanced technology projects it is frequently the presence of this man—the best technical talent in a company—that is required to secure the contract. The contract will frequently go to the organization with the one specialist who has impressed the customer best with his grasp of the customer's problem and his approach to solving the problem. This tendency, to give a contract to the organization exhibiting the greatest technical strength, is emphasized the more the product depends upon the scientist for its success and the more complicated and demanding the system interrelationships.

Problems in exposing technical talent to the potential customer

If one accepts the proposition that the exposure of top technical talent to the potential customer is a must, the problem becomes one of determining the proper procedure to insure optimum exposure, one that does not compromise the engineer's and scientist's primary interest and responsibility. The preceding statement implies that the engineer and scientist is a necessary sales ingredient. He is. However, this is a long way from saying that he must become a salesman. The technical man does not want sales as a primary function and he is not so trained.

The need for direct customer contact with technical personnel is one of the forces that is shaping the responsibilities of the marketing function. The optimum presentation of a corporation's strength and the optimum exposure of engineers and scientists to a potential customer are difficult assignments and should be considered major responsibilities of the marketing man. The technical man may be flat in his presentation. He may talk a minor technical point to death. He may be ill at ease and tongue-tied. His presentation may be so terse as to be incapable of being followed. He may resent being asked to make "sales" presentations. The point is, he is not practised or trained to plan a total presentation, or to sense and respond to the more subtle customer reactions which develop during a presentation. It should be the function of the marketing man to understand the total approach required to secure and retain a customer. He is the conductor, and like an orchestra conductor he may not be the performer, but he is totally responsible for the performance. The presentation shortcomings of the scientist in the hands of a good marketing man can become an asset. Aren't they evidence of the dedication and competence of the scientist? We are all aware of the value, at times, of a foreign—for example German—accent in a technical presentation. The words seem to take on a deeper technical significance. This is one example of the effectiveness of presentation technique in creating a desired response.

The problem, in general, is that the marketing man must resist the temptation to be a soloist and must concentrate on the effective presentation of the available technical strength.

THE MARKETING FUNCTION

The marketing function is responsible for much more than the effective presentation. It involves a great deal of pre-conditioning and post presentation control. The customer is to be conditioned to expect and to believe he received a significant presentation. The defects in the presentation of the engineer or scientist are to be bypassed, shored up, camouflaged, reinforced, irradicated, or otherwise circumvented.

Most of the preceding discussion was presented from the viewpoint of making a favorable technical impression on the customer in order to obtain the contract. Once one has received a contract for an advanced technology product, one has the problem of translating the contract into a product which will satisfy the customer. Here again the interdependence of the marketing personnel and the engineer and scientist is of major importance. Direct contact between the leading engineer and scientist and the customer is invaluable. The product specifications, a portion of the newly won contract, may contain over a hundred pages but be incapable of transmitting the real performance goal of the product. False starts, misdirected engineering, and improper interpretation of expected environmental conditions can result in costly, unnecessary engineering and are major contributors when a contract for a high-technology product goes sour and losses begin to pile up. Lack of an intimate understanding of the product's requirements in relation to other products and to the environment can result in the product either not fulfilling application requirements, or in being grossly overdesigned. It is not too unusual for some of the specifications to be unknown or unrecognized at the start of the contract and to be established as the design progresses.

The continuance of contacts between the customer and the technical men, which were initiated in the selling phase, are the best assurance that the detailed technical interpretations of the contract will be acceptable to the customer. This detailed interpretation of the contract is an area in which much time and money can be lost. Again, as in all customer contacts the marketing man is the coordinator, but he is most effective when he encourages proper direct contact between the parties involved.

The most successful marketing man that I know of in this area began as an engineer. He has become a master in whetting the appetite of the potential customer for the words and approach of the scientist and engineer. In his capable hands the lack of presentation polish by the scientist became another indication of the technical dedication and strength of the scientist. The meetings are set up, designed, and controlled by this marketing specialist, who acts as coordinator of the customer contacts required to secure the contract and to perform within the contract. Visits of the customer to the scientist's laboratory are encouraged. The goal of direct contact between the customer and the engineer and scientist is admirably met.

CONCLUSION

In summary, the advanced technology product has forced a second change in marketing techniques which places new, and sometimes unwanted, responsibility on the engineer and scientist. When we are selling an advanced technology product, the salesman and sales engineer must be replaced by, or assume the role of, a marketing man who has overall responsibility for customer relations and takes on the role of the orchestra conductor, and not the role of the soloist, in customer contact.

The all-too-frequent marketing attitude, that customer contact is the sole prerogative of the sales or marketing man, must be abandoned.

GROWTH OF INDUSTRIAL ADVERTISING — FROM 1916 TO THE PRESENT

By Christopher Swan
Contributing editor

The history of industry in the U.S.A. is a story of inventions. In the technological revolution that began about 1916, inventions became the energy of industry. Through them markets were captured and won, and industrial reputations were made. Technological progress became, to borrow a long-advertised phrase, industry's most important product.

Like any important product, technological progress was advertised. Corporations rushed to put into print the accomplishments of their expensive r&d programs. And, over the years, this advertising itself became a sort of history of the technological revolution, a collection of artifacts that graphically tell how this country grew from a nation of workshops to a land of industrial giants.

The wooden barrel, for instance, is not a very progressive and forward looking product in itself. But in a 1916 advertising campaign it symbolized the beginning of the end of backwardization and resistance to tech-

nology. The steel barrel had become commercially practical as a means of shipping oil, and the advertising pages of *National Petroleum News* were all agog with the virtues of the all-steel barrel.

In desperation, a group of wooden barrel manufacturers launched an advertising campaign under the banner, "The Why of the Wooden Barrel." The results are a good example of the best advertising strategy somehow not fulfilling the marketing objectives. The steel barrel triumphed.

The times were changing. Old markets were disappearing. New markets were emerging. This was, after all, the decade of the multiple cylinder car, the x-ray tube, stainless steel and assembly line techniques. Anything was likely to happen. The country was converting to electricity. And central stations—electric utilities—were looking everywhere for new markets for their product. One company that thought it had an answer was Anderson Electric Car Co., Detroit.

"Electric car recharging pays a

profit," the company proclaimed. "It is mostly done in garages, so it is a wholesale business. It is almost entirely off-peak business. Drive this car from the back or front."

Somehow the electric car bonanza never materialized for the central stations. The product disappeared, and the market evaporated.

One market that did not evaporate was the night-time store window business. Store lighting, and promotional night-time lighting in general, were to become a heavy source of revenue for electric utilities. One company that foresaw this was National Mazda, a light bulb manufacturer. It urged the central stations to "Pluck the Profits in Store-Lamping and Store-Lighting." This was a merchandising campaign, designed to sell more products by opening up new uses for them. And it worked.

Electricity was the endless frontier in those days. It was the fuel that America was growing up on. Thomas Edison was a national hero. And companies that pioneered in electricity earned themselves an important fran-

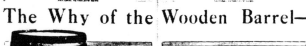

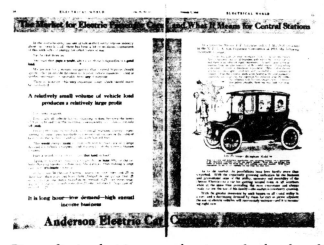

Despite the efforts of a group of wooden barrel manufacturers who placed this ad in National Petroleum News *in 1916, the steel barrel triumphed.*

Big profits in electric car recharging and other benefits were promised by Anderson Electric Car Co., Detroit, in this Electrical World *ad, 1916.*

Reprinted with permission from *Industrial Marketing* (now *Business Marketing*), vol. 61, pp. 74, 75, 78, 79, 80, and 82, Mar. 1976.
Copyright © 1976 by Crain Communications, Inc.

Early merchandising advertising from National Mazda, in Electrical World, 1916.

History-in-the-making ad, one of oldest and best, in Electrical World, 1916.

Early IBM ad in Business Week, 1929, features machines, rinky dinky image.

TeleType promised increased productivity in this ad in Business Week, 1929.

Condit Electrical touts newly developed circuit breaker, via Electrical World, 1929.

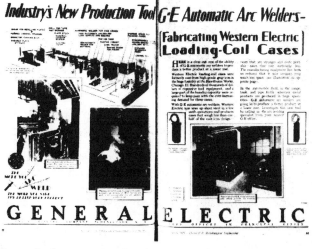

General Electric capitalizes on the drama of a technological first in this ad for its automatic arc welders, in Chemical & Metallurgical Engineering, 1929.

GE uses its reputation in technology to lure the plastics market, via Plastics, 1929.

chise on the public imagination and the pocketbooks of their industrial prospects.

In a timeless *coup-de-grace*, General Electric ran an ad that not only strengthened its electrical pioneering image, but also laid claim to an event of national moment: the opening of the Panama Canal. (This was, in its own way, equivalent to North American Rockwell laying its claim to the moon shot about 50 years later.) The ad is a classic example of technological-history-in-the-making advertising.

Then came the 1920's and Prohibition, Calvin Coolidge and Herbert Hoover. Charles A. Lindbergh flew solo non-stop from New York to Paris. The Holland Tunnel was opened. The stock market crashed. Color tv was

demonstrated. And the photo-electric cell was invented. Wonderful and cataclysmic things were happening in the country, and marvelous machines were helping to make them happen.

IBM was there, with a collection of business machines that looked like old grandfather clocks and a rather rinky-dinky image for a company that was to become the awesome, futuristic giant that we know today. Its pitch to business: "Closer supervision and increased profits." Copy explained, "A recent analysis made by 18 leading engineers disclosed the fact that 20% of the resources and energies wasted by American business as a whole is occasioned by management itself."

TeleType Corp. was there too, with a brand new invention that sent type-

written messages by telephone. The company promoted this year-old invention in the third issue of *Business Week*. With the improbable hook, "No gossiping on the company's time," it ran an application case-history ad showing how the communications capabilities of the TeleType reduced employe idleness among Studebaker assemblers.

Other companies were there as well —Condit Electrical Mfg. Co. somewhat lamely promoted the circuit breaker, which had just been developed, with the modest headline, "A new breaker for underground service."

And General Electric Co. ran two more groundbreaking ads, one promoting a new technological develop-

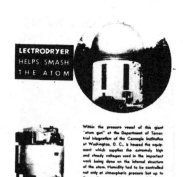

"Lectrodryer helps smash the atom": Chemical & Metallurgical Engineering, 1939.

Television is born: International Nickel is one of the midwives; Electronics, 1939.

IBM ad offers information as a product in Business Week ad, 1935.

Monarch Machine Tool resisted U.S. entry into WWII; American Machinist, 1939.

ment and one captivating an emerging industry.

It was a time of unprecedented development and prosperity. And this was reflected in the ads and in the vehicles that carried them. The first magazines for their industries, *Plastics, Packaging, Control Systems, Product & Design Engineering*—all appeared in the mid to late '20s.

The Great Depression somehow never surfaced in industrial advertising. If you restricted your historical research on this era to the advertising pages of the business press, you would conclude that there never had

been a Depression. What does emerge in the industrial advertising of the '30s is the birth of a whole new technological age. There was the age of atomic power. The age of information. The age of television. All were briefly foretold in the '30s, and then snuffed out just as quickly by the gathering winds of war.

"Lectrodryer helps smash the atom" is the simple unequivocal proclamation of a little Pittsburgh company that does not appear to have become as famous as the event it is trumpeted. But its 1939 ad is a stunning example of technological history captured in a piece of advertising artifact.

Another company heralded the coming of the age of tv: "RCA swings into production on television tubes . . . using nickel and nickel-base alloys," proclaimed International Nickel Co. in a 1939 issue of *Electronics*. Television itself had been around since the '20s but in the late '30s it was just becoming commercially practical.

And, finally, the beginnings of information as a product were trumpeted by IBM in a 1935 issue of *Business Week*. "More information in greater detail," the company promised in an ad promoting mechanical tabulation as a method of gathering vital business information.

But all of this was a bit premature,

"Battle cry!"—by Bendix Aviation Corp., via Business Week, 1941.

U.S. technology and equipment are vital during both times of war and peace, according to Elliott Co. ad in Electrical World, 1943.

because war was brewing—and, despite the best efforts to keep us out of it, we were going in. "When cannon grow cold" was an example of the kind of hope for peace that many companies publicly held out in their advertising. This ad was prophetic of the age of prosperity that was to follow, but not until after a long, grueling and costly war.

The story of World War II filled the ad pages of industrial magazines. The nation was at war, and industry had gone with it. "They're all Bendix equipped," was the battle cry of the Bendix Aviation Corp. And one could see in the omnibus illustration all the horrible machines of destruction that "When cannon grow cold" decried, and then some.

The inexorable Allied march to victory was borne along by one irresistible factor, according to the Elliott Co.: the "combined might of American manufacturers. The trademarks of industrial America" were on the move. And the "Axis powers do not know production as we know it," the ad said. American factories were winning the war.

These factories had to be refitted for peacetime, when the time came. But long before V-E Day, Black & Decker admonished American industry to "Standardize now on Black & Decker tools for easier postwar retooling." The end was in sight. And, with it, a new technological age was emerging.

All the promises of the '30s soon were to materialize, and, with them,

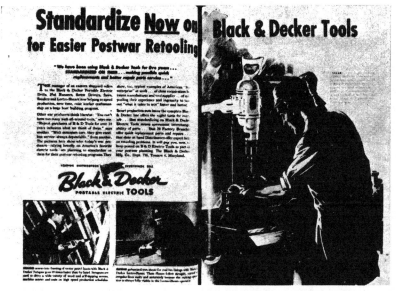

Standardize on Black & Decker Tools, for easier postwar retooling, urges this spread in American Machinist, *1943.*

Texas Instruments heralds age of miniaturization; Electronics, *1958.*

Buy your own atomic power plant: Alco Products in Power, *1956.*

Space Technology Laboratories sets its sights on the New Frontier, in this ad headed, "Space flight and nuclear propulsion," in Aviation Week, *1958.*

Westinghouse ad asks, "Are we ready for automation?" in Power, *1956.*

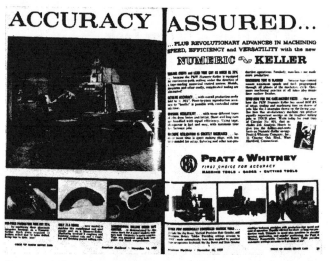

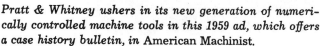

Pratt & Whitney ushers in its new generation of numerically controlled machine tools in this 1959 ad, which offers a case history bulletin, in American Machinist.

IBM recruits for the new field of computer manufacturing in American Machinist, 1959.

TRW ad ties in with the technological event of all time, in Business Week, 1969.

a new age—the age of power: power in miniaturization, power from atomic fission, power to conquer space. All were products of the '50s, even if the fulfillment of much of their potential would still be in progress two decades later.

With the age of power, came also the age of astounding mechanization that made Henry Ford's mass production techniques seem antiquated. And an altogether new kind of product that was to change the way business and society itself was to operate—the computer.

Texas Instruments gave a big bang to power in transistors in its advertising. But perhaps one of the best examples of history-in-the-making ads

on power was Alco Products' ad for atomic power plants for industry. Space Technology Laboratories in its advertising gave a thrilling view of the newest frontier—space, and the power needed to conquer it—nuclear propulsion.

Then in the November, 1956, issue of *Power,* Westinghouse asked the big question: "What would you say if your boss asked . . . 'Are we ready for automation?'" Automation itself was a new word, coined by *Automation* magazine only two years earlier to describe the new mechanization that had come of machine computerization. In another big, bold spread, Pratt & Whitney showed one of the developments characteristic of this

new mechanization—n u m e r i c a lly controlled machine tools. And IBM itself ran advertising in *American Machinist* to attract skilled production workers to the new business of computer manufacturing. It was, to coin a phrase, a whole new ball game.

Then, men were on the moon. And TRW was on the ground to guide them safely home. Like a hundred other companies, TRW was grabbing a piece of the moon shot, probably the biggest technological event ever.

At the same time that TRW was promoting its futuristic accomplishments, General Electric Co. was combining a little of its past history with some of the present technology to try

Ad that tried to use old-time refrigerators to sell new-fangled computers is an example of General Electric know-how that never paid off, in Business Week, 1969.

Sony gives executives a new toy —personal electronic calculators; Business Week, 1969.

The newest—and most expensive—industrial product: social responsibility, as exemplified by this Combustion Engineering ad that appeared in Business Week, *1969.*

Big problems arrive in the '70s, as noted in this Pullman Inc. ad; Business Week, *1975.*

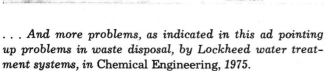

. . . And more problems, as indicated in this ad pointing up problems in waste disposal, by Lockheed water treatment systems, in Chemical Engineering, *1975.*

Sarco ad zeroes in on still another problem: excessive fuel consumption, in Power, *1975.*

Grand Rapids Grinders offers some answers from the past in American Machinist, *1975.*

to capture a slice of the computer pie. GE used old refrigerators in an effort to break into the crowded computer market place, but like many other would-be computer gains, the company did not measure up to IBM.

Not everything was big in the '60s. This was still, after all, the age of miniaturization. And new tiny wonders were everywhere. Wonders like the Sony Answer Box, forerunner of a long line of ever tinier machines that gave men answers to mathematical questions.

And, finally, the newest "product" of all surfaced in the '60s, one that was to cut across industry and become one of the most discussed, heavily advertised ever: social responsibility. The '60s began the age of anti-industrial-

ism, and the student riots that attended it. Companies including Combustion Engineering were quick in response to proclaim their fondness for pastoral scenes and the preservation of wild life.

Hard on the heels of early anti-industrialism came an almost universal realization of some of the problems that gave it force—traffic congestion, water pollution and energy waste all became paramount in the '70s.

Everybody was—is—looking for solutions. And one of the places that people look is in the past. Back in the good old days, people thought, there were simpler, cleaner ways of doing things. We had not yet inherited all of the marvelous children of industrial expansion, but then we had not

inherited some of its unwanted stepchildren either. Besides, didn't things get done better when they were done more slowly?

In an eloquent advertising statement, Grand Rapids Grinders summed up the nation's hankering for the quality of the past. And, even if the company said it still does things that way, it said they were done very well then, too. ■

The editors express their appreciation to McGraw-Hill Publications Co., New York, whose archives provided an excellent source for illustrations of historic industrial advertising. ■

PSYCHO-MARKETING

Industrial Advertisers
Lag Behind State-of-the-Art

by Marianne Paskowski

It's sometimes said in consumer marketing circles that people consume the advertising as much as the products. Show the TV viewer an emotionally powerful commercial linking a deodorant to sex appeal. When he buys it and uses the brand, he'll actually feel sexier.

Serious marketers haven't suggested that the same process benefitting a $1.79 deodorant applies with a $79,000 machine tool. But emotion does coexist with logic even in the industrial buying decision, experts recognize. "Buyers are not always as rational as we'd like to believe," concludes Mel Prince, Marsteller Inc.'s New York-based research director, who has probed many an industrial buyer's attitudes through his agency's "focus group" interviews on behalf of Marsteller clients.

Still, industrial advertisers have yet to seize upon the insights of behavioral research which are common to consumer advertising planning. Researchers blame the industrial ad campaign's limited budget, the different role advertising plays in the industrial sale compared with the consumer goods sale, and a general lack of behavioral sophistication among industrial marketers.

Nonetheless, understanding the emotional needs of buyers can help industrial advertisers tailor messages to specific audiences. For example, business publisher Penton/IPC reports strong continuing interest in a study it sponsored, where psychologist Bruce Morrison found four main personality traits distinguishing dif-

ferent types of industrial buyers. Mr. Morrison also demonstrated ways in which advertising could be tailored to each group. (See story, this book, p. 14.)

Yet the Morrison study was completed in 1974. Its standing as one of the best among a thimbleful of industrial ad psychology studies illustrates the slow pace at which business-to-business advertisers have copied the more potent theories and research techniques used in the consumer arena. Motivation, attitude and personality theory have established themselves as the stuff of serious marketing inquiry on Madison Ave. Aside from growing adoption of the directed interview "focus group" technique, the same hasn't happened on industrial row.

WHY THEY DON'T

Industrial advertisers shy away from psychological research primarily because it's costly. "An industrial advertiser isn't going to spend $6,000 to pretest an ad, which might only cost $10,000-$20,000 to run," remarks Walt Wesley, president of Walt Wesley Co., a Sierra Madre, Cal.-based advertising research firm.

Most industrial advertising research dollars are spent finding out exactly who has the buying power. "Research is very expensive, and although there's a body of psychological research on consumer advertising," explains Alden Clayton, managing director, Marketing Sciences Institute, Cambridge, Mass., "it's often not transferrable to industrial, where it's more difficult to identify the actual buyer."

Furthermore, while it may be possible to transfer findings from beer consumption research to other consumer products, "it probably wouldn't work in applying research results from steel, for example, to computers because of the differences in the two audiences," Mr. Clayton speculates.

There isn't much psychological research generated for industrial advertisers because there is no demand for it. "We don't get any demand for that type of research from industrial advertisers," relates agency Griswold Eshelman's research director Mary Lou Schooley. "In fact," she adds, "we don't do any research of this type any more, not even for consumer, because it's too costly." Psychological research is one of those dormant hot topics of the future, she says.

Although academic advertising and marketing journals routinely report limited experiments on psychology/advertising research, journal articles do not mirror the real world, charge firing-line practitioners.

"A lot of this research comes straight out of academia," observes Ms. Schooley, "applications are hard to come by and the samples are just too small" for practical use.

DICHTER, ET AL

Consumer and packaged good companies, in contrast to industrial advertisers, have adopted psychological research for advertising effectiveness since Ernest Dichter aroused interest with his motivational theories in the '50s. Subsequently, consumer researchers have wrestled to apply theory to phenomena.

Motivational theory addresses the psychological needs underlying behavior. Those needs and wants can be used to explain and develop appropriate advertising and sales strategies. Mr. Dichter, founder of the Institute of Motivation Research, and credited with fathering motivational research, did his first motivational research study for Procter & Gamble's Ivory Soap. (A recent example of the Dichterian approach appears on p. 48 of the July 1981 issue of *Industrial Marketing*.)

Instead of asking people why they used a particular brand of soap, which was the common research tactic, Mr. Dichter described the problem in terms of bathing habits.

He reasoned that the Saturday night bath still had a ritualistic meaning, which is "getting rid of all your bad feelings, your sins, your im-

morality, and cleansing yourself, baptism, etc." Mr. Dichter's Ivory soap slogan, "Be smart, get a fresh start with Ivory soap," translated that analysis into a successful advertising campaign.

Motivational research waned in the early '60s, as advertising researchers turned to attitudinal studies, focus groups and "psychographic" lifestyle studies. At that time classic attitudinal-change theories became popular, among them Leon Festinger's theory of cognitive dissonance.

Cognitive dissonance theory explains how advertising could change or reinforce existing attitudes. It offers an explanation of how people seek out advertising messages that allow them to reduce dissonance —or conflict—between what they actually do and what they think.

That theory proposes that people try to reduce conflict between their attitudes, behavior and the information they receive. In terms of advertising messages, a consumer can accept wholly or partially the communication depending upon the strength of his attitude and the credibility of the communication. To reduce dissonance he might alter his attitudes or actions; ignore the communication; discredit the source; or seek reinforcing information that supports his existing attitude.

For example, if a consumer just purchased a Chevrolet he might ignore Ford ads because those ads could create conflict over the Chevrolet purchase. The Chevrolet ads might gain the consumer's attention because they reinforce his past buying decision and raise no conflict.

Similarly, cognitive dissonance theory explains what happens in the industrial marketplace because an important function of business-to-business advertising is to keep customers sold. Many industrial products involve repeat purchases. Industrial advertising reinforces the buyer's decision and helps reduce dissonance.

FOCUS GROUPS

For advertising to reinforce or change attitudes, advertisers must know what the prospects think. Hence the most widespread attitudinal research technique with industrial advertisers is the focus group, a directed interview technique which reveals buyers' subsurface attitudes.

A focus group is a small group discussion led by a trained moderator who directs conversation to reveal attitudes.

Focus groups can be very useful for

"gathering indepth, subsurface thinking and motivation behind buyer behavior," explains Marsteller's research director Mr. Prince. He says that the majority of Marsteller's industrial clients conduct focus groups.

Mr. Prince cites the experience of a chemical company's focus group as a good example of how the technique helps to explain the buying process.

Marsteller questioned a group of owners of small companies, management from large companies and distributors in the processed food industry about its perceptions of FMC's industrial chemicals division's food phosphates. Buyers of food phos-

---

'Industrial advertising reinforces the buyer's decision and helps reduce dissonance.'

---

phates, for example, were more interested, or "romanced" by the image or positioning of a product than they were with price considerations. Important to those buyers was that FMC's chemicals, which would ultimately be used in food products, were "pure and specialized," compared with bulk commodity chemicals.

Once the advertiser knows what the buyer sees as important, in that case high quality, Mr. Prince explains, the advertiser can highlight those product traits in the advertising or sales presentation.

Purchasing agents, for example "want to make maximum impact while minimizing hassle, struggle and risk," Mr. Prince concludes.

PSYCHOGRAPHICS

Psychographic data is used to segment an audience into useful divisions for emotional appeals.

Researchers have questioned if psychographic data, or knowledge of personality and "style" traits such as authoritarianism, passivity, aggression, etc., could be more effective in predicting purchasing behavior than by simply using demographic data, such as age, sex and income. But the predictive value of psychographics differs depending on the degree of emotion which enters into the buying decision.

Nonetheless, researchers continue to be surprised translating theory to the real world. For example, copywriters have long assumed that

FOCUS / *Marketing Psychology*

people have strong emotional preferences among coffee and beer brands.

Researchers from the University of Pennsylvania, Stanford University and Cornell University found that personality characteristics added little when combined with demographic data in predicting a household's purchase of coffee, tea and beer. Sex or age, rather than specific personality traits, were the key factors correlated to brand choice. The researchers acknowledge, however, that their findings could not be conclusive on the beer or coffee brand decision.

Indeed one study does not conclusively answer all the questions. Operational problems with personality research—how to translate findings into effective copy and media strategies—confound the usefulness of behavorial research. Also, critics question the validity of the personality tests used in behavioral studies.

"The absence of empirically validated bases for personality theory, the ambiguity and arbitrariness of theoretical language and the lack of real-world references have all made personality theory an ineffective tool in marketing and advertising practice," commented one critic on problems with personality research.

Another study illustrates the complexities of personality research.

That study, in 1977, explored the relationship between personality, physique and advertising. Cornell University researchers Irene Rosenfeld and C. Samuel Craig wondered if an ad message, tailored to a subject's body type and temperament, could be more effective.

While the researchers found a significant relationship between temperament and type of advertising preferred, there was little correlation between physique and type of advertising preferred, even though physique and temperament correlated strongly. Even if physique could be correlated with advertising preference, it would be difficult to segment a market by body type for many kinds of products. While *Weight Watchers* magazine may offer a market segment of fat body types, rarely are market segmentation opportunities so obvious, especially among trade publications.

PHYSIOLOGICAL MEASURES

Advertising researchers find it's often difficult to nail down consumers' true attitudes about products. What consumers say about products

in testing situations often doesn't reveal their true attitudes. Researchers frequently observe that people give a classic "yea-say" bias, attempting to either please or impress the researcher.

That difficulty in getting beyond the words, or lip service, prompted researchers to measure autonomic responses to gauge the emotion or conviction behind the words. Advertising researchers have used a variety of physiological techniques to measure consumers' attitudes. Voice pitch analysis, brain wave analysis and galvanic skin response are three of the more popular techniques in use today.

But they are controversial techniques most strongly defended by researchers selling their physiological measurement studies. (See story, page 50.)

Savvy marketers say that as buyers become more sophisticated, it will become more critical than ever to address individual needs. "Buyers are more professional and they expect you to be sensitive to their individual needs," comments Jack Raymond, FMC Corp.'s ad manager in the industrial chemicals division. His experience with focus groups confirms, he says, "that the backslapping days of selling to industry are gone." ∎

Know the Buyer Better

"The industrial buyer is much more human in his business buying decisions than we may have realized," concludes a 1974 study commissioned by Penton Publishing (now Penton/IPC). That study has been one of the few efforts by industrial marketers to apply psychological research to industrial advertising and sales.

Psychologist Bruce J. Morrison interviewing 200 industrial buyers for the Penton study found that fear of looking bad or losing face strongly influences industrial buying. Buyers fear displeasing stockholders, board of directors, superiors and associates.

The study has never been updated, says Penton/IPC's marketing director Gordon B. Guest, "because there's just no need to update it." Penton claims continuing interest from its customers since the study was published seven years ago. Mr. Morrison is now research director at the New York-based agency, Nadler & Larimer.

Mr. Morrison studied four groups of industrial buyers: managers, purchasing agents, design engineers and production engineers and found that each group had distinct personality traits.

More importantly, the study demonstrates that different buying influences did not react in the same way to selling and advertising appeals. For example, design and production engineers, who exhibit low anxiety levels and a sense of personal control over their environments, prefer an advertising approach that stresses end-use consequences, solutions to problems, and specific engineering information.

Managers and purchasing agents exhibit a different set of personality traits. They rank high on the authoritarian scale; have higher levels of anxiety than design and production engineers; and believe that they are controlled by their environment. Advertising campaigns to management, the study concludes, should be "modern, aggressive, idea presentations—the big picture approach" because managers have anxieties to succeed which propel them to take risks to move their companies ahead.

Purchasing agents like facts and figures and are fond of wheeling and dealing. The purchasing agent believes he has the greatest influence on selecting suppliers and that he shares with management the responsibility for the final approval of the purchase.

Mr. Morrison found that the average number of persons involved in a purchasing decision is 12. But, purchasing agents, when asked how many people were involved in the buying decision, and believing themselves more influential in decisions than they actually are, said eight. They tended to single themselves out as the most important link in the purchasing decision chain. Mr. Morrison finds that purchasing agents are "subjective fellows striving for status."

Penton/IPC produced a 22-minute film which summarizes the results of the Morrison study, called "Know the Buyer Better." That film emphasizes the importance of targeting sales presentations and advertising messages to specific audiences, relates John W. Hogan, director of communications, Elco Products, Rockford, Ill.

The Penton movie "shored up what we already knew," Mr. Hogan explains. Elco manufactures specialty metal components, "so we view the design engineer's function as most important," relates Mr. Hogan, "but a company that sells standard stock items, would probably place more emphasis on the purchasing agent's function."

Although Elco did not change its advertising strategy as a result of seeing the Penton film, Mr. Hogan says the film "reinforced what we were already doing." For example, in advertising tailored for design engineers, copy stresses the full range of capabilities of Elco's custom engineered metal components. While advertising directed at purchasing agents for the same service, Mr. Hogan explains, emphasizes delivery, quality, reliability and the image of the company.

Johnson Controls, Oakbrook Ill., invited Penton to show the movie at its national sales meeting. "The human element of selling is very important," says David Firszt, marketing communications manager of the control products division. Mr. Firszt says that although they didn't change advertising strategies as a result of seeing that movie, the movie, does fit in very nicely with another sales training technique the division uses.

That technique is based on a psychological model which classifies buyers into four personality groups: drivers, amiables, analyticals and expressives. (See story, page 60). That model, coupled with the findings from the Penton study, is very useful in reaching buyers, Mr. Firszt notes. "You can learn a lot about the buyer within 30 seconds by the first few words and a handshake."

— MCP

Harnessing Engineers and Scientists to the Sales Effort

R. P. Andelson*

In marketing technical products, engineers and scientists are frequently used in a sales capacity. Necessity for such usage is examined as a function of the character of product and market. Relationship between the marketing man and the technical man during the course of a sales campaign is developed. A philosophy and a technique for motivating and preparing the engineer and scientist to act effectively in the alien marketing capacity is then presented. The author further explores development of a marketing technology program designed to place all aspects of the marketing plan and concept on a factual base fully intelligible to the engineer and scientist.

INTRODUCTION

A topic such as "Harnessing Engineers and Scientists to the Sales Effort" may imply that a marketing man is in a position to harness someone for some purpose. The truth is that he is more often the harnessee than the harnessor. In any event, it is the thesis of this article that it is possible to motivate the engineer and scientist in such a manner that he will accept the marketing harness without being subject to duress. The technique is relatively simple: engineers and scientists are experts in the organization of fact and in application of physical laws. By establishing a marketing technology, which is to say a body of fact and "laws" applicable to a specific market, the marketing function becomes comprehensible to the technical man. When he understands a specialized field, he is comfortable. When he feels comfortable in an activity, he becomes effective. When he's effective in marketing, your sales or win rate can show increases of a most gratifying nature.

In discussing the engineer in marketing, it is first necessary to define the kind of market to which the procedures apply. Second, it is necessary to determine why the engineer finds himself thrust upon the marketing state. Finally, it is necessary to develop the philosophy and the technique that can make him a good performer on that stage. The procedures and conclusions should be of interest to any

*Director, Marketing Group Office, Hughes Aircraft Company, Fullerton, California.

Reprinted with permission from *Proc. World Congress*, 1966, pp. 204–215, J.S. Wright and J.L. Goldstucker, Eds. Published by the American Marketing Association.

marketing man or manager who may have the problem of asking a working engineer to be amiable to a customer.

CHARACTERISTICS OF THE MARKET FOR THE COMPLEX TECHNICAL PRODUCT

In a discussion of harnessing engineers, it is necessary first to consider the vehicle to which they are to be harnessed. That is, what kind of a market is being considered? What are its character-istics? In the context of this discussion the answers are simple. The market is aerospace; the product, electronic systems.

There have been a number of articles pointing out the presumed peculiar characteristics of aerospace or defense marketing. It is true the product is not a consumer goods. It is also true that the customers are the governments of the world. Above all, it is true that in dealing with domestic government agencies it is necessary to work to a set of synthetic constraints. Despite constraints, defense marketing problems are actually much the same as those encountered in any industry dealing in a complex technical product. The product is the criterion.

Figure 1 - Market and Product

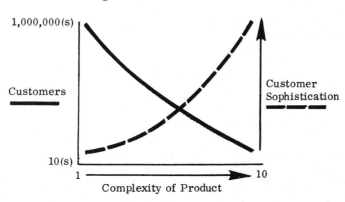

Figure 1 serves to illustrate that point. In that diagram product complexity is noted on a scale of ten, where "one" is presumed to equal the product complexity of for example, shoelaces or mechan-ical can-openers. "Ten," then, equals the complexity of a product such as electronic defense systems or the commercial equivalent for example, process control computer systems.

It is manifest that at the "one" level of complexity there are generally many, many customers: the classic mass market. At the other end of the scale customers are numbered in the small tens and hundreds. That simply says that not too many people or agencies buy defense systems but then not too many people or agencies buy TV transmitters or hydroelectric turbines either. Thus the size of the market can be said to bear an inverse relationship to the com-plexity of the product. Figure 1 also illustrates another factor defense industry and the equivalent commercial activity have in common. For both, the sophistication of the customer is in inverse proportion to his numbers. In dealing with a mass market, it can generally be said that the customer is more concerned with perform-ance than with design.

The customer for the complex technical product (all two or three hundred of him) is certainly concerned with performance, but fre-quently he knows just about as much concerning design as do the engineers developing and producing the product. That latter fact is the crux of the marketing problem. Certainly those engaged in the marketing effort must be just as knowledgeable and as technically sophisticated as are their customers. That requirement is the compelling reason for using engineers and scientists in the marketing effort for the complex technical product.

Figure 2 - Market and Marketeer :

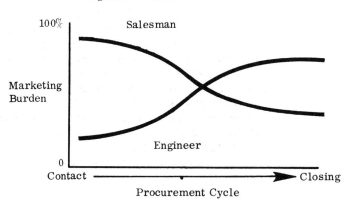

Figure 2 shows the relative role of the salesman and of the engineer during a protracted sales effort. Again, their involvement varies with the complexity of product. For a product of complexity of "one," it is generally true that the marketing burden can be borne almost entirely by the salesman, by the advertising agency and by the public relations people. The engineer can pursue his morose ways in his office, in the laboratory and in the shop, all the while designing better machinery for making shoelaces and better mechanisms for opening cans. Both of these pursuits it should be emphasized, may well demand just as much skill, education, and ability as do the activities of his colleagues in organizations concerned with products of greater complexity. The only difference is that the shoelace and can-opener engineers can stay in the plant. It is only when customer sophistication mounts that it is essential that technical people be sporadically called forth from their normal habitats to support the marketing effort.

Figure 2 further illustrates that when product complexity reaches a scale factor of ten, and when intensive customer contact is required, the salesman as we know him in the mass marketing arena can carry only a part of the marketing burden. The principal effort must rest upon the engineer. Again, that statement must be qualified. The salesman and the engineer in the marketing environment have a symbiotic relationship. Neither could survive in the technical sales jungle without the other. In view of that relationship, the problem then becomes one of effective utilization of individuals who by temperament and training are neither facile in, nor fond of the interpersonal dynamics essential in sales. Technical men are slow to respond to the stimuli and rewards that normally motivate a marketing man. What then, can be the motivational harness?

The first step, as described above, is to recognize the fact that the engineer is of necessity the only credible salesman in certain marketing situations. The second step is to attempt to reduce the marketing "art" so far as possible to a technology. If certain "laws" can be formulated, and if experimental evidence can be advanced to support them, the engineer will accept them, apply them, and begin to feel comfortable in his marketing function.

It may seem "marketing" in the sales aspect is too subjective a matter to be reduced to a "science." However, as Will Durant has said ". . . what does any discipline do but try by rules to turn the art of a few into a science teachable to all?" Even an approximation of a science will serve to increase the effectivity of the engineer as a marketeer. A method which will serve to develop the necessary factual foundation for a specific marketing environment is the institution of a Marketing Technology Development Program.

MARKETING TECHNOLOGY AND THE ENGINEER

A Marketing Technology Development Program in not necessary in marketing all types of products. However, the marketing technology elements as discussed below probably exist, in an embryonic form, within the marketing concept and marketing plan for many concerns. They need be emphasized to the degree noted only in the marketing of the complex technical product.

What are the elements of a marketing technology? In this instance they fall into three categories: Needs Analysis, Sales Research, and Feedback Studies.

"Needs Analysis" comprises four elements:

(1) Market Conditioning Surveys
(2) Market Intelligence Research
(3) Market Projection Studies
(4) Product/Program Selection Analyses.

The "Sales Research" phase of the development program comprises three elements:

(1) Proposal Format Development
(2) Persuasion Engineering
(3) Presentation Research and Education.

The "Feedback Studies" has but one element:

(1) "Marketing Effectiveness Analyses."

It is very easy, it seems to me, to misunderstand this distinction 3 within the Sales Research category is specifically applicable to the engineer's function in a sales effort. Before discussing the application of that information to motivate and indoctrinate the engineer/marketeer, it would be well to enlarge briefly upon the significance of each of the other elements within this program. Such a discussion will place the two items of special interest into the proper context. It will also help relate the program to the problems which generally may be encountered in any marketing, whatever the industry, whatever the activity, and whatever the product.

As all marketing men know, sales are made by satisfying needs and perhaps the first need of any customer is for belief in the competency of the people with whom he does business. Thus the first element within the "Needs Analysis" category is "Market Conditioning Surveys." The work here is directed to determining those techniques which will favorably influence customers to accept the concern's programs and products. If this should happen to read as though it had a public relations flavor, the conclusion is exactly right. In the classic sense, however, "public relations" is not particularly applicable to the "Ten" complexity level of product. As earlier noted, customers here are relatively few and keenly sophisticated. In this area public relations must be considered to be simply a general, or nonspecific marketing program. The objective is to present the capabilities and competencies of the concern in such a manner

and through such media as to create a responsive audience when the occasion for a specific marketing effort arises.

"Market Intelligence Research" is another element within "Needs Analysis." Existing market intelligence sources are here codified, and a formalized search made for new, effective, and ethical means of securing information concerning customer needs and plans. Concomitantly, data on competitive efforts and products must be secured.

"Market Projection Studies" concern the "preview" aspect of marketing. These studies look into the future, ascertain customer problems, and attempt to forecast the programs and products on which the concern may be working in near and distant future. Such projections are extremely important because they form the foundation for the decisions which establish internally funded research and development programs. They also strongly influence plant and other capital investments.

In "Product/Program Selection Analyses" an attempt is made to use such tools as operations analysis to evaluate specifically which product lines will be of greatest benefit to the concern at minimum risk. Basically this is a considered appraisal of the concern's capacity to respond to a customer's need.

In a sense, "Needs Analysis" paves the way for sales. Within a marketing technology program, the next logical category is that of "Sales Research" since in most defense-oriented industries the proposal carries most of the technical burden of sales. "Proposal Format Development" is the first element. Proposals comprise a substantial part of the marketing effort since they may run to several thousand pages in a number of volumes. Continued development of formats has led to entirely new and more efficient communication in the proposal medium. One technique, now in use, is termed "Sequential Thematic Organization of Proposals" (STOP) and is demonstrably an improvement over conventional proposal techniques.

As earlier noted, "Persuasion Engineering" is one of two items which is particularly pertinent in the marketing of technical products by technical people. In this area the applicable behavioral sciences are explored and the various processes which are effective in group and interpersonal communications selected and evaluated. It can be demonstrated that much of what salesmen have learned empirically can be stated as laws. Indeed, with reference to groups and audiences, many mathematicians are found to be applying stochastic mathematical processes to develop formulas which well predict the response of a given group to a given set of stimuli. Many salesmen may vehemently deny that prediction is possible because it seems to indicate that men are simply biological mechanisms. It further implies that the hard-won abilities of the salesman may one day no longer be needed. Those working with persuasion engineering have concluded however, that in a measure, people can be mechanically manipulated.

The second element of special interest in increasing the efficiency of the technical man in the sales function is "Presentation Research and Education." For a complex technical product, the presentation can be considered to be the point of sale, if any product which experiences a sales cycle measured in months can be considered to have a "point" of sale. Research here is directed to determining what factors influence a successful presentation. As the factors are developed, programs are evolved to educate engineers and scientists in the pertinent laws and procedures.

Completing the elements of this specimen Marketing Development Program is within the category of "Feedback Studies." Here are developed the formalized techniques and procedures which permit evaluation of why some campaigns are successful and others are not. These analyses are extremely important because if the "why" of a win or loss can be ascertained, it is inevitable that the marketing effort will become increasingly effective. After conducting analyses for some years, it has become evident that given enough data it should be possible to construct a mathematical model for any given marketing effort and retroactively evaluate strengths and weaknesses. Conversely, it may well be possible to program a computer to give odds on winning new competitions.

A marketing technology program keyed to a marketing concept and a marketing plan is one approach to the effective utilization of technical personnel in a sales effort. It may be well at this juncture to indicate just how some of the findings of such a program can be applied. Perhaps the best example is the presentation. The presentation is the point at which most engineers first become aware of the marketing concomitant of their chosen profession.

POINT OF SALE: THE PRESENTATION

To indicate where the function of the presentation falls, it is useful to trace briefly the chronology of a typical marketing effort for the complex technical product. First, by market conditioning, or by conventional public relations, and by formal submittal of qualifications, a concern is established as capable of handling certain categories of defense business. The organization is then placed upon a qualified bidders list for products and programs within those categories. If market projection studies have been valid, the concern should be reasonably cognizant of the products and programs the customer is seeking. Consequently, it should seldom or ever be a surprise when a Request for Proposal (RFP) is received.

The response to a RFP is to mobilize a task force of engineers and scientists, marketing men and administrators, production men and accountants. The team works with an intensity and dedication which, by and large, is unmatched elsewhere in industry. Their product, at the conclusion of three or four, hundred-hour weeks, is a proposal. This is a formal document looking much like a text book and may run up to several thousand pages of text, photographs, and drawings. The customer evaluates the proposals in a formal fashion, using teams of specialists who report their findings numerically on a weighted scale which emphasizes those factors which are of most importance to the user. Technical portions and price are evaluated separately.

No matter how dispassionate a customer attempts to be and no matter how knowledgeable his team of experts, there must always remain a substantial area of ambiguity. The scores usually fall within a fairly close range because the competence of the large firms in the defense industry (and the commercial equivalents) is fairly evenly distributed. There is also one other point. The customer owns no universal genius: no one man who can read through 4,000 pages of complex technical information and involved mathematics, synthesize the data, and objectively determine whether a proposed system is good, better, or best.

Therefore, it frequently comes to pass that the presentation becomes the point of sale. What is the function of the presentation in this context? It is really to evaluate personal competencies. Two factors dictate this requirement. They might be expressed as

Proposal Size + Complexity of Content = Ad Hominem Emphasis.

This situation leading to this emphasis is not unusual; everyone has experienced it as reflected by the slogan, "If you don't know diamonds, know your jeweler." *Ad hominem* simply means "to the man." If a procurement agency has digested as much of the information concerning a proposed multimillion dollar project as it can, and if the decision is difficult, and if it cannot be quite certain that details of system function are really understood, or if it cannot clearly establish what the high-risk development items are, then it must look to the man, or men, who presumably do know. And the vehicle or ad hominem evaluation is the presentation.

The presentation is thus the means of evaluating the caliber of individuals that will be assigned to a program in either a technical or managerial capacity. It is a means of determining from the designer specifically what he considers the problems to be and how much confidence he has in tentative solutions for them. It is a means of determining whether the contractor is completely aware of the needs of the user of the proposed system or product, and whether he is motivated to response to those needs.

Just as the point of sale is usually those critical moments when the housewife stops in front of a section of supermarket shelf and the pretty package or the advertising to which she has been exposed tips the balance in favor of a given product, so can the presentation be the point at which the final decision may be reached in the marketing of the complex technical product. In one sense, the presentation can be said to be the point at which the customer inspects the merchandise. Fundamentally, the product is not the hardware or system. The product is the brains, training and creative ability of managers, engineers, and scientists. Thus, the vehicle of the presentation showcases the basic competencies of a company dealing in products of great complexity and great value. For that reason, the presentation must be effective. It must present a true picture of the capabilities and competencies of people as well as of the virtues of the product.

As might be surmised many engineers and scientists, and indeed many technical managers, have a reluctance to function in what they may conceive as a marketing capacity. Certainly it is difficult to say that it is not marketing to stand in front of an audience and describe the capabilities and peculiar virtues of a product. At this time in the program cycle, however, it is essential that the technical man gracefully wear his marketing harness.

Many marketing men are effective speakers and can present information succinctly and well. It might be thought that the appropriate information could be given to one of these speakers and permit him to impress the customer audience. As has been noted, only the technical man is credible at this point. However, he will be credible and he will be effective only if he has been given the appropriate facts which govern effective communication at the lectern.

What are the appropriate facts? Figure 3 is one chart taken from a lecture termed "Presentation Physics." It demonstrates what an audience will retain of information presented verbally, the same information presented visually, and when both channels of communications are used simultaneously in a reinforcing mode. Given these data as part of the presentation research and education element of the marketing technology program, the technical man will accept the desirability of using visual aids in a presentation and will accept the necessity of closely cued verbal reinforcement of the information presented visually. It is unlikely that he would accept the necessity for such a procedure had he simply been told to do so by an accomplished speaker or by an experienced marketing man. His professional skepticism would lead him to reject any opinion or direction which was unsupported by fact.

Figure 4 illustrates a sample of the kind of information that is useful to the technical man in another arena: the interpersonal or group situation. The chart illustrated is drawn from another lecture termed "Engineering of Persuasion." This chart gives the experimental evidence supporting the contention that it is better to state the conclusion which is desired to be drawn from a series of facts. If the individual or the audience is allowed to infer the conclusion, in most

Figure 3 - The Effect of Reinforcement

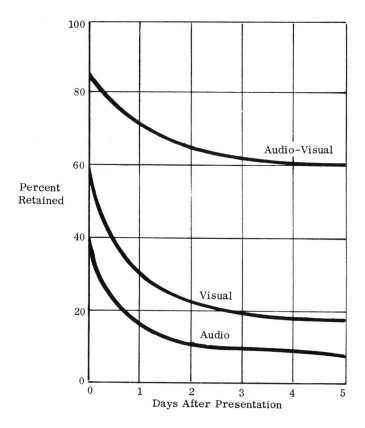

Figure 4 - State the Conclusion

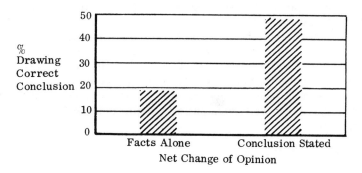

instances there will be no conclusion, or worse, the wrong conclusion will be drawn.

Neither of the educational programs from which the specimen charts were taken would of themselves make a marketing man of a technical man. They will, however, cause him intellectually to accept the techniques of good sales communications practice that marketing men normally accept either intuitively or pragmatically.

CONCLUSION

In effect what has been discussed here is that the information derived from a Marketing Technology Development Program, is particularly effective in convincing a technical man why he must function in a marketing capacity. The program also provides the information he must have and accept if he is to be efficient in that capacity. It can be stated almost as a truism that a technical man cannot be retreaded into a marketing man by the use of exhortation and "sloganeering." The average engineer at the average marketing rally would become actively nauseous. The reason is generally accepted. It has become almost platitudinous to mention that engineers, by and large, are "thing" or hardware oriented and salesmen are "people" oriented. There is something else however that is more to the point. Engineers are professional skeptics. They undergo a long and rigorous training directed toward the goal of ensuring that they will always ask "why?" or "prove it!" Thus while many persons can accept certain marketing techniques as being effective and do the things that professional speakers state must be done, the engineer will ask "why do we do it that way?" If there are no facts or experimental evidence to support a given marketing method, he will certainly conceive that his opinion of the method is just as good, if not better, than anyone else's.

In summary then, the transition of engineer to marketeer takes the form of a four-point program. Step one is to analyze the market. In essence, this was essentially what has been done in the first part of this article. Figures 1 and 2 indicated the special market and the special role of the technical man in that market. Step two is to attempt to reduce specific marketing procedures and plans to as quantitative and factual a base as possible. Such an exercise, discussed here as a Marketing Technology Development Program, serves to develop marketing objectives in terms that are comprehensible and meaningful to a technical man.

Step three is to structure the quantitative data derived from the program. Two examples of this structuring have been given. There are many other instances of structuring, which is simply the organization of marketing information in such a form that it can be expressed as a "law" or "axiom." The fourth and most important step is to educate. Time must be devoted to present formally the information developed to those technical people who will be required to support the marketing effort.

It will be seen that the construction of a marketing harness for a technical man is not a simple matter. It takes time, it takes effort, and it takes long and intensive analyses. The results, however, are rewarding. In many markets the technical man makes an exceptionally effective salesman and the team of marketeer and engineer is a combination that can well substantially augment the efficiency of any marketing effort.

ANALYZING THE MARKET POSTURE
FOR A TECHNICAL PRODUCT OR IDEA

John A. Ledingham
University of Houston

When at long last a product is finally completed — having grown from the conceptual stage to a finished innovation — the real work has been done from the perspective of the research and development team. All that remains is to "market" the product, whatever that means, and have someone write a few advertisements to sell the product.

From the perspective of the creator of the product, that seems to be the case. For the marketing/advertising professional, however, the work is just beginning. Hundreds of new products are created each year. In fact, 75 percent of Proctor and Gambles' revenues since World War II have come from products that have been developed and introduced into the marketplace since 1945. Most companies would envy P&G's record. Most new products are not successful, and many companies created expressly to market a new product fail every day. In fact, most of the companies that fail do so within a year and a half of being created are the victims of poor planning or undercapitalization.

The somewhat obvious point is that the creation of a product in no way assures its success in the competitive marketplace. That success is linked to a marketing effort that is based on solidly planned strategies that encompass a thorough knowledge of the prospective buyer, a clear understanding of the way in which potential consumers view the product, realistic budgeting, effective creative, efficient media placement, and campaign evaluation. It might help to realize that when a viewer sees a commercial or print ad, he is seeing the end result of a campaign rather than the beginning of it — the embodiment of careful analysis and planning of the market and the ways in which those advertisements can help achieve the goals of the campaign.

The first step is to evaluate or establish a marketing posture. This is, in effect, a review of all you know about important factors that will ultimately affect the success of your marketing effort, or a checklist for analysis.

Part of that review, or development, includes careful analysis of more than a dozen marketing factors. Those factors have been conveniently lumped together under a term common in marketing — the "4 Ps." Those 4 Ps are Product, Price, Place (meaning the distribution of the product) and Promotion (including advertising and public relations, and other promotions such as trade shows, sales pieces, and convention materials). Actually, there is a fifth "P" and it is the most important one of all: "People."

In planning your marketing strategy, everything starts with the potential buyer. To be successful, a marketing effort must include a clear understanding of who the product is being "targeted" to and what that consumer is like. Marketing

This article was prepared specifically for this anthology.

and advertising professionals generally discuss that consumer group in terms of age, income, family size, and the like (demographics); the part of the country or even the subdivision in which the consumer group resides (geographics); the collective attitudes and predispositions of that market segment (psychographics); and, the ways in which the group interacts with its environment (lifestyle). That last category can tell the marketing planner whether the group is active in outdoor recreation, and what they do with their leisure time.

A thorough understanding of who the consumer is, what the consumer is like, and other characteristics (such as the publications read and television watched) provides clues on how to "position" a product (the way you want the product to be perceived in the mind of the consumer) to construct the most effective advertising messages. As marketing expert Roger Blackwell has noted, people do not buy a drill because they want a tool; they buy it because they want a hole. Understanding the needs and wants of your market is necessary for any successful marketing effort.

Professionals use the term "market" to cover a number of meanings.

A "market" may be a country, a section of a country, or a part of a community. It may be subteens or senior citizens. A market is almost never everyone. Few goods are used by everyone. Most products are targeted for segments of that mass market based on the characteristics discussed. However, there is also another characteristic that is critical — past purchase behavior.

The best indicator that someone will buy your product is the fact that they have already bought a product similar to it.

In political advertising, the importance of past behavior is obvious. It is axiomatic that political campaign professionals try to ensure the vote of their own party members as their primary effort. Asking voters who have already voted a certain ideology to continue to do so is immeasurably more effective than trying to convince voters to change political camps. But, this is not limited to political behavior; it is true for essentially all our behavioral decisions. When looking for a segment of the market that you would expect to want your product, find those who have already purchased a product exactly like yours or similar to it. That is the best evidence — behavior — that they belong in that market segment. Even if they already have a product like yours, it will not last forever. Even large items like automobiles are traded in every few years. Sources to help you find out about consumer behavior are plentiful. The most obvious is the U. S. Census. Numerous indexes are housed in the library of most universities that tell you who has purchased various products locally, regionally, and nationally. The Simmon Marketing Research Bureau provides information about products and in-depth information about consumers of those products. Direct mail operations (there are even advertising agencies that specialize in direct mail) are another source of consumer information, as are the books of lists you can rent that can be found listed in Standard Rates & Data's publications. Direct mail brokers are experienced in working with these lists and can help you test out your product and creative efforts with a sample of consumers, or launch an all-out campaign. The Direct Mail Marketing Association is eager to help those who may be making their initial foray into that area of marketing.

<u>Try out your ideas or products first with potential consumers.</u>

Marketers have found pre-campaign research saves money. They often sample consumers from probable market segments for in-depth interviewing, either with one individual at a time or in "focus groups." In that way, they gain some expectation of probable reaction to that new product (or service) prior to entering into a full campaign. That kind of research helps to identify what the consumer thinks about your product, and lets you know what is important to the consumer.

<u>What you or your advertising agency thinks about the product is not important. What is important is what the potential buyer thinks about it.</u>

To you, the outstanding feature of your product may be obvious — and it may be wrong. In a situation where all products are similar, the slightest variation may be the key selling point for one of them. To you, a master light control switch may be perceived as an evergy-saving device. To consumers, it may be a way to protect against burglary when the residents are away. That is true whether your product is targeted to an industrial, corporate, or retail market. Obviously, the more you know about the probable market for your product, the better opportunity you have of selling that product by identifying the attributes that are most important to the consumer and couching your advertising message in terms that promise to (and will) solve a problem for that consumer.

An example of how important it is to know the ways in which you and your product are perceived is seen in the case of a Midwest chemical manufacturing operation. The manufacturing concern knew that the particular chemical it manufactured was purchased by industries on the Atlantic Coast and in the Northeast part of the U. S. through easily available secondary source materials. However, the Midwest company did not know if any of these companies were disposed to change suppliers, let alone what might affect that decision. The Midwest company did not even have a mailing list. However, from working with a list of industry publications, the chemical company was able to put together a survey list that ultimately provided titles, names, and information. Through that survey, the Midwest firm found that, indeed, a market was there and ready to move toward new suppliers. However, the cost of the chemicals produced by the Midwest company was not the major benefit as perceived by the potential buyers, but rather guaranteed delivery dates. Next most important was the quality of the product. Price was last on the list, and then those buyers were only concerned that the price be "competitive." In short, the chemical company was able to find out the most important attributes of its product. In addition, the chemical company developed a mailing list from the survey for a direct mail effort, and also identified the industry publications read by those prospective buyers. Ads placed in those publications were immensely successful.

<u>After the consumer, the most important factor is the product itself.</u>

Just as the product developer may not perceive a product in the same way as a consumer, products need to be pre-tested with the market segment to make certain that the product will do what it claims <u>for that segment</u>. A company seeking to market a product to reduce water use in the home plumbing system attempted to market that product without first pre-testing it with prospective buyers. The product had been installed in less than an hour by its developers, all of whom had a thorough knowledge of its workings. And, the product was advertised as being able to be installed in that time. However, non-experts who purchased the product found it took hours for them to complete the job, with frequent trips to a hardware store for parts. The complaints made further distribution through local outlets impossible in that region.

It is just as important for the advertising agency to understand the product, which it obviously did not in the case of the plumbing innovation. A large ad agency was in danger of losing a major client, a portable computer firm, because of the agency's inability, from the perspective of the manufacturer, to properly market the product. After a senior copywriter spent several days with the client examining the way the product was built and the workings of that product, he was able to translate those benefits into copy that addressed the problems of the targeted market segment. The agency still has the account.

But, do not discount the power of creative intuition.

Sometimes, the most brilliant efforts are the result of bringing together seemingly unrelated facts. There is a story that a fundraiser in the presidential campaign of Senator Barry Goldwater was looking at some direct mail lists and noticed one that was comprised of consumers who had spent $15.00 to purchase a chamois cloth through the mail. It seemed to the fundraiser that $15.00 was a considerable investment (remember, this was in the early 1960s) for a cloth with which to wash a car. He intuitively realized the compulsive nature of such a person. Further, he thought that such a person might be extremely conservative because of that compulsiveness. The subsequent fundraising letter to those on that list was one of the most successful political fundraising letters of all time.

One of your most important decisions to be made concerns the price of the product. The potential market is known, and the product advantages are known, what about price? Price must be set, of course, to make a profit (marketing is often defined as "meeting consumer needs at a profit"). That still leaves a wide range of possible prices.

Let your market help you in establishing the price.

Think of the interviewing process again. In that person-to-person interview, or in discussions with the focus group, ask those consumers what they would "expect" to pay for such a product, or what the product would "be worth" to them. That is exactly the way prices are being set for the emerging text-on-television systems (videotex, teletext, viewdata) that are being introduced by home computer companies and cable television systems around the country. In fact, many of the services on those systems are the direct result of asking consumers to imagine the kinds of services they think might be possibly made available, and then developing them. Direct mail advertisers have found through testing of different prices that the highest price is often the one that produces the most sales because low-priced products are often thought of as being of low quality and having little value.

<u>When it comes to establishing your budget, there are a number of approaches.</u>

It is common to base that budget on a percentage of actual sales. If you have a company that has been selling the product long enough to have sales, that works fine. But, if you have a new company, it presents a problem. Another approach is to base the marketing budget on a percentage of future sales. There again, a lot of guesswork is going on. Also, you have to be flexible to respond to downturns and gains that occur. Yet another way is to look at historic records of the company (when they exist) and identify through statistical analysis those variables that seem to most affect sales, and then concentrate on those variables. Once again, an obvious problem is that many companies do not have this historic data to analyze. Finally, parity is a very common approach. Set your budget the same as your competition, plus $1.00, is the guideline of parity. The problem with that approach is that it essentially is letting someone else dictate your budget, and their situation may be far different than yours.

<u>The best approach to budgeting is to develop a clear idea of exactly what you need to do and then plan your budget around it.</u>

Your marketing plan may include advertising in several "test markets" before rolling out a campaign. By analyzing the results of those test efforts, you can articulate a rationale for future efforts, and you have some reasonable expectations on which to construct a budget. For example, it may be that you varied the creative approach in the different test markets. All else being equal, you then know which approach worked best and can maximize that effort. It may be that television worked better than print, or that a combination was most successful. At the least, you have data for decision making based on your needs and your situation — not someone else's.

<u>Your distribution efforts depend on the nature of your product.</u>

Products are generally divided into hard goods, soft goods, package goods, and services. In most cases, these products must be "sold" to outlets before they can be sold to consumers. The exception is direct response advertising, in which the consumer buys directly from the advertiser, rather than going through an outlet (direct response, by the way, is the fastest growing marketing technique in the U. S.). Sales representatives, then, must be the front line of attack if your product is being sold through an outlet. When approaching these outlets, think of them as your "target." Find out their interest just as you would for consumers. A strong promotional campaign is generally the key to getting your product onto the shelves of the outlet. Packaging that takes the place of the personal sale, along with a brand name that lends itself to creative advertising, are especially important for retail sales.

<u>Promotion usually means advertising rather than public relations.</u>

There are a number of activities that are included under "promotion," and all are important. Sales literature, trade shows, premiums — all are part of promotion. Public relations is also part of promotion, but PR generally concerns news of the company, not information about the product. It is important to remember that when it is crucial that something be said exactly the way you want it said, then advertising is the only approach to use. Too often, news releases are not used or are used in an altered form. When you pay for space and time, you control that message.

Advertising can be done through an in-house agency or an independent agency.

There are essentially two ways to create advertising messages: through your own in-house agency, and/or through an independent agency. There is no "right" way.

In-house agencies offer a number of advantages and disadvantages. They can develop a thorough understanding of the product because they work with it closely and on a day-to-day basis. They do not have other clients to be concerned with. However, some feel that they tend to lose their objectivity because of their closeness to the product manufacturer and that being in-house lessens the flow of creative juices. Certainly, an in-house agency is another area that needs administration and management, but you may find this offset by the convenience of having your marketing/advertising staff at your fingertips.

Independent agencies tend to be objective and highly competitive. However, you may be but one of a number of clients that are important to that agency. On the other hand, that fact alone may stir their creative juices and result in more effective advertising for you. If you decide to work with an independent agency, make certain that you know of the agency's track record with other clients. Find one that has experts in your field (some retail agencies will not work on an industrial campaign, and vice versa). Most importantly, make certain you are comfortable with the Account Executive assigned to your account. That is the person you will be working with on a daily basis. And, that is the person in which you must have confidence.

In addition to the in-house agency and the independent agency, there is a third form — the boutique agency. Such an agency specializes in one aspect of the marketing/advertising process. A boutique agency may only work on commercials, leaving print advertising to others. Or, that agency may only provide graphics. Some agencies only conduct research for their clients, and for other agencies. Still others only handle certain kinds of promotion.

Many companies have an in-house ad manager that works with an independent agency. In many instances, that ad manager utilizes boutique agencies to develop creative and effective advertising while maintaining responsibility for the campaign effort in-house.

There is no set rule for paying for advertising work. Some companies prefer to work on a retainer arrangement with their agency, and others pay on a project basis. Similarly, some agencies will only work on a retainer, while others refuse to do so. Find the arrangement that is comfortable for you and be flexible. Remember that independent agencies are entitled to a commission on the media they place in many instances. That commission is theirs. As a non-agency company, you are not eligible for the commission.

<u>Media planning and placement are another specialty in advertising.</u>

Once you know the characteristics of a market segment, and have advertising concepts that will address the advantages of your product as perceived by the consumer, you need to produce and place those ads and commercials. The agency generally has its own media planner and buyer. If not, there are media "houses" available — firms that only do media planning and placement. While the creative staff of the agency produce the advertisements, those on the staff of the media department (or house) see to it that the advertising messages are placed in media that will be seen by your target audience. This is essential. The best conceived advertising is worthless if it is not seen by the market segment to which it is targeted.

<u>The decision on which media to use depends on the product and the goals you have set.</u>

Generally, television is excellent for demonstrating a product. That is why you see so many commercials for kitchen items. Television also supplies the largest audiences. Television is excellent for campaigns that are designed to create awareness of a new product or to increase memory of brand names. However, television is also the most expensive medium for advertising, and those large audiences may or may not include your market segment.

Radio has been called the "personal medium" because the messages depend so heavily on the imagination of the listener. This need not be a disadvantage. The sound of surf, a bad muffler, or a dying battery all evoke mental images that are rich in detail. Radio also works with short lead times so you can put a message on the air within days after you conceive of it. Radio stations generally are helpful in producing those messages, too. And, radio is a specialized medium with particular audiences for different musical and non-musical formats allowing you to target in on particular segments. Radio is also relatively inexpensive compared to network and even a good deal of local television.

Cable television is increasingly offering the advantages of television at less than the price of radio. And, the multiplicity of channels seems to be fragmenting that medium so that it is slowly building audiences that are defined more like radio audiences than those of television (emphasis on the type of audience rather than on the size of that audience). Major agencies are watching that medium closely. When those agencies begin to place more commercials with the cable systems, that medium will finally emerge as a forceful advertising medium.

Newspapers and magazines are excellent for supporting television and radio ads and for coordination with other media for special sales. In addition, magazines have been highly specialized since the 1950s and enable the advertiser to reach market segments effectively and efficiently. Newspapers are purchased for their advertising content as much as for their news coverage (some say more for the ads than the news), so they are seen as an informational service rather than instrusive (as commercials are sometimes thought to be). And, newspapers are increasingly specializing. Neighborhood newspapers are, in fact, the fastest growing medium in the U. S.

Another print form, direct mail, is the least inhibiting advertising medium available. With direct mail, you can target to your market segment and personalize the envelope to include the prospective buyer's name as well as address. And, from the order forms or telephone calls, you know exactly who acted on the promotional messages. Direct mail marketers also conduct split tests of their envelopes, cover letters, and offers continuously. They are experts at knowing what works in direct mail.

<u>Now, you need to know why the marketing effort worked so you can do it again next year.</u>

Having found your market segment, utilized your knowledge of the consumer and the product to develop effective as well as creative advertising, and placed that advertising in appropriate media, you need to analyze the results.

It is not enough simply to know that sales were good. You must know why. It may be that sales could have been a lot better. It may be that those who bought the product were not satisfied and will not buy another one in the future. You need to know how many of the product are being sold per consumer and if the product is being used in the way you intended it to be used (the use of baking soda as a deodorizer for refrigerators was discovered in the post-testing and analysis of a campaign).

The idea, of course, is to maximize that which worked and minimize that which did not work as well. Research firms are increasing throughout the U. S. in the major population centers, and increasingly research is part of the service available through full service advertising agencies. As noted earlier, some boutique agencies only do research. In addition, many faculty in universities are available to consult with companies regarding their research needs. The main point is that there is no reason to not utilize research to find out if your strategy was on target, and why or why not.

This brief summary of some of the factors that require attention in putting together a marketing effort is not exhaustive. It is intended as a basic framework. Other chapters of this anthology expand on many of the points mentioned in passing here. However, the basics are here with which to begin thinking about a marketing effort and to provide a marketing perspective. In the process of marketing and advertising a technical product or idea, reviewing these points can greatly enhance the probability of success. While no one of these factors can cause a marketing effort to succeed by itself, neglecting any one of them will greatly reduce the opportunity for success.

_____

The Marketing Concept Can Aid, Not Erode, Business Efficiency

A. Parasuraman

Recent criticism of the marketing concept may be leading many managers to mistrust it. Firms that are willing to implement the marketing concept wholeheartedly, however, can reap handsome dividends through improved business efficiency.

D ue to a variety of factors, the pressure on U.S. firms to improve their efficiency or productivity is greater today than ever before. The maturing U.S. market, the increasing competition from abroad, and the recent ills of the U.S. economy are some of the major factors. Steady improvement in business efficiency is becoming essential for ensuring the profitability, if not the survival, of many firms. Consequently, the need for cutting costs and boosting output is clear. In their eagerness to improve efficiency, however, firms should avoid the temptation to label the marketing concept, and the resources needed to implement it adequately, as excess business fat. Doing so may be tantamount to killing the goose that lays the golden eggs.

The Misunderstood Marketing Concept

The gist of the marketing concept is really quite simple: A firm that wants to be a winner in the marketplace must consider customer needs as its primary focus and must coordinate all its operations to ensure the satisfaction of its customers—without, at the same time, giving the company away. Intuitively, such a philosophy should make a lot of sense in today's highly competitive business world. But have U.S. firms wholeheartedly adopted the marketing concept? Unfortunately, the answer is *not* an unequivocal yes. Even more disturbing is a recent rash of criticism against the marketing concept that is perhaps leading many managers to mistrust it.[1] For instance, the marketing concept has been accused of being impractical and the root cause of the decline in U.S. product innovativeness.[2] A scrutiny of the arguments against the marketing concept, however, leads me to believe that it is perhaps ill understood and grossly underrated by its critics.

First, let us examine the argument that it is not practical to expect business operations other than marketing—such as R&D, production, and purchasing — to have customer satisfaction as their primary focus. Proponents of this argument are perhaps still living in an era when various functional departments within a firm focused on their own self-interests and were apparently difficult to coordinate. In such an era, however, when firms (not customers) had the upperhand in the marketplace, there really was no great incentive for them to strive toward a coordinated focus on customer satisfaction. Today customers (not firms) have the upperhand, due to the wider choice of products and the greater "protection" that they have compared to just a couple of decades ago. In the present marketing environment, not only is a well coordinated customer orientation desirable, it is also quite feasible to implement, as will be demonstrated below.

Searle Diagnostics, Inc. has set up a system through which R&D personnel can directly monitor the firm's markets to provide proper direction for its R&D efforts.[3] The still-growing reputation of McDonald's as a purveyor of truly fast food, reasonably priced and of reliable quality, is no fluke. McDonald's success is the result of a well-planned production process that originated as a means of satisfying customers' needs, rather than as an end in itself. While many other fast food outlets are currently struggling to stay profitable, McDonald's—due to its early and wholehearted adoption of the marketing concept—has a comfortable niche in the market and is continuing to open new outlets in the United States as well as overseas.[4] As these examples illustrate, considering the marketing concept as being impractical, on grounds that it is impossible to achieve a unified customer focus across various departments within a firm, is no more than a cop out.

What about the accusation that the increasing degree of customer orientation is stifling the product innovativeness of U.S. firms? Recent empirical evidence suggests that firms that have adopted the marketing concept are no less likely to be truly innovative than those that have not.[5] Furthermore, the philosophy of customer orientation can actually *aid* the development of innovative products that are likely to be winners when introduced.[6] The development and highly successful introduction of AIM toothpaste, the first "regular and gel toothpaste in one" product to appear on the market, is a case in point.[7]

Mistrust of the marketing concept is the result of misconceptions rather than any basic flaws in it. The marketing concept can be valuable in ensuring a firm's success in the marketplace. What may not be readily apparent, however, is the fact that it also can make significant contributions towards improving business efficiency. This point deserves careful attention, especially from firms that have doubts about adopting the marketing concept. Firms not fully committed to the marketing concept also are likely to be skeptical about marketing research, which is a key ingredient in implementing the marketing concept. Such firms, when pressured to improve the efficiency of their operations, are likely to ax their expenditures on marketing research, thinking that it will be a sound cost-saving measure. Ironically, they may actually squeeze the last breath of life from whatever customer orientation they have; hence they may inadvertently pass up the potential contributions that a customer orientation could make towards improving the efficiency of their operations. Nothing could be more penny-wise and pound-foolish.

The Link with Business Efficiency

What is business efficiency or productivity? The most frequently mentioned measures of business efficiency are stated in production terms. Output per manhour, units produced per employee, and dollar value of output per dollar of investment are commonly found in discussions about business efficiency. Although these measures serve as useful yardsticks, business efficiency can, and perhaps should, be viewed from a much broader perspective. A firm may manufacture products very efficiently at the lowest possible cost per unit; however, if it *sells* very little of its output, can it be considered efficient? Most likely not. The costs of carrying large quantities of inventory, and the costs associated with ultimately scrapping unsold units, can be viewed as inefficiencies on the part of the firm. In order to appreciate fully the contributions of the marketing concept to business efficiency, it should be viewed as being multifaceted.

Firms that wholeheartedly embrace the marketing concept ultimately will have a solid sales advantage over their competitors. Increased sales volume can lead to a stream of benefits, such as production economies of scale, faster inventory turnover, and better utilization of marketing as well as manufacturing resources. No one can deny that benefits like these will contribute to improved business efficiency. Thus, the marketing concept can augment the general efficiency of a firm through improved sales performance.

A sincere concern for customer needs often can offer an extra bonus by suggesting useful changes in a firm's operating procedures—changes that can simultaneously result in improved operating efficiency and increased customer satisfaction. Until recently, IBM Corporation had three sales divisions (data processing, general systems, and office products) that independently called on customers. This product-oriented approach was causing a lot of confusion and annoyance among IBM's customers. With rapidly evolving technology, the product offerings of the three divisions started to overlap, and the same customers were often confronted by three separate salespeople selling seemingly similar products. Fortunately for IBM, its keen sense of customer satisfaction and service enabled it to detect and remedy this problem. As part of a recent reorganization of its sales operations, it decided to merge its three sales divisions into a single information systems group which would sell and service all products manufactured by IBM.[8] The merging of the three divisions, which apparently was initiated by a concern for customers, is not only likely to increase customer satisfaction, but also likely to improve operating efficiency.

The AmEx company, which issues the well-known American Express card, is another firm in which the pursuit of a customer-oriented philosophy resulted in substantial operating efficiencies. Based on an analysis of inquiries from customers applying for an American Express card, AmEx found that these customers got impatient if they did not receive a response within three weeks. AmEx also discovered that it took an average of *five weeks* to process credit card applications. Acknowledging that the credit card applicants had every right to become impatient, AmEx took measures to tackle this problem. For instance, a task force was appointed to examine the entire application-processing operation. This task force broke the operation into discrete elements, measured how long each one took, set performance standards, and recommended ways of meeting them. As a result, AmEx was able to cut the average application processing time to a mere two weeks. Similar scrutiny of other operations led to significant reductions in the time it took AmEx to replace lost cards and to respond to enquiries from merchants. Together, these measures boosted AmEx's sales revenue by $2.4 million, of which $1.4 million was profit.[9] That is profit return of over 58 percent on the incremental sales. What better testimonial could there be for the capability of a customer orientation to contribute to improved business efficiency?

Boosting Employee Morale

The marketing concept's potential for improving business efficiency is not limited to the kinds of direct operating efficiencies that have been discussed so far. Adopting the marketing concept also can add indirectly to a firm's efficiency by boosting the morale of its employees. The organizational literature is replete with research results that show a positive link between employee morale and productivity. A number of rather obvious factors can influence the morale of employees in a firm: the degree of job security provided by the firm, the firm's pay policy, working conditions in the firm, and so on. However, when a firm ignores its customers and undervalues their needs, it may not be readily apparent that it may simultaneously be sowing seeds of frustration among its employees.

Employees like to take pride in their firm and its products. They may be unable to do so if their firm is not customer oriented. The lack of customer orientation and the resulting customer dissatisfaction ultimately can lead to undesirable outcomes—ranging from a drop in sales, at best, to serious public accusations against the firm, at worst. Employees of a firm with a lackluster performance record and a tarnished public image would find it difficult to be in high spirits. Consequently, their morale and productivity will most likely wane. Of course, adopting the marketing concept cannot in itself guarantee high employee morale; as already pointed out,

employee morale is a function of a variety of factors. A genuine customer orientation, however, ultimately can make a significant contribution to employee morale and productivity.

Let me illustrate my preceding arguments with some features of the U.S. auto industry, which is severely affected by Japanese competition. Although we hear a lot of talk these days, especially from U.S. auto companies, about unfair Japanese competition, it is hard not to notice that the Japanese auto makers are more customer oriented than their U.S. counterparts.[10] Contrary to what the accusation of unfair Japanese competition would lead us to believe, Japanese cars in the United States do not have a price advantage over similar U.S. cars. Indeed, based on actual selling prices, U.S. cars perhaps sell for less than comparable Japanese models.

Why then have the Japanese been so successful? The answer lies in their turning out high-quality cars (at least as perceived by customers) with the features deemed important by customers. More relevant is the fact that Japanese auto workers take great pride in their firms and their cars, which in turn may be reflected in their high productivity and product quality. How many U.S. auto workers can be said to be genuinely proud of their firms and their cars? Seeing U.S. auto workers driving to and from work in Japanese cars is not unusual. The apparent lack of customer orientation of U.S. auto firms, and their dismal performance in the marketplace, perhaps do not offer much to be proud about. If so, it is doubtful that the morale and productivity of U.S. auto workers are currently as high as they could be.

Reap Handsome Dividends

Firms that are willing to make the commitment to implement the marketing concept, especially by providing adequate resources for researching customer needs, can reap handsome dividends through improved business efficiency. Firms that have misconceptions about the marketing concept may only pay lip service to it, however. Less than full commitment to the marketing concept may lead to haphazard customer research, which can be counterproductive. For such research may not provide the kind of comprehensive information needed to implement

potentially productive strategies. Worse still, it may provide erroneous information and hence lead to wrong strategies.

In either case, the end result is likely to be wasted resources and increased skepticism about the marketing concept. Hence, firms must assimilate the substance of the marketing concept wholeheartedly if they want to derive maximum benefits from it. To perceive the marketing concept as merely a cover that a firm can use to conceal its product-oriented blemishes would be unwise. Rather, a firm will do well to view the marketing concept as a potent elixir that it can use to rid itself permanently of any product-oriented blemishes. The marketing concept, if properly conceived and put into effect, can aid—not erode—business efficiency.
∎

1 To get a feel for recent criticisms of the marketing concept, see, for example, Peter C. Riesz, "Revenge of the Marketing Concept," *Business Horizons* 26, no. 3 (June 1980): 49-53.
2 William S. Sachs and George Benson, "Is It Time to Discard the Marketing Concept?," *Business Horizons* 21, no. 4 (August 1978): 68-74; Ronald W. Stampfl, "Structural Constraints, Consumerism, and the Marketing Concept," *MSU Business Topics* 26, no. 1 (Spring 1978): 5-16; Edward M. Tauber, "How Marketing Research Discourages Major Innovation," *Business Horizons* 17, no. 3 (June 1974): 22-26.
3 William White, "The Research Survey—A Way to Bridge Gap Between Lab and Market," *Research Management* 21, no. 4 (pp. 14-18).
4 "McDonald's: The Original Recipe Helps It Defy a Downturn," *Business Week*, May 4, 1981, pp. 161-162.
5 Leigh Lawton and A. Parasuraman, "The Impact of the Marketing Concept on New Product Planning," *Journal of Marketing* 44, no. 1 (Winter 1980): 19-25.
6 For further discussion of this point, see A. Parasuraman, "Hang On to the Marketing Concept!," *Business Horizons*, 24, no. 5 (September/October 1981): 38-40.
7 "Close-Up, Aim Not Ovate, but They Were Nest Eggs for Lever: Johnson," *Marketing News* 10, no. 24 (June 2, 1978): 7-8.
8 "An Overhaul That Will Strengthen IBM's Hand," *Business Week*, October 19, 1981, pp. 46-47.
9 "Boosting Productivity at American Express," *Business Week*, October 5, 1981, pp. 62+.
10 "U.S. Autos Losing Big Segment of the Market—Forever?," *Business Week*, March 24, 1980, pp. 78-88.

A. PARASURAMAN is an associate professor of marketing at Texas A&M University.

Keith K. Cox

Marketing in
the 1980s—Back to Basics

The profession of marketing will be facing some difficult environmental trends in the forthcoming decade. To adapt to the demands for greater marketing productivity, marketing managers need more than 'business as usual' attitudes.

AS THE business world moves into a new decade, probing questions are being raised concerning strategic planning and marketing strategy. How valuable is the strategic-planning process for an organization? What environmental opportunities and threats will influence managers in developing their corporate strategies? How should the functional area of marketing be integrated into the broader organizational concept of strategic planning? What specific marketing strategies will be appropriate? This article addresses these four questions and assesses their impact in the marketplace during the 1980s.

Dr. Cox *is Professor of Marketing at the University of Houston, Texas and President of the American Marketing Association.*

What is strategic planning? Contrary to some conceptions, it is not a fancy type of forecasting, a bundle of statistical techniques, or the making of future decisions (although it deals with future viability of present decisions). Strategic planning determines how organizational decision makers use planning over a period of time. Ideally, a strategic plan should start with an organization's environment—

Environment → Organization

This means that the organization first studies the environment in which it is operating, with emphasis on inherent opportunities and threats. It then formulates a strategy that promises to achieve the corporate objectives.[1]

However, because an underlying premise in strategic planning is that organizations should adapt to environmental changes, organizations usually plan in reverse order—

Organization → Environment

Thus existing organizational structure and systems are assumed to be sound because they worked successfully in the past. Then, using strategies that are manageable within that framework, the organization scans the environment for the best opportunities. For instance, a hospital sets up its objectives and organization to attract a certain number of tubercular patients. Then it searches the environment for that type of patient. The irony is that there are fewer such patients today, thanks to miracle drugs.[2] Therefore, the hospital has set up an efficient, but not an effective, operation. However, as Peter Drucker has observed, it is better to do the right thing than to do things right.

The strategic-planning process involves articulating basic goals and missions of an organization and then matching them up with existing environmental opportunities (Exhibit 1). Through this matching process key leverages are identified for exploitation.

Finance, marketing, production, logistics, and other major functional areas then should develop and adapt strategies that are consistent and supportive of these key leverages.

Basic Missions

An organization needs to define the basic business it wishes to be in. Equally important, in many cases, is to identify what business the organization does *not* want to be in. Marcel Bich, president of Societe Bic, stated that the basic mission of Bic was to "manufacture and sell only products that can be made cheaply, used relatively briefly, and then thrown away."[3] Bic's product line of ball-point pens, disposable lighters, and disposable razors logically fits into the company's overall mission.

The American Marketing Association developed a formal mission statement in 1979: "The American Marketing Association is a professional society of individual members with an interest in the study, teaching, or practice of marketing. Our principal roles are first, to urge and assist the professional development of our members, and second, to advance the science and practice of the marketing discipline."[4] The first role clearly identifies continuing education and professional development as basic to the organization's mission, while the second role implies that the existing diversity of publications (*Journal of Marketing*, *Journal of Marketing Research*, *Marketing News*) is directly germane to the mission of the organization.

Unfortunately, many mission statements are so general or broad that they are not helpful in strategic planning. Examples are:
● To serve humanity in a profitable way. (What does this exclude?)
● To maximize long-run profits. (Great mission, but how do we attain this ideal?)
● To educate young people who are critical thinkers.[5] (How would you implement this general platitude?)

As many organizations turn to strategic planning as a useful concept in the new decade, they must increasingly describe their basic mission in clearer operational terms.

Environmental Assessments

Vast environmental changes will take place in the 1980s. This discussion will examine a few of the major areas that will have an impact on organizations in general and on marketing specifically.

Economic Environment: I predict that one of the major economic threats for organizations in the next 10 years will be continued inflation, for a number of reasons—
● Inflation rates (13.3% in 1979) are the highest since immediately after World War II.
● Productivity growth (−0.9% in 1979) has leveled off.
● The energy crisis will continue, with OPEC influencing a spiraling increase in gasoline prices.

One of the major challenges of organizations in this decade will be to adapt to institutionalized inflation. This will have tremendous implications for both organizational and marketing strategies. Potential harmful effects of adapting to inflation include—
● Reduced usage of entertainment industries, like theme parks, ski resorts, and summer camps, that are located far from major population centers.
● Reduced housing demand in suburbs far from central business districts.
● Elimination of large gas-guzzler automobiles (in spite of the fact that many Americans still want them).

Potential positive effects of adapting to inflation are—
● Resurgence of business growth in cities, relative to suburbs.
● Increased sales of energy-saving products.
● Increased emphasis by many buyers on price as a major consideration in their buying behavior.

Political Environment: Conflicting trends seem to be occurring in the area of government regulation of business. On one hand, a tremendous growth of government regulation in business is evident—
● The cost of complying with governmental regulations continues to rise rapidly.

● Corporate decisions increasingly run into a law or a regulation.[6]
● Managers are being implicated in criminal actions, even though they may not have participated directly.

One noticeable countertrend is the movement toward deregulation, especially within some of the older federal government agencies—
● Deregulation of the airline industry, providing more managerial flexibility in pricing and routing decisions.
● Cutback of a number of controversial proposed rules by the Federal Trade Commission (FTC).
● Elimination of many Interstate Commerce Commission rules affecting the railroad and trucking industries.

The logic of this deregulation is, "If the costs of federal rules appear too burdensome and if the marketplace is working reasonably well, cut back on existing regulations and avoid imposing new ones."[7]

A series of recent legal court decisions in the area of professional services should have major impact in the 1980s—
● Professional groups such as doctors and lawyers are not exempt from anti-trust regulation.
● Commercial speech (advertising) has received the protection of the First Amendment, and many state laws banning prescription advertising have been eliminated.[8]
● First Amendment freedom has also been extended to advertising by lawyers.[9]
● The American Medical Association has been barred by the FTC from restricting advertising by doctors.

In the 1980s the changing legal environment should have a major impact on the marketing strategy of professional service organizations.

Cultural Environment: Organizations will continue to have difficulty assessing the cultural environment during the next 10 years. Values of individuals continue to change as a result of experiences and interactions with such institutions as the family, church, and school. Some of the major changes include—
● The changing influence of the family with the rise of single parents, more mobility, changing roles of women, smaller families, more working wives, and the impact of television on children.
● Religion's declining influence in

instilling traditional values and attitudes in people.[10]

● The expansion of educational opportunities to the middle and lower classes, especially at the junior-college and university level; and the increasingly analytical approaches to teaching, encouraging students to question many existing values.

Given the changing values in society, the major life-styles of people in the 1980s will continue to reflect different values of individuals—

● People want instant gratification in their consumption of goods and services. Couples no longer want to wait to buy a home until they "can afford it."

● The use of credit is seen as necessary by consumers in their 20s and 30s in order to achieve instant gratification, as opposed to the traditional protestant ethic of earning money before spending it.

● People want life-simplification products with both time- and labor-saving features. The minimization of search-time in buying products and services should continue.

The net effect of these economic, legal, and cultural environmental changes implies that strategic planning should become more important as organizations attempt to cope with environmental trends in the 1980s.

Organizational Assessment

After a company assesses future environmental trends, it must assess its strengths and weaknesses in order to match up organizational strengths with environmental opportunities.

Organizational Leveraging: The results of matching an organization with its environment are referred to as the key leverages of the organization. Exhibit 2 summarizes the estimate of the leveraging strength of eight different organizations in terms of four functional areas—production, marketing, finance, and distribution. Some general observations are—

● Organizations in different industries have varying leveraging strengths in the functional areas.

● Finance is almost never a low-leverage strength in a successful organization.

● Retailing firms and organizations selling mass consumer products have marketing and distribution strength.

● Organizations selling industrial products have production and finance strength.

● Organizations selling services rather than goods have production (expert service) strength.

A major implication of leveraging is that any functional area may be less important than others in achieving its strategic-planning objectives, depending on the organization. Therefore, no functional area should set its strategy in isolation from the strategic planning of the total organization.

Role of Marketing: The marketing concept holds that the key task of the organization is to determine the needs and wants of target markets and to adapt the organization to deliver the desired satisfaction more effectively and efficiently than its competitors.[11] In an article on marketing myopia, Ted Levitt has vividly articulated the value of the marketing concept as a way of thinking.[12] Yet, what if an organization's basic strength lies not in strong consumer markets but in production technology, finance, or distribution? In this situation, pushing the marketing concept could be inappropriate or dangerous in terms of key organizational leverages. Sometimes the production technology of an industry may dictate that management take an existing

product and look for a customer need, rather than start with the need and develop a product.[13] By-products in a chemical company, for instance, can be viewed as products for which a need has not yet been identified.

In the 1960s many forest-product companies lost sight of the fact that their chief asset was their timberlands. However, those companies that made a serious effort at strategic planning and took careful stock of their strengths and weaknesses discovered that their production and logistics strengths were much more appropriate for organizational leveraging than their marketing strengths.[14] Even when marketing has strong leveraging strength in an organization, the problem of satisfying needs in the marketplace still exists. How do decision makers determine what needs will be addressed to which target audiences? Without a basic mission statement, there frequently is a lack of consensus regarding the basic goals and objectives of an organization.

Marketing in the 1980s

From a strategic viewpoint, the marketing discipline needs to adapt to a number of strong environmental trends in the 1980s. The dual impact of increased energy costs and high inflation means that marketing executives must place increased emphasis on marketing productivity. Small retail businesses and

Exhibit 1: Strategic-planning model

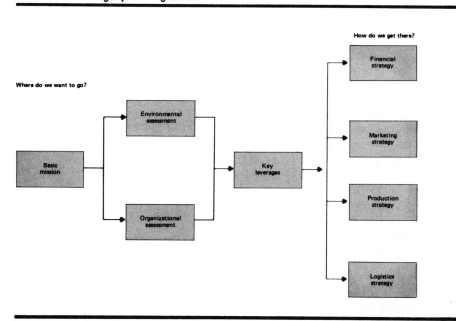

Exhibit 2: Leveraging strengths

Organization	Functional area			
	Production	Marketing	Finance	Distribution
Exxon	High	Low	High	Medium
Coca-Cola	Low	High	Medium	High
Bank of America	Medium	Medium	High	Low
U.S. Steel	High	Low	High	Low
Sears	Medium	High	Medium	High
Price Waterhouse	High	Low	Medium	Low
7-Eleven Stores	Low	High	Medium	High
IBM	High	Medium	High	Medium

organizations with a low share of market will be particularly vulnerable to continued inflation. Specific marketing tactics that may be appropriate for the 1980s include competing with fewer segmented target markets, pruning existing product lines, and expanding standardized products and services.

Marketing Productivity: More emphasis should be placed on the whole area of marketing productivity. Marketing decision makers should become more profit-oriented than sales-oriented. The challenge for increased marketing productivity is perhaps greater than for production efficiency in the 1980s. As many writers have suggested, there is substantially more inefficiency in marketing than in production. Even though it may be difficult to measure marketing efficiency, there is a desperate need to develop "quick and dirty" tools that produce at least satisfactory if not optimal answers. As one seasoned marketing manager put it, "Why use a scalpel when a meat-ax will do?" We need to take less sophisticated tools and examine at least some of the major marketing expenditures for inefficiency.

Vulnerability of Small Retailers: While the "mom and pop" grocery store and the corner gas station may be part of the American dream, if small retailers continue trying to be everything to everybody, they will also continue to be vulnerable to inflation, technological changes, and lack of adequate finances. Choices available to small retailers who still want to be their own boss appear to be—
● Specialize and concentrate on a specific core market.
● Do nothing and attempt to survive in a hostile environment.

● Push for special legislation that would protect small retailers.

In the long run, the most feasible retail strategy may be to concentrate on a small core market and attempt to be as efficient as possible. Small grocery stores could specialize and custom-tailor their operations to a specific neighborhood market. For independent gas stations, one tactic would be to increase personalized services and attempt to build a hard core of loyal customers.

The problem of continuing to do business as usual in retailing goes beyond the threat of inflation. The growth of mail-order retail business seems likely in the 1980s. With the increase in working women and the technological advances in home computers and two-way communication television, mail-order retailing should become more attractive. Large chain and variety stores will enter the 1980s in a fighting mood with emphasis on more productivity.

The push for special legislation to protect small retailers is a likely possibility in this decade. Unfortunately, much of this type of legislation will result in more inefficiency in the marketplace. For example, current state laws that protect independent service stations should slow the decline in the number of service stations. However, now that the general public has accepted self-service at the gas pump, having large numbers of service stations is obsolete and inefficient. In the long run, political solutions may be self-defeating, as small retailers become less competitive.

Companies With Small Market Shares: Organizations that have a low share of market and continue to compete in the total market will be very vulnerable in

the 1980s. The marketing expenditures required to support this strategy are usually large, and the productivity is generally very low. Chrysler Corporation is an example of an organization that refuses to recognize that it can no longer efficiently compete across the board with Ford and General Motors. Companies with small shares of market should practice more concentrated marketing strategies whereby they can develop a dominant niche or segment of customers. For example—
● American Motors is concentrating on the Jeep four-wheel-drive vehicle instead of competing directly with GM and Ford.
● Southwest Airlines has developed a dominant core of commuter businessmen rather than competing with Braniff for all business in its geographical territory.
● United Parcel is concentrating on business customers in competing with the U.S. Postal Service.

Less Market Segmentation: Fewer market segments may be economically viable in an era of energy shortages and inflation. To the extent that organizations have to move closer to an undifferentiated strategy and away from extreme segmentation, the satisfaction of customers' needs could be adversely affected. Yet this may be a price that the American consumer has to pay. As the cost of products and services continues to soar, the values and attitudes of many consumers may change. In return for a lower price, consumers may be willing to buy a product or service that is not as precisely tailored to their desires as it presumably would have been in an era of stable prices.[15] Some home builders have been successful in selling houses stripped down to basic necessities for a cheaper price. Many foreign corporations entering the U.S. market have appealed to much broader market segments than the existing competitors and then charged lower prices.

Pruning Product Lines: Closely related to the strategy of less segmentation is the increasing pressure to streamline existing product lines. The reluctance of many marketing managers to enthusiastically spend time on problems relating to product elimination is well recognized. Somehow, it is much more exciting and rewarding to develop new products. But at what point does a marketing manager abandon the obsolete nine-sided pretzel machine, even though the original founder of the company personally invented it 58 years ago? I'm not sure a company can afford the luxury of keeping outmoded products in an inflationary era. Here are some examples of how companies have pruned product lines—

• White Industries reduced its 40 models of refrigerators to the 30 that represented 85% of sales.

• Grocery "box" stores like Jewel T are offering approximately 500 fast-moving grocery items at significant price savings by minimizing operating costs.

• General Motors has standardized its automobile engines, and the number of options have been reduced.[16]

Growth of Standardized Products and Services: The 1980s should see an increased acceptance by many consumers of generic products and standardized professional services, which appear to be natural growth areas in an inflationary environment.

Generic food products are expanding in the marketplace in spite of strong opposition from the sellers of both national brands and private labels. Increasing their line of generic food products continues to be a viable strategy for a number of supermarket chains.[17] Yet this phenomenon seems to violate the first principle of retailing: Retailers should always trade the customer up to more expensive products, not down to cheaper ones. Most of the supermarket trade magazines like *Progressive Grocer* and *Chain Store Age* have editorialized that the expansion of generic food products is an undesirable retailing practice. Only the buyers seem to like generic food products.

Generic drugs also look like a big growth area in the 1980s. Following the legal challenges to state laws that have prohibited retailers from advertising prescription prices, and the growing pressure to allow pharmacists to fill prescriptions generically, many buyers will probably elect to buy generic drugs instead of the more expensive branded drugs. Since many branded drugs have traditionally had very high markups, this pricing strategy may be increasingly vulnerable. With overall health-care prices rising faster than the rate of inflation, consumers may be very willing to substitute generic drugs for the expensive branded ones. In fact, the armed services and many state agencies have bought generic drugs for years.

The use of standardized professional services should increase greatly in the 1980s. Legal clinics, hospital clinics, and dental clinics that specialize in standard, routine services at a cheaper price will be received with enthusiasm by many consumers. The cherished tradition prized by almost all professional-service associations is a reliance on the one-to-one customized relationship between the professional and his client. But like some organizations' extensive, inefficient product lines, customized professional services are very expensive to the customer. With standardization and simplification, many services can be priced more cheaply and still be profitable because of volume—

• Dental clinics will become popular for routine services like cleaning teeth. Both Sears and Montgomery Ward set up dental clinics in California in 1979.

• Legal clinics will increasingly provide services like uncontested divorces and simple title searches at a cheaper price.

• H & R Block has pioneered the use of standardized income tax services in the accounting profession.

Now that advertising professional services is no longer illegal at the state level, their use becomes a significant opportunity, which should expand as inflation continues and consumers are willing to make the tradeoff of accepting more standard service for a cheaper price. People will increasingly resist paying $300 a day to treat an infected toenail in the hospital when an outpatient clinic is available at a much cheaper cost.

Conclusion

The 1980s may be a difficult time for marketing decision makers. First, emphasis on marketing productivity should be the name of the game for marketing in this decade; increased questioning of marketing cost will be frustrating for marketers. Second, the marketing concept and its orientation toward buyers' needs must be more fully integrated into the strategic-planning process. This, in turn, implies that *all* functional areas (including marketing) must develop and operate their strategies more closely, within the broad strategic guidelines of the organization. Third, no major marketing innovations appear to be on the horizon to revolutionize the marketing discipline in the near future.

In summary, "back to the basics" may be an appropriate philosophy for marketing in the 1980s.□

1. Philip Kotler, *Marketing Management: Analysis, Planning and Control* (Englewood Cliffs, New Jersey, Prentice-Hall, 1980), p. 96.

2. Ibid., p. 97.

3. "Bich: A Strategy Based on a Single Idea," *Business Week*, February 28, 1977, pp. 60-61.

4. American Marketing Association, *Strategic Plan for the American Marketing Association* (Chicago, American Marketing Association, 1979), p. 71.

5. Kenneth Mortimer and Michael Tierney, *The Three "R's" of the Eighties: Reduction, Reallocation, and Retrenchment* (Washington, D.C., American Association of Higher Education, 1979), p. 55.

6. "Complaints About Lawyers," *U.S. News and World Report*, July 21, 1978, p. 44.

7. "Federal Agencies Ease, Lift Some Regulations That Burden Business," *The Wall Street Journal*, September 4, 1979, p. 14.

8. Virginia State Board of Pharmacy v. Virginia Citizens Consumer Council, Inc., U.S. 96 S. Ct. 1817 (1976).

9. Bates v. State Bar of Arizona, 45 U.S. L.W. 4895 (1977).

10. David Kollat and Roger Blackwell, *Direction 1980—Changing Life Styles* (Columbus, Ohio, Management Horizons, Inc., 1975).

11. Kotler, *Marketing Management*, p. 31.

12. Theodore Levitt, "Marketing Myopia," *Harvard Business Review*, July-August 1960, pp. 24-47.

13. Keith K. Cox, "Marketing Concept May Be in Some Danger in 1980's," *Marketing News*, August 24, 1979, p. 5.

14. Stuart U. Rich, *Marketing of Forest Products: Text and Cases* (New York, McGraw-Hill, 1970).

15. Alan Resnik, Peter Turney, and J. Barry Mason, "Marketers Turn to 'Countersegmentation,' " *Harvard Business Review*, September-October 1979, pp. 100-106.

16. Ibid., p. 102.

17. "Generic Products Are Winning Noticeable Shares of Market From National Brands, Private Labels," *The Wall Street Journal*, August 6, 1979, p. 6.

Part II
The Marketing Program

Section II-A
Premarket Planning

"The Dimensions of Industrial New Product Success and Failure," by R.G. Cooper, reports the results of an investigation on what separates successful from unsuccessful new industrial products.

"Committing Economic Suicide: A Review of the Status of Industrial Marketing Planning," by R.J. Voorn, stresses the need for careful, formal industrial marketing planning.

"The Role of Planning in the Marketing of New Products," by M.P. Peters, describes product planning guidelines and alternative strategies that should be considered throughout a new product's development.

"Planning for Technological Innovation—Developing the Necessary Nerve," by E.P. Ward, addresses long-range product planning concepts and procedures.

"The Adoption of New Industrial Products," by G. Hayward, reports on research findings in the areas of product diffusion research and the characteristics of product innovations.

"Designing a Long Range Marketing Strategy for Services," by C. Grönroos, presents a three-stage model used as a frame of reference for long-range marketing strategy.

R.G. COOPER

This article reports the results of Project NewProd, an extensive investigation into what separates successful from unsuccessful new industrial products. Multivariate methods are used to probe this success/failure question. The dimensions underlying success and failure are identified. The dominant role of product strategy and the need for a strong market orientation clearly are demonstrated.

THE DIMENSIONS OF INDUSTRIAL NEW PRODUCT SUCCESS AND FAILURE

THE high incidence of industrial new product failure has long been acknowledged (Booz, Allen, and Hamilton 1968). The call has been for a greater marketing orientation, more marketing research, and improved marketing launch efforts as the route to stemming the tide of new product failures (Cooper 1975; Crawford 1977; Hatch 1957; Hopkins and Bailey 1971). However surprisingly little has been done in the way of empirical research to probe the question of what makes a successful new product. In this article, we report the results of such an empirical study whose purpose was to identify the major factors which differentiate between successful and unsuccessful new industrial products.

Being able to "predict a winner" in the new prod-

R.G. Cooper is Associate Dean and MBA Director, Faculty of Management, McGill University, Montreal, PQ, Canada. This research was funded by the Associates Research Workshop, School of Business, University of Western Ontario, London, Canada; and by Office of Science and Technology, Department of Industry, Trade, and Commerce, Ottawa, Canada.

uct game has been an elusive goal. A variety of tools and techniques have been provided to assist in screening new product ideas, including rating scale and checklist models to judge the overall suitability of the product idea to the company and concept test models to screen ideas for market acceptability (Wind 1973). One of the problems with the rating scale or checklist approach is that neither the screening variables included nor their relative weightings, whether variable or fixed, have been empirically derived; they simply are based on subjective estimates (Shocker, Gensch, and Simon 1969). Thus, a major impetus for research into new product success/failure discriminators is the desire to provide an empirical base to new product screening models.

An equally important reason for investigating success versus failure is the potential for developing prescriptive guides for the new product process. Many of the variables which might separate the "winners" from the "losers" are within the control of the firm. A knowledge of what these variables are and their relative importance would lead to corrective action to improve the way the firm develops and launches new products.

Reprinted with permission from J. Marketing, vol. 43, pp. 93–103, Mar. 1979.
Published by the American Marketing Association.

What Separates the "Winners" From The "Losers"

Recent years have witnessed several research thrusts into industrial product innovation. The Booz, Allen and Hamilton studies (1968) in the mid 1960s provided an overview of the field and highlighted many of the problems faced by product developers. Another research direction was the investigation of new product failures (Cooper 1975; Davidson 1976; Hopkins and Bailey 1971; Lazo 1965; NICB 1964). The rationale for this research was that an understanding of one's past deficiencies is the first step to a prescriptive solution. Shortly after, a number of researchers began to probe case histories of new product successes with the goal of uncovering the key to success (Cooper 1976; Globe, Levy, and Schwartz 1973; Marquis 1969; Myers and Marquis 1969; Roberts and Burke 1974). Such research, typified by the Myers and Marquis studies, identified the need for a strong market orientation, even in the case of complex and moderate to high technology innovations.

More recent research has focused on comparing and contrasting new product successes and failures. Such research is based on the premise that only through a direct comparison of successes with failures will the variables that differentiate the two be identified. Project SAPPHO[1] in 1972 was the first of these success versus failure studies (Rothwell 1972). The results of it, and several other European studies that followed, identified a number of key facets of product innovation — variables that described the process, venture, organization, industry, and environment — which were related to successful new product outcomes (Gerstenfeld 1976; Kulvik 1977; Rothwell 1974, 1976; Rothwell et al. 1974; Utterback et al. 1976).

These success/failure comparison studies, while the most fruitful in terms of useful and interesting results, have not been without their problems. There have been the usual methodological ailments which commonly plague any new research field. Operational definitions are often vague or inconsistent (for example, how does one define "a new product success"?). Evidence of conceptual model building is rare; as a result, there appears little logic or consistency in the variables any particular researcher chooses to measure. Sample sizes are typically small; their method of selection is often suspect; the data analysis techniques are naive. And finally, from a North American and marketer's perspective, the studies lack some relevance. Virtually all of the research is set in a European context, while the researchers themselves are nonmarketing people (industrial economists, technologically-oriented researchers, and so on). Hence the variables probed are not ones of greatest interest to marketers.

The current research was designed to overcome many of the problems that have beset previous work. First, a conceptual model was outlined, and from this model a set of variables was identified that were expected to impact on new product outcomes. Next, a substantial and randomly-selected sample — about 100 successes and 100 failures — was utilized. Data analysis techniques used were the multivariate ones familiar to marketers. Finally, the study was set in North America, and focused on variables of particular interest to practicing marketers.[2]

The Research

Previous research has uncovered a great diversity of variables which are related to new product outcomes. A sampling of these findings is provided in Table 1 where correlates of success versus failure are summarized.

A review of the many variables that were found to influence new product outcomes led to the development of a conceptual descriptive model (Cooper 1975, 1979). This communicative model lent structure to the research area by identifying as its elements the main blocks or groups of variables that impact on new product outcomes. Six blocks of particular interest to marketers were singled out for investigation in the current research. These include:

- **The Commercial Entity:** that with which the firm enters the marketplace. This block includes the attributes and advantages of the new product, its price, the nature of the launch efforts, and the production or manufacturing effort underlying the launch. The Commercial Entity is the *result* of the new product process.

- **Information Acquired:** the nature or quality of information acquired (or known) during the new product process. For example, whether the firm had accurate data on market potential, on buyer behavior, on production costs, etc.

- **Proficiency Of Process Activities:** how well certain activities were undertaken during the new product process (if at all), from idea generation to launch. For example, whether or not a detailed market study, pilot production, or a test market were expertly undertaken, or undertaken at all.

---

[1]SAPPHO is an acronym for Scientific Activity Predictor From Patterns With Heuristic Origins.

[2]Although the study was undertaken in Canada, the proximity and similarity with the United States both geographically and in terms of industry structure; nature of firms (many were MNCs); tariff structure; and market characteristics (albeit much smaller than United States) suggest that the research results are likely to be applicable in the United States.

TABLE 1
Recent Findings From Success Versus Failure Investigations

Variables Discriminating Between Success And Failure	Research Study[a]	Type Of Variable
Understanding user needs	1,2,3,6	
Extensive customer-producer interfacing	1,2,3,4,6	
Efficient performance of development process (e.g., few "bugs"; fewer modifications; better planning, etc.)	1,2,3,6	New Product Process
Sales forecasting carried out	1,2,6	
Strong selling (and marketing) effort	1,2,3,6	
Product and/or price advantages	4,7	Launch Effort
Strong promotional, user education effort	1	And
Fewer after sales problems	1,2,3,4,6	Product Offering
No initial marketing difficulties	4	
Market pull (idea derived from market)	1,2,3,4,5,6	
Technology push (for major successes)	5,6,7	Nature of
Good fit with company potentials, resources	3	Venture
Close to current market (familiarity with market)	1,3,4	
Better internal and external communication	1,2,3,4,5,6	
Better coordination of R&D, Marketing, Production	1,2,3,6	Organizational
Product champion or top management support	1,2,4,6	Descriptors
Better planning and systematic approach to innovation	1,3,4,5,6	
Industry maturity (affects nature of venture)	4,6	External:
Business cycle (influenced efforts)	5,6	industry,
Government role (induced efforts)	4,5	market,
Government support insignificant (except for major innovations)	1,4,6	environment

[a]Studies refer to:
1: Rothwell 1972; Rothwell et al. 1974
2: Rothwell 1974 (Hungarian SAPPHO)
3: Kulvik 1977
4: Utterback et al. 1976
5: Gerstenfeld 1976
6: Rothwell 1976
7: Davidson 1976

- **Nature Of The Marketplace:** the characteristics of the new product's market. For example, degree and nature of competition, market-size and growth rate, and product life cycle characteristics.

- **Resource Base Of The Firm:** the compatibility of the resource base of the firm with the requirements of the project; that is the "company/product fit" in terms of a variety of resources, including R&D, production, distribution, and sales force capabilities.

- **Nature Of The Project:** the characteristics of the new product project or venture. For example, the magnitude of the project, the level and complexity of the technology, the innovativeness of the product, the source of the idea.

The delineation of these blocks permitted the development of a list of 77 variables that were expected to be related to new product outcomes. The number of variables and the exploratory nature of the research precluded individual and detailed statements of hypotheses. Nonetheless, a set of general propositions was developed to indicate the expected impact that each major block of variables would have on product outcomes (Table 2). An overview of the 77 variables considered in the research is obtained from Table 3.

A mailed questionnaire was utilized to measure these variables for a large sample of new product successes and failures. A random sample of 177 firms was first selected from a government listing of active industrial product producers.[3]

Firms initially were contacted by telephone to solicit cooperation, identify the appropriate respondent, and provide direction. Respondents within firms were selected to be "functionally neutral" and have an overall knowledge of the firm's total new product efforts. (In smaller firms, the president or owner was typically the respondent; in larger firms, the division manager or

[3]Firms were located in Ontario and Quebec, Canada. The survey was conducted in the latter half of 1977.

TABLE 2
Research Propositions

New product success is expected to be positively related to:

1. products which are superior, have a differential or economic advantage, or are unique relative to competing products; ⎫
2. products where the other elements of the Commercial Entity — selling, distribution, production, etc. — are proficient; ⎬ Commercial Entity

3. projects where considerable technical and market knowledge is acquired; ⎬ Information Acquired

4. projects where the technical, marketing, and evaluative (process) activities are proficiently undertaken; ⎬ Proficiency Of Process Activities

5. products entering mass, large, growing, dynamic, and uncompetitive markets, with a high but unsatisfied need for such products; ⎬ Nature Of Marketplace

6. projects where a high degree of resource compatibility exists between the needs of the project and the resource base of the firm; ⎬ Resource Base Of Firm

7. familiar projects to the firm (do not involve new technologies, new markets, etc.); ⎫
8. market-derived projects (product idea came from the marketplace). ⎬ Nature Of The Project

In addition, other characteristics of the project — for example, whether a custom product or not; whether a true innovation or a "me too" effort; etc.—were expected to impact on product outcomes, but in a moderating way.

corporate new product development officer provided the data.) A detailed questionnaire, which had been extensively pretested (to check clarity, operationality, etc.[4]), was mailed to each respondent. He was requested to select two typical, recent new product projects: one a commercial success, the other a failure. Success and failure were defined from the point of view of the firm, and in terms of profitability (that is, the degree to which a product's profitability exceeded, or fell short of, the minimum acceptable profitability for this type of project or investment, regardless of the way the firm measured profitability). Because of selection errors which could result from difficulties in the use of this operational definition, managers were asked to select products which were clear-cut successes and failures.

The respondent then was asked to characterize each venture on each of the 77 variables that made up the six major blocks. Variables were measured by presenting a phrase or sentence, and requesting the manager to indicate whether the description applied to the project (agree/disagree, 0 to 10 scales).

The eventual sample numbered 102 successes and 93 failures (195 projects) from 103 firms, which represents an effective response rate of 69% after correction for inappropriate or nonexistent firms. A review of the industry categories and sizes of the responding firms revealed no evidence of a response bias.

Results

Preliminary analysis revealed the need to collapse the many variables measured into a more useful and manageable subset (Cooper 1979). The correlation matrix of the 77 characteristics measured for each new product project showed that the great majority were highly intercorrelated, often with correlation coefficients in excess of 0.50. This network of correlations suggested that the 77 variables could be explained by a handful of underlying dimensions.

The Dimensions Of New Product Projects

Eighteen dimensions or factors that describe new product projects were identified and labeled. Factor analysis[5] was utilized to reduce the 77 variables to their underlying factors.[6] All 18 factors had eigenvalues in excess of 1.0; 11 had eigenvalues greater than 2.0 The factors explained 71.3% of the variance in the original 77 variables, and thus appear to describe new product projects fairly well.

The 18 dimensions, in spite of their numbers, proved quite easy to label. In all but the last factor, variable loadings of at least several variables were strikingly high, mostly over 0.60. The factors are identified and labeled in Table 3, which summarizes the important factor loadings and provides an indication of

---

[4]Pretest respondents were personally interviewed following completion of the test questionnaires.

[5]Varimax rotation, SPSS routine.

[6]Although variables were not continuous, the fact that all scales were 11-point (zero — 10) with anchors at each end suggests that an interval scale assumption is not a bad one. Data appeared normally distributed along the scales.

TABLE 3
Factors Underlying New Product Projects

Factor Name (% Variance Explained)*	Variables Loading On Factor	Type Of Variable	Variable Loadings
1. Technical & Production Synergy & Proficiency (28.8%)	Had compatible engineering skills for project	Firm Resources	0.638
	Had compatible production resources for project	Firm Resources	0.601
	Undertook preliminary technical assessment well	Activity	0.691
	Undertook product development well	Activity	0.642
	Undertook in-house prototype test well	Activity	0.639
	Undertook pilot production well	Activity	0.635
	Undertook production start-up well	Activity	0.687
	Knew product technology well	Info. Acquired	0.669
	Knew product design well — no "bugs"	Info. Acquired	0.672
	Knew production process and technology	Info. Acquired	0.794
	Production facilities well geared up	Comm. Entity	0.719
2. Marketing Knowledge And Proficiency (11.7%)	Undertook preliminary market assessment well	Activity	0.470
	Undertook market study well	Activity	0.570
	Undertook test market well	Activity	0.421
	Undertook market launch well	Activity	0.451
	Understood customers' needs, wants	Info. Acquired	0.583
	Understood buyer price sensitivity	Info. Acquired	0.612
	Understood competitive situation	Info. Acquired	0.616
	Understood buyer behavior	Info. Acquired	0.761
	Understood/knew size of potential market	Info. Acquired	0.740
	Were confident about success	Info. Acquired	0.425
	Had a strong sales force launch effort	Comm. Entity	0.408
	Sales force effort well targeted	Comm. Entity	0.507
3. Newness To The Firm (10.1%)	Potential customers were new to firm	Project	0.649
	Product class new to firm	Project	0.758
	Product use (need served) new to firm	Project	0.746
	Production process new to firm	Project	0.516
	Product technology new to firm	Project	0.514
	Distribution, sales force new to firm	Project	0.745
	Advertising, promotion new to firm	Project	0.750
	New competitors for the firm	Project	0.668
4. Product Uniqueness/ Superiority (9.0%)	Highly innovative product, new to market	Project	0.449
	Product had unique features for customer	Comm. Entity	0.799
	Superior to competing products in meeting customer's needs	Comm. Entity	0.832
	Product let customer reduce his costs	Comm. Entity	0.410
	Product did unique task for customer	Comm. Entity	0.564
	Product higher quality than competitor's	Comm. Entity	0.691
5. Market Competitiveness and Customer Satisfaction (6.7%)	Highly competitive market	Market	0.754
	Intense price competition in market	Market	0.765
	Many competitors in market	Market	0.797
	Customers satisfied with competitors' products	Market	0.402
6. Marketing & Managerial Synergy (5.1%)	Had adequate financial resources	Firm Resources	0.576
	Had necessary market research resources	Firm Resources	0.677
	Had needed managerial skills	Firm Resources	0.727
	Had compatible sales force/distribution resources	Firm Resources	0.655
	Had adequate advertising skills	Firm Resources	0.562

the strength and clarity of the evolved factors. The factor analysis was validated using a split-half method: the structure of the factors — variables and loadings — was essentially the same for the two halves of the sample. A total of 19 and 20 factors were generated in the two factor analysis runs (eigenvalues ≥ 1.0), and 14 of the factors were virtually identical to each other (and the same as those in the full-sample run, Table 3).[7]

A review of this list of 18 underlying dimensions reveals that many of them are both familiar and intuitively obvious. The first two dimensions describe a *production/technical* orientation and a *market* orientation, which have been the topic of much discussion and research into product innovation (Kulvik 1977; Rothwell 1974). The current research supports the notion that both dimensions are important characteristics of product projects. Of particular interest is the fact that these two orientations are not mutually exclusive; the dimensions are independent of each other.[8] A project

---

[7]Additionally, percent variance explained by each factor was almost identical at equal number of factors. For example, after 16 factors, 72.0% variance was explained in one half (94.2% after rotation) versus 74.0% in the other half (95.5% after rotation).

[8]Factors are orthogonal (at right angles).

TABLE 3 (continued)

Factor Name (% Variance Explained)*	Variables Loading On Factor	Type Of Variable	Variable Loadings
7. Product Technical Complexity & Magnitude (4.4%)	A high technology product A high per unit price — "big ticket" item Mechanically, technically complex product	Project Project Project	0.820 0.623 0.875
8. Market Need, Growth and Size (3.5%)	Customers had great need for product type Market size (dollar volume) was large High growth market	Market Market Market	0.558 0.570 0.634
9. Strength of Marketing Communications & Launch Effort (3.1%)	Had adequate advertising skills Had a strong sales force launch effort Had a strong advert./promo launch effort Advertising effort well targeted Undertook market launch well	Firm Resources Comm. Entity Comm. Entity Comm. Entity Activity	0.464 0.544 0.762 0.668 0.457
10. Product Determinateness (2.8%)	Market determinateness (product clearly specified by marketplace) Technical determinateness (technical solution clear at start)	Project Project	0.689 0.577
11. Production Start-Up Proficiency (2.5%)	Production facilities geared up (for launch) Production volume adequate to meet demand	Comm. Entity Comm. Entity	0.422 0.526
12. Product Uniqueness (First to Market) (2.2%)	Product did unique task for customer Company first into market with product Existence of potential demand only (no actual demand)	Comm. Entity Comm. Entity Market	0.400 0.616 0.586
13. Existence of a Dominant Competitor/Customers Satisfied (2.1%)	Existence of a dominant competitor Loyalty to competitors' products Customers satisfied with competitors' products	Market Market Market	0.586 0.793 0.494
14. Market Dynamism (1.8%)	Frequent new product introductions in market Users' needs change rapidly in market	Market Market	0.441 0.435
15. Relative Price of Product (1.7%)	Product let customer reduce costs Product priced higher than competing product	Comm. Entity Comm. Entity	−0.457 0.608
16. Proficiency of Precommercialization Activities (1.6%)	Undertook initial idea screening well Undertook preliminary market assessment well Undertook preliminary technical assessment well Undertook market study well Undertook product development well Undertook financial analysis well Role of government in marketplace	Activity Activity Activity Activity Activity Activity Market	0.401 0.374 0.336 0.284 0.212 0.338 0.436
17. Product Customness (1.6%)	Whether product was a custom product Existence of a mass market	Project Market	0.552 −0.542
18. Source of Idea/ Investment Magnitude (1.4%)	Relative magnitude of investment in project Market-derived idea	Project Project	0.288 0.280

*After rotation, add to 100%

simultaneously can have both a strong market orientation *and* a strong technical/production orientation.

Three of the 18 factors identified describe the innovativeness of the venture:

- Newness to the Firm: A project which takes the firm into new markets, new technologies, etc.

- Product Uniqueness: A product which is truly unique; firm is first into the market with type of product.

- Product Uniqueness/Superiority: A product which has significant improvements over previous products making it unique and superior.

Previous literature has often referred to "product innovativeness" as an important descriptor of new products (Davidson 1976; Marquis 1969; Rothwell 1976).

But on closer inspection, it appears that the term "innovativeness" is perhaps too global; there are at least three dimensions of newness quite independent of each other.

A number of dimensions describe the nature of the product or project. These include (references are to previous work identifying similar variables):

- Technical Complexity and Magnitude (Marquis 1969; Myers and Marquis 1969);
- Product Customness (Little 1970);
- Product Determinateness (Globe, Levy, and Schwartz 1973; Roberts and Burke 1974);
- Relative Price of Product (Calantone and Cooper 1977); and
- Source of Idea/Investment Magnitude (Marquis 1969; Myers and Marquis 1969).

That these descriptors evolve in a study of product innovation is not surprising. Indeed all have been mentioned or alluded to in previous work, although not all in one single investigation.

Similarly, some of the market descriptors, namely:

- Market Need, Growth, and Size (Globe, Levy, and Schwartz 1973; Marquis 1969; Rubenstein et al. 1974, 1976);
- Market Dynamism (frequency of new introductions);
- Market Competitiveness (Cooper 1975); and
- Existence of a Dominant Competitor (Cooper 1975).

are also the types of dimensions one might logically expect in a study of new product projects.

Finally, several factors describe the company and its proficiencies, particularly as they pertain to the new product under investigation. The first two — a market orientation and a production orientation — have already been mentioned. But there are others, namely:

- Marketing and Managerial Synergy (Kulvik 1977);
- Strength of Marketing Communications Launch Effort (Rothwell 1972; Rothwell et al. 1974);
- Proficiency of Production Start-Up (Cooper 1975);
- Proficiency of Precommercialization Activities (Cooper 1975).

The 18 dimensions identified help to clarify and simplify the set of variables that describe the new product situation. Instead of working with 77 or more interrelated project characteristics, the problem has been reduced to more manageable proportions: 18 independent dimensions. Not only were the dimensions readily identified and labeled from the results of the factor analysis, but they also appear to be valid. And most important, the dimensions make sense and have meaning to managers.

Success And Failure

The next logical question concerns the relationship between success/failure and the underlying dimensions identified above. Linear discriminant analysis was utilized to relate group membership (success or failure) to the 18 factors in Table 3.[9] Factor scores were calculated for each of the 195 project cases and used as the variables in the discriminant analysis. A total of 11 of the 18 factors entered the discriminant solution, and appeared to differentiate between new product successes and failures. In order of inclusion, these were:

- introducing a unique but superior product;
- having market knowledge and marketing proficiency;
- having technical and production synergy and proficiency;
- avoiding dynamic markets with many new product introductions;
- being in a large, high need, growth market;
- avoiding introducing a high-priced product with no economic advantage;
- having a good "product/company fit" with respect to managerial and marketing resources;
- avoiding a competitive market with satisfied customers;
- avoiding products "new to the firm;"
- having a strong marketing communications and launch effort;
- having a market-derived idea with considerable investment involved.

The coefficients of the discriminant function are shown in Table 4 along with group centroids for the two groups, Success and Failure. The discriminant relationship is a particularly strong one, with 84.10% of the cases correctly classified. (The model had greater accuracy predicting successes than failures, with 89.2% of successes correctly classified.) The Wilks' Lambda criterion for the ability of the variables to discriminate was 0.51 with an associated F statistic of 15.95 (d.f = 11; 183), significant at the 0.001 level.

The discriminant analysis results were validated using Montgomery's (1975) V_3 method for small samples. The limited sample size, the extremely high cost of collecting data, and the focus of the research (on description and explanation, not prediction) pointed to the use of a validation technique which tests for spurious results (as opposed to a hold-out sample valida-

---

[9]Stepwise discriminant analysis, SPSS routine; Wilks' method for selection of variables.

TABLE 4
Discriminant Analysis Results: Determinants Of New Product Success

Factor	Factor Name[a]	Standardized Function Coefficients	Wilks'[b] Lambda	F To Enter or Remove
F4	Product Uniqueness/Superiority	0.527	0.859	31.66
F2	Market Knowledge and Marketing Proficiency	0.465	0.730	33.95
F1	Technical/Production Synergy and Proficiency	0.325	0.680	14.13
F14	Market Dynamism (Frequency of New Product Introductions)	−0.264	0.644	10.65
F8	Market Need, Growth, and Size	0.271	0.610	10.49
F15	Relative Price of Product	−0.252	0.576	10.62
F6	Marketing and Managerial Synergy	0.193	0.557	6.49
F5	Marketing Competitiveness and Customer Satisfaction	−0.186	0.540	5.88
F3	Newness to the Firm	−0.170	0.526	4.93
F9	Strength of Marketing Communications and Launch Effort	0.137	0.517	3.24
F18	Source of Idea/Investment Magnitude	0.114	0.510	2.27

Group Centroids:			
Successes:	0.666	(N = 102)	
Failures:	−0.731	(N = 93)	

[a]in order of inclusion in the discriminant solution.
[b]significant at the 0.001 level.

tion). Observations were scrambled randomly into arbitrary groups, and then the performance of the discriminant analyses observed. The results of the five V_3 runs undertaken stand in sharp contrast to the original discriminant findings: correct classifications around 60%; F values in the low 2.0 to 3.0 range; Wilks' Lambdas equaling 0.90 to 0.95; and relatively few variables entering the solution. These V_3 validations confirm that the figure of 84% correctly classified in the original discriminant analysis is not spurious. The successful validation of the discriminant and factor analyses, the lack of a response bias in the sample, and the nature of the population (see footnote 2) suggest the results can be generalized to industrial product innovation in North America.

Implications To New Product Management

The research provides a vital insight into the factors which separate the successes from the failures in industrial product innovation. The complex problem of new product outcomes has been greatly simplified by identifying 18 underlying dimensions that capture much of the new product situation.

The Keys To Success

- **The single most important dimension** leading to new product success is Product Uniqueness and Superiority. Unique, superior products were typically highly innovative and new to the market (Table 3); incorporated unique features for the customer; met customers' needs better than competing products; allowed the customer to reduce costs or to do something previously impossible; and were of higher quality (tighter specifications, stronger, lasted longer, more reliable, etc.) than competing products. That product uniqueness and superiority is such an important ingredient in new product success is so obvious and truistic that it tends to be overlooked. The product is the core or central strategy in most industrial new product ventures; and it is through the product that the firm must seek its differential advantage.

- **Market Knowledge and Marketing Proficiency** plays a critical role in new product outcomes. Projects which were strong on this dimension were those where the market-oriented activities were proficiently undertaken (market assessment, market studies, test market, market launch). The firm had a sound understanding of the important facets of the market: customers' needs and wants, price sensitivities, buyer behavior, market potential, and competition. Finally, the sales force and distribution effort was strong and well-targeted at launch. The obvious point needs reinforcing: the commercial viability of a new product rests in the hands of its potential customers; and therefore a solid understanding of the marketplace together with an effective market launch effort is vital to new product success.

- **The third most important new product dimension** which impacts on success/failure is a technical one, Technical and Production Synergy and Proficiency. Projects where such synergy and proficiency existed were undertaken in firms with a particularly strong and compatible technical engineering and production and resource base. The technical and production activities were carried out proficiently: preliminary technical assessment, product development, prototype testing, pilot production, and production start-up. In addition, such firms had a thorough understanding of the product and design technology, and also the production process. That all of these technical and production facets are important to new product success has long been taken for granted. Perhaps the most noteworthy conclusion is that this technical dimension, although very important, does *not stand alone* as the most critical dimension to new product success, even in a study of industrial product innovation.

Three Barriers To Success

Another six dimensions are closely related to product outcomes, although not as strongly as the first three. Of these, three are considered to be barriers to success since they are negatively related. These are:

- having a high-priced product, relative to competition (with no economic advantage to the customer);
- being in a dynamic market (with many new product introductions);
- being in a competitive market, where customers are already well satisfied.

The high-priced product dimension and the competitive "brick wall" factor have both been identified as barriers in studies of new product failure (Calantone and Cooper 1977). The dynamic market dimension is somewhat surprising: one might expect that such markets are particularly receptive to new ideas; hence facilitating new introductions. But dynamic markets, characterized by many new product introductions, can become a quagmire of problems and hidden obstacles, and a breeding ground for competitive one-upmanship (Calantone and Cooper 1977). Intense product competition results, often with deadly outcomes for the new product launched into the market.

Three Facilitators

Three contributors to new product success are:

- Marketing and Managerial Synergy
- Strength of Marketing Communications and Launch Effort
- Market Need, Growth, and Size

All three describe the marketplace or the marketing function. That a strong Marketing and Managerial Synergy is critical to success simply echoes the importance of a market orientation in product innovation. This synergy factor (people and skills) complements the more important determinant of success, Market Knowledge and Marketing Proficiency, which focuses on market information and activities.

The strength of the Marketing Communications and Launch Effort also is related to new product outcomes. Again the need for careful attention to the marketing function — sales force, advertising, promotion, and distribution — as a part of the innovation process is reinforced.

The final dimension — being in a high need, high growth, large market — is an obvious and expected result. More surprising is the fact that large, high growth, high need markets do not play an even more pivotal role in new product successes than the research results suggest. One might speculate that such lucrative markets also are attractive to others, making success a competitive and up-hill battle; in contrast there may exist many smaller, apparently less lucrative markets which also offer unique opportunities for new products.

Weakly-Related Factors

Two additional dimensions appear related to new product outcomes, but in a somewhat weaker fashion. Newness to the Firm is a dimension which was clearly identified in the factor analysis and is frequently cited as a proxy for synergy in the literature. Yet the factor entered the discriminant solution towards the end of the analysis, and in other analyses (correlation and multiple regression) did not stand out as a significant factor in product success. One must conclude that although newness is a familiar dimension, it it probably more useful as a moderating or classifying variable than as a direct predictor of outcomes.

Another weakly-related dimension, Source of

Idea/Investment Magnitude, also yielded an unexpected result. Previous work by Marquis (1969) and Myers and Marquis (1969) showed that the majority of innovation successes were market-derived. The implication was that market-derived products are clearly more successful. The current research also revealed that successful products tended to be market-derived (mean of 7.19 on a 0 to 10 scale, 10 = market-derived). The problem is that *failure products are also largely market-derived* (7 out of 10), and that whether a product is market-derived or not — the source of the idea — simply does not differentiate all that well between success and failure.

Dimensions With No Impact On Success

Of particular interest is a review of the many strong dimensions that do not differentiate successes from failures:

- One hotly debated dimension is the "first to market" factor. The current research found that although Product Uniqueness (first to market) is an important dimension describing new product projects (factor analysis results), it is *not* a determinant of success or failure. The results suggest that the advantages of being "first in" are almost equally balanced by the many pitfalls and disadvantages.

- Another important dimension not related to success is the Proficiency of the Precommercialization Activities (market assessment, technical assessment, detailed market study, product development, financial analysis). Note that the market activities did load heavily on other factors that were related to success. The message is that proficiently executing the "front end" of the development process alone is not a condition for success. In contrast, the commercialization phase, or "back end" of the process *was* found to be of particular importance.

- The Intensity of Competition was found to be a barrier to new product success (above); in contrast, the mere existence of a dominant competitor does not impact on product outcomes. Both dimensions are commonly lumped together in a global measure when a manager speaks of "strong competition." The conclusion is that these are two quite independent dimensions; and that only Intensity of Competition is a barrier to success.

- Another factor that has no direct bearing on success/failure is the proficiency of production start-up. The two variables which load most heavily on this dimension, "adequacy of production volume" and "smoothness of start-up," are also highly loaded on another dimension that did impact on success, Technical And Production Synergy and Proficiency. The discriminating factor included production facilities *as well as* a number of other variables, such as technical and engineering proficiencies and synergies. Production capability alone is not the key variable, but must be considered in concert with other vital ingredients as a determinant of success.

Finally, several remaining factors simply describe the product or project, and a priori were not expected to impact directly on success/failure. These include:

- Product Technical Complexity and Magnitude (Big Ticket Item);
- Product Determinateness (degree to which product was predetermined, i.e., market specifications, technical solution); and
- Product Customness.

Such dimensions are likely to be of greater use as classifying or moderating variables, and not so much as determinants of product outcomes.

Conclusion

The secrets to success in industrial product innovation remain a mystery, for the problem is very complex. What this research has done is identify a set of underlying dimensions that can be used to characterize and perhaps cluster new product projects. The identification of the relative importance of each dimension as a determinant of success provides valuable inputs into the screening decision. Moreover, a knowledge of which dimensions are critical to success can be used to suggest needed improvements — which activities need attention, what information is critical, etc. — to individual firms' new product processes.

The research suffers from a number of limitations. A lack of descriptive model building, questions of reliability of the data (after the fact, scaled measures), and issues of predictability are some of the unresolved problems. Overriding all of these is the basic issue: is there really an answer to what makes a new product a success? Perhaps the problem is so complex, and each case so unique, that attempts to develop generalized solutions are in vain.

The research question — what makes a new product a success — is an important one, and so the search will continue. Future research will aim at the development of an empirically-based predictive screening model to improve the idea selection decision. Another research thrust will focus on the moderating impact of other variables: for example, are the determinants of success the *same* for high technology versus low technology areas; for big versus small firms; etc.? Finally, future work should also bring together the type of model derived from this research (empirically derived, based on management opinion) with market concept test methods (Wind 1973) to yield comprehensive new product screening models.

The message from the current research is gratifying to marketers. The critical role of a market orientation, marketing information, marketing communication, and marketing launch strategy was strongly demonstrated. Indeed a review of the nine factors closely linked to success shows that all but one directly or indirectly pertain to the marketing function or to the marketplace. The wisdom of the marketing concept, even for industrial, often high technology new products, prevails.

There are words of warning for marketers as well. The dominant position of product strategy as the central or core strategy in new industrial products was made clearer than ever. While marketing communications, promotion, sales force, and launch strategies certainly were important, *product* stood out above all. Those marketers, often with consumer goods backgrounds, who believe in the preeminance of communication, promotion, and sales force (at the expense of product), are on dangerous ground in the field of industrial production innovation. Similarly, while market dimensions did dominate the results, the need for a strong technical/production orientation to complement (rather than to detract from) a strong market orientation also was revealed. The research results provide both encouragement and warning to the technically-oriented and the market-oriented product developer.

REFERENCES

Booz, Allen & Hamilton (1968), *Management Of New Products*, New York: Booz, Allen & Hamilton, Inc.

Calantone, Roger J. and Robert G. Cooper (1977), "A Typology Of Industrial New Product Failure," in *Contemporary Marketing Thought*, Greenberg & Bellanger, eds., Chicago: American Marketing Association, 492-497.

Cooper, Robert G. (1975), "Why New Industrial Products Fail," *Industrial Marketing Management*, 4 (January), 315-326.

————— (1976), "Introducing Successful New Products," *MCB Monographs*, European Journal of Marketing, 10, Bradford, England.

————— (1979), "Identifying Industrial New Product Success: Project NewProd," *Industrial Marketing Management*, 8 (May).

Crawford, C. Merle (1977), "Marketing Research And The New Product Failure Rate," *Journal of Marketing*, 41 (April), 51-61.

Davidson, Hugh J. (1976), "Why Most New Consumer Brands Fail," *Harvard Business Review*, 54 (March-April), 117-122.

Gerstenfeld, Arthur (1976), "A Study of Successful Projects, Unsuccessful Projects, and Projects in Process in West Germany," *IEEE Transactions On Engineering Management*, 23 (August), 116-123.

Globe, Samuel, Girard W. Levy, and Charles M. Schwartz (1973), "Key Factors and Events in The Innovation Process," *Research Management*, 16 (July), 8-15.

Hatch, R.S. (1957), "Product Failures Attributed Mainly to a Lack of Testing, Faulty Marketing," *Industrial Marketing*, 43 (February), 112-126.

Hopkins, David S. and Early L. Bailey (1971), "New Product Pressures," *The Conference Board Record*, 8 (June), 16-24.

Kulvik, Hanser (1977), *Factors Underlying The Success or Failure of New Products*, Helsinki: University Of Technology, Report No. 29, Finland.

Lazo, Hector (1965), "Finding a Key to Success in New Product Failures," *Industrial Marketing*, 50 (November), 74-77.

Little, Blair (1970), "Characterizing The New Product For Better Evaluation and Planning," *Working Paper Series*, No. 21, University of Western Ontario, London, Canada (July).

Marquis, Donald G. (1969), "The Anatomy of Successful Innovations," *Innovation Magazine*, 1 (November), 28-37.

Montgomery, David B. (1975), "New Product Distribution: An Analysis of Supermarket Buyer Decisions," *Journal Of Marketing Research*, 12 (August), 255-264.

Myers, Summer and Donald G. Marquis (1969), "Successful Industrial Innovations," *National Science Foundation*, NSF 69-17.

National Industrial Conference Board (1964), "Why New Products Fail," *The Conference Board Record*, New York: NICB.

Roberts, R.W. and J.E. Burke (1974), "Six New Products — What Made Them Successful," *Research Management*, 16 (May), 21-24.

Rothwell, Roy (1972), "Factors For Success in Industrial Innovations," from *Project SAPPHO-A Comparative Study Of Success And Failure in Industrial Innovation*, Brighten, Sussex: S.P.R.U.

—————(1974), "The 'Hungarian Sappho': Some Comments And Comparison," *Research Policy 3*, 30-38.

—————(1976), "Innovation In Textile Machinery: Some Significant Factors In Success and Failure," *SPRU Occasional Paper Series*, No. 2, Brighton, Sussex, United Kingdom, (June).

—————, C. Freeman, A. Horsley, V.T.P. Jervis, A.B. Robertson, and J. Townsend (1974), "SAPPHO Updated-Project Sappho Phase II," *Research Policy 3*, 258-291.

Rubenstein, Albert H., Alok K. Chakrabarti, and Robert D. O'Keefe (1974 ed.), "Field Studies of The Technological Innovation Process," in *Progress in Assessing Technical Innovations* by H.R. Clauser, Technomic Publication, Westport, CT.

—————, —————, —————, W.E. Sounder, and H.C. Young (1976), "Factors Influencing Innovation Success at The Project Level,"*Research Management*, 16 (May), 15-20.

Shocker, Allen D., Dennis Gensch, and Leonard S. Simon (1969), "Toward The Improvement of New Product Search and Screening," *AMA Conference Proceedings*, (Fall), 168-175.

Utterback, James M., Thomas J. Allen, J. Herbert Holloman, and Marvin H. Sirbu (1976), "The Process Of Innovation in Five Industries in Europe and Japan," *IEEE Transactions on Engineering Management*, No. 1 (February), 3-9.

Wind, Yoram (1973), "A New Procedure For Concept Evaluation," *Journal of Marketing*, 37 (October), 2-11.

COMMITTING ECONOMIC SUICIDE: A REVIEW OF THE STATUS OF INDUSTRIAL MARKETING PLANNING

Randall J. Voorn

INTRODUCTION

This article is concerned with the present lack of industrial marketing planning and the corresponding effects on effective industrial operations. Careful, formal planning is essential for maximizing the chances of success: in new product development, in setting up an international marketing program, in establishing a distribution system, and in countless other aspects of a total marketing system. Today, forward-looking industrial competitors are adopting the systems approach to marketing their products. Firms are using sophisticated computer technology to help management optimize its use of quantitative analytical techniques. In such a setting, a firm may be committing economic suicide if it relies on haphazard, informal planning.

MARKETING PLANNING IN PERSPECTIVE

Planning, as the most basic of all managerial functions, has been referred to as "fundamentally choosing," and a planning problem or situation arises "only when an alternaive course of action is discovered."[1] If marketing planning is deciding in advance what, how, when, and who is to carry out the marketing function for a firm, then marketing planning is fundamentally choosing the strategic and tactical marketing alternatives for the firm and then successfully implementing them.

Marketing planning should facilitate the accomplishment of enterprise purpose and objectives. Goetz aptly states this in the following quote:

"Plans alone cannot make an enterprise successful. Action is required; the enterprise must operate. Plans can, however, focus on purposes. They can forecast which actions will tend toward the ultimate objective . . . which tend away, and which will likely offset one another, and which are merely irrelevant. Managerial planning seeks to achieve a consistent, co-ordinated structure of operations focused on

desired ends. Without plans, action must become merely random activity, producing nothing but chaos."[2]

Given this importance of marketing planning, most industrial marketing managers have found that it is better to plan their activities before they start accomplishing them. However, in everyday business situations, this is rarely the case. More often than not, marketing managers permit themselves to drift into situations which place them at the mercy of chance and circumstances. Typically, only about "20 percent of the major industrial companies that are thought to be good marketing planners are good marketing planners."[3]

Every manager knows that planning is equally important as organizing, staffing, directing, and controlling, and simple logic tells us that planning should precede all other managerial functions. This principle is known as the "primacy of planning." But in today's constraint-filled industrial marketing environment, with fierce competition and shrinking profit margins, managers are taking action without first planning the proposed action. The results can be catastrophic! One would think that the industrial marketing managers of today would focus more attention on marketing planning, particularly with the dynamic nature of our economy. If planning is essential to contribute to, and facilitate the accomplishment of enterprise purpose and objectives, then why is there a lack of adequate industrial planning, especially marketing planning?

OBSTACLES TO SUCCESSFUL PLANNING

Typically, today's marketing manager justifies this lack of sufficient planning by stating that: "There just isn't time for planning," or "I don't have enough people or the right people to plan ahead anymore," or "I had to act immediately." Let us carefully examine each of these reasons.

Today's marketing manager cannot delay his planning indefinitely. He must make commitments for the future, and these commitments can be critical in terms of earnings and market share if the plans are successfully executed over a long period

RANDALL J. VOORN is Sales/Marketing Manager, Jewel Companies, Inc., Melrose Park, Ill.

Reprinted with permission from *Industrial Management*, vol. 23, pp. 3–7, Nov.–Dec. 1981.
Copyright © 1981 Institute of Industrial Engineers, 25 Technology Park/Atlanta, Norcross, GA 30092. (404) 449-0460.

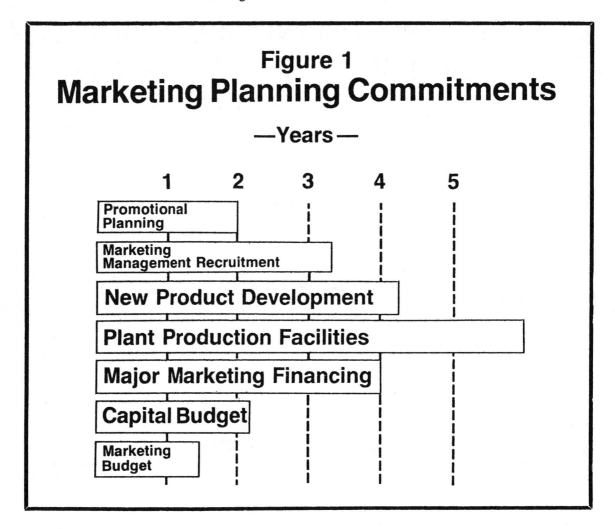

Figure 1
Marketing Planning Commitments
—Years—

	1	2	3	4	5

Promotional Planning

Marketing Management Recruitment

New Product Development

Plant Production Facilities

Major Marketing Financing

Capital Budget

Marketing Budget

of time. For example, some typical marketing commitments with their lead time periods are shown in *Figure 1.* Obviously these periods will vary according to the kind of business, but one can readily see the decision areas that involve planning ahead for differing periods of time.

Equally as important to the time factor of planning is the people factor. Effective marketing planning involves the proper utilization of human resources and the efficiency with which a marketing department can be operated will depend to a considerable measure upon how effectively its personnel are utilized.

One must have a marketing planning staff to carry out this function, and this staff must possess the experience to plan effectively. Good management requires the development of a program that will permit employees to be selected and trained for positions that are most appropriate to the developed abilities. In order to maintain an effective marketing department, the firm must have accurate and continuing information as to the number and the qualifications of personnel needed to perform the various marketing tasks. This includes marketing

planning — if the people are presently not there, then select them and train them!

Aside from the requirements of making commitments and utilizing trained marketing personnel, marketing planning is also time-consuming.

Deliberative thinking, the acquisition and analysis of market data, the consideration of alternative courses of action, and the development of comprehensive marketing plans and programs cannot be hastened. Good industrial marketing planning is usually discarded when time is of the essence. And even though the complete planning process is neglected, marketing managers still employ some degree of planning. However, the lack of time, as well as the shortage of trained marketing personnel, should never be a valid excuse to ignore planning. Never should the necessity for immediate action circumvent the need for planning. If this happens, then one's actions follow a reactionary approach, and not a systematic, planned approach. One approach to planning that is becoming more commonplace is "contingency planning," where contingency plans are made, held in abeyance, and put into effect when and if needed. Even in the better managed firms, most of the planning is of this sort.

When an industrial marketing manager insists that action must be taken immediately, to the extent of abandoning planning, the situation is probably one where action is being confused with accomplishment. Form a production standpoint, a man running around in circles can be working as hard as a man running down the street. This important difference is due to the usefulness of the achievements. Taking marketing action without planning is basically due to an apathy toward thinking.

Most marketing people do not reflect or cogitate enough, and do not produce required plans; we let others do our thinking for us. If marketing planning is the "exercise of analysis and foresight to increase the effectiveness of marketing activities,"[4] then the motto of all marketing practitioners should always be to "Think-Think-Think!" All marketing managers should set aside at least one hour each day to think about what his actions should be for the following day, week, or some definite period of time.

If marketing managers, as well as other middle and upper management managers, are to spend proportionately more time using conceptual skills than human or technical skills, then it would follow that managers should devote an adequate amount of time to the planning function.

Managers in middle management and upper management positions should be dealing with long and short-range planning, modeling, and other abstractions, more than human or technical tasks.

Just think how much better our marketing efforts would be if we set aside one hour per day for planning? Psychologists tell us that our actions are influenced by our thoughts. Any accomplishment requires physical action, and action must be preceded by thinking if one desires optimal results. Always remember that accomplishment requires two steps: (1) thinking, (2) then acting.

PLAN TO AVOID ENTROPY

Planning enables the marketing manager to avoid entropy, or the tendency to let things run down, and to see things as they could be, not as they really are. Planning gives expectation and stimuli for higher objectives of the firm. Planning gives a consciousness to the marketing manager relative to opportunities and shows the way to their realization. Industrial marketing planning provides the connecting structures between what one expects and the realization of those expectations. Even though there are many obstacles to successful planning,[5] planning must be accomplished. Not only does planning provide solutions to problems, it also opens up new avenues, new operating methodologies, and reveals opportunities previously unknown to the marketing planner.

Also, one's action of planning activities on paper provides one with guidance and purposiveness. Searching for relevant facts, considering and determining various courses of action, and calculating the time, people, and material needs are of themselves positive actions toward good management. By its very nature, industrial marketing planning assists in the achievement of enterprise results. Predetermined objectives, accomplishments, and mutually agreed actions are stressed by planning. Always remember that planning reduces random activity, needless redundant actions, and irrelevant actions.

Furthermore, and of paramount importance, marketing planning is important because it reduces and/or minimizes costs. Even some planning, though poor, will reduce random, expensive, irrelevant, and inconsistent activities. Reduced costs are the consequences of good marketing planning since coordinated departments within the firm, and those outside the firm, must work consistently together to minimize costs. For example, a firm's costs can be reduced, such as those in a milk bottling plant, by coordinating the raw materials and ingredients in such a manner that "down-time" is minimized. The proper timing of packaging, ingredients, labor, and other product components, at strategic manufacturing points, happens as a result of sound, detailed planning. But for this planning, the production costs per unit would be high, and the production lines would be in a confused, unorganized state.

PLANNING AND THE NEW PRODUCT DEVELOPMENT PROCESS

The importance of planning can also be highlighted by using an example familiar to most industrial marketing managers — that of the "new product development process." Planning is the most critical element of every new product development process. It is in the planning stage that the degree of success is determined. This importance is highlighted by the stages in the new product development process as illustrated in *Figure 2*, where each stage involves important planning activities. Even though in outline form, one can readily see where planning is of paramount importance, especially in the concept and product tests, in the marketing mix decisions, in marketing forecasting, and in the market test. Marketing managers should formalize planning questions that need to be answered at each phase (and at each subphase) to assist in the planning process. If answers are provided to these questions, and if these phases are planned and

Figure 2
Stages In New Product Development And Implementation

Phase 1

Corporate Research

Activities:

1. Establishment of corporate objectives
2. Continuous surveillance of "marketing situation"
3. Analysis of corporate strengths and resources
4. Characterization of "the business of the corporation".
5. Specifications of criteria for new product fields
6. Generation of "pool of product ideas"
7. Screening, selection and preliminary validation of new product idea

Phase 4

Market Test

Activities:

1. Planning
   a. Selection of geographic area and accounts
   b. Complete schedules and budget.
   c. Establishment of standards to judge test performance
2. Experimental production for market test.
3. Final production planning
4. Execution of market test
5. Analysis and review
6. Final plans for launch with budgets and fixing of responsibilities

Phase 2

Feasibility Research

Activities:

1. Experimental technical research
2. Market research
3. Analysis and integration of findings
   a. Time
   b. Costs
   c. Manpower

Phase 5

Market Introduction

Activities:

1. Build-up
2. Launch
3. Follow-up and review

Phase 3

Development

Activities:

1. Technical development
2. Production costing and planning
   a. Materials
   b. Labor
   c. Equipment
   d. Space
3. Market evaluation of product prototype
4. Marketing mix plans
5. Market forecasting
   a. Demand analysis
   b. Cost analysis
   c. Price analysis
6. Break-even analysis

Phase 6

Commercial-ization

Activities:

Program absorbed by established organization and operating system as a going enterprise

Source: Adapted from T.A. Staudt and D.A. Taylor, **A Managerial Introduction to Marketing,** 2nd Ed. (Englewood Cliffs, N.J.: Prentice-Hall, Inc., 1970), pp. 242-243.

strictly followed, then the new product development process will progress on time. And, the new product development process is only one of numerous marketing functions that require good, detailed planning.

NARROWING THE UNCERTAINTIES

Effective marketing planning and the decisions about the composition of future marketing plans/ programs are time-consuming activities. Marketing managers, especially in industry, must analyze a wide spectrum of products, concepts, and programs, and the alternative courses of action that are available to fulfill them. This also involves interfacing with people, and infers that immediate action might be required in given situations. All in all, planning must take place to make the future more manageable — and more profitable.[6]

Igor Ansoff and others[7] concluded in a study viewing the effect of planning on the success of acquisitions that:

(1) On virtually all relevant criteria, . . . planners . . . significantly outperformed . . . nonplanners.

(2) Not only did the planners do better on the average, they performed more predictably than nonplanners. Thus, planners appear to have narrowed the uncertainties in the outcomes of . . . behavior.

These same conclusions of planning would be true for a study measuring the effect of planning on the success of industrial marketing research, or industrial new product development, or promotional planning, or any marketing function aspect for that matter.

SUMMARY

This article has examined characteristics of unsuccessful industrial marketing planning and their effect on effective industrial operations. It has focused on the reasons why today's marketing managers are planning in an informal, haphazard way. Three reasons for this lack of planning have been suggested: (1) lack of time for formal planning activities, (2) the lack of well-trained marketing staffs, (3) the need for immediacy of action.

Even though planning is time-consuming and involves the effective use of human resources, and even though industrial marketing managers might have to act extemporaneoulsy in certain situations, none of these reasons are valid excuses to ignore planning! Clearly, we all can and need to improve our planning. The benefits of planning far exceed the reasons for not planning. Economic suicide could be a reality if good industrial marketing planning is not a reality.

ENDNOTES

1 Billy E. Goetz. **Management Planning and Control** (New York: McGraw-Hill Book Company, 1949), p. 2.

2 **Ibid.,** p. 63.

3 "Shortcomings Predominate in Marketing Planning," **Industrial Marketing** (July 1967), p. 60.

4 Wendell R. Smith, "The Role of Planning in Marketing," **Business Horizons** (Fall 1959), p. 54.

5 See "Long-Range Planning: Séance or Science?" **Sales Management,** 15 Jan. 1969, p. 31.

6 "Plan or Perish," **Sales and Marketing Management,** 18 May 1981, pp. 45-46, provides an excellent synopsis on the importance of marketing planning.

7 H. Igor Ansoff, Jay Avner, Richard G. Brandenburg, Fred E. Portner, and Raymond Radosevich, "Does Planning Pay? The Effect of Planning on Success of Acquisitions in American Firms," **Long Range Planning,** (December 1970). p. 7.

THE ROLE OF PLANNING IN THE MARKETING OF NEW PRODUCTS

By Michael P. Peters

THE NEED FOR PRODUCT PLANNING

An inherent part of long term business planning is the development of new products and services. Its importance has been particularly evidenced during the 1970s, a decade of increased challenges for business executives. The 1980s will serve as a further test of the ability of corporate executives to successfully generate, develop and market new products and services within the context of a changing complex environment. In particular, management must be concerned in product planning with changes in consumer tastes and at cultural life style changes, competition, government and economic changes.

Even though conditions are rapidly changing, there appears to be continued emphasis in many industries on new product planning and development. It is apparent that the period of instability caused by the energy crisis has fostered the development of new products and services to satisfy the new demands of consumers under these changed environmental conditions. Energy saving products and services have saturated the marketplace in the past few years. Electric appliances, machinery, automotive accessories, insulation, clothing, micro-processors, are just a few categories that have been significantly affected by the changing economic environment.

All of these trends lead to an important conclusion for business executives that new-product planning and development is an important function in the overall business planning process and that long term growth hinges largely on change through a well organized product planning and development process.

The new product planning process can be divided into two major stages. First is the development planning function where management determines alternative development strategies through changes in technology or market segments. The effects of new technology on development of new markets on the existing product line must also be evaluated. Second is the evaluation of the major issues inherent in strategic product planning prior to a final decision to introduce the new product. Each product plan or proposal may be evaluated using specific guidelines that serve to identify crucial issues and problems relating to the marketing mix and ensure comprehensive product planning prior to its introduction.

Reprinted with permission from *Planning Rev.,* the bimonthly journal of the North American Society for Corporate Planning, 300 Arcade Sq., Dayton, OH 45402, vol. 8, pp, 24–27, Nov. 1980.

The Development Planning Function

The development planning function is generally carried out at high management levels, particularly in medium and small firms. In larger organizations the development planning function may be implemented as a staff function or as a line function depending on whether product planning advisory committees are used or the firm employs a product/brand management organization.

Inherent in all organizations in the development planning function is the ability of management to respond to changes in customer needs and market conditions such as those described earlier in this paper. The firm's response to these changes can take one or a combination of the following development strategies.

- Technological development planning — improve utilization of the firm's existing scientific and production skills or acquisition of new skills.
- Marketing development planning — exploitation of existing markets or new markets with present products or new products.

Figure 1 illustrates possible development and planning strategies that can be initiated through the combination of technological development or market development.

The minicomputer provides an excellent example of the use of technological or marketing development planning. With little or no new technological development, the manufacturer of a minicomputer may choose to further exploit the marketplace. The same computer system may be marketed through OEM's to reach new markets such as banks and insurance firms. Another alternative would be to solicit international markets, again without any significant technological development.

Medium technological development has been significant in the computer industry and can be achieved through modification of either hardware or software. For example, technological development may involve modular software such as the Honeywell Level 6 GCOS or hardware modification such as the DEC XVM series, which adapted accessories such as a video terminal and graphic system. IBM's reduction of a memory bit to about 1¢ from 17¢ or Data General's reduction of computing power required for its systems has resulted in lower prices and new market opportunities. Improved user capacity for distributive network systems such as the DEC Datasystem 500 or the Honeywell Level 60 series provided expansion of sales to both existing customers as well as to new customer/markets. Higher speed printers, expanded memory, disk, cassette or batch adaptability all would allow the manufacturer to expand its capability in existing markets or reach totally new markets with moderate technological development.

High technological development in the computer industry has recently involved the personal computer or microcomputer. New technology affecting price, quality, reliability, simplicity, etc. has resulted in the potential mass marketing of these products for households. These systems could be marketed to existing customers (low market development) for distributive network or office use; they could be marketed to small businesses such as doctors, lawyers, real estate brokers (medium market development); or they could be marketed to the homeowner (high market development). In each instance where there is high

FIGURE 1   DEVELOPMENT OPPORTUNITIES THROUGH TECHNOLOGY AND MARKET PLANNING

TECHNOLOGICAL DEVELOPMENT PLANNING

MARKET DEVELOPMENT PLANNING		Low	Medium	High
	Low	no changes	modified products to same market	totally new products to same market
	Medium	same product to expanded market	modified products to similar but new expanded markets	similar but new expanded markets with totally new products
	High	same product to new markets	modified products to new markets	new markets with totally new products

technological development the planning involves more complex marketing decisions particularly in distribution of product, price, and promotion. The problems with high technological development focus on the firm's ability to reach these new markets without any prior market experience. The need for new facilities, skills, distribution outlets and communication sources are only a few important planning tasks that will require substantial analysis of the various alternatives before management is able to commit the firm to a specific strategic market plan.

Figure 2 illustrates some of the effects of market development or technological development on the product line, moving from an initial product unit to the various alternatives. Thus, a firm that initially markets product A_1 may decide to remerchandise the existing product by increasing sales through a new merchandising program such as an expanded salesforce, use of OEMs or special trade promotion. If product improvement is initiated then the firm may expect increased sales because of the improvement. These improvements such as higher speed or increased memory could have been initiated as a reaction to competition, from customer complaints or from research and development.

If a new minicomputer A_2 is developed having greater flexibility, more power and a lower cost central processing unit the firm may consider replacing A_1 or using it to satisfy the needs of more than one market (market extension) such as the education market or laboratory research market. A product line extension would occur through planned product variations or modifications such as a graphic system, video terminal, disk operation or multiple user adaptability. In this instance product A_2 along with its variations (A_3 and A_4) may be marketed to one or more markets.

Development planning through diversification would likely include a situation where a firm offers variations of A_2 to one or more markets and also has added a different product B_1 (personal or microcomputer) to the product line.

The development planning classification system illustrated in Figure 2 provides an important basis for estimating or planning the marketing mix decisions. In the development planning process, management may use the classification model to interpret its specific internal or external needs to achieve any of the chosen strategies.

Once the alternative opportunities such as remerchandise, reformulate, extend the market or diversify are analyzed, management should consider which strategy should be employed and then begin to develop a product strategy plan. Inherent in the product strategy plan are critical marketing decisions which must be considered prior to market introduction. Guidelines that might be used to effectively enhance the decision making process are discussed below.

PRODUCT PLANNING GUIDELINES

As management begins to seriously evaluate where a new product or service should be considered further for development and eventual market introduction it is important that a decision framework be used to ensure that the product planning process is implemented. The format of such a guide may vary for each management team. One effective planning tool that has been previously used is described below in the form of questions or instructions.

1. Evaluate the industry in which the product or

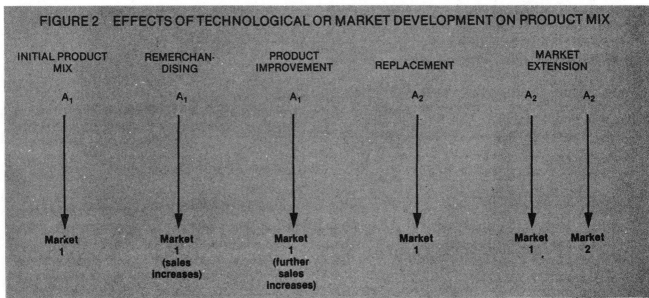

FIGURE 2 EFFECTS OF TECHNOLOGICAL OR MARKET DEVELOPMENT ON PRODUCT MIX

service will be marketed.

2. Evaluate the alternative target markets for the product or service by preparing a market grid and identifying the unique characteristics and approximate size of each.

3. Identify and analyze the nature of the competitive environment. What advantages or benefits does the new product or service have over the competitive products or services? What reaction can be expected from competition if the new product or service is introduced?

4. Set goals (units) for the new product or service for the next three years. As the marketplace changes, be prepared to modify the goals.

5. How well does the existing organizational structure satisfy the needs of implementing and managing the new product or service? Determine if new personnel are needed and what qualities these individuals should possess.

6. Carefully weigh the pros and cons of patenting the new product.

7. Consider the possible governmental regulations that may have an impact on the successful market planning of the new product or service.

8. What is the most effective means of distributing the new product? An analysis should include possible costs, existing distribution networks, margins, competition, future expansion and selectivity.

9. Establish a price that considers the company's objectives, profit targets, quantity purchases, competition and image. If possible, consider the sensitivity of price to demand particularly when capacity is limited or raw materials or labor restricted.

10. Consider alternative means of packaging, particularly when product display is an integral part of the selling process.

11. Develop a promotion plan for the new product or service that considers costs, effectiveness, media, and alternative appeals. Include fact sheets, special introductory premiums, or displays where appropriate.

12. Future planning decisions related to product line expansion, design modifications or reactions to competition should also be given initial consideration.

All of these questions require careful consideration prior to the introduction of a new product or service in the marketplace.

CONCLUSIONS

An understanding of the alternative strategies in the planning function as well as the use of planning guidelines such as those discussed previously can ensure the future success of any new product or service. Without careful planning throughout the development and introduction stages, a new product or service may never achieve its potential or may result in a financial disaster. □

Michael P. Peters is Associate Professor and Chairman of the Marketing Department at Boston College. He is also Director of H & P Associates, a marketing consulting firm. Dr. Peters has experience in all phases of strategic marketing planning, marketing research and product planning and positioning. Author of numerous articles and a book *Marketing a New Product: Its Planning, Development and Control.* Dr. Peters holds a Ph.D. degree in Business Administration from University of Massachusetts, Amherst.

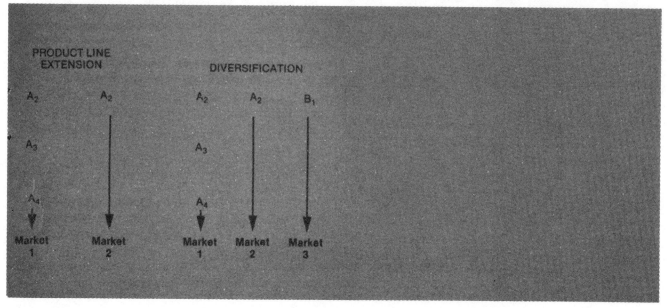

Planning for Technological Innovation—Developing the Necessary Nerve

E. Peter Ward, New Product Management Group, London

Adaptation is a condition of survival, affecting companies as much as other organisms. Survival in industry depends on innovation, in products, processes and management. The principles of adaptive or dynamic planning were outlined in an article published in the December 1980 issue, where the conditions or characteristics favouring innovation were described as generative, receptive and selective. A methodology serving to optimize these conditions is described in this article, with some case material.

Fundamental to dynamic planning is a functional structuring of corporate identity (see previous article in *Long Range Planning*, Vol. 13, No. 6), together with a procedure whereby a company may usefully interact with its technical, commercial, economic and social environment, keeping abreast of changes through innovation. These concepts are readily translated into practical tasks.

Iterative Dialogue

Once identity has been adequately formulated, the iterative dialogue between a company and its environment which I have called successive focusing may be put in hand. In practice, the simplified representation shown in the earlier article (Figure 2) needs to be elaborated. Such a dialogue may be seen as a cycle of stages, providing a framework or procedure whereby alternate consideration of company and environment successively focuses attention on a diminishing field of interest until products are identified which optimally reconcile inherent capability with emerging needs.

A typical product study embraces the six stages itemized in Table 1. Stages 2 and 3 are normally performed concurrently. A procedural chart is reproduced in Figure 1. The first, or planning stage is particularly important and comprises the six tasks reviewed in Table 2, not necessarily carried out in order.

Table 1. The six stages of a typical product-planning study

(1) Planning	Define say eight functional dynamic (or search) areas, consistent with the group's or company's resources and experience, embracing but not limited to existing technologies; develop screening criteria; formulate tentative strategy
(2) Exploration	Explore sectors of the market corresponding to the agreed dynamic areas, to identify emerging or unsatisfied requirements and check the probable demand; record possible parallel developments by competitors; and note attractive product-market sectors
(3) Search	Conduct a carefully defined and systematic worldwide search within dynamic areas for self-contained (and ideally proprietary) product opportunities which might be introduced under licence, by joint venture, continuous subcontracting, creative imitation or independent development
(4) Analysis	Evaluate the opportunities brought to light, technically and commercially, with reference to competitive activity, standard codes and any potential hazards, through a procedure ranging from coarse screening to research in depth, identifying trends
(5) Acquisition	Investigate prospects for acquiring companies or agencies, serving to extend the business of the group or company, reinforce available facilities, introduce new lines or provide appropriate sales and marketing resources
(6) Action	Recommend a positive course of action and introduce proposed associates, with a detailed programme for implementation, advising generally on the negotiation of agreements and identifying resources necessary for implementation; also finalize long-term strategy

Market Exploration

Market exploration (Stage 2) should be distinguished from market or marketing research, terms which themselves tend to be used indiscriminately. Presumably market research is concerned with knowledge of the market itself (size, structure, etc.), while marketing research is intended to yield information on how a market

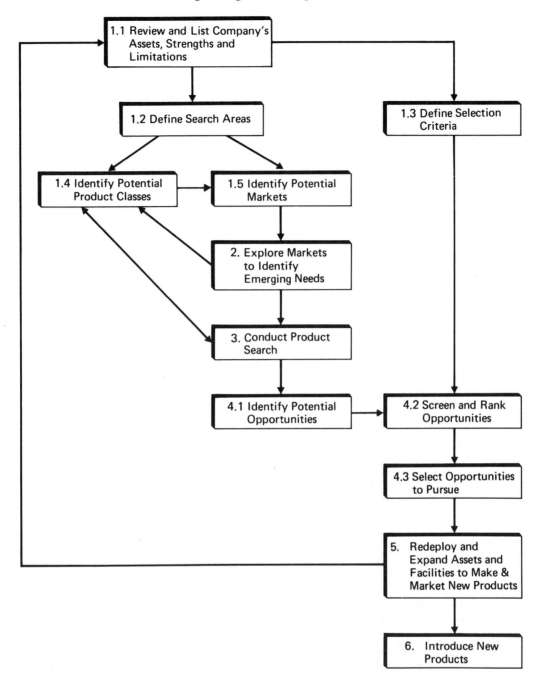

Figure 1. Simplified procedural chart, with reiteration, for product-planning study

may be exploited, embracing the items listed in Table 3.

Both market and marketing research are usually concerned with a single product or service or coherent group of products. Market exploration, on the other hand, is conducted to identify emerging needs within a given dynamic area and so may involve a great variety of products.

Taking separation plant again as an example, we may interview technologists and marketing executives in companies or other organizations active in such industries as mining and mineral-

extraction, oil and chemicals (an oil refinery is only an elaborate separation plant), food, nuclear-fuel, plant-contracting, process-consulting and others where problems of separation are likely to arise.

The interviewer first defines what is meant by 'separation plant' in the present context, then enquires: (1) what kinds of separation plant are used at present; (2) what features the users approve or find unsatisfactory; (3) what materials are separated; (4) what are their physical and chemical properties; (5) what are the physical and chemical properties of products which might be separated in the future; and so on.

Table 2. Tasks conducted in the first stage of a product-planning study

(1) Review pertinent facilities, skills, technical and manufacturing experience, the special knowledge of senior executives, with product technology and applications (as in original equipment manufacture or process engineering), also marketing and sales experience: in order to draw up a characteristic table summarizing the available or accessible assets and potential

(2) Record the underlying thinking affecting earlier attempts to diversify (including any which were abandoned), also experience of licensing, acquisition and market development, establishing the reasons for success or failure (or perhaps transfer to other Group divisions) and to what extent the same conditions still apply

(3) Consider the activities of external companies making products similar to those supplied by the Group or company (including products which compete functionally), to uncover prospects for parallel diversification, noting developments envisaged by suppliers, competitors and customers

(4) Collect information on technical and commercial developments related in any way to present capability, including applications data on existing products, other uses of manufacturing equipment currently installed and the wider use of existing, particularly sophisticated, technology

(5) Conduct, in the light of information assebled so far, a preliminary market exploration to establish possible areas of opportunity for further search (see Criteria for Dynamic Areas, Article 1, some of which may not apply), classifying products in associated groups and listing (from the technical and trade press) typical proprietary items to help determine the scope of the enquiry

(6) Select, in consultation, approximately eight (dynamic) areas of search, half defined broadly in terms of the available technical and commercial resources, the others derived more indirectly by generalization; and establish, again in consultation, comprehensive screening criteria for evaluating potential new activities within the eight dynamic areas

Table 3. Questions to be resolved in a marketing survey

Marketing may be described as the utilization of processed information in order to place a company in an optimum relationship with its environment, now and in the foreseeable future. Marketing research may clearly assist in the collection and interpretation of such information to determine for example:

(1) The applications in which any given product, material or service may be expected to yield a cost–benefit advantage

(2) The size and structure of corresponding markets and their projected growth, bearing in mind the influence of legislation or local regulations

(3) Alternative ways of meeting the demand or satisfying the same requirement; and factors governing demand

(4) The identity, character and strength of competition (including names and market shares of principal competitors)

(5) The market share likely to be captured by a newcomer or new development, given appropriate engineering, design and marketing effort

(6) Preferred specifications and features; optimum range of types and sizes, on introduction and at later stages; factors affecting preferences

(7) Acceptable prices and price elasticity, with any traditional discount structure or special terms in the user industries concerned

(8) Channels, methods and conditions of sale; standards and other factors which may limit or prohibit sale or determine selling methods

On the basis of this information, it should be possible to recommend the product, specifications, types, sizes, market sectors and customers on which the company should concentrate its efforts, initially and in the longer term; also to select the most effective methods and channels of sale, with pricing; and to prepare estimates of cash flow, margins and profitability over a period of years

A hundred controlled exploratory interviews, with cross-checking and correlation of results, may generate any number of technoeconomic perspectives within a given dynamic area. The interviewer must himself be sufficiently well informed to maintain a dialogue, which is a small learning process embodied in the major learning process of the study as a whole. The order in which informants are approached is therefore critical.

Conducting Research

Strictly, market exploration and market research are simply categories of marketing research, the main objectives of which are stated in Table 4. Reduced to a minimum, the function of marketing research, as defined by my former colleague, Henry Novy, is to help decision-makers in resolving: what to make and how to sell it.

Information may be assembled by: (1) literature searches, (2) statistical analysis, (3) postal questionnaires, (4) telephone interviewing, (5) direct interviewing and (6) designed seminars.

Interviewing itself may be by questionnaire, presubmitted or used as a checklist, structured or unstructured; of an exploratory nature; or conducted as the pilot preparation for an extended programme.

Market research differs from much other research (as scientific research or R & D) by virtue of the information it is expected to yield. Research generally is concerned with discovery and the interpretation of facts or patterns of facts. The special nature of market research follows from the facts with which it deals and awareness that fact and interpretation are, in practice, inseparable.

Many primary facts, corresponding in scientific research to observations, are reasonably firm, relating to historical data, sequences or behaviour. Secondary or derived facts in market research differ, at least in degree, from the deductions or findings of scientific research, as I have suggested earlier,[1] in that they are:

☆ usually about a contingent future,

☆ often of a transitory nature,

Table 4. Actions dependent on market or marketing research

	Objectives of market research
To judge	Whether present or potential markets are large, accessible and durable enough to justify entry on any scale consistent with company policy; and if so
To decide	What investment should be allocated to technical development, manufacture and marketing, over what period and in what stages, for maximum continuing return
To select	Those developments, specifications and product ranges likely to be most acceptable to users and most competitive in performing the functions envisaged
To define	The market sectors, geographically and by applications, users, OEM's etc., on which selling and other effort should be concentrated, initially and progressively
To plan	A market-development and sales strategy, with channels of sale, pricing policy, methods of promotion, targets and schedules, for optimum penetration and overall profitable growth

☆ frequently based on opinion,

☆ vulnerable to subsequent action,

☆ subject to sharp discontinuities,

☆ fraught with uncertainty,

☆ seldom susceptible to proof.

Not very encouraging. But market research is relatively cheap, compared with, say, scientific research (perhaps involving the construction of a proton synchrotron), while an error in appreciation of a market can be extremely costly, at worst totalling all other investment in a project put together.

Where a market situation is unfamiliar or the sum at risk substantial, the market cannot usefully be quantified until it is fully understood, with progressive identification of factors likely to prove significant.

Decision Making

Decision makers sometimes even fail to do their sums. Examination of figures for purchases and total stock of steam, diesel and electric locomotives in the United Kingdom (and overseas) from 1955 onward was a fairly straightforward task; but there were still companies in the early 1960s making steam locomotives and very little else. Results come from asking questions; but what questions? Sums certainly need doing; but what sums?[2]

I recall a market study to determine the potential for an alarm system which would warn the driver of

a heavy vehicle when the diesel-engine coolant had fallen to a critical level. Many considerations had to be resolved but possibly the most unfavourable was the almost universal preference of fleet operators, not for aids in the driver's cab, but for vigilant drivers. The situation may have changed by now. Lead time is not confined to tooling or other schedules but also embraces the lag of general acceptance behind demonstrable advantage. The time horizon is too often overlooked.

Although checklists are employed, interviewing tends to be unstructured in exploratory work, with information interpreted progressively, to make the most of any leads uncovered. Questioning is so directed as to discern the underlying facts, significance and reasoning. By correlation in a matrix, data which may prove unobtainable directly may be inferred and then confirmed. Such information serves as an aid in decision-making but must also lend conviction—and so provide the necessary nerve for innovation.

Market versus Technology

Market-led and technology-led innovation are not as simple to distinguish as has sometimes been suggested: consider the development and exploitation of gas turbines, float glass, glow-discharge welding, nickel alloys, videorecorders, child-proof drug bottles, thermonuclear power, rechargeable fuel cells, microprocessors and recombinant DNA technology.

The ideal innovative product calls for the combination or fusion of technical and marketing inputs; technology and marketing are not in conflict but partners in the same enterprise. Properly processed information of both kinds, brought together in an interactive relationship, provides a sound basis for planning and decision-making, improving the quality of insight and minimizing risk.

Where information is assembled in a pattern or matrix to be internally consistent and where it is essentially qualitative, as in the case of the coolant-level alarm, data interpretation involves what my colleague, Balint Bodroghy, calls a synoptic, as distinct from a numerical, approach. Qualitative is quite as important as quantitative information; and the task of reconciliation (though it might seem an attempt to solve n simultaneous equations with 2^n unknowns) is not quite as formidable as it first appears. A convincing set of recommendations may, in the event, be so self-evident that confidence limits are meaningless, while credence and sensitivity analysis are quite unnecessary.

Underlying Reasoning

On the other hand, it is essential to establish, and be seen to establish, the ground rules and fundamental arguments. Interviewing is therefore performed as a ranging dialogue, designed to elicit, sooner or later, key considerations and parameters. Not only is the interviewer looking for the unexpected; he must also spot the significant aside.

The principal, and possibly most delicate, problem is to recognize the stage at which all significant factors have come to light: 'a little learning' can be dangerous, as, conversely, can the residual unknown. Two tests I have found useful are convergency and matrix interlock, while a third checking procedure is to approach the same results via different routes.

Provided we are careful not to accept a glib or superficial coherence of results too early in a study, there comes a time when the sudden recognition of interlocking data illuminates reality. As William Blake observed in *The Marriage of Heaven and Hell*, 'Truth cannot be told in such a way as to be understood, and not to be believed'.

Envelope Parameters

It is always difficult to comprehend in advance of an enquiry all the factors worth investigating. The only satisfactory solution is progressive elaboration of a questionnaire as work proceeds. I remember when I prepared a report on the diversification of the British aircraft industry in the light of reduced defence requirements for *Engineering* in 1958, that I started with 16 questions and finished with 45.[3]

At the same time, it is important to identify as many considerations as possible at the beginning. A study was conducted for Lucas Industries Limited to investigate the commercial prospects for a group of new ceramic materials known as sialons, the properties of which could be tailored to requirements, within reason, by varying the composition. Essentially, they consist of silicon nitride, with substitutionally dissolved aluminium and oxygen.

Potential applications were numerous, embracing, for example, metal cutting, continuous casting of alloys, medical equipment and microelectronics. The company were seeking information on the markets for these materials and wanted, in particular, to:

(1) Identify specific applications and products, both by substitution for existing materials and through the conception of entirely new

Table 5. Envelope checklist for family of new materials

Envelope factors and parameters		
Cost–benefit relationship	Price	Refractory qualities
Cost–life relationship	Quantities	Impact resistance
Price sensitivity	Size limits	Creep resistance
Conditions for switch	Strength	room temperature
Ease of fabrication	(Rupture)	high temperature
Dimensional accuracy	Hardness	Chemical stability
Dimensions as finished	Stiffness	oxidation
Complexity of fabrication	Toughness	sea water
cubes, spheres,	Fatigue	chlorine
annuli, splines,	Finish	Surface quality
grooves, helices,	Adhesion	Wear resistance
re-entrant forms	Clamping	Crater wear
Mechanical properties	Machining	Edge (flank) wear
Consistent properties	speeds	Abrasion resistance
Production repeatability	removal	rolling
Predictable properties	rake	sliding
Operating reliability	coolant	slurries
Materials cut or formed	Drawing	sand, etc.
ferrous alloys	die life	Corrosion resistance
cast iron	die cost	Erosion resistance
mild steel	Profiles	molten metals etc.
medium carbon	strip	Heat absorption
high speed steel	rod	Thermal diffusivity
hardened steels	tube	Thermal conductivity
copper alloys	section	Thermal gradients
nickel alloys	Thin forms	Thermal shock
aluminium alloys	Economies	Thermal degradation
with silicon	energy	Thermal expansion
nitralloy	materials	Differential expansion
nimonics (no)	process	Electrical conductivity
titanium (no)	manpower	Dielectric properties
Materials transmitted	Homogeneity	Magnetic properties
Blood compatibility	Uniformity	Optical properties
Tissue compatibility	Variations	Arcing problems

developments arising from the unique properties of the sialons considered.

(2) Determine the envelope of properties and parameters, for any given application, whereby the economic advantage of a sialon over competing products would be sufficient to achieve initial market penetration.

(3) Evaluate the corresponding markets, both existing and potential, in unit and financial terms, with 5-year annual growth projections, as these markets are effectively developed, with emphasis on volume manufacture.

In order to secure the assignment, it was necessary to demonstrate an understanding of what was clearly a formidable research problem. To this end, I prepared a checklist reproduced in Table 5. The condensed single-page listing is similar in appearance to the characteristic table which I first devised in 1961 for G. & J. Weir, covering in three columns, products, technologies and outlets. Depth interviews were subsequently conducted in order to assemble the information specified in Table 6, which may be compared with the more general listing in Table 3.

Table 6. Exploratory market survey for new materials

Research will be carried out in depth in order to validate and quantify particular markets. It will be borne in mind that specialized items made in small numbers will not be so attractive as products or components required in commercial volumes. Interviews will be carried out in order to establish

(1) Applications outside the automotive and other industries traditionally served by Lucas, subdivided into high-temperature and room-temperature requirements

(2) Corresponding market sectors, classified in terms of immediate and longer-term accessibility, level of technology and potential

(3) The criteria which a particular sialon would need to meet in any given application to be markedly competitive with other materials

(4) The annual volume (units) and value of demand by market sectors, also by grade of sialon, with corresponding market structure

(5) The anticipated rate of expansion or decline in each sector over the next 5 years (annual estimates), with underlying reasoning

(6) Factors likely to influence demand in each sector during this period, with trends, including evolving technology and changing practice

(7) Prices which the market will bear in each sector, related to likely sales (number of units), with price sensitivity and elasticity where possible

(8) Strength of emerging competition, with extent of design-stage co-operation and methods of marketing, noting procedures likely to be most effective

Statistical data for grossing up will be assembled through desk research if the study proceeds. The approach is iterative, with successive focusing for maximum cost-effectiveness.

Generative Stimulus

Although I have emphasized that successful innovation will involve a union of technology and marketing, it is still useful to ascertain where innovation starts, reviewing the partly artificial distinction between technology-led and market-led innovation. A more realistic dichotomy may be obtained by asking: who starts innovation?

In this context there are two potential sources: (1) a technologist with a commercial appreciation of the market; and (2) a marketing executive who understands technology. The key lies in identifying such people; stimulating them to think and experiment in the duplex mode proposed; and helping them to focus their activity in accordance with corporate perspectives.

Much has been written concerning the roles of individuals in innovation,[4] notably with regard to independent inventors, creative research technologists, managers and the institutional environment.[5] Similarly, much case material has been assembled on sources of invention[6] and generative methods identified. Typical procedures include the delineation of a three-dimensional lattice, with axes

representing respectively: (1) manufacturing processes, from say cold-forming to electrolysis, (2) raw material, from thermosetting resins to ferrous alloys and (3) market segments, from the automotive industry to building construction.[7] Unit cubes within the lattice may help to recognize or highlight opportunities.

Receptive Context

Again for successful innovation, a receptive context is essential, without the various negative syndromes, long familiar and grievously inhibiting. It might be better to adopt the policy of agreeing to proceed with a development, unless good reason is found to the contrary; instead of only deciding to go ahead if an attractive and convincing case can be presented.

It would naturally be foolish to disregard sensible criteria for decision-making[8] and control[9] but the sooner we develop the necessary nerve for innovation, the better. Again an appropriate three-dimensional lattice can contribute, this time where the axes represent: (1) technological risk, (2) market risk and (3) operating risk, defining a board's responsibility in terms of dominant resource pattern.[10] Today, not only must a development be cost-effective, but it must also be socially acceptable.[11]

The way in which research is managed[12]—across the whole spectrum, from the fundamental search for knowledge to the improvement of a production process—critically determines the level of acceptance encountered by novel technology.[13] Table 7 lists many of the important considerations in evaluating the performance of a research establishment or laboratory and judging the effectiveness of research in a commercial context.[14]

Selective Procedure

Optimum selection is the third requirement for successful innovation and perhaps the most difficult. The cubes of clarification, which figure as three-dimensional lattices under the generative and receptive headings which appear above, can also assist in the selective process and illustrate (as does the diesel-engine coolant-level example earlier) the extent to which selection is qualitative, rather than quantitative.

The hazards of quantitative screening have long been recognized and continue to be repeated.[15] There is no case whatsoever (yet) for switching off brain and plugging in computer, in product evaluation.

Table 7. Checklist for proposed study on the management of research and development

---

Assessment of research effectiveness

---

(1) To what extent does control inhibit scientific creativity? Can industry afford to offer scientific freedom?

(2) Are fundamental and applied scientists simply distinguished by their motivation, in that one wishes to understand nature, the other to improve on it? Will they work happily together? Can a useful distinction be drawn between pure research and practical development?

(3) When should research projects, which have their own peculiar momentum, be terminated so as to minimize misapplication of effort and hoarding of manpower?

(4) On what basis should decisions as to penumbra limitation or extension be made? How can a company ensure that spin-off opportunities or research byproducts are recognized and properly exploited?

(5) Which of the following elements are considered to play a significant part in the successful management and planning of research:
  (5.1) Recruitment policy and methods of selection; staff mobility
  (5.2) Academic breadth compared with working field
  (5.3) Staff motives and attitudes, especially on research
  (5.4) Expenditure: budget allocation per head: company turnover
  (5.5) Manpower and cost ratios, materials and equipment
  (5.6) Preparation of budgets and financial control
  (5.7) Organization, incentives and management
  (5.8) Liaison and communication with other departments
  (5.9) Liaison and communication outside the company
  (5.10) Channels of communication: internal and external
  (5.11) Information storage, retrieval and distribution
  (5.12) Selection and planning of research programmes
  (5.13) Review procedure and period of review
  (5.14) Duration of projects and policy on termination
  (5.15) Definition of objectives; freedom to digress
  (5.16) The recognition and exploitation of peripheral discoveries
  (5.17) Routes from concept to commercial product
  (5.18) Follow-up procedures: production and marketing
  (5.19) Policy on licensing and co-operative projects
  (5.20) Effects of taxation and Government policy

(6) Distinguish between successful and unsuccessful research projects. What factors, in real cases known to the informant, have contributed to research effectiveness?

(7) What form does communication take at present between technical research and marketing departments? How can such communication be improved in practice? How can excessive preoccupation with the present be redressed in favour of the future and the planner be given adequate authority?

(8) Can planning be so conducted that a company may benefit at the same time from changes in the environment and from internal innovation? How can the two be constantly related?

Selection may also take place at many different stages in product development and introduction. Choosing research projects, in the context of limited resources, can present a problem[16] and it may sometimes be desirable to discontinue a project, even when the prototype has flown. For this reason, I am always puzzled when a new-product success rate is quoted, without definition, as one in a hundred or some other arbitrary figure. Whatever does it mean?

Alien Theology

It is usually the research arms of advertising agencies who explore the problems of new-product development in the consumer field, where there may be universal yardsticks for measuring success rate. Perhaps, because of their origin, practices seem foreign to my own experience in the engineering field.

It is commonplace to suggest that basic principles apply overall, though questionably where the same words mean different things. Once, for no apparent reason, I was invited by an advertising agency to attend a presentation on product planning, where I found myself the only member of the audience. After four contributions, much sophisticated language and the explanation of many subtle techniques, my hosts announced their conclusion: their figurative client should market a pink cereal.

This occasion was some little time ago but I note in the supplement on New Product Development to the March 1980 Market Research Society *Newsletter* that, under 'Launches of 1979' are listed a number of curious innovations, including 'Square crisps'. I have also read in the *Financial Times* of an 'unusually methodical analysis' (often a euphenism for pedestrian) conducted on behalf of a tobacco group, leading to the acquisition of an American hotel chain. The almost equally pedestrian movie *Blazing Saddles* might have brought the acquisitive principals, rather more quickly, to the same conclusion. No wonder, in the illustration, the victim wears a sardonic smile. Still, the ways of the consumer industry remain mysterious and clearly most expensive.

Although industrial marketing[17] owes something to consumer methodology, industrial product planning is something else again. The difference is apparent: a new industrial product can only be justified if it fulfils more cost-effectively some recognizable function; a new consumer product may involve no more than a change in colour, shape or presentation.

Systematic Sources

It would be churlish and unwise to dismiss the systematic efforts of reasonable people. The appropriation of product planning by the marketing lobby, instead of say the proponents of strategy or operational research, means that much constructive thinking has come from the (academic) marketing side.[18] I was however prompted to describe marketing somewhat whimsically at a conference in 1969 as a management function first devised by salesmen (and progressively redefined until it became a synonym for business) such that they might either escape the rigours of measurable performance into comfortable staff positions or predispose their peers to accept them as future chief executives. Selling, I suggested, was the measured use of truth.

There are several useful texts on product planning with a technical or innovative bias, plus a few attempting universal coverage, including consumer products. They range from excellent short manuals[19] to collections of published articles.[20] The diversity of methods and sources used in conducting a product search is indicated in Table 8.

Case Examples

As I hope has been established, diversification is usually best directed in relation to a company's established capability, qualified by any weaknesses. The totally alien activity is seldom successfully assimilated. Three studies conducted by the Metra Consulting Group show that this condition need not be restricting and that the solutions to diversification problems are as diverse as the companies themselves.

A component manufacturer supplying parts to the automotive industry was fully occupied in current manufacture and development but foresaw a decline in turnover during the early 1980s. A search for acquisitions was defined in sectors of industry having at least minimal affinity with present operations, as in terms of purchasing or manufacture. Using simplified criteria, in keeping with available data storage and retrieval systems, a search was completed, yielding, after visits, some 15 potential acquisitions. Negotiations with two were put in hand.

Either acquisition could provide a base in four or five new markets, also forming a nucleus, such that a significant step in expansion might be achieved through inputs from the client company. The client in turn would be able, in terms of technology and quantity, to assimilate the resulting surplus of workload over capacity.

Limiting Criteria

In a second case, the company made a variety of semi-finished items in a wide range of materials for a multiplicity of markets, but was excluded by group policy from introducing end-products of its own. The intention was to increase added value.

The company had itself devised sets of components which could be assembled by a particular group of installers. Based on familiarity with the company's

Table 8. The scope and coverage of typical product search

Checklist of internal and external product sources	
Existing products	Departments of Trade and
New applications	Industry
New markets	Departments of Commerce
Existing markets	Other government departments
Adapted products	Embassies
New products	Commercial Attaches
	Government laboratories
Research departments (R & D)	National agencies (as NRDC)
Marketing departments	Foreign trade organizations
Market research departments	
Brand managers	Sponsored research laboratories
Advertising departments	Research associations
Advertising agents	University research departments
Planning departments	Trade associations
New product departments	Makers of complementary
Purchasing departments	products
Sales staff	Byproducts of other companies
Production staff	Spin-off departments
Other employees	Companies relinquishing products
	Companies for sale
Customer requirements	Potential acquisitions
Written enquiries	Existing partners or licensors
Written complaints	
Distributors and agents	
Competitors' customers	Monopoly breaking
Component suppliers	Parallel diversification
Original equipment	
manufacturers	Precursor markets
	Historical reiteration
Sales literature	Import statistics
Trade and technical journals	Portfolio scanning
Product journals	Secondary portfolios
Mail order catalogues	Market exploration
Press releases	Functional analysis
Exhibition catalogues	Molecular examination
	(chemicals)
Inventors	Substitution products
Patent agents	Multiple assemblies
Licence brokers	Complementary products
Industrial designers	Gap filling
Merchant banks	Tool and product
Consultants	
	Characteristic tables
New product centres	Brainstorming
Exhibitions and fairs	Technological forecasting
Direct mail	Normative methods
On-line terminals	Exploratory methods
Viewdata systems	Extrapolation
	Projection
Patent office files	Delphi
Patents expired	Relevance trees
Foreign patents	Morphological analysis
Competitors' patents	Foreign travel

technical competence, a search by scanning was undertaken for analogous sets or combinations of parts, leading to a uniquely versatile system, developed in France, acquirable by taking up an agency and permitting concentration in one of the client's existing markets.

A third company's plastics building products sold in a notoriously cyclic market. Any new product was to be manufactured using existing plant and to sell through present outlets. These conditions seemed at first intolerably restrictive, but the answer soon became self-evident. Troughs in the cycle could theoretically be filled by a shift to components used in improvement, maintenance, repair or extension, as distinct from original structures. Of the 120 products found, 4 were subsequently studied in depth with a view to licensing or creative imitation.

Technology Transfer

No company is able to exploit every opportunity uncovered, every innovation brought to its attention, every unsatisfied commercial need. Effort is necessarily concentrated on selected opportunities, ideally on opportunities where the company's inherent capability provides competitive advantage. Similarly, no company, however large, can afford to maintain a research and development activity embracing every technology of present or potential interest.[21]

It follows that technology transfer has a part to play even in the most industrialized societies.[22] Much has also been written concerning the transfer of appropriate technology from developed to developing countries.[23] The mechanism of transfer may involve sale of patents, licensing,[24] the formation of joint companies or even acquisition; and procedures exist for comparing and evaluating such agreements.[25] Licensing, for example, now has a long track record.[26]

Minimal Search

Methods of conducting product searches have already been itemized (Table 8) but, without the formulation of dynamic areas, searches of this kind are difficult to focus, allowing that a company's combined differentiated assets provide its only continuing competitive advantage.

A disarmingly simple approach I have developed recently has proved successful. Indeed, with increased financial stringency, many companies would like to see an early indication of practical results before committing substantial funds to a full programme of business development.

Those products in a company's portfolio produced using under-utilized facilities are first identified, followed by manufacturers, especially overseas, of all competing products (primary companies). From sales literature provided by these companies, details of their manufacturing portfolios are then established, on the assumption that some of their product lines at least, though not within the subject company's existing range, might fall within its capability.

The next step is to identify further groups of companies having appropriate products in common with the primary group but not competing with the subject company. These secondary companies are also approached for product literature. The literature from both primary and secondary companies is then examined and their products screened with particular reference to the company's surplus capacity. Residual items are then classified in order to formulate product categories of potential interest, providing a basis for a systematic search, employing, for example, the following methods:

(1) On-line scan of opportunities, using computer terminal;

(2) Courteous enquiries to relevant trade and technical associations;

(3) Similar requests to publishers of representative trade journals;

(4) Interrogation of government trade and other agencies;

(5) Approaches to competent licence brokers;

(6) A focused review of pertinent corporate and other patents;

(7) Direct mailing to selected manufacturers (using word processing);

(8) Also to suppliers of associated (as control) equipment or complementary products.

The aim in all tasks itemized above is to elicit information on licensable products, ideally involving some unique or innovative element, plus requirements for local manufacture such that siting in the district of the subject company merits consideration. Opportunities are finally listed, with any pertinent information assembled incidentally during the enquiry. Implementation need not be confined to licensing, since there is a wide range of companies and other establishments ready to undertake contract development and design.

Formal Implementation

It is often said that finding a new product is far easier than driving it through to a commercial success. Certainly, conception tends to be easier than labour and labour easier than rearing the results. Still, it has frequently been done and postnatal prototypes transformed into talented, well adjusted and mature products. Given adequate raw material, it is, I suppose, a matter of doing the right thing at the right time, for which most of us are reasonably well equipped, whether through

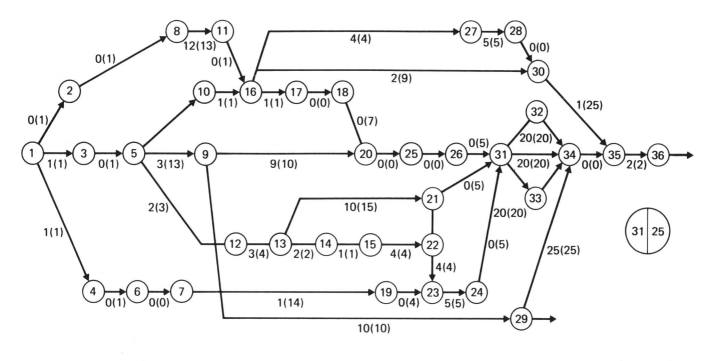

1–2	Approve Product Proposal and Expenditure	13–14	Clear Areas and Prepare Foundations	20–25	Select Materials and Subcontractors
1–3	Prepare Detailed Three-year.Programme	14–15	Civil and Electrical Contracts	25–26	Place Orders for Materials
1–4	Review Terms for Buying or Leasing Tools	10–16	Analyse Batch Requirements from Sales Leads	16–27	Plan Initial Sales Approach
3–5	Approve Three-year Programme	11–16	Report Market Research and Review Project	27–28	Staff and Organize Task Force
4–6	Decide to Lease or Buy Tools	16–17	Select Product Specifications	9–29	Continue Technical Development
6–7	Place Orders for Machine Tools	17–18	Decide Quantities and Batch Sizes	16–30	Continue Market Consultation
2–8	Plan Market Exploration for Further Applications	7–19	Order Ancillary and Test Equipment	21–31	Install and Commission Tools
5–9	Continue Technical Development	9–20	Prepare Detailed Designs	31–23	Produce Prototype Batches
5–10	Follow-up Sales Contacts and Inquiries	13–21	Select and Train Machine Operators	31–33	Plan and Conduct Field Tests
8–11	Conduct Market Exploration	15–22	Complete Workshop Preparation	31–34	Modify Designs in Consultation
5–12	Allocate Works Area to Machines	22–23	Install and Test Electrical Plant	34–35	Define Machining Tolerances
12–13	Plan Production Flows and Layout	23–24	Install Ancillary and Test Equipment	35–36	Decide Further Batch Specifications

Figure 2. Implementation network for new-product introduction (J. M. Pick)

instinct, our own experience or the vicariously accumulated and synoptic wisdom of others.

Timing has often been considered in terms of the largely sterile product life cycle, with unit profit passing its peak somewhat in advance of unit sales.[27] I have come to regard it as a device whereby consultants frighten potential clients into buying their services.

In my view, it is a dated and not very useful concept. The curves can only be drawn retrospectively and have no mathematical significance. The cycle could only serve a practical purpose, were it possible to derive the first and second differentials at the present instant. Otherwise, it has no predictive value. Just think about the wheel, which unlike non-alcoholic beer, has clearly had an exceptionally long, if somewhat erratic, life cycle, foreseeably coming to an end—though I doubt it.

Other models include the long abandoned exponential and the S-curve or logistic, modelled on the introduction of a new species into a given ecological environment, corresponding to the commercial exploitation of technology in con-

ditions of opportunity and constraint, with growth levelling off with the approach of saturation.

The implementation of a decision to introduce a new product is not too formidable, provided that steps are taken systematically and in the right order. My former colleague, Joan Pick, prepared the network diagram shown in Figure 2 to plan the introduction of a hydraulic motor. The critical path is 1–3–5–12–13–21–22–23–24–31–34–35–36.

Abstract Formulation

The task becomes more difficult when the launching concerns something more abstract, such as a service: setting up a consultancy business provides a typical example. Perhaps the most interesting venture in my recent experience relates to a service for design and drawing-office staff of consulting and contracting engineers or original equipment manufacturers. Before the case can be related, some explanation of the principle is necessary.

The Universal Drafting and Specifying (UDS) System is an important new marketing concept for manufacturers of components used in engineering or construction. It encourages specifiers to select the products of manufacturers participating in the system, also providing sales leads and demand forecasts.

The designer usually arrives at a basic concept for his scheme relatively quickly. He then selects components from a range of competing products by consulting catalogues. Having made a selection, he then spends considerable time arranging the components in space, detailing their location, interconnection and exact specification. Manufacturers of components spend much money and effort to ensure that their catalogues are noticeable, convenient to use and available to the specifier. So far they have done little for their potential customers to ease the tedium of detailing and specifying the components they supply.

Patented Process

In UDS, a supplier's comprehensive range of components is detailed in drawings, which are made available to contractors and original equipment manufacturers, free of charge, in the form of dry transfers. The transfers are designed by licensed graphics studios, using uniform standards of drafting (covering line width, presentation, lettering and materials identification) in carefully selected standard scales. The dry transfers are made by the patented Hona process suited to draftsmen rather than graphic artists (it is non-sticky, non-peel, as permanent as drafting ink 'but erasable' and susceptible to over-drawing).

The Hona transfers are inserted, along with the catalogue and specification sheets, in a distinctive folder and distributed by, or on behalf of, participating component manufacturers. Mailing lists are carefully chosen to suit the sales profile of each product. As dry transfers are used, replacements are despatched centrally and the replacement requests analysed (by manufacturer and product) for feedback of marketing data to the participants.

Users and Specifiers

For users or specifiers: UDS saves much effort and valuable time, by eliminating up to 75 per cent of the work associated with detailing and specifying. This aid generates goodwill and encourages the specifier to search his shelves for the distinctive catalogues of manufacturers participating in the scheme.

For component suppliers: UDS is (1) an effective way of ensuring that their catalogues are consulted whenever there is a chance of their products being specified; (2) an efficient method of distributing catalogues and other sales literature; and (3) an important marketing aid, improving the control and deployment of salesmen and enhancing the ability to anticipate and forecast demand. The cost of the service (including transfers) might therefore come from the component supplier's promotional budget.

The dry transfer revolution is already under way in drafting offices, in advance of or complementary to computer aided design. Only through the adoption of UDS (with controlled standards of presentation and scales, the benefits of Hona technology, plus the economy and analytical advantages of central distribution) is it possible, so the principals claim, to exploit the potential fully and turn it to the benefit of participating companies.

It is also said that the UDS system, being comprehensive, achieves economies of scale in artwork, printing and distribution, which no individual component manufacturer could approach, even remotely, using his own resources, while relying on other and (from the draftsmen's point of view) inferior dry-transfer technology.

Market Evaluation

A market study was commissioned from the Metra Consulting Group, who had the problem of presenting a complex and recondite idea to component suppliers and potential users before any level of probable acceptance could be determined. The problem was compounded on one occasion when, for some reason verging on the arcane, the dry transfers did not work. The fault has since been found and rectified.

The findings of the survey were encouraging. The potential market was large and likely to survive at least 10 years. The snag lay in the time projected to develop sufficient sales commensurate with a payback period short enough to satisfy the proposed partner resposible for purchasing the dry-transfer printing machinery. My present employers were therefore invited to draft a marketing plan.

Marketing Plan

For present purposes the schedule can only be reproduced in outline. Even without allowance for

Table 9. Annual action and sales projection

	Month	Sales	Cumulative	Action	Comment
(1)	January	—	—	Planning	Begin trial
(2)	February	10	10	Plan + Trial	(trial mktg.)
(3)	March	45	55	Mailings	(selective)
(4)	April	55	110 (110)	Mailings	(selective)
(5)	May	55	165 (55)	Advertisement	(mail analysis)
(6)	June	30	195 (85)	Response analysis	(hol. period)
(7)	July	25	220 (110)	Sector mailing (1)	(hol. period)
(8)	August	25	245 (25)	Sector mailing (2)	(hol. period)
(9)	September	45	290 (70)	Advertisement	(mail analysis)
(10)	October	60	350 (130)	Advertisement	(resp. analysis)
(11)	November	60	410 (60)	Sector mailing (3)	also advert.
(12)	December	30	440 (90)	Annual analysis	(resp. analysis)
(13)	January	60	500 (150)	Annual analysis	(assume cont.)

(1), (2) and (3) = First, second and third mailings, respectively.

holidays, sickness etc., the maximum number of working days per salesman per quarter was 65 (13 × 5). For one salesman to achieve the target of 110 participating component manufacturers, he would need to make two sales a day. Such a target could not be achieved by casual selling (even one sale a day by two salesmen working in parallel), but a strike rate in this region was just conceivable on the basis of pre-promoted and prepared selling, with administrative support.

Since rapid build-up of subscribing or participating companies was critical, it was sensible to use every sales aid in the early stages, with a 1 month preparatory and promotional period. At the same time, it was undesirable to act in such a way that lateral competitors were prompted to intervene on any appreciable scale. Selling methods and sales aids considered, with some overlap and mutual reinforcement, included:

(1) Selective selling based on directories;

(2) Identification of candidates through end-users;

(3) Prestigious informative advertising (self-selection);

(4) Complementary promotion through editorial copy;

(5) Direct mail with descriptive enclosures;

(6) Conferences on Universal Drafting System.

Market development was not expected to proceed at a rate determined simply by the number of salesmen employed but was likely to be cumulative, with various contributory effects (bandwagon, extension of range coverage, etc.). Conversely, the same number of sales might be achieved with diminishing effort. Six different stages, in two groups, were identified, with step increases followed by stability, as shown below.

Group 1: Build-up

(1) Initial sales (scattered and experimental).

(2) Encouraged sales (after say 10 participants).

(3) Make-up sales (so service to user is comprehensive).

(4) Second round (keeping up or me-too).

Group 2: Stability

(5) Reordering (dependent on consumption by users).

(6) Revision (redesign of component, say every 2 years).

It is impolitic to reveal the underlying assumptions dictating 110 sales (participants) a quarter for the first 12 months and the details provided here are drawn from an initial draft, intended in part to evoke a more realistic attitude in the sponsors. Activity and sales are projected by months in the first 12 months and January of the succeeding year (Table 9).

The charge per sheet and the percentage revenue to cover marketing cannot be disclosed, or the average income, based on the number of sheets, from each customer. The cash-flow calculation, based on a calculation of receipts to marketing, both shown in Figure 3, may however be illustrative. The assumptions and calculations were later modified.

BUDGETED CASH FLOW FOR MARKETING THE HONA SYSTEM

Months	1	2	3	4	5	6	7	8	9	10	11	12	13
Income					(sums in £'000)				8	21	35	41	36
Expenses													
Payroll	2.5	2.5	3.5	3.5	3.5	5.0	5.0	5.0	5.0	5.0	5.0	5.0	5.0
Accommodation	0.6	0.6	0.6	0.6	0.6	0.6	0.6	0.6	0.6	0.6	0.6	0.6	0.6
Equipment Hire	0.8	0.8	0.8	0.8	0.8	0.8	0.8	0.8	0.8	0.8	0.8	0.8	0.8
Services	0.5	0.5	0.5	0.5	0.5	0.7	0.7	0.7	0.7	0.7	0.7	0.7	0.7
Advertising					7.0				7.0	8.2	1.2		
Set-up Costs	2.5	1.5											
Total Outgoings	(6.9)	(5.9)	(5.4)	(5.4)	(12.4)	(7.1)	(7.1)	(7.1)	(14.1)	(15.3)	(8.3)	(7.1)	(7.1)
Profit	(6.9)	(5.9)	(5.4)	(5.4)	(12.4)	(7.1)	(7.1)	(7.1)	(6.1)	5.7	26.7	33.9	28.9
Cumulative	(6.9)	(12.8)	(18.2)	(23.6)	(36.0)	(43.1)	(50.2)	(57.3)	(63.4)	(57.7)	(31.0)	2.9	31.8

CALCULATION OF RECEIPTS TO MARKETING UNIT OR INCOME

Months	1	2	3	4	5	6	7	8	9	10	11	12	13	14	15	16	17	18	19	20	21	22	23	24	25
Sales (participants)	–	10	45	55	55	30	25	25	45	60	60	30	60												
Cumulative (quarters)	–			110			110			130			150			130			140			150			160
Sheets sold (×10⁶)	–			6.5			6.5			7.7			8.8			7.7			8.3			8.8			9.4
Distribution (×10⁶)	–	–	–	–	–	–	–	2.4	3.9	4.2	4.2	2.4	4.2	4.0	4.2	4.2	4.2	3.2	2.4	2.4	4.2	4.2	3.2	3.0	3.2
Marketing Invoices (£10³)	–	–	–	–	–	–	–	24	39	42	42	24	42	40	42	42	42	32	24	24	42	42	32	30	32
Marketing Receipts (£10³)								8	21	35	41	36	36	35	41	41	42	38	33	27	30	36	38	35	

Apart from exceptional items, selling costs will, if anything, diminish in the second year. Annual profit will therefore exceed £360 000

Figure 3. Share of projected income due to marketing unit and budgeted cash flow

Business Regeneration

A healthy economy does not depend solely on the creation of new businesses; existing businesses must be capable of survival and regeneration, at least until the situation becomes entirely hopeless—if indeed it ever does. Solutions for larger companies are numerous and many of considerable contributory value, including: the managerial grid approach[28] or matrix management, multilayered management,[29] strategic management,[30] with strategic business units (SBU's),[31] and most recently what Igor Ansoff has termed 'surprise management'.

Surprises are best accommodated through an adaptive posture. Again, business units, based on market-oriented product groupings prove less appropriate in a context of innovative technology, where multiple cross-linkages are of critical importance. Each functional responsibility—research and development, production and marketing—calls for an organizational structure suited to its own activity.

Acknowledgment—This is the second of E. Peter Ward's three articles on Planning for Technological Innovation. The third will appear in August 1981.

References

(1) E. Peter Ward, The Contribution of Market Research, Paper presented to scientific and technical staff at Lucas Research Centre, September (1978).

(2) Tom Stoppard, *Albert's Bridge*, Faber and Faber, London (1969).

(3) Report of Inquiry into the British Aircraft Industry, *Engineering*, **185,** May (1958).

(4) Michael Shanks, *The Innovators*, Pelican (1967).

(5) J. Langrish, M. Gibbons, W. G. Evans and F. R. Jevons, *Wealth from Knowledge: Studies of Innovation in Industry*, MacMillan (1972).

(6) J. Jewkes, *Sources of Invention*, MacMillan (1958).

(7) R. C. Parker, *Guidelines for Product Innovation*, British Institute of Management Foundation (1980).

(8) Rex V. Brown, Andrew S. Kahr and Cameron Peterson, *Decision Analysis for the Manager*, Holt, Rinehart and Winston, New York (1974).

(9) Stafford Beer, *Decision and Control*, John Wiley, London (1966).

(10) Edward P. Hawthorn, *The Management of Technology*, McGraw-Hill, London (1978).

(11) H. Igor Ansoff, *Corporate Strategy: an Analytical Approach to Business Policy for Growth and Expansion*, Penguin, London (1968).

(12) R. E. Seiler, *Improving the Effectiveness of Research and Development*, McGraw-Hill, New York (1965).

(13) Denis Gabor, *Inventing the Future*, Penguin, London (1964).

(14) E. Peter Ward, Research Effectiveness in a Commercial Context, Lecture presented for Polytechnic School of Management Studies, London, April (1968).

(15) Jan Buijs, Strategic planning and product innovation—some systematic approaches, *Long Range Planning*, **12**, 23–34, October (1979).

(16) T. S. McLeod, *Management of Research, Development and Design in Industry*, Gower Press (1969).

(17) Aubrey Wilson, *The Marketing of Industrial Products*, Hutchinson (1965).

(18) Philip Kotler, *Marketing Decision Making: A Model Building Approach*, Holt Rinehart & Winston, New York (1971).

(19) Peter J. T. Gorle and L. T. James Long, *Essentials of Product Planning*, McGraw-Hill, London (1973).

(20) Thomas L. Berg and Abe Shuchman (Eds.) *Product Strategy and Management*, Holt Rinehart & Winston, New York (1963).

(21) Thomas J. Allen, Michael L. Tushman and Dennis M. S. Lee, Technology transfer as a function of position in the spectrum from research through development to technical services, *Academy of Management Journal*, **22**, 694–708 (1979).

(22) J. A. Jolly and J. W. Creighton (Eds) *Technology Transfer in Research and Development*, Naval Postgraduate School, Monterey, California, June (1975).

(23) C. V. S. Ratnam, Technology Transfer from Developed to Developing Countries: Experience in India, presented at International Conference on Technology Transfer in Industrialised Countries, Estoril, November (1977).

(24) D. Edmunds Brazell, *Manufacturing under Licence: a Handbook*, Kenneth Mason (1967).

(25) *Guidelines for Evaluation of Transfer of Technology Agreements: Development and Transfer of Technology*, Series No. 12, United Nations Industrial Development Organization, Vienna, United Nations, New York (1979).

(26) Basil J. A. Bard, *Historical View of Licensing*, Licensing Executives Society International Conference, December (1975).

(27) David R. Rink and John E. Swan, Product life cycle research: a literature review, *Journal of Business Research*, **148**, 219–242, Elsevier, North Holland (1979).

(28) R. R. Blake, J. S. Mouton, L. V. Barnes and L. E. Greiner, A managerial grid approach to organization development: the theory and some research findings, *Harvard Business Review*, **42** (1964).

(29) Wilbur M. McFeely, The Conference Board Record, March (1971). Revised and republished in *Changement: Understanding and Managing Business Change*, Peter H. Burgher (Ed.), Lexington Books, Lexington, Massachusetts (1979).

(30) H. Igor Ansoff, R. P. Declerck and R. L. Hayes, *From Strategic Planning to Strategic Management*, John Wiley, London (1976).

(31) Clifford H. Springer, General Electric's Evolving Management System, *Organization for Forecasting and Planning: Experience in the Soviet Union and the United States*, William R. Dill and G. Kh. Popov (Eds.) John Wiley, Chichester (1979).

Theory

THE ADOPTION OF NEW INDUSTRIALPRODUCTS Anything that can be done to ensure that new products are accepted and accepted quickly must have a major effect on the profits from innovation. Dr George Hayward reports on important new techniques that have been developed on the basis of research sponsored by a grant from the Social Science Research Council

Dr Hayward worked for eighteen years in North America, Finland and Denmark as well as in the UK with three international engineering companies before entering academic life. He holds the Diploma in Marketing and postgraduate awards from three UK Universities. He is Director of the Innovation Research Group, North East London Polytechnic (NELP), and Head of the Higher Degree Unit, Anglian Regional Management Centre, formed by NELP and Essex County Council

The length of time taken by new machines and new ideas to spread throughout industry is an area which equally concerns academics and marketing practitioners: the research findings discussed in the present article may help to bridge the ever narrowing gap between the 'academic' and 'practical' workers.

In his book *Diffusion of Innovation* Everett M Rogers gave a fresh insight into many of the problems confronting marketing men, drawing heavily on work carried out in North America by rural sociologists. The farming community is one in which products are readily observed, as anyone will know who has been stuck behind a farmer on rural roads keeping his eyes on crops and stock as he drives along. He can identify every fellow farmer and he can see if the stock look particularly good or the grain is standing well and fields are weedfree. The farmer soon comments to the owner of the stock or field and finds out just what method of feeding is being used, what varieties of cereal are being grown, or what brands of weedkiller are in use. The local weekly market day often assists in this social exchange of ideas.

When this activity is compared with the study of industrial products, mostly hidden behind factory walls, it can readily be appreciated that rural sociologists can and have made a tremendous contribution to marketing literature. However, little work had been carried out in the industrial sector and B E Cook, in a dissertation for the degree of Master of Science from Bradford University, mentions that out of seven hundred and eight publications under fourteen headings only five could be attributed to the industrial field. This then seemed an area worth following up and research was undertaken by the writer into the diffusion of technological innovations in industry. The investigation was carried out in two stages, first diffusion research, and second, the characteristics of innovations.

1. Diffusion research
It was considered that the work already done by the American rural sociologists could be adapted to the marketing of industrial equipment in the UK and a

research project was developed to examine their findings. It was decided to study the time taken for technological innovations to spread throughout all the factories of a food processing industry within the UK, composed of both large groups and small independent plants and well served by both engineers and consulting chemists, with a good trade journal available.

Having selected an industry, the next problem was to choose the innovations to study, and due to the length of time it was anticipated that some products took to spread, immediate post-war innovations were decided on. Managers within the industry established the five innovations (see *Exhibit 1*) which they considered to be most important.

The research method was carried out with personal interviews and postal questionnaires, and the response rate for the returned questionnaires was very high:

Group plants	92%
Independent plants	72%
Total industry	81%

Time taken for adoption
The completed questionnaires were analysed and the time taken for the five innovations to diffuse throughout the industry calculated. The research showed that none of the five innovations approached the 100% adoption figure, so the study was based on the time taken for 50% of the industry to adopt. Even then one of the innovations failed to reach that stage.

It can be seen that the variation in time for adoption was very great in all cases, but that there was a significant variation in time taken to adopt between the innovations (this difference between individual innovations was to be the subject of future research). A further study was initiated into separating the plants according to the number of innovations which they adopted. The plants were grouped into three categories of innovators: low (with none or one only of the five innovations), medium (two or three of the innovations) and high (four or five of the innovations). The results shown in *Exhibit 2* were

Reprinted with permission from *Marketing* (UK), pp. 44, 45, 47, and 48, Nov. 1977.

obtained and it can be seen that the independent plants scored favourably in the high innovator category as against the group plants. This could be interpreted as evidence of a 'survival strategy'.

The innovations were also studied in relation to the plant capacity and it was apparent that both for the group and independent plants, a small capacity range existed in which the greatest amount of adoption of innovations took place. This information was of especial interest to marketing managers with engineers serving the industry and, in particular, the fact that independent plants with capacities below the optimum range showed a high rate of failure and subsequent closure.

Cumulative adoption curves were drawn up for all the five innovations but did not always follow the 'S' shaped curve so well documented in existing literature. In *Exhibit 3* the 'S' shaped curve (A) and the Bell shaped curve (B) are used frequently in diffusion research but may require some explanation. The 'S' shaped (or *cumulative*) adoption curve denoted the number of adopters of the innovation on a *cumulative* basis. The curve rises gradually as the innovation becomes accepted, rises more steeply, and then tails off as the last few remaining organisations adopt the innovation. On the other hand, the 'Bell' shaped curve shows the *annual* adoption of the innovation, starting slowly, rising to a peak, and again tailing off.

Information sources
The sources from which managers obtained information about new plant and techniques were studied; the two major ones proved to be technical sales engineers and managers of other plants. Virtually 100% of the managers read the trade journal (only one manager stated that he did not read it at all), and it appeared that managers used the journal as a means of gaining initial awareness of new machines or ideas, but then sought further information from either the engineers serving the industry or from other plant managers. These findings were of interest in view of the innovation-decision process described by Rogers and Shoemaker in their book *Communication of Innovations*. This was suggested by a committee of rural sociologists in 1955 and consisted of five stages:—

1. *Awareness stage:* The individual learns of the existence of the new idea but lacks information about it.
2. *Interest stage:* The individual develops interest in the innovation and seeks additional information about it.

3. *Evaluation stage:* The individual makes mental application of the new idea to his present and anticipated future situations and decides whether or not to try it.
4. *Trial stage:* The individual actually applies the new idea on a small scale in order to determine its utility in his own situation.
5. *Adoption stage:* The individual uses the new idea continuously on a full scale.

EXHIBIT 1: TIME TAKEN FOR 50% OF THE PLANTS TO ADOPT THE INNOVATIONS	
Innovation	*Time for 50% to adopt*
Pneumatic conveying (a method of conveying products by using air)	19 years
Bulk outloading (a method of delivering the final product in bulk rather than in sack)	12 years
Silo (a method to store final products)	13 years
Short Surface System (a new method of processing)	19+ years
Special dust collector (an improvement in existing dust collection)	8 years

EXHIBIT 2: CLASSIFICATION OF PLANTS INTO INNOVATION CATEGORIES			
Innovator category	*Group plants %*	*Independent plants %*	*Total plants %*
Low (0 or 1)	12	21	17
Medium (2 or 3)	59	30	55
High (4 or 5)	29	49	28

This concept of the adoption process implies that the process always ends in adoption, whereas rejection may be the eventual outcome. Also the stages do not always take place in the order outlined and the trial stage may be omitted in many cases. This was particularly the case in the research outlined above because the independent plants were often in a 'Go' or 'No Go' situation and either had to adopt the innovation on a full scale or reject it, whilst the group plants could install an innovation in just one of their production units and study it at leisure before adopting it in other units. Thus the trial stage could be used by the group plants, but was not always possible for the independent units.

Opinion leaders
Following on from the study of sources of information, it became possible to identify opinion leaders in the industry by setting out various criteria such as:
□ the number of innovations introduced into the plants under their control
□ the number of plants they controlled
□ their degree of responsibility in introducing the innovations studied
□ their reading habits (trade journals)
□ the degree to which they were 'cosmopolitan' ie how often they paid visits to plants overseas or in this country, and to consultant chemists and engineers.

Based on these criteria, eight opinion leaders were identified and on interviewing

them it was found that they played major roles in influencing other managers to adopt innovations. It was thought that this identification of opinion leaders could be of great benefit to sales engineers and technical representatives.

Conclusions from the diffusion research
The research highlighted the lengthy times taken for innovations to spread throughout

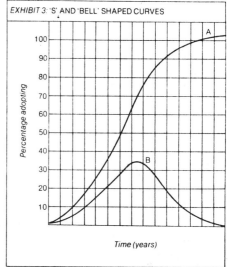

EXHIBIT 3: 'S' AND 'BELL' SHAPED CURVES

industry and the importance of identifying opinion leaders. The different stages of the innovation process were of major importance, particularly in distinguishing the roles played by trade journals, sales engineers and managers in other plants. From the point of view of the marketing manager, the different adoption patterns between group plants and independent plants was of value. It was felt that the research work was worth extending and the reasons not only for the time taken for innovations to diffuse, but also the variation between the different innovations, should be studied in greater detail. The research then carried on into the second stage.

2. Characteristics of innovations
The non-cumulative adoption curve shown in *Exhibit 3* has been stated by many authorities to be bell shaped, and using simple statistical techniques Rogers has suggested the following classification of adopters on this basis:

Innovators	2.5% of adopters	
Early adopters	13.5% ,,	,,
Early majority	34.0% ,,	,,
Late majority	34.0% ,,	,,
Laggards	16.0% ,,	,,

These categories are, of course, arbitrary but have been found of value in the diffusion of agricultural innovations, since it has been possible to ascribe certain characteristics to farmers who fall in the different categories outlined above.

Theory

However, for the purposes of industrial innovations it was felt that the reasons for the time taken for innovations to diffuse were rather more complex than could be explained by categorising adoptors.

In the case of technological innovations, it was thought possible that the innovations

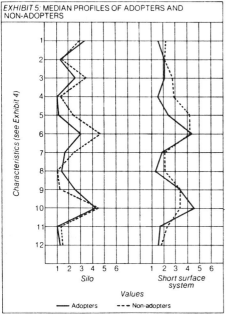

EXHIBIT 4: CHARACTERISTICS OF INNOVATIONS

Identification number	Characteristic
1	Initial cost
2	Running cost
3	Pay-off period
4	Saving in time
5	Reduction in dust (two industries) Easy to clean (one industry)
6	Reduction in noise
7	Mechanical advantage
8	Easier in operation
9	Flexibility
10	Trial on a small scale
11	Reliability in operation
12	Ease of understanding

EXHIBIT 5: MEDIAN PROFILES OF ADOPTERS AND NON-ADOPTERS

themselves had certain characteristics which could be perceived by adoptors and potential adoptors and that these perceived characteristics could influence the rate of adoption. In fact, not only were innovation characteristics of interest in their own right, but it was apparent that a relationship might exist between the perceived characteristics of the innovations and the length of time taken for them to diffuse throughout industry.

The research was widened to examine three industries within the UK, all of them being concerned with food and drink processing, but varying in their degree of management sophistication. Again, the method of research was to establish the areas of study following interviews within the industry and then to obtain the information required by means of postal questionnaires.

The three industries provided for study a total of fourteen major post-war innovations, and senior managers from the three industries selected twelve characteristics which they considered to be of importance when deciding whether or not to adopt an innovation. These characteristics are listed in *Exhibit 4*.

Managers in the three industries were requested to rate their perception of the importance of each characteristic by rating them on the following scale, circling the number which most approximated to their personal evaluation:

1. Strongly agree
2. Agree
3. Neither agree nor disagree
4. Disagree
5. Strongly disagree
6. Not applicable

These scores were made in relationship to the previous machine or process which the innovation was to replace. The median was taken for the various responses, and profiles were drawn up to demonstrate the variation in responses, not only between one innovation and another, but between adoptors and non-adoptors of the various innovations, and also to illustrate the differences of the characteristics as perceived by managers in the group plants as against managers in the independent plants. *Exhibit 5* shows how the 'profiles' may be used to determine the differences between adoptors and non-adoptors for two of the innovations studied. This demonstrates how both machine designers and marketing managers may use 'profiles' either to improve design or increase sales by working on characteristics which show unfavourable responses. In the profile for the Silo, characteristic number 5, reduction 'in dust', is seen by adoptors to be more favourable than by non-adoptors. This

shows an area that can be covered by designers of future plants and used by marketing men to advantage. Similarly, with the Short Surface System, characteristic number 4, 'Saving in time', is seen as a very favourable characteristic by adoptors but non-adoptors feel neutral about it. Characteristic number 10, 'Trial on a small scale', is viewed unfavourably by adoptors and non-adoptors for both innovations. This type of analysis can be undertaken for all the twelve characteristics.

Exhibit 6 demonstrates a further method of using profiles: the 'clockface' method. From it Bulk Outloading and the Silo are seen to be very similar, but the variations between Pneumatic Conveying and Short Surface System (non-traditional innovations) are great. Characteristic number 6 'Reduction in noise' is very favourable for

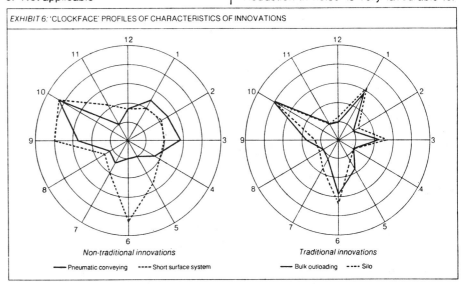

EXHIBIT 6: 'CLOCKFACE' PROFILES OF CHARACTERISTICS OF INNOVATIONS

Non-traditional innovations
— Pneumatic conveying   ---- Short surface system

Traditional innovations
— Bulk outloading   ---- Silo

Pneumatic Conveying, but very unfavourable for the Short Surface System. Characteristic number 6 is therefore one on which designers of future Short Surface Systems could concentrate and in the meantime marketing managers should note the very unfavourable response to it.

Characteristics numbers 9 'Flexibility' and 10 'Trial on a small scale' also rate very unfavourably for the Short Surface System, and *Exhibit 1* shows that the Short Surface System has taken the longest time of all the innovations to diffuse. Attention to the unfavourable points could well speed up its rate of acceptance by customers, whilst emphasis on the favourable characteristics would also have the same effect.

Innovations and their rate of diffusion
The work started under the early stage of the programme on diffusion research was extended and two types of cumulative adoption curves emerged; one which rose

very sharply without tailing off at a high figure for adoption, and the other which clearly showed the traditional 'S' shape but at a very low percentage of adoption. The innovations under study formed separate groups according to the curve shape and these were termed 'traditional' and 'non-traditional' innovations.

The traditional innovations were those which were an improvement on existing practice rather than a technical 'break-through', whilst the non-traditional inno-vations were completely new machines or changes of process and gave no basis of previous experience on which to judge them. The traditional innovations diffused fairly rapidly within their industries, whilst the non-traditional innovations with the 'S' shaped curves took a long time to reach a 50% adoption figure.

The benefit to the marketing manager of being able to predict the rate of diffusion of new products is significant, especially if he can discuss with designers the need to develop traditional innovations or to move in that direction. In one of the products under study the innovation was just moving from the non-traditional stage to the traditional stage, i.e. sufficient adoptors had experience of the innovation in use for evaluation of its application to be made.

EXHIBIT 7: SUM OF MEDIANS RELATED TO TIME TAKEN FOR A 50% ADOPTION FIGURE FOR THE 5 INNOVATIONS				
Innovations	Sum of medians	Rank	Time 50% to adopt	Rank
Special dust collector	21.7	1	8 yrs	1
Bulk outloading	22.1	2	12 yrs	2
Silo	23.9	3	13 yrs	3
Pneumatic conveying	27.1	4	19 yrs	4
Short surface system*	30.8	5	19+ yrs	5

*This is an estimated time but cannot be less than 19 years as the total ad option rate is only 40% in eighteen years

Also, a non-traditional innovation may require an intermediate product before it can gain acceptance, for example firms that weigh products manually may adopt semi-automatic weighers before moving to fully automatic weighers.

Characterstics in relation to time
It had already been suggested that the per-ceived characteristics of innovations bore a relationship to the time taken for them to diffuse within industry. *Exhibit 7* indicates the relationship of the sum of the median scores for all twelve characteristics of the five innovations and the time taken for them to be adopted by 50% of the total industry. It will be seen that the rank order is identical for both the sum of the medians and for the time taken in reaching a 50% adoption figure.

This aspect of the research is covered in some detail in report HR2269/2 of the Social Science Research Council entitled *Study of the Characteristics of Innovation in the Capital Equipment Field* by Hayward and Masterson. The findings were sup-ported in the other two industries examined in the later research.

Conclusions from the research
Innovations possess characteristics which may be translated into profiles. These can enable designers and marketing managers to reach conclusions concerning the prob-ability of adoption of the innovations. They also make it possible to determine different perceptions of innovations according to market segments. Innovations may be classified as traditional or non-traditional, each with their own characteristics and differing times for diffusion. The research also demonstrated links between the characteristics of innovations and the time taken to spread them. □

References
Cook, D E A *Review of Some Methodological Aspects of Dif-fusion Research*. M Sc dissertation. University of Bradford, 1970.
Hayward, G 'Diffusion of Innovation in the Flour Milling Industry' *European Journal of Marketing*. Vol 6, No 3, pp 195-202, 1972.
Hayward, G, Allen D H and Masterson J. 'Characteristics and Diffusion of Technological Innovations.' *R & D Management*. Vol 7, No 1, pp 15-24, October 1976.
Hayward, G, Allen D H and Masterson J. 'Innovation Profiles: A New Tool for Capital Equipment Manufacturers.' To be published in the *European Journal of Marketing*.
Hayward, G and Masterson J. *Study of the Characteristics of Innovation in the Capital Equipment Field*. Social Science Research Council Report No HR2269/2, 1977.
Rogers, E M *Diffusion of Innovation*. Free Press of Glencoe, 1962.
Rogers, E M and Shoemaker F F. *Communication of Innovations: A Cross-cultural Approach*, Collier-Macmillan, London, 1971.

Designing a Long Range Marketing Strategy for Services

*Christian Grönroos**

The purpose of the article is to develop a frame of reference for long range marketing strategy, labelled the Three Stage Model which could benefiti the attempts of service firms and institutions to successfully introduce marketing and eventually achieve marketing-orientated operations. The author stresses some organizational aspects especially concerning the use of traditional marketing departments for handling an organization's marketing function. The views on service marketing are supported by a substantial amount of empirical evidence from the industrial and the consumer service sector. The frame of reference and the organizational views of the marketing of services will be equally valid for industrial marketing of services and for marketing consumer services.

Introduction

Marketing orientation means that a firm or organization plans its operations according to market needs. The objectives of the firm should be to satisfy customer needs rather than merely to use existing production facilities or raw material. The organizations' marketing activities will be concerned with analyzing and revealing customer needs, developing products which will satisfy those needs, and demonstrating the need-satisfying qualities of the products in order to make the customers buy them.

In the goods-producing sector marketing activities have often been organized by establishing separate marketing departments, which have been made responsible for the marketing activities of the firm. The marketing department has been used as a means of making goods-producing companies marketing-oriented. In many cases, such firms have been accused of merely paying lip service to the so-called marketing concept. However, the organizational solution which has been used still seems to have a fair chance to succeed.

At least this is the case for firms producing consumer

*The author is acting professor of marketing at the Swedish School of Economics and Business Administration, Arkadiagatan 22, SF-00100, Heisingfors 10, Finland.

goods. In the industrial sector there is a stronger interdependence between different departments of the companies, and therefore, the marketing activities cannot be as well planned and implemented within a marketing department as in the context of consumer goods.[1] Marketing seems to lead to some organizational problems.[2]

In the context of services there is very little explicit marketing knowledge today. Most frequently the marketing establishment, both academicians and practitioners, strongly resist the view that the marketing of services in any critical dimension could differ from that of physical goods. There are, however, some signs of a shift in thinking.[3,4,5,6,7,8] This will, in my opinion, benefit firms and institutions in the vast and growing service sector of Western economies. There the service sector counts for almost 50 per cent—and in some countries for much more—of total employment and gross national product. Indeed, we are moving into a post-industrial society,[9,10] where the impact of services to welfare and the total economy is substantial, and yet, we know almost nothing about how to manage marketing of services and about how to organize for marketing in service organizations.

Today, there is some evidence supporting the opinion that marketing is a difficult task in the service sector, and that service companies are less marketing-oriented than firms in the goods-producing sector.[3,6,11] Moreover, marketing executives which are experienced with consumer goods marketing in many cases seem to feel uncomfortable when coming into a service business. Marketing is often a small and marginal business function, and their past experience somehow does not seem quite applicable.[6,7]

Characteristics of Services

Services are immaterial and physically intangible. The customer cannot see, feel, or taste a service, and therefore, there will be substantial evaluation problems for him. As he is not able to evaluate the abstract service, he

Reprinted with permission from *Long Range Planning,* vol. 13, pp. 36–42, Apr. 1980.

will look for tangible clues in the service context, which he can use as a basis for an evaluation. Furthermore, services are frequently to a great extent consumed as they are produced. Because of this characteristic of services *buyer/seller interactions* emerge. The producing firm and its representatives gets in contact with its customers. In some cases one is only confronted with machines and other non-human attributes of the organization, but most frequently human representatives of the service provider are also involved in the buyer/seller interactions.

Finally, services are activities, not things, although physical goods or things may be needed either to support or facilitate the service consumption.[12] This means that a service is produced in a process which simultaneously *is* the service. The output of the production process cannot be separated—more than to some extent—from the process itself. Moreover, this process takes place in the presence of the consumer and with the cooperation of the consumer.[13]

The characteristics of services discussed above lead to some important conclusions about what actually is the service in the opinion of the consumer. His evaluation of a given service's capability of satisfying his needs will depend on several components in the service context.[4] *First* of all, the *means of production*, the technological resources and the human resources of the organization are important. A customer's preferences towards a given service will be influenced by the exterior and interior of offices, by the condition of transportation vehicles, by machines, documents and other items, as well as by the company employees. *Secondly*, the customer's opinion of a service depends on the *production process*, i.e. it depends on the way in which the production resources are used in order to produce the service. For instance, the capabilities and behaviour of consultants, bank tellers and travel agency representatives, and their way of taking advantage of the other means of production, will have an impact on the customer's evaluation of the service. *Thirdly*, other people simultaneously purchasing or consuming a service may influence the preferences of a given customer. In the next section I shall discuss the marketing consequences of this view of the service offering content.

The Three Stage Model

In order to satisfy the needs of its target market the *Three Stage Model* holds that the service organization will have to consider three stages in the customer's opinion of the need-satisfying capabilities of the service offerings provided by the organization. These are:

(1) *interest* in the organization and its service offerings as possible means of satisfying the customer's needs;

(2) *purchase* of a service offering in order to get the particular need satisfied; and

(3) *repeat purchase* of the same or similar service offerings provided by the organization whenever needed by the customer.

These three stages will have substantial consequences for the marketing of services, especially for designing a long range marketing strategy. At each of the stages the objective of the marketing efforts and the nature of marketing will be different. The objective of marketing at each stage should be

(1) to *create interest* in the company and its service offerings;

(2) to *turn the general interest into sales* by activities during the *purchasing process*, i.e. from the moment the potential consumer has come to the company or its representative up to the moment he has made the purchase decision; and finally;

(3) to *guarantee resales* by activities during the *consumption process*, i.e. when the service is consumed usually in a very close contact with the service provider and the production process.

There is a very clear difference between the marketing activities at the second and third stages as compared to the activities at the first stage. Interest is mainly created by developing an attractive company image, by advertizing and other mass marketing efforts, and in industrial marketing to firms and institutions by personal sales activities by more or less professional salesmen. Furthermore, interest can be created by offering services at a certain price level.

The mass marketing activities cannot, however, result in much more than customer interest. A potential traveller may decide to get in contact with a given travel agency, a company may get interested in approaching a particular advertizing agency, or a factory manager may find it suitable to ask for an offer from a security and maintenance company. Such an interest is also heavily influenced by external sources such as colleagues, family members, and friends. The personal selling by professional salesmen, on the other hand, cannot lead to more than the creation of interest and perhaps sales. Resales is not, however, guaranteed by such efforts. One should notice that this kind of personal selling normally only exists in industrial marketing of services, and not in marketing to ultimate consumers.

In most cases sales and certainly resales are achieved by other marketing activities than those which have been considered so far. These activities are frequently not thought of as marketing today, but nevertheless, they do influence the preferences of the consumers towards a given service offering, and therefore, they are marketing activities. I here refer to activities in the buyer/seller interactions, which emerge in the buying and selling of services.

When a potential customer has come to the service company or its representative and is about to make up his mind about buying the service or not, he is confronted with the point of purchase, the employees, various kinds of documents, etc. These certainly have an impact on his opinion of the service. For example, when choosing among administrative consultants the buyer will be influenced by the consultants themselves, their capabilities and behaviour, by the technological resources provided by the consulting agencies, etc; when choosing among different banks the potential customer will be influenced by the location of bank offices, the capabilities, appearances and behaviour of the tellers, the supporting technological resources, documents, etc.

When the customer finally is consuming the service, he is in close contact with the service provider. He will be confronted with the means of production—both human and non-human—and with the production process. The means of production consist of *resources*, and in the production process *these resources are utilized*. The consumer's future purchasing behaviour, i.e. possible resales, is to a great extent influenced by what happens during the consumption process.

Consequently, managing the buyer/seller interactions of the purchasing and consumption processes is a marketing task and not solely an operational, technological, or personnel problem. It can be labelled the *interactive marketing function* of service organizations. In the following section I shall turn to the problem of

fitting together the objectives and activities of marketing at the various stages into a long range marketing strategy for services.

The Marketing and Need-Adaptation Circle

According to the *Three Stage Model* the service company has to respond to the needs of its customers throughout the process. When interest is created, the customer in many cases has a rather vague idea of his actual needs. He is looking for some kind of transportation or bank account in general, or for some sort of factory maintenance or office cleaning. In the purchasing process, the scope of the needs is narrowed, and finally the customer decides to buy a certain service offering as the 'best' means of satisfying the needs he feels that he has at that moment. During the consumption process he can evaluate how the service which he gets actually corresponds to his perceived needs. As a result he will be satisfied enough to come back, or he will be disappointed and become an ex-customer.

Figure 1 illustrates this process and demonstrates the place of the marketing functions in the process. In order to attract customers and turn an initial interest in the service offerings into sales and finally into resales and lasting customer contacts, a *continuous adaptation* of the operations to the customers' needs is required. Throughout the whole process the organization will have to demonstrate its capabilities to offer services, which really can satisfy these needs. This fact leads to substantial marketing consequences.

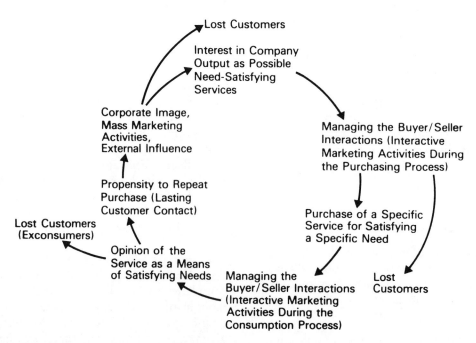

Figure 1. The marketing and need adaptation circle

82

The marketing and need-adaptation circle in Figure 1 illustrates the need for various kinds of activities throughout the process. By these activities the service firm tries to create customer interest in the services, turn this interest into sales, and in the long run establish lasting business contacts with satisfied customers and clients. The traditional mass marketing activities and the personal selling by professional salesman are by no means unimportant to the success of a service organization, but in my opinion however, managing the buyer/seller interactions—i.e. the interactive marketing function—is the most important marketing function of service organizations. Neglecting them may in the future be disastrous, in the increasing competitive environment of many service industries.

It should be noticed that managing the interactive marketing function is not only handling the human resources of the firm. The buyer/seller interactions involve technological resources as well. Planning such resources should also be a marketing task, so that, for instance, the location and interior of offices, computer systems, fee-collecting systems, transportation vehicles, and documentation systems benefit marketing instead of restricting or even counteracting it, as oftens is the case today. Moreover, the buyer/seller interactions also involve contacts between customers. Other customers may have an immense impact on a person's opinion of a service, which he is about to buy or which he is consuming. They may by their appearance or behaviour increase the quality of a service, but their influence can also be very undesired. Then their activities lead to a deterioration of service quality. Clearly, managing the interactions between customers should be a marketing task, too.

As an illustration of a long range marketing strategy based on the marketing and need-adaptation circle concept, let us consider the activities of a transportation company offering transportation services by sea. The company is operating on a consumer market as well as on industrial markets, offering both transportation services and conference arrangements to business firms and other organizations. This example describes the company's marketing of conference services.

Through advertizing efforts and various kinds of PR activities the company attempts to make potential clients interested in it as a possible conference operator. Occasionally, personal selling efforts are also used. Moreover, it relies heavily on external influence on potential clients by satisfied customers promoting the idea of using its ships as a possible conference site. The marketing activities used at this stage are mostly mass marketing efforts, and indirect promotion drawing on the company's reputation and on word-of-mouth communication.

When a potential client contacts the transportation company, the marketing activities become more specifically directed towards the unique needs of the client. The purchasing process starts. At this stage a conference service which corresponds to the wishes of the client and to his conference budget must be designed. Here the output of the process, sales, is to a great extent a result of personal selling efforts. The salesman will have to find out what the client really desires. His ability to negotiate is considered critical to the success of the marketing efforts. The client should be offered a conference design, which he will feel satisfied with during and after the conference, rather than merely a minimum budget design which seems to correspond to his initially expressed needs, but in the long run will be a disappointment to him. The salesman is, therefore, encouraged to think of himself more as a consultant than as anything else.

If the purchasing process comes to a successful end, the potential client will buy a conference service from the company. The marketing manager does not, however, stop being concerned with the client as soon as the purchase decision has been made. Marketing activities are carried out until the end of the conference. The company attempts to produce a service, which corresponds to the expectations of the client. The conference facilities, arrangements for meals and accommodation, the appearance and performance of the personnel onboard, etc. are considered to be of utmost importance to the success or failure of the company as a conference operator in the mind of the client. By appropriately designing the conference facilities as well as other necessary technological resources—e.g. cabin design, access to telex and telephone communication—and by conducting internal marketing programs in order to improve the marketing performance of various categories of employees, the company tries to guarantee that the client, the conference participants, and of course, other passengers, too, leave the ship in a state of satisfaction and with a favourable image of the transportation company and its services in mind. Eventually, the client and conference participants will probably return to the company, when a need for conference services or transportation services occurs. Moreover, they are expected to have a considerable impact on the word-of-mouth influence on potential customers that exists about the company, resulting in increased interest in the company and its services.

Thus, generally speaking, marketing services can be viewed as a continuous process, a circle. Successful marketing attracts customers who get into the circle and stay there, because they are satisfied with the performance of the firm. A customer may, however, break out at any stage of the process, if the company is not capable of giving him what it has promised to do. A client may be lost, because the company in an advertizing campaign makes promises, which the interactive marketing function cannot keep, or because the organization cannot successfully manage the buyer/seller interactions of the purchasing and/or consumption processes. Moreover, external influence by colleagues or friends may also have an impact on the customer's behaviour.

The marketing and need-adaptation circle concept demonstrates how the preferences of a customer towards a certain service depends on an enormous part of the service company and on the operations of the company. Consequently, it demonstrates the importance of the marketing function in the context of service. In the next section of the article I shall turn to the question how marketing has been introduced in service companies and how one could organize for successful marketing in the service sector.

The Misuse of Marketing Departments

When service companies have introduced marketing to any greater extent, separate marketing departments have frequently been established. The model has been taken from the goods-producing sector—especially consumer goods—where the marketing activities of the firm to a high degree can be initiated, planned, and implemented by and within the marketing department. What has happened in service firms? Other departments, such as operations, personnel, technology—as well as top management in many cases—have given up all their responsibility for the marketing performance. Before the marketing department was established, more or less spontaneous initiatives by various departments and persons in the firm were taken in improving the quality of the service and meeting the wishes and expectations of the consumers. Such activities tend to disappear in the new era of the marketing department.

What earlier was service production combined with often unconscious marketing efforts tends to become just plain service production. The firm has a separate department of specialists in marketing, so let them handle the marketing function and be responsible for the marketing performance of the organization. At this moment the real problems of the company start. It is now that the firm will start losing customers. What has happened?

It is my opinion that the main reason for the company becoming increasingly production-oriented instead of marketing-oriented is a failure to see the nature of service marketing. The marketing of physical goods has been applied to service firms without noticing that the marketing of services seems to be different. Indeed such a difference is not commonly recognized even today.

The difference between the *marketing function* of an

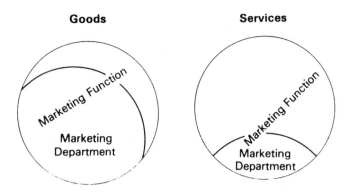

Figure 2. The relationship between the marketing function and the marketing department

organization and its *marketing department* should first of all be distinguished. The marketing function, as has been said in the article, is all activities which influence the preferences of the consumers towards the offerings and, therefore, also the success of the company and its chances to stay alive in the long run. The marketing department, on the other hand, is the organizational entity which is responsible for some, but not necessarily all marketing activities performed by the firm. In Figure 2 the relationship between the marketing function and the marketing department of goods-producing firms and service companies, respectively, is illustrated.

In the goods sector, and especially as far as consumer goods are concerned, the marketing department can plan and implement most of the marketing activities, i.e. the marketing department is able to control almost the total marketing function. It can, therefore, also be given a total marketing responsibility. Only personal selling efforts by top management is normally outside the marketing department. In the industrial sector of goods-producing industries the situation is somewhat different, because of the greater interdependence between different business units.[1]

In the service sector the situation is entirely different. A traditional marketing department can only control a minor part of the marketing function. The marketing manager is in an off-side position in the organization. Usually he does not have the necessary authority to manage the buyer/seller interactions. He cannot, therefore, plan and especially not implement activities within the interactive marketing function during the purchasing and consumption processes. Furthermore, people in the personnel department, operations department, and other departments often are quite prejudiced against their activities simultaneously being the concerns of the marketing department and the marketing manager.

Consequently, the marketing department is mainly engaged in mass marketing activities: planning advertizing campaigns, designing brochures, etc. Moreover, personal selling to industrial buyers, some pricing decisions, and sometimes also some marketing research and analysis are performed by the marketing department. This means that the department which has been made responsible for the marketing activities mainly is concerned with creating customer interest. Those parts of the marketing function which influence sales are the responsibility of others, who are not particularly interested in marketing. Clearly, this is a most unhappy situation, but it is merely a consequence of the misuse of an organizational arrangement, which has been developed for the goods-producing sector and not for service companies.

Organizing for Marketing

It is quite clear that establishing marketing departments is not a useful means of introducing marketing in a service organization. It must be realized, though, that *the marketing function is a key function in the service sector. Even if the term marketing is not used in connection with the activities in the buyer/seller interactions, managing these activities is a marketing function.* The responsibility for this marketing function must, therefore, be taken by someone, who is concerned with the total marketing performance of the organization. This person may be the marketing manager, but as the head of a traditional, decentralized marketing department he will probably continuously come into conflict with other departments and their heads. It will, for instance, be difficult for him to avoid conflicts with the personnel department, but nevertheless, the personnel policy, including hiring, rewarding, and promoting almost every employee, as well as the design of job descriptions, should be a marketing task like, for instance, advertizing.[3, 14, 15]

Successful service companies often do not have any marketing department at all, or they have very small marketing departments. In both cases the total marketing function is not expected by top management or by any part of the organization to be initiated and implemented within a marketing department. If there is no marketing department, top management will take the responsibility for the marketing performance of the firm, and there will be a fair chance that the different parts of the organization accept their duty to assist top management in serving the customers. Of course, the managing director must realize the importance of the total marketing function, and especially of the interactive marketing function.

If the marketing department is comparatively small and top management keep the total marketing responsibility, the other departments of the organization may accept that they still have marketing tasks to perform, although there are marketing people in the company. It is

essential that such a small marketing department either is concerned with the overall co-ordination of marketing activities and assisting other parts of the organization to perform their marketing tasks, or only is treated as a specialist on some marketing activities and not as marketing specialists responsible for the total marketing function. As soon as the rest of the organization, and indeed top management, start to think of the marketing department as overall marketing specialists the movement towards a production-orientation begins.

As a conclusion, top management should never delegate the responsibility for the total marketing function to any department head. Preferably the top executive should keep it with himself. Unfortunately, when the company grows, the managing director will be so busy with other duties that it will be quite difficult for him to give the marketing function as much attention as would be necessary. It seems as if it would be almost impossible to solve the problem which follows within the organizational structure of today's service companies. Perhaps this is not so surprising, because the organizational structure has also been inherited from the goods-producing sector.

In order to illustrate the organizational aspects of service marketing, let us consider another transportation company, which is engaged in urban mass transit. When the company in the past started to perform organized marketing activities, a traditional marketing department was established. The marketing activities of the company were delegated to this organizational unit headed by a marketing manager. What could the new department do? Mainly it was made responsible for advertizing, some public relations activities, and some market research. The marketing department became a rather weak unit within the organizational structure. Other parts of the company stopped being particularly concerned with the ways in which the company responded to the customers' wishes and transportation needs. A change in a production-oriented direction seems to have occurred.

The marketing department's attempts to influence the operational and personnel functions in a more marketing-oriented direction were resisted. The marketing manager's colleagues, to whom the responsibility for other business functions had been delegated, could, of course, not be expected to report to him and to be managed by him.

Eventually, the organizational structure was changed. The various functions were regrouped, and as part of this process the status of the marketing department was changed. It became merely an information department responsible for both external information, such as advertizing, PR and personal selling, and internal information. On the other hand, the marketing manager was removed from the marketing department to the board of directors, where he became a member responsible for co-ordinating the activities of all company functions and units in a marketing-oriented manner. Thus, the reduced marketing department *and* other organizational units are now expected to report to him. Instead of merely preparing marketing plans within the former marketing department, he is now responsible for developing a corporate plan of operations including advertizing, pricing, and other traditional marketing activities according to a goods-oriented philosophy, as well as technological resources, personnel planning, corporate image activities, etc. The new organizational structure is considered a more appropriate means of marketing-orientating the transportation company than the structure of the past.

In general, some sort of an *organizational innovation* seems to be needed. As the managing director most frequently is too busy and the head of the marketing department is in an off-side position, some kind of marketing co-ordinator on the top management level may be the solution: a person to whom both a possible manager of market research, professional salesmen, advertizing and other mass marketing activities, and those responsible for personnel, operations, technology, etc. are reporting. Then not only the traditional mass marketing and personal selling activities, but also the interactive marketing function could be managed with a responsibility for their marketing consequences. In such a case the result might be a marketing-oriented service organization, where not only lip service is paid to the marketing philosophy, but where the company really is adapting its operations to satisfying the needs of its target market.

Summary

In order to design a long range marketing strategy, a service organization will have to recognize the stages, through which its customers proceed, from merely being interested in the company and its services to becoming loyal to the company. The marketing activities to be used in the different stages are not the same. Traditional mass marketing efforts and personal selling by professional salesmen can only create customer interest and in some cases, when marketing to industrial buyers, also turn this interest to sales. However, sales and, above all, resales and lasting customer contacts cannot be achieved by these means. In spite of this fact the traditional marketing activities from goods marketing mentioned above are usually the only activities of the service company, which are considered to be marketing tasks.

Much more important to success are the activities performed in the buyer/seller interactions, which emerge during the purchasing and consumption processes. By these activities, which have been labelled the interactive marketing function of the service organization, sales and, eventually, resales are promoted.

Establishing traditional marketing departments does not seem to be an appropriate way of handling the total marketing function, because such a department usually cannot plan and implement activities within the interactive marketing function. As a matter of fact, marketing departments seem to be a bad means of making a service company marketing-oriented. Instead of becoming marketing-conscious the rest of the organization rather tends to be come production-oriented, thus leaving the total marketing responsibility to the marketing manager, who generally has not the necessary authority for such a responsibility. Therefore, an organizational innovation may be needed, if marketing-orientation is to be successfully introduced in service organizations.

References

(1) E. Frederick Webster, Jr., Management science in industrial marketing, *Journal of Marketing,* January (1978).

(2) Håkan Håkansson and Claes Östberg, Industrial marketing. An organizational problem, *Industrial Marketing Management,* Nos. 2–3 (1975).

(3) Christian Grönroos, A service-oriented approach to marketing of services, *European Journal of Marketing,* No. 8 (1978).

(4) Christian Grönroos, *The Nature of Service Marketing,* Swedish School of Economics and Business Administration, Helsingfors, working papers, No. 11, 1978. (Report presented at the Seventh Annual Workshop on Research in Marketing, European Academy for Advanced Research in Marketing, Stockholm, May 1978.)

(5) Evert Gummesson, Toward a theory of professional services marketing, *Industrial Marketing Management,* April (1978).

(6) Christian Grönroos, An applied theory for marketing industrial services, *Industrial Marketing Management,* No. 1 (1979).

(7) G. Lynn Shostack, Breaking free from product marketing, *Journal of Marketing,* April (1977).

(8) Pierre Eiglier *et al., Marketing Consumer Services: New Insights,* Marketing Science Institute, Cambridge, Mass. (1977).

(9) Peter K. Mills, *New Perspectives on Post-industrial Organizations,* Akademilitteratur, Stockholm (1977).

(10) Victor P. Fuchs, *The Service Economy,* Columbia University Press for National Bureau of Economic Research, New York (1968).

(11) William R. George and Hiram C. Barksdale, Marketing activities in the service industries, *Journal of Marketing,* October (1974).

(12) John M. Rathmell, *Marketing in the Service Sector,* Winthrop Publishers, Cambridge, Mass (1974).

(13) Pierre Eiglier and Eric Languard, Une approche nouvelle pour le marketing des services, *Revue Francaise de Gestion,* No. 2 (1975).

(14) William R. George, The retailing of services—a challenging future, *Journal of Retailing,* Fall (1977).

(15) David S. Davidson, How to succeed in a service industry . . . turn the organization chart upside down, *Management Review,* April (1978).

Section II-B
Entering the Market

"Target Marketing: The Key to Successful Entrance into Technical Markets," by J.A. Muncy and M.A. Humphreys, points out advantages of target marketing and the effect it has on customers.

"Evaluating the Role of Advertising," by C.H. Patti, addresses the advertising management process.

"An Applied Theory for Marketing Industrial Services," by C. Grönroos, suggests frameworks concerning the marketing of industrial services.

"Marketing Industrial Technology in the Small Business," by L.M. Lamont, is based on an investigation of marketing problems and programs of 76 small enterprises.

"A Systems Approach for Developing High Technology Products," by G. Miaoulis and P.J. LaPlaca, highlights three important phases in the development process of high technology products.

"How to Approach Export Markets," by W.E. Littler, includes five informative steps for entering export markets.

"A Professional Approach to Exporting," by A.G. Davis, offers more practical advice on exporting.

"Creating a New Product: Two Paths to the Same Marketplace," by S.E. Currier, describes two different approaches to marketing two brands of the same product.

"Ten Questions to Ask Your Advertising Agency," by V. Wademan, gives worthwhile tips on how to select and work with an advertising agency.

"How to Work with Your Agency—An Agency Man's Manifesto," by G.D. Shorey, states what he believes both an agency and client must do to make a relationship work.

TARGET MARKETING:

THE KEY TO SUCCESSFUL ENTRANCE INTO TECHNICAL MARKETS

James A. Muncy and Marie Adele Humphreys

University of Oklahoma

Sandra Kurtzig took a $2,000 investment and in ten years turned it into $66,000,000. She did so in the computer software industry. Why was she so astonishingly successful in an industry that almost daily sends firms into bankruptcy? One Hewlett-Packard executive attributed her success to the fact that "she did not try to be all things to all people." In essence, he was saying that she did a good job of target marketing.

The concepts of market segmentation and target marketing have had a more fundamental impact on corporate strategic market planning than any other developments in modern marketing. The practical importance of these concepts is reflected in the impressive level of corporate resources that have been, and continue to be, committed to segmentation studies and to the development and evaluation of target market strategies arising from these studies.

Prior to the mid-1960's the dominate theme in strategic planning was "mass marketing." However, since that time, markets have become increasingly fragmented. Few firms can compete profitably in today's marketplace without the guidelines which segmentation research provides for the development of target marketing strategies and the allocation of the firm's resources among markets and products.

The history of business development in the U.S. is replete with examples of entrepreneurs who developed potentially viable technical innovations but failed to profitably bring their products or ideas to the marketplace. Instead of using the concept of target marketing, many of these entrepreneurs relied on commonly held but fallacious views in developing their marketing plans.

Three Major Marketing Fallacies

Before describing the basic principles of target marketing and presenting suggestions which may be helpful to the individuals or organizations who wish to profitably market technical innovations, it will be useful to review three of the major marketing fallacies. Many entrepreneurs have believed strongly in these marketing fallacies and have adhered strictly to them— all the way to the bankruptcy court.

The Mousetrap Fallacy

Emerson once contended that "If a man... makes a better mousetrap... the world will beat a path to his door." Emerson's contribution to literature is unquestionable; however, it is questionable how successful he could be as a

This article was prepared specifically for this anthology.

businessman in today's competitive environment. A recent study by the Denver Research Institute of 200 innovations that failed found that only 13 did so due to technological problems. The majority failed due to marketing and management related problems and the majority of the management problems were closely tied to the marketing problems. There are three dangers in believing in the Mousetrap Fallacy. First, because one develops a better mousetrap, that does not mean the world needs a better mousetrap. Second, because the world needs a better mousetrap that does not mean that it will automatically know when one is developed and available. Third, the mousetrap that is better for one group of people may not be better for another.

The Marketing-Is-Selling Fallacy

Another common marketing fallacy is equating marketing with selling. The entrepreneur who accepts this view believes that high-powered personal salesmanship and aggressive advertising are the key to business success.

Marketing, contrary to this popular view, is not selling. In fact, Peter Drucker, today's top management theorist, states correctly that, "the aim of marketing is to make selling superfluous." If marketing is not selling, then what is it? The successful marketer is the one who views marketing as process by which a firm identifies a homogeneous group of customers (consumers or organizations) whose needs are not being met satisfactorily, develops a product to meet these needs at a price that the customers are willing to pay (while still making a profit for the firm), tells them about it, and then gets it to them. Certainly selling is a part of this process, but selling is not the focus of the process. The process focusses on the identification of a group of customers with a unique set of needs and the meeting of these needs. Marketing is not selling any more than computer programming is keypunching. A realistic view of marketing is necessary for an organization to be a viable competitor in today's marketplace.

The Majority Fallacy

In an article which appeared in the Harvard Business Review, Kuehn and Day noted that larger markets attract a disproportionately large number of entering firms. One of the primary reasons for this phenomenon is belief in The Majority Fallacy. According to this belief, larger markets are more profitable markets.

The Wall Street Journal in discussing the nature of competition in high tech fields noted that:

Small companies can succeed in the land of the giants by staying out in front technologically... and by picking a niche. "But you have to pick your niches carefully so they're small enough that it isn't of interest to a big guy" says Richard Munn, a marketing consultant to firms in high tech industries. (September 13, 1982, p.1)

The secret of competing in technological markets is not in always entering the biggest market but rather in carefully picking the niche in which one can be the most successful. The best niche for a firm is not necessarily the biggest one.

What is one able to conclude if it is true that 1) even a good product does not ensure success without good marketing, and 2) marketing is more than picking the biggest market and having a good sales force and advertising campaign to sell to that market? One is left to conclude that the organization must have an overall marketing strategy for the product and that the first step in developing such a strategy is to choose the proper market (not always the biggest market) to which to target the firm's efforts. This is a two step process which requires a firm to first segment the market and then to develop a target marketing strategy.

Marketing Segmentation

Realizing the potential benefits of a target market strategy requires first that management accept the concept of market segmentation. This concept is based on the view that so-called mass markets are usually made up of segments, composed of separate groups of customers, whose differences in attitudes toward and susceptibilities to marketing efforts are more important than their similarities.

Even a cursory look at the marketplace will reveal that the vast majority of successful marketing efforts are designed to serve market segments rather than the mass-market. Today, the opportunities are rare for a Henry Ford, who effectively entered the marketplace with a black Model T, to meet the needs of all the potential customers in a mass market. The successful entry into the market today is more likely to emulate Digital Equipment Corporation. It picked a specific market segment, the minicomputer market, which was initially ignored by the established computer manufacturers. DEC successfully defended its niche in the computer market by constantly improving its products and, as a result, grew into a major corporation with annual sales of more than $3 billion.

This implies that an organization must identify those niches in the market which can be potentially profitable. Market segmentation is the process by which the market is divided into homogeneous groups. Success of a marketing plan is almost always dependent (at least in part) on the development of a viable market segmentation schema.

The above definition of market segmentation gives a firm the criteria with which to evaluate a particular segmentation schema. The dimensions chosen in a particular market should divide the market into homogeneous groups. Figure I graphs three hypothetical market segmentation schemata. In this example, the market is segmented based on two dimensions (1 and 2) and can be represented by a two-dimensional graph. Customers can then be represented as points in this two-dimensional space.

In Figure I, Segmentation Schema A would not be satisfactory because it did not adequately divide the market. The customers are homogeneous in relation to both dimensions 1 and 2. Segmentation Schema B was sufficient in dividing the markets (the customers were not homogeneous on either dimension 1 or 2). However, this would not be an acceptable schema because the customers were not divided off into homogeneous groups; clusters did not develop. Segmentation Schema C was successful in dividing the market into homogeneous groups. Therefore, it is this type of segmentation schema that would be desirable.

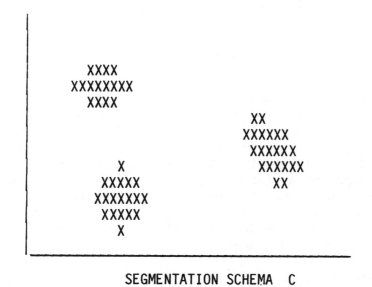

SEGMENTATION SCHEMA A   SEGMENTATION SCHEMA B

SEGMENTATION SCHEMA C

FIGURE 1.   THREE POSSIBLE SEGMENTATION SCHEMATA

91

Segmentation requires the organization to identify the appropriate dimensions along which the market is to be divided. Most dimensions relate either to the customer (e.g., age, income, etc. in consumer markets or size, location, etc. for organizational markets), or the product-usage situation (e.g., emphasis on file manipulations vs. emphasis on data analysis in the computer industry).

How does a firm go about selecting the most appropriate dimensions along which the market should be segmented? While intuition may well suggest potential bases, the more successful firms usually rely, at least partially, on market research. Such research usually follows one of two research patterns. One pattern is an a priori segmentation study design in which the firm already understands which groups exist (i.e., segments) in the market and conducts research to determine the characteristics which are most important in differentiating between these groups. Another pattern is post hoc design in which the firm first collects data which describe potentially relevant characteristics of possible customers and then places the customers into homogeneous groups in relation to these characteristics.

Two statistical techniques that are used extensively in these types of market research studies are cluster analysis and discriminant analysis (for a discussion of these techniques, see Paul Green's Analyzing Multivariate Data, Hinsdale IL: The Dryden Press, pp. 142-184, 296-316, and 423-433).

Target Marketing

Once the market is segmented, the firm is ready to consider how to develop a target marketing strategy. It should be noted that, at this point, the firm has not yet decided who its customers will be. Segmentation simply divides the market. Target marketing occurs when the firm chooses one or more of these groups (which will be its target markets) and then develops a marketing strategy to reach each group. If more than one market is chosen, a unique marketing plan (i.e., product, promotional, distribution, service, and pricing strategies) is developed for each group. This does not mean that product, promotion, distribution, service, and pricing all will differ across each group. What it does imply is that each will be decided in the context of each group.

The process of target marketing requires the firm to choose one or more target markets. How is this done? Each group can be evaluated with regard to certain criteria for a good target market and the selection is made from the ones that meet these criteria. The firm should use three criteria when evaluating whether or not a particular group should be chosen for a target market.

Criterion One: Is the Segment Unique?

The first criterion states that a target market should be unique. Unique in relationship to what? A target must be one that is unique in how it buys the product, why it buys the product, or what it buys. For example, Timex Corporation recently announced that it was entering the at-home health-care market with digital devices to measure blood pressure, weight and temperature. They are directing their marketing efforts toward three different market segments: the elderly, younger families with small children, and active physical fitness consumers. Obviously they have well thought out their marketing strategy based on the unique need for ease of use of these segments of the medical products market.

An organization is successful in marketing because it is able to develop a competitive advantage - that is it can do something for someone better than anyone else. The identification of a unique segment can result in a firm being able to develop such a competitive advantage. If a firm can identify such a market, it can focus its efforts on meeting the unique needs of this market (thus developing its competitive advantage).

Criterion Two: Can Selling to This Segment Be Profitable?

The second criterion states that the market must be profitable. In any marketing segmentation schema, there will be market segments that are not being fully satisfied. However if selling to this segment cannot result in long-term profitability to the organization, then there is no reason to choose it as a target market. When evaluating a segment in relation to its profitability, the firm must consider several factors. An actual or potential need must exist, and the size and purchasing power of the segment must be large enough to represent a potentially profitable marketing opportunity for the firm.

As was stated earlier in this paper, a firm is not always wise to go after the largest segment of a market. However, that does not mean that size is not a factor when considering to what target market to which a firm should sell. The target market must be large enough to justify a commitment of the firm's resources. Another factor to consider is the margin (i.e., the revenue minus the costs) at which the firm can sell at within this market. This does not imply that the target market which can produce the largest margin should be chosen. However, margin is an important factor which directly affects profitability.

Consideration should also be given to how intense the competition is within a particular market. Established firms have several advantages (e.g., reputation, knowledge about a market, an existing customer base) which makes it difficult for a new firm to carve out and defend a profitable market niche in existing markets. The most successful newer firms often attempt to fill an unmet need in the market by offering a unique product.

Criterion Three: Is the Segment Economically Accessible?

The third criterion states that a firm must be able to reach the target market it has chosen. The firm needs to develop a product that will best meet its target segment's particular needs. But it must also pay considerable attention to the costs associated with the other elements of its marketing plan which are needed to satisfy this market. Distribution, pricing, after-the-sale service and promotion, as well as the product itself, are all critically important factors in determining the success of the firm. If, for example, an economical method of promotion or distribution cannot be found, then the marketing plan will be a failure.

Advantages of Target Marketing

As stated above, the success of an organization can depend on its ability to divide the market into segments and then target its products at one or more of these segments. One may wonder why this strategy is so superior to a mass marketing strategy. The two major advantages of target marketing are that it is more efficient and that it is more effective.

Something can be viewed as more efficient than something else if it results in the same or more output for a smaller amount of input. In these terms, a target marketing strategy is almost always more efficent than a mass-market strategy. Distribution outlets can be selected to reach certain segments of the population. In many cases promotional strategies can be even more refined to effectively and efficiently reach precisely the right market by publishing in special interest publications. Target marketing allows the organization to analyze audience profiles of TV, radio stations, and magazines so as to get the widest exposure possible for a given promotional budget. If a firm accepts a target marketing strategy, they need not distribute or promote their products everywhere. The firm needs only use those media that best reach its target market.

Target marketing is generally more effective in reaching customers. People do not buy products; they buy solutions to problems. This implies that firms do not market products, they market solutions. Firm A will successfully market their product only if customers see firm A's solution to their problem as being superior to the one offered by firm B. If one assumes that all of the problems people buy products to solve are the same, then there is no need to target market. However, this is rarely the case. More often, the problems are similar within certain groups of customers. Contrast, for example, IBM's marketing strategies for the large main-frame and personal computer markets. Every element of their marketing strategy—pricing, service, distribution, promotion and product—is designed to provide a specific solution to the unique problems of each target market. If a firm develops a marketing strategy that is uniquely suited to solving one group's problems, they will be more successful at solving that problem than the firm that tries to solve all of the problems of everyone. In trying to reach everyone, the firm successfully reaches no one.

Evaluating the Role of Advertising

CHARLES H. PATTI

Charles H. Patti, received his Ph.D. from the University of Illinois in 1974. Prior to returning to graduate school, he spent more than eight years in industry working for Bliss & Laughlin Industries as Assistant Director of Marketing Communications, Director of Advertising and Promotion for USI-Clearing, and as Director of Communications for U.S. Industries, Inc., a large industrial conglomerate. He is a member of several professional associations and the main emphasis of his research interests is on a determination of the role of advertising. Dr. Patti is now Assistant Professor of Marketing and Advertising at Arizona State University.

ABSTRACT

This paper presents a procedure useful in assessing the probability of an individual marketer profitably employing advertising to stimulate demand for products or services. The procedure is based on the classic factors which affect the ability of advertising to stimulate demand originally identified by Neil Borden (*The Economics Effects of Advertising*). This managerial approach provides strategic insights into the extent to which an individual firm should invest in advertising. In addition, the results of the procedure — an advertising opportunity score — provide the strategist with guidance in establishing advertising objectives and determining the portion of the total selling task which should be assigned to advertising.

INTRODUCTION

In 1959, the National Industrial Conference Board conducted a survey among advertisers to determine the common areas of concern for advertising management. As a result of their survey, the Board initiated major studies dealing with the following topics:

1. evaluating spending strategies;
2. pretesting advertising;
3. evaluating media; and,
4. measuring advertising effectiveness.

Although each of the above topics are obviously important to advertising management, they all concern questions or issues that develop after the firm has decided to advertise. In other words, all of these decision-making areas are concerned with improving the efficiency of the advertising effort, but they presume that the firm's strategic decision to advertise was sound.

Most of the research done in advertising since 1960 has been concentrated in the four areas isolated by the National Industrial Conference Board's survey. Although there are continuing attempts to explain, understand, and isolate the effects of advertising on sales, profits, and share of market, little formal attention has been directed to the appraisal of the basic opportunity to use advertising effectively. This lack of concern with an assessment of the advertising opportunity exists despite the fact that common sense and past case histories clearly indicate advertising is a much more effective promotional tool for increasing brand demand in some product/market situations than others (3).

Thus, the first task facing advertising management should be to determine the extent to which advertising can be used to help accomplish the marketing goals of the firm. As Wedding and Lessler so aptly point out, this task is analogous to that facing the farmer in comparing the relative fertility of one field with that of another.

When a given amount of seed, fertilizer, and cultivation effort are applied to two fields of different fertility, with the same climatic conditions for both, the field with the higher relative fertility will produce the greater yield. Similarly in the case of advertising, a comparable amount and quality of advertising effort put on products facing different advertising opportunities will also produce different sales and profit results. (7).

The strategic importance of the appraisal decision in the sequence of advertising management decisions is illustrated in Figure 1. The determination of the advertising opportunity should be the fundamental decision which helps formulate advertising objectives. A determination of the advertising budget can take place only after objectives have been set. Decisions about creative strategy (product attributes to emphasize, product and brand positioning, etc.) and tactics (message content and execution) and media must be made within the constraints of the budget. The last step in the sequence, measuring advertising results, provides feedback on the degree of success/failure and assists advertising management in re-assessing the advertising opportunity for the next campaign period.

Figure 1

ADVERTISING MANAGEMENT SEQUENCE OF DECISIONS

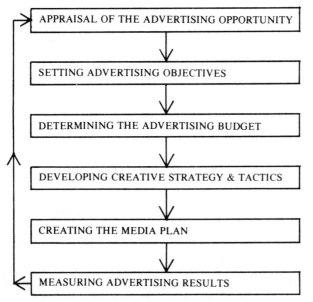

A PROCEDURE FOR EVALUATING THE ADVERTISING OPPORTUNITY

The primary questions facing advertising management in evaluating the advertising opportunity are:

1. Under what conditions is advertising most likely to help expand demand?
2. How can these conditions be evaluated?

Factors Affecting the Advertising Opportunity

In his book, *The Economic Effects of Advertising*, Neil Borden observed that (1)

. . . the opportunities for the successful use of advertising vary widely. Advertising is not a business stimulator which can be turned on and off at will with the assurance that results will be commensurate with expenditures. Successful advertising depends on the right combination of numerous factors.

To Borden, the most important of these factors include:

(1) The trend of demand in the particular industry should be rising.
(2) There should be an opportunity to stimulate selective demand — brand preference for the particular product. This opportunity is most likely to be present when:
  (a) there is substantial chance for product differentiation
  (b) consumer satisfaction depends on hidden qualities that can't be easily judged at the time of purchase
  (c) strong emotional buying motives exist
(3) The combination of potential unit sales times rate of gross margin must be high enough to permit necessary advertising expenditures in the particular product.

During the late 1930's, Borden conducted a number of studies on the economic effects of advertising in several industries (sugar, shoes, cigars, refrigerators, domestic sheeting, dentifrices, et al.) and concluded that the opportunity for advertising to stimulate brand demand for consumer goods generally depends upon the presence of a combination of these conditions. Advertising for consumer goods has a greater chance of being effective under such conditions than when the conditions are not present.

For most companies, to use advertising effectively and efficiently usually means whether or not the use of advertising can succeed in bringing about a sales increase large enough to cover cost, including advertising, and still make a contribution to net profits. The decision to allocate funds for advertising is ultimately a matter of executive judgment and should depend on an appraisal of the opportunities to use advertising effectively.

Enlarging on Borden's original list of conditions, Wedding and Lessler suggested the following factors for appraising the advertising opportunity for stimulating brand demand (7):

product differentiation
hidden qualities
strong advertising appeals

market potential
favorable generic demand trend
favorable economic conditions
strength of competition
sufficient funds
adequacy of marketing/distribution system

The work of both Borden and Wedding-Lessler is based on the assumption that under certain conditions, advertising can shift the demand schedule of a branded product. When a company finds it possible to do so through advertising, the brand can then be considered "advertisable," or at least, presents a good advertising opportunity. The extent to which a company's advertising is successful varies widely and depends on the circumstances under which the company operates. A company must consider both the conditions that affect generic demand as well as those which affect brand demand. The primary interest of any individual company is to expand demand for its own brand — whether through attracting new users to the product class or by attracting customers from competitors.

The basic conditions or factors which are considered to have an important effect on how profitably advertising can be used to expand brand demand fall into two major categories: product factors and marketing/financial factors (1, 2, 7). Each of these categories and the major questions under each which affect the basic opportunity to effectively employ advertising are briefly described in the following paragraphs.

Product Characteristics

1. *Does the product or service possess unique, salient attributes?*
Although parity products (cigarettes, gasoline, beer, etc.) have been advertised successfully, it usually requires considerably more effort and expense to do so. On the other hand, products which are differentiated on physical rather than psychological dimensions are much easier to advertise. However, rarely is simply "being different" enough. The advertisability of product features are enhanced when prospects perceive the unique features as being important and useful.

2. *Are "hidden qualities" important to prospects?*
If by viewing, feeling, tasting, or smelling the product, the prospect can learn all there is to know about the product and its benefits, advertising will have less chance of increasing brand demand. Conversely, if all the product's benefits are not apparent to the consumer on inspection and use of the product, advertising has more of a story

to tell and the probability that it can be profitably employed increases.

The "hidden quality" of Vitamin C in oranges once helped explain why Sunkist oranges could be effectively advertised while the advertising of lettuce has been a failure. With lettuce, the complete decision process can be made by physical inspection of the product.

3. *Is the product/service bought largely on the basis of powerful, emotional motives?*
If the basic motivations for the purchase involve strong emotional drives — such as parental affection (baby care products) or social enhancement (deodorants, colognes, etc.) — the possibilities for the profitable use of advertising are increased.

Marketing/Financial Characteristics

4. *Is the generic demand trend for the product/service favorable?*
Although many billions of dollars are invested in advertising annually, the powers of advertising are not limitless. If the generic product category is experiencing a long-term decline, it is less likely that advertising can be used successfully for a particular brand within the category. It is often unwise to use advertising to attempt to stimulate brand demand amid a declining generic demand trend.

5. *Is the market potential for the product/service adequate?*
The use of advertising to stimulate demand can be an expensive undertaking and unless the potential for profit is sufficiently large, advertising should be avoided. That is, mass media communication with prospects is profitable only when there are sufficient actual or prospective users of the brand in the medium's audience.

6. *Is the competitive environment favorable?*
The size and marketing strength of competitors, their brand shares and loyalty will greatly affect the possible success of an advertising campaign. For example, to compete successfully against Kodak Films, or Morton Salt, or Campbell Soup requires considerably more marketing effort than simply advertising. Such firms are large, knowledgeable, hold substantial market shares, and possess strong brand loyalties. These advantages are difficult to overcome and argue against the successful use of advertising by these firm's competitors.

7. *Are general economic conditions favorable for the marketing of the product/service?*
The effects of an advertising program and the sale

of all products are influenced by the overall state of the economy and by specific business conditions. For example, it is much easier to advertise and sell luxury, leisure products (stereos, sail boats, recreation vehicles, etc.) when disposable income is high. However, even when unemployment is high and discretionary income reduced, the environment is conducive to the successful advertising of some products — distributor brands (substitutes for higher priced, manufacturer's brands), for example.

8. *Is the organization financially able and willing to spend the amount of money required to launch an advertising campaign?*

As a general rule, if the organization is unable or unwilling to undertake an advertising expenditure which as a percent of the total amount spent in the product category is at least equal to the market share it desires, advertising is not likely to be effective.

9. *Does the firm possess sufficient marketing expertise to market the product/service?*

The successful marketing of any product/service involves a complex mixture of product and buyer research, product development, packaging, pricing, financial management, promotion, and distribution. If the firm is weak in any of the areas of marketing, this is an obstacle to the successful use of advertising. For example, if the firm does not have a reasonable assurance of obtaining fifty-percent distribution the use of advertising is usually highly questionable.

Evaluation of the Appraisal Conditions

A Simple Procedure. The most basic method of determining the advertising opportunity is to answer the above questions with a "yes" or "no." Figure 2 presents a worksheet for evaluating the advertising opportunity in this fashion. If, for example, the particular product/service possesses physical differentiation, answer "yes" (meaning in favor of advertising) for question number one. By analyzing all nine conditions and responding with an answer that is either in favor of advertising or against it, an objective appraisal can be made of the opportunity for advertising to contribute to the stimulation of brand demand.

In situations where "against advertising" responses dominate the analysis, a decision to rely on advertising heavily will very likely fail. Whenever "for advertising" responses dominate, marketing management's confidence in the ability of advertising to make a substantial contribution to company profits should be strengthened. In those situations

where the "fors" or "againsts" are fairly equally balanced, judgment becomes even more important.

The purpose of this analysis is to assist judgment and while a thorough review of the product, market, and firm helps reduce the possibility of error, there are two major shortcomings in the analysis just described.

First, a simple "yes-no"/"for-against" procedure treats all nine factors with equal importance. Rarely does this accurately reflect the business environment. Usually, an organization considers an advertising program because its management believes there is a market opportunity.

Because each firm operates with varying management styles, objectives, competitive environments, and levels of human, financial, and physical resources, the nine-factor appraisal model described above must be adapted to the individual peculiarities of every organization and the market situation it faces. Every firm must evaluate the relative importance of each factor in its own situation.

A second shortcoming of the "for-against" procedure is that it does not account for degrees or extent of existence of the factors. Business conditions are sometimes highly favorable. Some products

Figure 2

A SIMPLE MODEL FOR APPRAISING THE
OPPORTUNITY FOR EXPANDING BRAND
DEMAND THROUGH ADVERTISING

Product Factors	For Advertising	Against Advertising
1. The Presence of Unique, Salient Product Qualities	_____	_____
2. The Existence of "Hidden" Qualities In the Product	_____	_____
3. The Possibility of Appealing to "Powerful" Buying Motives through Advertising	_____	_____
Marketing and Financial Factors		
4. Adequacy of Market Potential	_____	_____
5. The Generic Demand Trend	_____	_____
6. Economic Conditions	_____	_____
7. The Competitive Environment	_____	_____
8. Adequacy of Funds for a Sustained Advertising Program	_____	_____
9. Possibility of Developing and Implementing an Effective Marketing Program	_____	_____
	_____	_____
	_____	_____
TOTAL	_____	_____

Evaluate each of the factors as either being favorable or unfavorable to the use of advertising to stimulate brand demand, and place a check in the appropriate column. Add the number of checks in each of the two columns to make an initial judgment about the role advertising should play in the marketing program.

are experiencing a rapidly declining generic demand trend. Occasionally, a product is introduced that is a technological innovation (micro-wave ovens, for example) and therefore possesses an unusually high degree of product differentiation. The for-against procedure does not allow the evaluator to make allowances for such situations.

A More Sophisticated Procedure. To help advertising management overcome these two problems, the procedure presented in Figure 2 can be expanded in two ways. A more sophisticated version of the procedure is presented in Figure 3.

First, each of the nine factors are assigned a score between 1.0 and .00. The more strongly the factor is in favor of profitably employing advertising the higher the assigned Factor Score. For example, if a small manufacturer of citizen's band radios was assessing his advertising opportunity in the spring of 1976 on the "Generic Demand Trend" factor he would probably give that factor a relatively high score, perhaps a .85.

Second, each of the nine factors is given a Factor Weight which reflects the relative importance of the factors in the advertiser's particular situation. If the potential advertiser felt that all factors were of equal importance, he would assign each a weight of 1.0. If he felt that each of the Product Factors was twice as important as the Marketing/Financial Factors he would assign factors 1 through 3 weights of 2.0 and factors 4 through 9 weights of 1.0. To continue our small manufacturer of CBs example, if he felt that the "Adequacy of Funds" factor was twice as important as the "Generic Demand Trend" factor which in turn was twice as important as the "Powerful Buying Motives" factor, he would assign these factors weights of 4.0, 2.0, and 1.0 respectively.

An *Advertising Opportunity Score* may then be determined by multiplying each *Factor Score* by its *Factor Weight* summing these nine products and dividing by the sum of the nine *Factor Weights*. This overall score may be interpreted in the same way as an individual Factor Score. That is, 1.0 - .90 = extraordinary; .89 - .80 = excellent, and so on (see footnote, Figure 3).

ESTABLISHING ADVERTISING OBJECTIVES

The basic purpose of the advertising appraisal procedure described above is to determine what role advertising should play in accomplishing the marketing goals of the firm. Figure 4 presents some general guidelines for appropriate advertising goals and the percentage of the total selling task that should be assigned to advertising based on an Advertising Opportunity Score.

Figure 3

A MODEL FOR APPRAISING THE OPPORTUNITY FOR EXPANDING BRAND DEMAND THROUGH ADVERTISING

	(a) Factor Score*	(b) Factor Weight	(a)	(b)
Product Factors				
1. The Presence of Unique, Salient Product Qualities	___	___	___	
2. The Existence of "Hidden" Qualities In the Product	___	___	___	
3. The Possibility of Appealing to "Powerful" Buying Motives through Advertising	___	___	___	
Marketing and Financial Factors				
4. Adequacy of Market Potential	___	___	___	
5. The Generic Demand Trend	___	___	___	
6. Economic Conditions	___	___	___	
7. The Competitive Environment	___	___	___	
8. Adequacy of Funds for a Sustained Advertising Program	___	___	___	
9. Possibility of Developing and Implementing an Effective Marketing Program Total	___	___	___	

$$\text{ADVERTISING OPPORTUNITY SCORE} = \frac{\sum_{i=1}^{9} (a_i b_i)}{\sum_{i=1}^{9} (b_i)}$$

*Factor scores range from 1.0 to 0.0. Assessments fall on the following continuum: 1.0 — .90 = extraordinary; .89 — .80 = excellent; .79 — .70 = very good; .69 — .60 = good; .59 — .50 = average; .49 — .40 = poor; .39 — .30 = very poor; .29 — .20 = weak; .19 — .10 = extremely weak; and .09 — .00 = a negative consideration.

Although the stimulation of brand demand is the long-range goal of most advertising, it is now generally accepted that more modest communications goals must first be achieved. Despite a controversy surrounding the appropriateness of using communications tasks as the basis for setting objectives for advertising (6), the work of Colley (4), Lavidge and Steiner (3), and others have encouraged the adoption of a communications hierarchy-of-effects orientation.

Nevertheless, advertising management is concerned with the amount of the selling task assigned to advertising. Through an analysis of the advertising opportunity, management can set more realistic, attainable advertising objectives. As shown in Figure 4, if the advertising opportunity is good — that is, majority of the factors strongly favor the use of advertising — then advertising can be assigned tasks closer to the ordering of action end of the communication hierarchy. This method of setting advertising objectives has the advantage of assisting management in setting objectives which are sensitive to conditions within the firm, the market, and the economic environment.

Figure 4

RELATIONSHIPS BETWEEN THE ADVERTISING OPPORTUNITY SCORE AND ESTABLISHING ADVERTISING OBJECTIVES AND SELLING TASK

Advertising Opportunity Score*	Appropriate Advertising Goals	% of Total Selling Task Assigned to Advertising
GOOD	encourage direct sales response from customers and prospects / promote expanded use of company products and services	50 — 100%
FAIR	demonstrate that company products and services have want-satisfying qualities generate sales leads for personal sales staff / encourage customers and prospects to request product and service information	10 — 50
POOR	communicate favorable image throughout the distribution system / increase awareness of company existence / inform important publics of company philosophies, purposes, etc. / increase familiarity of company brands among customers and prospects / inform customers and prospects of product and service developments	0 — 10

Advertising Opportunity Scores may be interpreted as follows: 1.0 — .70 = Good; .69 — .50 = Fair; and, < .50 = Poor.

Additionally, having appraised the advertising opportunity and established advertising objectives, the advertising budget can then be related directly to the established objectives. This method of budget determination is far superior to other methods (percentage of sales, competitive-comparison, arbitrary) and relates advertising directly to an assigned task — an objective that has been determined after an appraisal of the role of advertising.

CONCLUSIONS

The formal procedure described above is suggested as an aid to managerial decision-making. Obviously, the validity of the procedure hinges on the soundness of the judgment of the individual(s) using the procedure. The value of the methodology lies in forcing the decision-maker to systematically consider the likely effect of major factors which have a direct bearing whether or not an investment in advertising will be a profitable decision.

This structured procedure provides useful strategic insights into the answers to several major questions facing the marketer who considers using advertising. By systematically evaluating the advertising opportunity, establishing advertising objectives in light of this evaluation, and setting a budget in line with these objectives; the advertising management process can be made more rational and easier to defend to top management.

REFERENCES

1. Borden, N. *The Economic Effects of Advertising* Homewood, Illinois: Richard D. Irwin, 1942.
2. Borden, N. and M. Marshall. *Advertising Management: Text and Cases* Homewood, Illinois: Richard D. Irwin, 1959.
3. Borden, N. "The Concept of the Marketing Mix." *Journal of Advertising Research*, (June 1964), pp. 2-7.
4. Colley, R. *Defining Advertising Goals for Measured Advertising Results.* New York: Association of National Advertisers, 1961.
5. Lavidge, R. and G. Steiner. "A Model for Predictive Measures of Advertising Effectiveness." *Journal of Marketing.* (October, 1961) pp. 59-62.
6. Palda, K. "The Hypothesis of a Hierarchy of Effects: A Partial Evaluation." *Journal of Marketing Research.* (February, 1966) pp. 13-24.
7. Wedding, N. and R. Lessler, *Advertising Management* (New York: The Ronald Press, 1962).

An Applied Theory For Marketing Industrial Services

Christian Grönroos

When the area of industrial marketing is discussed in the literature on marketing and marketing management, only the marketing of goods to industrial buyers are considered. However, a vast amount of services are also marketed in the industrial sector. There is some, although very limited, literature on professional or consultancy services, but the area is usually not thought of as a part of industrial marketing [1–3]. Recently, a few papers have been published where these services are treated as an integral part of industrial marketing [4, 5]. The purpose of this article is to suggest some frameworks concerning the marketing of industrial services.

CLASSIFICATION OF SERVICES

Services can be classified either by the kind of market where they are sold, or by the service provided. First, we have *producer services* and *consumer services* (4). Producer services are offered to industry and other institutions, whereas the latter kind of services are marketed to households and to individual customers. The first category should be treated in the context of industrial marketing.

Second, professional or consultancy services are nor-

mally discussed separately and not in the same context as other services [2–4]. In identifying such services, four criteria are usually used: (1) the service should be provided by qualified personnel; (2) it should be advisory and focused on problem solving; (3) the professional should have an identity, such as a "lawyer" or "management consultant"; and (4) the service should be an assignment given from the buyer to the seller [4].

In Fig. 1 the two ways of classifying services discussed above are combined, resulting in a 2 × 2 matrix. In cell 1 of the matrix we could put services offered by computer firms, management consultants, and advertising agencies. A lawyer could render his professional services to either industrial buyers or individual customers. In the latter case he would be providing consumer services, and thus these services would be placed in cell 2. A physician also renders professional services, but only consumer services. Consequently, his services are in cell 2. As can be seen, the same professional or the same consultancy firm can operate either in the industrial sector providing producer services, or both in the industrial and consumer sector, thus rendering either producer or consumer services.

Usually one gets the impression that there is a quite clear distinction between professional and other services, and that the criteria presented above would discriminate

*Present address: Department of Marketing, Swedish School of Economics and Business Administration, Arkadiagatan 22, SF-00100 Helsingfors 10, Finland.

Reprinted with permission from *Industrial Marketing Management,* vol. 8, pp. 45–50, Jan. 1979.

	Producer services	Consumer services
Professional (consultancy) services	1	2
Other services	3	4

FIGURE 1. **A classification of services.**

well between these two types of services. This is, however, not the case. For instance, a company using a bank or a cleaning and maintenance firm demands some kind of professionalism, and a firm dealing with a travel agency or a company offering car hire services looks for some advisory help and consultancy guidance. Nevertheless, these services are rarely thought of as some kind of professional or consultancy services and, indeed, their providers do not do that either. However, most of the services that are considered other than consultancy services involve, or at least should involve, a substantial part of professionalism and advisory help.

For the sake of convenience we shall, however, make a distinction between services traditionally labeled "professional" or "consultancy" services and other services. Most of these other services, such as those provided by banks, travel agencies, hotels, restaurants, transportation companies, car-hire firms, and cleaning and maintenance companies, are rendered both as producer and consumer services, and thus we can find them either in cell 3 or cell 4 of the classification matrix. There are, of course, some services that solely belong to cell 4, such as hair cutting and personal care and, on the other hand, some services that almost solely are producer services, such as security services.

Within the area of industrial marketing of services, both the marketing of traditional professional services to

CHRISTIAN GRÖNROOS. who received his Lic B.A. from the Swedish School of Economics and Business Administration. Helsinki, Finland, is a researcher at the Research Institute of the Swedish School of Economics and Business Administration and a marketing consultant specializing in the service sector. His research has for the last few years been concerned with the marketing of services and has been conducted in cooperation with the Marketing Technique Center in Stockholm, Sweden. He has written two books on marketing problems and co-authored and edited two other marketing texts. He has published articles on the marketing of services, in British, Finnish, and Scandinavian journals.

industrial buyers (cell 1) and the marketing of other services as producer services (cell 3) should be considered. Today there is at least some knowledge about marketing in cell 1 (1, 2, 4–6) and in cell 4 (7–9), although the total area of service marketing is still quite unexplored. Relative to the two other cells, including the industrial marketing of "other services," there is very little published indeed [10]. There are, of course, some books and articles concerning specific industries, but these reports usually deal with quite detailed problems specific to a given industry, and they seldom have an overall managerial view of marketing. The following sections of this article discuss the marketing of producer services other than traditional professional services, although the views put forward to some extent may be used in the marketing of professional services, too.

PROGRESS OF CLIENT NEEDS

The need for financing, business trips abroad, transportation of goods, or cleaning will emerge in a rather vague and unspecific form in a firm. The firm starts to look for banks, travel agencies, transport operators, or cleaning companies and thus becomes a potential client for enterprises in those industries. The potential client gathers information about the reputation and specific offerings of the firms that provide the services. The industrial buyer exposes itself, in an active manner, to advertisements, word-of-mouth information, gossip by colleagues, and possible personal selling efforts. Eventually the company decides to purchase or, more usually, to ask for an offer concerning the type of service demanded from one or a few providers of those services.

Thus the needs of the potential client proceed from an *initial stage* to a following stage, where the scope of the needs is narrowed. The buying firm decides whether it should choose a particular service company as provider of particular services. It exposes itself to sales efforts by professional salesmen, to other service-firm employees, to service-supporting equipment and documents, and to the service-production environment, including location of offices, appearance of transportation vehicles and offices, and so on. This stage in the progress of client needs could be called the *purchasing process*. Finally, the firm makes the purchasing decision, and the next stage in the process follows. The client has committed itself to one company, which produces the service. The service is now consumed by the client, and it is to a great extent simultaneously produced. Therefore, buyer/seller interactions emerge, as in the industrial marketing of goods

[11, 12]. The client will consider whether the services really satisfy the perceived needs. It exposes itself to the resources used in producing the service and to the service production process itself. For example, on a business trip the company executive will observe the location of the hotel where he lives, the exterior and interior of the hotel and its rooms, the equipment and extra services provided by the hotel, the hotel employees, their capabilities, appearance and behavior, and so forth. All these components of the service will have an impact on the executive's preferences toward the hotel service, and thus they will influence the company's future use of the hotel. This stage in the progress of client needs could be labeled the *consumption process*.

The progress of client needs can be summarized as follows: (1) an *initial stage*, where the potential client develops a general *interest* in a service company and its services, (2) the *purchasing process*, where the client

on, will perform activities that can be characterized as marketing activities. This fact leads of course, to a rather complicated situation because the service operations, administration of human resources, and technological development are usually not thought of as marketing problems today. They are rather merely managed as operational, personnel, and technological problems, respectively, and correspondingly, they are made the responsibility of people, who usually do not care to any great extent for their marketing consequences.

Competition may increase in most service industries in the future, which, in turn, may demand a thorough recognition of the total marketing function, if the service company is to be successful. A company that stays at the production-oriented stage of today will soon have to leave the marketplace, whereas firms that succeed in making their operations marketing oriented (i.e., spreading their marketing activities throughout the company)

"The marketing function of a service company will have to be spread throughout the whole company."

decides to *purchase* a service from a particular service company as a means of satisfying specific needs, and (3) the *consumption process*, where the service offering and service company can prove its need-satisfying capabilities and thus lead to an enduring client contact. In the next section we examine the marketing consequences of this three-stage process.

MARKETING OBJECTIVES AND EFFORTS AT DIFFERENT STAGES

The client's preferences toward a service firm and a given service offering will be influenced by what different representatives of the client experience throughout the whole process. The objectives of marketing should be to manage all sources that have an impact on these preferences. Consequently, the marketing function of a service company will have to be spread throughout the whole company. Not only a traditional marketing department, but also organizational units, which are mainly responsible for operations, personnel, technology, and so

will have a fair chance to prosper and grow.

A service company cannot, however, expect to become marketing oriented by merely developing its mass-marketing activities and personal selling efforts by professional salesmen, especially with the use of the marketing literature of today, which is overwhelmingly concerned with consumer goods and to a minor extent with producer goods. In such a case one is only concerned with a part of the marketing function, whereas the most important part still remains outside the marketing-orientation efforts. As a result, only lip service is paid to the marketing concept, which states that the firm should design its operations according to the needs of its targeted client. It should be recognized that the objectives of marketing differ between the three stages of the progress of client needs, and that different kinds of marketing activities should occur at the three stages. Generally, the objectives at the various stages can be stated as follows: (1) the initial stage—to develop *interest* in the firm and its services, (2) the purchasing process—to turn the general interest into *sales,* and (3) the consumption process—to secure resales and thus develop *enduring client contacts*. The nature of marketing will be quite different at the th : stages, the activities will differ, and various parts of the organization will be engaged in the marketing efforts.

Marketing at the Initial Stage: Stage I

At Stage I the service company wants to become recognized by potential clients as a possible provider of services, which they might need. A basic effort in creating interest among prospective buyers is to develop an attractive corporate image. If the image is too negative,

selling only occurs at the second stage, whereas interest is developed merely by mass-marketing activities.

In some cases stage I and the purchasing process are separated from each other. When the potential buyer physically contacts the service company, he is already interested in the service provider and its services. Stage I has come to an end, and the purchasing process starts. The buyer gets in touch with salespeople of the service firm, but probably he is also confronted with the service-production resources, including employees other than professional salesmen, with the technological resources,

---

"Different kinds of marketing activities should occur at the three stages."

---

the market may not even notice marketing activities such as advertising and personal sales calls. At this stage traditional mass-marketing efforts, such as various kinds of advertising, can be used in order to put the service company on the list of possible firms that the potential client may contact for an offer. This may be a critical list, because if the company cannot reach such a list, it often has no chance to get the business. Personal selling by top executives and professional salesmen can also be used to develop client interest. Public-relations activities and sales-promotion efforts are also important. Key employees of prospective buyers, either the purchasers or users, which often are not the same people, can be invited to take part of some activity where they can get acquainted with either the service provider and its representatives or the service itself. Of course, pricing is also important.

Marketing during the Purchasing Process: Stage II

At stage II the general interest of potential clients has to be transformed to sales. The service company wants to become the firm that is selected from the list and given the assignment. Frequently, stage I and the purchasing process cannot, in industrial marketing of services, be totally separated. Whereas the advertising and possible other mass-marketing activities of stage I can do no more than create client interest, the personal selling efforts will also turn this interest into sales. Sometimes personal

and with the physical setting of the service company, including the location of offices, and so on. There is a buyer-seller interaction involving some representatives of the prospective buyer and the means of production of the service provider, including human resources other than those engaged in the traditional personal selling activities. These interactions will also have an impact on the buyer as well as the personal selling efforts and, of course, the contents of the offer regarding price, service delivery, and so forth.

Marketing during the Consumption Process: Stage III

Marketing must not stop as soon as the service company has succeeded in selling a service once. This is, however, usually the case today. When a service has been sold, marketing is not responsible for what happens subsequently. In the service sector, this can be a disastrous mistake. If there is no interest in the marketing consequences of the service operations in the company, the client is likely to become unsatisfied with the service, and the service company gets, in the long run, an uncomfortably bad image. Finally, the company will lose the customer.

At stage III the service provider should demonstrate for the client that it is able to render a service that is really satisfying the needs of the client. As a result, a lasting client contact can be achieved, and the assignment will probably be prolonged. This process is normally separated from the purchasing process, as well as from the initial stage. The company's salespeople and its mass-marketing efforts cannot do much to show the client that it can handle the business. Instead, the management of the *buyer–seller interactions* of the consumption process will be of utmost importance to the success or failure of the service provider.

At stage III at least, if not already at stage II, these interactions will emerge. The contacts between the client and its representatives and the means of production and the production process, respectively, will strongly influence the client's future purchasing behavior. In some cases these interactions may involve other clients or customers of the service company. For instance, on a business trip by air the executive will get in touch with the other passengers, as well as with the aircraft, its equipment, the air hostesses, supporting services such as meals and drinks served, and with the way in which the various resources, pre-, in-, and post-flight, are utilized in order to produce the total transportation service.

In other cases the situation will be somewhat different. For instance, cleaning and maintenance services are, to a considerable extent, sometimes totally, produced at a time when no human representative of the client is present. The *direct* interaction will be minor, but there will be an *indirect* interaction with the service provider. The client will notice the result of the cleaning and maintenance service. However, there will usually be at least some direct confrontation between the buyer and the seller and their representatives during the consumption process. These buyer–seller interactions, whether direct or indirect, will to a considerable extent influence the client's perception of the service company and the service rendered.

TWO FUNCTIONS OF INDUSTRIAL MARKETING OF SERVICES

In industrial marketing of services there are, as has been demonstrated by the previous sections, varying types of marketing efforts to be used. Two different marketing functions can be distinguished. The first function could be called the *traditional marketing function*, which mainly consists of mass marketing activities, advertising, public relations, sales promotion, personal selling by top executives and professional salesmen, and pricing. Most of these activities can be managed and implemented by a traditional marketing department assisted by top management.

The second function could be labeled the *interactive*

marketing function [10]. Every component—human and nonhuman—in the service-production context, every production resource used, and every stage in the service-production process should be the concerns of marketing, and not considered merely as operations or personnel problems. Their marketing consequences have to be recognized in the planning process, so that the production resources and the operations support the company's marketing efforts and not, as is often the case today, restrict or even counteract them.

The interactive marketing function is most frequently not considered to be marketing today, and clearly a traditional marketing department will not be able to handle this function. Major parts of, for instance, the administration of human resources and the development of technological resources will belong to this marketing function, which will involve other organizational units and their heads.

The traditional marketing function can create client interest and, to some extent, also transform this interest into sales. Consequently, activities within this function can be used to advantage at stages I and II (i.e., at the initial stage and in the purchasing process). Resales, prolongation of assignments, and finally, enduring client contacts cannot, however, be achieved by such efforts. At this stage of the process—the consumption process—the interactive marketing function will be of profound importance. Activities within this function can also, in some cases, influence the purchasing decision at the preceding stage.

Although developing client interest is very important, managing the buyer–seller interactions is, in the long run, more critical to the success or failure of the service company. Therefore, it must, in my opinion, be realized that a successful development of industrial marketing of services demands that service companies recognize the immense importance of the interactive marketing function (i.e., of the management of the buyer–seller interactions), and give high priority to developing this marketing function instead of just hiring another salesman or increasing the advertising budget.

SUMMARY

The marketing of industrial services, and indeed the total area of service marketing, is quite underdeveloped today. The traditional marketing activities, which firms in the service sector seem to have inherited from the theories of consumer goods marketing, can only to some extent be used in marketing services. Moreover, they cannot be used to advantage in developing enduring client contacts. Instead, another kind of marketing activity, the interactive marketing function, can be much more important. In this context the literature on industrial marketing of goods has some, though limited, help to offer [12]. The interactive marketing function means that the marketing consequences of buyer–seller interactions are considered. The company must continuously demonstrate its capability of handling these interactions throughout the whole purchasing and consumption processes. If it fails to do that, it will probably lose its clients, whereas a competitor that successfully manages its interactions with the clients and their representatives will get a positive reputation and an attractive corporate image followed by satisfied clients and lasting business contacts. Such a reputation and image will, moreover, be a powerful means of creating interest in the company among new potential clients.

REFERENCES

1. Wilson, Aubrey, *The Marketing of Professional Services*, McGraw-Hill, New York, 1972.

2. Wittreich, Warren, How to Sell/Buy Professional Services, *Harvard Business Review* (March–April 1966).

3. Kotler, Philip and Connor, Richard A., Marketing Professional Services, *Journal of Marketing* (January 1977).

4. Gummesson, Evert, Toward a Theory of Professional Services, *Industrial Marketing Management* (April 1978).

5. Gummesson, Evert, *The Marketing of Professional Services—An Organizational Dilemma*, research report presented at the Seventh Annual Workshop on Research in Marketing, European Academy for Advanced Research in Marketing, Stockholm, May 1978.

6. Turner, Everett B., Marketing Professional Services, *Journal of Marketing* (October 1969).

7. Grönroos, Christian, A Service-oriented Approach to Marketing of Services, *European Journal of Marketing* (8) (1978).

8. Shostack, G. Lynn, Breaking Free from Product Marketing, *Journal of Marketing* (April 1977).

9. Eiglier, Pierre et al., *Marketing Consumer Services: New Insights*, Marketing Science Institute, Cambridge, Mass., 1977.

10. Grönroos, Christian, *The Nature of Service Marketing*, Swedish School of Economics and Business Administration, Working papers No. 11, Helsingfors, 1978, research report presented at the Seventh Annual Workshop on Research in Marketing, European Academy for Advanced Research in Marketing, Stockholm, May 1978.

11. Webster, Frederick E., Jr., Management Science in Industrial Marketing, *Journal of Marketing* (January 1978).

12. Håkansson, Håkan and Östberg, Claes, Industrial Marketing. An Organizational Problem, *Industrial Marketing Management* (2-3), (1975).

MARKETING INDUSTRIAL TECHNOLOGY IN THE SMALL BUSINESS

Lawrence M. Lamont

SUMMARY

This article examines the role of marketing in small technology-oriented business and is based on an extensive investigation of the marketing problems and programs of 76 small enterprises located in a large scientific complex in the mid-western United States. All the firms considered are "spin-offs" of large corporations, nearby universities and other technology-based firms. The author hopes that this paper will provide a conceptual framework for management and aid their development of an effective marketing capability.

1. INTRODUCTION

The small technology-based business (often called a spin-off) continues to play an important role in the development and marketing of industrial technology. In many regions of the U.S.A., the formation rate of technical enterprises is expected to continue at a high level during the 1970s (see Danilov, 1969). However, a changing market environment will make it more difficult for the current group of potential entrepreneurs to reach the levels of success achieved by those of the previous decade. Rapid technology transfer and renewed corporate interest in internal spin-off mean increased competition. The managements of the technology-based firms of the 1970s will have to place more emphasis on the development of a strong marketing capability.

This article is based on an extensive investigation of the marketing problems and programs of 76 small technology-based enterprises located in a large midwestern scientific complex in the U.S.A. All the firms are spin-offs from large corporations, nearby universities and other small technology-based firms. New businesses having sales of less than $100,000 are included, as well as firms with annual sales of several million dollars. Technologies represented include electronics, computers, optics and engineering materials.

Despite differences in size and technology, the marketing problems are remarkably similar. The entrepreneurs of new firms will be confronted with the task of developing a marketing capability consistent with current business and flexible enough to change with the rapid development of the firm. This statement of the marketing problem agrees with the existing literature. Few of the published articles, however, go beyond the generalization that a major weakness of the small technology-based enterprise is the lack of effective marketing. The research findings confirm this fact, but they also indicate that the capabilities required for effective marketing are different for certain types of businesses. The objectives of this article are:

1. To examine the role of marketing in the small technology-oriented business by relating it to the nature of the business activity.

2. To provide a conceptual framework for management, to aid in the development of an effective marketing capability.

2. THE BARRIERS TO EFFECTIVE MARKETING

2.1. Technical Orientation

The majority of technology-based enterprises are founded by scientists and engineers who have little knowledge or interest in marketing. At the time of formation, less than 37 % of the entrepreneurs studied had previous experience in marketing and only 44 % of the firms had any employees (founders included) with marketing experience. In many firms the situation was perpetuated by hiring only engineers or scientists whose interests were compatible with those of the original entrepreneurs.

Having inexperienced personnel is not always a barrier to effective marketing. In certain instances the firm's business is primarily research and development, and a high degree of sophistication is simply not required. Some experience, however, is valuable in evaluating the significance of the market opportunity prior to formation. Several examples were observed where technology-based firms began business only to discover that the anticipated customers no longer existed and the market was too small to support a profitable level of operations.

2.2. Limited Financial Resources

Most of the technology-based firms in this study were undercapitalized at the time of formation and throughout the early stages of development. Many entrepreneurs were unable to secure adequate initial financing while others underestimated the amount of capital required to finance an extensive technology development cycle.

The implications for effective marketing are clear. By the time the technical development work was completed, insufficient capital remained to effectively perform the marketing task. A compromise strategy in product-oriented firms was to license the manufacturing rights or manufacture for another firm who assumed the marketing responsibility. The alternative was to develop a marketing program; but in firms under financial pressure this resulted in products that did not reflect market requirements, inadequate product service, poorly–selected marketing channels and ineffective sales promotion.

2.3. Multiple Business Activities

Technology-based firms engage in a variety of business activities. They include consulting, research and development, engineering and manufacturing on a contract basis, and the provision of proprietary products and services (hereafter referred to as products). Some firms begin business by performing only one activity–such as contract research and development, while others engage in a combination of two or more activities. As the firms grow, their development is frequently marked by dramatic changes in the nature of the businesses. Alpha

Technology (fictitious name) illustrates the concept and a common development pattern: Alpha began business as a contract research and development firm performing environmental studies for the government space program. Two years after formation, Alpha had developed two electronic measuring instruments using technology transferred from the previous research. In a short period, Alpha's business had changed dramatically from a research and development orientation to a product orientation.

A number of development patterns were observed during the research. Some firms began operations with the intention of developing proprietary products, but financed the development cycle by consulting. Others started business by obtaining contracts to design and build custom products and then developed proprietary items. Several performed only one activity—such as research and development or engineering—and resisted the tendency to progress in the direction of a product orientation. Beta Engineering (fictitious

Lawrence M. Lamont joined the University of Colorado School of Business in 1970 as an Assistant Professor of Marketing. From 1962 to 1966 he was employed by the Dow Corning Corporation as a technical sales representative. From 1966 to 1969 he worked as a research associate at the University of Michigan's Institute of Science and Technology. In addition to his research duties, he consulted for several small, technology-based firms in the Ann Arbor, Michigan area. Dr. Lamont received his B.S.E. in Chemical Engineering, M.B.A., and Ph.D. from the University of Michigan. His research and publications concern industrial marketing, small business management, corporate responses to consumerism and consumer purchase behavior for durable goods.

name) illustrates this development pattern: Beta does a nation-wide business designing and fabricating custom medical electronic instrumentation for researchers with highly specialized applications. The president views the firm as an interface between the medical researcher and the large medical equipment manufacturers. If marketable products are developed, they are turned over to some other firm for manufacture. Beta has no intention of manufacturing and marketing proprietary items.

Rapid changes in the business orientation of many technology-based firms makes the development of effective marketing programs a confusing and difficult task. Existing programs are quickly outdated and the need for a changed emphasis is either not recognized or is implemented well after it becomes apparent. The task of developing a marketing capability can be further complicated. Depending on the mix of contract and proprietary business, the firm may be involved in several different marketing efforts, each requiring a unique capability. A conceptual framework is needed to help the managements of existing technology-based firms— as well as prospective entrepreneurs—determine the proper role of marketing in their businesses.

3. A CONCEPTUAL APPROACH

It is helpful to view the business activities of technology-based firms as falling across a spectrum.

This spectrum, illustrated in Fig. 1, includes contract activities at one extreme and proprietary activities at the other.

New firms can begin business at either end of the spectrum or engage in a combination of contract and proprietary activities. Generally, companies working with new technologies start in contract research and development, while firms using well-developed technologies begin at the product end of the spectrum. The initial position may be occupied permanently (the case of Beta Engineering), or the firm may move along the spectrum to a new position by developing technology into proprietary products (the case of Alpha Technology).

Fig. 2 shows the development patterns of Alpha and Beta superimposed on the business activity spectrum. In reality, a variety of development patterns is possible. The point to be emphasized is that the marketing capability required depends on the position occupied by the firm at a particular time as well as the direction of development. Visualizing the various business activities as a spectrum provides a conceptual reference point for management in the development of marketing programs.

3.1. *The Marketing Program—Contract Activities*

Marketing programs at the contract end of the spectrum are characterized by the need to sell a technical capability. They consist of the ability to analyze and solve problems using specific technol-

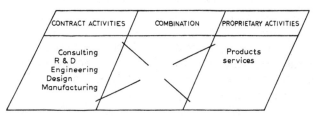

Figure 1. The spectrum of business activities.

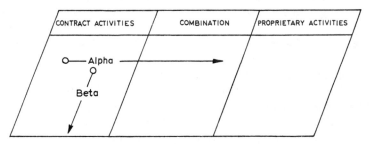

Figure 2. The business development patterns of technologybased firms.

ogies. The dimensions include the firm's people, technology, facilities and research equipment, and record of technical achievement. Because technical capability is intangible, it is difficult to market. Therefore a marketing approach quite different from that used to market a proprietary product is required.

Technical selling is the key component in the marketing program. The management and technical personnel of a technology-based firm must identify the potential customer and sell the contract capability of the company. A sale is initiated by an unsolicited proposal, or a proposal is sent in response to a request from a prospective customer. Prior to the proposal, however, extensive personal selling is required by the entrepreneur and his technical staff to help the prospective customer define his needs. Additional follow-up is necessary to modify the proposal and reinforce the firm's ability to successfully complete the project. Entrepreneurs reporting success in marketing research and development, design and engineering, and contract manufacturing were submitting pre-sold proposals that reflected the customer's problem and ideas in terms of the firm's technical capability. They confirm that a truly market-oriented approach is needed. (For a similar viewpoint see Murphy, 1968.)

The technical proposal reflects the firm's marketing activity and is the primary form of sales promotion. It contains a suggested approach to solving the problem and an estimate of the cost to complete the contract. Many firms supplement the proposal with a capability brochure. The well-designed brochures contain a description of the firm's people, facilities and special equipment, areas of technical competence, and pictures of completed projects involving technical achievements. The capability brochure can be of significant value to the marketing program of the small technology-based business engaged in contract activity. Not only does the brochure make an intangible capability more meaningful to the customer, but it also helps the firm bridge the credibility gap that plagues new businesses.

When the government purchases a technical capability, it is bid competitively whenever possible. However, corporations purchasing to supplement an in-house capability often negotiate with selected suppliers. Contracts are usually fixed-price or cost-plus-fixed-fee. The perceived risk in the project and the willingness of each party to share that risk determine the specific contractual form. A cost-plus-fixed-fee (risk sharing) contract is used when the risk is high or difficult to estimate. Fixed-price contracts result when the problem is well-defined or the supplier's bargaining position is weak. Naturally, most entrepreneurs preferred risk-sharing contracts, but because of competition they were not always successful in negotiating them.

Technology-based firms marketing a technical capability generally confine their activity to local or regional markets. This reflects the need for frequent contact with the customer. The technical uncertainties in the projects often require modifications in the scope of the contract. When customers are located a great distance away, the process becomes prohibitively expensive and time-consuming. Regional markets also restrict the use of advertising in the marketing program. The use of mass media such as industrial trade journals is expensive because of the wasted circulation. In addition, advertising is ineffective because of the difficulty of making specific buying appeals and communicating an intangible capability in a limited space.

3.1.1. The marketing problem. The marketing program for a contract activity is relatively simple. Primary emphasis is on personal selling. Yet the failure to effectively market the firm's technical capability was an important reason for poor corporate performance. New firms have a tendency to operate in a technical vacuum. Entrepreneurs believe that a superior technical approach to a problem is all that is necessary to win a contract competition. Because of insufficient market contact, new firms fail to reflect the customer's ideas and preferences in their contract proposals. Opportunities for the development of proprietary products are also missed. The corporate philosophy of some firms such as Beta Engineering discouraged the development of technology into proprietary items. In others, the entrepreneurs simply preferred a small, highly technical scale of operations typical of a contract-oriented business.

Some technology-based firms are unable to overcome the credibility gap. Poorly-designed capability brochures, weak technical proposals, poor credit ratings and a lack of familiarity with selling techniques contribute to the problem. Few entrepreneurs recognized that at least two years would be required to land a major contract and establish the firm as a going concern.

Contracts were frequently priced below the cost to complete the work. The absence of historical cost data and the failure to allow for contingencies often meant rapid depletion of capital. Some entrepreneurs intentionally priced below full costs to generate revenue to cover overhead. In many cases it was necessary to win the contract and begin establishing a reputation.

3.2. The Marketing Program–Proprietary Activities

Firms selling proprietary products have a greater opportunity for creative marketing. Products are tangible and specific buying appeals can be made. Markets are national in scope and defined in terms of potential customers and product applications. The marketing programs require a broad range of activities and a considerably higher level of expenditures.

The crucial component in the program is the marketing channel used to reach the market. Products such as computers, electronic instruments and lasers are typically sold by a direct sales force or through a network of manufacturers' representatives. Most electronic components and minor accessories are marketed through industrial distributors. The specific channel depends on the product and the size and financial strength of the firm. Many small firms use manufacturers' representatives.

Entrepreneurs concede that a line of at least five items is required to make a direct sales force profitable. Alpha Technology found this to be the case. When faced with the decision of market representation, the firm had only two products and less than $500,000 annual sales. Financial and market considerations made the manufacturers' representative the only viable alternative. However, Alpha's president believed that direct sales would eventually be possible with the addition of new products and the development of a stronger financial base.

The need to reach national markets increases the role of advertising and sales promotion in the marketing program. Technology-based firms marketing products with geographically scattered markets can use trade journal and trade paper advertising, trade shows, direct mail, sales brochures and news releases to support the selling effort. The extent of their use varies with the marketing orientation of the firm and the financial resources available. Small firms frequently design their own promotional items; they are often marked by a technical orientation and poor design. Larger firms seem to recognize the need to reach different buying influences in customer firms and use professionally prepared

literature directed specifically to the decision-makers for their product.

Compared to the intangible technical capability, proprietary products are well-defined in terms of physical characteristics or performance specifications. Price comparisons with competitive products are possible and pricing strategy plays an important role in the marketing program. Negotiation and competitive bidding are used to determine prices when large purchases are involved. Both the government and large industrial buyers use these techniques to bring competition into the procurement and assure a fair price. When a number of competitive alternatives are available, prices are set by the forces of the market and standard commercial prices prevail. Entrepreneurs determined these prices using costs and the prices of competitor's products as reference points, and then adjusted the price to reflect differences in performance or quality.

3.2.1. The marketing problems. During the process of developing marketing programs for proprietary products, entrepreneurs failed to realize that the various marketing tools are designed to be used in combination, rather than individually, as a complete marketing program. In many firms, the entire marketing program consisted of a trade show or advertising in a few selected trade journals. These programs were doomed to failure or at best, only marginal success. To successfully market high technology products, personal selling either by a direct sales force or manufacturers' representatives is almost always required. Firms having this basic capability can then add sales brochures, direct mail, advertising and trade shows to increase the effectiveness of the marketing channel selected.

In most of the technology-based firms studied, the pricing process for new products tended to be cost-oriented. Most entrepreneurs estimated manufacturing costs and added a fixed percentage for profit. Using this approach, products and services are underpriced. Technology-based firms which have unique items and a strong competitive position miss profit opportunities by failing to price the product as close to its value in use as possible.

3.3. The Programs Reviewed

The essential elements of the marketing programs for a technical capability and a proprietary product are combined with the spectrum of business activities in Fig. 3. Beta Engineering's marketing program is essentially personal selling by the principal foun-

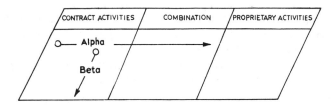

Figure 3. The marketing programs for contract and proprietary activities.

ders. In addition, a capability brochure is used to support the selling activity. Alpha Technology is involved in two marketing programs: the firm's contract capability is sold by the management, while the electronic instruments are marketed by manufacturers' representatives, sales brochures and national trade journal advertising.

4. THE MAJOR MARKETING ADJUSTMENTS

Technology-based firms having development patterns similar to Alpha Technology face a series of critical marketing adjustments as they change from a contract-oriented business to a product-oriented business. These include obtaining market representation and developing a formal marketing organization to implement the marketing program. The analysis is concluded with a discussion of these adjustments.

4.1. Selecting Initial Market Representation

One adjustment takes place when the firm develops its first proprietary product and is faced with the problem of selecting marketing channels. In addition to product and market considerations previously mentioned, an important factor in the channel-selection decision is the nature of the selling effort required to market the product. Technically, complex products are best marketed through a company sales force because of the difficulty of finding manufacturers' representatives with the technical knowledge to perform the selling task. This works an additional hardship on small companies. Because they are unable to finance a direct sales effort, they are often forced to use manufacturers' representatives not having the necessary technical background. About 60% of the firms studied used manufacturers' representatives. Another group of firms indicated that they had attempted to secure representation but were not successful in attracting an organization under conditions satisfactory to both firms. Overall, this marketing channel played a key role in the marketing programs of a large number of firms.

The success of the firms' products depends almost entirely on the ability of the entrepreneurs to attract and select a strong representative organization. Most entrepreneurs, however, performed the selection process in a haphazard manner. Very few even bothered to develop a list of criteria and candidates to increase the chances of selecting a capable organization. Improper selection resulted in a rapid deterioration of the relationship between the representative and the firm. In some cases the representative simply did not perform well for the company because of lack of ability or interest. Just as often, the problem was due to inadequate support from the firm; failure to meet delivery schedules, restrictive prices, product problems and poor sales support were reasons mentioned by manufacturers' representatives.

Entrepreneurs should begin the selection process by examining the nature of the selling effort required and the prospective customers to be reached. Ideally, the representative's customers should be the same as the firm's prospects, the representative should have sales contacts with the key decision-makers for the product, and the geographic market coverage should be the same as that needed by the firm. In addition, entrepreneurs should evaluate the compatibility of the representative's line with the firm's product, his facilities for handling sales promotion, his standing in the business community and the importance of the firm's product to the representative's existing line.

To attract the best possible organization, the entrepreneur must also market his company, its management and the sales prospects for the product. Technology-based firms that can provide market data, sales and technical support, promotional literature, demonstrators, and after-sales service are in a better position to attract good manufacturers' representatives.

4.2. *Organizing for Marketing*

As the sales of the firm's products expand, the time required to manage the marketing program increases to the point where the principal founders can no longer perform the administrative duties without assistance. Marketing becomes a full-time job and the firm hires an experienced marketing executive.

The formation of a formal marketing organization is often the first step in a direct selling program and the beginning of a transition from a technically-oriented firm to a market-oriented business. The decision to sell direct signals an important adjustment in marketing strategy. It is the most important marketing decision that the firm will make (see Germeshausen, 1968).

The evolution of a direct sales organization was observed in many companies during the study. Generally, the shift in responsibility occurred about the time the firm's sales volume reached the

$500,000–$750,000 range. Usually, the decision was made when the company was facing serious marketing problems. Some of those most frequently observed are mentioned below:

1. A reduced rate of sales growth caused by the firm's inability to increase its market penetration with existing marketing channels.

2. The threat of competition from larger corporations with national distribution and a superior marketing capability.

3. A recognition of the need for a broader customer base, increased brand recognition and greater control over markets.

4. Increased price competition from direct selling competition, making it difficult to maintain commission margins on indirect sales to large customers.

Two fundamental considerations in the decision to develop a company sales force are cost and control. How does the cost of direct selling compare with the cost of the present marketing channels? Which method provides the required degree of control over the marketing effort?

The cost of keeping a direct salesman on the road is one of the most important considerations. This cost can run between $25,000 and $40,000 per year, depending on the sales territory and the arrangements made for compensation and the sharing of expenses. Thus, if a manufacturer's representative is paid a sales commission of 10%, sales territories producing $250,000 to $400,000 a year will have to be available to make the change feasible from an economic standpoint. Very few companies were able to satisfy this condition when confronted with the decision of whether or not to sell direct. The analysis also assumes that the company salesmen will be able to gain acceptance and maintain the existing customers in the sales territory. This is not always assured, since if a representative's contract is cancelled he may take the firm's customers to a new client. In this case, additional expenses will be incurred to rebuild the sales territory.

In new technology-based companies where there is pressure to obtain marketing channels, little consideration is given to the need for control over markets and the representative's selling effort. Exclusive representation arrangements are made and products are sold under restrictive private brand agreements. If it becomes apparent that the manufacturer's representatives cannot perform the selling job or the firm is unable to exert much control over their selling techniques, the need for an alternative selling approach such as direct sales is more urgent. This need is reinforced when one representative or distributor accounts for a high proportion of the firm's sales volume.

Another problem encountered in implementing a program of direct selling is the need for a broad product line. If the technology-based firm has only one or a few products, it is difficult to define sales territories with enough sales volume to be economically handled by one salesman. Alpha Technology solved this problem by adding the products of other small manufacturers to its line. The company actively searched for new products to complement their existing line. When they were discovered, Alpha licensed the exclusive marketing rights. Several new products were obtained in this manner.

A contract engineering firm solved the problem by establishing a separate sales company to market the products. By taking this approach, the new sales company was also able to act as a representative for other manufacturers. This strategy not only increased the number of products available for the company's salesmen, but it also made direct selling economically feasible much earlier in the firm's development.

4.3. The Marketing–Technology Partnership

Several of the entrepreneurs estimated the minimum costs of developing a direct sales force at $500,000. Others believed that this adjustment in the marketing program could take as much as five years to complete. When these facts were combined with the risk in phasing out existing marketing channels and the need to develop the sales potential of new products, many firms searched for an alternative approach. The most popular involved assigning the exclusive marketing rights for a new product to a large corporation having a national marketing organization.

The contractual arrangements for this alternative vary, but usually the firm receives cash advances (to be credited against future product sales), or part of the firm's equity is sold for cash. These funds are then used to finance the start-up and production costs for the firm's product. Many large corporations have benefited from these arrangements. Some are technologically obsolete compared to their more aggressive competition and they view this as an opportunity to remain competitive or enter new markets. More importantly, they usually obtain exclusive rights on the products to be developed in the future to assure product improvements and

an expanding line.

Financially, these arrangements have advantages for both parties. The technology-based firm has the technology, the corporation has the marketing capability, and both are needed to make the venture a success. Beyond this, however, it is difficult to see how this arrangement solves the long-range problem of developing a direct sales force. If the agreement is terminated by either party, the firm is left without a marketing capability and a much larger scale of operations to support.

4.4. The Evolving Marketing Department

Along with the development of marketing channels, technology-based firms must begin to build a formal department for marketing management. This final adjustment in the marketing program starts after the first proprietary product has been developed, or when the volume of referrals is not sufficient to sustain the existing level of operations. Technology-based firms usually began their marketing department with the addition of a sales manager or a vice-president of marketing. Subsequent additions were along functional lines and typically included regional sales management, advertising and sales promotion, and customer services such as order processing, bids and proposals and field technical service. These changes occurred while the firm's sales were in the $750,000 to $2,000,000 range. Additional marketing functions such as product management, product planning and market research were considered peripheral to the everyday operation. They were structured into the marketing department when the sales and financial strength made it possible. Most of these organizational changes took place in the $2,000,000 to $8,000,000 sales range.

4.5. The Marketing Adjustments Reviewed

Fig. 4 completes the conceptual framework. It highlights the major marketing adjustments required and integrates them into the technology-based firm's marketing program. The problem of selecting and developing initial market representation, the decision to sell direct and the development of a formal marketing department can be viewed as barriers to the transition from a contract-oriented firm to a product-oriented business. As illustrated in Fig. 4, Alpha Technology and other successful entrepreneurs must anticipate these major marketing hurdles and integrate them into their business operations.

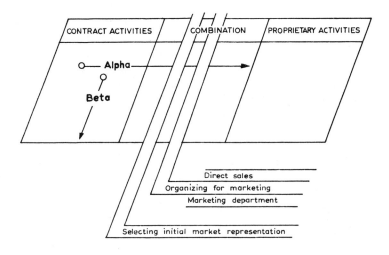

Figure 4. The major marketing adjustments and the marketing programs.

5. CONCLUSIONS

The small technology-based firms of the 1970's will be conducting business in a market environment marked by increased competition. To be successful, entrepreneurs must place greater emphasis on the development of a strong marketing capability.

Most entrepreneurs do not recognize the need for a marketing capability during the early stages of the firm's development. As a result, they are unable to anticipate marketing problems. All entrepreneurs would benefit from a careful analysis of the marketing requirements for the items they plan to sell. This would also lead to a more accurate evaluation of the market opportunity prior to the commitment of resources to a direction of corporate development.

Marketing programs must reflect the nature of the business activity and the direction of the firm's development. The discussion indicates that the marketing program required to market a technical capability is entirely different to the program needed to market a proprietary product. Firms moving across the spectrum of business activities toward a product orientation must recognize that the capabilities required for effective marketing change rapidly. A continuous evaluation and adjustment of the firm's marketing program is required. The major problems in this transition include selecting and modifying marketing channels and formally organizing for marketing management. The conceptual model developed in this article is designed to assist entrepreneurs in specifying the role of marketing in their firms.

Ind. Mark. Manage., 4 (1972)

ZUSAMMENFASSUNG

Marketing industrielle Technologie in kleinen Unternehmen

Diese Abhandlung beschäftigt sich mit der Rolle des Marketing in kleinen, technologisch orientierten Unternehmen und basiert auf einer eingehenden Untersuchung der Marketingprobleme und Programme von 76 kleinen Unternehmen, die in einem großen wissenschaftlichen Komplex im Mittelwesten der Vereinigten Staaten liegen. Die in Betracht gezogenen Firmen sind aus großen Gesellschaften hervorgegangen und liegen nahe Universitäten und technologisch basierten Firmen.

Professor Lamont zielt mit seinem Artikel auf ein anschauliches System für das Management und auf die Entwicklung einer effektiven Marketingfähigkeit ab.

RÉSUMÉ

Le marketing de la technologie industrielle dans la petite entreprise

Cet article examine le rôle du marketing dans les petites entreprises s'orientant plus particulièrement vers la technologie et est fondé sur des recherches approfondies sur des problèmes et programmes marketing faites auprès de soixante-seize petites entreprises situées dans un vaste complexe scientifique du middle-west américain. Toutes les entreprises étudiées sont des "spin-off" de grandes compagnies, d'universités avoisinantes et d'autres entreprises à orientation technologique.

Le professeur Lamont espère que son article fournira un cadre conceptuel de gestion et favorisera le développement d'une capacité effective de marketing.

REFERENCES

Danilov, V. J. (1969). "The Spin-off". *Industrial Research* (May): p. 58.
Germeshausen, K. J. (1968). "A Product Line for a Government-Oriented R & D Company". *IEEE Transactions on Engineering Management*. Em-15: 85.
Murphy, R. F. (1968). "Selling Aerospace Technology to the Federal Government". *Journal of Marketing*. XXLII: 46.

A Systems Approach for Developing High Technology Products

George Miaoulis   Peter J. LaPlaca

Product development for high technology products is comprised of the three stages of assessment, development, and execution. In addition, all three stages consist of information and decisions involving technological, product, and market dimensions. This article presents a systematic approach for integrating these three dimensions by which a go—no—go decision can be reached prior to the expenditure of large amounts of funds for research and development.

INTRODUCTION

Many industrial firms continue to be preoccupied with the technology surrounding their market offerings. Industrial manufacturers frequently cite inadequate market knowledge as the primary reason for their newly introduced products to fall short of expectations. Industrial advertisers do not seem to understand the major considerations that influence the purchase of their product. Earlier marketing appraisals would reduce investments in

Address correspondence to: Peter J. LaPlaca, Associate Professor of Marketing, University of Connecticut, Storrs, Connecticut

bad research and development projects. These situations point to a lack of customer orientation.

High technology companies frequently lack a systematic approach to product evaluation and product planning [1]. Specifically, the industrial marketing manager needs accurate information on the product characteristics or features required by prospective customers. This includes the exact function to the performed, the value placed by prospective customers on performance, and the varying requirements of different customer groups. Accurate demand information is also needed in terms of the market's present and future size, trends, and segments. Finally, knowledge is needed concerning industrial channels of distribution and how to operate successfully through them with direct sales and promotional programs.

It is often difficult for the high technology firm to know what market application to pursue in developing new products and in defining them. This is especially true if several potential applications for the same technology appear attractive at the outset. The problem is further compounded if the product concept is entirely new to the company and if many of the potential applications are external to its served markets. Therefore, a comprehensive marketing development model is presented that ad-

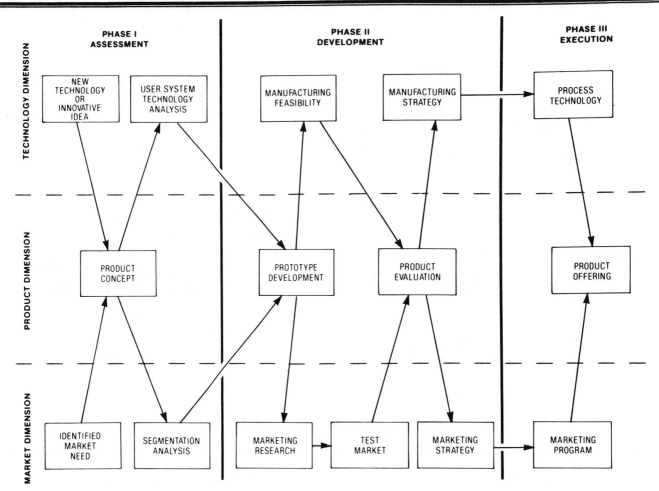

FIGURE 1. Overview of the high technology product development process

dresses the problems facing high technology firms. The model presents systematic guidelines to:

1. Provide enough information for a "go, no–go" decision on specific product-market applications within a reasonable period of time and cost.

PETER J. LAPLACA is Associate Professor of Marketing at the University of Connecticut, Storrs, Connecticut. He has conducted numerous research and consulting projects for companies engaged in new product development and is a frequent speaker at professional marketing conferences and seminars. Dr. LaPlaca received his degrees from Rensselaer Polytechnic Institute.

GEORGE MIAOULIS is Professor and Chairman of the Marketing Department at the University of Hartford, West Hartford, Connecticut. Since receiving his doctorate from New York University, he has had extensive experience as a consultant in the field of new product development for high technology companies.

2. Provide the information for a complete market program in terms of product development, prototype testing, overall marketing strategy, and feedback and control.
3. Provide sufficient flexibility to be useful in developing an interactive relationship between existing products and potential new ones.

HIGH TECHNOLOGY MARKET DEVELOPMENT PROCESS

Within a high technology industrial firm, the market development process evolves naturally in three phases: (1) assessment, (2) development, and (3) execution. The model presented here structures those processes by identifying key information needs and decisions. The end result (see Fig. 1) is a marketing development process which allows management to effectively assess market opportunities and risks, and to integrate technological resources and marketing programs necessary for market entry.

In each phase of the process there is an evolution and interaction among technological, product, and market dimensions. The *technology* evolves over three phases:

1. from technological innovation
2. to user systems analysis
3. to process or manufacturing strategy and technology

The *product* concept develops from:

1. a product concept
2. to a prototype
3. to a marketable product and an extended product line.

The *marketing* function evolves from:

1. identification of market needs
2. to market segmentation and marketing research
3. to development of marketing strategies and programs

As the technology, product, and market dimensions evolve, they continually interact and feed back until each is sufficiently developed to be accepted by the target markets.

Phase I—Assessment

The assessment phase (Fig. 2) is designed to provide a timely, low cost evaluation of the technological innovation's viability as a marketable product. Central to the assessment phase is the product concept. This serves not only as a crystallization of the original innovative idea or proposed answer to an identified market need, but also as an integrative point for engineering feasibility, analysis of potential user systems, market segmentation, application research, market screening, and market analysis. The primary purpose of the assessment phase is to reach a decision for further development before the project has absorbed significant amounts of research and development funds.

There are three principal analyses which are undertaken on the technology dimension. The first concerns

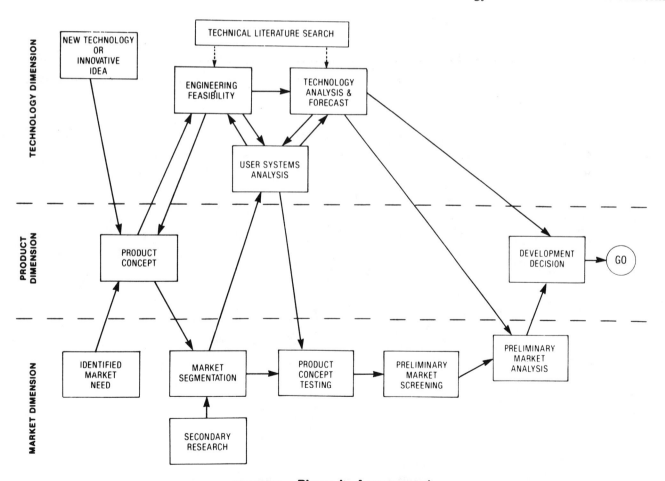

FIGURE 2. Phase I - Assessment

the engineering feasibility of the product concept. This provides information on how the product should be configured to best provide the anticipated benefits/functions and the design alternatives. The second analysis investigates the appropriateness of state-of-the-art technologies for meeting market needs as well as the rate of change for these technologies (Is there a significant chance of the proposed technology becoming obsolete before an adequate return on the investment is obtained?). Most of these two analyses can be accomplished by means of secondary (i.e., published) data with a modicum of engineering effort. The third technological analysis requires an understanding of how the proposed product concept could become part of the user's overall system. Will the anticipated product benefit actually result, to a significant degree, when the product is applied by the user? A thorough understanding of the possible applications of the product concept in each potential market segment is required to complete this analysis.

Several types of analysis must be undertaken along the market dimensions. One is the identification of alternative market segments [2–7]. All too frequently, the technological firm investigates only one potential use of the product concept; if this market proves to be too limited to support the growth expectations of management, the project may be terminated. However, if multiple applications (at least of the basic technology) in a variety of markets are identified, there are frequently opportunities for greater cost reductions (due to the effects of shared experience and learning curve factors) in future stages of the product life cycle.

Once the appropriate market segments have been delineated it is necessary to conduct product concept tests in each segment. The product concept test asks the questions, "Is this product concept viable?" and "What adjustments are necessary to enhance its marketability?" The product concept test should present a holistic concept rather than separate components of the concept. In this way, various trade-offs can be made (i.e., reduced speed for lower operating cost) and prospective users can

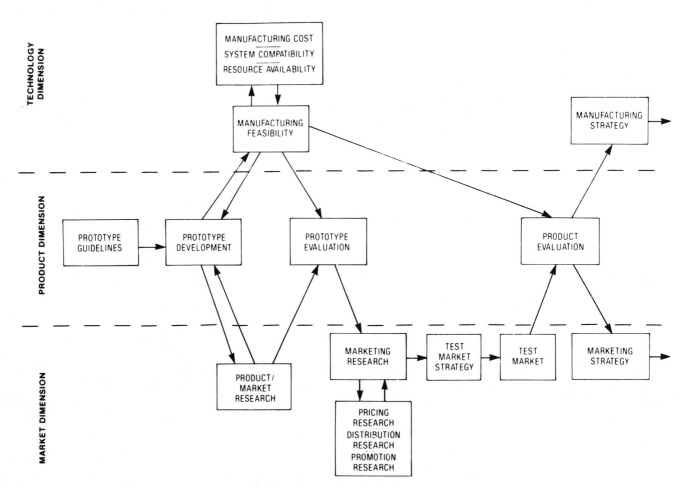

FIGURE 3.   **Phase II - Development**

better visualize the product concept in use [8]. Positive feedback from the product concept tests are followed by market screening—a quick appraisal of the potential match between the product concept and user needs. This will eliminate those market segments for which there are limited product applications, and hence, limited sales potentials. Those segments which pass this initial screening are subject to a more thorough analysis to determine current and anticipated market trends as well as a rough estimate of total market potential. This market analysis, in conjunction with the technology analysis and forecast, forms the basis for the decision to drop the project or to proceed with prototype development (Phase II).

In several recent applications of this process dealing with high technology electronics and environmental products, the ''go, no-go'' Phase I assessment decision was made in less than two months and for under $5,000. By focusing on the external environment and integrating all elements, the likelihood of success or failure can quickly become obvious.

Phase II—Development

In Phase II (Fig. 3) the technology, product, and market dimensions of the assessment phase are expanded and tested. The decision to proceed to this phase precipitates the development of prototype guidelines from which one or more prototypes are produced.

what independently until the end of Phase II when they are integrated with the product for test marketing.

During test marketing, when previous estimates of market response and required marketing effort can be refined, the opportunity exists to conduct financial analysis, quality control studies, and other quantitative assessments of proposed marketing strategies. Consideration for marketing, competitive, financial, portfolio, technological, and regulatory risks must also be incorporated into the overall decisions analysis [9]. The test market may result in a go–decision, recycling within Phase II for further development, or an abort–stop decision. A go–decision will require comprehensive marketing and manufacturing strategies.

Phase III—Execution

The execution phase (Fig. 4) focuses on the matching of product characteristics and market delivery systems to meet customer needs. On the technology dimension, manufacturing strategies must be translated into specific process or manufacturing technologies. This occurs simultaneously with the development of detailed marketing programs for each targeted market segment. To control the total marketing program, a marketing monitoring system must be established. This includes measurements of market penetration and growth, customer usage and satisfaction, and other elements of market dynamics.

The development of detailed marketing programs for each targeted market segment.

These prototypes are put through a complete manufacturing feasibility analysis including full scale cost projections (at multiple volume levels), tests for compatibility with present manufacturing systems (and determination of possible shared experience factors), and determination of resource availability and stability (such as raw materials and components, certainty of supply, and dependence on restricted sources).

Market segmentation progresses to customer identification and usage and delivery systems. Prototypes are field tested and necessary modifications are made. In order to speed up the development process, pricing, distribution, and promotional research proceed some-

Additionally, the impact of the firm's product, pricing, promotional, and distribution programs must be carefully monitored to provide information for strategy adjustments and new product opportunities.

Continuous monitoring of customer applications (by means of the sales–and–service force) can yield useful information on customer initiated product modifications or unmet customer needs. Product modifications should be subjected to a technological assessment to determine the impact of the proposed changes. These modified products can be offered to other customers as alternative models of the basic product. Customer monitoring can also help identify related product opportunities which,

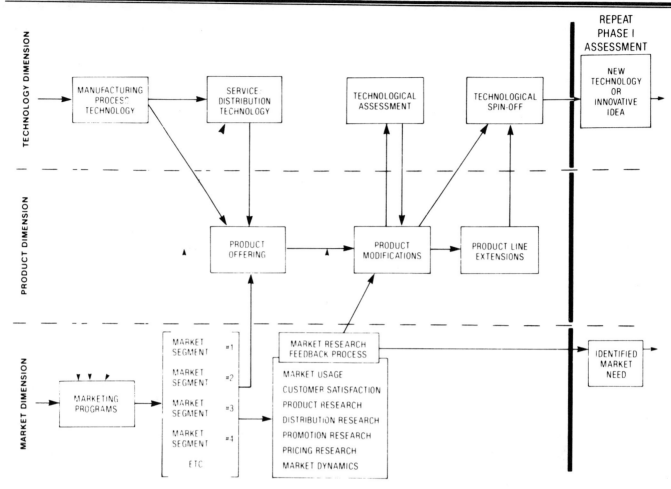

FIGURE 4. Phase III - Execution

subject to favorable technological assessment, can also be offered. Gradually these modified and related products will constitute a complete product line.

Product modifications can sometimes be significantly different from existing products as to require new technologies or the application of new technologies to customer problems. In either case, a technological spin-off can be organized using a venture management concept [10–12]. These spin-offs and identification of new market needs provide a direct linkage back to Phase I.

COMPLETING THE MARKETING MIX

The high technology development process emphasizes the need for internal and external communication systems to introduce new products. Often industrial management's support for a new product overlooks several basic communication opportunities before, during, and after introduction, materially affecting the product's suc-

cess [13]. In fact, overlooking them repeatedly can adversely affect a company's future ability to mount successful new product efforts [13]. The integration of pricing, distribution, and promotion research offers opportunities for improved organizational communication and for more effective marketing.

Pricing Research

Since price alone is often not the most important criteria in the selection of a *new* product, pricing research in industrial market research should include an analysis of customer purchase needs. The importance of price as a choice criterion differs from organization to organization [14]. A variety of other factors, such as a value-in-use warranty and service, add to the value of the product and should be considered elements of price. Although choice criteria differ from organization to organization, the industrial buying process for new products involves common steps across organizations. In a new product decision an industrial organization will tend to delay purchase decisions [15] in attempting to reduce risk [16]. Industrial purchase risk contains two major components:

1. The ability of the buyer to accurately predict negative outcomes based on an affirmative adoption decision.
2. The amount of loss associated with each negative outcome [16].

Pricing research can be used to measure the trade-off between these two risk components. Various packages of product performance, service, and guarantees can be associated with different price levels, and market response to these offerings can be measured, segment by segment. In certain market segments buyers may accept higher degrees of risk than in other segments. Appropriate product price strategies can then be designed for each segment. Analysis of the value of the product to the buyer may be used to determine the competitive advantage of the new product, even at a higher price, and can improve the company's image as a supplier of high quality high technology products [17]. Therefore, pricing research can be used to help the marketer better understand the buyer's behavior and perceptions, and also help manage the buyer's risk. While pricing research may not necessarily be aimed at analyzing customer purchase behavior, it can be used to define the perceived components of price for a given product offering.

Promotion Research

In the development of marketing strategies for high technology products, the industrial salesperson has been virtually ignored as an integral element of the marketing mix. For example, there are few organizations that provide a sales support program based on adequate market research of what is needed to assist the sales force to reach the organization's marketing and sales goods. Yet, numerous studies of buying practices in industry have shown that personal selling is 2 to 3 times more accepted by industrial customers than any other marketing technique [18]. As Wilson and McFarlane discuss, there is an opportunity to combine pricing and promotion research for better organizational integration and more effective marketing:

Research can identify the typical decision-making unit in an industry buying situation, and it can designate the criteria to enable the salesperson to recognize a particular type of buying situation and the steps which will be followed by the buyers. This enables the salesperson to ensure he is visiting the real decision makers, not just the purchasing officer

(who so frequently is totally constrained by specifications designed by others), and is providing the information required to the right people at the right time in the right way [19].

Although personal selling seems to be preferred by industrial markets, Greyser cautions that "pull through" advertising for industrial products appears to be increasing [18]. He states that research can be used in making communication decisions regarding the most effective allocation of organizational resources between personal selling, advertising, and other promotions. For example, Greyser suggests advertising research to optimize media scheduling. He proposed research that ". . . would investigate alternative approaches to scheduling advertising, such as steady pressure, fighting with short, but intense, "on" periods and long "off" periods. Also, how should these strategies vary with low, moderate, or high advertising budgets?" [18] These questions must, of course, be answered within the context of the total promotion and marketing strategies.

One promotional tool often underutilized by high technology industrial firms is public relations. Public relations is a promotional tool important to the timing of the introduction of a high technology product. It can be used to give a new product a "presence" leading to eventual acceptance [20]. Additionally, public relations can be used to reduce the newness of an introduction and to make the introduction more believable and acceptable. Press releases and feature articles in highly credible publications (e.g., respected trade newspapers and magazines, scholarly journals, and so on) contribute to risk-reduction and copies can be used by the salesforce as well as part of proposals submitted to purchasers. Secondary research conducted during Phase I can identify important informational sources for prospective purchasers and can provide the basis for an effective public relations strategy.

Distribution Research

Distribution research can result in effective and efficient channel development. Here, again, marketing mix elements interrelate. If rapid delivery is defined as a price component, it seems logical that research in that area would have an impact on the channel development for a new industrial high technology product. Stacey and Wilson emphasize the importance of industrial distribution research:

The very lack of ready-made reference emphasizes the importance of distributive data especially tailored to the individual requirements of the firm. In this respect the industrial marketing research is in a position to provide valuable information and perhaps original and exclusive market data for the formulation of distributive policy. Further, in providing such information on distribution, the value of marketing research can impress itself more readily upon management than it would perhaps in any other field of marketing activity [21].

In many high technology fields, key distributors may actually be larger than the high technology manufacturers; their role in developing the market must be determined. Are distributors expected to provide technical assistance to the purchaser? What are the promotional roles played by distributors? Do distributors increase or decrease perceived purchase risk for new high technology products versus a direct-to-user channel of distribution? How will the chosen distribution system affect total cost to the purchaser? What is an appropriate means of controlling distributors? What interaction can be anticipated among company sales personnel, distributors, and customers? Answers to some of these, and other questions can be gleaned from secondary research conducted during Phase 1. However, a sound primary research effort during test marketing and other Phase II activities is usually required to develop an effective distribution component to the overall marketing strategy.

IMPLEMENTING THE MODEL

Two key considerations in implementing this systematic new product development process are: what are appropriate organizational structures to use to increase the success of application of the system, and what are reasonable expectations of the financial resources required to satisfactorily complete the process.

Organizational Alternatives

Although there are numerous alternatives for controlling and coordinating the company's efforts used for high technology product development, perhaps the two best approaches are the project task force and the venture team [11]. Both of these organizational concepts involve the use of various experts (i.e., patent, marketing, engineering, various technical specialists, legal, and so on) brought together to further the product development process. The chief differences in these two concepts are the degree of autonomy from the continuing operations of the organization and the degree to which personnel involved with the product development process are removed from other functions and responsibilities.

In general, the venture team is a separate organizational entity reporting directly to senior management or a committee. A project task force may report to the lab director, new product director, or a divisional manager. While engaged on the new product development project, members of a project task force may also be involved with other responsibilities and therefore not direct all of their attentions to the development project. However, members of the venture team are assigned full time to the project as long as their particular expertise is needed. The venture team concept appears to be more appropriate when the technology involved is quite different from the firm's existing technology and when the principle applications of this technology are in markets removed from those already served by the company. When either of these conditions are absent, the project task force is a more common approach.

Regardless of the organizational form used, there are several responsibilities which should be assigned to the group:

- Determine the immediate, mid-range, and long-range obstacles facing the introduction of the new concept.
- Determine the most advantageous product for integration of the new concept.
- Develop a set of alternatives for marketing new programs with associated budgets to be reviewed by management.
- Establish time lines for the implementation of the program—the task force will relinquish responsibility for the project when it enters the manufacturing start-up phase and the production can be phased into normal operations. The venture team may have to assume production responsibility if there is no similar process in place.
- Submit periodic status reports on the progress of the project.

Financial Considerations

Technical obstacles, current research, and development momentum, and even luck can impact the final total cost of the product development process. The early involvement of market assessment advocated in this system as described in this article will help minimize the total new product development cost of the firm by eliminating those concepts with little or no probability of commercial success.

Assigning relative costs to each of the three major phases of the development process is by necessity a flexible process. Although the functions that must be performed are constant, the relative cost intensity of each step will shift as various technologies, products, and markets are considered. The nature of activities that must be accomplished will depend heavily upon how closely aligned a new product concept is to the existing product line, the technical expertise the corporation has to draw upon, and the nature of the marketplace. In general, the industrial marketing cost breakdown for activities, that preceed actual market introduction, should be closely aligned to the following:

- Phase I—Assessment   10%
- Phase II—Development   60%
- Phase III—Execution (planning, research, and assessment)   30%

These guidelines do not include technological research and development costs, nor additional fixed costs such as new production capacity.

The developmental phase incurs the heaviest cost because it requires the commitment of corporate resources to develop and test prototypes, extensive marketing research, and associated test market budgets. Promotional and distribution expenditures are dependent on the size of the test market and the degree of confidence required by corporate management.

It is suggested that a formalized return on investment evaluation be included in the prototype evaluation stage of Phase II. Appropriate burden rates should be established for each of the division's products. This rate should reflect the product line's return as forecasted for a period consistent with the life cycle of the innovation.

The assessment phase can conceivably be accomplished with relatively minor direct internal involvement. Outside marketing research, concept testing, and other marketing and/or technical consultants can be used to provide information and establish prototype guidelines for managerial review. Since these consultants are specialists in their field, they usually can accomplish these tasks at a lower cost and in a shorter time span that can be done using corporate personnel.

The execution phase has the second lowest developmental cost because much of the activity scheduled is not an integral part of the new product concept. A large portion of this expenditure is for marketing research, information retrieval, and feedback conducted for the entire product line. Although some funds may be diverted from other budgeted programs, only limited additional funds will be directed solely at the new product in the final phase.

In part, the results of an project will be dependent upon what basic assumptions are made at its inception. The relevant items to be addressed regarding the cost of developmental programs are:

- When does the product become independent of the general level research and development effort?
- What is the appropriate cost approach for the projects? Should it be fully loaded costs, variable costs, or some other mix?
- How to budget for these projects—can an appropriation system be used? If so, who will be held responsible for the detailing of expenditures and maintaining internal controls?
- Is market research contracted on a bid basis, a cost plus percentage basis, or authorized dollar limits?

To further help in an appraisal of the true costs of developing a high technology product, it is recommended that the following corporate policies be adopted with regard to high technology development projects:

- The R & D effort should be considered a corporate expense until the technology is developed to a stage that it can be limited to a specific segment of the business sector or product class.
- Projects should be cost-based on the productive capacity of the corporation or the appropriate product division. If there is excess capacity available, or expected to be available by the time the product can be developed, a variable cost approach should be implemented. If a new capacity must be acquired, the project should absorb fully loaded costs.
- Budgets for these projects should be integrated into the annual capital budgets. General funds should be made available for new concept development and allocated to specific projects as they emerge. Once these funds are exhausted, the projects should be absorbed into other general budgets or deferred until the following year. Only one individual should be made responsible for allocating these fun   nd an appropriate channel for requests shou   be established.
- Market research should be contracted on a maximum dollar limit basis. A bid process will minimize cost, but might not achieve the desired results. A time plus cost basis is uncontrollable.

This approach should provide a systematic means of internal control, coordination of internal and external effort, and timely managerial review while not requiring additional personnel to be hired.

CONCLUSIONS

A systematic development process for high technology products is critical in reducing the high mortality rates for new industrial products. A model comprised of assessment, development, and execution phases has been described which involves an integrated approach among the technology, product, and market dimensions of the new product process. A shift in the traditional focus of high technology product development to include an early and continuous interaction with the market place is also encouraged. The approach described here can help in allocating funds for continued product development on a more rational basis. If carefully conducted, the process should reduce many of the risks inherent to the selection and development of high technology industrial products.

REFERENCES

1. Zarecor, William D., High Technology Product Planning, *Harvard Business Review*, January–February, pp. 108–115 (1975).

2. Barnett, Norman L., Beyond Market Segmentation, *Harvard Business Review*, Jan.–Feb., pp. 152–166 (1969).

3. Choffray, Jean-Marie, and Lilien Gary, A New Approach to Industrial Market Segmentation, *Sloan Management Review*, Spring, pp. 17–29 (1978).

4. Cordozo, Richard, Segmenting the Industrial Market, *American Marketing Association Proceedings*, 1978.

5. Johnson, Hal G., and Flodhammer, Ake, Some Factors in Industrial Market Segmentation, *Industrial Marketing Management*, July, pp. 201–205 (1980).

6. Spekman, Robert, Segmenting Buyers in Different Types of Organizations, *Industrial Marketing Management*, Feburary, pp. 43–48 (1981).

7. Wind, Yoram, and Cardozo, Richard, Industrial Market Segmentation, *Industrial Marketing Management*, April, pp. 153–166 (1974).

8. Wind, Yoram, Grashof, John, and Goldhar, Joel, Market-Based Guidelines for the Design of Industrial Products, *Journal of Marketing*, July, pp. 27–37 (1978).

9. Shah, Kiran, and LaPlaca, Peter J., Assessing Risks in Strategic Planning, *Industrial Marketing Management*, February, pp. 77–91 (1981).

10. Cook, Frederick, Venture Management as a New Way to Grow, *Innovation* October, pp. 27–37 (1971).

11. Hill, Richard, and Hlavacek, James D., The Venture Team: A New Concept in Marketing Organization, *Journal of Marketing*, July, pp. 44–50 (1972).

12. Hlavacek, James D., and Thompson, Victor, Bureaucracy and New Product Innovation, *Academy of Management Journal*, September, pp. 360–372 (1973).

13. Linehan, Thomas A., Communications Boosts Chance of New Product Acceptance, *Industrial Marketing*, September, pp. 46–52 (1977).

14. Kelley, J. Patrick, and Coaker, James W., The Importance of Price as a Choice Criterion for Industrial Purchasing Decisions, *Industrial Marketing Management*, May, pp. 281–293 (1976).

15. Chenu, Pierre, and Wilemon, David, A Decision Process for New Product Selection, *Industrial Marketing Management*, October 1973.

16. Barnes, Jim, and Ayars, William B., Reducing New Product Risk Through Understanding Buyer Behavior, *Industrial Marketing Management*, March, pp. 189–92 (1977).

17. Forbis, John L., and Melita, Nitin T., Value Based Strategies for Industrial Products, *Business Horizons*, May, pp. 32–42 (1981).

18. Greyser, Stephen A., Academic Research Marketing Managers Can Use, *Journal of Advertising Research*, April, pp. 9–14 (1978).

19. Wilson, Aubrey, and MacFarlane, Ian, Research as an Aid to the Industrial Field Salesman, *Industrial Marketing*, August, pp. 73 (1977).

20. McDonald, Morgan B., Jr., Appraising the Market for New Industrial Products, in Vinson, Donald and Sciglimpaglia, Donald (eds), *The Environment of Industrial Marketing*, Grid Press, Inc. Columbus, Ohio, pp. 131–140 (1975).

21. Stacey, Nicholas, A. H., and Wilson, Aubrey, *Industrial Marketing Research*, Hutchinson and Co., London, pp. 92–93 (1963).

How to approach export markets

FIVE CAREFUL STEPS FOR BEGINNERS

by W.E. (Ted) Littler
Vice-president, Sales
Kleen-Flo Tumbler Industries, Ltd., Toronto

This article is aimed at the smaller Canadian company that is thinking about entering into foreign trade but has only a vague concept of export market approach. They may not be too sure whether they really want to take the plunge at all or doubtful about how to develop a basic marketing plan/philosophy.

That is exactly the position my employer was in about seven years ago.

I should tell you a little more about Kleen-Flo, since you will have a greater appreciation of the marketing techniques utilized if you know about the products that we sell.

Kleen-Flo sells automotive chemicals—radiator sealers, gasket compounds, anti-rust compounds, car polishes, oil and gas additives. The market for these products in both Canada and around the world is very competitive, so that strong merchandising approaches must be used to promote them.

Kleen-Flo entered the export market in 1973 for several reasons. . . .

- We had excellent penetration of the Canadian market and felt that future growth could be reduced due to limited population and vehicle expansion rates.
- Our packages were bilingual.
- We suspected that with the rapidly growing world vehicle population (mainly in underdeveloped countries) of about 288 million cars and 79 million trucks and buses, our products would find ready buyers.
- We felt that we had something to sell in terms of technology and promotional know-how since our products had

Kleen-Flo Tumbler Industries Limited of Toronto is one of Canada's largest automotive specialty chemical companies. Over the past six years Ted Littler has been responsible for the total redesign of more than 100 automotive products, the creation of product catalogues and the concepts used in their point-of-purchase and national advertising campaigns for export markets. Kleen-Flo entered the field of foreign trade seven years ago and today sells in more than 60 countries.

been used in one of the toughest markets in the world for more than 30 years. (Toughest in terms of wide temperature range, from sub-zero winters to scorching Prairie summers, and toughest in terms of the end-market application since most vehicles manufactured around the world are available in Canada.)

So, we went into the export business . . . and started to re-educate ourselves!

STAGE ONE

We discovered that our packaging was outdated; we didn't know anything about international price levels for products such as ours; we were too generous with credit; our printed matter was drab and uninteresting. We did one thing right, however, we didn't go all over the world all at once. We chose the Caribbean area because it was English- and French-speaking, it was near Canada and regularly serviced by Canadian shipping lines. In addition, it did not have insurmountable trade barriers since it was a member of the Commonwealth and had strong ties with Canada.

Obtaining Statistical Information

Few underdeveloped countries are able to provide statistical information on particular products. However, in industrialized nations, this task is not such a challenge.

For instance, the United States and most European countries are able to supply the exporter with relevant information.

International trade magazines, especially those published by the Americans and British, can often provide useful product information. "Automobile International" magazine published in New York issues annually an analysis of the automotive industry worldwide, identifying car, bus and truck populations by country.

Commercial Officers at Canadian embassies are useful contacts. However, be sure not to overload them with intricate questions which would take a major market survey for them to answer! Remember, you are only one of the companies they are assisting to enter into their particular area. The U.S. publishes excellent foreign trade information. A list can be obtained from the United States Consulate General office.

Often your local agent can obtain access to importation records in his particu-

Ted Littler

Reprinted with permission from *Sales and Marketing Management in Canada,* vol. 22, no. 3, pp. 7, 9, 24–26, Apr. 1981.

lar country, but of course, you have to have a contact before this method can be utilized.

Obtaining Sales Leads

After you have selected the particular geographical area to begin your export activities, prepare a short, concise letter addressed to the Commercial Officer of the Canadian Embassy in that particular area encompassing the following:

- A description of the product range.
- Important sales features, size of market, probable profit ratios.
- C.I.F. prices for a major central port within that particular geographical area, perhaps in the form of a typical pro forma invoice.*
- Your payment requirements—i.e. open account, irrevocable confirmed letter of credit, sight draft.
- Your manufacturing ability, availability of the goods, and the approximate time from receipt of order to the arrival of the goods.
- Type of distributor you are looking for—a manufacturer's representative who would work on commission, an agent who would import and pay for the goods for redistribution, or a large, retail-oriented organization, i.e. a mass merchandiser.
- Illustrated catalogues or sales sheets, preferably in colour, on your product range and promotional techniques.

(In South America, most buyers wish to be quoted F.O.B. Miami or New York in U.S. dollars. Arrangment for the C.I.F. is negotiated later).

Trade Fairs

Lufthansa publishes an excellent booklet titled "Calendar of Events—Trade Fairs and Exhibitions," which is an international listing. (Available from Canadian German Chamber, 480 University Avenue, Suite 1510, Toronto, Ontario M5G 1V6.) Attending trade fairs, whether you are an exhibitor or not, provides excellent contacts.

Federal and provincial government trade fairs provide an excellent method of reaching foreign buyers and offer the advantages of reasonable cost, plus instant credibility.

Advertising for Agents

Design your own advertisements and place them in major trade magazines—both British and American. (Canada, unfortunately, does not have many internationally known trade magazines.)

Make the advertisements small and concise and don't try to be clever with snappy expressions or gimmicks! Choose only international magazines that are read the world over. Tell them why your products are unique, show them which packages you sell, indicate that you have competitive prices, and that you can deliver. Nothing more. International businessmen are far too busy to wade through your company's history or aspirations!

Advertisements of this nature have yielded my company up to 70 replies per issue.

Package/Product Design

Take a long hard look at the products you intend to sell abroad. Your design and brand name may be quite popular in this country, but it's probably unknown abroad. The moral here, then, is not to fall in love with your 20-year-old product design! Don't try to do a redesign of the product yourself, since there are many young professional designers ready to do the job for you.

When redesigning your products, use the "show and tell" technique—try to design them in such a way that the foreign consumer does not have to read the copy. In this way, the language problem is overcome and an accelerated buying decision obtained.

When redesigning your products, use the "show and tell" technique—try to design them in such a way that the foreign consumer does not have to read the copy. In this way, the language problem is overcome and an accelerated buying decision obtained.

Try to use as much colour as possible, and, in the case of smaller products, consider self-contained display cartons.

Since Canada enjoys an excellent image abroad, Kleen-Flo has for several years incorporated the Canadian flag on all its packages and export publications. Apply to the Secretary of State for permission to use the Canadian flag.

Don't forget to include on all products and publications, "Made in Canada," for customs purposes.

When visiting a country, check any problems which could occur in package design. For instance, your colours or symbols could unwittingly conflict with religious or cultural taboos. Your local agent will be able to advise you.

Negotiating Your First Sale by Correspondence

Let us assume that you've now found an interested buyer and are entering the negotiation phase.

First of all ask that he indicate to you a typical order to enable you to generate a pro forma invoice that will allow him to raise an irrevocable confirmed letter of credit.

Almost without doubt he will ask you for an exclusive agreement.

Do not give in to him!

Under no circumstances enter into a long-term agreement with a party that you have not met even though he has written the best commercial letter you've ever read! Instead, indicate in your reply that you would much prefer a "gentleman's agreement" in the first phase of your negotiations, and that after the second order has been shipped, you will be willing to discuss firmer commercial arrangements with regard to exclusive territories, etc.

For safety's sake, insist upon an irrevocable confirmed letter of credit and try not to sell on an open account basis.

Let's assume that the irrevocable confirmed letter of credit arrives at the bank and you now have to prepare the documentation. For newer companies, I would suggest that you contact one of the excellent freight forwarders available in Canada and leave the sometimes difficult task of documentation entirely in their hands. For this, a nominal charge will apply. However, for companies with inexperienced personnel, it is the most effective method of completing the transaction.

STAGE TWO

Visiting the Foreign Territory

We have now reached the stage where your products have been shipped abroad and you have received payment. By this time, the agent may have indicated his lack of product knowledge and its effect upon sales or expressed some doubt as to which path he should take for developing his market or that he wants a special discount to develop an advertising campaign.

It is difficult to answer questions of this nature, therefore a visit to the particular country is essential.

"Confucius say, exporter who covers chair seat rather than foreign territory—will always remain on bottom!"

Visits abroad are obviously the best way to get your story across. Both the provincial and federal governments have excellent schemes and the co-operation and encouragement that we have received from both governments has been superb.

Pre-organization of your export visit is vital. When you, or your employee, visit a particular territory, make sure that he knows all about your products, your prices and your policies. He will be landing in some countries where the importer expects the President or Vice-President to visit him and expects the company representative to have all the answers.

- Develop C.I.F. prices for that particular territory on all products.
- Prepare a photograph album showing close-ups of your products, typical Canadian in-store displays, photographs of the manufacturing facility and office arrangements—these often interest potential buyers.
- Carry a schedule of sailings from major Canadian ports taking into consideration the closing of the St. Lawrence Seaway.
- Indicate the difference in price between a typical export pack and shipping your goods in container load quantities, if applicable.

Arriving in a country well-equipped and well-informed will allow you to increase your own sales if you are fortunate enough to have already obtained a distributor. Being well-prepared will also allow you to make clear, concise presentations to the interested organizations recommended by the local Canadian Embassy.

Before entering into any firm negotiations in a new country, I much prefer to spend a day or so looking at the market on my own—visiting service stations, garages large retail stores, large fleets. This is not as difficult as it appears since I usually walk out of the hotel, hail a cab and explain to him that I want to visit "as many service stations and large department stores in the next five hours as possible!"

The taxi driver, I suspect, often shakes his head in disbelief but I usually obtain a much firmer "feel" for the local market before I enter into firm negotiations with a potential distributor.

Call on agents who are distributing your competitors' products as part of your market survey. There is always the possibility that he is dissatisfied with his present supplier and would like to obtain a more attractive, or profitable, line.

Choosing a Distributor

Aspects which influence your choice of distributor will include the following:
- his grasp of the local market, business contacts, acceptance
- financial reliability
- other lines carried
- warehousing, office facilities
- familiarity with importing requirements and ability to correspond in English.

We have found from experience that the biggest agent is not always the best since products can often get lost in his crowded line-up.

STAGE THREE

Let us assume that you have decided upon a particular company, shipped and received payment for your first order, and now, since you are visiting that particular country intend to intensify the marketing of your goods there.

Price Lists

Do not simply issue your Canadian price list and tell him that it's "40 per cent off!"

Try to control every piece of paper that the local foreign representative carries. For instance, try to design your price lists so that they inform the buyer, rather than simply tell him the price.

Include. . . .
- A small illustration of the product.
- A one sentence sales message, in three languages, of that product.
- Package dimensions, weight and volume (preferably metric measure).
- Local price, i.e. after all import duties have been paid, agent's mark-up, etc.

We make our export price lists available in two editions, the first edition is our prices F.O.B. Toronto and the second is a "price blank" edition, which allows the local agent to fill in his local prices.

In this way we can control what the foreign salesman carries with him, ensuring that all the essential details are available to him to close the sale.

Product Catalogues

Here again, try to use the "show and tell" technique.

If your budget allows it, have your product catalogues, sales sheets and so on printed in full colour: a well-designed, colourful publication can pre-sell the buyer before he actually sees the goods. In addition to showing the product, try to show it in use, and again include copy in three languages (English, French and Spanish).

Kleen-Flo uses the same product catalogue in the Canadian market as it does in the export market. Our export sales could not support a full colour product catalogue. None of our Canadian customers has objected to the presence of Spanish in our catalogues!

Attractive publications are very important in the export business since you will be judged by your "paper." If your publicity material is poor and uninspiring, you can expect your sales to reflect it.

Foreign Representative Training

Of course, it is more difficult to train salesmen in foreign countries than it is in Canada. To overcome this problem, generate an "Export Newsletter" on a regular

basis to inform your foreign customers of the latest product development, a new technique for selling an old product, the sales prize for a particular campaign, etc.

Secondly, generate a product sales sheet designed to provide the local salesman with more information than the product catalogue carries. Do not make it too long-winded, and again, show both the product and the product being used.

To educate foreign salesmen on our line of products, we issue booklets called "Five Minute Facts." As the name implies these are designed to be read in not more than five minutes. They all have the same paragraph headings . . . What? Where? How? When? Why? and then Buyer Benefits—listing up to 10 features of the particular product.

This approach to salesmen's education has been so successful that we now make them available in five different languages, most of which have been translated and printed locally, at no charge to us.

A salesman cannot sell effectively if he does not know his product!

Advertising

Of course, advertising is essential with consumer products and this will be one of the first financial commitments you will have to make when you appoint a foreign distributor.

We have never believed it sensible to launch a strong advertising campaign in the expectation of receiving business. That is a risky method of opening up a market!

It is not wise to advertise until you have obtained reasonable distribution.

When you obtain that distribution, and your products are placed on the shelves of the stores, the shop assistants will know very little about your product, and the consumer will not recognize your brand. How do you solve the publicity problem?

We have found from experience that well-designed, informative point-of-purchase information systems not only attract the consumer but educate him into purchasing our brand names.

Let's look a little more closely at why we stress point-of-purchase promotional techniques so strongly in the export market.

With practically any commodity today the range of choice for the buyer is vast. In most retail stores, knowledgeable assistance is rarely at hand to help the consumer make a choice.

The usual method of overcoming this problem is to launch a national advertising campaign. The challenge, then, is to develop a successful method of moving consumer goods without a national advertising campaign.

To make an intelligent buying decision, the consumer needs information.

The advantages of an attractive, well-designed, point-of-purchase consumer information system are:

- They are efficient, since information is available when the consumer is actually making the buying decision.
- They can promote both high gross margin and high volume products.
- They persuade the retailer to allocate you shelf space and reduce the chance of him "cherry picking" your line; if the product is mentioned on the point-of-purchase charts, it should be on the shelves.
- Consumer information systems trigger the spontaneous purchase and remind the consumer that he has a "problem" or a "need."
- They are usually of moderate cost.

This approach to product advertising/promotion helps to sell technical products to non-technical buyers.

To illustrate the technique, Kleen-Flo supplies four-foot (1.2 m), double-sided illuminated screens, which, when attached to the top of existing product displays, answer most "car care" questions without any sales help.

They provide accurate, up-to-date information aimed at a specific market segment and are available in different languages. with every $6,000 order, the customer receives an Auto Data Centre—free. In this way, our products, our trade and consumer education program and our advertising enter the market at the same time.

We have found that this form of merchandising increases our gross margin, sells a wider mix of products, and has materially assisted us in obtaining an increased share of shelf space and markets.

Financing Local Advertising
When suitable distribution has been achieved, fortified with a strong point-of-purchase consumer information system, the next approach is to promote in other advertising channels.

Cinemas are a popular medium abroad, utilizing colour slides which are displayed on the screen during the intermission. Advertising in foreign trade magazines, billboard campaigns and of course, television, can quickly consume large amounts of your advertising dollar. A good rule to adopt if you do not generate the advertising yourself is to be very cautious about the size of the budget for a particular territory. If possible, allow a promo-

This is an example of a well designed "see and tell" POP display from which the customer can obtain all the necessary information about the products without the help of a salesperson.

tion/advertising amount based on total annual sales, which is payable when the amount is matched equally by the agent or the distributor. Three to five per cent, depending on your product line, is a good starting point.

Of course, before your half of the bargain becomes payable, you will require full details of how the money was spent, in the form of actual newspaper or magazine advertisements, photographs of billboards, tapes of radio and TV promotions, copies of handbills and posters, etc.

Over the years we have found it advisable to only suggest to the agent the basic design of the advertisement and the copy. We leave it to them to obtain a local translation to ensure that the right "accent" is obtained.

STAGE FOUR

Developing the Local Marketing Program
Try not to rush in and out of a great many countries in one trip. Make as many customer calls as possible while you are visiting a particular country to see the market for yourself. This first-hand experience will be invaluable to you when you return to Canada.

While you are with your new distributor, organize a sales seminar for the local sales force. Before you start your sales seminar, tell the salesmen that you will be sending around a questionnaire at the end

of the session to determine how much they have learned—even if you have no intention of it! In this way, perhaps you can hold their attention for most of the time!

Show the product, how to use, it, where and how to sell it and emphasize its main features and benefits. Show your sales incentive, preferably produced in North America, i.e. a company-identified wrist watch, sportswear, etc., or, in the even of an annual sales target, describe a trip to Canada and a visit to your operation.

If your budget can handle it, a cocktail party, with major purchasing agents of the local country, is often a good way to get your marketing program show on the road.

Your earlier marketing exposure will allow you by now to clearly define the market you want. Do you want to emphasize sales into retail stores only? Which trade route will you be taking—through major distributors or direct to the final retail outlet?

"Show and tell" the sales force about your price list, catalogue and sales sheets, and ensure that they know how to use them.

Before you leave the country, agree with your new distributor on an annual sales target. If this is achieved, you would allow him, say, a one per cent discount, retroactive to the first dollar, on reaching target.

STAGE FIVE

You will find that after awhile your existing agents and new agents will want to visit you. Ensure that both you and your staff are organized to make an excellent impression. Perhaps this will entail showing the manufacturing facility; allowing him time with your engineers or chemists to discuss particular product problems; indicating to him new products you have on the drawing board and exposing him to your advertising/marketing people and the approach they take in developing new techniques.

Our involvement in the export business has definitely improved our domestic activities. It is safe to say that we are well ahead of our competition in marketing because we have faced much tougher sales problems than the Canadian market.

By making use of the techniques described above, our problem today is not "How can we sell more products abroad," but "How can we ship enough to those export agents who have ordered the goods!" ⚛

Conclusion

- **Select one area of the world to spread your wings before you tackle the rest—don't attempt too much, too fast.**
- **Wherever possible use attractive, full colour, informative literature, preferably in the three major languages—English, French and Spanish.**
- **Try to design your products so that the package sells itself.**
- **Advertise for export leads.**
- **Use point-of-purchase advertising to save money and to control the promotional techniques used abroad.**
- **Be sensible in your initial targets and gross margin requirements.**
- **Be prepared to sell at varying margins, at varying discounts, in different countries.**
- **Don't send your domestic price list and tell him it's "40 per cent off!"**
- **If at first you don't succeed, analyze, change, and try again.**

(This article was originally published in Canada Commerce)

A Professional Approach to Exporting

Is your firm ready to take its first tentative steps into international markets? Alvin G. Davis, Senior International Trade Specialist with the U.S. Department of Commerce District Office in Chicago, has some practical advice to get you started. He has distilled his years of experience in assisting U.S. firms develop export programs into a few simple steps that can help your company take a professional approach to exporting.

The process of determining whether your company should develop an export program involves a few simple steps that will take time but little or no expenditure of funds. You, or someone else in your firm, will have to do some research in a library and visit a trade specialist at your nearest Commerce Department District Office. The steps involved in a professional approach to exporting are outlined below.

1. Define your objective. What do you hope to achieve, both in terms of immediate additional volume as well as long-term development of your business worldwide? Put this in writing—you will be referring to it many times.

2. Decide which member of your firm will assume the responsibility of fulfilling the international marketing objectives of your company.

3. Examine your product or service characteristics so that you know what to search for from available research profiles and statistics. This process involves several steps:

A) Find the Standard Industrial Classification (SIC) number of your product(s). This is essential in order to classify your product for statistical and market profiling purposes. You can find your SIC number in one of two places. Look in your copy of the last Census of Manufactures, submitted during some previous year ending in 2 or 7; your accounting department should have it, if you were in business during those years. Failing that, refer to Dun & Bradstreet's Credit Reference Book; look up your firm name and note the four digits preceding the listed name. This may give you the basic clue as to where to begin.

Visit your local library or nearest U.S. Department of Commerce District Office (listed on the inside back cover of this magazine) to obtain further detailed information to complete your international profile. Verify the exact description of your firm's product category. Be sure the nomenclature is as close as you can get. If you are not satisfied, contact a commodity specialist at the U.S. Bureau of the Census to assist you in pinning the exact number down.

A number of descriptions may be needed to fully cover your product and its applications. It may not always be exactly as you believe it to be. Care should be taken in exploring alternative classifications.

B) When goods are exported, the Schedule B number is used to classify the commodity description for statistical purposes, and to record units shipped and value. In 1978, the Schedule B numbers were modified and the nomenclature changed to conform to the Tariff Schedule of the United States (TSUS), used for import commodity classification. While there are minor differences, the descriptive ranges are minimal.

Locating these numbers requires precise clarification of the product by its usage, or of the material of which it is made. If you are already exporting, you may have it; if not, you will have to locate it. At this point, it may be well to recheck the information to make certain you have the correct number. Again, this is an important information base. Having the right number assures the statistical information you give and receive is accurate.

A good source is your shipping department. Get descriptive information as to the nomenclature they use. If your own shipping department does not have the information, take the descriptions you have to a freight forwarder. They are listed in the business section of your telephone directory. If you're still having problems, call your nearest Commerce Department District Office for advice.

C) Armed with your Schedule B and SIC numbers, research your product's position in this country and worldwide. Do this in a library's business reference room or at a Commerce Department District Office; if you're visiting Washington the Commerce Department has a Foreign Trade Reference Room in its main building at 14th St. and Constitution Ave. NW. The room number is 2314 and telephone number is 202-377-4855. The data you're looking for is in the reference books *Foreign Trade Statistics, FT135 Imports* and *FT410 Exports*. It will be necessary to cross-reference from the Schedule B numbers to the Schedule E number for exports and the Schedule A number for imports. The statistics will establish the location of currently active markets for the products you have to offer. You'll find the number of units shipped and the value of the shipments; in some cases, the average value of units can be calculated.

D) To obtain the statistics for the market shares of other major supplying countries, you will need the Standard International Trade Classification (SITC) number. This is the numbering system used by the United Nations in compiling worldwide statistics. United Nations statistical publications are available either at your library or at a U.S. Department of Commerce District Office. Copies may be purchased directly from the United Nations Publication Office, New York, N.Y. 10017.

Market Share Reports can show how products similar to your's have been doing against the competition in world markets. These reports, prepared by the Com-

Reprinted with permission from *Business America*, vol. 4, pp. 11–12, Aug. 24, 1981.

merce Department's International Trade Administration, are available by both country and commodity. The country reports provide data on imports of more than 900 manufactured products into a market from the world, the United States, and the eight leading suppliers for a five-year period. The U.S. share percent of the import market is shown. The commodity reports enable exporters to analyze world growth trends for their products, identify fast-selling products in emerging markets, and evaluate shifts in supplier performance. The *Market Share Reports* are available from the National Technical Information Service, U.S. Department of Commerce, Springfield, Va. 22161; telephone 800-336-4700.

The *Census of Manufactures* can help you evaluate where your product stands in the U.S. market. Using the SIC number, check the available figures nationally or by state, or down to counties or even census tracts.

Guidance on how to use government information sources for profiling domestic and international markets is contained in the publication *Measuring Markets,* available from the Superintendent of Documents, U.S. Government Printing Office, Washington, D.C. 20402.

E) The Customs Cooperation Council Nomenclature (CCCN) is now used by most countries of the world in place of the Brussels Tariff Nomenclature to classify goods for import tariffs. It is important to know what these are and to include them in your correspondence and literature. This helps the buyer determine what his import duties will be. Furnishing weights of products and sizes of cartons is needed for development of the "landed cost," or c.i.f.—cost, insurance, freight.

The BTN/CCCN numbers are found in a directory—"duanes"—published by the International Tariff Bureau of Brussels. Copies are available in most libraries and chambers of commerce. The basic code consists of the four numbers 80.00, followed by one or more suffix numbers, depending on how precise a particular country wishes to classify products. Once you have these numbers, current import tariffs can be rapidly determined. Commerce Department country specialists can furnish general "guides" for current duties; however, latest determinations should be made directly with each country.

The buyer has primary responsibility for the payment of all duties and taxes based on the cost of goods imported. When you furnish your f.o.b. price (free-on-board—your dock, city or port of export) with size and weight of product, the buyer should be able to calculate the landed costs and determine what his cost and selling price will be.

4. Having established some basic facts, it is now possible to begin developing a working budget of operation, based on these factors. Another alternative is to assume that exports could be 10 percent of domestic volume and then develop your working budget and international marketing program. You will need the company financial statement and general ledger accounts structure. Eliminate those items that make no contribution to export volume and recalculate a gross profit base. From these figures, you can produce a budget for international sales and marketing activities.

5. Restructure the company table of organization, indicating international operations as either equal to the domestic marketing department, or a part of it. It should be constituted as an important part of the company.

6. Developing international marketing policy is essential to the preparation of any program. The prices, terms and conditions must be suited to both the industry and the marketplaces. Market conditions for each of the trading areas of the world should be appraised. An analysis of the trade statistics should indicate the general starting direction.

When you reach this point, it would be wise to arrange for a consultation with a trade specialist at a U.S. Department of Commerce District Office.

7. Compile your program, with all of the supporting data, for presentation to management, complete with your recommendations as to starting dates, funding, personnel requirements and, most of all, the authority to carry out the objective.

Product Classification

The number assigned to his product under various international classification systems is the first and most important thing a new exporter needs to know. Numbering systems discussed in the accompanying article are listed below.

SIC—Standard Industrial Classification; used for statistical and market profiling purposes.

TSUS—Tariff Schedule of the United States; duties assessed on imports into the U.S.

B—Schedule B numbering system; exports from the United States.

E—Schedule E numbering system; exports from the United States, reported monthly in FT410 trade statistics.

A—Schedule A numbering system; imports into the United States, reported monthly in FT135 trade statistics.

SITC—Standard International Trade Classification; numbering system and nomenclature used by the United Nations for gathering, compiling and comparing statistics worldwide.

BTN—Brussels Tariff Nomenclature; used by most countries until replaced by CCCN.

CCCN—Customs Cooperation Council Nomenclature; used by most countries to classify goods being imported for duty determination.

CREATING A NEW PRODUCT: TWO PATHS TO THE SAME MARKETPLACE

By Susan E. Currier INC. Assistant Editor

Take two brands of the same product—yogurt. Both are introduced about the same time in different parts of the country, by two entrepreneurs who have had their share of marketing experience. One bet on his intuition, on *his* judgment of what his customers wanted. The other bet on research and testing, on what his *customers* said they wanted. Each knew the odds were against him; at least two out of every three new consumer food products fail.

Bill Bennet bet on intuition; his brand of yogurt was Yoplait. It's now the second-best-selling brand of yogurt in the country. Though he succeeded with his product, Bennet made some mistakes and lost his company to a big corporation.

David Goldsmith bet on research; his brand was New Country. Although it sold big when introduced in 1975, New Country started to falter two years ago. Goldsmith still has his company, but now he's introduced another new product to augment New Country's sales.

Both Bennet and Goldsmith say they would still use the methods they used the first time if they had it to do over again. Their stories, along with the commentaries that follow, make it clear that there's no one right way in the risky business of developing new products.

BILL BENNET SAYS FOLLOW YOUR INSTINCTS

Bill Bennet is tenacious when he's convinced he's on to something good—like French-made yogurt. "Once I get fired up with an idea," he says, "I just put the blinders on and keep moving in one direction."

Bennet's single-mindedness paid off. His Yoplait (pronounced yō-play) yogurt is outsold only by Dannon and will bring in estimated revenues of $50 million this year. Un-
(continued on page 135)

DAVID GOLDSMITH SAYS ASK YOUR CUSTOMERS

David Goldsmith doesn't like assumptions. So he tested his new yogurts every which way and back again. "We felt it made more sense to let consumers tell us what they liked," he says. "That way we could be sure that we weren't going to make any disastrous mistakes. I believe in the old carpenter's adage: Measure twice, cut once."

Goldsmith and his partner, Robert Finnie,
(continued on page 136)

BENNET

(from page 134)

fortunately, Bennet won't share in the bonanza. He was forced to sell out to General Mills two years after Yoplait's successful introduction left his company in serious financial straits.

When he first tasted French yogurt ten years ago, Bennet was already in the dairy-manufacturing business. He had bought Michigan Cottage Cheese Co. in Otsego, Mich., in 1967 after leaving Jewel Cos. Inc., a Chicago-based supermarket chain, where he had been a buyer and marketing specialist. Although his high-priced, premium products were bringing in $8 million a year, Bennet knew the cottage cheese market would never grow dramatically.

A large French dairy manufacturer offered Bennet his first taste of French yogurt—and the chance to introduce its products to Americans. Other U.S. dairy manufacturers (including large ones like Borden) had turned the company down, because they didn't feel American consumers would buy the product. Bennet was convinced they would. He spent two years in Paris working on the U.S. introduction, only to watch the deal fall through when the French dairy maker was bought out by a conglomerate.

But Bennet didn't give up. His instincts told him the product had tremendous potential. The flavor was full and fruity, the texture creamy yet thin enough to make the yogurt drinkable. Health-conscious Americans were just discovering yogurt, and Bennet simply knew that the French version would be a hit.

He began developing his own French-style yogurt, which he called Mais Oui. On a trip to France to get ideas for packaging Mais Oui, Bennet discovered that Yoplait, a major competitor of his first French partner, now wanted to get into franchising. He jumped at the chance to move French yogurt into American hands sooner than he had planned, and dropped plans for manufacturing Mais Oui. Michigan Cottage Cheese became Yoplait's first licensed manufacturer and distributor in the United States.

Nine months later Bennet had altered the product to meet his own vision of what would capture the American consumer. Yoplait's French parent had commissioned product research, both in France and then in its new U.S. market. The report on the American market came to a basic conclusion: Yoplait's taste would be appealing to consumers, who actually preferred it to Dannon, but the peculiar shape of the tapered package would not.

Bennet didn't entirely agree. He'd worked with product research during his stint at Jewel, but he was never completely sold on its validity. "I'm cautious about research," he says. "You can't be blind to it, but you can't be its prisoner either."

Bill Bennet: He's cautious about research.

So he ignored some of the research conclusions. He was pleased that the research confirmed his own judgment about Yoplait's taste appeal, but he liked the odd-shaped container. He wanted his product to stand out on the supermarket shelf. So he made only one minor change, expanding the size of the cup from four to six ounces. He could still advertise a lower shelf price than Dannon, whose standard cup is eight ounces, even though Yoplait sold at a higher price per ounce.

Bennet was convinced that the product had to be "all natural" to capitalize on the American consumer's preoccupation with healthful foods. So he eliminated the taste enhancers and stabilizers used in the French product.

Finally, to keep the French connection right in front of consumers' eyes, he had the cup printed with English on one side and French on the other.

Bennet had neither the money nor the temperament to conduct methodical tests on any of his changes.

He focused his resources on those aspects of the product that he viewed as most critical, relying, as he says, "on what was in my head and my heart, based on observing the marketplace for years."

Once he had a product and product presentation, Bennet hit the road to find investors. The money he had used from Michigan Cottage Cheese to finance the Yoplait franchise was running low. He'd had to invest $1.5 million in a plant and equipment, and only part of it was financed through French and U.S. government loans. Finding investors took much longer than he'd expected, almost two years.

At the same time, he and his sales manager visited retailers in Michigan to sell them Yoplait. Their basic technique was simple, says Bennet. "We just made everyone we talked to—venture capitalists, dairy buyers, bankers—taste it. I didn't care if they were allergic to milk or hated yogurt. I was so convinced that I had the right product that I was sure it would sell itself once someone tasted it."

As Yoplait moved into a few supermarkets, sales proved Bennet right. Consumers and retailers were happy, but Bennet needed cash for production, advertising, and promotion more than ever. His equipment loans and the profits from Michigan Cottage Cheese couldn't take Yoplait the rest of the way. Finally, in February 1976, Bennet sold 51% of his company to a group of investors in return for the $1.5 million he needed to keep going.

Then came a setback. Some of the waxed-paper cups began to leak. The problem surfaced only intermittently, making the task of finding the cause and a solution difficult. "It would come and go, and we couldn't even track it down to a specific phase of production or design," says Bennet. "We even had the French packaging equipment manufacturer flying back and forth, and their people couldn't come up with a solution either."

Meanwhile, sales continued to grow stronger. But as they increased, so did the instances of Yoplait oozing onto supermarket shelves and inside consumers' refrigerators. It began to get an awful reputation as a "leaker."

Bennet now knows that the leaking was caused by a combination of problems: a seal that wasn't strong enough, warehouse distribution, and the material of the cup. When Bennet took the stabilizers out of Yoplait, he hadn't thought to check how the new formulation would behave while held in a warehouse in waxed-paper packages. In 1977 he was faced with the consequences of his oversight. Putting the stabilizers back in the formula would have been an easy solution. But he was determined to keep the product "natural." So Bennet turned to his last hope: changing the package from waxed paper to plastic and designing a better seal. His solution came too late. Unlike Bennet, his nervous investors lost confidence in the product. Out of funds and out of time, they accepted an offer from General Mills in October 1977.

General Mills proceeded with changing the Yoplait cup from waxed paper to plastic. It took 6 months to come up with the right cup that would hold the yogurt in its place. Within another 12 months, H. Brewster Atwater, Jr., president of General Mills, announced that during its introduction in Southern California, Yoplait had outsold Cheerios, General Mills's longtime bestseller in terms of units. And today Dean Belbas, vice-president for corporate communications, puts Yoplait's market share at 10% of the retail foodstore market, which he pegs at $450 million.

So Bill Bennet's instincts were right. He beat the two-to-one odds against finding a successful new product. But in the process of bringing that new product to market, he lost his company. Could he have done it any differently? Probably not, says Bennet. "The cup problem was a bad break," he says. "I still feel that when you see an opportunity and believe that it's right, you should go for it. I ask a lot more questions now, but basically I like to shoot from the hip."

Bennet is still shooting from the hip. In 1980, he and a partner bought the Michigan franchise for King Cola, the latest entrant in the cola soft-drink market. No other buyers had been interested because of the distribution problems caused by Michigan's strict bottle bill. His solution? Michigan Container Redemption Service, a new Bennet company that picks up returnable soft drink bottles and cans. □

GOLDSMITH
(from page 134)

unveiled their New Country yogurt in March 1975 only after they had spent 18 months and over $200,000 testing the product in focus groups, testing the package, the concept, and the taste with consumers, and testing whether it would sell. When they put New Country on the market, it did sell; it captured a 7% share of the New York metro market after a year on supermarket shelves. But New Country ran into problems on the way to a solid share of the yogurt market. Now its New York metro market share is down to 2.1% and it's listed under "all other" on most A. C. Nielsen's market reports because its share is so small.

Goldsmith didn't make any disastrous mistakes such as those that cost Bill Bennet his company, but some people might say he lost perspective. Goldsmith and Finnie were used to doing market research. Be-

fore they formed Venture Foods Inc. to develop New Country yogurt, they worked together as business consultants for large consumer-product companies. Goldsmith had been an account manager for an advertising agency and Finnie a product-development manager at Procter & Gamble.

In May 1973, they formed Venture Foods with the help of one of their consulting firm's former clients, The Sentry Insurance Co., which invested $1 million in the company. "We looked for a joint investor," says Goldsmith, "because we knew we were going to get involved in some very expensive product development and testing. We decided that if we could come up with innovative packaging, create some exotic flavors, and give yogurt a whole new fun feeling, we had a reason for being."

Once they had a market, a company, and financing, all they needed was the product. They felt market research would serve them well in developing one. All the testing they

David Goldsmith tested his new yogurts every which way and back again.

did over the next 18 months hinged on their belief that the customer knows best; to create the perfect product, you need to ask your customer what he wants and then produce it.

Despite their mixed success, Goldsmith thinks they got their money's worth. "Market research saves time, saves money, saves people, and above all, it saves emotional anguish," he says. "It's basically risk reduction. You spend a little money early on to toss out the bad ideas—the ones that consumers tell you won't make it—before those ideas see the light of day."

Before they could start eliminating any ideas, they had to come up with some. They went straight to the consumer to get them. The first step they took was to gather focus groups of 12 yogurt eaters in three cities—72 yogurt eaters in all—to talk with a moderator about what they wanted in a yogurt. While Goldsmith and Finnie listened behind mirrored glass, the moderator started with a broad topic and then "focused" down to yogurt.

The focus groups produced more than 60 ideas for new kinds of yogurt as well as a general idea of consumer perceptions about the product. "The consumers said to us, 'This is what we want,' " says Goldsmith, "and we had to take their ideas and translate them into products. That was our mission."

They spent the next few weeks going over the list of ideas with a team of seven consultants whose specialties ranged from packaging to food technology. When they had narrowed the field down to those ideas that sounded interesting and could be produced economically, the partners asked the food technologist to create small batches of each of eight different product concepts. Then they taste-tested these product concepts on groups of 200 consumers in New York City, upstate New York, Boston, and the Hartford/New Haven area.

Three of the concepts were panned; one was a yogurt made with soybeans that tasted as bad as it sounds, and another was a yogurt flavored with carob that reminded at least one taster of sour chocolate milk. The three that got the most enthusiastic response—a fruit-and-nut yogurt; a rich, custardy yogurt with fruit rippled through it; and a fruit-

salad yogurt—were sent back to the dairy to be mass-produced in different flavors.

Meanwhile, the packaging consultant tested different shapes and graphics on 500 consumers. He ended up with a standard shape for the cup to keep production costs down. It was made of heavy-gauge plastic with brightly colored graphics. He recommended that the product be a "natural" one, because of trends he saw in consumer tastes. But he was voted down by Goldsmith and Finnie. They wanted to use stabilizers in the yogurt to enable them to keep it in warehouses and to get an edge with retailers who

Goldsmith didn't make any disastrous mistakes but some people might say he lost perspective.

didn't want to worry about quick spoilage.

As soon as the food technologist was ready with the flavor variations of the three winning concepts, the market research consultant set up taste-testing booths in five shopping malls in the Northeast, where more than 500 consumers tasted flavors like Date Walnut, Hawaiian Salad, and Blueberry Ripple.

"At each stage of testing," says Goldsmith, "we were making what I call 'go/no go' decisions. The most important one came at the very beginning when we had to decide whether there was room for a new product in the yogurt market. There were minor 'go/no go' decisions on each of the eight product concepts, the flavors, and the packaging. If we began to get negative feedback anywhere along the way, especially if New Country hadn't sold well in test market, we were prepared to pull out."

The last measure Goldsmith took of New Country was to place it in 30 supermarkets in Binghamton, N.Y., in order to track sales during a six-month period. It was like opening a show on Broadway. "The critics had to review it," he says, "and our critics were consumers paying dollars to buy the product."

The results were encouraging. New Country actually attracted new

users and expanded the yogurt market in Binghamton by 30%. There were also some negative results. One of the ideas that had come out of the focus groups was to segment New Country yogurt into three product lines: Rich 'N Ripply yogurts made with the creamy base were supposed to be eaten as a dessert; Fruity-Nutty yogurts were meant to be eaten as snacks; and Sunshine Salad was supposed to be a lunch yogurt. Attitude and usage tests showed that the Binghamton shoppers completely disregarded this marketing ploy and ate the yogurts whenever they felt like it. Goldsmith dropped the segmenting and at the same time changed the Rich 'N Ripply formula to the more typical low-calorie yogurt since it was no longer going to be marketed as a dessert. "The original Rich 'N Ripply formula ate so well," he says, "that I had to restrain myself from producing it."

After these final touches to conform with consumers' reactions, Goldsmith unveiled New Country yogurt in the Northeast in March 1975. Although sales started out strong, New Country's performance in the last two years has been disappointing. Goldsmith points to three reasons: a growing demand for plain, not fruited, yogurt; a proliferation of brands; and serious problems with the food broker Venture Foods first used to distribute its product. To make New Country stand out on grocery store shelves and to increase sales, he decided to lower the price of his yogurt from the standard 49¢ a cup to 39¢ a cup in January 1979.

Goldsmith still hasn't given up his belief in market research: "It's easy to say that we may have gone overboard with our market research, but there are a lot of guys who have tried to make it in this business who aren't around anymore. We're still here, and it's because we did market research."

Would he do anything differently if he had another chance? Goldsmith had that chance in early 1979 when Venture Foods acquired the license to the brand name Sweet 'N Low and began developing a new, low-calorie yogurt. "We took a short cut on some of the testing, because we already had the basic data," he says, "but essentially we followed the same market research and testing procedures that we had used for New Country." □

The head of an ad agency gives some tips on how to deal with him and his colleagues.

Ten Questions to Ask Your Advertising Agency

VICTOR WADEMAN

There is no other area in business where it is so costly to be wrong as in advertising. Most unsuccessful capital investments are recoupable to some extent, but bad advertising is money down the drain.

And year after year, the risk factor gets remorselessly higher, what with rising media rates, rising production costs, and more intense competition demanding heavier advertising outlays. Furthermore, the process of managing the advertising function is becoming more complex. Consumers keep getting more and more difficult to fathom, the media are becoming more fragmented, and many companies' product lines are downright Byzantine in scope.

While the soul of advertising remains simple salesmanship, suc-

---

"The agency that aspires to be 'the world's largest' has an unworthy and unproductive objective, from the advertiser's point of view."

---

cess in the function now involves a major managerial effort that must be wisely conceived, strongly directed, and sensitively controlled.

With this in mind, I would like to advance a set of simple ideas that companies with products or services to advertise might want to consider in selecting, or in working with, their advertising agency. If I were an advertiser, in other words, the questions I would definitely ask my agency or prospective agency would be:

1. What are your corporate objectives?

Normally, we think of the *advertiser's* objectives as the critical factor in shaping advertising. Yet, subtly, the agency's hopes, dreams, and plans have at least as much impact on the final result.

For example, the agency that aspires to be "the world's largest" has an unworthy and unproductive objective, from the advertiser's point of view. Even an agency that wants to "grow at a 10 percent compound annual rate" probably should be approached carefully. In fact, to keep faith with the advertiser, there is only one thing an agency *should* aspire to—namely, constantly increasing professional skill, placed against marketing problems of increasing scope and difficulty. (This is the "bake-better-bagels-and-profit-will-take-care-of-itself" approach.)

Now clearly, an agency that cannot make money for itself cannot be expected to make money for its clients either. But the paradox of an excellent advertising agency (like an excellent management consulting firm) is that it is the exception to the rule that every business needs a business plan. It needs only a manpower development plan and adherence to professional goals.

2. Who will work day to day on my account?

The vast majority of new-business presentations made to advertisers are handled by the ad agency chairmen, presidents, and copy chiefs. Were I an advertiser reviewing agencies who wanted my business, I would insist that these agencies place their presentations almost entirely in the hands of the people who would actually run my advertising.

Knowing the quality of the people who will "bail out" an account when it gets into trouble can only be of secondary concern to an advertiser. What you really need to know is who will create profits for you from day one.

3. What are your creative principles?

Clients can go daffy listening to a series of new business presentations. *Is* there an agency, for example, that doesn't have a boringly infallible creative "formula"?

The trouble with these things is that they are so artificial. They pretend the Muse will operate on a highly structured, demand-deposit basis. But the Muse usually won't cooperate on those terms . . . just as agency executives who promulgate such stuff don't use it themselves to evaluate a piece of copy. Therefore, predicting the kind of advertising a client is going to get is up to the client.

What I would do is ask for tearsheets on all the ads the agency has done recently, then in privacy ask myself these questions:

• Is there *substance* to their stuff? Do their ads tell each product's real story, or do they fool around with irrelevant phrases that merely flatter the brand?

• Is the selling point of each ad dramatized? And is it delivered in the vernacular of the audience I'm trying to reach?

• If each of the agency's ads were put up on a billboard, and I sped past it at 60 miles an hour, would I get the point?

At the heart of what makes ads sell in this busy, media-saturated world is simplicity. If the prospect cannot understand the proposition an ad presents to him within the flick of an eyelash, the chances for making a sale decline geometrically.

4. To whom are you writing my advertising?

The reason this question is so important is that advertising research on target audiences is so inadequate. Demographic information, for example, is like a skeleton. You see the approximate size and shape of the target consumer, but not how he thinks and acts. It is hard to establish rapport with a skeleton.

In other words, demographics tell you who buys the product, but nothing about the cause of the purchase. A good way to get around this problem is to think of the target audience in terms of a representative individual. Chances are, the agency copywriter will do this anyway. And it will be the single most important premise the agency will make.

"Irrelevancies and inconsistencies must be avoided. Irrelevant humor, for example, is the work of a lazy copywriter."

---

5. What character are you trying to build for my product?

For years, Madison Avenue talked about brand image. The world has passed that idea by; what appeals to us today is character. And the advertiser who fails to reflect the inherent character of his product fails totally.

Projecting the character of a product involves several things:

• The product must stand for something. Its physical composition or benefit may be similar to that of other products, but its inherent uniqueness must be articulated, and then sold without compromise. This uniqueness can be the way the product serves a specific public, the way it performs, or the precise extent and nature of its benefit.

• Irrelevancies and inconsistencies must be avoided. Irrelevant humor, for example, is the work of a lazy copywriter. Inconsistent media spending is the work of a lazy agency president who fails to chastise the client for it.

• Advertising must speak the language of the prospective customer. If you had a nickel for every ad written in advertisingese rather than people-talk, you would be rich.

6. What kind of marketing services can you offer?

For the past decade, Madison Avenue has supposedly been divided into two camps: the big full-service agencies and the small creative boutiques. Popular wisdom has it that you go to a big agency if you want solid marketing help, a small one if you want outstanding creative services. This is type-casting. Excellent creative abilities exist in some big shops and equally excellent marketing skills exist in some small ones.

The critical thing, therefore, is to decide what specific marketing help you need: backup in market planning? assistance in devising organization structure? a sales deployment or compensation plan? Having done this, you can then probe the agency's marketing competence in depth, to see whether there's a fit.

Keep in mind too that profit-producing creativity comes a lot easier when you have your marketing thinking straight.

7. How much should I spend?

The question of how to determine the most advantageous spending level for a product has received shockingly little attention from the advertising fraternity. Most penetrating agency discussions on finance center on the fruitless argument of media commission versus fee remuneration (or, how the agency gets its cut).

As a practical matter, it can be far worse for an advertiser to spend too little than too much. In fact, the failure to recommend a higher advertising spending level, when appropriate, can be the most heinous thing an agency can do to a client.

I recommend forgetting all the textbook theories on percentage of sales, a competitive level, and the objective-setting method as ways of determining a budget. These approaches view advertising as something defensive, related more to accounting considerations than to a knowledge of the company's underlying profit economics and risk-taking preferences. Advertising exists to make money, and only a careful review of the results of historical (or test) spending levels and the approximate message weight they delivered, plus a feeling for the company's profit sensitivity and breakeven characteristics, really put an agency in a position to spend sensibly.

8. How can I measure the contribution of my advertising?

Forty years ago, George Washington Hill, president of the American Tobacco Company, said, "Half my advertising is wasted. The trouble is, I can't tell which half." Even today, people tend to view advertising as a "black box" operation.

Baloney.

What has happened to advertising is that people have fallen into the trap of trying to measure it by scientific standards, rather than prudence. The fact is that the value of perfect information is hardly ever worth its cost in business. Yet there is one way to get a handle on probable advertising effectiveness: memorability research. Endless experience establishes that the probability of sales success is infinitely higher when people can simply remember the ad.

Of course, the purists can't stop arguing that advertising memorability is one thing, persuasive power another. True. But the two are highly correlated, and memorability research is as effective a performance-evaluation tool as you'll find in any area of a business.

9. How much time do you spend with my sales force?

Some of the shrewdest people in business are salesmen—probably because they have to use their wits practically every minute of every working day. Consider what salesmen can do for an advertising person:

- They can let him know whether the advertising is really working.
- They can take him out and show him how the market operates.
- They can tell him why the product does, in fact, sell.

It's strange, therefore, that Madison Avenue's attitude toward salesmen frequently involves condescension or boredom. From time to time, a client should remind the agency that marketing, done well, is a highly integrated function.

10. What operating procedures do you recommend to keep mickey-mouse out of our relationship?

Most clients feel that agencies are dropouts as far as management systems are concerned, and agencies feel that much client work is just gunk that fouls their motor.

A client can solve this problem the way he solves it within his own organization: by canny dedication to a management-by-objectives system—in which client and agency determine the objectives together. Indeed, the history of the advertising business is full of 40-year relationships that are based as much on good management as on good advertising.

The great secret of effective advertising is that advertising agencies are waiting to be sold something, just as eagerly as anyone else. But it must be a good product, well packaged and promoted. Systematic, fair-minded management fits that description perfectly.

VICTOR WADEMAN is president of his own advertising agency (Victor Wademan & Co.) in New York. Prior to founding this firm, he was vice-president—marketing of Texfli Industries, a soft-goods company. A graduate of Harvard Business School, he has done advertising and marketing work for a number of large U.S. packaged goods and industrial companies while in the agency business and with the management consulting firm of McKinsey & Co.

HOW TO WORK WITH YOUR AGENCY
An Agency Man's Manifesto

by Gregory D. Shorey

Gregory D. Shorey, for the last eight years chairman of Shorey & Walter, Greenville, S.C., started his agency at age 50 following 25 years on the client side. Now, running a $5 million shop with some 20 accounts—all industrial—Mr. Shorey talks of "the frustrations we encounter as agencies in dealing with many industrial clients who are wedded to old-school ideas."

Understandably, he says his perspective on the agency-client relationship has changed dramatically since his client-side days.

For example, "I didn't understand fully the need to set communications goals and strategies, and not be faint of heart in following them."

Mr. Shorey wrote the following "manifesto" for his clients, declaring his philosophy and practice. It states what he believes both the agency and client must do to make the relationship work.

By following it, he says, he's avoided unhappy incidents such as when a regional dairy client demanded a certain media buy. "I told them they could buy media for us, if they let me milk their cows," he recalls. "We weren't going to be somebody's job shop."

The successful client/agency relationship has many foundations, complete mutual trust being foremost. No one area of the agency's activity on behalf of the client tests that basic trust more than agency production and creative costs. It is misunderstanding of what constitutes such costs that is the number one cause of controversy and disruption of the relationship.

Understandably, most clients are accustomed to buying tangibles. When paying for professional services or advertising production elements, they have great difficulty comprehending the dollar value. Thus, agency creative services and production billing are frequently suspect. Some confuse a few paragraphs of ad copy with what they pay per word for a telegram, or the cost of a product photograph with what a snapshot costs at the Fotomat, and the agency is then unnecessarily subjected to justifying its production billing.

Interestingly, media costs are rarely ever questioned. We don't mind justifications, and we should be held accountable. But if our integrity is suspect, we should not have been engaged.

This memo is prepared for our clients in the hope that by providing creative service and production cost guidelines, signed by our clients, that most misunderstandings in these areas can be avoided. Although our agency agreement deals clearly with this area, this information seeks to provide clarifying detail. (See box.)

In simple terms, it's worth spending the time and the money to do it right. Too much advertising looks the same, sounds the same and is dull and not impressive. Thus its fundamental meaning and mission are lost.

The advertiser uses the proper agency for many valuable reasons. First and foremost, not because you get your work for less cost, but because the communications produced are better, more effective, more crea-tive, more objective—and work.

Internal client time and all other attendant costs are rarely considered when comparing agency work with in-house "do it yourself" work. The mechanics are often confused with real creativity. Like comparing an amateur song to an Irving Berlin hit, an appreciation for a good creative product and the imagination of the agency must exist.

Do not make the mistake of telling your agency as little as possible and expecting a proper result. It can't operate in a vacuum, nor can it play guessing games. Instead of worrying about the cost of a single element of advertising materials, one should be concerned with getting all the needed and agreed-upon tools necessary to achieve predetermined marketing goals within the annual allocated budget.

"You get what you pay for" applies to good advertising production. Short cuts and bargain costs just will not work. Using any professional service

No production or media is undertaken by the agency without written prior approval for the described work and the preproduction cost estimate furnished to the client. With such approval, the client agrees that the estimated costs are fair and acceptable. If the nature and/or scope of the job is changed, requiring an amended cost estimate, that too is provided to the client.

All elements of such production work will be procured by the agency, employing all of its expertise, at the best possible costs for the circumstances. The agency's judgment and experience must be trusted in selecting the best and most competitive resources. We operate a purchasing function, every bit as important and involved as those of most businesses.

In view of rapidly increasing supplier costs, often subject to change without notice, all preproduction cost estimates must have a contingency, and estimates may be subject to revision after 30 days. A National Advertising Agency Network survey reveals that production costs have risen 60% since 1975.

No production estimate will include tax (where applicable) or delivery charges, nor do they provide for any client changes or revisions to the job as first conceived. Extra proofs or reprints, repro of mechanically-finished ads or duplicates for broadcast spots carry an extra charge, plus shipping costs.

It is understood that all agency staff time devoted (logged) to the production of a particular job will be charged to that job at the prevailing hourly rate of that professional function.

Furthermore, all source contact costs, including long distance phoning and correspondence, photocopying and other agency costs likewise will be charged against each production job. Such normal services are considered in preproduction cost estimates. But extraordinary services as may be required by client revisions will be an extra charge.

As production work progresses on approved work, we will bill progressively on the first of each month for all costs incurred in the preceding month. Terms are *Net 10 days*. While the agency's credit lines are used to procure production elements and media, its role is not a financing one.

It is understood that any and all actual outside supplier materials or services furnished on a production job will be marked-up by the agency to insure the necessary gross margin income to the agency in procuring such outside materials or services. There are no other mark-ups or surcharges to the client.

Any prompt-pay cash discounts, rebates or volume discounts extended to the agency by a supplier will be made available to the client.

No two production jobs are the same; thus no scale of charges can be predetermined. Jobs that resemble each other may have very different costs for many reasons, so comparisons will not be a fair basis for cost determinations.

Often deadlines require use of delivery services such as Purolator, Federal Express or other special handling for next-day guaranteed, insured delivery service. Those charges may appear extreme, but may be required to meet media or delivery commitments and are charged as encountered only when lead times require such special handling.

No agency mark-up is applied to tax, delivery charges, phone, source contact charges, postage or Qwip (telecopier) line charges. But such costs are charged.

In considering production costs, remember that the people who perform all the necessary functions (i.e., artists, illustrators, mechanical artists, photographers, creative directors, copywriters, proofreaders, copy services, researchers, librarians, production supervisors, traffic managers, account services) all play a role in producing any piece of advertising or collateral material. Those are skilled, specially trained and experienced professional talents who are paid well to be a part of our regular staff and always available to our clients. Their talents are time-logged into every job we handle at a rate to cover their salaries, plus fringe benefits. Their hourly cost must also be at a rate adequate to cover the balance of the supportive and administrative staff whose time is not possible to bill against any specific client jobs. Thus they become overhead like other operating costs of running and supplying a business office (like your own) with indirect overhead, operating and administrative costs.

is like riding a cab. While you ride, the meter runs. The more input you provide, the better the finished product with valuable time and money saved.

Too often the advertiser believes that he knows good advertising, perhaps as much or more than his agency. So he uses the agency to just "grind-out" his needs, stifling any initiative by the agency.

Good agencies, even small ones, do not function as job shops. While many clients are inclined to use them in a such a way, I would suggest that when an agency allows itself to simply respond to the "I want a . . ." request, they function little differently than the local print shop, perhaps contributing to the client's misunderstanding of the real costs of engaging a full service and truly creative agency.

When a client confronts us with an "I want a . . ." we ask, "Why?" That usually gets us back into the process and reason for having a full service agency deeply involved in the total marketing communications effort, using all the resources and abilities of the agency.

If the client has doubts about his agency's capability or cost integrity, or if the agency is incapable of performing with full service creativity, a change would seem to be in order. The right agency will control costs and can be trusted to help you be who you want to be and get where you want to go. ∎

Section II-C
Cost Factors

"How Media Men Buy Media—Six Factors for a Good Plan," by H. Maneloveg, gives a summary of how advertisers buy and sell media and how much it costs.

"How Much to Spend for Advertising," by T.K. Parrish, includes eight points to consider when formulating advertising budgets.

"How to Develop an Industrial Advertising Budget for Smaller Companies," by D. Hosman and D.L. Fugate, provides more information on advertising budgets.

"Kicking Perrier in the Derriere," by J. Sharkey, explains how to get free publicity without spending a nickel on advertising.

"Industrial Advertising Effects and Budgeting Practices," by G.L. Lilien, A.J. Silk, J.-M. Choffray, and M. Rao, examines available research relating to the effects of industrial advertising and budgetary practices.

How the advertising business works

Advertising media

One of the marks of our democratic society operating in a capitalistic economy is the great variety of media for delivering news, information, entertainment—and advertising messages—to the public. There are endless ways to deliver messages to masses of people, and advertisers have at one time or another used most or all of them. But a handful of media have demonstrated their ability to carry advertising messages to masses of people economically and efficiently. Here is a summary of how advertisers use media, and a brief description of each, explaining how it is bought and sold, how much it costs, and why advertisers select it.

How media men buy media— six factors for a good plan

BY HERBERT MANELOVEG
EXECUTIVE VICE-PRESIDENT
McCANN-ERICKSON, NEW YORK

Advertising, one of the fuels that moves the free enterprise system forward, is often complex to describe and/or implement. However, in order to simplify, let me suggest that an advertising effort is broken down into two basic components.

First, we must create a compelling sales message that helps establish or reaffirm a positive attitude towards a product or service. That's the function of copy. Second, we must determine who the prime customers might be and then select vehicles in a way that the best prospects are reached a sufficient number of times to foster awareness of the copy claim. That's the function of media. Together, both formulated in concert, they produce a successful selling campaign.

What are the factors that go into determining a sound media proposal? There are basically six: The communication requirement, an emphasis on the prime prospect, geographic sales analysis, efficiency/effectiveness balance, the pressure of competition, and the budget.

Not all receive equal emphasis. Certain categories take precedence over others because of unique problems involved in the total marketing mosaic. The order of priority changes, depending on the nature of the marketplace. This must be recognized in order to fashion a sound media effort; there is no "pat" formula for formulating the plan. Let's examine the six points:

1. The communication requirement.

This is normally the most important element in choosing the various media for our sales messages. It's obvious; the selling proposition itself remains the principal ingredient of advertising. If we find it valuable to have a demonstration, to visually compare the advantages of one brand over another television becomes a most logical contender. If study and an articulation of sales points are required, print (magazines and newspapers) comes to the forefront. If mood through music lends credence to certain sales points, then radio holds promise. If all we require is package

identification and a short sales idea, then outdoor could make sense.

The selection of media is always tied to the message (and while this may be contrary to Marshall McLuhan, it remains a fact of marketing life). Accordingly, before a media planner starts building his proposal, it becomes essential that he knows what the copywriter is trying to say and in what media form it can best be said.

If you wish to demonstrate the holding action of one hair spray over another, or the absorbency of a cleaning tissue compared with competition, then television is the way to go. On the other hand, if you're trying to inform an audience about all the features one automobile has over another, or let a housewife secure new recipe ideas to use with canned soup, magazines perform a splendid job. If you have a cents-off promotion, or desire to announce a price reduction, newspapers are a superb medium. Again, the communication idea is the key element.

2. Emphasis on the prime prospect.

Here is where the media man must do his best work— analyzing media vehicles in order to maximize concentration on the product's prime prospects. Here he becomes a market expert rather than just a media man. Before a planner develops his proposal he must secure a fund of knowledge about who buys the product or service being advertised. Market and media research data is his primary source of information.

Through client and agency consumer research studies, Target Group Index, Simmons Research data, Audits & Surveys, and others, the media planner learns who the heavier users of the products are and he explores media to determine which will deliver these prospects.

For a campaign aimed at selling insurance policies, he may be trying to key against young males 18 to 34. For a European airline, men and women, upper educated, higher income groups from 18 to 49 years of age. For a soap or detergent, women only, with primary emphasis on ages 18 to 49. If he's selling records or slacks or cosmetics, young gals 12 to 24.

Each product has a demographic profile that pinpoints

COMPARISON OF ADVERTISING OF MAJOR MEDIA IN 1971 AND 1972		1971**		1972*		
		Millions	% of total	Millions	% of total	Per cent change
Newspapers	Total	$ 6,250	30.0	$ 6,960	30.2	+11
	National	1,140	5.5	1,240	5.4	+9
	Local	5,110	24.5	5,720	24.8	+12
Magazines	Total	1,399	6.7	1,480	6.4	+6
Television	Total	3,590	17.2	4,110	17.9	+14
	Network	1,593	7.6	1,780	7.7	+12
	Spot	1,201	5.8	1,375	6.0	+14
	Local	796	3.8	955	4.2	+20
Radio	Total	1,440	6.9	1,530	6.6	+6
	Network	63	0.3	75	0.3	+19
	Spot	395	1.9	395	1.7	+0
	Local	982	4.7	1,060	4.6	+8
Direct Mail		3,050	14.6	3,350	14.5	+10
Business Papers		720	3.5	770	3.3	+7
Outdoor	Total	261	1.3	290	1.3	+9
	National	172	0.9	190	0.9	+9
	Local	89	0.4	100	0.4	+10
Miscellaneous	Total	4,102	19.7	4,541	19.7	+11
	National	2,237	10.7	2,445	10.6	+9
	Local	1,865	9.0	2,096	9.1	+12
Total	National	11,970	57.4	13,100	56.8	+9
	Local	8,870	42.6	9,960	43.2	+12
Grand Total		$20,840	100.0	$23,060	100.0	+10.7

*Preliminary **Revised Source: McCann-Erickson Inc.

the primary customer. We concentrate mainly on age, income, sex, education and life style.

■ And the data we have on our media possibilities is geared to the market profile information. Thus, if we're aiming at both men and women and have decided that television does the best creative job, we often go for prime time television, 8 to 11 in the evening. (Yet this makes sense only if our budget permits the cost of prime time national television; the size of the budget could move us to other day parts.)

But assuming the budget is ample, within the top viewing hours (8–11 p.m. EST) when 55 to 65% of the homes of the nation are tuned in, again the demographic requirements of the brand determine our selection of specific media vehicles available through the network. (And it must always be remembered that the networks in almost all cases determine the programs to be put on the air; we select from these; we, like shoppers, buy from the available stock.)

The audience of a program such as the perennial "Lucy" show is oriented more towards the middle and older age groups, and products with that kind of skew purchase accordingly. The old "Lawrence Welk" program (now in syndication) was a natural for a denture cream because most of its audience was over 45 years of age. Movies, late night talk shows, programs like "MASH," "Kung Fu" and "Flip Wilson" attract younger adults. "Room 222," "Partridge Family" speak best to the teen age audience. Men gravitate to sports. Affluent, better educated men to certain movies and sports. And even in the female-dominated daytime, there is a way of looking at properties to fill specific prospect needs. Daytime serials aim at the younger housewife, quiz shows at the older.

The media man must pore over all the demographic data supplied by A. C. Nielsen and other syndicated sources to select properties that target in on his specific audience. He does the same when analyzing print as well.

3. Geographic sales analysis.

Here he must decide where to place his weight, across the nation or regionally. And in what proportion. Often he chooses a thin layer of national weight and then supplies additional units where he has favorable sales conditions. It is in this area that he decides whether he should be on network television, which covers the nation with a hook-up of 175 to 200 stations, or utilize spot in ten or twenty more markets. Or if he should lean towards national magazines or regional editions of same. If a small group of newspapers in selected markets makes more sense than a national Sunday supplement. Here is where demography (target audience), geography and budget mesh together.

Take magazines, for example. A media planner can use *Time* on a full run national basis or he can select certain geographic regions in which to concentrate. And if his budget is small and his target audience a top income, highly educated group, the planner may desire to "husband" dollars by only running in four or five key marketing areas (say, New York, Chicago, Los Angeles, San Francisco and New England) in *Time* regional rather than *Time* national. Said another way, if the plan is frequency-oriented, the regional route may be the best way to go; if he wants to reach as many different but not concentrated people as possible in one shot, then the full-run *Time* route might be best.

In determining vehicles, the planner must always keep in mind how the public spends its time with media. There is much criticism about the advertiser's idolatry of television and the attendant fostering of clutter. But there's a reason for that. The people spend their time there. Look how men divide their hours of the week with the major media. They spend 25.1 hours with tv, 21 with radio, 2.2 with magazines, 4.8 with newspapers. Women, specifically the better educated, higher income women, spend 29.1 hours a week with tv, 21.5 with radio, 2.5 with magazines and 5 with newspapers.

As advertisers, we must logically go where the people are. And the people are with the mass electronic media. People will argue that we are missing a good bet by not supporting educational television; it certainly warrants support. But the public doesn't seem to gravitate to these types of programs. Research proves that.

The vital ingredient, though, is to be where the sales are. And often the majority of sales fall into a few major markets. We must learn to build the proper balance by national/local weight in order to make the media plan most productive.

4. Efficiency/effectiveness balance.

When exploring various media alternatives, we must take into account unit costs and attendant efficiencies. In the past we measured cost value in relation to *homes* delivered. But today, in an age of market segmentation and product proliferation, as we concentrate on specific audiences, we now view media vehicles in relation to the cost of delivering our prime *customers.* Our criterion is cost-per-thousand *prospects* delivered.

Prices vary dramatically. A 30-second announcement on NBC daytime's "Jeopardy" costs $3,600, delivers 2,360,000 women between 18 and 49, and the cost-per-thousand is $1.52. A 30-second announcement on CBS "Thursday Night Movies" costs $27,150, delivers 7,510,000 women between 18 and 49, and the cost-per-thousand is $3.62. A 1,000-line newspaper ad in the top 50 markets costs $104,000, delivers 20,668,000 women 18 to 49 for a cost-per-thousand of $5.03. A four-color page in the *Ladies' Home Journal* costs $35,000, delivers 9,479,000 women between 18 and 49 for a cost-per-thousand of $3.69. A four-color page in *Parade* costs $84,450, delivers an estimated 11,337,000 women between 18 and 49, which is a CPM of $7.45.

On the surface it would appear that the lowest cost property should receive most of our advertising dollars. But here again one must weight the communication requirement and the geography of the brand to decide which vehicle is best for a specific effort.

■ This—whether it be network, spot, magazines or newspapers—is where media people end up. After the planning stage we must go out and buy. Our purchases, hopefully, conform to the statistical thrust of the plan, yet as we buy in each market, it is the medium that tells us what is available and what the going price is for each item. The selection from all availabilities should be equal to the efficiency goals set by the plan. And while efficiency—especially if the budget allows for adequate frequency—is a major factor, it is not necessarily synonymous with effectiveness. There are many times when we are willing to break the norm and buy high-cost specials over minutes in movies, spreads in magazines over single pages, sports sponsorship over prime time minutes, an eight-page insert in a Sunday newspaper rather than a number of insertions in a daily newspaper.

Marketing requirements of certain products—beyond just audience goals—often dictate a change in strategy and a desire to be "big" at one moment in time to support a promotion, a new product introduction, a change in product formulation, or as a weapon to gain wider distribution.

While the popular belief is that we worship the rating and only purchase the lowest-cost properties, that is not always the case. First of all, we are moving more and more towards prime customer concentration. Thus, our efficiency goals are against this group, and it is quite possible that a lower-rated show or a higher-priced special could and does deliver more *prospects* for us, rather than merely homes.

5. The pressure of competition.

In our competitive economic system we need to position our brand or service so that it talks to key customers as often as similar brands in the marketplace. Before a media plan is developed we examine the delivery of our own previous efforts as well as that of competition—and weigh both against usage information. In this manner we decide where best to apply pressure in the upcoming plan. Coverage and frequency patterns vis-a-vis competition form a framework for many of our media decisions.

6. All this must be measured in relation to the dollars allocated to advertising: The budget.

It must be remembered that advertising budgets are determined within the framework of the over-all marketing expenditure. Sales promotion, merchandising, packaging, point of sale material and the like blend together into the total cost of selling a product. Advertising is but one facet. And the media man, given his budget, must work within the constraints of that dollar figure to deliver maximum pressure—*but effective pressure as well.*

There is a belief that most advertising budgets are large and that the message weight is such that the population is bombarded dozens of times with a sales message. This is not truly so. Most budgets for individual products or brands are not large for the job at hand, and people are not as overwhelmed by messages as one might expect. The cost of sending one letter to all 60,000,000 American homes now comes to $6,100,000. Few national advertising campaigns for individual brands come in at this figure. My own agency's breakdown is as follows:

Six accounts spend over $5,000,000; seven are between $2,500,000 and $5,000,000; 24 are from $1,000,000 to $2,500,000; and 74 are under $1,000,000.

And what kind of over-all message pressure does a large account produce? Take a grocery manufacturer with a healthy expenditure of over $18,000,000. Its mix of media presents this pattern:

Television gets $11,900,000 for a major product and reaches 88% of the public an average of 120 times; radio receives $1,800,000 and reaches 50% about 30 times. The magazine figures: $3,900,000 and 75% and 28 times. Newspapers: $850,000 and 55% and two times.

Media Mix Keeps Changing

Add it all together and you'll notice that our messages only talk to our total public about three times a week. Certainly in the peak selling season the frequency goes up, but not as much as critics will have you believe.

The planning and budgeting of media is a difficult job. The mix constantly changes. In 1966, national advertisers spent their appropriations like this: 20% in newspapers, 26% in magazines, 7% in radio and 47% in tv. In 1972, newspapers got 18%, magazines 24%, radio 8% and tv 50%. Local advertisers' figures in 1966 were 78% in newspapers, 13% in radio and 9% in tv; in 1972, 74% in newspapers, 14% in radio, 12% in tv.

This, of course, becomes a reflection of how people

150

Newsprint Consumption

COMPARISON OF NEWSPRINT CONSUMPTION TO NATIONAL ECONOMIC GROWTH

Year	Newsprint Consumption (thousands of tons)	Growth Index	Real Gross National Product* (billions)	Growth Index
1946	4,296	100.0	$312.6	100.0
1968	9,244	226.0	706.6	215.2
1969	9,741	231.8	724.7	226.7
1970	9,545	230.3	720.0	222.2
1971	9,601	236.6	739.5	223.4
1972	10,271	252.6	789.5	239.1

*Gross National Product in 1958 prices.
Source: American Newspaper Publishers Assn.
U.S. Department of Commerce

NEWSPAPER GROWTH AS MEASURED BY CHANGES IN NEWSPRINT CONSUMPTION
Thousands of Tons

Source: American Newspaper Publishers Association.

---

spend time with the various media. They are, as I mentioned earlier, normally oriented to the electronic vehicles. The national advertiser moves more and more to radio and television, and the local retail advertiser, still heavily in newspapers, is moving in this direction as well.

■ Even within the electronic media the way of buying is shifting somewhat. Take television. While the networks control most of the programming that's put on the air, advertisers attempting to be more selective in their audience requirements are now moving to more varied types of programming. Entertainment will, of course, continue to fill 70% to 80% of the time, but many astute advertisers are buying differently than in the past. Advertisers in my own agency—still requiring a base of low-cost frequency against prime audiences though—are going that route; they are willing to sacrifice some frequency at specific periods of time and are now willing to pay more for programs of stature.

Computers Help, but Aren't All

The cycle of media planning is a never-ending one. It's something like this: Initial fact finding, then building alternatives, evaluating alternatives, working to a final recommendation, then final modification, after that, execution and post-buy evaluation, and finally, back to initial fact finding for the next year's effort.

Computers, new technology and more sophisticated research lend information to help make better media plans. But with it all remains the judgment of the media man and his intimate knowledge of the brand's require-ments. The new science has only led us a part of the way in our media knowledge. For example, we still do not know how to measure perception or the direct relation to sales.

But as media people, we stick to the basic six points to determine what is the best medium for a sales effort: The communication requirement, an emphasis on the prime prospect, sound geographic sales analysis, a proper efficiency/effectiveness balance, understanding the pressure of competition, and the budget. The delicate balancing of all these is the key to sound media planning and buying. #

Classified is big—$2.1 billion in 1972

Newspaper classified advertising is a medium within a medium, and a growth phenomenon as well. According to Classified International Advertising Services, classified's dollar volume has grown from $1.1 billion in 1964 to $2.1 billion last year, and the expectation is that continued growth will take it to between $3.5 and $4.5 billion by 1980. Classified furnished daily newspapers with 21% of their total advertising revenues in 1950, a figure that increased to 28% in 1972—and which is expected to grow 1% a year to 1980.

The Newspaper Advertising Bureau has calculated that some 40,000,000 people turn to something in the classified sections each day: 45% look at ads for goods and merchandise, 42% at real estate listings, 35% at car offers, 33% at employment offers. One result is that last year 58 newspapers carried 100,000,000 or more individual classified ads. #

The president of a

major cosmetics firm

reviews eight ways to decide . . .

HOW MUCH TO SPEND FOR ADVERTISING

T. Kirk Parrish

People associated with the marketing management of companies are accustomed to getting many types of data from market research. These may have to do with brand shares, product ratings, media data, awareness/attitude/usage studies, and many others. Such data is expected from researchers as a matter of course. It seems to me, however, that market research has stayed away from an extremely important marketing issue, namely, how much to spend on advertising. The issue, without question, is loaded with politics, irrationality, opportunism, and vanity—to mention some of the lesser sins. Why should science risk becoming tarnished in such an environment?

The purpose of this paper is to invite the greater participation of market research people in the issue of how much to spend on advertising.

The manager of an advertised package goods business has several key variables with which to deal over the short run. They are: unit sales, pricing levels, advertising dollars, and profits. How often, however, have marketing managers asked for the use of market research disciplines to help determine the very critical variable of advertising dollar level? Obviously, I am excluding the kinds of decisions in which market researchers do participate far more closely, such as product formulation, packaging, advertising copy, even new product introductions, but these tend to be operative only over the longer run.

Over the years I have made a practice of assigning trainees and junior marketing personnel to the project of developing a list of the different ways by which advertising budget amounts can be established. I have always specified that the list should not be a recommendation of the best ways to set budgets, but simply a categorization of the available means—both good and bad. Following are eight

methods of setting advertising budgets—consider for each of them whether market research could be brought to bear in a constructive way. The number eight is not magic. Depending on how precisely definitions are drawn, the number could be less or far more. I do not distinguish between good and bad, usual and unusual, short run and long run, aggressive and defensive.

1. *Advertising-to-Sales Ratio.* This is perhaps most common of the eight methods of setting advertising expenditure levels, and it is generally used when brand categories seem to have evolved into fairly well-established advertising-to-sales ratios. Obviously, this varies with new product introductions, brand milking, importance of private label, or other such special factors. This method is, nevertheless, one of the safest and most frequently used bases for setting advertising expenditures. The system is so straightforward that there is very little opportunity for market research to participate, other than through the

T. Kirk Parrish is president of Lanvin-Charles of the Ritz, Inc., a subsidiary of Squibb Corporation. Previously, he was president of Life Savers, Inc. and before that president of the American Chicle Division of Warner-Lambert. Mr. Parrish started his business career in 1955 with Vick Chemical Company where he was a salesman, then a copywriter, and a product manager. He was also on the staff of Benton & Bowles. Mr. Parrish received his A.B. degree from Princeton University.

Reprinted with permission from *J. Advertising Res.*, vol. 14, pp. 9–11, Feb. 1974.
Copyright © 1974, by the Advertising Research Foundation.

simple gathering of competitive sales and advertising spending data.

2. *Competitive Level.* This system of setting advertising expenditure levels is based upon departing from a category's traditional advertising-to-sales ratio or the established relationship between share of market and share of advertising. In a situation where a brand has an opportunity to gain share of market, it logically follows that the brand should have a significantly larger share of spending than its existing share of market. Conversely, a well-entrenched Number One brand can probably afford to spend somewhat less than its share of market, particularly if the market category is a relatively mature one. Market research, I believe, can be tremendously constructive in identifying situations where overspending or underspending traditional advertising-to-sales ratios are in order. Tracking studies can help by measuring brand awareness, trial, and frequency of usage, as well as by relating these factors to advertising levels, distribution, display, and pricing.

3. *"Left-Over" Funds."* Setting advertising expenditures by the use of left-over funds is hardly scientific. It is not an unusual business practice, however. It occurs in situations where rigid profit goals are set and where sales volume projections are based upon fairly stable patterns. Since cost of goods and brand pricing are usually fixed factors over the short run, the advertising appropriation may simply be whatever is left over after the profit requirement has been met. About the only constructive role that market research can play in the company where this system is used is to track and analyze the effects of underspending on the part of competitive brands, or underspending by your own brand in past test situations.

4. *Trade Impact.* This is another rather unscientific way to set an advertising budget. Someone who establishes a consumer advertising spending level, in order to have an impact on trade listings, distribution, display, etc., is almost by definition misusing advertising. On the other hand, particularly in a few fashion or cosmetic categories, one must admit that persuading the buyer may be the name of the game. Perhaps there is room for market research to step more fully into this murky and ill-defined area of persuading the buyer. Maybe market research could measure the relative effectiveness of persuading the buyer by different means, such as allowances, trade advertising, trade shows, consumer sampling, couponing, or simply frequency and level of sales force contact.

5. *Minimum Effective Spending.* I am convinced that, in aggregate, massive amounts of advertising dollars are wasted on budgets that are well below minimum effective levels of spending. These levels can be arrived at from some of the formulas mentioned already, and can simply be an outgrowth of management conservatism when caught in the trap of being afraid to spend large amounts and afraid to spend nothing. There are certainly case histories in which small advertising budgets have worked.

I do believe, however, that most of these have been aimed at very specific audience targets, so that the dollar spending behind any given message directed at some prospect group has been at a level which would be equivalent to many millions of dollars if directed to a full national audience, comprising the major demographic groups. Naturally, minimum effective spending levels will vary, depending on brand category, audience target, advertising medium, and, of course, the advertising copy itself. I believe that market research could perform a truly professional service if it were to speak out and clearly warn companies who are in danger of spending at below minimum effective levels.

6. *Consumer Impact.* Until now, I have been referring to advertising levels in terms of dollar spending levels. I could also, of course, have been converting these to message delivery levels. But what about measuring levels of advertising communication and setting budgets based upon consumer measurements? One might set advertising spending levels in terms of either absolute or share measurements of brand, copy, or key benefit awareness. Obviously, this is an area where market research has already made very significant contributions. I believe, however, that more experimentation and measurement should take place as a guide to using consumer measurements in setting advertising expenditure levels.

7. *Experimentation.* It is critical that any company with large advertising budgets should experiment to determine optimum effective levels. Everyone has heard the claim that spending tests don't work. Let me suggest that only spending tests conducted under certain circumstances don't work. A few of these circumstances are making too small a change in the spending level itself, or increasing spending behind a copy story that is already very well known, or decreasing spending and not waiting long enough to see the effect. Running a market test to measure reduced levels of spending, admittedly, may take several years to conduct.

Certainly any experimentation should follow a

few rules, such as: tests should be in a large, representative share of the country; tests should be run over a prolonged period of time; tests should be measuring significantly different circumstances.

Finally, let me caution that the finest experiment in the world is going to be ruined if there is a major product innovation, a new product introduction, or a radical change in pricing—or even just a major copy change by an important factor in the category. Market research people should be far more aggressive in encouraging advertising spending level tests, even if they must declare a large portion of their tests aborted prior to completion.

8. *Incremental Margin.* When sales are plummeting, it takes a rare, brave, and possibly stupid man to greatly increase his advertising expenditures. At such a time, it may be wise simply to recognize that brands have life cycles. On the other hand, when sales are increasing significantly, it is a common fault to accept this event with gratitude and do nothing about it. It is always a tough decision to move into uncharted waters, but when sales begin to exceed budget, that's where you are. It is the time to capitalize on your good fortune by spending a major part, or all, of your incremental margin on top of your established advertising budget. I call upon market research disciplines to participate much more actively in the role of making the sales projections that lead to such decisions. Bringing a fully-disciplined approach to this very tough job would greatly enhance a company's ability to set advertising levels.

I hope these eight points confirm your suspicions that no inspired intelligence, mystical or otherwise, prevails in the establishment of advertising spending levels. Some do it well, some do it poorly. But let me suggest that the task is of central importance to marketing. The attempt is challenging. Success is rewarding.

Mr. Parrish gave an earlier version of this paper as a speech to the Market Research Council in late 1973.

How to develop an industrial advertising budget for smaller companies

**While there may not be a "right" way to formulate
an advertising budget, there certainly is a better way.**

**DAVID HOSMAN
DOUGLAS FUGATE**

SMALL AND MEDIUM-SIZE companies have traditionally viewed industrial advertising as a necessary business expense. Advertising professionals were called in, they developed an ad campaign, and money was provided. Recently, however, this unquestioning, uncritical attitude has changed dramatically. Advertising is now seen as an investment that requires careful management and financial control by high-level executives.

There are several reasons for this radical shift in thinking. First, the rapid escalation of costs has forced companies to seek greater efficiency in all areas of business, including advertising. For example, the McGraw-Hill Laboratory of Advertising Performance estimates that the cost of an industrial sales call has

climbed to $137, up nearly 42 percent since 1978. At the same time, the amount of face-to-face contact between salesmen and clients has dropped by 23 minutes per working day.

Faced with this situation, many industrial managers are turning to advertising as a less expensive way of reaching potential customers. Actually, researchers have found that using advertising in conjunction with personal selling can yield significant results. For example, the average dollar volume of sales generated per salesman's call on buyers who have been exposed to advertising is approximately 20 percent higher than the level generated by calls on customers who have not.

However, optimum levels of advertising are critical to the success of any ad campaign. Research indicates that small doses of advertising (below five exposures per year) have little or no effect on buyer preference. Yet there is a diminishing return on advertising above a certain level.

The second reason for the shift in attitude is the rapid changes that have taken place in advertising production and the execution and measurement of advertising performance. The quality of graphics, typesetting, and photographic separation techniques have improved substantially in recent years. Advertisers now enjoy a wider range of visually attractive options in developing an ad program.

For some time, the industrial advertising sector was regarded as the stepchild of marketing in terms of the amount of research devoted to its problems. However, recent research efforts have greatly increased management's understanding of the interaction between customer preferences and ad content and placement with different information sources. A

David Hosman, president of Trend Graphics, Inc. of Pittsburgh, Kansas, is an expert on the marketing and advertising needs of smaller businesses. Donald L. Fugate is assistant professor of marketing at Pittsburgh State University.

marketing group at M.I.T. has developed a highly successful interactive computer model that produces a set of norms that serve as guidelines in setting advertising budget levels and allocating expenditures among space media, direct mail, trade shows, and sales promotion. The guidelines were formulated by surveying industry practices and examining factors influencing the advertising-to-marketing expense and marketing-to-sales ratios.

Research at the micro level has also produced useful findings. For example, company reputation is favorably enhanced by image-building campaigns. According to comprehensive studies, this reputation makes it easier for a salesman to get a favorable first hearing for a new product with both purchasing and technical personnel. In a related finding, as buyers move from initial product awareness toward the actual purchase decision, they rely more on word-of-mouth than on impersonal sources such as advertising.

Common budget-setting techniques

The growing sophistication of industrial advertising should cause managers to constantly monitor the actual and potential efficacy of their advertising programs. This evaluation is particularly important during inflationary periods when the rising costs of message production and media insertions can quickly outpace budgetary outlays.

Unfortunately, many smaller companies use outdated and ineffective methods of budget determination. The most common of these techniques are:

• *The historical method.* The manager takes the total budget from the previous year (amount x) and adds a certain amount (a) that is usually expressed as a percentage of x. The budget formula is therefore $x + ax$.

• *The competitive method.* Companies usually like to gear their spending to what the competition is doing. The budget is formulated by using the various comparative ratios on the effect of average advertising on gross sales figures for the industry. These figures are often available from trade associations. This form of budgeting is justified by assuming competitive parity or by accepting the old saw that "advertising share equals market share of the total market."

• *The management mandate method.* Managers draw up a budget using an intuitive method based on past experiences and current hunches.

• *The percent of sales method.* Companies often determine their advertising budget by using a fixed percentage of anticipated gross sales. This involves a circular reasoning process that reverses the conventional view that advertising should help determine sales.

When used in isolation, these traditional techniques usually result in impractical budgets. The reasons are simple. First, they presume a continuation of the status quo in a dynamic marketing environment. Certainly, during boom times, these methods provide little guidance. Conversely, advertising expenses are often a natural target for trimming during an economic slowdown.

Second, most executives don't have the expertise needed to anticipate and project time and money costs associated with realistic industrial advertising expense variables. Under these circumstances, any relationship between budget allocation and realized expectations is mostly coincidental.

Third and most important, these methods do not establish appropriate marketing objectives before the budget process begins. In advertising, the makeup of the final program—the selection, mix, and

use of many alternatives—is directly affected by the budget level. Advertising programs, unlike production schedules, cannot be scaled down without jeopardizing much of their effectiveness. Therefore, for advertising goals to be fully realized, the budget must reflect the money needed to achieve these objectives.

Another widely used budget-setting technique is the "objective and task" method. Managers allocate funds by establishing specific marketing objectives, determining the best communication mix, and estimating the money needed to meet these goals. Taken at face value, this is a valid approach, which has shown more satisfactory results than the other methods. However, it requires accurate cost estimates for the various communication options and a thorough knowledge of the relationship between purchase behavior and communication mixes. This informa-

tion is usually available to only the largest advertisers.

A partial solution

In view of the limitations of the traditional methods, the natural question arises: Is there a way for small and medium-size businesses to competently establish an advertising budget? The answer is a qualified yes.

An adequately constructed advertising budget should consist of two cost components:

● *Maintenance costs.* Research indicates that a minimum level of exposure is needed for advertising to have a measurable impact on industrial buyers. Therefore, enough money must be provided to maintain a threshold level of continuous advertising activity.

Managers can determine the maintenance component of the

budget by using a variation on the historical method of allocation. Although the figures will be different for each industry, it should be possible to find an amount, x, that will pay for a minimum of five yearly ad exposures for target buyers. This base figure should be adjusted for each fiscal year by adding a cost escalation factor, a, that covers increased in production and placement costs. The necessary cost data are usually available from advertising firms and/or media services.

● *The cost of meeting specific marketing objectives.* The advertising budget should also include the funds needed to achieve a defined set of marketing goals and to meet environmental challenges. This involves the use of a step-by-step approach, which is a variation on the objective and task method.

The starting point of this phase of the budgetary process is the estab-

157

vertising efforts.

At the same time, managers must select the specific production projects that the company will pursue in its ad program. Determining what formats contribute to the achievement of marketing goals is a fairly subjective process. It is best to try to blend the views of company managers with those of outside advertising professionals. This combines the pragmatism of the industrial manager with the more comprehensive technical know-how of agency personnel.

The final stage of the budgeting process is the cost analysis of the individual projects that will make up the company's ad campaign. The production and media checklist with prices (see Figure 1) is designed to help managers assess necessary expenditures. The final budget is formulated by adding the costs of the various promotional activities to the maintenance cost. If the budget is too large to support, cuts can be made by retracing the steps used to determine the costs of meeting specific marketing objectives.

lishment of a list of realistic marketing objectives, which provide direction, magnitude, and evaluative dimensions to any marketing mix. These objectives are determined by asking a standard set of questions, such as: What are the gross sales for the upcoming year? What are the target markets? What percentage increase in gross sales are assigned to each market segment?

The next step is the most difficult of the entire budgeting process—the determination of the selling effort expected from each portion of the marketing mix. It is usually impossible to measure directly the impact of advertising on sales responses in the industrial market. Larger firms can sometimes develop workable econometric advertising response models. For smaller companies, the best approach is to rely on the past experiences of managers in developing effective ad campaigns. Some companies keep a log of such experiences. The collected information is combined with information gleaned from the client/agency relationship, trade journals, research reports, and other sources to form an individual correlation between sales responses and advertising.

A final warning

Clearly, advertising is a business investment that merits careful management. It is vital that advertising activities be coordinated and implemented within an integrated framework. When this is done, managers are better prepared to make strategic and tactical decisions because they can be fairly certain of the interaction between advertising and sales. Careful budgeting makes every promotional dollar more efficient, reduces wasted coverage, and lays the groundwork for future budgeting efforts.   •

KICKING PERRIER IN THE DERRIERE

A genius for free publicity got Rick Scoville's Artesia Waters off and running without spending a nickel for advertising.

By John Sharkey

When Rick Scoville began calling on Texas food brokers almost two years ago, many found him downright amusing. His plans to compete with Perrier, the French sparkling water that dominates the U.S. market, by marketing a Texas sparkling water, no less, raised more than one eyebrow and elicited some good-natured laughs, but no orders.

Undaunted, the 36-year-old San Antonio entrepreneur shrugged off the laughter, loaded a few cases of his Artesia mineral water into a van, and set out for Texas's lucrative urban markets. He personally introduced his bottled water to grocery store chains and chic discos. Before long the nightclubs and supermarkets were placing large orders for the amber bottles bearing Artesia's "pure Texas spirit." Scoville wrote dozens of letters to media organizations touting his product, and stories appeared in Dallas, Houston, and San Antonio newspapers. Scoville soon found himself behind radio talk show microphones, and finally on TV.

"I went out and aggressively marketed myself," says the curly-haired, bearded Texan, "and it worked."

Perrier flatly denies that Scoville's Houston-based company, Artesia Waters Inc., is chipping away at its Texas market, but Scoville has established a definite presence in the state. Gross sales for 1980, Artesia's first year, were $102,000. Revenue in 1981 jumped from $12,200 in January to $80,000 in May, and Scoville predicts Artesia will post total 1981 sales of $1.5 million. And he contends Artesia has already taken up to 30% of Perrier's sales in Texas and will overtake the French bottler in the

John Sharkey, a reporter for the Dallas Morning News, *writes frequently on business matters.*

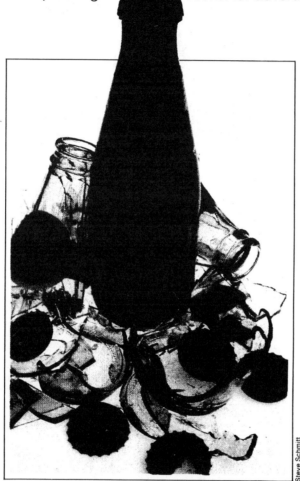

Steve Schmitt

state this year. "Au revoir, Perrier," his advertising slogan bids his competitor, but he's fond of putting it another way. "I'm out to kick Perrier in the derriere," Scoville says.

His success rests largely on his marketing strategy. He has combined self-promotion with a classy ad campaign and a healthy dose of confidence in his product. He has focused his campaign by taking direct aim at the French company, whose groundbreaking efforts several years ago virtually created the U.S. market for sparkling water. "When I started I was riding Perrier's coattails," Scoville admits. "Now, in Texas, I'm halfway up their back."

Scoville had his marketing ideas but little money when he launched the venture in early 1980, with a $25,000 loan and a small, aging bottling facility in San Antonio. Without a nickel for advertising, he created his own crafty

public relations assault that snatched headlines for the "Texas Hill Country" spring water.

One of the first and most valuable bits of exposure for the young entrepreneur came from a business writer at a Houston newspaper, who wrote a success story about Artesia when it was still too early to determine the company's future. Scoville made copies of the clipping and sent it to other publications. It was the best press release anyone could write—and it was free.

He wrote letters to major magazines and newspapers touting his product. Follow-up calls produced a one-paragraph front page story in the *Wall Street Journal* and a new product feature in *Texas Monthly* magazine. The *Texas Monthly* piece, in turn, earned him an invitation to compete in a locally sponsored bottled water taste test. The taste test, which Artesia won, was filmed by a Dallas TV station, and suddenly Scoville was on the air, reaching thousands of Texans. Artesia sales in the Dallas area tripled one day after the broadcast.

The regional character of Scoville's public relations efforts is deliberate. He emphasizes that Artesia is a Texas product ("Texans are very loyal," he says) and plays up Artesia as an American product made by a small company that's taking on a big, foreign company. "We tell Perrier drinkers, 'We're chic. We're American. We're Texan. We're good. *And* we cost less.'"

Scoville says the amber seven-ounce and quart bottles help, too. Looking like beer bottles, they stand out on the tight shelf space in convenience and grocery stores, where 70% of his water is sold. The fancy Artesia label adds to its sales appeal; Scoville spent three months on the label design alone.

All the media coverage sent the young company into a spin. "My PR was taking off faster than my distribution," says Scoville. Bottling his brew was slow as well, because the intricate Artesia label had to be applied by hand. Last fall he finally mechanized the labeling process and set up a distribution system. That, with a shot of venture capital, enabled Scoville to begin direct mail, outdoor, and print advertising.

His print ads feature a sexy cowgirl reclining on a saddle, with a saddlebag containing two iced-down bottles of Artesia. "It's a Texas theme," says Scoville, "and the campaign has generated a lot of favorable response." It has been costly, though. He has already spent $200,000 of the $270,000 budgeted for advertising this year. "Our sales are better than we expected," he says, "so the cost hasn't been a problem, yet."

Even with his big ad budget, Scoville still considers himself a master of free PR. Even Ron Davis, the president of Perrier's American distributorship, has to agree: "He's a good promoter. He's getting a lot of good, free publicity in a tough category." □

Rick Scoville and his Texas challenge to imported bottled water.

HOW SCOVILLE DID IT

Rick Scoville got his business off the ground by generating mounds of free publicity. "Basically, I wouldn't pay for anything if I didn't have to," he admits candidly. The methods below have worked for Scoville— other entrepreneurs can modify them for their own success.

□ First, take your story straight to those who can give you free exposure to thousands of people—newspapers, trade magazines, radio and TV stations. Keep in mind local radio and TV talk shows looking for "people" stories. Find out the names of editors and program directors in your area so you can send letters directly to them. Write short letters, getting to the point very quickly without being pushy. Include any supplementary information that could be useful. Scoville, for instance, tested the mineral content of his water and published his findings in a series of press releases.

□ Once you have the free press, use it. Make quality reproductions of any newspaper clippings, even if you have just one, and include the copies in future mailings to news organizations. The *Wall Street Journal* wrote only a paragraph about Artesia, but it was on the front page. When someone opens Scoville's press packet, he sees the familiar logo of one of the most prestigious newspapers in the world.

□ Create a business or feature angle for telling your story. Scoville emphasized the small company vs. big company and the American vs. the foreigner aspects of his company's competition with Perrier. If you emphasize unique qualities, however, you should steer clear of gimmicks.

□ Design packaging for maximum consumer appeal. Scoville conducted intensive market research to determine what graphics to use. He concluded that mineral water consumers want to drink out of elegant bottles, so a sparkling waterfall is pictured on his logo and on the amber bottles containing Artesia.

□ Be patient but persistent and flexible. Don't worry if someone says no. If your story is worth telling, someone will take an interest in it sooner or later.

Gary L. Lilien, Alvin J. Silk,
Jean-Marie Choffray, and Murlidhar Rao

Industrial Advertising Effects and Budgeting Practices

*What is known about the effects of industrial advertising?
And how does this information affect
budget decisions?*

THE industrial sector has long been regarded as the stepchild of marketing in terms of the amount of research effort devoted to its problems. There are, however, indications that the situation may be changing. Research on industrial/organizational buying behavior is growing, and a considerable body of empirical knowledge about processes surrounding the innovation and diffusion of industrial technologies and products has been developing.[1] This article is concerned with a different set of issues: those surrounding the determination of expenditure levels for industrial advertising. The purpose here is two-fold: (1) to review the available research relating to the effects of industrial advertising, and (2) to examine practices currently used in budgeting industrial advertising in light of what is known about advertising response and costs in this field.

Estimates of total industrial advertising volume are not readily available because of the lack of relevant aggregate data and the vagaries of defining what constitutes "industrial advertising." However, N. W. Ayer estimated that industrial advertising totaled $925 million in 1973;[2] and Marsteller, chairman of one of the major advertising agencies in the industrial marketing field, has indicated that there are 300–500 firms with annual industrial advertising budgets exceeding $1 million.[3] Surveys of industrial advertising budgets show that outlays for research have been running at about 1% of expenditures for several years.[4] Considering that the top 100 national advertisers alone spent $5.68 billion in 1973,[5] one can readily appreciate why the cumulative body of studies bearing on industrial advertising effects appears so slight in comparison to that available on consumer advertising.[6]

The advertising budget for the industrial marketer is typically too small to justify or support the kind of research effort required to assess the impact of advertising in a manner that would yield information relevant to expenditure decisions. This condition contributes to the skepticism of many industrial executives toward the effectiveness of advertising. Thus, advertising expenditure policy continues to be a perplexing problem for industrial marketing managers, and it becomes important to ask what is known about the process and effects of industrial advertising and how that knowledge relates to current budgeting practices.

---

1. See, for example, Frederick E. Webster, Jr. and Yoram Wind, *Organizational Buying Behavior* (Englewood Cliffs, N.J.: Prentice-Hall, 1972); and James M. Utterback, "Innovation in Industry and the Diffusion of Technology," *Science*, February 14, 1974, pp. 620-626.

2. N. W. Ayer & Sons, Inc., *Industrial Advertising: Past, Present and Future* (Philadelphia, 1974), p. i.

3. William A. Marsteller, "Field of Industrial Advertising Gets More Competitive," *Advertising Age*, June 17, 1974, p. 23.

4. See, for example, Sally Strong, "Ad Budgets '74: Trend Is Still to Spend, Spend, Spend," *Industrial Marketing*, Vol. 59 (February 1974), p. 57.

5. Merle Kingman, "Top National Advertisers Hike Ad Total to $5.68 billion," *Advertising Age*, August 26, 1974, p. 1.

6. Advertising Research Foundation, *Measuring Payout: An Annotated Bibliography on the Dollar Effectiveness of Advertising* (New York, 1973).

Reprinted with permission from *J. Marketing,* vol. 40, pp. 16–24, Jan. 1976.
Published by the American Marketing Association.

Research Design

		Correlational	Experimental
Measure of Response	Sales	Occasional	None?
	Attitude and Other Nonsales	Most Common	Rare

FIGURE 1. Current state of industrial advertising research.

Industrial Advertising Effects and Costs

At the heart of the problem of budgeting expenditures for advertising is the lack of understanding of the nature of advertising response. This section presents a selective review of published empirical studies that provide information or clues about the effects of industrial advertising. The body of material that meets these criteria is quite small. Release of research undertaken by individual firms is infrequent, with the exception of brief, informal accounts that occasionally appear in the trade press.

Arthur D. Little, Inc. and N. W. Ayer have both recently issued reports surveying the literature in the industrial advertising field.[7] The Arthur D. Little report claimed that 1100 studies were uncovered, but many of the references listed dealt with consumer advertising research. In fact, only 8 studies were singled out for detailed discussion. The impression gleaned from those reviews, as well as from the present one, is that, from a methodological viewpoint, the current state of industrial advertising research can be described as indicated in Figure 1.

While only a very limited amount of empirical research is available in this area, some evidence exists that bears on each of the following important phenomena:

1. *Economies of scale.* Is there some relevant range in which additional increments of advertising yield increasing returns?

---

7. Arthur D. Little, Inc., *An Evaluation of 1100 Research Studies on the Effectiveness of Industrial Advertising,* A report to American Business Press, Inc. (Cambridge, Mass., 1971); and same reference as footnote 2.

• *ABOUT THE AUTHORS.*

Gary L. Lilien is assistant professor of management science, Alvin J. Silk is professor of management science, and Jean-Marie Choffray and Murlidhar Rao are doctoral students in the Alfred P. Sloan School of Management, Massachusetts Institute of Technology.

2. *Threshold effects.* Is there some minimum level of exposure that must be exceeded for advertising to have a discernible effect?
3. *Interaction effects.* Does advertising interact with other elements of the marketing mix (personal selling in particular) to produce effects that are greater than the sum of their separate effects?

This section will examine the current literature in industrial advertising with respect to the effects and costs of such advertising. Particular attention will be paid to the sales and nonsales effects and to specific cost considerations, in an attempt to answer the three questions posed above.

Sales Effects

The published literature is almost devoid of either correlational or experimental investigations of sales response to industrial advertising. A noteworthy exception is a regression analysis discussed by Weinberg.[8]

Weinberg reported empirical evidence on the marketing effort–sales relationship which implied diminishing returns for that effort. He developed a multiple-equation corporate planning model that was applied to several industrial goods manufacturers. Weinberg reported that a submodel of the system relating changes in a firm's market share to its "advertising exchange rate" (the firm's advertising expenditures per dollar of sales divided by the corresponding ratio for its competitors) had been successfully used in some of this work. He presented an example in which data consisting of seven observations for an unidentified glass container manufacturer were used to estimate the relationship between annual changes in market share and the exchange rate for advertising expenditures. An excellent fit was obtained ($R^2 = .966$), and the form of the relationship (linear in the logarithms of both variables) implied diminishing returns to ad-

---

8. Robert S. Weinberg, "Multiple Factor Break-Even Analysis: The Application of O.R. Techniques to a Basic Problem of Management Planning and Control," *Operations Research,* Vol. 4 (April 1956), pp. 152-186.

vertising effort. Weinberg also demonstrated how the model could be incorporated into a procedure to determine the company's relative advertising effectiveness per dollar expended and, more importantly, to find the advertising level that would maximize profit in the next year given a forecast of competitive activity and economic conditions.[9]

What is perhaps most interesting about the Weinberg study is that it remains a rarity. It showed how quantitative advertising-sales relationships could be *developed* and *used* to help set advertising budgets. Yet there are no reports in the literature of follow-up work.

There are, however, two other areas of sales effects of advertising that have received some attention in the literature: the effect of advertising on competition and advertising's effect on sales call effectiveness. Each of these is examined below.

Effect of Advertising on Competition. The effect of advertising on competition has long been a subject of considerable interest to economists concerned with industrial organization and economic performance. The debate has centered on whether or not heavy advertising helps raise entry barriers and thereby leads to diminished levels of competition and the earning of monopoly profits. Schmalensee has reviewed a number of "direct tests" of the proposition that advertising adversely affects competition, but interpretation of the available evidence on this question remains controversial for a variety of reasons discussed by him and others.[10] One of these studies, however, deserves mention here because it treated producer and consumer goods separately.

Miller reports a positive correlation between advertising intensity and industry profit rates. He examined the relation of profit rates to advertising intensity (advertising-sales ratios) plus two other variables: concentration (share of industry output produced by the largest firms) and diversity (the extent to which firms specialize in one industry or are diversified into other industries).[11] Multiple linear regressions of profit rates on these three variables were reported for a sample consisting of 71 "Internal Revenue Service minor industries" (roughly the three-digit standard industrial clas-

sification level of aggregation) that were manufacturers of producer goods. The regression coefficient for the advertising intensity variable was positive and statistically significant, which implies that those producer goods industries that spent more on advertising tended to be those that realized higher rates of profitability. An unresolved issue here is whether profits determined advertising rather than vice versa.

Effect on Sales Call Effectiveness. Morrill reports results that seem to indicate that advertising increases sales call effectiveness. He has carried out a large body of relevant industrial advertising research sponsored by a dozen major industrial sellers.[12] Some reports have appeared that summarize his results from studies involving 129 brands of 23 products drawn from five industries (utilities, commodities, electrical/electronic, metalworking, and chemical).[13] Over 40,000 telephone interviews at 17,000 buying locations were conducted during the period 1964 to 1969. In each case, an attempt was made to locate one or more "brand-deciders" and to assess purchase behavior, attitudes toward various brands, and magazine reading habits from which advertising exposure could be inferred. Analysis of these data revealed a strong positive association between amount of advertising exposure and various measures of attitudinal and sales response. Figure 2 illustrates some of these relationships using average data for the five industrial classifications.

Morrill also found that dollar sales per salesman's call were much higher for calls made on customers who had been exposed to advertising, as compared to those who had not. Based on estimates of the average costs of an industrial salesman's call ($50.00) and an advertising exposure ($0.16), a subsidiary analysis showed that for the average brand studied, an index of personal selling expense as a percentage of sales declined from a level of 100 with no advertising exposures to a value of 74 for 30 exposures.[14]

Taken at face value, Morrill's results make a strong case for industrial advertising, indicating that advertising pays off by making personal selling efforts more productive. However, certain methodological questions surrounding Morrill's

9. Robert S. Weinberg, *An Analytical Approach to Advertising Expenditure Strategy* (New York: Association of National Advertisers, 1960).

10. Richard Schmalensee, *The Economics of Advertising* (Amsterdam, Netherlands: North-Holland, 1972), pp. 219-228 and Chap. 7; see also, Julian L. Simon, *Issues in the Economics of Advertising* (Urbana, Ill.: University of Illinois Press, 1970), Chap. 9.

11. Richard A. Miller, "Market Structure and Industrial Performance: Relation of Profit Rates to Concentration, Advertising Intensity, and Diversity," *Journal of Industrial Economics*, Vol. 28 (April 1969), pp. 104-118.

12. John E. Morrill, "Industrial Advertising Pays Off," *Harvard Business Review*, Vol. 48 (March-April 1970), pp. 4-14.

13. McGraw-Hill Book Co., "How Advertising Works in Today's Marketplace" (New York, January 1971); and McGraw-Hill Book Co., "Advertising's Challenge to Management: A Second Report on the Morrill Study" (New York, September 1971).

14. McGraw-Hill, "Advertising's Challenge," same reference as footnote 13, p. 6.

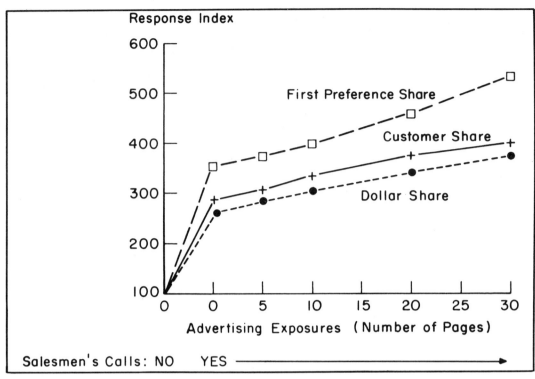

Source: Plotted from data pesented in "Advertising's Challenge to Management: A Second Report on the Morrill Study" (New York: McGraw-Hill Book Co., September 1971), p. 8.

FIGURE 2. Levels of response associated with varying amounts of exposure to advertising and salesmen's calls.

studies deserve mention. Morrill's inferences about the effectiveness of advertising are derived from *ex post facto* comparisons of exposed and unexposed groups. It is well known that this "preexperimental" design is prone to several threats to internal and external validity.[15] Morrill refers to a computer-based method for "matching" the exposed and unexposed groups.[16] Since Morrill's conclusions about advertising's impact depend on the equivalence of such groups (exclusive of advertising exposure), the adequacy of this matching procedure is critical and it is unfortunate that details of the method have not been published. Further, the practice of obtaining response data and self-reports of exposure in the same interview can lead to spuriously high associations between these two types of measures.[17]

Nonetheless, the sheer bulk and consistency of the evidence from Morrill's studies is impressive, and by no means can it be overlooked. The most important finding is that advertising used in conjunction with personal selling can reduce total selling costs. Morrill also refers to evidence of threshold effects in response to advertising. He

suggests that less than a certain (small) level of exposure (a frequency of about five advertising pages per year) seems to have no effect.[18]

Attitudinal and Nonsales Measures of Response

Research that focuses on attitudinal and other nonsales measures of response to industrial advertising is, as noted earlier, by far the most common type undertaken. Proprietary studies of this kind are done routinely, and occasionally partial accounts of them are made public.[19] Although these studies are seldom reported in sufficient detail to permit analysis and to provide a basis for generalization, there are some notable exceptions.

Morrill's comprehensive studies provide support for the widely held view that a principal function of industrial advertising is to make buyers more receptive to the advertiser's salesmen by creating a favorable impression of the

15. Donald T. Campbell and Julian C. Stanley, *Experimental and Quasi-Experimental Designs for Research* (Chicago: Rand-McNally, 1963), pp. 12-14.

16. Same reference as footnote 12, p. 6.

17. Same reference as footnote 15, p. 67.

18. Same reference as footnote 12, p. 14.

19. See, for example, James W. Mason, "The Communication Effect of an Industrial Advertising Campaign," *Journal of Advertising Research*, Vol. 9 (March 1969), pp. 35-37; and Harry D. Wolfe, James K. Brown, and G. Clark Thompson, *Measuring Advertising Results* (New York: National Industrial Conference Board, 1962).

firm as a supplier.[20] This concept constitutes one of the major rationales for the image-building campaigns frequently undertaken by industrial marketers.[21]

Levitt conducted a controlled laboratory experiment that demonstrated the positive influence of company reputation on the effectiveness of industrial salesmen.[22] Experienced business personnel (113 practicing purchasing agents and 130 engineers and scientists) were used as subjects. Participants were exposed to a ten-minute filmed sales presentation for a fictitious, but plausible, new product. Company reputation was manipulated by varying the name of the firm that the salesman was identified as representing. Immediately after viewing the film, and again five weeks later, subjects responded to a questionnaire that asked if they would recommend that the product be given further consideration by others in their organization and whether they themselves would favor adoption. As anticipated, company reputation was found to influence the favorableness of response on these measures. However, some unexpected differences were detected between the reactions of the purchasing agents and the reactions of the technical personnel. The results suggested that a seller's reputation made a difference in a salesman getting a favorable first hearing for a new product with *both* purchasing and technical personnel. But when it came to making an actual purchasing decision, the advantage of reputation manifested itself with the technical personnel but not with the purchasing agents.

There has been some research on industrial buyers' use of, or preferences for, different information sources in connection with studies of the adoption of new products.[23] The results suggest a pattern of diminishing reliance on impersonal sources such as media advertising and increasing influence of salesmen and other personal sources as buyers move from the initial awareness stage through the evaluation and decision stages of the adoption process. In this regard, Turnbull, in a study of marketing communication policies of ferrous components producers in the United Kingdom, reports "a failure of the companies to understand that buyers may have different communication needs and channel preferences at different stages in the buying process, and in different industries."[24]

Advertising Cost Studies

The preceding discussion focused on how industrial buyers and markets respond to advertising. This section examines research related to the other key element that enters into advertising expenditure discussions: cost considerations.

The issue of whether or not there are economies of scale in advertising is highly relevant not only to determining advertising expenditure levels, but also to allocating these funds among media and markets and over time. The occurrence of economies of scale in advertising implies that over some range of advertising, an additional unit of advertising input produces a greater marginal return than the previous equal increment yielded.

Schmalensee distinguishes between two sources of varying returns to scale in advertising.[25] The first he terms "technical economies," to refer to differences in the effectiveness of successive exposures. The data from Morrill's studies, plotted in Figure 2, would seem to indicate essentially constant returns to scale and hence reflect the absence of any technical economies. The second variety are "pecuniary economies," which may arise if the cost of advertising exposures changes with the total number of exposures used, such as might occur as a consequence of the media offering quantity discounts.

Economies of scale in advertising are treated to some extent in the economics literature. Increasing returns to scale constitute one mechanism whereby advertising might help raise barriers to entry. The available empirical studies tend to be based on cross-sectional samples consisting either entirely of consumer goods industries or of a combination of consumer and producer goods fields. Only occasionally has the latter distinction been recognized in the analyses reported. Most of these studies are consistent in failing to support the notion of economies of scale in advertising.[26]

---

20. Wolfe et al., same reference as footnote 19, p. 7.

21. See, for example, Wolfe et al., same reference as footnote 19, pp. 40-101.

22. Theodore Levitt, *Industrial Purchasing Behavior: A Study of Communications Effects* (Boston: Division of Research, Graduate School of Business Administration, Harvard University, 1965).

23. See, for example, Frederick E. Webster, Jr., "Informal Communication in Industrial Markets," *Journal of Marketing Research*, Vol. 7 (May 1970), pp. 186-189; John A. Martilla, "Word-of-Mouth Communication in the Industrial Adoption Process," *Journal of Marketing Research*, Vol. 8 (May 1971), pp. 173-178; and Urban B. Ozanne and Gilbert A. Churchill, Jr., "Five Dimensions of the Industrial Adoption Process," *Journal of Marketing Research*, Vol. 8 (August 1971), pp. 322-328.

24. P. W. Turnbull, "The Allocation of Resources to Marketing Communications in Industrial Markets," *Industrial Marketing Management*, Vol. 3 (October 1974), pp. 297-310.

25. Schmalensee, same reference as footnote 10, pp. 231-232.

26. George J. Stigler, "The Economies of Scale," *Journal of Law and Economics*, Vol. 1 (October 1958), p. 66; and Julian L. Simon and George H. Crain, "The Advertising

However, some contrary findings have turned up in cross-sectional studies of marketing costs of individual firms.

Turnbull obtained information on marketing communications expenditures and sales for a set of firms producing ferrous components whose combined output accounted for 51% of the industry total in the United Kingdom.[27] He found a rank order correlation of −.512 between firm size (sales) and the ratio of marketing communications expenditures to sales. Although based on only eleven observations, the coefficient approaches significance at the .05 level.

Bailey found evidence of economies of scale in a 1969 study of manufacturers' marketing costs that was conducted by the Conference Board. This study involved data obtained for 828 products, a large proportion of which were industrial goods.[28] Although detailed results were not presented, Bailey states that "the large-volume marketing unit dealing either in consumer or industrial goods generally gives up less of its sales dollar to the cause of marketing than does a small-volume competitor." He goes on to observe that "there is a certain point at which differences in sales volume become critical" and indicates that for industrial products this point is "just below $30 million."[29]

It was noted earlier that Morrill demonstrated a strong interaction effect between personal selling and advertising. Evidence of this phenomenon was also found in a study of industrial firms' marketing costs carried out by McGraw-Hill and reported by Kolliner.[30]

Kolliner reports that the larger the role of advertising in the marketing budget, the lower that budget seems to be as a percentage of sales. In 1961, marketing cost data were obtained via a mail questionnaire from 893 industrial advertisers. The sample contained firms of various sizes from three broad industrial product categories (machinery, materials, and equipment and supplies). Consistent with the view that advertising can increase the efficiency of personal selling, it was found that as the proportion of total sales expense spent on advertising and promotion increased, total sales expense as a percentage of sales tended to decline.

Interpreting this relationship is somewhat hazardous, inasmuch as it was formed by grouping and averaging the original observations on two variables which were ratios whose numerators and denominators contain common elements. It is unfortunate that more disaggregated analyses were not undertaken. Yet some additional results were reported which tend to confirm the basic notion that advertising contributes to marketing efficiency. The relationship between firm size (annual sales volume) and total sales expense as a percentage of sales was examined separately for firms that had expended "high" (more than 20%) and "low" (less than 20%) proportions of total sales expense on advertising and promotion. Figure 3 shows these relationships, which are also based on averages of grouped data.

For all four size categories, total sales expense (as a percentage of sales) was less with "high" advertising and promotion than with "low." Note that the results indicate economies of scale. The same pattern of results was observed in data from a second, smaller study of 227 firms conducted by McGraw-Hill in 1963.[31] Thus, the results from these cost studies appear to be consistent with the research on advertising response reviewed above in indicating that industrial advertising can serve to enhance the effectiveness of personal selling efforts.

Budgeting Practices

In light of the dearth of available empirical knowledge about market response to industrial advertising, management in this field must ordinarily depend on some blend of judgment, experience with analogous situations, and simple rules-of-thumb guidance in setting budgets. Heuristics like "X percent of expected sales" and the "objective and task" method are the principal approaches to budgeting that industrial advertisers report using.

Among 557 subscribers to *Industrial Marketing* who responded to a 1968 mail questionnaire, the following distribution of budgeting practices was found:[32]

Method	% Using
% of sales	24.8
Task	35.6
Arbitrary	27.7
Other	11.9
	100.0

Ratio and Economies of Scale," *Journal of Advertising Research*, Vol. 6 (September 1966), pp. 37-43. For a review, see Schmalensee, same reference as footnote 10, pp. 228-237; and Simon, same reference as footnote 10, Chap. 1.

27. Same reference as footnote 24.

28. Earl L. Bailey, "Manufacturers' Marketing Costs," *Conference Board Record*, Vol. 8 (October 1971), pp. 58-64.

29. Same reference as footnote 28, p. 60.

30. Sim A. Kolliner, Jr., "New Evidence of Ad Values," *Industrial Marketing*, Vol. 48 (August 1963), pp. 81-84. See also, McGraw-Hill Laboratory of Advertising Performance, "Advertising and the Cost of Selling" (New York: McGraw-Hill Book Co., July 1964).

31. McGraw-Hill, same reference as footnote 30.

32. Murray Harding, "Project Future: More Advertisers Mad than Glad about Budget Policy," *Industrial Marketing*, Vol. 53 (August 1968), p. 58.

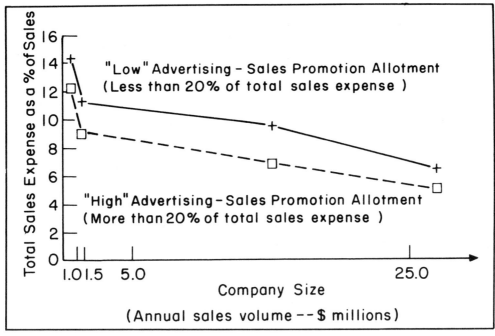

Source: Plotted from data presented in Sim A. Kolliner, "New Evidence of Ad Values," *Industrial Marketing*, Vol. 48 (August 1963), p. 82.

FIGURE 3. Relative selling costs and company size for high and low advertising-sales promotion allotments.

Heavy reliance on rules of thumb and the task method has also been reported in other budgeting studies on firms outside the industrial marketing sector.[33] In recent years, however, measurement programs and models have made some inroads on budgeting practices in the consumer goods field;[34] it is, therefore, surprising to find that Weinberg's work is the only documented account of a comparable analytical method for budgeting industrial advertising that has appeared in the literature.[35]

Heuristics

Percent-of-sales decision rules are a pervasive influence in setting advertising budgets. Schmalensee has analyzed the conditions under which it might be optimal for a monopolist or an oligopolist to maintain a constant advertising-to-sales ratio.[36] However, there have been no empirical investigations to demonstrate that the behavior of industrial advertisers' expenditures indeed are sensitive to key limiting requirements (e.g., the constancy of certain demand elasticities) of such a policy.

The weaknesses of percent-of-sales decision rules are well known,[37] but the most fundamental objection is that they implicitly make advertising a consequence rather than a determinant of sales and profits and can easily give rise to dysfunctional policies. For example, budgeting advertising as a percentage of expected sales would ordinarily lead to reduced expenditures in an economic downturn. Yet the Buchen organization, in a correlational study, indicated that industrial advertisers who maintained their expenditures during recession periods realized better sales performance than those who did not.[38] Nonetheless, some mechanism to control advertising expenditures is required, and in the absence of concrete and current measurements of advertising results, top management frequently establishes some percentage of sales or profit as a budgeting guideline.[39]

DeWolf used the results from the aforemen-

33. See, for example, David L. Hurwood, "How Companies Set Advertising Budgets," *Conference Board Record*, Vol. 5 (March 1968), pp. 34-41; Albert W. Frey, *How Many Dollars for Advertising* (New York: Ronald Press, 1955); and Walter Taplin, "Advertising Appropriation Policy," *Economica*, Vol. 26 (August 1959), pp. 227-239.

34. Seymour Banks, "Trends Affecting the Implementation of Advertising and Promotion," JOURNAL OF MARKETING, Vol. 37 (January 1973), p. 24.

35. Same reference as footnote 8.

36. Same reference as footnote 10, Chap. 2.

37. See, for example, Philip Kotler, *Marketing Management*, 2nd ed. (Englewood Cliffs, N.J.: Prentice-Hall, 1972), pp. 669-670.

38. Buchen Advertising, Inc., *Advertising in Recession Periods: 1949, 1954, 1958, 1961—A New Yardstick Revisited* (Chicago, 1970).

39. See, for example, George A. Perce, "How Kendall Prepares Its Advertising Budget," in *The Advertising Budget*, Richard J. Kelly, ed. (New York: Association of National Advertisers, 1968), pp. 52-54.

tioned McGraw-Hill study of industrial firms' marketing costs to establish a "yardstick that can apply to advertising budgets, present or proposed, to see if they are of the proper magnitude." De-Wolf recommended that if a company wanted to take full advantage of the potential of advertising, it should spend more than 20% of its marketing budget on advertising. As he put it, "the magic figure seems to be 20%—until you get above 20%, you are in the lower half of all companies in selling efficiently—and you can safely go up to at least 33%."[40]

Much could be learned from a study of the determinants of industrial advertising expenditures. The question of why "advertising intensity" (measured by the ratio of advertising to sales) varies across product categories has attracted some attention from economists.[41] However, this work appears to have been focused exclusively on consumer goods industries with no comparable analyses of data for industrial goods.

Other heuristics, such as "matching" competitive expenditures, also frequently enter into budgeting decisions. All of these methods share some common characteristics in that they serve as a management control device but are difficult to justify. Reliance on simple rules of thumb by industrial marketers appears to have declined over time. A 1939 survey of industrial advertising budgeting practices reported by Borden showed greater use of such methods than was indicated by the 1968 *Industrial Marketing* study mentioned above.[42]

Task Method

The task method focuses on communication rather than on sales effects of advertising. A budget is developed by summing estimates of the costs of activities and programs required to accomplish the particular functions assigned to advertising. The essential steps involved in applying the method are:

1. Establish specific marketing objectives for the product in terms of factors such as sales volume, market share, and profit contribution, as well as target market segments.
2. Assess the communication functions that

must be performed to realize the overall marketing objectives and determine the role of advertising and other elements of the communication mix in performing these functions.

3. Define specific goals for advertising in terms of the levels of measurable communication response required to achieve marketing objectives.
4. Estimate the budget needed to accomplish advertising goals.

Underlying the task method is the notion that the influence of advertising on buyers appears through some type of hierarchy of effects ranging from creating product or company awareness and knowledge through developing favorable supplier or product attitudes and preferences. Implementation of these ideas grew markedly in the early 1960s following the appearance of Colley's oft-cited volume on "DAGMAR."[43] Several examples of applications of this version of the task method and the accompanying use of intermediate measures of communication effectiveness in industrial advertising have been discussed in the literature.[44] *Industrial Marketing*'s 1968 survey found that users of the task method were more likely to be satisfied with their budgeting practices than respondents who relied on other approaches.[45]

The practical difficulty of isolating advertising's impact on sales, plus recognition that advertising's function is to communicate, have motivated adoption of the task method and accompanying measures of intermediate response. The latter provide a basis for some modicum of management control over advertising operations. The great stumbling block in using this approach as a planning tool, however, is that it requires knowledge about how levels of expenditures and various communication response measures are related, and how the latter are linked to the purchase behavior that is relevant to the attainment of marketing goals.[46] The existence and nature of

---

40. John W. DeWolf, "A New Tool for Setting and Selling Advertising Budgets" (Paper presented at the Eastern Regional Meeting of the American Association of Advertising Agencies, November 7, 1963), p. 21.

41. Lester G. Telser, "Some Aspects of the Economies of Advertising," *Journal of Business*, Vol. 41 (April 1968), pp. 166-173; and, for a review, see Schmalensee, same reference as footnote 10, pp. 18-20.

42. Neil H. Borden, *The Economic Effects of Advertising* (Chicago: Richard D. Irwin, 1942), p. 722.

43. Russell H. Colley, *Defining Advertising Goals for Measured Advertising Results* (New York: Association of National Advertisers, 1961).

44. William P. Raines, "Setting Advertising Goals for Industrial Products," in *The Advertising Budget*, Richard J. Kelly, ed. (New York: Association of National Advertisers, 1968), pp. 47-51; Patrick J. Robinson and David J. Luck, *Promotional Decision Making* (New York: McGraw-Hill Book Co., 1964), pp. 168-177; Saul S. Sands, *Setting Advertising Objectives* (New York: National Industrial Conference Board, 1966); and Wolfe et al., same reference as footnote 19.

45. Same reference as footnote 32, p. 68.

46. See, for example, the papers on "Advertising Research—DAGMAR Revisited," in *New Directions in Mar-*

such relationships are highly controversial matters.[47] Progress is being made in understanding and using these relationships for purposes of planning and controlling marketing communications, but these developments appear to have occurred largely in the consumer field.[48]

Conclusions

A review of the existing literature offers some insight into the existence of economies of scale, threshold effects, and interaction effects in the field of industrial advertising. It also points up the need for additional research in this area.

Evidence exists that supports the notion of economies of scale in industrial advertising, that is, that in some region of advertising expenditure, additional increments of advertising yield increasing returns. However, evidence has also been found that is not supportive of this hypothesis. Definitive information about the existence and location of this region would be of great help to budgeters in determining the level of advertising expenditures.

The existence of threshold effects, a minimum level of exposure needed for advertising to have a measurable effect, is supported by the literature. A manager should not expect to see advertising effects until the level of expenditure is sufficiently high. But *where* that threshold is found has not been established.

Finally, despite methodological problems in many of the studies, the volume of evidence suggests that industrial advertising and personal selling perform complementary and synergistic roles. Most managers might expect that a split of the industrial marketing budget between advertising and personal selling categories would be more

efficient than a total allocation to a single category. But there is no indication about either what the overall budget *should* be or what split between advertising and personal selling expenditures would be most efficient.

Thus, the study of the effects of industrial advertising has not yet provided guidance to industrial advertisers faced with specific expenditure decisions, and current budgeting practice reflects the lack of knowledge about response. Simple heuristics and the task method are the most common budgeting approaches used. Both methods provide a control mechanism for spending, but they may lead to inappropriate policies.

This review points to the need for a better understanding of how industrial advertising can be effective. A major field study of advertising response would be desirable, but the small size of industrial advertising budgets makes an upsurge of activity in this area appear unlikely. Opportunities do exist, however, for econometric work concerned with developing response functions for individual firms. Another fruitful research direction is to identify and exploit managers' existing knowledge about advertising effectiveness, an approach Bowman and others have shown to be empirically valid in other decision areas.[49] One such study is underway[50] and may help provide a basis for new forms of industrial advertising norms and guidelines.

keting, Frederick E. Webster, Jr., ed. (Chicago: American Marketing Assn., June 1965), pp. 333-358.

47. Kristian S. Palda, "The Hypothesis of a Hierarchy of Effects: A Partial Evaluation," *Journal of Marketing Research*, Vol. 3 (February 1966), pp. 13-25; and Michael L. Ray, "Marketing Communications and the Hierarchy of Effects," in *New Models for Communications Research*, Peter Clarke, ed. (Beverly Hills, Calif.: Sage, 1974), pp. 147-176.

48. Michael L. Ray, "A Decision Sequence Analysis of Developments in Marketing Communications," JOURNAL OF MARKETING, Vol. 37 (January 1973), pp. 29-38.

49. E. H. Bowman, "Consistency and Optimality in Managerial Decision Making," *Management Science*, Vol. 9 (January 1963), pp. 310-321; and Howard Kunreuther, "Extensions of Bowman's Theory of Managerial Decision Making," *Management Science*, Vol. 15 (April 1969), pp. B-415–439.

50. For details of the study, see Gary L. Lilien, "How Many Dollars for Industrial Advertising? Project ADVISOR" (Working Paper 735-74, Sloan School of Management, M.I.T., September 1974); and John D. C. Little and Gary L. Lilien, "How Much for Industrial Advertising?" (Talk before the Advertising Research Foundation Conference, New York, November 18, 1974).

This paper was prepared with the support of a research grant made to M.I.T. for Project ADVISOR, a study of industrial marketing communications funded by a group of participating companies and coordinated through the Association of National Advertisers. Thanks are due to Donald Gluck and John D. C. Little for stimulating this work.

Part III
Marketing Methods

"12 Quick Ideas to Get What You Want in the World of Business & Industry," by A. Adair, summarizes 12 successful ways to communicate your marketing objectives.

"How to Make Technical Publicity Work for You," by J. Sill, explains how to synchronize a technical publicity program with a company's business objectives.

"Effective Technical Publicity," by L.R. Greif, describes some methods and mechanics involved in producing technical feature articles.

"A Neglected Form of Technical Communication—The New Product Release," by H.K. Mintz, covers the content, style, format, and proprietary considerations of product announcements.

"How to Make a Book That Sells—The Fastest Growing Medium in Industrial Marketing: The Mail Order Catalog," by H.G. Ahrend, contains some "do's and don'ts" of direct response selling through the mail order business.

"A Medium Whose Time Has Come . . . Again!" by A. Goldenberg, reveals the effectiveness and cost of business press advertising.

"New Journals Tell the Local Business Story." *Business Week Magazine* reports on publicizing products in business journals.

"Tips on How to Prepare an Effective Firm Brochure," are given by T. Eisenberg.

"Writing Better Industrial Catalogs," by N.H. Brown, explains how to plan, write, and produce better catalogs.

"How to Design a More Memorable Exhibit," by R.K. Swandby and J. Cox, describes several factors to consider in planning an exhibit.

"Do You Need a Film?" by S.M. Shelton, presents advantages and disadvantages of using the motion picture as a communication medium.

"Radio: The Neglected Medium for Scientific Communication," by E. Garfield, although published in 1979, still contains valuable information that can be applied to today's marketing programs.

"Effective Use of Television to Popularize Science," by J.G. Richardson, presents the results of the first international meeting on the use of television to popularize science and technology.

"Comparative Evaluation of Sales Tools," by G. Black, presents a comparative analysis approach to determine the most effective means of evaluating investments in sales methods.

EFFECTIVE WRITING: THE BOTTOM LINE

a continuing series

12 QUICK IDEAS TO GET

IN THE WORLD OF BUSINESS & INDUSTRY

A company's success is usually judged by the goods/services it sells. And by the company's concept of "doing its job."

Communicating is integral to every company's job — to every key individual's. Every department must communicate information at all times. Either in conjunction with your own corporate communications department... or with outside professional services.

Here are some ways to communicate your objectives when performance counts.

NEWSLETTER

Keep in touch with your employees through a newsletter. Quarterly. Monthly. Weekly. Tell them what the company's doing and what their fellow employees are doing, too.

Newsletters also can be used as sales, marketing, recruiting and public relations tools. Good news is hard to beat.

MANUAL

Translate your manuals into plaintalk.

You've sold the equipment, but who's maintaining it? How well can they read? Will their mistakes come back to haunt you?

All the directions in the world go down the drain if the users can't understand them. With reading levels plummeting each year, plaintalk manuals are no longer an option; they're a requirement.

TRADE ARTICLE

Generate a trade journal article. Advertising's not the answer for everything. Become known as an authority in your field.

VIDEO PROGRAM

Control losses through video. Human. Product. Plant. All loss control comes down to prevention: practice proper safety and production habits. Through video you can pinpoint bad practices and focus on the good ones. Consider TV one of your safety tools.

FILMSTRIP

Advance your sales/ideas through advanced techniques. Filmstrips no longer mean an old roll in a plastic cannister and a bulky projector, with a script read aloud at each "beep."

Carry your story in a briefcase, with the filmstrip/sound cartridge and projection screen inside.

Set it up on a desk to show to one key person or project it on a wall for a greater audience. To tell and sell.

BOOKLET

Invite queries. Prepare a booklet that shows your basic equipment line. Showcase the selling points, explain why "many may imitate, but none can duplicate."

Distribute the booklets through your branch offices, to your field sales force. Have them available whenever and wherever customers want a reference on your company at their fingertips.

WHAT YOU WANT

ANNUAL REPORT

File an annual report that goes beyond replication of your 10-K.

Are you merely following minimum SEC requirements? Or are you using the opportunity annually to reach an audience of interested parties — stockholders, analysts, customers/clients, employees and prospects on all counts — with a readable presentation that keeps them interested?

If you're private, you can forget the SEC, but not those interested parties. A report to them annually can keep them interested.

SALES LETTER

Formulate well-crafted sales letters.

Analyze your customers' needs and determine where you best serve. Develop a series of letters to cover the most important opportunities. Use them to introduce, follow-up and keep in touch.

Each augments personal sales calls. And they don't have to read like form letters either. Good ones don't.

FILM

Show your customers around the world, or just around the corner, what makes your goods/services the best on the market — in live action. Make a film about your company's capabilities.

BROCHURE

Stack your track record against the competition. A brochure tells why your people are the best professionals in your business.

Emphasize their depth of experience and the impressive projects they've completed. Then give it to customers who want to know. And make it a keeper.

SLIDE SHOW

Explain your employee benefits package in a slide presentation. Include it in new employee orientations and use it as a refresher for others. Key the accompanying looseleaf notebook to the slide show. Update both periodically.

PRESENTATION

Turn a presentation into an invitation to do business. Use a scripted presentation that skillfully includes audio-visual media.

To proceed with these or 1001 other ideas unique to your company, or to simply notify us of any address corrections, contact:

Art Adair
Partner
THE WRITING COMPANY
3303 Louisiana, Suite 211G
Houston, TX 77006
713-521-9436

THE WRITING COMPANY

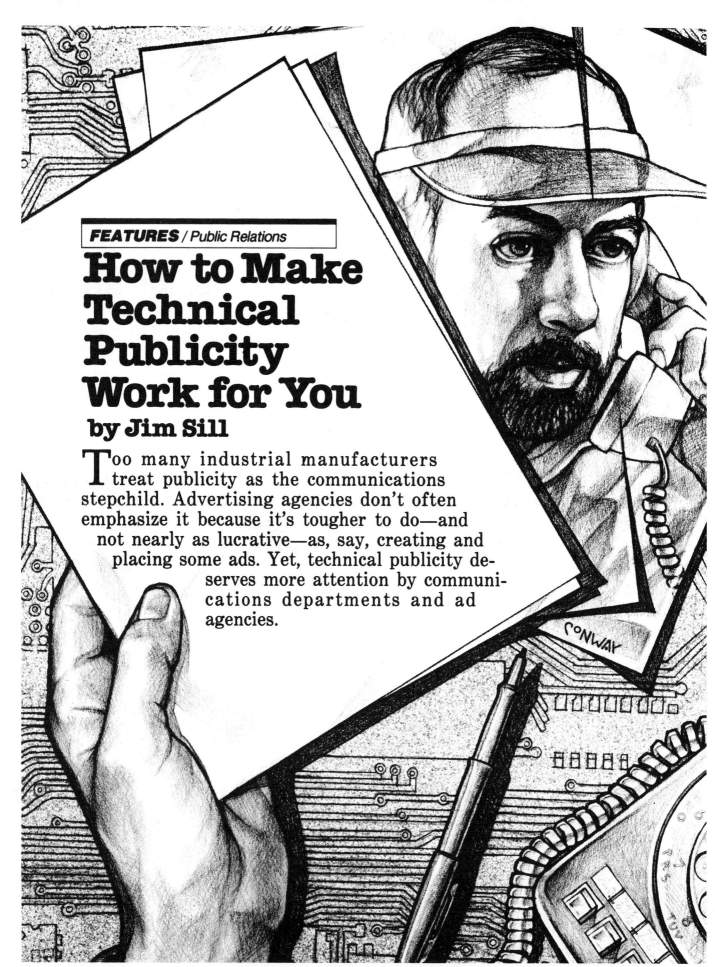

How to Make Technical Publicity Work for You

by Jim Sill

Too many industrial manufacturers treat publicity as the communications stepchild. Advertising agencies don't often emphasize it because it's tougher to do—and not nearly as lucrative—as, say, creating and placing some ads. Yet, technical publicity deserves more attention by communications departments and ad agencies.

Reprinted with permission from *Industrial Marketing* (now *Business Marketing*), vol. 67, pp. 94–98, and 100, June 1982.
Copyright © 1982 by Crain Communications, Inc.

How to sell technical publicity to management

Top management doesn't always understand or feel completely comfortable with a marketing element like publicity over which they have less-than-full control of both message and timing. They may also balk at a technical publicity program's price tag because some slick publicist may have tagged it as "free advertising."

But with that saving comes the obvious risk. Independent editing by the publication might leave some of the best parts of your company story on the cutting room floor. Even worse, your story might not run at all, for reasons well beyond your own control.

Yet, a successful technical publicity program is more dependent on active, company-wide support than perhaps any other marketing communications tool. There are a few good ways to demonstrate the efficacy of your program to management.

Synchronize your technical publicity program with your company's business objectives.

Your program needs measurable objectives—such as how many full feature stories will be placed (in contrast to those which are written), how many short news items will be placed, and so on. But certainly include how your program will further your company's goals.

For example, if your company has a market share goal, you may want to preface presentation of your program with, "To reach our widget market share of 20%, a technical publicity program, designed to demonstrate our technical capabilities, will be implemented . . ."

Turn the skeptics into your supporters.

Don't expect everyone to love your program—especially before you've had time to tuck a few tangible results into your hip pocket. A good way to gain support is to aggressively seek out the skeptics and get them into print. An easy way to do this is to respond to one of the many calls for editorial assistance you may receive—if you're running your program correctly—during the course

of a year.

Once published, skeptics often become the most vociferous of supporters, just as recent proselytes sing the loudest in church.

Get your numbers together.

Upper management typically relies on cost estimates to help make decisions. So give them some numbers which may mean something to them.

But remember, cost figures may not be the only way to assess the total effectiveness of your publicity program.

It may be that management finds it convenient to equate a dollar spent on publicity to a dollar spent on advertising.

Just remember, advertising buys space which is completely under the advertiser's control. Barring unethical or distasteful copy, what the advertiser writes appears in print. Publicity, of course, might well be edited by a publication. Exact wording is beyond the publicist's control. Comparing advertising costs to publicity costs provides only another frame of reference.

If you should provide management demand a direct cost comparison, calculate it this way:

For the cost of an ad program, add the space charges of all ads run, plus the estimated production and direct personnel time costs of preparing the program. Divide by the number of pages run to calculate the average cost per page.

For the publicity program, estimate a two-page article ghost written and placed by a competent technical editorial specialist might cost $2,000 to $4,000—the latter if there are lots of changes and rewrites. Figure another $1,000 for developing camera-ready art such as schematics, graphs, etc. If someone in your company writes the story without the help of a specialist (now it's down to a $500 incentive) and you edit and place it, and the magazine furnishes the camera-ready art—as many do—you've saved even more, compared with the the substantially higher cost of buying space to advertise your company.

— Jim Sill

Technical publicity can be a very effective way to achieve your marketing communications goals. It has some inherent advantages:

● Unlike its higher priced cousin, paid ad space, technical publicity carries the implied editorial endorsement of the publication in which it appears.

● Technical publicity, on the surface, is more believable than most other marketing communications tools. The reader depends on the publication's editorial integrity to keep the facts straight. That credibility spills onto the company when an executive bylines an article or when the editors report on company developments.

● It is one of the most economical (but certainly not free) marketing communications tools available to the industrial equipment marketer. The accompanying article (left) can help you figure publicity costs when compared with paid advertising space, an especially useful exercise when selling your publicity program to management.

● If you're judged on how many inquiries you can generate, a good "new literature" blurb, or feature story can pull more leads than an ad occupying the same amount of space.

● Technical publicity increases the flow of information which helps industrial technology progress. An industry that communicates well with itself and its customers is an industry most likely to survive and prosper.

For example, in the rapidly-evolving electronic data processing technology there are lots of embryonic stories just begging to be told across the pages of an industry's trade press. However, other industries may not be as lucky. But by digging and developing a "nose for news," you can discover some pretty good stories at nearly any manufacturing plant.

TRADE-OFFS

Publicity is not free, although page for page, it is usually less expensive than advertising space. The trade-off there, of course, is that with an ad, you pay to say exactly what you want to say. You retain control of your message with an ad. Although publicity is probably less expensive than advertising, control of the message is in

Jim Sill is president, Marketing Communications, Cypress, Cal. At the time this article was written he was manager, marketing communications, Pacific Valves, Long Beach, Cal.

the hands of the editor, not you.

Editorial space is solely dependent on the perceived interest of a given readership as interpreted by an editor. Because reader interest, not payment, determines the message, readers are likely to spend more time with that message.

Editorial space does not depend on a *quid pro quo* arrangement with an editor or an advertising space salesman. The purchase of paid space has no bearing on the placement of company sponsored editorial. Either the editorial material is of interest to a given readership or it isn't. That is, on the part of most high-quality, high-integrity publications, the sole basis for placement.

Perhaps there is a special "advertisers literature" section, or a special directory issue in which an advertiser can buy a little extra editorial mention. But the standard of all high quality, ethical publications reads like the Constitutional reference to church and state. Space reps sell space, editors keep readers interested, and neither rep nor editor encroaches on the other's turf.

Another trade-off is really a spin-off. Editors select editorial material on the basis of its newsworthiness. It's a tough idea for some advertising managers and agencies to accept if they don't understand the editorial function. Creating genuine news is a lot harder than just digging out a bunch of technical facts, sifting through them, then turning them into cogent prose.

You can sometimes burn an editor with a story about a "new product" that isn't, about a superior design feature that isn't necessarily superior, and so on. The editor may inadvertently run the story. Once. But editors generally have memories longer than a trip to the moon, and that's probably what you'd have to take in order for them to run another story from you or from the company you represent.

Learn to tell the difference between real news and the sales promotion materials you commonly use. And if you're candid in your approach, editors can often help you turn some sales promotion information into bonafide editorial material.

WHERE'S NEWS?

It's easier to start with where you won't find news. You won't find it at your desk. You won't find it at the agency. And you won't find it by waiting patiently for your telephone to ring. You've got to get up and track it down.

A good place to begin is that most reticent department of all, Engineering. Check the R&D lab for any unusual tests—or test apparatus. A visit to Design Engineering may reveal a new design innovation of which you were previously unaware.

Then, there's old Wayne who is about to retire after 37 years at the plant. As a senior statesman, he usually has the time to help you, and he'll generally have more stories to tell than you have time to listen. Find the old Wayne in each department.

Quality Assurance often buys or leases state-of-the-art equipment used in your plant in an unusual way which is newsworthy. That can lead to a good industrial process story for you.

Manufacturing is usually looking into new and better machine tools, such as the new breed of robot-like computerized numerically controlled (CNC) machine tools. They're often customized to produce a certain kind of product or component. Again you have an opportunity for another industrial process story if it's genuinely newsworthy.

Personnel is a good place to check for new hires and recent promotions.

Marketing and sales—the part of the company where you're usually involved anyway—are areas ripe with leads. Sales people are routinely exposed to customer problems. Customer problems often translate into some good opportunities for the company that solves them and for the publicist who tells about that solution.

Unusual application case histories are also worth exploring, especially where a new application is discovered for an existing product.

New product projects are the most obvious source for a technical story. But in the case of heavy industrial equipment, there aren't too many genuinely new products. More times than not, new product stories, when stripped of all their hoorah, are really stories about the modification of an existing product. It should be honestly depicted as such to the editors.

THE PUBLICITY PROGRAM

There are different types of editorial opportunities. By recognizing how the objectives and implementation of each differs from the others, you increase your success by synchronizing your technical publicity program with the other vehicles in your communications mix.

A **major feature story** is an in-depth explanation of a process, product, trend which is, from the editor's viewpoint, either newsworthy or otherwise of great interest to readers. From your company's viewpoint, the feature story is the best way to give a complete explanation of your company's strengths. It's a very important goal of any publicity program. The feature story can illustrate the company's expertise, or that of the key executive whose byline appears in the piece.

Features are also written by a publication's editors, of course. You want to be sure that they have every piece of information they might need to dwell on your company's contribution and your key personnel at length.

Feature stories that carry a company byline can be planned and initiated at the beginning of each calendar year—just about the time that editorial schedules come out. By basing your editorial contribution on editorial emphasis already planned by each publication, you increase your chances of placement. This kind of prior planning makes everybody's job easier.

A **short feature** is a less than complete explanation of a process or a company. It's used to focus on a particularly newsworthy or interesting portion of a company or a process. Major and short features must jibe with the editorial focus of the publication. In both cases, editors expect that features they have agreed to publish will be provided to them on an exclusive basis.

A vitally important but frequently overlooked element in a publicity program are **news stories and items.** News releases may be individual stories in their own right or short announcements such as personnel promotions. Either way they are timely, immediate news. They are pegged to an event.

They are more generally written to suit a variety of readerships, and they are sent out *en masse* and not on an exclusive basis. Most high quality publications will rewrite your announcement or news story to suit their style and their perception of reader interest. Most likely they will print less material than you provide. But if you make sure that they have all the pertinent information, you are more likely to get your item in print. How much background material to send with a news release is matter of

What editors look for
(. . . and what they'd rather not see)

Editors often desire bylined articles from company execs as much as companies desire the editorial space and editing skills that editors provide. The editor-exec relationship is fragile and the rules pertaining to it aren't always understood or practiced.

It's a partnership. And editors generally prefer a good company contact as a partner instead of an agency contact. Al Gaines of *Chemical Processing* reports, "Some agencies apparently write their 'news' releases more for the benefit of their client's management than for our readership. I'd like to see company communications managers exercise more control over, and provide more direction to their agencies; not just cut (the agency) loose. For example, we've received releases that talk about the company for the whole first page. We don't use puffery. We don't care if the company was founded in 1884."

Oil and Gas Journal technical editor John Kennedy adds that "about two-thirds of our technical articles come from our readers, because of the highly varied areas of expertise required."

Often, if the idea for a story is compelling enough, editors will volunteer to dig out and write the story themselves. In this situation, a knowledgeable company representative can help the editor reach the right people, obtain the appropriate drawings, and get accurate information.

Oil Daily editor John Moore imparts his pendulum theory: "It seems we've swung from engineers who know their subject but who have difficulty writing, to admen who can write, but who don't know that subject."

CRITERIA FOR ACCEPTANCE

"Will it provide information of value to our readership?" asks Mr. Kennedy rhetorically, "That's our chief criterion." Editors agree that practical information exclusively directed at a given publication's readership is what they wanted to see.

"We prefer a pre-contact," says Mr. Gaines in referring to the preliminary steps of submitting an exclusive technical subject for publication. A telephone call and/or an outline of the article usually suffices. He also indicates, as did the other editors, that ". . . a person should study a publication first . . ." for style, slant, tone, and compatibility with other editorial material.

"Be familiar with your target publication, its readers, its editorial content. Each book has its own 'personality,'" notes Mr. Kennedy.

"Use straightforward English," advises *Hydrocarbon Processing's* Frank Evans. "Although English is the international language of the oil industry, many of our overseas readers don't understand colloquial English." A good rule of thumb is to concentrate more on *what* you want to say, and less on *how* to express it. For prospective contributors who may feel comfortable with their subject, but who may feel uncomfortable expressing it, *Hydrocarbon Processing* offers a free Author's Handbook.

Other editors' suggestions:
● Meet your deadlines. Deliver what you promise.
● Pay attention to timing. For example, you're more likely to get a frost protection article published in January than in August.
● Always identify a knowledgeable contact on the first page of the release so an editor can obtain additional information and still meet his deadlines. Date the release.
● To save time, send material to the editor by name. Material addressed to "editor" often takes longer to reach the right person. And keep your names current. For example, INDUSTRIAL MARKETING regularly receives news releases addressed to an editor who left the magazine 15 years ago.

CRITERIA FOR REJECTION

As far as editors are concerned, there are three kinds of news items that will get you and your company or client in deep trouble:

1. Self-serving promotional puffery disguised as news. "We probably get several hundred (company-sponsored news items) a week," guesses Al Gaines. "I think of the millions of trees that are wasted because some companies want us to publish what amounts to free advertising."

2. Material that is of little or no interest to a publication's readership. For example, observes Bill O'Keefe, there are likely better places than the pages of *Power* magazine to inform culinary practioners about a new duck plucker.

3. "'Please publish this release. The response to this release will determine whether we buy advertising space in your publication.' Obviously, we didn't—and won't—respond . . . to an arrangement like this," says Al Gaines.

You can do other things to irritate your editorial partners; things that will guarantee a grumpy reception for your editorial publicity.
● Send the same story from the same company to the same publication four or five times a year. A variation of this act is to copy your agency, which then duplicates your efforts.
● Issue a retraction or correction to a story that was sent out several months ago.
● Get that good looking secretary down the hall to straddle the suction nozzle of a new pump while you photograph the event for a new product release that won't attract a dime's worth of ink. Cheesecake is strictly yesterday.
● Once your story has been scheduled for a particular issue, demand that your ad be placed in direct proximity to it.
● When an editor can't give you a definite commitment regarding editorial placement, call him every other day to "remind" him.

ILLUSTRATION

Whether or not to illustrate, and to what extent, can double or halve the cost of your article, depending on your decision. Illustration enhances the communicability of your article. But some publications prefer to develop camera-ready art from rough approximations while others would prefer that you provide camera-ready art.

The best thing to do is to ask the editor. For non-exclusive mass releases, use simple black-on-white line art or a black and white glossy photo that was shot originally on black & white film.

—Jim Sill

judgement. Be sure that editors know whom they can call to get whatever else they need as quickly as possible. Also, be sure to date your releases.

News exclusives. Editors will often give your news story or items more prominent play if you promise that you won't tip off other publications. There is an important trade-off that involves careful judgement. While you may get more prominent play in publication A (and there is no guarantee that you will), editors at publications B, C etc., may not ever run your item if doing so makes them appear to be late with the news. In extreme cases, you may alienate those editors, which hurts your chances of placing future stories with them.

Hence, dealing in news exclusives can be risky unless you're experienced in working with editors and you know the competitive publications in a given market well. Editors can be very competitive. Caution is advised.

Unplanned feature stories can be a fortuitous opportunity when you have discovered something of possible news value in your company. If at first glance the subject matter matches no known editorial style or requirement, but you would like to try and get mileage from it nonetheless, call editors who might be interested. Discuss it candidly with them. If one

shows interest, write the article to that editor's expectations and send it to him on an exclusive basis.

Editorial requests. Editors have a habit of helping the hands that help them. So if one calls looking for information, be as helpful as you can be without violating company confidentiality. In every case, respond quickly.

The trick is to get on editors' "call lists" to which they refer when doing industry round-up stories. Of course the more publicity your company generates, the more likely you will be called in the future. The important thing is that editors know of your willingness to share your company's expertise and make company personnel available for interviews.

Finally, coordinate your efforts; especially if you're using a combination of suppliers. For example, you might assign all blurbs (news stories) to the PR arm of your ad agency, while you—the manager of marketing communications —respond to all editorial requests. A technical feature writing specialist could handle the feature stories.

An ambitious program like that should be clearly documented. All parties, including your management, should know exactly what's expected of whom, and how each contribution helps fulfill a larger, common goal. How many blurbs or articles are expected to

be written? That is a much different goal than a goal based on the number of items placed. Remember placement of items is not in your control. It's always the decision of an editor. But in order to be placed, an editor must receive the information from you, so a goal of items written is probably much more realistic than items placed.

Some PR people and firms will guarantee placement. Great! Just make sure that you insist to your PR people that placement be in the publications important to your communications objectives, not obscure, irrelevant journals.

A good way to gain internal interest and assistance is to provide incentives to people who provide you with story leads, and for the technical people who write their own. Five hundred dollars isn't a bad price to pay for thousands of dollars worth of publicity.

When you gain a commitment from an editor to run your story, publicize it extensively within your company before it runs. People will watch for it, read it, and look for a way to participate in "such an important program."

Get the most mileage from your technical publicity that you can. Most publishers can furnish very reasonably priced reprints. Use them in your direct mail campaigns, as sales handouts, and in other ways to *demonstrate* your company's technical competence. ∎

EFFECTIVE TECHNICAL PUBLICITY

Lucien R. Greif, President
Greif Associates, Inc.

Nowadays, use of the word "semantics" automatically establishes you as a person of great learning and superior intellect. Permit me, therefore, to delve immediately into the semantics of publicity, and the other two terms with which it is often confused: public relations and advertising.

Definitions

Publicity--Getting your name (or that of your company or client) before the public, where it can be seen or heard and, hopefully, remembered.

Public relations--Doing the right thing and getting credit for it. That's our favorite definition, and about as good as any. Others we've heard: "Public relations is not treating the public like relations." Or, "Public relations is the letter you don't write when your're angry, and the nice letter you do write the next day, after you've regained your sense of humor."

Would you like a nice, long, formal one? "The activities of an organization in building and maintaining sound and productive relations with special publics such as customers, employees, stockholders, and the general public, so as to adapt itself to its environment and interpret itself to society." Take your pick.

If your wondering why we're spending so much time defining public relations, when right along we've made a big point of the fact that we'll be talking only about publicity, the answer is simple.

Public relations encompasses tremendous scope. Not only does it include the kind of publicity we'll shortly describe in greater detail, but it also covers radio and TV publicity, internal and external house organs, a well-stocked cafeteria, sponsoring a bowling or baseball team, large and well-publicized contributions to the Red Cross, scholarship funds, quarterly reports, annual reports, and speeches such as this one. There really is no limit to what you can do to enhance your "image"--pardon the use of this much overworked expression--if you have the time and the resources. But it also means you can't hope to tackle this vast subject in one short session-- and that's why we're limiting ourselves to only one small facet, technical publicity.

Advertising--Admittedly, it's difficult to see how or why anyone would confuse publicity with advertising, but it happens frequently. One minute, then, to differentiate. In advertising, you say exactly <u>what</u> you want to say (within the bounds of decorum) exactly <u>when</u> you want to say it. And you pay for this privilege, by buying space or time. On the other hand, in publicity you don't pay for the space or time, but you have no control over exactly what will be said, or when it will be said. In fact, you may end up with nothing at all. Your only weapons are your own good sense, a knowledge of what is newsworthy, ability to develop a good story, knowing who will be interested, a sense of timing, and a willingness to subdue your crassly commercial instincts. <u>That's</u> all you need!

Reprinted with permission from *Proc. 5th Annu. Inst. Tech. Industrial Commun.*, 1962, pp. 58–66.

So now, at long last, let's get to the meat of this speech.

Feature Articles

In our opinion, technical feature articles are one of the best ways of enhancing the reputation of an individual or his company. What does it take to produce such an article? Several things.

First of all, an intimate knowledge of the subject matter. Stick to what you know. Don't write about a subject that is quite foreign to your daily endeavors, unless for some reason you really know a lot about it. It's hard to say things clearly if you don't fully understand them yourself, and the article will show it.

Another reason for sticking close to your knitting is that your sources of basic information are more accessible. Some factors you may wish to bring up in an article may not be fully resolved in your own mind, or you may be just a little bit doubtful about some of the statements you wish to make. You can always check with an associate or supervisor, and then have the assurance that some reader will not tear your article apart for lack of technical accuracy.

Having chosen the subject and gathered all the necesary data, the next step is the actual writing. There are several approaches, though perhaps the most widely used and accepted is the problem-solution-result sequence. You tell what particular difficulties were encountered in a machining operation; how a plastic was substituted for a metal, or a forged part for a sub-assembly; how an optical instrument replaced tedious hand measurements; and then the happy end results. Less time, fewer rejects, better product, high profits.

Simple.   Short.   Terse. Punchy. Factual.

That's the best way to put an article together. Much has already been written on this subject, yet a lot of copy is still being turned out that is stilted and archaic; it tried to impress the reader through the use of fancy vocabulary, and in so doing forgets to put the real points across.

Use words so that your secretary can understand the story, not so that an old college chum will say, "My, doesn't Freddy have an esoteric vocabulary."

A chap we know, who used to like involved sentences, once got a memo from his boss. It pointed out the shortcomings of his article, then suggested that the writer constantly ask himself these three questions: (1) Can I say it in simpler words? (2) Can I say it with fewer words? (3) Do I need to say it at all? Somewhat piqued, mostly because there was so much truth in the memo, the writer retorted, "No, I don't have to say it at all. But will you continue to pay my salary?" Its too bad may former boss had no sense of humor.

Next, the matter of length. Most of you are probably familiar with Lincoln's answer to the question of how long a man's legs should be. "Long enough to reach the ground," quipped Abe. Makes sense.

The same yardstick may be applied to the article. Don't approach it the way most of us tackled certain calculus problems in school--working from the back of the book, by first looking up the answer and then carving the equation to fit. A much more sensible approach consists of making an outline--to be sure you've covered all the important thoughts--then writing the article to whatever length it turns out. When you've said all you want to say, quit. Don't embellish, and don't artifi- cially puff up a good story. The extra fat will ruin it.

As for organization, consider the article an inverted pyramid. The most important thought at the top, then the next most important idea, and so on all along the line. Think of the typical editor or reader for whom this is intended. If the editor has to cut your story to fit his space allotments, or the reader gets tired or called away before reaching the end of the ar- ticle, at least he will have ab- sorbed the gist of it. Don't save the strawberries for last.

Use paragraphs lavishly. Don't crowd ideas. Just as we recommend keeping sentences short for easy understanding, so with paragraphs. When you've analyzed one thought sufficiently, go to another; start a new paragraph. And don't keep coming back to the same idea. You'll confuse your reader by a Mexican-jumping-bean style--back and forth--and he'll grow weary. And when you've annoyed him enough, he punishes you. He turns the page to someone else's easier-to-follow article.

Actually, we can give you one rule of thumb, at least to provide some guidance in the matter of length. Feature articles published by business publications usually run to about two pages. They may, of course go to three, four, some- times even six, but that's not too usual. Most stories can adequately be covered in a two-page spread. Allowing space for photos and cap- tions, that leaves room for an average of 1500 words of copy. Figuring 250 words per double-spaced page--and all manuscripts <u>must</u> be double-spaced--that's the equivalent of about six pages.

Sub-Heads

Immediately preceding, we had a sub-head. Use them generously, but don't overdo it. And how do you like that for an explicit instruction?

You'd like some specific num- bers? All right. Use a sub-head after some five or six paragraphs, or at least one per typewritten page. Again, apply this "rule," just as any other we suggest, with intelligence. Don't put a sub-head right in the middle of a flowing idea simply because you've reached your sixth paragraph, and Greif said "after every six." As a matter of fact in writing, <u>don't</u> be rigid. Rules are meant to be a general help; but don't let your style be- come cramped because you're writing according to a rule book. It'll never work.

The sub-head should be rela- tively short--3 to 4 words--and convey the key idea of the para- graphs to follow. A very busy reader, and most readers are, should be able to reconstruct your entire story, or be able to tell whether he should spend time on it, by sim- ply scanning your headline, the deck (which is a secondary headline sometimes used) and the sub-heads. It's like looking at a skeleton to figure out whether the girl is likely to be shapely enough for a second look.

Headline

It may occur to some of you that we've sequenced our topics backwards, having now arrived at what would normally seem to be the beginning of the article: the headline. But to most writers, the headline is distinctly <u>not</u> the beginning, any more than the title of a book is the first thing most authors will write. Not till you're well through the article, have lived with it and tried to pour it onto paper, will a really incisive head pop into your mind.

Although we cannot offer you an all-purpose headline, which will suffice no matter what the subject, we can certainly give you a hint. Talk about money, in one form or another. Whether the widget or method you're promoting saves time, speeds production, eliminates rejects, reduces the labor force--and watch that one, because it leads to trouble--lowers inventory, implies substitution of a cheaper material, simplifies machining or assembly, reduced to the rock-bottom idea you're saying "less money." Want to whet the reader's interest? Mention money.

Length of headline? No longer than a telegram. Like so: HEADLINE TRIMS WORDS, USES COMMAS FOR LENGTHY CONJUCTIONS. MAJOR THOUGHTS EXPRESSED WITH MINIMUM VOCABULARY. Even better: NEW HEADLINE REDUCES MAJOR THOUGHTS TO FEWEST, SHORTEST WORDS.

The Deck

Sometimes a feature article will have one really major idea, and a second, almost as important. Trying to cram both into one headline may be impossible. Then use a deck, a sub-head in a smaller type.

Releases

Most of the comments we've expressed about feature articles will probably apply to news releases as well. Certainly, good style for one is good style for the other. And that applies to the headline, the deck, the sub-heads, and body copy.

Wherein, then lies the difference? Mostly in length, and in distribution.

A feature article must have enough meat to provide 1500 well-chosen words, without artificial expansion. A news release usually has but one idea to express--a new product, a promotion, a company building program, a new application--and you're lucky if you can squeeze out two pages.

The second major distinction between a feature article and a news release is distribution. Ideally, a feature article is prepared exclusively for a single publication We say "ideally," because lately we've backed away just a bit from this exclusive exclusivity, and sent individual feature articles to more than one journal--about six. However, we've made it a point to pick only those that do not overlap in readership, each servicing an entirely different audience; and we made sure that each editor knew that the others were also getting the same data. Don't _ever_ do it any other way.

The news release, on the other hand, is truly designed for mass mailing. You make out a release list which includes just about every conceivable magazine that might be interested in the story. In this case, you should certainly include competitive publications, and you can do so without qualms, because the format of the release (and its general heft) will clearly indicate that this is being sent to everybody. Also, because if used, it will be given only a few column-inches of space, there's no problem in having it appear in two or more competitive publications.

Whenever possible, send out at least one good 8x10 glossy photo with a news release. Chances of pick-up will be considerably improved. If you have them, and if your budget will permit, send out more than one photo. Either send two each to every editor, or as a refinement--and to save costs-

-alternate your photos as you mail. This will give more variety to the printed version, and may increase your impact. Inasmuch as most of us recognize photos we've seen before very quickly, a differ- ent photo may cause the reader to be drawn to your copy a second time, before he realizes he's already seen it.

List of Outlets

There are well over 3000 busi- ness and technical publications, ranging from those printed on news- print stock, such as Daily News Record, to the very slick on coated stock, such as Industrial Design. Some are daily, more are weekly, most are monthly. Subject matter ranges widely, and there is almost no industry which does not have a least one business publication. There is even one called Prison World--for the wardens, not the prisoners--and another called Diapason--and that has nothing to do with what you're thinking either. Mostly, there is one acknowledged leader for a particular field, then maybe one or two close seconds, finally a few more also-rans.

In addition to the vertical publications addressed to only one field, there are horizontal publi- cations which cover a lot of terri- tory. Mill & Factory, for example, will handle any topic from air- conditioning to welding, with a diverse range of subjects in be- tween. Obviously, there is never a dearth of markets for well-written, well-illustrated articles. You can find all of them listed in Standard Rate and Data Service, or Industrial Marketing's Market Data Book.

Editorial Contact

If you're not certain that the feature article you have in mind will fit a particular publication, write to the editor, and ask him. Give him an outline, if possible, or at least describe the scope of the article. He won't commit himself by promising absolutely to accept your article, but at least he can say whether or not he'd like to look at it. If he says yes, you can refer to previous correspondence when you send the article, which is better than sending it "cold" or unasked for. If he says no, you've saved postage, and don't have your manu- script and photos unnecessarily roughed up in the mail.

Better yet, try discussing your article idea during a luncheon meeting with the editor. Admit- tedly, that isn't always easy, par- ticularly for those not located in the major publishing centers: New York, Chicago, Philadelphia, and Cleveland, In fact, if we be per- mitted one small commercial for our organization, and we promise no more than that, this is the place for it. We consider any luncheon by ourselves, when we haven't dis- cussed business with an editor, waste motion. Don't misconstrue. This approach is never meant as a form of graft. ·In fact, editors treat us almost as often as it's our turn to buy. However, the re- laxed atmosphere and absence of telephone interruptions, means ability to concentrate on the story propositon at hand, and a willing- ness to investigate, discuss, take apart, rebuild the basic idea into acceptable scope and format.

If luncheon is not possible, visit the editor at his office. In any event, keep in mind that he's a busy man. Repay him for his time by bringing a workable idea, one that you've thought out completely, and one for which you're willing to do extra work. Don't pout if he doesn't agree to your proposition exactly as you offer it. Be alert to suggested changes; if you possibly can, be ready to accept them. And don't ask for any guarantees.

Getting Along with Editors

Editors are men who, above all, insist on fair play. Treat them with courtesy and consideration, help them as much as you can, make sure they can rely on your word, and they will be the most valuable friends that you will ever have.

Contrary to common belief, it is not necessary to ply editors with expensive luncheons, boxes of cigars, night clubs, or other little trifles in order for them to publish your material. The answer is much simpler. If the story is good for their readers, they'll use it. If not, six kegs of beer won't save it. Granted, there are borderline stories where the answer could easily be yes or no, and where your past services to the editor might induce him to say yes. But these instances are rare.

If wine, women and song won't do it, what will? Integrity. Follow "The Four Bees" below, and editors not only will be glad to receive material from you (and use it), but, more important, they will often ask you for stories.

1. Be honest. Make only legitimate claims. Call it new only if it really is new. If the editor asks an embarrassing question, tell the truth. Don't give him an "exclusive" which he'll read in a competitive publication before his own comes out.

2. Be on time. An editor has deadlines to meet. If you've promised a story by a certain date, have it ready by then. If you find you can't make it, tell him as soon as you know, not at the last minute. Give him a chance to make other arrangements.

3. Be useful. If the editor asks for data or photos you have, supply them promptly without fuss. Don't first haggle for a 72-point credit line. If the editor deems it necessary, he'll say "photos courtesy of XYZ Plastic Company." If not, insisting on it will only force him to say forget it, and he'll never call you again.

4. Be thoughtful. If you happen to know the editor's birthday, send him a card. If he's mentioned in the local paper and you see it, drop him a short note. If he has a hobby and you see something that would interest him, let him know. Or, if you happen to run across a story he could use, even if it has nothing to do with your company's products or services, tell him about it. He'll appreciate the lead.

Timing

For best results, learn something of publishing schedules and procedures. For instance, most monthly publications close on the 10th of the month preceding. That means we are today too late to make most August issues, even if we have a complete package ready for the editor. In rare cases, when you really have an unusual newsbreak, this deadline may be extended a bit. As a matter of fact, occasionally an editor will hold space open when he knows a story is coming through. But Lord have mercy on the publicity man who fails to deliver under these conditions!

Keeping editorial deadlines in mind should help our planning. First, allow about one month to complete a story, get the photos you need, caption them, and have all auxiliary data (charts, graphs, diagrams) prepared. Next, conservatively, allow one month for the approvals you need, from your company or client, and any others who may have contributed. If government agencies or the military services are in any way involved, allow two to three months for the necessary clearances. Put them all together, and what is the picture? Simply this: If you get started on a feature article today, July 11, you may see it in print in a November issue. If you're lucky. And if the editor uses it in the next upcoming issue. Which is not always the case. We have seen stories held for nine months without a word, have then received an urgent telegram for some additional data, because the story was suddenly being rushed into print in the next issue, for which the deadline was practically past.

The timing of news releases is also a bit of an art. You have to schedule them intelligently. You can probably send one or two new product announcements, one personnel change, one company news, and one new literature release in one month, but you're pushing your luck. The editor gets several hundred releases per month, but has space for only some 50. Obviously, out of those 50, he can't pick 5 of yours!

When possible, don't mail your material for arrival on Monday or Fridy mornings. These are the two busiest days. Also, keep the closing date in mind. Arriving just a day or two before means you're almost certain to miss the current issue; and with several hundred more releases to come in, it's unlikely that the editor will take great pains to save this month's leftovers.

Mechanics

One of the facets of correct manuscript preparation has already been mentioned: always double-space, and allow ample margins. The reason is simple. Editors like to edit. But if you single-space your story, either the editor has no room for his comments--very frustrating--or he has to have your material retyped. When you realize how crowded his day is, you understand that anything you do to create work for him will not be appreciated. And the most effective means of showing his lack of appreciation is a flick toward the round file.

Some many years ago, in an effort to put releases and articles on a more scientific basis, we sent out a questionnaire to more than 250 editors who often receive material from us. Ninety-two replied.

Several questions may have seemed very basic, yet we had to ask them. Even though we felt we knew the answers, they were not official until editors confirmed them. Here, then, are some of the key questions, and the results.

1. Which color of paper do you prefer?

   White, 69 (86%) green, 3 buff, 2 yellow, 4 blue, 1 pink, 1

2. <u>Which color of ink do you prefer?</u>

Black, 76 (96%) green, 0 red, 0 blue, 3

3. <u>Which method of reproduction do you prefer?</u>

Ditto, 3 Mimeograph[1], 23 Multigraph, 32 (55%)

4. <u>Should the release have a printed, formal masthead?</u>

Yes, 29 Not necessary, 56 (66%)

5. <u>Does presentation influence choice of material?</u>

Not at all, 72 (79%) Slightly, 18 Very much, 1

AVOIDING THE WASTE BASKET

Flushed by the success of this first questionnaire, we have since sent out five more, dealing with the following major topics: Why releases are discarded; front covers; press conferences; abbreviations; and, our most recent, photo captions. Although complete surveys are available to anyone wishing them, below are the main results.

Why Releases are Discarded

Do not pertain to field of interest	87.5 %
No real news value, puff	66.0

---

1. We believe most editors thought of conventional mimeographing, which tends to be slightly smudgy. There are some mimeograph machines, using two drums and a silk screen, which are capable of reproduction almost as good as offset.

Too commercial	48.2
Too many from same company	35.7
Badly written, too much rewrite	25.0
Too long	12.5
Incomplete	12.5
No illustrations	5.4
Poor illustrations	1.8
No source quoted for additional information	1.8

How Many Releases are Discarded

Percent of editors replying	Percentage of releases they throw out
24	90 or more
39	75 - 89
30	50 - 74
7	less than 50

Preferred release length

The same editors, when asked what they consider an ideal working length of a news release, replied:

Less than one page	4.2 %
One page	43.7
Two pages	20.8
Three pages	23.0
No preference indicated	8.3

Mastheads

One of our questionnaires elicited the answer that a printed, formal masthead is not necessary. By this, editors meant that a fancy, four-color, printed masthead, screaming the words "News Release" will have no effect on their selection or rejection. However, there are several basic bits of information which must be provided in the masthead of every release. Their absence immediately labels the sender as a non-professional.

First--and please don't laugh because this information <u>has</u> been omitted in some prime examples we've seen--the name of the company (or client) must be shown. Second, the company's address.

So far, so good. Next, two items which are overlooked more frequently: (a) the telephone number, and (b) the extension and name of the person who wrote (or sent) the release, or someone who can provide additional information should the editor desire it. These data are particularly vital when releases are sent out by large companies, possibly having several divisions. If you'll only visualize the royal run-around possible when you try to fight your way past the usual switchboard operator to find an "informed source," you'll see why.

Another plaint often heard from editors is that releases are not dated. You may consider this to your advantage, hoping the editor will find it "new" whenever he comes across it, but in actual fact it's likely to work the other way.

In many publishing offices, the mail-room opens all mail, and routes it, sans envelope, to the proper editor. Sometimes mail is date-stamped on receipt, more often it's not. Assuming the editor is out on a trip or the mail is mixed up or routed from one desk to another, there will then be no way of knowing how old your information actually is when it finally comes to rest. Because no editor wishes to be accused of using "old hat" material, his only safe recourse is to throw out the questionables. Therefore, be sure to include a date.

In most instances, the line "for immediate release" is adequate. As a purely personal opinion, we have always considered this a little on the presumptuous side--almost as if we were telling the editor he

must use it right now--but perhaps we're too sensitive on this point. The line isn't interpreted in this manner, it's widely used, and there really isn't any better way to say the same thing.

Sometimes the release should be dated for release on a specific date, rather than the usual "fire at will." For instance, if your company president is about to address the Rotary Club, or American Management Association, or some other well-known, important group, you may wish to prepare a release including excerpts of his speech. Obviously, the release should not be published until after his presentation, In that event, mail the release two or three days prior to the event, but incorporate a specific release date and time.

This matter of time is not greatly significant when releasing only to business publications. However, should you wish to include local and/or national newspapers, then the release time is important. It would never do to have the New York Times quote your president on the same day that he appears as the key-note speaker at an important luncheon. Timing, in that case, is a very vital factor in the success of your placements.

The next two suggestions seem painfully obvious: number all your pages, and include your company name on all pages. Similarly, if you send releases out on a fairly regular basis, develop some type of coding system, so that each may be designated by a few letters or numbers. It's much easier--in your own shop as well as during telephone conversations with others--to establish the identity of a particular release by referring to it as "BR-275," rather than having to say "the release that talks about the installation at the Buffalo plant."

There may have been several releases about the Buffalo plant. Which one? Be sure to show this code number on each page. Then there should be no way for pages to be improperly collated, misfiled, or otherwise confused. At least, theoretically.

When you come to the last page of the release, let the editor know. The designation "-30-" is rather archaic by now. Instead use one or more cross-hatches (####).

Photos

A single word--a tremendous subject. Enough, actually, for an entire speech. We'll try to crowd as much as we can into the time allowed, and will gladly answer any additional questions later on.

First of all, what makes a good photo for a technical article or release? More than anything, the composition. Editors like a photo with dramatic appeal. In fact, we've often been told that some of our articles have been used only because of the photos were good. It hurts our ego to admit it, but we know it's true. A good photo can sell the story.

Photos must meet two criteria to be acceptable. One, they must be technically perfect. Focus, lighting, exposure, development and printing must be combined to give as sharp and crisp a picture as the situation permits. Under technical perfection we would also include the absence of extraneous equipment in the background, highlighting of the machine or process that you're trying to illustrate, and a careful eye toward good housekeeping. Editors are rather critical on this point. Therefore, in planning plant photos, watch out for empty soda bottles, unswept floors, spilled liquids, carelessly scattered tools, or obvious violations of safety

rules. Common sense will tell you what has to be eliminated, although some of these may be overlooked in the haste to get the pictures taken and the men back to work. Enough minor flaws may detract so much from the final photo that it can not be used.

The second requirement for a good photo is that it tell a story. Particularly in industrial photography is this of grave importance. After all, a machine is a pretty dead thing, and a photo of a perfectly clean, brand new molding machine sitting on the floor is about as exciting as a political speech (or this one).

"Human interest" is what the editors call it. Whereever possible, include a man or woman in the photo doing something. But for heaven's sake, don't let them ham it up by smiling at the camera. They don't have to look grim as if their work were completely distasteful to them; but if they're operating an extrusion press, or filtering a chemical solution, or running a lathe, let them really look as if they were operating, filtering, or running.

If a product is small, or if only a portion of a larger unit is to be photographed, close-ups are wonderful. In that case, and if the situation permits, someone's hand alone would provide the human interest. Show the hand pouring, or fastening a screw, or pushing a button, or-and this is absolutely the last resort because it's so trite--have it point to something with a pencil. In any case, do your best to get the still-life qualities out of the photos you take.

Incidentally, in macro-photography, be certain to include some known object for size comparison. Paper clips and dimes are pretty "old hat" by now, so try to think of something new. For example, when photographing a miniature die-cast nutcracker for one of our clients, what could be more appropriate than placing it inside a peanut shell. The headline, "Nutcracker in a Nutshell" almost writes itself.

Front Covers

If your photo is particularly good, you have a chance of seeing it as a front cover. Out of 94 publications responding to another of our surveys, 78 always use a photo as front cover, 3 do sometimes, and 13 never do. It's certainly worth some extra effort to make the cover, and if you'll approach every shot with this goal in mind, you'll undoubtedly have a high batting average. Not only that, but even if the photos don't develop into a cover, they'll at least be so good that they'll make use of the story almost mandatorily.

Additional data gleaned from the front cover survey are shown below:

1. How much space does the photo occupy on the cover?

   Entire page (12) Partial page (58) Either (10)

2. Are photos black and white, or color?

   Black & White (49) Color (12)

3. If color photo, do you use Duotine, or full color?

   Duotone (10) Full color (16)

4. If full color, do you prefer print or transparency?

   Print (6) Transparency (14) Either (4)

5. What size should prints or transparencies be?

	Black & White	Color	Transparency
Preferred	8x10	8x10	8x10
Minimum	4x5	4x5	35 mm

6. How much personnel should be included in photo?

   One (7) A few (14) A lot (0) As situation requires (62)

7. Do you accept cover photos from publicity departments or agencies?

   Yes (70) No (3) Depends (5)

8. Is product identification permitted, if reasonable?

   Yes (56) No (21) Depends (5)

9. Must cover photo tie in with feature story inside publication?

   Yes (46) No (27) Depends (8)

10. Is explanatory paragraph concerning cover featured in publication?

    Yes (60) No (12) Sometimes (3)

A word of explanation about question 8. Note the stress on the phrase "if reasonable." We once worked for a manufacturer of welding rods, where no photo was considered good unless a box of the welding rods, bearing company name and a photo of the company president, was prominently displayed. Yes, that's right. Every photo. Needless to say, not many of them were printed, though we could never convince the company's president of the validity of our explanation.

Learn, if you can, from this classic error. Show the company name if you must. But be polite about it. It does not have to be in the foreground, nor does it have to be turned full-face to the camera. Innocuously displayed in the background, your chances of seeing the exemplary box of welding rods in print are much enhanced. Even so, don't include your commercial in every photo. Permit the editor a choice, and don't bludgeon him into submission.

Retouching

Sometimes, despite your best efforts, the finished photo will not be all you had hoped for. One of those omnipresent soft drink bottles did creep into the picture, or the operator is smoking a chewed-up stogey which the photographer hadn't noticed, or some other problem suddenly shows up. Your quickest way out is a good retoucher. But make sure he really is good, because some are so heavy-handed that the retouching is apparent to six-year olds.

Editors are quite specific as to the type of retouching they'll allow. Anything done to make the product look a lot better than it really is, no. Anything to improve housekeeping, eliminate unnecessary detail or poor backgrounds, or a general clean-up, all right. Their answers to the question, "How much retouching do you consider permissible?", were as follows:

Highlights (38) Separation (37) Removal of oil spots, etc. (47) Accentuating item (26) Removal of burrs, etc. (34)

CAPTIONS

Every photo you send to an editor should have a proper caption. This is particularly true for feature articles, where you would expect to supply about half a dozen different shots from which the editor may make a suitable selection. The only permissible exception is in the case of a new product release, where, in effect, the entire release is a caption for the accompanying photo. Even so, it is better to include a caption, certainly at least a code number of the photo to identify it in case it is separated en route.

By and large, editors want persons shown in photos identified by name, title, and company affiliation. On the question of arrows in the photos, most editors do not like them, or if they do permit use of arrows, they want to have them shown in grease pencil, or on an overlay. In other words, let the publication's art department insert arrows, if the editor considers them necessary. Once arrows are made part of the print itself, the editor no longer has the choice of leaving them out.

Press Conferences

Press conferences can either make or ruin your company's friendship with trade press and business editors. Use them intelligently.

Unless you really have something to say that can't be covered by a news release or a more complete press kit, don't waste your money, and the editors' time, on a press conference.

In one of our surveys, devoted to press conferences, five key points stood out clearly:

1. Carefully select the time and date of a press conference.

2. Don't be concerned about the distance an editor must travel to attend.

3. Don't try to do too much.

4. Arrange things for the editor's convenience.

5. Consider the value of a tour of your facilities.

Purpose

Almost to a man, editors agreed that a press conference is valueless unless you are certain to accomplish more than you might with the conventional release. Promotion of a company officer is not enough reason for a busy editor to travel 3000 miles to your plant; nor is a minor change in a machine which has been available for 15 years.

But if you are introducing a really new product which will be of vital interest to the readers of many publications, and if it would take too many pages of writing to explain all the possible story angles, then consider a press conference.

Despite the demand for something of real value from a press conference, editors commonly agree that press conferences are sometimes useful for background information. One manufacturer has a conference once every two or three years for this purpose.

Here's a thought to remember: a poorly conceived conference will do more harm than good if those who attend go away with the feeling that the expense in time and money did not contribute to the content of their publication or to their knowledge.

According to the survey results, the best time to hold a press conference is the second Tuesday of the month, starting in the morning and ending with luncheon.

If Tuesday is not suitable, Wednesday or Thursday ran a close second choice. In any event, don't plan for Monday or Friday. Only one third the number of editors who replied thought these were good days for such an affair.

If the second week of the month is not feasible, pick any other. There isn't much choice between the first, third, or fourth week; all of them lagged about 30% behind in popularity.

It is commonly believed that editors prefer to attend only those conferences close to home. However, out of 93 replies, 55 editors said they would travel more than 100 miles, whereas only 17 confined their activities to city limits.

Analysis shows that half a day is about all most editors would like to spend at a press conference. In fact, answers to the question on how long a press conference they can afford to attend indicated that half the respondents considered one to two hours sufficient for most purposes. Twenty-four editors thought half a day was justifiable, and only 13 were willing to spend the day.

Though long speeches are definitely undesirable, editors will sit still for a knowledgeable technical man who knows how to make his subject come alive. A rule of thumb suggested by T. W. Black, The Tool Engineer, was this: "Oratory and introduction, 45 seconds; technical discussion by a qualified expert, 20 minutes; question and answer session, as long as questions are being asked."

Remember that the editor is your guest; be helpful and do all you can do to make him comfortable. This does not necessarily mean the most lavish (and time-consuming) luncheon you can think of--a point made specifically by several editors.

One way to help is to provide the press kit before you start the formal program. Seventy per cent of the editors surveyed said they prefer it this way; it gives them a chance to bone up on the material, get ready for the questioning session. (Obviously, don't have the speaker read the material in the kit. That's a pointless waste of effort.)

Another major help is the presence of a photographer, strictly at the disposal of the editors who might wish to avail themselves of his services. No matter how good your planned photos, each editor will have his own ideas of how best to present the equipment to his readers. Help him.

Although some editors were rather strongly against plant tours, the majority (71 to 19) favored them. T. W. Black of The Tool Engineer made several suggestions: "For a plant tour, figure two hours at the most (some editors have fallen arches). Have editors go through in small groups, each with a qualified guide. Make sure the supply of safety glasses (where needed) is ample. Have a briefing session before the tour, using a comprehensive plant layout or three-dimensional model. Then the tour itself will make some sense."

Do's and Don't-s for Press Conferences

Send invitations early, as much as a month ahead of the planned conference. Follow up with one or two suitably timed reminders.

Avoid conflicts with trade shows and large conventions.

Start on time, and stick strictly to the announced schedule.

Rehearse your program. Make sure everyone knows what he's supposed to do. Have plenty of pencils, paper, ashtrays handy.

Provide badges. Use different colors for press and company personnel.

Have enough technically-informed personnel mix with the guests. Don't let staff people bunch up at one table, or talk only to each other.

Provide a complete press kit, which answers all key questions and includes a workable selection of photos, charts, diagrams, other illustrative material, and company literature.

Offer a small gift, if you wish, preferably one which has an appropriate tie-in with the product.

Above all, be a considerate host. Accede to editorial requests quickly, and make sure their needs are met.

RESULTS

"What's in it for me" might well be the question of any client, or the front office when reviewing the cost of a technical publicity program. What return may we expect for our investment?

There are several benefits that accrue from a well-planned, continuous publicity program. Among them are the following:

1. Repeated appearances of your company's name in the trade press help to familiarize the reader still further with your organization, its products, its service facilities, particularly its technical competence and experience.

2. Articles under the by-line of the company executive or engineer enhance his reputation, and help to establish him as a person of authority in the industry.

3. Industrial publicity cements relations with current customers, who will be called upon to supply the experience data needed for case-history articles.

4. New uses are found for your products or services because the reader of a technical article tries to adapt the advantages described to his own particular problems.

5. Publicity lowers sales resistance. Articles are good talking points when your representative calls; they help to show that you disseminate all available data which might prove of benefit to your client or customer.

6. Publicity in the trade press attracts capable engineers and technical personnal. Prospective staff members are more likely to accept a position if they feel that they know the company and its policies; that, in turn, the company is known and respected in its field.

Total results will vary considerably with the type of product or service being publicized, the time devoted to this effort, the amount of actual working data that can be made available with each case-history, number of competitors making the same or similar item and extent of their publicity activity, general interest in the particular topic at the moment, and the skill of the publicity man. Given a normal situation--if such there be--it should be possible to prepare and place a completely illustrated feature article every month. As an alternate, if product releases are desired more than feature articles, one or two of these (different types) should be mailed every other week. Ideally, of course, you combine both activities. You then have a first-class publicity program going, combining both prestige items (articles) with quick salesgetters (product releases). At this pace, potential customers should be unable to pick up any technical publication without reading something about your company or client.

A Neglected Form of Technical Communication— The New Product Release

HAROLD K. MINTZ

Abstract—The engineer may be called upon to write product announcements for his company and although in some cases he may have available professional public relations advice, in other cases he must proceed virtually alone. This paper briefly describes the type of content, style, and format of such announcements that trade journal editors are most likely to publish, and touches on some widely used company procedures established to ensure that legal and proprietary considerations are not neglected.

PRODUCT announcements in technical and business journals are part of the family of technical communications, although they often are treated as stepchildren. An engineer's touch, or an engineering concept is frequently necessary to ensure the adequacy of such communications. It becomes obvious that new product announcements, or "releases," are poorly done when almost two-thirds of more than 1200 releases submitted to 14 magazines were either rejected outright or accepted by only one magazine.[1] Those that do get published result, on a page for page basis, in more inquiries than display advertising.

The engineer may find himself teamed up with advertising, marketing, and public relations specialists in the production of product announcements, or he may find that his company has no such specialists and that he is expected to fill in for all of them. This paper presents information for such an engineer on the contents, style, and format of releases that editors are most likely to publish.

DISTINCTIONS BETWEEN ADVERTISING AND PUBLICITY

The distinctions between advertising and publicity are crucial to an understanding of this discussion. Advertising space is purchased, and therefore one can say *what* he wants *when* he wants and in the magazine he selects. There is no charge for publicity, and therefore the originator does not control *what* will be said in print or *when*.

Feature articles and new product releases, the major written media of publicity, differ in length and distribution. Where most feature articles run between 1500 and 3000 words, releases usually highlight a new product in 250 to 500 words. Articles are prepared for one magazine (if prepared for more than one, the magazines should be noncompetitive); releases, on the other hand, are designed for all magazines (competitive and noncompetitive) that may be interested. Occasionally, even wire services (Associated Press and United Press International) run releases on products that have a wide popular appeal.

Since most magazines do not publish releases on ad- vertised products, a guideline worth following is to distribute such releases before advertising is placed. This approach is probably the most cost-effective way to get the broadest possible customer exposure.

To find the names of receptive magazines, see N. W. Ayer. and Son's *Directory of Newspapers and Periodicals*. The section entitled "Trade, Technical, and Class Publications" lists publications with state, regional, and national circulations.

CONTENTS OF AN EFFECTIVE NEW PRODUCT RELEASE

By the time a new product is ready to be unveiled, the engineer should know better than anyone else its functioning, performance factors (should these be shown by graphs?), applications, and user benefits. From his studies and consultation with marketing specialists, he should know how the product compares with competition.

The engineer can stress the high level of design and the quality assurance tests which confirmed it. He should remember to specify, when of significant interest:

1) the dimensions, weight, volume, portability, (and relative improvement in these characteristics);
2) the materials, components, maintainability, operating or functional limits (and any relative improvements);
3) conformance to military, federal, or ASA specs;
4) requirements for government approval (such as an FCC license);
5) a reasonable warranty (in conjunction, of course, with the marketing and legal departments).

Product release copy should be restricted to one or two typewritten pages. If all the essential information cannot be reduced to fit, another page entitled "spec sheet" or "supplementary information" may be included.

Since trade magazine editors may not always know when a new product represents an advance or an authentic breakthrough, state the facts without window dressing. Be wary of the words "new," "unique," "revolutionary," and "breakthrough" unless the product justifies such terms—and few products do. Explain why the product is an advance. Some sales pitch is acceptable, but don't try to "snow" the editors with puffery; if you try, they will most likely "file" your release in a wastebasket. And the fact is that most releases meet that fate either because they are mere frosting on the cake or because the companies concerned use a fly-by-night, con man approach.

The succinct, factual information for a product release should be initiated by the design or production engineer directly concerned. Usually, however, he will find that it is reviewed and modified for communications efficiency and conformance to company policy, related to photographs or

Manuscript received February 3, 1969.
The author is with the RCA Airborne Systems Division, Burlington, Mass.
[1] *Ind. Marketing*, pp. 70–72, February 1967.

Reprinted from *IEEE Trans. Eng. Writing Speech*, vol. EWS-12, pp. 69–70, Oct. 1969.

194

drawings (or supplemented by them), and prepared in the format acceptable to the recipient journals by the advertising–marketing–public relations specialists or their engineering stand-in. Signed approval from the responsible management official is advisable before the material is released, but after the originating engineer has checked both the text and the artwork to ensure engineering accuracy and relevance. Many companies require a signed "release" from any person shown in a photo. Verify that such requirements have been met if you have major responsibility for new-product publicity.

ILLUSTRATIONS

Given two identical new product releases, one with dramatic, informative illustrations and the other without, a magazine editor is much more likely to publish the illustrated release.

Include sharp, black-and-white, 8-by-10 glossy photographs (if color photos are available, say so) that tell a story. If an indication of product size is advisable, show a familiar object of standard size in the illustration: a pencil, a key, or a hand. Avoid trite, cliche-type photos of an engineer smiling self-consciously at the product. For a very large product, consider using a close-up highlighting its outstanding features.

The cabinet illustrated in Fig. 1 could be 4 inches or 4 feet in height. If this were photographed on a bench top with a meter or knob lying beside it, the size would be implied to within a small tolerance. Fig. 2 shows the cabinet equipped with meters and knobs, which indicates a cabinet height of close to 12 inches.

Since most industrial magazines use photos on their front covers, an unusual, dramatic photo may "make" the cover. Such publicity is worth many advertising dollars to your company. But even if your photo does not rate cover treatment, the editor may run it to buttress the text in the magazine's new product section. And a photo there may well convert some readers into customers—the chief objective of publicity.

Caption and number all photos (indicate the top if ambiguity exists), refer to them in the text, and identify any persons in them as well as the company name and address. Type this information on paper that you *paste on the back* of each photo. Do not write on the backs of photos; the embossing may appear on the printed illustration. Insert a cardboard stiffener in the mailing envelope and mark on the envelope face: PHOTOGRAPH, DO NOT FOLD OR BEND!

WRITING STYLE

A straightforward, unadorned style is preferred by most industrial magazine editors. Avoid inverted sentence structure, unfamiliar abbreviations, jargon, and marathon sentences and paragraphs. In the first paragraph, the most important one in a product release, the outstanding customer advantages of the product should be summarized. The remaining discussion should supply key pertinent information.

Fig. 1.

Fig. 2.

Suitable similes or comparisons are always good to use for explaining operations, concepts, and size. For example, if you state that a plane carries 18 000 gallons of fuel, you might add "enough gasoline to power your car for the next 20 years."

Include, directly on the release, the name and address of the initiating company, the telephone number (including the area code), and the TWX number if your company has one. Also, name the person to be contacted if a magazine editor wants more information.

All copies should be clear and legible. An electric typewriter produces the best master copy; reproduction by automatic typewriters (to make each release look like an original) should be considered.

HOW TO MAKE A BOOK THAT SELLS
The Fastest Growing Medium
In Industrial Marketing:

THE
MAIL
ORDER
CATALOG

by Herbert G. Ahrend

A major revolution is taking place in industrial marketing, albeit with a minimum of publicity.

Products as varied as $1,390 precision lathe bed optical benches and $925 point diffraction interferometers, visual control boards, $795 electronic cash registers, office furniture, staples and electronic typewriters, even computers, are being sold through mail order catalogs, without the intervention of salesmen.

Not only small firms are involved. Xerox, NCR, Digital Equipment and IBM are just a few of the big name manufacturers now in the field. They're joining long-established business-to-business mail order catalog firms, each with hundreds of thousands of customers, such as NEBS (New England Business Service), Demco, Business and Industrial Furniture, and Caddylak Systems.

Clearly, mail order catalog selling to business and industry has come of age.

"It is essential to find marketing techniques which are less expensive than a personal call ... The cost of a sales call is up 33% from 1978 to 1981," says Chuck Francis, director of advertising at IBM, explaining one of the main reasons for the phenomenal growth of business-to-business mail order sales.

With the cost of an average industrial sales call at $137.02, and 4.3 calls needed to close the average industrial sale, it cost $589.18 to close that sale in 1980, according to McGraw-Hill. Those figures probably are much lower than current costs. It's no wonder that alert industrial firms are turning to catalogs to reduce sales expense and to insure repeat business.

Many firms find that their mail order catalog rapidly becomes a major profit center, permitting them not only to increase the number of their active customers, but also to broaden the lines of products they sell.

Others have been disappointed in the results achieved by their catalogs

Herbert G. Ahrend is president of Ahrend Associates, New York.

—poor results which in many cases could have been predicted.

KEY FACTORS TO SUCCESS

Let's examine some of the factors which create success or failure in the specialized catalog field.
● It is essential that your marketing posture be determined clearly, even before merchandise is selected.

Are you aiming for overall market leadership or at a particular segment of the market? Top of the line, or the low-price buyer? The sophisticated executive, or the person first investigating your type of equipment? The firm with 30,000 employes, 300, or 3?
● Although there are exceptions, it is wise to direct your catalog to a carefully selected, limited audience.

Issue different editions for different lines of business you serve. The difference in the book may be as slight as changing the black plate to include the name of the prospects' industry on the cover and key inside pages, or it may extend to merchandise selection and even terminology. It is particularly important to use the vocabulary of the industry which you are addressing.
● Regular industrial catalogs are *informational*, but mail order catalogs are *selling machines*.

They must not only inform, but also convince and bring about sales action. Every square inch must carry its weight in sales. The industrial mail order catalog writer and designer cannot afford the luxury—so often indulged in by industrial publication ad creators—of devoting two-thirds of available space to art or photos of possibly doubtful relevance.
● Your catalog must be user-oriented,

not product-oriented.

Give all the data the potential buyer needs to make sure your product meets his requirements, told in terms he understands.
● The catalog must also take advantage of every appropriate technique possible to encourage the prospect to place an initial order—from special offers (with a reasonable cut-off date) and bonuses to increase order size, to the use of 24-hour "800" telephone services.
● In striving for that first order, never neglect to promote your "best sellers."

They will often be your best door openers. Promote them hard; give them prominence of place; make joint offers with items with which they are used.

And if they fall into the category of supplies that are used up, encourage repeat business by giving special rates, bonuses, or other benefits for ordering regular shipments on either a fixed term or a "t.f." ('til forbid) plan.
● Catalog copy must be clear, leaving no room for uncertainty.

Terms such as "large size," "extra length," or "superstrength" (all taken from current industrial mail order catalogs) should be avoided.
● Every word must serve a vital function.

There is no room in a selling catalog for pointless puffery. But be sure you have included all essential statistics, not only as to the size, capacity, durability and other features of the product, but also as to its function. If, for instance, your catalog includes similar supplies of different sizes to fit different makes and models of machines, or for which the standards vary in different industries, be sure you indicate clearly the exact uses of each size or type.
● Bear in mind at all times that you are writing to human beings, or, even better, to *a* human being.

Getting in all the facts will not create a selling catalog if they are presented in a dry-as-dust manner. The human being who is your prospect for industrial goods is the same man or woman who probably regularly purchases, by mail, a wide variety of merchandise from magazines to garden equipment, from coins and collectibles to cheese and clothing. His choice of mail order suppliers, in every instance, is influenced by the tone in which he is addressed.

● Build confidence in your firm and products in appropriate ways.

The industrial catalog house faces one major hurdle which the consumer goods supplier avoids. With consumer goods, the worst that the potential buyer must contemplate before reaching a decision is possible dissatisfaction. In the industrial case, however, the question often arises, "Am I putting my job, or future advancement, on the line by purchasing from these people, instead of from the usual source?"

It's vital, therefore, for you to build confidence with the style of writing and design, and ironclad guarantees of satisfaction or money back. Don't give that fear a chance to arise to ruin the sale.

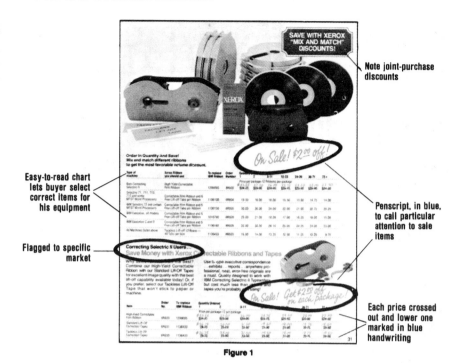

Figure 1

Note joint-purchase discounts

Easy-to-read chart lets buyer select correct items for his equipment

Penscript, in blue, to call particular attention to sale items

Flagged to specific market

Each price crossed out and lower one marked in blue handwriting

COPY DO'S AND DON'TS

● Build a benefit into every headline. Headlines should reach out to qualified readers, those able to buy your product. Don't aim at cuteness or try to catch everyone's eye. Don't overuse your trademark or company name in headlines.

● Know your products and their manifold uses. Explain fully differences in use, quality, durability, etc., of seemingly similar items. Don't scatter superlatives throughout the book; avoid such terms as "extra-long".

● Stress key features which are of interest and value to your prospects. Those may differ for each prospect group such as CEO's, purchasing agents, and plant managers, or for various industries which may use your product for different purposes.

● Talk specific user benefits, emphasizing those which are most important to the group addressed. If your widget saves money for the user, state precisely how and to what degree. Don't generalize or say "You save 8 ways" unless you can prove it clearly.

● Make your explanations understandable to non-technical persons whenever possible. Don't use "private language" your customers may not recognize.

● Call your catalog "Fall-Winter 1982-3", or a similar time span, even if you intend to issue another within that time. Make clear the time limits within which price quotations will remain valid.

● Be sure to tell all; don't leave the prospect wondering if your product will do.

FORMAT AND DESIGN

● Provide an easy-to-use, selling index to make it simple for prospects to locate what they need.

Use symbols for different types of products. Provide adequate cross-references.

● Group products by usage wherever appropriate. Don't drop products in at random.

● Make it easy to order. If you use an 800 number, build it up.

● Always include at least two order forms.

● Put specials and "hot" items on, near and facing the order forms.

● Make your cover as dramatic as possible, but not at the expense of hiding what it is you're selling.

Show your products in use by believable people, not obviously professional models.

● Use a paper stock which will stand up in the mails. If it's a multi-page book, consider that a separate, heavier cover may allow using lighter-weight inside stock with resultant postal savings, at the same time permitting a change of cover design on a re-mailing without remaking large plates.

● Don't hide your catalog in an envelope or wrapper. (There may be exceptions for certain personalized wraparounds to special groups such as inactives.)

● Clearly identify those items which are "in-stock for immediate shipment," if some are not.

● Flag plainly the types of products on each page.

● Strive for clarity of presentation, not for "prettiness" *per se*.

● Use easy-to-read typefaces and a body type with sufficiently large point size. Remember, many potential customers are past 40 and don't like to read fine print.

● Avoid surprints against dark backgrounds. Shun reverse type, white on black, for body copy. Especially avoid reversing type against color. Registration problems in the four-color process can make copy totally illegible.

● Make all tables as open, clean, and uncluttered as possible.

● Use sunbursts, arrows, imitation handwriting in blue, or other attention-getting techniques to flag specials.

● Call attention to vital or unique features of major products with "callouts," such as those used by the marketer whose catalog page appears in Figure 1.

Those suggestions are offered as guidelines, not as absolutes. Mail order techniques are not universal in their effect. Some firms have found the way to success by ideosyncratic approaches.

In general, however, any industrial firm engaging in direct response selling for the first time would be well advised to heed those proposals and warnings. ■

BUSINESS PUBLICATIONS

A medium whose time has come . . . again!

by Allan Goldenberg

If your image of trade or, more broadly, business-to-business advertising is that it all looks like catalogue pages or garage calendars, you could be surprised. Today, Canadian business press advertising and editorial are looking better, sounding better and communicating better than ever before.

Unlike descriptions which were used just a few years ago, a recent special report on the business press called it:

"More voluminous, diversified, creative, specialized, political, sexy, experimental, technical, socially significant, and profitable than you thought it was . . ."

Why? Money is one answer. Dollars invested in business publications in 1981 totalled $113 million. Add another $30 million

Allan Goldenberg is President & Chief Executive Officer, Canadian Business Press.

for corporate advertising (a lot of which is business-to-business advertising), and pretty soon you are talking about "big bucks"!

Perhaps most important, however, is how the people creating the advertising, those writing the editorial copy and the people reading and being influenced by the business press have changed. Statistics Canada has reported that in 1961, just under 12 percent of Canada's population had been educated at a level beyond high school. Twenty years later, in 1980, that number approached 30 percent.

And further, according to **AD-WEEK** (May 1981): "On the other side of the desk, purchasing agents once characterized as guys with a green eyeshade and a sharp pencil, learned through a time of shortages to be purchasing men for all seasons — and they're not always men anymore". Business press advertising and editorial content are both changing from blue collar to white collar, because the people who buy and sell are better educated and demand better information, presented more intelligently.

A recent study conducted of Canadian Business Press members, showed that that group alone accounted for almost 36,000 pages of advertising in 1980. That's a lot of advertising. More advertising than one person could look at, let alone read, in a year.

Now, it's true that much of what is included in business publication advertising is of interest only to professionals in a particular field. And this obscurity often creates the impression that what is going on is dull. But that is seldom so.

The vitality of the periodicals market makes it a difficult one to do a superficial analysis of or to predict with "crystal ball" efficiency the potential growth and development in the coming year.

However, given the current competition in the rugged marketplace — or the current rugged competition in the marketplace — the scope and effectiveness of business publications and proof that advertising in business and professional publications is a sound investment must be made here.

There are 588 periodicals with a total circulation per issue of 7,345,848 in the publishing category known as the business press in Canada. Each is directed to a specific sector of business, industry, commerce and the professions. Their function is to assist decision makers in reaching right decisions. To do this they report and exhort — reporting on trends and developments, on new techniques and new products, on successes in problem-solving; and exhorting governments and industry policy-setters to create the conditions under which everyone can prosper. For the corner merchant or the nation-wide corporation, the name of the game is profit, and profit is what the business press is all about. All advertisers want to increase market share, decrease selling costs and increase profits. The UNIQUE selling proposition of the business press is geared to achieve these objectives through its circulation characteristics, research initiatives, and its editorial quality.

Dozens of individuals are involved in almost every industrial or business purchasing decision. The numbers vary with different

Reprinted with permission from *Sales and Marketing Management in Canada*, vol. 23, no. 1, pp. 22 and 23, Jan.–Feb. 1982.
Copyright © 1982 by Ingmar Communications Ltd.

purchases and so does the degree of influence. But ALL of them are critical when you want to sell your products and services. You must have contact with them, have them on your side, when purchases or quotes are being considered.

These "influential" people are critical to any sales success. They *receive* business publications — and read them! In fact, recent readership studies have shown that a large majority (72 percent) read three out of four issues of those received and spend over one hour reading these issues, and not only the editorial content! The same study showed that 68 percent of those business press readers read the advertising — intentionally! They read those advertising messages containing useful, practical information that helps them do their jobs more profitably or easily.

It's difficult to ascertain exactly *who* has what degree of buying influence. They aren't always

obvious, and many are unknown, or cannot be reached, by a sales force. In most markets, sales forces reach only one-quarter of the buying influences, and for business publications, circulation quality is as important as circulation size. Identifying these "influential readers" is an important part of business press research — and it's an ongoing process with lists continually being updated and revised. The combination of the sales force and the market coverage through business paper advertising produces consistent contact with 60 percent of the buying influences. The selling/advertising combination provides a dramatic opportunity to "influence and sell", and to gain a distinct competitive edge over companies that invest their marketing dollars in a sales force alone.

Canadian Business Press member publishers' circulation records are also required to meet the discipline of an **external** audit so that the integrity, quality and

reliability of the circulation of these highly specialized and targeted books are verified when use is made of *audited* business publications.

The unique ability of business publications to maximize coverage among "the influentials" or prospects and not just an "audience" as in the consumer publication sector, (an audience is **not** a market!), positions the business press as the most effective and economical medium in the marketplace.

The effectiveness of business press advertising is indisputable — but ... at what cost? Here lies the real beauty of business press advertising, for not only is it highly effective — it's economical.

Recent Canadian Business Press analysis revealed that the average cost of reaching a single potential purchaser via the business press is approximately 11-1/2 cents. That's compared to $3.50 for a phone call; 30 cents (just for the stamp!) through direct mail and $160 for a personal industrial sales call. Hundreds of research studies prove that advertising in business and professional publications is a sound investment. It produces measurable returns: *more sales volume and reduced sales costs*.

To reach and influence specialized business, technical, merchandising, agricultural or professional markets, there is simply no other medium that even comes close — in cost or effectiveness — to the business press.

Oh yes, my crystal ball gaze for the future! "The business press will continue to be an economical means of quick and effective dissemination of essential information".

Biased? — You Bet!!! ❧

New journals tell the local business story

Cities across the U. S. are suddenly being inundated by local business publications. This month alone two brand-new weeklies—*Pittsburgh Business Journal* and *Pittsburgh Business Times*—will be hitting the newsstands in the nation's steel capital. They arrive on the heels of yet another business journal, the monthly *Executive Report*, which made its debut in Pittsburgh just five months ago. And the Association of Area Business Publications, which began three years ago with 15 members, now boasts

Journalist Gray: From a backyard startup to four weeklies and a merger with Scripps.

a roll of 53 publications. "Everybody and his brother is trying to get into this business," says President C. Robertson Trowbridge, who predicts that by 1983 the association will have 100 members.

Business has been the big national news story ever since the Arab oil embargo of the early 1970s and the subsequent quadrupling of energy prices. Now regional publishers are capitalizing on heightened interest in local economic and financial coverage. George H. Walker III, president of Stifel, Nicolaus & Co., a St. Louis-based brokerage, believes that the city's new weekly, *St. Louis Business Journal*, "fills a void of cover-

age the daily papers ignore—namely, smaller companies." Erwin E. Coleman, president of New York Business Publications Inc., which owns three business monthlies, adds that one reason the local approach works is that business communities are close-knit. "Business people want to read about their neighbors, their peers, and the people they're doing business with," he says.

The most aggressive company in this market is E. W. Scripps Co.'s Cordovan Corp. Cordovan itself was started by Bob Gray, a former newspaper reporter who began publishing *Horseman Magazine* out of his Houston garage in 1959. Gray launched *Houston Business Journal* in 1971 and added three more business publications before merging with Scripps last year. "The only way we could get into other markets in a hurry was to merge with someone with financial clout," he explains. Since the merger, Cordovan, aided by seed money from Scripps, has started a paper every three months, and its 10 business weeklies have a combined circulation of 118,000. These Cordovan publications had a total of nearly 3,000 advertising pages in 1980, a 60% jump from 1979.

So far only three of the weeklies—*Houston Business Journal*, *Atlanta Chronicle*, and *Dallas/Fort Worth Business*—are profitable. "Our concept has been to take all profits and plug them back into new startups," says Scripps's president, Edward W. Estlow.

Inexpensive to launch. Scripps's toughest challenger is longtime publisher Crain Communications Inc., which puts out *Advertising Age* and several other trade magazines. *Crain's Chicago Business* started three years ago with an investment of $3 million. Last year the magazine chalked up 849.3 pages of advertising, 70% more than in 1979. This year circulation stands at 40,000, and with revenues expected to reach $4.5 million, the publication is making a profit. "That's a pretty good move into the black in just three years," boasts Crain's president, Rance Crain, who says the company will launch another business weekly in a new market next year. Although he will not say where, industry sources believe Crain is planning a paper for Detroit.

The success of publications such as *Crain's Chicago Business*, together with the relatively low startup costs for new journals, has attracted an increasing number of entrepreneurs. John Burkhart, a retired insurance company chairman who is the co-owner of business weeklies in St. Louis, Indianapolis, and Pittsburgh, says that startup costs run from $1 million to $2 million. Capital expenditures amount to no more than $500,000, including the cost of the computer equipment that produces print-ready pages. The biggest expense is for staff, which typically is small.

One entrepreneur, Paul L. Parshall, previously a salesman for Litton Industries Inc., started his Parex Co. with a $2,000 investment. The Ohio company now publishes business monthlies in Columbus and Cincinnati with a combined circulation of 18,000, and Parshall says they will bring in advertising revenues exceeding $340,000 this year.

All types. While a handful of these publications—such as Riverview Publication

Regional papers spring up to exploit the interest in economics and finance

Inc.'s *Executive Report* in Pittsburgh—are full-color magazines, the majority are black-and-white tabloid newspapers. Editorial philosophies vary. Some coverage has been criticized as puffery, but a number of business papers have been lauded for in-depth reporting. *St. Louis Business Journal*, for example, is credited with some of the best stories on Apex Oil Co., a privately held, publicity-shy St. Louis company with yearly revenues of $8 billion. And a Houston banking executive praises the *Houston Business Journal*. "It's a good source, probably the best source, for a lot of basic information about all the local companies," he says.

Although these papers receive some of their revenues from circulation—subscribers normally pay 50¢ an issue or about $26 per year—most money comes from advertising. Local business publications are receiving $1,000 or more for a full-page black-and-white advertisement, compared with roughly $400 for ads in consumer-oriented suburban weeklies.

These rates are still well below those charged by daily metropolitan newspapers, and apparently the buy is attractive. Nine of the 11 city, state, or regional publications whose advertising volumes are tracked by *Advertising Age* reported

1981 first-half increases in total ad pages: Cordovan's *Dallas/Fort Worth Business* led the group with a 43% gain, while *Crain's Chicago Business* showed a 38% jump. By contrast, advertising volume in several national business publications has declined.

Even more first editions. The majority of advertisers are companies that offer services and products to businesses. Cordovan, for instance, counts among its advertisers such national names as Delta Air Lines, American Airlines, Sheraton, and Avis. American Airlines Inc., which is ballyhooing its expanded air freight service, went to the local business journals because they provide market penetration in "a cost-efficient manner," says Willard J. Dreslin, an advertising executive for the airline. Cordovan now offers combined rates for ads that run in more than one of its weeklies.

The success of these regional publications in both attracting advertisers and gaining readers has triggered some maneuvering by local general-interest newspapers. The Cleveland *Plain Dealer* reacted to the arrival of *Crain's Cleveland Business* last year by increasing its coverage of business news. Other newspapers have adopted the tabloid format. Last year, one month before Cordovan started its *Miami Business Journal*, Knight-Ridder Newspapers Inc.'s Miami *Herald* launched a weekly business tabloid supplement called *Business Mon-*

The newcomers prompt some old-line newspapers to widen their coverage

day. The section has attracted enough advertising to average 36 pages, and its peak has been 52. "It has surpassed our expectations," says Beverly R. Carter, the *Herald*'s general manager.

Richard M. Scaife, publisher, Tribune-Review Publishing Co. in Greensburg, Pa., has taken a slightly different tack. He not only distributes his *Pennsylvania Economy*—a monthly statewide business-news tabloid—to the 80,000 readers of his *Sunday Tribune-Review*, but he also sells the section as a supplement to other newspapers for $6.50 per thousand. In August, 16 newspapers took *Economy*, giving it a statewide circulation of 500,000.

Neither the expansion of business coverage in local newspapers nor the current lead by Cordovan has discouraged other publishers. Burkhart and Mark B. Vittert, a St. Louis entrepreneur, for instance, still launched *Pittsburgh Business Times*. "We hope to be adding anywhere from two to three weeklies a year," says Burkhart. Adds Vittert: "We're going to shoot it out with Cordovan all over the country. You can call Pittsburgh the O. K. corral." ∎

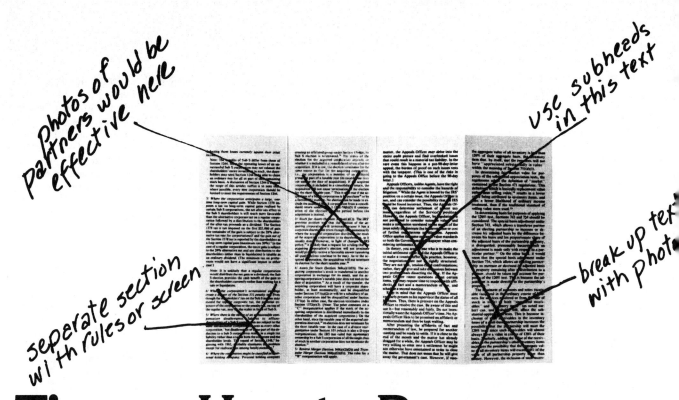

photos of partners would be effective here

seperate section with rules or screen

use subheads in this text

break up text with photos

Tips on How to Prepare an Effective Firm Brochure

by Ted Eisenberg

Although firm brochures have become an indispensable marketing tool, many accounting firms still do not have one or use an ineffective brochure. Here are some pointers on how to prepare a firm brochure that can be a powerful catalyst to practice development.

Despite the growing competition for clients, many accounting firms are failing to take advantage of the marketing clout of a firm brochure. Either they do not have a brochure or they use a brochure that is inadequate for the job. (A good brochure should distinguish a firm in a way that invites further consideration by prospective clients; yet, most brochures seem *alike.)*

This article will suggest how to produce a brochure that works and how much it might cost.

CONSIDER THE PROSPECT'S PERSPECTIVE

A firm brochure is, in effect, an expensive, illustrated calling card. It offers a unique opportunity to put into a prospective client's hands an impressive presentation of the firm. (Yet, many firm brochures are *not* impressive because they fail to consider the potential client's perspective.)

Potential clients want to get a basic picture of

your firm and the services it provides. They want to know such things as:
- The firm's reputation,
- The quality of its service,
- The qualifications of its people,
- The range of services,
- The size of its office,
- The industries in which it specializes,
- The names of some clients, and
- How well it meets deadlines.

Prospective clients are *not* particularly interested in a firm's history or philosophy. (Yet, many brochures start with the saga of the firm's dynamic growth and the philosophy.) You should use the opening pages of the brochure to

TED EISENBERG heads a New York City marketing communications firm, Ted Eisenberg Associates, that specializes in brochures for professional firms.

Reprinted with permission from *The Practical Accountant,* vol. 15, pp. 29–32, June 1982.
Copyright © 1982, by the Institute for Continuing Professional Development, Inc.

make the *first,* and usually the *strongest,* impression on the reader. These pages should pique the reader's interest and provide information about the firm that is clearly relevant *to the reader.* The brochure should be written *for the reader.*

> EXAMPLE: Summarizing a few specific problems your firm has solved for clients will go a long way toward catching the interest of your prospect. This is also an effective way of communicating the firm's benefits. By including the essential information your prospects are looking for, you will stimulate their interest in your firm.

Consideration of a prospect's needs extends beyond the *contents* of the brochure; it also involves how the material is *presented.* Prospects usually are pressed for time and are anxious for a quick picture of your firm to help them determine whether it is worth further serious consideration. Most prospects are not likely to read your entire brochure. They will flip through it in a few minutes. Therefore, it is best to have few, if any, long blocks of text. Keep in mind that a brochure is a *visual* presentation, a marriage of graphics and words that should balance each other and work together. Headlines and graphics, pictures and captions, and the use of subheads should all catch the eye and spark reader interest.

TELL YOUR STORY

Once you have presented what potential clients want to know, you can tell the story of your firm. But, here too, the emphasis should be on the story—the attitude or special services, the exceptional ability or experience—that is most likely to interest prospective clients. At the start, you want to communicate the single most important characteristic of your practice. In deciding how to do this, consider what you might say informally to an acquantance to describe your firm in one or two short sentences. This is what marketing and advertising people call a ''positioning statement''—a statement that tells your story in a way that separates you from competing firms. Again, from the perspective of the prospect, what is *different* about you? For example:
• Do you offer the same services but with more partner involvement?
• Are your firm's partners younger and more energetic or older and more experienced? Or are they a mix of both?
  • Is your practice based on specific industry expertise?
• Are your clients particularly satisfied with your firm's work and service?

• Are your auditing teams supervised to produce timely reports?

Naturally, you will want to convey more than one important characteristic in your brochure. However, in formulating your positioning state-

---

"A good brochure can be designed to do double duty."

---

ment, select only a single idea—and actually write it down. This statement will provide the theme for your brochure. And it will give you a conceptual yardstick for evaluating everything that goes into the brochure. If just one relevant and distinguishing concept about your practice registers on a prospective client as he looks through the brochure, you will have communicated effectively. You will be much more likely to do this if you can express your position on paper.

PROJECT YOUR FIRM'S PERSONALITY

Thus far we have dealt with the *information* a prospective client is looking for and the *story* you want to tell. However, distinguishing your firm from any other in the client's mind requires something more: defining and conveying your firm's *personality.*

While your firm's services and professional characteristics can be more or less matched by other firms, your firm's personality is unique. Precisely for this reason, your firm's personality can ultimately be its strongest selling point.

What exactly is a firm's personality? It is an amalgamation of the many attributes of the firm: key personalities, attitudes, goals and style. It is the impression your firm makes. In a word, it is your firm's *image.*

No two firms have the same image. While their professional abilities may be similar, the way they are perceived by clients and the ways they think and work are always different. For example, some firms center around a single dominating personality while others reflect a character derived from a variety of personalities. Also, each firm's history affects its personality. Some firms generate a more dynamic image while others are known for their dignified, traditional style. Since professional firms are selling services, and not a product, these differences usually are the crucial factors in winning engagements. Moreover, firms that are ''finalists'' in the competition for the engagement are usually statistically equal, competing on the basis of personality and nothing else.

When looking through your brochure, a prospect should be able to get a distinct sense of your firm's personality. The image you wish to convey will affect how you organize your presentation and how you use text, typeface and graphics.

> EXAMPLE: If client involvement of the partners is the key element of the firm's image, their pictures and biographies should be used in a way that signals this involvement, i.e., the photos should be informal and spontaneous-looking, perhaps including clients and/or staff members, and done in a reportage style. Placing these pictures near the front of the brochure will also contribute to the desired impression—as will their position on the page and their size and shape.

There is, of course, no "formula" for a brochure. How you prepare the brochure depends on what you want to convey. For example, if you want to emphasize that your audit team managers are the best in the business, you would take a different approach from the one you would use for emphasizing client involvement of the partners. Just how to project a firm's image is the art of communication.

Keep in mind that a good brochure will not only impress clients—because it projects an image you want to be associated with—but also recruits. Keep the recruiting function in mind as you plan your brochure, and it can easily do double duty.

PRODUCING THE BROCHURE

Your firm brochure can be prepared in-house, by an outside consultant or by a combination of both. The selection of an outside consultant is very important. Here are some pointers for making this decision:
• Since advertising agencies are mainly experienced in selling *products,* try to get a sense of their orientation to marketing *professional services.*
• Public relations and marketing communications firms are often too wordy or tilted to "interesting" but distracting graphics, since many of these people are editorially oriented.
• Consider the personal element—select someone you feel comfortable with and have confidence in. Your gut reaction here is important.

The brochure will be expensive—from $1,000 to $2,000 per page, depending on how it is produced and whether it is printed in full color. For example, 1,000 copies of an eight-page brochure, with a half dozen photographs, can cost $12,000 if printed in black and a second color and about $16,000 if printed in full-color.

The number of pages, not the number of copies printed, is the single biggest cost factor. However, this should not cause you to limit your brochure to just a few pages, since a too-short brochure of limited effectiveness may be less "cost-effective" in the long run than a brochure with the "right" number of pages. The "right" number of pages is a balance between your budget and the number of pages required to deliver your message effectively.

Incidentally, pages are counted by the number of sides, i.e., a single sheet with material printed on both sides is two pages. Four pages constitute a folder, which is a single sheet folded in half to provide front and back covers and a two-page "spread" on the inside. Six pages is also a folder—a four-page folder plus a fold-out giving two more pages. These formats might be called mini-brochures. The smallest number of pages for a brochure to feel like a "publication" is eight, which requires binding the pages together.

A full-color brochure is not always best. A brochure might be printed in one or two colors on the inside, with only the covers in full-color. For some effects, such as a very dignified look, black-and-white, perhaps with gray or tan as a second color, can be particularly elegant.

A pocket inside the back cover can be added to the brochure to hold current and other relevant material. If the brochure is 8-1/2" × 11" make the cover one-eighth inch larger in each dimension to allow the pocket to take standard size 8-1/2" × 11" sheets without sticking out. The cost of the pocket should be only a few hundred dollars.

The image you present in your brochure should be fresh and up to date when you address the market you seek. In three or four years, your market or your firm will likely have changed, and you will have a somewhat different story to tell. Therefore, you can consider your brochure to have an active life of three or four years.

*   *   *

The needs of your prospective clients, the story you want to tell and the image you present are the three essential concepts to have clearly in mind before you start to create a brochure.

Because of the expense, many firms delay producing a brochure as long as possible. However, as a primary marketing tool, a firm brochure is an investment in a firm's growth, and no growing firm should be without one. ▪

204

Writing Better Industrial Catalogs

N. H. Brown

AN EFFECTIVE TOOL *in many offices and plants is the industrial catalog. But there are good catalogs and there are bad ones. How to make the good ones is the subject of this article. The author tells you in a few easy steps how to plan, write, and produce catalogs that are not destined for the wastebasket . . . but rather, fulfill their basic purpose – to serve buyers seeking sellers.*

Catalogs are used by many potential buyers. Every time a man reaches for a catalog, a sale hangs in the balance. If the catalog contains the information he wants, there's a good chance the sale will be made. If the catalog doesn't have the data, the sale is lost.

The catalog must give enough data for the reader to decide quickly whether he wants to know more about the product. A skimpy, poorly prepared catalog implies an inferior product.

What is a catalog? The simplest answer is that a catalog is a basic source of information about products. It must tell the user what you have for sale. And it must help him to decide if your product can be of use to him.

Users refer to a catalog to get answers to basic questions *before* the salesman is called. So you must write your catalog to give a user the answers he wants. How can you do this? It isn't easy, but it can be done.

PLAN YOUR CATALOG

Why is the catalog being written? Ask yourself this question before you put a single word on paper. The answer will tell you the purpose of the catalog.

A catalog for an electronics technician has a much different approach from one for a research scientist. Unless you know exactly who your readers will be you can't decide what approach to use. So investigate your readers. What is their favorite reading matter? What is their average education? What do they want from a catalog? Prices? Design data? Dimensions? Weights? Only when you know the answers to these questions can you plan an effective catalog that will help sell your product.

Make a list of these needs. Then include answers to as many of them as you can. Don't overlook items like finish, color, materials, sizes, capacities, allowable loadings, discounts, dealers addresses, and phone numbers.

Choose the best way to present your data. Determine what your reader is accustomed to using. Charts? Tables? Circuit diagrams? Include those he is most familiar with and he'll find your catalog easier to use and more helpful.

Remember – the catalog indirectly reflects your company and its products. Write a serviceable catalog and the users will buy your product. Don't use extravagant colors, complicated foldouts, or cheap emotional appeals. If your reader wants these, he won't turn to a catalog. He'll buy a publication that provides these better than any catalog ever could. Catalogs are not designed for leisure reading – they're tools, just like a hammer or saw.

WRITING THE CATALOG

There are six steps in writing effective catalogs: (1) collect your data and illustrations, (2) make an outline, (3) write a rough draft, (4) check your facts, (5) polish the draft, and (6) send copy and art to the production department.

Get data and illustrations from the engineering, sales, and advertising departments. Try to get the latest data and illustrations. If you get old material, you'll have to change it before the catalog is published, which means wasted effort, lost time, and misunderstandings. And don't overlook customers as potential sources of illustrations. Many of your customers will be glad to supply photographs of your product in use. Or they'll allow you to visit their plant to take photographs.

Don't cut costs on illustrations. Get the best. Remember – you're after sales.

PLAN THE CATALOG   KNOW YOUR READER

CHECK YOUR FACTS   COLLECT DATA

MAKE AN OUTLINE   WRITE AND REWRITE

(Adapted from Westinghouse Electric Corp.)

Steps in writing a catalog.

BANDSTOP FILTERS

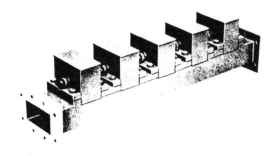

FIVE-SECTION WAVEGUIDE BANDSTOP FILTER

There are usually fewer specifications in the design of bandstop filters than bandpass filters. The practical requirements can be stated very simply. A given amount of rejection must be provided for the unwanted signals while the loss at the desired signal frequency must be kept low.

Ripple and time delay are rarely specified since they are of consequence only around the resonant frequency. The desired signal is usually far outside of the 3-db points where ripple and time delay are both negligible.

AIL engineers, using high rejection and low loss as their principal objectives, have developed the optimum in bandstop filters — the equal-element filter.

Parameters such as the number of resonators, type of transmission line, stopband rejection, and passband loss must still be determined to satisfy particular requirements. As with the bandpass filters, it is impossible to list all of the combinations. However, the table on the opposite page lists some typical characteristics of five-section equal-element filters. It shows, for example, that in the 3.95 to 5.85 Gc band a waveguide bandstop filter can provide 50-db rejection over a 5-Mc band with only 0.15-db loss for all signals at least ±25 Mc from band center.

There are many applications for bandstop filters. The tunable bandstop filter is a valuable, versatile piece of test equipment. Bandstop filters can be used to eliminate spurious outputs of multiplier chains and at the input of parametric amplifier receivers to eliminate saturation from close-in transmitter signals. Cryogenic tunable bandstop filters have been developed to eliminate intermodulation problems in high-frequency receivers.

AIL's unique experience and background in every phase of filter theory and design ensures the best possible solution to your filter problems.

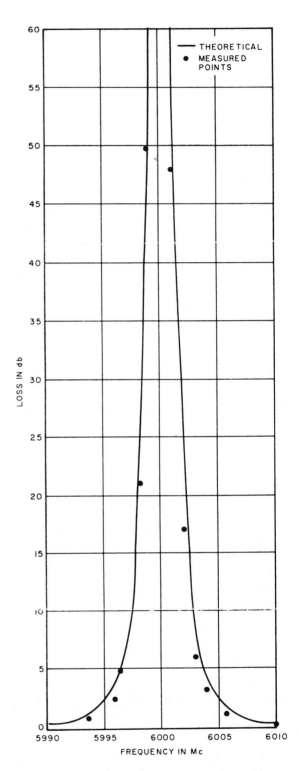

FIVE-SECTION WAVEGUIDE BANDSTOP FILTER RESPONSE

The better the appearance of your catalog, the greater your chances of making the important sale.

Insist on being supplied *all* data related to the product. True, you may use only a tenth of it. But having the data on hand will help you write your text. This will show up in the greater assurance your writing reflects.

Before you make an outline, study other catalogs to see how they're written. And don't overlook your competitors! Some of your best ideas may result from reading poorly executed catalogs. (Not your own, of course.)

MAKE AN OUTLINE

When preparing your outline, try to visualize the information the typical user will be seeking. Arrange the outline so the needed information is given in the sequence the user will need it. Though there are no fixed rules, many engineers prefer to see the information presented in the following order: (1) catalog contents; (2) product uses; (3) product features; (4) ratings, capacities, loads, etc.; (5) selection procedure; (6) dimensions, weights, finish, etc.; (7) product prices; (8) ordering information; and (9) sales representatives.

Study your outline and revise it until you're satisfied it's the best you can prepare. Indicate where you'll use illustrations. Specify which illustration will be used where. It's amazing how quickly you can forget which photograph you intended to use on page 2, or page 20.

When you write the rough draft, keep these rules in mind. Be specific. Be concise. Leave the adjectives at home the day you write your catalog. Give enough information to the catalog user to invite further action on his part. Relate the illustrations to the text. Use specific captions for the illustrations.

Don't discourage your reader with pages of formidable text. Break up your text with illustrations, tables, and lists of applications.

Be sure your reader knows exactly what the catalog covers. Keep the text short enough to encourage reading. But give the needed facts. Catalog users are looking for a quick, exact answer. Forget the history of your company, or how long the firm spent testing the product. The salesman can supply this information if the customer wants it.

Make all detail drawings large. Be sure the user can read the dimensions. And give those important limiting dimensions — like how much clearance is needed for installation or how close two units can be placed. Don't overlook

weights, colors, finishes, materials, and special considerations. They're extremely important to the user of your catalog. Show illustrations of related products. But use judgment in this. Don't show antennas in a catalog on filters.

Use tables, charts, and formulas, in that order, to present selection and product physical data. Arrange the data so that it can be read easily without squinting. The catalogs that get the most use are those that save the user time.

If your product has limitations — and almost all do — state exactly what these limitations are. Then your users will make fewer mistakes, and there will be less dissatisfaction with your product. Though catalog writing is less restrained than the style used in articles and reports, watch the superlatives. They can get you into trouble.

OBTAIN APPROVALS

Once your rough draft is finished, type it neatly and collect all your illustrations. Send the copy and art to the engineering and sales departments for checking. Never begin final production of a catalog until you've done this.

Engineering and sales will probably have comments. Listen to them. Then make changes they request. But don't let sales people inject too many adjectives or superlatives into your copy. The back-slapping that gets into many catalogs annoys most engineers. Why? Because they are usually modest people who state the facts and go on from there. So be clear, be brief, and give the facts. That's enough for most users of catalogs.

When you are ready to polish the rough draft, try to be as critical as possible. If a sentence or paragraph is not clear, mark it. If there is information missing, supply it. While you are reading, write in the margin any ideas that occur to you.

If you find that a rewrite is necessary, don't hesitate — do it at once. If you put the rewrite off, you will probably forget what was wrong. Remember that it is not shameful to rewrite — all good writers do.

Some faults to check are (1) yard-long sentences, (2) big words, where shorter ones will do, (3) unrelated illustrations or tables, (4) too much material on one subject, and (5) missing material. Any of these faults can mean the difference between a sale and no sale.

Finally, don't ever skimp on catalog production. Use the best paper, printer, and binding your budget will stand. Your

catalog subtly reflects your company. So settle for only the best. You'll never regret it.

CATALOGS ARE IMPORTANT

Catalogs are one of the strongest links between your firm and the purchasing public. And since most purchasers today are well-trained technical personnel, the importance of good catalogs will continue to grow.

In a survey of a committee of 100 prominent engineers, *Consulting Engineer* magazine made these findings:

"Somewhere between half and two-thirds of the catalogs received in the mail or directly from salesmen are filed in the wastebasket. This is because too many catalogs contain more sales story than pertinent technical data. The consulting engineer does not want the two combined.

"Some manufacturers seem to have a tendency to include not only promotional material, but also maintenance and operation manuals and perhaps histories of their companies or detailed reports of the preliminary research required for development of their product. Most of this is superfluous from the consulting engineer's point of view. His primary concern is preparing good specifications for his client."

The really good catalog is an effective tool in the office or plant. Remember that buyers seeking sellers will use your catalog and you'll write better industrial catalogs with far less pain. Ω

About the Author . . .

NORMAN H. BROWN *received the B.S. degree in writing from Columbia University in 1959. He is a technical editor with the Airborne Instruments Laboratory Division of Cutler-Hammer, Inc., Deer Park, New York. During his six years with the company, he has worked in all areas of technical writing and editing, including reports, proposals, brochures, catalogs and handbooks. Formerly a technical writer for the McGraw-Hill Technical Writing Service, he is the author of articles in national magazines as well as trade publications and has conducted in-plant seminars on engineering writing.*

How to Design a More Memorable Exhibit

by Richard K. Swandby
and Jonathan (Skip) Cox, Exhibit Surveys, Inc.

There are many factors that go into making a most remembered exhibit. Some are within your control, others are not.

Among the controllable factors are the size of the exhibit, product presentations and demonstrations, the design of the exhibit, and the personnel working the exhibit.

Size of the exhibit in relation to the size of the show is probably the single most important factor in becoming a most remembered exhibit. In fact, we have found a precise relationship between the two.

There is a very high degree of correlation between the size of the show and the amount of space needed to become the most remembered exhibit. The mathematical equation to determine the optimum space for maximum impact is $y = 0.0075x + 720$ square feet; where y equals the size of exhibit in square feet needed for maximum impact, and x equals the total net square footage of a show (paid space).

For example, in a show with 100,000 net square feet of space, 750 square feet (100,000 x 0.0075) plus 720 square feet is needed to become a most remembered exhibit.

Two limitations to this equation exist. First, the equation may not apply to shows with less than 40,000 net square feet of exhibit space, simply because we have insufficient data from smaller shows. Second, the equation provides too conservative an estimate of the space needed in shows where many companies display very large pieces of equipment, because a large amount of space is needed to accommodate the products themselves.

Product demonstrations and presentations will positively influence your score as a most remembered exhibit, assuming they are effective. As a rule of thumb, seven to nine of the top 10 most remembered exhibits in

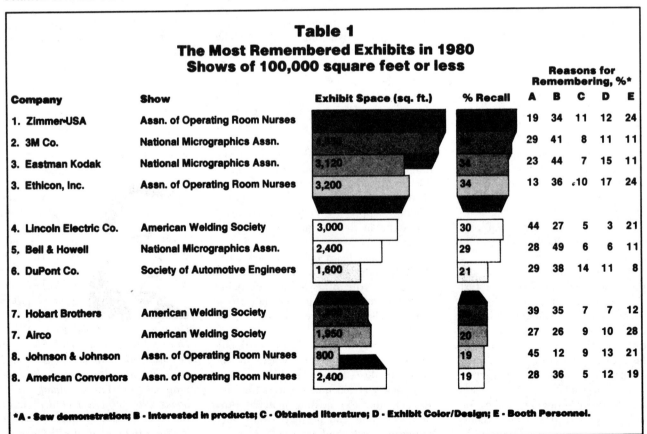

Table 1
The Most Remembered Exhibits in 1980
Shows of 100,000 square feet or less

Company	Show	Exhibit Space (sq. ft.)	% Recall	Reasons for Remembering, %* A	B	C	D	E
1. Zimmer-USA	Assn. of Operating Room Nurses			19	34	11	12	24
2. 3M Co.	National Micrographics Assn.			29	41	8	11	11
3. Eastman Kodak	National Micrographics Assn.	3,120	34	23	44	7	15	11
3. Ethicon, Inc.	Assn. of Operating Room Nurses	3,200	34	13	36	10	17	24
4. Lincoln Electric Co.	American Welding Society	3,000	30	44	27	5	3	21
5. Bell & Howell	National Micrographics Assn.	2,400	29	28	49	6	6	11
6. DuPont Co.	Society of Automotive Engineers	1,600	21	29	38	14	11	8
7. Hobart Brothers	American Welding Society			39	35	7	7	12
7. Airco	American Welding Society	1,950	20	27	26	9	10	28
8. Johnson & Johnson	Assn. of Operating Room Nurses	800	19	45	12	9	13	21
8. American Convertors	Assn. of Operating Room Nurses	2,400	19	28	36	5	12	19

*A - Saw demonstration; B - Interested in products; C - Obtained literature; D - Exhibit Color/Design; E - Booth Personnel.

Reprinted with permission from *Industrial Marketing*, (now *Business Marketing*, vol. 66, pp. 76, 78, and 82, Apr. 1981.
Copyright © 1981 by Crain Communications, Inc.

Table 2
The Most Remembered Exhibits in 1980
Shows Over 100,000 net square feet

Company	Show	Exhibit Space (sq. ft.)	% Recall	Reasons for Remembering, %*				
				A	B	C	D	E
1. Perkin Elmer Corp.	Pittsburgh Conference on Analytical Chemistry and Applied Spectroscopy	4,500	43	24	49	8	9	10
2. Cincinnati-Milicron	International Machine Tool	11,200	30	39	30	5	17	9
3. Kohler Co.	National Association of Home Builders	2,720	28	22	32	7	30	9
4. Varian Associates	Pittsburgh Conference on Analytical Chemistry and Applied Spectroscopy	2,700	26	19	52	5	12	12
5. Heidelberg U.S.A.	Print 80	16,500	23	33	37	11	9	10
6. Joy Manufacturing Co.	AMC Coal	22,000	22	17	51	9	6	17
7. Hewlett-Packard	Pittsburgh Conference on Analytical Chemistry and Applied Spectroscopy	1,400	21	23	58	7	1	11
8. Challenge-Cook Bros.	International Concrete & Aggregates	5,000	20	41	36	3	9	11
9. The Herman Corp.	AFS Foundrymen's Castings	1,200	19	52	41	2	–	5
9. Coca-Cola USA	NRA Restaurant, Hotel-Motel	2,275	19	14	15	6	65	–
9. General Electric Co.	Design Engineering	2,279	19	42	26	8	14	10

*A - Saw demonstration; B - Interested in products; C - Obtained literature; D - Exhibit Color/Design; E - Booth Personnel.

any given show are also listed among the 10 most impressive demonstrations or presentations in the show.

In some preliminary research, we're discovering that visitors prefer product demonstrations as the most effective method of presenting products. One recent survey found that over 80% of the audience preferred formal or informal product demonstrations to audio-visual presentations, professional entertainers, or other types of attention-giving devices.

The effect of color, lighting and design of the exhibit on overall impact is obviously important as evidenced by the reasons given for remembering most of the exhibits in Tables 1 and 2. To date, the degree to which each design element affects exhibit impact is not known. However, we've undertaken a five year study for the Trade Show Bureau to correlate such factors as light intensity, special effect lighting, color, and type of exhibit (backwall, island, etc.) with specific exhibit performance measurements. This study should begin to reveal the relative value of the various elements that comprise the design aspect of the exhibit.

PERSONNEL PERFORMANCE

A final factor in becoming a most remembered exhibit that you should have control over is the performance of your booth personnel. Booth personnel reinforce the memorability for visiting the exhibit. They may not be responsible for attracting visitors to the exhibit, but effective person-to-person contact is essential to maintain memorability over a long period of time.

There are two very important factors over which you have little or no control. One is the inherent level of interest in your types of products among the show audience. The second is the existing level of awareness for your company among the show audience. Invariably, companies on the most remembered exhibit list are leaders in their fields in terms of recognition among customers and prospects, and there is a high level of interest in seeing their types of products. ∎

DO YOU NEED A FILM?

S. Martin Shelton
Technical Information Department

Presented at the Twenty-Second International Technical Communications Conference Society for Technical Communications, 15-17 May 1975, Anaheim, California.

ABSTRACT. The information film is a communications tool. It may do other things also, entertain, for example, but its foremost function is to convey information. The information film offers a host of unique advantages as a communication medium. Conversely, in terms of the total scope of communications, it has many serious disadvantages—too often overlooked or not recognized by film zealots. Within the context of this paper "film" includes all forms of kinetic audiovisuals such as motion pictures, television, filmstrips, and slide-tape shows.

COMMUNICATIONS MEDIUM

Communications—that's a buzzword that'll guarantee fifteen minutes on the latest esoteric learning theory, nuclear arms race, or whatever. But unfortunately, considering all that's been said, written, and shown about it, there is still a great paucity of clear, concise communications. And, I suspect, there is no improvement in sight. It's something we all talk about, but no one does anything about it.

In today's high-energy visual and audio environment, we constantly are inundated with a myriad of miscellaneous and multifaceted messages—all competing for our time, energy, and thought processes. The barrage never ceases from birth to death. Alvin Toffler puts it this way: The waves of coded information turn into violent breakers and come at a faster and faster clip, pounding at us, seeking entry, as it were, into our nervous system.[1]

This information comes in waves of the spoken word, the written word, the electronic word, and the photographic and graphic-art word in an infinity of variations and combinations. These are the obvious media, the ones over which we as communicators have direct and creative control. But consider also the host of other communication media which make up the bulk of the waves: a color, a signpost, an abstract painting, a whiff of perfume, a uniform, a waltz, a traffic signal, a bikini-clad beauty, ad infinitum, to include every sensation our five senses receive. And each sensation contributes to the barrage of communication symbols and messages our audiences receive every day—each with its own influence on their daily lives, their attitudes, their mores, and from which the id and psyche are molded. Some are concise, some are subtle; but every one demands attention to some degree. Each sensation must be assimilated, associated, evaluated, collated, and stored; each requires a decision to act (mentally or physically) or not, now or in the future.

People communicate by talking and listening, by writing and reading, by broadcasting and viewing. In its simplest form, then, communication is the transmission of information from A to B and receipt of this information by B. Ideally this is followed by an acknowledgment from B to A that the information has been received. These processes of transmitting, receiving, and acknowledging require considerable skill. Unfortunately, the primary trouble with communication is that most people don't think there is a problem at all![2]

There is a multitude of media which can carry the information. Each has its special advantage and disadvantage. Each is best suited to specific applications depending on what the message is (information), who is to get the message (audience), and where and when the audience is to receive it (environment). As professionals in the communication business, our task is to exercise judgment and expertise in selecting the medium best suited to the information, the audience, and the environment. We cannot afford to be parochially comfortable in our own niches. All the media possibilities must be explored, even combinations, which in some instances are highly effective methods of communication.

[1] Alvin Toffler. *Future Shock*. New York, Bantam Books, February 1972, p. 166.
[2] William R. Van Dersal. "How To Be a Better Communicator—And a Successful Nurse," *Nursing '74*, December 1974.

S. MARTIN SHELTON
332 Iowa Court
Ridgecrest, CA 93555

Head, Film Projects Branch, Naval Weapons Center, China Lake, California 93555

Society For Technical Communication, Associate Fellow
Information Film Producers of America, National President
Delta Kappa Alpha (national honorary cinema fraternity) Vice President, USC Chapter
Society of Motion Picture and Television Engineers, member

B.S. (physics) St. Mary's University, Texas
M.A. (cinema) University of Southern California

FILM AS A COMMUNICATION MEDIUM

Film is an excellent medium to solve those communication problems which require strong, animated visuals. It is not, however, a panacea for all communications problems, far from it. It has many pitfalls too often overlooked or not recognized by the uninitiated and the zealots. Unfortunately, its tinsel glamour seduces too many of us. Its popular social and corporate acceptance is not challenged. Film has become a buzzword for instant gratification and solution. This heterodoxy is evidenced by the proliferation of film in today's mass communication arena.

Most of *these* films, I am convinced, have at best only marginal communication value and reflect a near total apostasy of communication canons and a squandering of scarce resources. They typify the age-old conflict of "Want" versus "Need." And what is wanted, more often than not, is not what is needed. Too frequently, however, the "Want" wins on spurious rationale. It is just too easy to make the snap judgment that "I need a film."

When this kind of judgment is made, the essential preproduction communication analysis, necessary to determine if the problem really can be or is best solved by film, is relegated to limbo. And the film is sponsored and produced by the uninformed, the biased, and the parochial without in-depth preplanning, precise problem statement, audience analysis, and synthesis of the essential elements of information into the communication message. Distribution methods and screening environment are thought of little, if at all. Yet, careful consideration and successful resolution of all these analysis elements are the very hallmark and foundation of successful films.

ADVANTAGES OF FILM

Our job, as professionals in the communication analysis process, is to evaluate all film advantages and disadvantages individually and together as they apply to the specific information problem at hand. An unbiased and professional look at this evaluation will determine if a film truly is needed or not. That is, a film will tender, at a minimum, a satisfactory solution to the communication problem, with maximum economy of resources.

Multimedia

Film's most important advantage is that it is multimedia. Both sight and hearing are stimulated in concert. (Some contemporary theatrical films claim to offer olfactory and tactile sensations.)

Each photographic scene, unless distorted for some purpose, is a faithful reproduction of the images and movements of an event (real or pseudo). This is a powerful communication faculty—illustrated by the old understatement "A picture is worth more than ten thousand words." And it signifies the primacy of film as a visual medium.

Approximately 70% of the information received from films comes from the visuals; only 30% is received aurally.[3] Stimulation of these dual senses with the right mix of sight and sound can have a powerful synergistic effect on audience comprehension, assimilation, and retention. However, some studies have shown that certain types of film commentary may interfere with communication.[4]

There is no absolute answer for the "right mix" of sight and sound. From my experience, however, I've found that audiences assimilate visual information at a significantly faster rate than auditory information. Also, the more familiar the audience is with the visuals, the more there is a progressively nonlinear, almost exponential, increase in assimilation and understanding.

The auditory information must not introduce communication static (interference) to the primary or visual element of this multimedia information tool. To be effective, auditory information must complement the visual information. If it is commentary, it must explain or amplify what the audience cannot perceive from the visual development.[5] Karel Reisz of the British Film Academy put it this way when discussing the robbery sequence in Carol Reed's 1946 film *Odd Man Out*: "... The dialogue track ... does not anchor the visuals by conveying important information, but adds to the total effect on a contributory rather than a primary level."[6] If the auditory information is music, sound effects, or background prattle (or a combination of these), it must be unobtrusive to the degree that its presence is not noticed. These sound elements set moods, add the dimension of realism, and amplify the pacing established by the visuals. Interference is established quickly when these aural elements become preeminent (in volume or importance), or incongruous, or not germane.

The primary interference, however, usually emanates from the commentary in the form of an incessant harangue of drivel or in a melange of technical trivia that dulls the senses. Attempting to comprehend what is being said, some audiences will concentrate on the commentary to the exclusion of the visuals. Since there is no time for reflective thought, they will fall farther and farther behind. Eventually they'll give up by escaping mentally (or physically) to a more comfortable environment.

Mass Medium

Another major advantage of film is its ability to reach the masses, simultaneously or sequentially over a period of time. From a film's internegative a host of identical release prints can be struck—tangible *end products* which *precisely repeat* the message. Prints can be projected (transmitted if over television) over and over again in a myriad of locations, each time *transmitting* the same message to new audiences. (All may not *receive* the same message, however.)

[3] S. M. Shelton. "A Writer Is a Writer Is a Writer—But a Film Writer Should Be More," *Proceedings, 21st International Technical Communication Conference, 15-18 May 1974*, St. Louis. Society for Technical Communication, Washington, D.C., p. 38.

[4] Charles F. Hoban, Jr., and Edward B. Van Ormer. *Instructional Film Research (Rapid Mass Learning), 1918-1950*. Pennsylvania State College, State College, Pa., December 1950.

[5] Shelton, op. cit.

[6] Karel Reisz. *The Techniques of Film Editing*. New York, Visual Arts Books, 1953, p. 265.

Or, for repeat audiences, the message is reinforced. In terms of overall audience manipulation, this is a powerful factor. The total audience is limited only by the film's distribution. And the cost per screening per person usually is the most economical, over the long term, of all media for any given message.

Visually Oriented Audience

Today's film audiences are attuned to receiving visual information—especially in film and television format. As a result of 30 years of incessant bombardment by the mass media of film and (later) TV, audiences are by and large highly visually oriented. They are capable of comfortably receiving copious amounts of (visual) information. And they can receive it quickly. The upper limit of the rate of reception is as yet undetermined, but I suspect it is several orders of magnitude faster than we imagine.

Capitalizing on this audience capability, we can design films to be shorter, faster paced, and more cogent, all with major increases in audience reception and with overall economy of production resources.

Captive Audience

Once the house lights dim and the projector starts, our audience is a captive in the darkened screening room. They can look only at the screen to see what we want them to see. They can hear only what we want them to hear. They have no other sensation choices. We've established near total control of their sensory environment (physical control also, for that matter). The only options our audience has are to adapt to the environment and follow the film, or to mentally turn off, or to leave the room.

To a lesser degree, these factors are true for other screening environments, such as television, individual teaching machines, and desk-top super 8-mm cartridge projectors. All factors considered, however, the captive audience remains as one of film's most potent advantages.

Passive Audience

The film audience is passive—a concomitant factor of the captive-audience advantage. A member of the audience doesn't have to do anything. Physically he settles in his chair, relaxes, and generally is comfortable. This sets a favorable environment for the reception of information.

Mentally he doesn't have to do much either, at least during the screening—that is, if the film is well-produced. He follows along easily as the film designer[7] mentally leads him by the hand through every facet and nuance of information. He is not strained, he likes it, and he is receptive. Hopefully, sometime after the lights come on, his mental processes will function favorably to the film's message. This can happen within seconds—or several days later. Some particularly well-made films of the attitude-changing or

motivation type can exert their influence for many years over some audiences. This is especially true of a well-designed film that causes the audience to become emotionally involved with it. They have empathy.

Empathy

Within our frame of reference, empathy is that close identification audiences have with a person, place, or event depicted in a film. This experience happens to all to some degree or another. It is almost inescapable by the captive and passive audience ensconced in their physical and psychological niches.

I've found that the more intense and enduring the empathy is, the higher the probabilities are that the audience will receive, process, and store the film's message (information), and take action if required. For example, in a training situation strong empathy causes significant increases in learning.[8]

As communicators (film designers) our task is to exploit this powerful advantage. Early in the preproduction phase, the film designer must conduct a comprehensive audience analysis. He needs to find out just *who* this audience is that he intends to influence, manipulate, motivate, or train. What are their motives (to be looking at his film)? What is their average education? Intelligence? Age? What are their interests? Mores? Attitudes? What is the screening environment? A host of other questions must also be asked. Each film is unique, requiring a distinct set of questions for a valid audience analysis.

From this analysis the film designer can plan and produce his film to fit the audience—not himself, which so often happens. Generally, I've found, the films which engender the strongest empathy are not patronizing or abstruse; they present just enough challenge to pique the interest. Admittedly, this is a fine line. But with careful evaluation, perception, and experience, the film designer usually will be successful.

Designer Selection

Designer selection is a phrase I've coined to denote the film designer's decision-making process in his synthesis of certain major film elements into a total communication package. Its overall advantage lies in the control the film designer has in *what* is shown to the audience, *how* it is shown, and *where* in the film it is shown. Designer selection can be thought of as the artistic and scientific blending of psychological and technical elements to achieve the level of communication needed to accomplish the film's goals.

• One elemental advantage of designer selection is that the film designer shows the audience *precisely* what he wants them to see and with the proper emphasis. The film designer has *total* image (and audio) control by his selection of scenes.

At a live stage play, the audience can choose by concentration and selective viewing what he sees—be it the

[7] Shelton, op. cit.

[8] S. M. Shelton. Unpublished master's thesis, "An Experimental Study To Determine the Effects of Comic Emphasis as a Means of Depicting Errors in Motion Pictures as a Help in Learning a Perceptual Motor Skill," University of Southern California, Los Angeles, June 1956.

entire scope of the stage or just the face of a speaking actor. In a film the audience can see only what is shown to him. Recognize that the audience has some selective viewing decisions in certain types of film scenes, a long shot for example, but this is severely limited in terms of the total viewing experience.

• *How* information is shown, in terms of scene types (LS, MS, CU, and ECU),* determines in large measure its relative importance. The more full-frame an action is (CU or ECU), the more emphasis it has. It is in these two scene types, and to some extent the MS, that the essential elements of information are most successfully transmitted. Additionally, two or three CUs or ECUs edited in sequence enhance significantly the importance of an action.

The technical techniques of how information is shown is another major factor influencing emphasis and importance. Some of these techniques are split screen, rack focus, multiple image, zoom, soft focus, perspective distortion, solarization, and color shifting. All, however, are image controlling devices that distort or enhance the visual perspective of the audience.

• The juxtaposition of information within a film influences greatly its relevance and importance. Juxtaposition defines *where* it is shown in terms of internal sequencing. For example, consider this fundamental sequence: LS, MS, MS, CU. All scenes depict related and sequential action (information). If the essential elements of information are contained *primarily* in the CU, the audience immediately should comprehend its relationship to the preceding ancillary information and ascertain its importance. This film element is akin closely to the sequencing of CUs mentioned earlier.

Also, scenes which are dissimilar, unrelated, or nonsequential can be joined into a pregnant relationship by juxtaposition and adroit screen direction manipulation. This technique is prevalent in historical documentaries composed of stock and newsreel footage.

Juxtaposition also can give scenes meaning which they inherently do not have.[9] Sergei Eisenstein noted, ". . . Two film pieces of any kind, placed together, inevitably combine into a new concept, a new quality, arising out of that juxtaposition."[10]

Another element which gives import to information is simply the amount of time it is on the screen. Generally, the longer the screen time an action has (up to a saturation point), the greater its importance.

• In summary, the result of designer selection is the physical and psychological compelling of the audience to receive the film's message completely and correctly.

Remote Locations

Film can take the audience to remote locations—on the earth's surface, under the oceans, and out in space. This advantage is not limited to geographical locations. It encompasses the total spectrum from micro- to astro-photography—from molecular structure to distant galaxies.

Within the frame of reference of this paper, this advantage also applies to all specialized and nonvisible-light types of photography, such as infrared, ultraviolet, X-ray, microwave, radar, and camouflage-detection. These kinds of photography have expanded the scope of our vision to as yet unbounded dimensions. We now see what the eye could never see before.

Time Manipulation

Through various film techniques, time can be compressed or expanded. Time manipulation is used for detail study of fast-happening sequential events, for scientific analysis, for understanding of natural phenomena, or simply for artistic purposes. Time-lapse photography compresses into a few seconds the hours or days some events take to complete—clouds building or flowers blooming, for example. Conversely, high-speed photography expands near-instantaneous events into seconds and minutes—an explosion or a staged automobile crash, for example.[11]

Time can be manipulated by simple editing. For example, depending on technique, inserting a CU or a cutaway scene or scenes into a master scene can either expand time or compress it.

Also, time can be distorted (or rectified) in optical printing. This occurs when the length of an original scene is shortened by skip-frame printing or lengthened by multiframe printing.

Abstract Visualization

Film is an excellent medium to visualize abstract ideas. However, this presents a severe challenge to the film designer, but it also is one of the best uses of film as a communication tool. Through a short animation sequence, for example, the economic concept of gold in international finance could be made understandable to tenth graders.

Film can visualize also that which is inaccessible by reason of location, size, or nonavailability. It can explore the inner workings of the human circulatory system, or it can look inside a vacuum tube to scrutinize the electron flow.

Tailor-Made

Every film is unique. Each is designed especially to resolve a particular communication problem. (A few films have multipurpose applications.) The precision communication thrust of the film can be concentrated on the essence of the problem. If the film is designed and produced with care, therefore, the probability is high that the tailor-made film will be successful.

---

* Film production parlance for Long Shot, Medium Shot, Close Up, and Extreme Close Up, respectively.

[9] Reisz, op. cit., p. 30.

[10] Sergei Eisenstein. *The Film Sense.* New York, Meridian Books, 1957, p. 4.

[11] Edgar Dale. *Audio Visual Methods In Teaching—Revised Edition.* New York, Henry Holt and Company, Inc., 1959.

Silver Screen Magic

All factors considered, I've found audiences generally tend to be receptive to messages contained in films. This acceptance stems from some "silver screen magic," which I've not been able to identify clearly. In some measure this is attributable to a glamour conjured by film audiences. It comes from an arcane inherent authority that is attendant on all well-produced films. And, simply, it springs from the fact that if a film was made at all, "it must be important."

DISADVANTAGES OF FILM

In film as in physics, for every action there is a reaction—not necessarily equal or opposite, however. The preponderance of "advantages" must not cloud the film designer's reasoning in his preproduction communication analysis. He also needs to examine the specific communication problem at hand in light of the numerous disadvantages film has. The final decision, if film is or is not a valid and economical solution ("Need"), results from a trenchant analysis of all pro and con factors.

Continuous Format

One major disadvantage of film in its traditional format is that it must be seen continuously from start to finish. The audience has *no time* for reflective thought, for review of difficult sequences, for detailed scrutiny of complex visuals, and for discussion. This reduces significantly the overall communication effectiveness of film. Too much information is lost and cannot be retrieved. Multiple screenings alleviate the problem only marginally—if they can be arranged at all.[12] However, too many film screenings can cause a reduction in learning as well as negative attitudes.[13]

Much improvement has been made with the use of new film formats and screening techniques that permit, for example, stopping and reversing the film.

The disadvantage of continuousness, and others discussed below, augur well for short films (five to seven minutes) with pinpoint communication thrust. I've found this type of film to be more effective than traditional ones, and it is a more efficient use of design and production resources.

Transitory Nature

Perhaps film's greatest disadvantage, when compared with the written word, is that it is transitory. After the screening, the audience has *no residual material* for perusal or for review next month. If they didn't get the message or most of it the first time, they are out of luck. The odds are that they'll not have another chance to see the film.

Except in a very few instances, this fleeting nature of films negates to a large degree most long-term retention of information. Usually, only a few impressive highlights are remembered after a few months. Detailed information is lost

so quickly that, if it is not reinforced in some other way, the printed word, for example, it has only marginal validity for inclusion in a film. Specifically for example, I'm referring to depicting a complex, sequential motor skill operation, or listing of exact numbers or items, or showing a complex drawing of any kind.

Linear Structure

As it is structured currently, film can unfold its message only linearly. That is, because film inherently is a time-based product, its information must be developed sequentially. And, perhaps more importantly, it must be seen sequentially. There is *no method* for the audience to skim, to concentrate, or to peruse at random. Linearity also poses serious problems for those who do not have the need, time, or inclination to see the whole thing—at least to see it the way the film designer shows it from his viewpoint.

Alien Perspective

In terms of information content, development, and pace, the film presents a perspective formed by the subjective judgments of the film designer—that is, a new or alien perspective for the audience. Film by its nature is a compendium of germane information the film designer has determined is necessary to solve the communication problem and has structured and paced. These elements define the film's informational common denominator. Because film is a mass medium, all who see it are exposed, for better or for worse, to the same interpretation of the information.

There is *no opportunity* for the audience to ferret out the essence of information or to evaluate, within their frames of reference, the truth, relevance, import, propriety, and perspective of each element of information. Also, other problems are caused for those who can not or do not want to follow the development set by the film designer as to what is seen, how it is seen, and where (in the film) it is seen. For others, the pace of the film may not be to their liking—either too fast or too slow for their individual comprehension rates.

Inflexibility

Films become obsolete quickly, especially those treating topical subjects. Any significant updating or revising of a film is almost impossible because it is an inflexible composite in which no element can be changed without changing all others. Only a simple scissoring of unwanted scenes and their accompanying sound track of a release print is possible. Any revision more than this requires a major expenditure in personnel, money, and time. This largely causes the proliferation of obsolete films which remain in circulation. It's just too expensive to change them.

---

[12] Chester L. McTavish. "Effects of Repetitive Film Presentations on Learning," in *Abstract of Doctoral Dissertation, the Pennsylvania State College, Vol. 16.* State College, Pa., 1954.

[13] J. C. Reid and D. W. MacLennan. *Research in Instructional Television and Film.* Office of Education, U.S. Department of Health, Education, and Welfare. Superintendent of Documents Catalogue Number FS5.234:34041. U.S. Government Printing Office, Washington, D.C., 1967, p. 10.

Logistics

Film is worthless without the integral parts necessary to hold a screening. And the logistics of putting these parts together successfully are deceptively complex—posing a challenge of major proportions. The film, equipment, projectionist, group (audience), and group leader all are required to assemble in near perfect "harmony" at the same time and at the same place. If they do not, a negative attitude can be generated, which seriously impedes audience reception. Additionally, the audience should be motivated that it's to their advantage to see the film here and now. One research study found the nearer the goal for using the film's information, the greater the learning (communication.)[14]

- The equipment, composed of a sound projector with attendant amplifier, speaker, takeup reel, and screen, is heavy, expensive, in constant need of cleaning and preventative maintenance, and prone to breakdown. Additionally, the projectionist needs specialized training and mechanical skills.

- The screening room should be designed especially for light and acoustic control, should be insulated from outside noise, and should provide enough comfort that the audience is not distracted. The complete setting should be conducive to audience reception of the film's message.

- Under all but ideal conditions, release prints deteriorate rapidly. Scratches, torn sprocket holes, missing sections, dirt (especially on the sound track), and incorrect threading all contribute to the deterioration and to negative attitudes.

Helping to solve logistics problems are new film formats and projection devices; for example, super 8-mm magnetic sound, Mylar film base, cartridge-loaded prints, desk-top and briefcase projectors, daylight screens, and individual teaching machines.

Cost

Films are expensive. Considering all communication tools, it probably is the most expensive in terms of cost per item. However, over the long term I suspect that it is the least expensive in cost per person per screening.

Of all the disadvantages, cost is the one that needs the most careful evaluation. It must be determined clearly that the expected accrual of information by the prospective audience is worth the resource expenditure necessary to produce the film.

Lead Time

It takes a relatively long lead time to produce a film and to get the release prints distributed. Of all communication tools, I suspect that film requires the longest lead time. If there are no compelling other justifications, this disadvantage alone seriously erodes the justification to produce films dealing with fast-developing topical subjects.

No Room for Error

Film by its inherent authority commands attention and, I believe, respect. Therefore, one absolute guarantee of failure in a film is to be dishonest or inaccurate in any way. Today's audiences are too sophisticated to be deceived. The film's *total* credibility is lost quickly if *any* misstatement of fact or deceptive visual distortion is detected.

Within my experience, I've found that one way to have a visual distortion accepted is to tell the audience unabashedly that the scene is a fake, for whatever reason; for example, "We're using a model now (instead of a real airplane) because it is easier to control in this demonstration of approach procedures." In this circumstance, the audience usually will extend their empathy and, by being more receptive, join the film designer in his efforts to communicate.

CONCLUSION

Film is an excellent communication medium for some types of messages; for example, general information, sales, motivation, orientation, and some kinds of teaching. It is not effective usually for messages that require detailed, long-term retention of specific facts or procedures. And generally it should not be produced to be used by itself. That is, it should be used with a group leader, teacher, or proctor.

Oftentimes, I've found there is no one "best" communication medium. Optimum communication (maximum influence over the short and long terms) is achieved best by use of an audio-visual medium, backed up by the printed word, illustrated, preferably.

---

[14] Malcolm McNiven. *Effects on Learning of the Perceived Usefulness of the Material To Be Learned.* Technical Report SDC269-7-54, U.S. Naval Training Devices Center. Port Washington. Long Island. N.Y., 1955.

Radio: The Neglected Medium for Scientific Communication

EUGENE GARFIELD, ASSOCIATE MEMBER, IEEE

Abstract—The advantages of radio as a medium for scientific information flow include its speed relative to printed material, the "live" aspect, simplicity and economy relative to television, and the ubiquity of inexpensive receivers. The licenses of commercial radio stations—to meet local needs—effectively preclude all-science broadcasting. Public broadcasting stations—nonprofit—are hampered by lack of financial support. The Physicians Radio Network in New York City is a for-profit operation that uses a sideband of an FM channel to broadcast special-interest news and information to a limited group. Funded by proprietary advertisers, it serves as an example of "scientific radio," but a drawback is the need for special receivers.

IT is 8:30 a.m. You have just reached your office. First you order some coffee. Then you turn on the radio. As you begin to go through the morning mail, there is a little Beethoven, Bach, or Basie. Then the news broadcast begins. Instead of the usual fire, tornado, or accident report the announcer tells you about a bill in Congress that may make your present research illegal. A few minutes of music and he introduces an interdisciplinary panel to discuss the waste disposal problems faced by your city. After more music there is a report on the meeting of the American Association for the Advancement of Science you couldn't attend. Finally, the announcer gives a brief summary of some recently published papers. The hour-long broadcast is over before you know it. If you came in a little late, you are informed that the broadcast will be repeated several times that day.

This scenario is fictional. It ought not to be. The potential value of radio as a means of scientific communication has been underestimated and certainly underutilized.

The amount of science programming on U.S. radio is amazingly small. In other nations it is probably more extensive. But in no country is it used to serve the specific needs of the scientific community. This is unfortunate because radio is a particularly appropriate medium for much scientific communication.

For one thing, radio is an almost painless way to be exposed to information. You don't have to devote your attention exclusively to it as you do with TV and print. You can listen while you are looking through papers, moving about, or setting up equipment in the lab. Even as you drive to work or sit on the beach, you could be keeping up with the latest scientific information. And it can also be a shared experience, during a coffee break or in the classroom.

A radio is an inexpensive purchase. It is easy to operate and maintain. You can take a small, battery-powered model virtually anywhere. By using an earphone, you can listen without disturbing others. Even the morning newspaper is more intrusive. Did you ever sit beside someone on a train who is leafing through the *New York Times* or the *Wall Street Journal?*

Radio offers several more advantages over other media as a means of scientific communication. Radio can transmit the latest news more quickly than print. It can provide the listener with all the energy and emotion of "live" discussion. Such human qualities are often lost in a printed transcript.

Radio is often more appropriate for science broadcasting than television because many programs of interest to scientists do not require video. Science news, discussions, talks by individual scientists, even educational courses often lose little or nothing by being aired on radio.

Moreover, the requirements of radio program production and transmission are less distracting to the participants than TV. For example, if a discussion at a conference is being aired, the members of the panel do not have to worry about makeup or to be subjected to hot lights. The broadcast equipment involved is not so cumbersome that it separates the panel from the audience. TV cameras necessarily do this.

With radio, scientists throughout the world could participate in a program merely by sending in audio cassettes of their talks. This would avoid the travel expenses and loss of time incurred by the need to appear in person at a TV studio. Even when an on-site broadcast is necessary, the cost of sending a radio crew is far less than the cost for a TV crew.

I have often wondered why the "simple" solution offered by radio is not used more often for communicating scientific information. However, on further investigation I found that there are very real difficulties facing anyone wanting to operate an "all-science" station or network.

Using a commercial radio station in the U.S. for this purpose would be out of the question except in a very few localities. All commercial stations are governed by a complex set of regulations, outlined by the Federal Communications Commission (FCC) [1]. These regulations require commercial stations to meet the needs of the local communities they serve. This geographic limitation most likely means that a science-oriented station would only be sanctioned in an area with a high percentage of scientists. Among the few communities which might qualify are Bethesda, Maryland; Cambridge, Massachusetts; or Palo Alto, California.

Commercial stations, of course, do carry short science programs designed for lay audiences, since these programs are

The author is President of the Institute for Scientific Information®, 325 Chestnut St., Philadelphia, PA 19106, (215) 923-3300.

Reprinted with permission from *Essays of an Information Scientist.* vol. 3. Philadelphia: PA: ISI Press®, 1980, pp. 517–521.
This material has also appeared in the *IEEE Trans. Prof. Commun.*, vol. PC-22, pp. 14–15, Mar. 1979.

deemed in the public interest. The American Chemical Society sponsors one such program called *Man and Molecules.* The ACS distributes tapes to over 500 stations in the U.S. and other countries. But this type of programming is designed for the public, not the professional scientist.

Public radio could carry programming aimed at scientists [2]. Stations run by colleges, universities, and public school districts fall into this category. Sometimes known as educational radio, public radio stations provide instructional programming to teachers and students, as well as cultural, informational, public affairs, and entertainment programs to the general public.

Unlike ordinary AM and FM, public radio stations carry no advertising and may be licensed only to non-profit organizations with an educational purpose. They are supported by funding from their parent institutions, state or local governments, foundations, private firms, or contributions from the listening audience.

Science programming for the professional would be a possibility on public radio only if it could be provided cheaply enough to fit public radio stations' budgets. I do not know if any large corporations have considered funding such programming. While they might be willing to support an occasional program, the costliness of a regular feature—without the chance to advertise—has probably deterred them.

With commercial or public radio seemingly beyond consideration, I did find one viable method for broadcasting science programs and one organization that has had the initiative to do so. The organization is the Physicians Radio Network (PRN), a New York based group that transmits news, short courses, live call-in shows, and reports from various medical associations to doctors.

PRN is a for-profit enterprise, financed by drug company advertising. It is permitted to broadcast its special-interest programs over Subsidiary Communications Authorization (SCA) sidebands. Ordinary FM broadcasting uses a main channel and two sidebands. However, in 1955, the FCC granted FM stations permission to sell the use of their SCA sidebands to those who wished to transmit programs of interest to a limited segment of the general public—such as a professional group. Broadcasts over SCA bands can be picked up only by a special receiver tuned to the SCA frequency. Ordinary FM radios filter out the broadcasts that are transmitted over these bands.

PRN distributes these special receivers to physicians within the 35-mile radius of their signal in 33 cities. About 75,000 doctors are now listening to the network. Certainly as many or more scientists in both university and industrial positions would listen to all-science stations.

A science radio network patterned after PRN could distribute receivers free of charge to qualified scientists. Revenue would be received from program sponsors. Certain advertisers should be eager to reach a guaranteed audience of scientists. Scientific and technical journal, book, and magazine publishers might be interested. They could attract new readers to their publications through commercials on an all-science station. Industry is also a potential sponsor. Science-oriented companies could attract new employees through appropriate spot announcements. Manufacturers of scientific instruments, too, might find radio an attractive supplement to journal and direct mail advertising. Of course, separation of advertising from editorial content would have to be strictly maintained.

PRN uses medical journalists to write and edit the material it presents. An all-science network would also require the services of senior science journalists able to report science news events in proper perspective. Short courses would be prepared by researchers and educators in the field, and most programs would have to be reviewed by qualified scientists.

In my opinion, one drawback to PRN is that doctors cannot as yet listen to these programs in their cars. The network has considered putting receivers in automobiles. The idea was dismissed because the task of installing them proved too difficult. The special receivers must be hooked up in addition to or in place of the regular car radio. Each installation job is different because each car maker has different specifications for installing the equipment. An individual listener, who was willing to go to the expense and fuss of having the radio installed, could do so. PRN is considering the use of portable receivers that doctors could take with them in their cars, but an appropriate antenna needs to be devised.

PRN has been successful by aiming its programming at practicing clinical physicians. These doctors face a wide variety of medical problems and make decisions based on current information. The counterpart to the clinician in science is the engineer. In some ways engineers might benefit even more than pure scientists from a science radio network. The engineer is an applied scientist. His or her need for continuing science education is perhaps greater than that of the academic scientist doing research.

If no one else is interested in starting the network, I suppose this might be another job for ISI®. Our basic objective is to communicate scientific information effectively through any appropriate medium. Radio will not replace print. But it can help us do a better job of digesting and communicating the results of research. I can even see the various media supplementing each other. For example, additional instructional materials for short courses via radio as well as programming schedules could be included in *Current Contents*®. I can also envision people using our TV-based SCITEL™ service to peruse the radio schedule for the day [3].

An ISI radio network could, of course, provide me with a new opportunity for ego gratification. I don't know whether my essays would be as well-received were I to read them over the air. But I am sure that items in our Press Digest could be interesting "hearing."

Perhaps the Science Radio Network can only be realized through a collaborative effort involving several organizations: government (National Science Foundation and/or National Institutes of Health), societies (American Association for the Advancement of Science), and private enterprise (ISI and other science-oriented corporations). Anyone out there listening?

REFERENCES

[1] Federal Communications Commission, "Broadcast Services," *FCC Information Bulletin Number 3.* Washington, DC: FCC, 1977.
[2] —, "Educational Radio," *FCC Information Bulletin Number 17.* Washington, DC: FCC, 1977.
[3] E. Garfield, "Viewdata and SCITEL Bring Interactive Information Systems into the Home," *Current Contents* (41):5–10, 10 October 1977.

EFFECTIVE USE OF TELEVISION
TO POPULARIZE SCIENCE

JACQUES G. RICHARDSON
Editor
Impact of Science on Society
United Nations Educational, Scientific, and Cultural Organization

ABSTRACT

The growing use of television to popularize science and technology has generated a trial examination of the motives, the dynamics, and the effectiveness of the process. Some results of the first international meeting held on the subject are presented by one of the participants.

Fifteen specialized communicators, meeting in Luxembourg in late Spring, held a week-long workshop on the problems of using television to popularize science.[1] The specialists — a few of whom did not represent the video medium directly — were concerned primarily with

1. the effectiveness of TV as a means to popularize science and technology; and
2. how the experience of industrialized countries might best be transferred to developing nations.

A first question asked was basic to the subject: What is popularization, and why should it be done? Nicolas Skrotsky of French television suggested that "we need more science to solve our daily, social problems." He added that it is "unfortunately, the 'technological fix' that gets science and scientists most in trouble

[1] Regional Working Group (Europe) on the Popularization of Science through Television, Luxembourg, 8-13 May 1978, organized by Unesco and cosponsored by the Ministries of Education and Culture, Grand Duchy of Luxembourg.

with the public." Sensational or even spectacular research results, as interpreted by the public, often derive from the undue emphasis placed on them during the popularization process. Alexander Beshkov of Bulgarian TV conceded that the popularization of all specialized subjects (engineering, comparative literature, esthetics) is challenging, and that popularization itself risks being a caricature of what is being interpreted, "just as irony may be the simplest popularization of philosophy."

As to *why* we popularize science (a question also raised by Dimitris Zois of the Development Division, Doxiadis Associates, a group of planning consultants in Athens), there was a consensual reply: "because science is real and with us every day." Bengt Feldreich of Swedish television, Fernand Seguin of Radio Canada-CBC, and Bent Henius of Copenhagen insisted that scientific research and technical innovation are now so much a part of man's general culture that they deserve a respectable amount of continuing attention by the electronic and other media — on news as well as on feature programs.

An unusual experiment in social psychology was presented to the workshop by Francoise Berdot of the University of Paris and the International Film and Television Council. A psychoanalyst by training, Ms Berdot had brought together five working people who had never been exposed to scientific training. She had them select five topics that had interested each of the five for various personal reasons. The five subjects were DNA, infinity, relativity, wave action, and psychosomatic medicine. Through a process of self-help, the five formulated the main questions they had to ask on each phenomenon. These sessions, filmed, were then shown to experts in the different fields; their explanations were then filmed and later shown to the five individuals. In a third phase, questioners and answerers met in a face-to-face situation in order to work out the unanswered or unsatisfactorily answered aspects of the dialog. The interesting feature of the experiment is the total lack of a specialized communicator in the process.

WHO WANTS TO KNOW WHAT ABOUT SCIENCE?

What should be popularized in science? Viviane Reding, a communication analyst from Luxembourg, cited some intriguing figures emerging from an official analysis made in 1977 by the then Ministry of Industry and Research in France. This is how the French public expressed its desires to be informed about science and technology through TV:

Medicine and health	23.6%
Agriculture and food	10.9%
Environment	7.5%
Atomic energy	0.5%
Other physics	0.4%

Among the persons questioned during this poll, 17 per cent said that they always watch television programs on science, but a comparable 16 per cent admitted never watching science shown on TV screens. Such figures will vary, of course, from country to country and culture to culture.

Another point of concern to the specialists meeting in the history-laden city of Luxembourg, now a major world financial center, was that of the impact of science-technology programs on viewers. Gerhard Sieler of the German Democratic Republic showed a video film "Are We Upsetting the Balance of Nature?" which concentrated on the possible global effects of a current Soviet plan to reverse the course of several major rivers (in order to reroute fresh water headed for estuaries in the Arctic Ocean to the parched regions of the southern U.S.S.R.). Alec Hughes, a visual aid specialist with the British Association for the Advancement of Science, believes that the growing ability of TV producers to induce spectators to analyze what they see and hear on the screen helps to broaden the medium's audience for specialized programs.

Both Hughes and Jacek Moscinski, a physicist from Cracow with experience on Polish TV, believe that today's most effective popularizers of science are often persons in their sixties or seventies — whereas many of the best classroom teachers of science and other technical subjects are often men and women younger than thirty-five years. Canada's Seguin believes, too, that the question of viewer ratings often gives rise to non-problems. "Is it not better today," he asked, "to have one million people out of a possible five million watching a science program when, before the advent of TV, a lecture hall with an audience of 150 was all that could be hoped for?"

As to the respective roles of researcher, communicator, and layperson, there seems to be a variety of opinion. In some cultures, the authority of the scientist or engineer is such that he or she commands much of the time on screen — an *ex cathedra* presentation outside the classroom, as it were. Sergei P. Kapitza of Moscow television's "The Evident and The Incredible" series cites the case of a subject most difficult to popularize, economics and economic planning. When Soviet television was preparing an interview with the

U.S.A.'s Wassily Leontief and the Soviet Union's Nikolay N. Inozemtsev, the two principals had such a telling forcefulness during rehearsals that, according to Kapitza, "all films were dropped in the final production." Fernand Seguin recalls a similar experience with the eminent biologist Jean Rostand appearing on CBC in 1969. The "talking head" was so impressive in this case that little supportive material had to be added. Still, there seems to be general agreement that that the talking head is a filming device to be avoided in most cases.

RELATING SCIENCE TO OUR DAILY ROUTINES

The communicator himself or herself (Henius of Danish television thinks that sex has no role to play in popularization) establishes his or her pedigree by both the level of interest and the degree of accuracy he can maintain in his TV presentations. Ms Reding, the Luxembourg communication specialist, maintains that "both film and word images must remain simple; redundancy and analogy to everyday life are essential." So, while the TV film on science or engineering begins to loom greater in the life of the audiovisual viewer, the very nature of the filmed message takes on new meaning. Suzanne Duval of the International Scientific Film Association reminds us at the same time that "the traditional scientific film is dead; it is being replaced by the contemporary television film depicting scientific or technological subjects."

Polish and Bulgarian experience has shown that a proficient communicator can win a wide audience with specialized productions on archeology and art history. A communicator can also enhance his effectiveness by the choice of accompanying music (if any). He can gain or suffer, as we know, from the day and hour when his program is scheduled — less a problem with his audience than with his own management. Gesinus Diemer, a physicist with Philips R&D Laboratories at Eindhoven (Netherlands), points out that the communicator has two options open for channelizing his message. One is what Diemer calls "radial communication," news of discovery emanating directly from a research center. The other is "tangential communication," an interdisciplinary approach which combines the results of research with common problems of current interest, e.g., energy sources, transport modes, improved consumer products. The first is normally practiced directly by a research scientist or engineer; the second filters through the presentation made by a specialized technical communicator.

International cooperation depends, in large measure, on how fully producers of specialized TV programs can gain access to sources outside their own countries. The free flow of information needs increasingly to take the form of loan or exchange of films, visits by TV teams, access to centers of research or technological development, exchanges of finished productions with suitably prepared sound tracks, and due compensation for copyright when required.

The participants at the European regional workshop on science popularization by TV were especially desirous that know-how on popularization be made available to apprentice specialists in developing countries who are launching or expanding their work in the popular communication of science and technology, and the influence of these on both traditional and evolving cultural patterns.

A FIRST CONCLUSION

In the words used in the final report of the working specialists, making their recommendations to the director-general of Unesco, this international organization "should provide funds and practical assistance to convene further working groups, seminars, symposia and [offer] training opportunities involving both countries already presenting science and technology on television and others wishing to introduce [these]." The Luxembourg workshop should prove to be a first step in this direction.

Other Articles on Communication by This Author

A French View of Technical Publishing, *Journal of Technical Writing and Communication*, 2:4, 1972.

Fifty Years After the Death of Flammarion, the Science Popularizer, with Y. V. Novozhilov, *Journal of Technical Writing and Communication*, 6:2, 1976.

	IMPACT OR IMPRESSION	SIZE OF AUDIENCE	COST PER CONTACT	SALES LEADS	MESSAGE CONTROL	FLEXIBILITY	TIMING CONTROL	REPETITIVE CONTACT	REACTION SPEED	CREDIBILITY	CLOSING THE SALE	
SALESMAN	5	2	1	4	4	5	4	2	5	5	5	(42)
MAGAZINE ADVERTISING	4	5	4	4	5	1	3	5	2	4	1	(38)
DIRECTORY ADVERTISING	3	4	4	3	5	1	2	3	1	4	1	(31)
DIRECT MAIL	5	3	2	4	5	3	3	2	3	3	3	(36)
PUBLICITY	4	5	5	5	2	1	1	3	3	5	1	(35)
EXHIBITS	5	2	2	2	3	5	1	1	5	5	5	(36)

Figure 1. Technical communications tools compared.

Comparative Evaluation of Sales Tools

To help marketers of process equipment evaluate their investments in sales methods, various promotion tools have been comparatively rated against 11 effectiveness and cost criteria.

George Black, Bozell & Jacobs, Inc., Union, N.J. 07083

Marketing executives responsible for determining the most effective means for launching a new product in the chemical or petrochemical field, or for sustaining and building the sales of an existing product line have to make a number of critical decisions. Some of these involve market research. Others involve sales and distribution policies. Still others are concerned with pricing, appearance, warranties and service. Another group of decisions involves product promotion and selling tools.

Top management seldom questions the allocation of funds involved with marketing functions. But when it comes to expenditures for sales promotion, everyone becomes an instant expert. One thing we know from experience. In spite of upfront analysis, intelligent positioning and pricing, and carefully planned selling and distribution policies, new product failure is more prevalent than is success. Ninety percent of all new products fail and are taken off the market within four years. Less than 3% of the more than 100,000 U.S. patents issued each year ever turn into profitable products.

The reasons are legion and synergistic. We can seldom pick out the straw that breaks the camel's back. But 40 years of living with process equipment on the manufacturing, buying, marketing, selling, and advertising fronts has provided me with a perspective not available in textbooks. It has helped me develop what I call the "fingerprint" theory. This theory is based on the observation that product success seems to come from identification of an area of significant difference (the product fingerprint) and then spreading the word about this difference to the right decision-makers. In my opinion, more products fail because this area of marketing is treated as a stepchild than for any other single reason.

Decisions, decisions

Marketing executives repeatedly face the need to make financial decisions on a wide variety of techical communications projects. The major subdivisions which require decisions are:

● Advertising in trade magazines (purchased space in media)

● Advertising in reference publications (purchased space in directories or prefile catalogs)

● Direct mailing to customers and prospects (printed matter mailed to select lists)

● Public relations/publicity (editorial space in various media)

● Exhibit participation (display space at conventions or exhibitions)

If you are involved with the marketing of process equipment, you have faced these decisions many times or delegated the responsibility to your advertising manager or advertising agency. In any case, the decisions on how much or how to spend it properly were made by asking one of these questions:

1. What did we do last year?
2. What is our main competitor doing?
3. How does the "boss" feel about it?
4. How would it look if we didn't do it?
5. Do we have the money?

Reprinted with permission from *Chem. Eng. Progr.*, vol. 79, no. 6, pp. 17–25, June 1983.

To some extent, each of these seemingly frivolous reasons for making a budget decision has some validity. Each is better than tossing a coin. Not much better, but better. Like the old-fashioned remedies, each is tied in some way to an observed pattern of success or at least not to a noticeable adverse reaction.

There ought to be a better way of arriving at a budget decision, and there is. Start with the listing of significant objectives or functions you want to accomplish with your promotion activities. Then, examine each of the sales or communication tools available and evaluate them against these objectives. Not in an absolute or academic sense but in a relative one, ask: How well does each method accomplish the specific objective? The result is a marketing management tool which helps you put your money and your efforts behind the methods which will accomplish for your product what needs to be done. It helps you fine-tune your promotion activities to your own product's fingerprints.

For comparative analysis to be valid, we need a norm that we can measure against. Since communications is not an exact science, we have to settle for the sales egineer, who, although not perfect, is the best all-around selling/communications tool.

Evaluation criteria

The key to this comparative analysis approach is a clear understanding of what it is you want the sales tool to do. Here are the most common objectives or functions of sales tools, stated in terms of criteria against which we can measure each tool:

1. Ability to penetrate the consciousness and be remembered (impact or impression)
2. Suitability for spreading the message to the entire prospect universe (size of audience)
3. Efficiency in reaching large numbers of prospects (cost per contact)
4. Suitability for securing inquiries or sales leads (sales lead development)
5. Capacity for telling the whole story, the way it should be told, and the same way each time (message control)
6. Facility in overcoming objections as they are raised (flexibility)
7. Ability to reach out and touch the prospect at your convenience and be there at the time of need, when the buyer or specifier is looking (timing control)
8. Suitability for repeating the message with frequency (repetitive contact)
9. Ability to sense the prospect's reaction rapidly (reaction speed)
10. Capacity for being believed (credibility)
11. Ability to get the signature on the order (closing the sale)

To evaluate each of the sales tools in terms of their strengths and weaknesses, we will apply a rating system from one to five with one being extremely weak and five being extremely strong, Figure 1. Your ratings might be different from mine and you may change them as you go from tool to tool, because these values have specific meaning for your product line and the tools ought to be rated comparatively as they fit your needs.

The Salesman

. . . best communications tool around. . .

No matter how you look at it or who does the looking, the salesman is the best communications tool around. Running down the line of evaluation criteria, here's how he stacks up for most marketers of chemical equipment.

Impact. He can surely penetrate the consciousness of a prospect and be remembered. His individuality, personality and appearance all set him apart. These characteristics are strengths, but they can also be weaknesses. He has to gain confidence, earn respect, and be liked. If he creates a negative image, however, the impact can work against him. Despite this, we have to rate him at the top of the heap for this objective. I'd give him a five.

Size of Audience. Here the salesman has a problem. He's one person and can only be at one place at a time. While he is shooting the breeze with Prospect A, Prospect B can be buying from a competitor. The universe he can reach is extremely limited. Even assuming he can make four calls a day or a 1,000 calls a year, the figure gets reduced rapidly when you consider the number of key accounts which are called on monthly and those hot accounts in the middle of a quote which require a number of repeat calls over a short span. For speading the message, I'd rate the salesman at two.

Cost per Contact. Here again the salesman suffers by comparison with other methods. The average cost per call is close to the $200 mark and that's a far cry from the cost of a letter, an ad, publicity item, or other sales tool. In terms of cost per contact, the salesman is the highest, which gives him the lowest score, one.

Sales Leads. The salesman does a good job of developing leads from the calls he makes. He can separate the wheat from the chaff and move from idea to idea, turning conversation into a product inquiry and an inquiry into an active sales lead. His numbers are small but his quality high. I would rate him a four in this area.

Message Control. The salesman can tell it like it is, like you wrote it, like you want it told. He can do pretty well at telling it the same way each time, particularly if he has audiovisual devices to help him. He's not perfect but he's right near the top. I'd give him a four.

Flexibility. There's nothing quite so flexible as the human mind. The salesman can overcome objections as they are raised. He can anticipate objections or sense them and get them out of the way before trying to close the sale. He leads the pack in this. A five.

Timing Control. The salesman can select his time in most cases. He can be there when he thinks there is a need or respond immediately to a call from a buyer or specifier. There are shortcomings, however. He may be at Prospect A when Prospect B has our immediate need. He may be on vacation or ill. In the area of timing control, he's very good but not perfect. I'd give him a four.

Repetitive Contact. When there's an active quote and invitations are extended, the salesman is welcome day-in, day-out. When he is trying to develop business, however, it's not quite as easy. It is costly. His customers are busy; unless he has something new to offer them, they may not have the time to listen. In rating the salesman's ability to repeat the same message with frequency, we have to give him a low score. I'd make it a two.

Reaction Speed. This is the time delay between the prospect's reaction and the sales or marketing department's awareness of that reaction. Here the salesman gets a high score, just as he does for flexibility. But don't forget that he can misinterpret and relay the wrong information. That's another story. For reaction speed I'd still rate him a five.

Credibility. Would you buy a used car from this man? Being believed goes hand in hand with building confidence. A good salesman, over a period of time, builds credibility. When it's built, nothing quite approaches its effectiveness. I'd rate him high in this area, particularly where custom equipment is concerned. My score in this category would be a five.

Closing the Sale. No question about it, the salesman has no peer in terms of getting the signature on the bottom line. I'd give him a five with no reservations.

Your scores may not agree with mine. They probably shouldn't. What is important is that your scores reflect your thinking in relation to your product and your markets. According to my chart, the salesman's total comparative score against a potential high of 55 is 42.

Magazine Advertising

. . . bold statements, and attractive graphics and colors penetrate our consciousness. . . .

The purchase of magazine space involves a number of selection criteria such as circulation verification, editorial evaluation, demographic percentages, readership, graphics, etc. These, however, are not our concern here. We want to review magazine advertising as a tool in comparison with other tools which might be used for the various objectives vital to the successful marketing of an engineered product.

Impact. Although the advertisement cannot be compared with the salesman in terms of the impact it can make, bold statements, and attractive graphics and colors penetrate our consciousness. For most products, when it comes to impact, I would have to rate magazine advertising just below the salesman. A four.

Size of Audience. The circulation of trade magazines in the process field runs between 50,000 and 100,000. When you consider that pass-along readership multiplies this by 3 or more, it is obvious that a single message in a magazine can reach a large prospect universe simultaneously. If we ignore the cost limitation, we would have to rate magazine advertising with a five for audience size. The only promotion tool which surpasses it is publicity, because more publications can be used with the same budget allocation. Since cost is considered in another category, I suggest leaving this with a top score. A five.

Cost per Contact. Here we have to weigh the judgment factors carefully. Compared with the $200-per-contact cost for the salesman, magazine advertising is measured in pennies. Three to 5 cents per contact is standard. However, not all of the contacts are prospects and that changes the figures. If you measure it by inquiries or responses, the cost goes up to approximately $25 or $30 per contact—still a lot lower than the salesman. If you measure it by impressions made, the cost is still lower, closer to $3 of $5 per prospect contact. For this function I would rate media advertising with a four.

Sales Leads. Sales leads result from repetitive contacts with prospective buyers and specifiers. As just stated, the cost of inquiries runs between $25 and $30 on the average. If you consider the untraceable ones which come through the phone and by means of letters, the figure drops appreciably. The trend in industry is to use the telephone when needs are current because it is faster and frequently less expensive. For future needs, the publication bingo card or the letter suffices. I would rate magazine advertising with four for its ability to stimulate and develop sales leads.

Message Control. Any printed piece automatically has absolute control over the message. You set in type what you want to say and the printing presses make sure that it is said the same way every time it appears. Memory plays no tricks, nor does individuality. In this area, the advertisement rates a five.

Flexibility. The converse of message control is flexibility. The finite nature of the printed word makes it completely inflexible. There is no way for an advertisement to overcome an objection that may be raised. Your ad may say that your design is trouble-free, but the reader who has had trouble with your product won't be impressed. Therefore, it is placed at the bottom of the heap, with a one.

Timing Control. Since the advertisement can be in a large number of places at the same time, the chances of it being there at time of need are better than that of a salesman. But it still must be at the publication a month before. I would give it a three.

Repetitive Contact. We all know from the wonders of television how the advertisement has a way of getting into our consciousness through repetition. The huge sum spent in consumer advertising can often lead to repetition *ad nauseam* and have an inverse effect. We may even learn to hate the product. But the odds are with the professionals. Repetition pays off and pays well. This is true even in industrial or technical advertising. Study after study shows that the same advertisement can be repeated over and over again with equally good results. If a message is right for the audience and it reflects what the company wants to say about its product, the advertisement can be used over and over again and find a welcoming audience with the same degree of effectiveness as on its initial insertion. For this objective, magazine advertising rates a five.

Reaction Speed. There is an automatic built-in time delay between prospect reaction and company awareness of what the reader may be thinking. Phone responses are relatively fast, letters take days, and bingo card responses weeks. Even then we only know the reaction of a small number of people, and for the most part they will be those who reacted favorably. When the salesman stands face to face with the prospect, the reaction is immediate, both favorable and unfavorable. The value is therefore much greater. In terms of reaction speed, magazine advertising rates no higher than a two.

Credibility. In spite of all the jokes about advertising and the news articles which expose occasional deceptive advertising, most people tend to believe the essence of an advertisement. This is particularly true in the advertising of engineered products where diagrams, curves, case history information, and other proof factors are often included. The salesman may still have an edge in this area, but advertising rates high. I would give it a four.

Close the Sale. With the exception of stock items, magazine advertising can't get the signature on an order. There have been some notable exceptions, particularly in the area of securing rentals or sample unit sales on memo billing for test purposes, but these are the exceptions. There is hardly enough room in a typical magazine advertisement to catch the eye and intrigue the reader. To think you can get the order as well is star-gazing. For this function, I would have to rate magazine advertising with a one.

Compared with the salesman's rating of 42 out of a possible 55, advertising shows a respectable figure of 38.

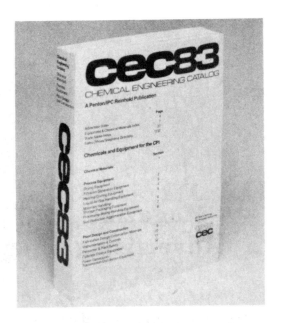

Directory Advertising

. . . credibility level is extremely high. . .

This category represents purchased space in directories or pre-file catalogs. Directories are generally annual or semi-annual publications which alphabetically list various products along with names, addresses, phone numbers and other information about the companies who manufacture those products. They are either horizontal across all industries such as "Thomas' Register," or they are vertical within an existing industry such as "Chemical Engineering Equipment Buyers Guide" and "Rubber Redbook." For the most part these directories seek to have the advertiser describe his product parameters with fractional ads close to the various headings. There is, however, a strong trend to using large advertisements and even inserts by the advertiser in directories.

Pre-file catalogs, such as "Chemical Engineering Catalog" in our industry and the Thom-Cat section of "Thomas' Register" for the horizontal market, attempt to get the advertiser to insert detailed catalog information in terms of sizes, construction materials, performance characteristics, etc.

We will treat directories and pre-files as a single advertising tool, but you should be aware that there are significant differences. The directory is primarily used when the purchaser or specifier knows what he wants but is looking for a source. It is also used when he knows what he wants and knows the source, but is looking for an address or phone number.

The pre-file catalog is more often used by central engineering personnel or project engineers who try to choose among various products with the same function. They are seeking comparative data. The need may not be an immediate one; it may be one on the drawing board. It is also used frequently as a replacement for individual company catalogs which may not be available. It is a convenient form and its value is related to the data made available by the advertisers.

Impact or Impression. A pre-filed catalog can make a better impression or have greater impact than a small ad or a single-page advertisement in a directory, but neither of these publications is thumbed routinely or regularly. Users are seeking specific information and the impact aspect is not as significant as the efficiency in which the advertisement or insert answers the need of the directory or catalog user. A score of three would be my decision.

Size of Audience. Certainly the directory or pre-file catalog can reach a larger audience than the individual salesman. Since it sits on a shelf, it is available at all times to a number of people in the company. It rates right up there with magazine advertising. The problem is that it can only make contact with this audience when the audience makes contact with it. It is not automatically looked at on a monthly basis the way a magazine is. For this reason, my rating in this category is slightly lower than an advertisement—a four.

Cost per Contact. In terms of contacts, directories and pre-file catalogs rate high. Their cost per contact is low. Many studies prove that people use them regularly. They are economical tools for making sure that your message is there when the buyer or specifier comes looking. I would rate them with a four.

Sales Leads. Unlike responses from magazine advertising, inquiries or sales leads which develop from directories or pre-file catalogs tend to be much closer to the actual sales or need. The numbers are small, but the quality is high. You can compare this to having your name in the phone book. When people want to reach you, the listing makes it easy. There is little generation of inquiry based on curiosity. My rating for this category would be a three.

Message Control. Directories and pre-files are printed material and as such provide absolute control over the message. As with advertising, since we are paying for the space, there are practical limitations to what we can illustrate and how much we can say. From this point of view, pre-file catalogs have the advantage in that they encourage us to give more data. For most pre-file catalogs, the costs go down rapidly as the advertiser takes additional space. Thus, a five.

Flexibility. The printed word is inflexible. This is even more of a problem with directories and pre-file catalogs than it is with advertisements. You can change an advertisement without too much difficulty. Altering the message, adding, subtracting or providing new figures, present no real problems. The short life of most magazines minimizes the danger of perpetuating a statement that is no longer applicable or harmful. On the other hand, directories and pre-file catalogs have a full-year life; since previous year's volume is generally moved down the line to others in the department, the life span is often appreciably expanded. The argument as to whether or not to show your complete agent list in an annual is perpetual. There is practically no flexibility for these tools, thus a one.

Timing Control. The advantage of the directory or the pre-file catalog is that it is always there when the buyer or specifier has the need. From the viewpoint of your control of timing, however, it is obviously weaker than the salesman or the advertisement. The message is fixed for at least a year. You just have to wait for the next issue if you have a new message to send. On a comparative basis I would give it a rating of two.

Repetitive Contact. Advertisements in annuals cannot reach out and make contact on a regular basis the way advertisements in magazines do. They have to sit there and wait for the interested party to come to them. Therefore, they are not an active tool for repeating the message you want to get across with any degree of frequency. They are there, but they can't call out. On the other hand, there is no need to change the message to attract attention. Change should be made to make the information more readily accessible and more meaningful. A rating of three is recommended.

Reaction Speed. Like any other piece of printed matter, there is no way for the advertiser to know the reaction of the reader unless there is a specific response. As with magazine advertising, we can't tell what they are thinking; so, for this function the rating is a one.

Credibility. Since the basic thrust of an advertisement in an annual is factual, the credibility level is extremely high. Your product better be able to do what you say it will do or you'll be wasting your money. This is not the place to encourage inquiries for products you don't make or are thinking of making. If you do this you will make more enemies than friends. The credibility rating is a four.

Close the Sale. With the exception of standard items, the directory or pre-file catalog doesn't close any sales. Advertisements may lead to phone calls or letters which result in sales, but the tool itself is just not built for the function. I'd give it a one.

Summing up the point score, we see that directories and pre-file catalogs show a total of 31 compared with 42 for the salesman and 38 for magazine advertising.

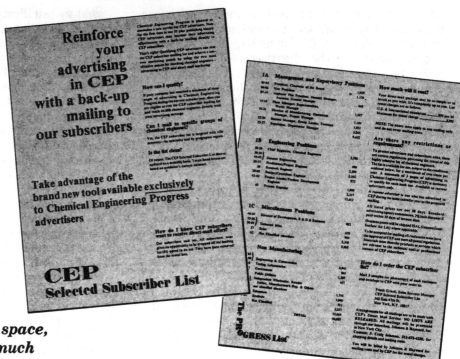

Direct Mail

. . . no limitations on space,
you can go into as much
detail as you want. . . .

Direct mailing or direct response refers to printed matter mailed to customers and prospects on lists we maintain or to "suspects" on purchased list. The forms are infinite from simple postcards to elaborate multicolor brochures and three-dimensional items which are decorative or useful. Creations are limited to the imagination of your advertising people as well as available funds. The most common items equipment manufacturers use are post-card packets, individualized letters, product flyers, and printed literature.

Impact or Impression. The tremendous variety in terms of size and graphics gives this tool a strong edge in terms of penetrating consciousness and being remembered. We have to rate it at the very top. A five.

Size of Audience. If funds were unlimited, audience size would be unlimited. Except for the post-card packet in which your product information is mailed along with a number of other product pieces, you pay for the creation, printing, envelope, handling and postage. In today's market, this is a considerable cost. It substantially reduces the size of the audience for which this sales tool can be used. "Target marketing" has become a byword. Audience selectivity is critical. In terms of audience size I would rate this tool a three.

Cost per Contact. As mentioned under audience size, the cost per contact is high. The post-card packet is very low, about the same as that offered by magazine advertising. But all other forms involve high preparation and mailing costs. I would rate it a two.

Sales Leads. Direct response is a good tool for developing inquiries or sales leads because it permits targeting or individualizing both the message and the audience so that the leads are very specific. You get what you ask for and you can ask for what you want, changing your request with each segment of the audience. For the development of sales leads, I would

rate direct response with a four.

Message Control. More than any other tool, direct mail permits you to tell the whole story, the same way everytime. Since there are practically no limitations on space, you can go into as much detail as you want. We have to rate it up there with every other printed sales tool, right at the top. Actually it has an edge over magazine advertising and even the salesman. I'd give it a five.

Flexibility. Once again we are dealing with the printed form, which means it is inflexible. It is finite. On the other hand, since we are targeting our mailing, the wording and inclusions can be varied with the audience, giving a degree of flexibility above that offered by media or directory advertising. Individual pieces may not be flexible, but the tool has flexibility potential built into it. For this reason I would rate it a three.

Timing Control. Direct mail may not arrive at the time of need, but it certainly is true that we can make our mailings when we want to and to whom we want them to go. From this point of view, we control the timing better than an annual directory or a monthly magazine. The problem is our timing may be off—a rating of three.

Repetitive Contact. Although it is certainly true that you can mail and remail the same piece of information over and over again, the cost factor comes into play. The message can be repeated frequently, but gaining attention with the same piece mailed on a repetitive basis is not so easy. We are all familiar with the junk-mail piles that hit the round file everyday. Experience seems to show that the second mailing of the same piece to the same audience will produce about the same results as the first mailing. Beyond that, results fall off rapidly. For repetitive contact, I would rate direct mail a two.

Reaction Speed. There is no way of knowing what the respondents think of our direct mail until we get a response. But with direct mail the response is much faster than with the other forms of advertising. If we specifically ask them to do something, we know whether or not they have done it. That's a pretty quick reaction. Mail questionnaires can often ask about product awareness and provide us with valuable research information. The time delay is slight. Response comes generally in a matter of days. For this function I would rate direct mail a three.

Credibility. The credibility is high. With direct mail you have the opportunity to tell a complete story, to illustrate it, to overcome objections before they are raised, and to build confidence. On the other hand, the general perception of mail pieces is one of suspicion. Although this is certainly not the fault of technical or industrial mailings, there is no escaping. And since we don't have the opportunity for sufficient repetition to build the credibility, I would rate direct mail for this objective with a three.

Close the Sale. Direct mail has a better chance of closing the sale than the other advertising forms. Although not as good as the salesman, it can incorporate an order blank and get the signature on the dotted line for standard or stock items, for special products, for laboratory test work, etc. My rating would be a three.

Direct mail gets a comparative evaluation rating of 36 compared with 42 for the salesman, 38 for magazine advertising, and 31 for directory advertising.

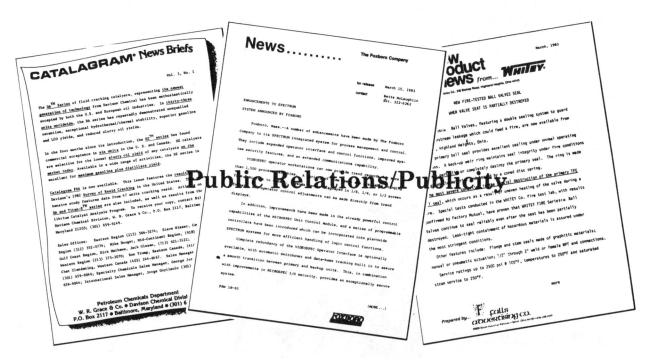

Public Relations/Publicity

. . . most economical for developing sales leads and inquiries. . . .

We now move into the area of editorial space in publications: feature articles, case histories, new product or new literature items, and a variety of other editorial insertions. This is exposure for our product message which is not related to the cost of the space. The cost to prepare these may be similar to the cost of preparing advertisements, but once prepared, there is no further cost other than mailing to a particular publication or group of publications and hoping it will be printed. Unfortunately, it is a tool too often handled haphazardly, since planned technical or industrial publicity activities are very closely related to the success or failure of products in our market place.

Impact or Impression. The impact of publicity is often made more by accumulation than by the individual insertion. Since the material is editorial in nature, there is a minimum sales thrust. Generally the illustrations are in black and white although there is a trend for publications to utilize color. Because of the accumulated impact, the rating is on the high side—a four.

Size of Audience. No tool can help us spread our message to as wide an audience as this one. Since we are not paying for the space, we can send our releases and stories not only to the most important publications, but to those in special or fringe areas as well. We can attempt to get our editorial message into publications much beyond the reach of our limited media budgets. Public relations/publicity rates a five in this category.

Cost per Contact. There is no sales tool that can make as many contacts at so low a cost. Companies keeping records of publicity exposures show related costs in mils. This tool has no equal in terms of low cost per contact—a five.

Sales Lead Development. Because of the extended exposure permitted by this tool, it is the most economical one for developing sales leads and inquiries. For this reason it is widely used where it is important to ferret out interest areas for further follow-up. Once again we have to rate it at the very top, a five.

Message Control. This is a category in which public relations/publicity finds itself on the low end. We can write the story or the release exactly as we want to; but since we are not paying for the space in the magazines, the editor is the boss. The story can be re-written, even distorted at times. Of course, it can end up in the waste basket and never appear. Fortunately, the advantages far outweigh the risks; the better your relationship with editors, the more certain you are that the message will be close to the way you want it. For this function, however, I would rate it a two.

Flexibility. As with every printed form, there is no flexibility. Objections cannot be overcome as they are raised. In this category we have to rate public relations/publicity at the bottom, with a one.

Timing Control. Although we can send out publicity releases whenever we want to, we have absolutely no control over when they appear. This is the province of the editor. There is no way to be sure that your message will be there at the time of need, when the buyer or specifier is looking for an answer to a problem. For this function publicity ranks low. A one.

Repetitive Contact. The message cannot be re-peated with any kind of frequency. Variations on the theme can be provided but the same message can be used only once. Repetitive contact is made through a multiplicity of releases; well-planned programs can

hope to get across predetermined messages with a high degree of frequency. I'd rate it a three.

Reaction Speed. Since publicity tends to generate many inquiries at low cost, it becomes an excellent tool for exploring prospect reaction. The time delay is about the same as that for magazine advertising, but the numbers are so much larger in relation to the cost that the tool has a greater value for this function. I would give it a rating of a three.

Credibility. Since the material is editorial in na-ture, representing independent third-party endorse-ment, the credibility is extremely high, particularly in the area of technical features. People tend to quote the statements included assuming the editor would not have permitted the information to appear with-out some verification. Credibility is at the top of the heap. A five.

Close the Sale. Public relations/publicity is not a sales closer. It is an image builder. An identity devel-oper. An inquiry producer. By its nature, it is low key and of no value in getting the signature on the bot-tom line. I would give it a one for this function.

The total score for publicity/public relations is 35, this compares with 42 for the salesman, 38 for adver-tising, 31 for directories, and 36 for direct mail.

Trade Shows/ Exhibits

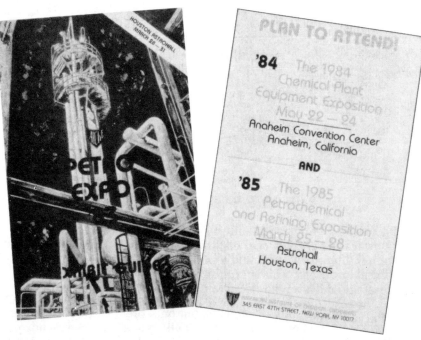

. . . advantages of the salesman can be multiplied at your booth. . . .

This sales tool provides an opportunity to put your products on display and to have your people meet customers and prospects face to face. It is not quite the same, but fairly close to having important deci-sion-makers seek you out and visit your facilities. It can multiply the effectiveness of the individual sales-man, because he can have on hand his technical sup-port and top management in addition to actual equipment.

Impact or Impression. Obviously a top rating for this function. You have your opportunity not only to put your best foot forward, but your best feet. All the attributes and advantages of the salesman can be multiplied at your booth. It rates a five.

Size of Audience. Limitations in terms of size of audience are severe. Exhibitions such as Petro Expo attract an audience of 35,000, but local exhibitions are sometimes numbered in an audience of a few hundred. There is no pass-along exposure as there is with printed advertising. The total potential is the audience. Even this figure is reduced somewhat by how many visit your booth and stop in for discussion. Compared with the mass circulation of most maga-zines, we have to face the fact that participation at exhibitions provides a more limited audience. A rat-ing of two would be adequate.

Cost per Contact. Here too, the limited audience size works against you. For an average show investment the cost per contact might be three to four times that of your media investment. On the other hand, in terms of cost per inquiry or sales lead, the cost might be very similar. For cost per contact, however, we would have to rate it on the low side, a two.

Sales Leads. Properly planned exhibits with booths manned by technically qualified personnel generally result in good inquiry development at a cost per inquiry lower than that of media advertising. One of the reasons is that the exhibit audience takes the action and starts the discussion. They come to you. Another is the fact that the equipment is on hand so that there is less guess work. Inquiries tend to be meaningful. The numbers may be small, but the quality, extremely high. As a tool for sales lead development I would rate exhibits two.

Message Control. Exhibits permit an opportunity to tell the story over and over again to the passing audience. There is absolute control of the message in terms of painted signs, audiovisual devices, and individual sales personnel properly trained. The opportunity for message reinforcement makes this an excellent tool for getting your message across properly. But there is frequently confusion—many voices over which you have limited control. I'd rate it a three.

Flexibility. Because you are face to face with a prospect, you have complete flexibility. You can overcome objections as they are raised. Because you have other people to call upon as well as equipment, it is a lot easier to prove your point. For this function, I would rate exhibits with a five.

Timing Control. Since exhibits are set up on an annual or semi-annual basis, or at the whim of a local association or group, the advertiser has no control over the timing. There is an advantage in that the buyer or specifier comes to you, but chances are he is looking in general not reacting to a specific need as he might be when referring to a directory or a pre-file catalog. For timing control, exhibits get a low mark. A one.

Repetitive Contact. At conventions or exhibitions you get one chance only. You state your message graphically and verbally, and that's it. You catch the prospect as he goes by or you've lost him. This tool offers no opportunity for repetitive contact with any meaningful frequency. The rating is one.

Reaction Speed. Because you are face to face with the prospect, and talking with him, reaction speed is instantaneous. There is no time delay. You ask the question and you get your answer; if you are perceptive, you read between the sentences. For reaction speed, I'd rate exhibits with a five.

Credibility. If ever you have an opportunity to be believed, this is it. You have the full arsenal of equipment and other personnel to bring to bear on your remarks. Exhibits rate at the top when it comes to credibility. A five.

Closing the Sale. At exhibitions you have an opportunity to get the signature on the bottom line. Although not very common in the United States, on the European scene the booths always have a separate room for private negotiations and sales closing. After all, what better chance could there be provided you are talking to the right people. You have your technical personnel, your sales personnel, and possibly your management. You have the equipment or reasonable facsimile. This should be the time for closing and the tool gets a high rating. A five.

Totalling up the scores we find exhibits earned a rating of 36 compared with a 42 rating for salesman, a 38 rating for magazine advertising, a 31 rating for directory advertising, a 36 rating for direct mail, and a 35 rating for public relations/publicity.

Black

In summary

RATE EACH TOOL FROM 5 (HIGHEST) TO 1 (LOWEST) TO INDICATE ITS VALUE FOR EACH FUNCTION

	IMPACT OR IMPRESSION	SIZE OF AUDIENCE	COST PER CONTACT	SALES LEADS	MESSAGE CONTROL	FLEXIBILITY	TIMING CONTROL	REPETITIVE CONTACT	REACTION SPEED	CREDIBILITY	CLOSING THE SALE	
SALESMAN	5	2	1	4	4	5	4	2	5	5	5	(42)
MAGAZINE ADVERTISING	4	5	4	4	5	1	3	5	2	4	1	(38)
DIRECTORY ADVERTISING	3	4	4	3	5	1	2	3	1	4	1	(31)
DIRECT MAIL	5	3	2	4	5	3	3	2	3	3	3	(36)
PUBLICITY	4	5	5	5	2	1	1	3	3	5	1	(35)
EXHIBITS	5	2	2	2	3	5	1	1	5	5	5	(36)

Each sales tool has a relatively high total score, but the strengths and weaknesses are obvious. The values, individually evaluated, should help you invest wisely in promotion tools. The numerical values may not agree with your own interpretation, but they can be used as a management tool for your advertising department or agency. You can weigh each function and rate each tool, keeping your product's fingerprint in mind. You can come up with the right answers, if you ask the right questions. It certainly beats flipping a coin.

Part IV
Producing Marketable Copy

Section IV-A
Writing to Sell

"Technical Communication in Marketing," by C.F. Rohne, explores some of the end products marketing-oriented communicators might produce.

"Keeping Your Trade Name or Trademark out of Court," by F. Delano, describes a procedure used for selecting a new corporate or brand name.

"Add Style to Your Technical Writing," by D.L. Plung, details some important ingredients needed to improve the style of scientific and technical writing.

"Technical Wording in Advertising: Implications for Market Segmentation," by R.E. Anderson and M.A. Jolson, presents results of studies made to determine whether technical language should be avoided in print media.

"News for Print," excerpted from *CH2M Hill Guidelines,* gives valuable information on content, format, and media relations concerning news releases.

"The Role of Technical Literature in Marketing Communications at Stelco: Standards and Style," by E. Zucker, describes how advertising and technical styles of writing can be reconciled.

"Three Vital Views for News Release Writers," by E. Mazzatenta, gives worthwhile suggestions for producing scientific and technical news releases.

"You Can Often Enhance Your Product by Using External Resources . . . . and Here's How," by L.K. Moore, points out the advantages of using supplemental external resources for the editing and production stages.

TECHNICAL COMMUNICATION IN MARKETING

Carl F. Rohne
McDonnell Douglas Automation Company

INTRODUCTION

The increasing technical sophistication of American industry, combined with ever-mounting competition for the available sales dollar, represents an important professional challenge for the technical communicator. In particular, the expanding service industries in the U.S., along with more traditional technical industries such as electronics, chemicals, and automobiles, offer the professional communicator a wide range of marketing-oriented job opportunities.

Technical products need technical communicators who can relate them to potential sales prospects. Increasingly the technical communicator can find himself a member of the marketing or product promotion team. In this role, the end product of his activities is geared to raising his company's share of available sales.

As many of our colleagues who are in marketing already know, the effort of promoting technical products is a highly competitive one. Your company's product line must be interpreted, explained, and finally "sold", and that is where we as professional technical communicators have a tremendously significant role to play. If we choose to capitalize on this opportunity, we are in the enviable position of being the interface between two worlds — our own in-house technical people, and the wide world of the customer. Our talents as intermediaries, as men and women who are able to translate highly complex ideas into readable prose and graphics, are in demand because those are precisely the talents required to create an effective technical marketing program.

SERVICE INDUSTRY MARKETING

The service industries in the U.S. (on which the observations in the paper are premised) have in common a high-technology product, an intensely competitive marketplace in which to operate, and potential customers who are both sophisticated in their own fields and familiar with the best in marketing and public relations. These factors pose a professional challenge for the technical communicator who hopes to succeed in technical marketing.

The service industries in particular, and high-technology industries in general, need technical writers/editors to produce a wide variety of marketing and product promotion literature, including manuals, proposals, brochures, and advertisements.

Technical marketing communicators should be writers who are sensitive to the nuances of language, who have some flair for design and graphics, who like to write as much as they like to do research, who enjoy (or at least accept) the give and take of criticism and compromise (salesmen can be hostile when their job depends on your literary efforts), and who can sort a complex technical idea into marketable segments.

Sensitivity to Language –
Marketing requires an ability to write not merely clearly, but with verve and excitement, to write with a feel for exactly the turn of phase which will relate product to potential customer.

Design and Graphics –
Because the atmosphere in the service industries is highly commercial, the successful marketing communicator has to comprehend the interrelationship of words and graphics, not simply recognizing "good illustrations" but knowing how to help the artist or designer to develop graphics that are appealing and integrated with copy.

Liking to Write —
A not so obvious quality as it might appear at first blush, since some technical writers much prefer research and blueprint reading to the mechanical act of creating text.

Service industry marketing shops are looking for writers who are willing and constitutionally able to spend many hours writing, polishing, rewriting, and redesigning sometimes only a very few lines of copy. The ability to produce a 2000 page manual in readable prose on exact schedule is of less value than a willingness to rewrite a brochure lead paragraph 20 times in order to achieve *precisely* the sales message that you and the marketing director both know you have to have.

Willingness to Listen –
A corollary of enjoying the act of writing is the willingness to engage in give and take over your literary *bons mots*. Salesmen, marketing managers, field reps, and many others who are part of (or think they are part of) marketing will have ideas to contribute to your work. The marketing-oriented technical communicator has to be willing to listen to, and often to accept, a new approach to *his* proposal, or product description, or favorite brochure. Furthermore, once a marketing piece is completed, it is seldom really finished. The technical communicator must be willing to revise, to add new concepts as they are

CARL F. ROHNE
1537 Ross Avenue
Creve Coeur, MO 63141

Specialist, Product Promotion
Hospital Services Division, McDonnell Douglas Automation Company, St. Louis, Missouri
Writing and editing brochures, newsletters; AV presentations; coordinating conventions and exhibits

Past Treasurer, St. Louis Chapter STC
Community College Social Science Association

Ph.D., University of Southern California; M.A., Stanford University; A.B., Washington University

Publications: "Editing the Small Study Proposal," ITCC Proceedings, 1973; "Phototypesetting for Proposals," Technical Communication, Third Quarter 1974.

Reprinted with permission from *Proc. 22nd Int. Tech. Commun. Conf.*, 1975, pp. 28–30.

developed by the Research staff, and to discard prose he thought was great but which fell flat in the field when used by the sales force. You must be prepared to rewrite and redesign quickly and without proprietary pride in your last offering.

Technical Interpretation –

Because they deal in high-technology products and services, the service industries require technical communicators who can translate highly complex, often abstract ideas into marketable concepts fit for client consumption. Tech writers have been doing this for years – the difference in the service industries is the breadth of the client base and the diversity of product comprehension levels. By way of example, my own company (MCAUTO Health Services)* sells shared computer services to hospitals under three rubrics, Hospital Financial Control, Hospital Data Collection, and Hospital Patient Care. The programming behind these concepts is extremely complex as is the hardware to make the systems work, both at MCAUTO and in the hospitals. These products are not like toothpaste: you cannot, as a communicator, assume that your audience understands what it is buying. An educational effort, long before a sale takes place, is implicit in our marketing campaign. This educational effort is partially the responsibility of the technical communicators (writers), who must sort out the "computereze" of the research and development personnel, find the marketable wheat in the mass of technical chaff, and then design marketing aids which educate the potential client on what the products, do, what they'll do for him, and why MCAUTO's products do those things better than someone else's.

Versatility –

Subsuming other characteristics, versatility is the real key to what service industry marketing departments are looking for. The service industries tend to be new and less organizationally specialized (read, "departmentalized"), than the industrial megacompanies with technical products.

The technical writer who has a broad background in industry should do well. Manuals, proposals, technical manuals which describe a product, brochures, and advertising may all be part of the marketing tech writer's weekly fare. To succeed, or even to enjoy this kind of work, requires a willingness to suffer frequent shifts of priorities and styles of writing.

With these requirements in mind, let us look at the areas in which a marketing-oriented technical communicator might be expected to work.

THE TECHNICAL COMMUNICATOR'S PRODUCTS

Technical communicators who have done well in other industries will find that marketing, especially in the service industries, represents a logical career path upwards. The products with which most of us are familiar are, with few exceptions (advertising probably being the greatest), exactly those which are used by service industry marketing and product promotion departments to sell their technical product line. Thus, the technical communicator who has done well with aerospace proposals, or electronics "overview" manuals, or who has been a versatile general editor, etc., will find that he has much to offer a marketing department. Let's look at some of the technical communicator's sales tools and see what the communicator has to offer the service industries.

MANUALS

The technical manual is increasingly regarded as a valuable sales tool, one whose content and appearance deserve careful attention. Why? Because the manual is a critical bridge between technical personnel and the customer. In MCAUTO Hospital Services, the manual bridges the often formidable chasm between, let us say, a computer system analyst and a hospital assistant administrator. The manual writer/editor must take complex materials from his tech people and turn them into understandable, yet intellectually sophisticated, prose and illustrations for an audience with demonstrated technical expertise in its own field.

The appearance of manuals is also considered important in the competitive environment in which most service industries operate, and the technical communicator with manual experience who can make the mental transition to marketing can prove an invaluable addition to the promotional staff. Because documentation can be an important element in winning a sale, and because customers will compare documentation for ease of use, readability, appearance, etc., the system-level manual is frequently used during early customer contacts to help explain the company product in detail. This implies that manuals must receive the closest attention from the technical communicator, who may often be asked to begin his marketing career in this area, helping the technical people tell their story in detail, while keeping a wary eye on the needs and requirements of the sales staff who will use the manual in the field as an important sales aid.

PROPOSALS

An important source of new business for many service industries is developing around the proposal, familiar to many technical communicators who have cut their teeth in aerospace, armaments, or government vending. The proposals which you, as a marketeer in a service industry, will be asked to write or edit are generally prepared to much less stringent RFPs than government proposals because the RFP frequently issues from a private (i.e., non-governmental) source. In my own case, MCAUTO's Hospital Services Division responds to over 250 requests for a proposal each year, most of them from individual hospitals or hospital groups who simply want us to "put it in writing". We have also responded to much larger and more complex RFPs, organized much as are those emanating from Washington, with the same kinds of restrictions on content, organization, style, etc. In most cases, however, there is a considerable degree of implied latitude in how you go about answering a proposal request, and this gives the technical communicator an important avenue for making known his skill as a technical interpreter and his talents as a writer. Design, prose style, and selection and type of illustration can be much better custom tailored to meet what you, the communicator (working closely with the field marketing representative), know the customer needs to see in order to evaluate your product intelligently and favorably. Many of the tricks of standardization which we have taught each other over the years in meetings such as this also apply, allowing the communicator to concentrate on honing a specialized and individualized message for that one particular customer. Often, you will find yourself in a competitive environment in which several of your competitors have

---

*Since this paper was published, the company name has been changed to McAuto Health Services.

been asked also to submit proposals. Because of the commercial atmosphere in which you are working, there is much more scope and opportunity to "pull out the stops" with imaginative use of color, clever page formats, photographs that convey mood as well as message, and other tricks which your experience and your personality will dictate.

ADVERTISING

Because advertising, particularly in specialized organs, is considered a major method of attracting sales prospects, the technical communicator in service industry marketing will devote a significant fraction of his time to writing and thinking about ads. Underneath the razzle dazzle of the professional advertising agency there is a solid core of help for your marketing effort. The agency (and, by the way, retaining an agency appears the best and most expeditious way of achieving your advertising goals) can be of inestimable help in preparing your ad campaign, from market potential analyses, through the preparation of a comprehensive ad plan, to design, layout, and final writing of copy for your ads. Through the whole process, the technical communicator can play the role of advisor on the subtle nuances of the technical message which he knows has to be part of the ad. Again, to restate an earlier premise, the technical communicator is a medium between the technical forces of his own company and the professionals of the ad agency. A note of caution: ad agency account executives *are* professionals, and in terms of what the ad should look like and how it should reach your audience they will insist on having (and should have) the final say. But no agency can have a staff large enough to be completely technically conversant with all of the complexities of every one of their clients' businesses. Therefore, they need the kinds of technical prose inputs which the technical communicator who is privy to his company's marketing philosophy has to offer.

BROCHURES

Perhaps the most exciting avenue for the creative technical communicator to really prove his ability as a member of the marketing team lies in brochures, those marvelous, multicolored, artistic productions which we dream of producing some midnight while huddled with irascible engineers finishing a manual for the XQ/P37 — Mark 6 — all 2,318 pages of it! Well, product promotion work gives the technical communicator the opportunity to live out his fantasy, and to draw a rather nice salary for it at the same time. Brochures are the *sine qua non* of technical marketing, especially in the service industries. Brochures also represent a good application of the technical communicator's skill as interface between customer and technical forces. Because a brochure, be it 2 or 20 pages, black and white or color, pocket size, tri-fold, or 8½ by 11, can be scheduled and planned for, it is the ideal foil for displaying the company product line to absolutely maximum advantage. The technical message (and there must be one) can be worked out through hours of reading, discussion, and close coordination

with your company's technical folk. After these necessary preliminaries, you the writer can really go to work, distilling the thousands of technical, often arcane, words on your product into the quintessential few hundred which make the customer understand not only what your product is, but what it will do for him, and why yours will do it better than anyone else's. And the guts of all of that argumentation is the technical message which we as technical communicators have generated from our interface with marketing and product development (or research, or advanced products or whatever your company calls its skunk works).

Brochures, if they are done right, represent a considerable investment in time and patience. Time must be spent in learning the technical personnel, their contributions to the product line, their thought processes, and their idiosyncracies of terminology and phraseology. Patience is required to listen through endless arguments and counter arguments between technical types, in hearing or seeing the buried word or phrase which triggers in the subconscious of a good marketeer that bell that says "Hey, that's a marketable idea if I can only get him to talk about it a bit more".

For many of us, there is a serendipitous spinoff from writing and producing brochures — the good feeling of being totally responsible for every aspect of your own creation, and the knowledge that you'll be around to watch the end product come rolling off the color press.

It is a good feeling to take a rough idea, which, quite possibly you as one of the marketing team thought of, do the research, coordinate the multifarious technical inputs, turn out eminently readable prose, and then move into the art and production cycle. Working with your own (or an agency's) art director and staff, you develop the kinds of illustrations to fit your conception of what the brochure is to look like, untrammelled by specs, regulations, or prior conventions. Good taste is what really matters, an innate sense of proportion and "fit" (for want of a more exact word), and it is up to you and the artist to establish the visual appearance. Finally, you can watch the mechanics of printing, often in three or more colors, itself a learning experience and the rewarding end product of your weeks of labor.

CONCLUSION

Not every technical communicator would (or will) find himself happy in the world of marketing, but for those who appreciate a creative professional challenge and who have the good fortune or the insidious wiles to get them into this area, there exists an important opportunity for growth and advancement. The technical communicator will not, by himself, solve his company's marketing problems, but his expertise in language and graphics, his publications skill, and his ability to deal with complex technical concepts and terminology can prove of real assistance in a progressive technical company, especially in the fastest growing segment of American business, the service industries.

Keeping your trade name or trademark out of court

Frank Delano

Mr. Delano is president of Frank Delano & Associates, Los Angeles, specialists in name development, corporate identity, and marketing communications.
His book, Total Corporate Identity, *will be issued this fall by the Whitney Library of Design.*
Illustration
by Richard A. Goldberg.

Selecting a new corporate or brand name no longer is as simple as in 1879, when Harley Procter, inspired by reading Psalm 45, named his company's hand soap Ivory. Not only has the process become complex from a creative standpoint, but also the sheer volume of needs for naming brought about by mergers, product proliferation, and other marketplace changes have created legal minefields.

Some 54,000 trademarks were filed with the U.S. Patent and Trademark Office in fiscal 1981 – the most ever. This figure compares with 32,803 filings a decade ago and 23,242 in 1960.

People in the business of developing names estimate that the volume will come close to doubling again in five years. According to a widely held view, corporations are "stockpiling" names for future use (or perhaps to sell to other companies at a premium). The idea is to secure a good name today rather than be forced to accept a less attractive one tomorrow.

When the trade names and trademarks in the world marketplace are added to the flood in the United States, we can easily envision great confusion in the consuming public by 1985, which will extend the chain of legal battles. Recently, for example, Western International Hotels (now Westin Hotels) brought suit against Best Western International for dilution of its trade name, and Vidal Sassoon, Inc. took legal action against jeans maker Sasson concerning television commercials that made the syllable sound more "soon" than "son."

Settlements in some of these battles are hardly penny ante, for legal fees, damages, and marketing repercussions may run into millions of dollars. Helene Curtis agreed to pay Church & Dwight Co. $2 million in damages and to surrender its Arm in Arm baking soda deodorant trademark because it too closely resembled the latter's Arm & Hammer baking soda trademark.

A common misconception on the part of the new or the small company is that the whale takes no interest in the minnow. Not so, as demonstrated by what happened to United Telecommunications Corporation. Between 1972, when it adopted its name, and 1979, the Latham, New York distributor of telecommunications systems was virtually unknown at the national level. Then its first public offering of common stock, coupled with an aggressive advertising effort, caught the eye of United Telecommunications, Inc., the big Kansas City telephone services enterprise. It sued the smaller company for illegal infringement on its name. Despite the fact that the New York company had the name first, its failure to claim ownership outside New York State and the overwhelming material advantages to the plaintiff for use of the name United Telecommunications in interstate trade obliged the New York company to surrender its corporate name and switch to UTC Group, Inc.

But its tribulations were not over. Within months, UTC was challenged by an even larger company, United Technologies Corporation, which claimed legal ownership to the initials when used in the telecommunications field. So the Latham company once again adopted a new moniker, Coradian Corporation, a name with no bridge to its past. A company official summarized the experience in these words: "It was disruptive and costly, and it has blurred ten years of industry identity."

The victory does not always go to the Goliath; witness Goodyear's encounter with a small Colorado tire company. A Denver federal district court ruled that Big O Tire Dealers had the rights under common law to a snowmobile track called Big Foot. The court assessed damages of about $17 million against the world's largest tire producer in connection with its introduction of Big Foot radials.

Such a decision need not be the outcome. For the company willing to do its homework and ask the tough questions –

How should we start?

How can we minimize the chance of infringing on someone else's name?

After we have chosen an identifier, what steps should we take to protect our investment in it?

– the outcome can be quite different. Let's see how to avoid problems.

Where to start

Before embarking on the journey, obviously you have to have some charts. First, taking into account future areas of corporate activity, compile a list of all trade names and trademarks in the subject field and related fields of endeavor. (A *trademark*, by the way, is a brand name used on goods moving in the channels of trade. A *trade name*, on the other hand, identifies companies and organizations. A trade name does not have to be a trademark, and vice versa.)

There are names with dictionary words like Spring Clean, initial names like AM International, surnames like Goldman, Sachs, and invented names like Nestea. Company and brand names in use can be obtained from directories, registers, journals, and magazines. A caution, however: for a variety of reasons, many names are not included in these publications.

To forestall rivals, many companies register names similar to those they have adopted. Ethicon, a health products subsidiary of Johnson & Johnson, holds rights to a shopping list of product names similar to Ethicon—Ethibond, Ethi-Pack, Ethilon, and so on.

The search through names already registered will reveal which companies have challenged others that have come too close to their identifiers. These companies should be noted on a separate list for use when the best prospects undergo review. Companies with track records for thwarting others from diluting their identifiers habitually peruse the white and yellow telephone directories in all cities and on a weekly basis review trademarks posted for registration.

Heading the list of trademark fighters is Coca-Cola, whose trademark research department employs some 25 investigators. The company files 40 to 60 trademark suits every year to prevent its trademarks from becoming generic words, which would depreciate 90 years and millions of dollars of investment in its identity.

Companies that have lost infringement suits or agreed to covenants limiting the use of their marketing names have learned the hard way that plaintiffs do not have to be direct competitors. The settlement of the trademark suit pressed by Vidal Sassoon—best known for hair-grooming products—against Sasson jeans stipulated that the jeans maker must make clear that *Sasson* is pronounced differently from *Sassoon* and that its logo bear no resemblance to Sassoon's. Sasson must also restrict its name to clothing and luggage, whereas Vidal Sassoon (the company's founder) can use his full name on a new jeans line.

Make it stand apart

A review of the lists of all trade names and trademarks in your field and related fields will help you decide what kind of name you should choose to make the company stand apart and minimize the chance of infringing on someone else's preempted nomenclature. An invented word may prevent infringement when an industry or a product group is overcrowded with names composed of dictionary words or initials. A dictionary word, on the other hand, may prevent infringement when the word is uncommon in the field of endeavor or in the product group.

The rapid growth of the health care industry, for instance, has created certain identity problems because of too many similar corporate names. National Medical Enterprises looks like National Medical Care, and American Health Services resembles American International Health Services. Advanced Healthcare, Advanced Health Systems, Americana Healthcare, and American Healthcare Management are more examples.

When Houston's Medenco, Inc., one of the largest hospital management companies, sought a novel corporate name, management and the board selected Lifemark, a neologism.

Obviously, an appropriate surname is often the safest direction to take in naming an organization. Such a choice would probably obviate the need for a modifying word, which federal and state registration requirements often demand.

It may be tempting to include one of the familiar words that convey high quality, professionalism, stature, or something else favorable. While one of those words might be an excellent marketing name, more than likely it already identifies a company or product in your industry.

The same is true for dictionary words related to industries or products. For instance, calling a new restaurant chain or line of prepared foods Escoffier or a brand of hunting equipment or razor blades Excalibur will only increase the odds for a trademark or trade name confrontation.

When the Helmsley hotel chain announced the grand opening of the swish Palace in New York City, it was promptly sued by the owner of a small hotel with the same name in lower Manhattan. Helmsley had already spent a considerable sum having the Palace logo inscribed on thousands of items. But the chain was forced to modify the name of the chic Madison Avenue hostelry to the Helmsley Palace.

Similarities in trade names and trademarks within a certain field or product classification may give rise to the dangerous assumption of precedent and the possibly faulty reasoning that "if a dozen companies are using XYZ, we can do it too." An investigation would probably show, however, that competition is not present, legal rights under common law (first use of the name in the channels of trade) cannot be proven, or companies have been casual about testing assumptions.

Remember that decisions on trade name and trademark disputes are decided on the basis of what is believed to be going on in the buyer's or the user's mind. Issues of registration and infringement are won and lost on consumer psychology. Also, the public is an unnamed third party in every lawsuit because of its right to protection from being misled or deceived.

Establish the choice

When the name has been chosen, its legal availability should be evaluated. Legal clearance cannot be ensured as easily as the name's novelty or adaptability for several reasons, the most important being that tens of thousands of identifiers are recorded at neither the state nor the federal levels (although under common law legal rights are well established through their use) and that a review of registered trademarks may prove inconclusive since the patent office is only now processing applications submitted 12 to 16 months ago.

Here are three suggestions to help determine if the new name is infringing on someone else's:

☐   Advertise the new name (without identifying the corporation) in national trade and business publications to invite a challenge.

☐   Retain a firm specializing in trademark law to make a search in your fields of endeavor or product and service classifications. A search of trademarks should include the federal registers, the *Official Gazette of the Patent Office*, and applications pending at the patent office.

☐   Review telephone directories, including the yellow pages, in all large communities.

The day that management or the board approves the name, the company should take steps to feature the name (without corporate endorsement) on products and business documents moving in interstate or foreign commerce channels. In this way the company can prove commercial adoption and the date of actual use. (Also, featuring a name in these channels is a requirement for obtaining a federal trademark registration.)

The company should also immediately reserve the name in the state of incorporation as well as in states and foreign countries where the company markets or plans to market its products.

Until legal counsel has verified that ownership under common-law has been properly declared and there are no indications of a name challenge, all persons knowing of the project must hold the new identifier in the strictest confidence. Recently a Southern financial institution prepared a name change ad campaign for print and television, fabricated branch signs, and printed engraved stationery.

When it asked legal counsel to file the new name, management was shocked to learn that only a month earlier an out-of-state competitor had reserved, in the company's home state, the identical name and almost identical logo. Obviously, too many people inside and outside the company had knowledge of the new name and logo design.

A name is basic to conveying all organization and product images. It deserves the same investment and protection afforded the most valuable of corporate assets. Given the realities of the courtroom and the marketplace today, making an effort to develop a truly distinctive name is the best legal and competitive defense. ▽

Add style to your technical writing

There is no reason for technical professionals to turn out writing that is dull and lifeless. 'Style' can add a dash of charm and readability too.

D. L. Plung, Exxon Nuclear Idaho Co., Inc., Idaho Falls, Idaho

TECHNICAL WRITING is typically recognized for its devotion to precision, conciseness and concreteness. Yet, the delivery and success of technical communications also require that each author develop a *style*. Style is an ability to use language and phrasing to assist rather than impede the reader's efforts to understand the information being communicated. Such a style for technical writing is accommodated by only one readability formula, the *Orwell Writing Success Number* (see Box). In addition to emphasizing the precision and conciseness not accounted for by other popular formulas, the OWSN is also the only readability formula that encourages the development of a true style.

What is style? There is certainly no shortage of quotations by great writers about style. For instance, consider Henry James' astute remark that: "It is by style that we are saved." Or the comment by E. B. White that style is "the sound words make on paper." However, enlisting these authors as spokesmen for the cause of improving technical writing might seem too strained for the skeptical author who has been repeatedly advised to stress objectivity and impartiality, and who senses intuitively that he should not embellish technical wisdom with fanciful words and phrases. Rather, it seems obvious when one considers the paucity of information on style provided by most texts on technical writing that such discourse has no use for style.

Yet, that assumption is definitely incorrect. It is that mistaken inference that originally led to technical writing's unwarranted reliance on first generation readability formulas such as the *Fog Index*. And it has been the willing godparent of a subsequent generation of readability formulas: computerized editors that "input" good writing and "output" lifeless, tedious prose.

Computerized Lincoln. Consider the following revision of Lincoln's "Gettysburg Address" produced by Bell Laboratories' computerized system:

Eighty-seven years ago, our grandfathers created a free nation here. They based it on the idea that everybody is created equal. We are now fighting a civil war to see if this nation or any similar nation can survive. On this battlefield we are dedicating a cemetery to those who died for their country. It is only right. But in another sense, the task is impossible, because brave men, living and dead, dedicated the place better than we can. Hardly anyone will notice or remember what we say here, but nobody can forget what those men did. We should continue the work they began, and make sure they did not die in vain. With God's help, we will have freedom again, so that the people's government will endure.[3]

ORWELL WRITING SUCCESS NUMBER (OWSN) SYSTEM

In July 1981 HYDROCARBON PROCESSING published *Evaluate your technical writing*, describing the OWSN.[1] The system proposed differs markedly from the popular readability formulas such as Robert Gunning's *Fog Index* and Rudolf Flesch's *Reading Ease Score*: 1. It is designed specifically for evaluating technical writing, 2. It accounts for the value of conciseness and precision, 3. It recognizes the need for technical terminology, and 4. It allows each author to develop a "style" of writing.

What is OWSN? The *Orwell Writing Success Number* (OWSN) system is predicated on the six writing principles discussed by George Orwell in his essay, "Politics and the English Language."[2] Therein, he neatly summarized the questions the "scrupulous" writer should ask himself:

1. What am I trying to say?
2. What words will express it?
3. What image or idiom will make it clearer?
4. Is the image fresh enough to have an effect?
5. Could I put it more shortly?
6. Have I said anything that is avoidably ugly?

These questions he then developed into six rules, rules that serve as the cornerstone of the OWSN system:

1. Never use a metaphor, simile, or other figure of speech that you are used to seeing in print.
2. Never use a long word where a short word will do.
3. If it is possible to cut a word out, always cut it out.
4. Never use the passive where you can use the active.
5. Never use a foreign phrase, a scientific word or a jargon word if you can think of an everyday English equivalent.
6. Break any of these rules sooner than say anything outright barbarous.

In the OWSN, these rules are weighted in terms of their contribution to sound technical writing and then coupled with a component called the "Superfluity Ratio": the number of words used divided by the number of words necessary to communicate the thought.

With these principles in mind, the reader can evaluate and thereby improve his technical writing. Two main features of excellent technical writing were stressed in that article: precision and conciseness. This article discusses some of the finer points of style OWSN accommodates.

Reprinted with permission from *Hydrocarbon Processing,* pp. 123, 124, 127, 129, 130, 132, and 135, May 1983.

Summary of "Highly Excited Atoms"

The test tube has provided many significant breakthroughs in the chemical sciences (metonymy).* In atomic physics, advances have been due in great part to Niels Bohr's hydrogen theory and to quantum physics. Now a new field of study has emerged: Rydberg Atoms. "It is the physics of atoms in which an electron is excited to an exceptionally high energy level" (alliteration).

"Rydberg atoms have been detected whose diameter approaches a hundredth of a millimeter. . . . The Rydberg atoms are so large that they can engulf other atoms. Rydberg atoms are also remarkably long-lived" (anaphora). A particular difference between Rydberg and other atoms is their responses to electric and magnetic fields. "Ordinary atoms are scarcely affected by an applied electric field or magnetic field; Rydberg atoms can be squeezed into unexpected shapes by a magnetic field" (epistrophe).

"Rydberg atoms are like hydrogen in their essential properties" (simile). And "according to the Bohr theory, the hydrogen atom is a solar system in microcosm" (metaphor). However, quantum physics needed to refine this model; "Bohr's simple model accounted for the most conspicuous features of the spectrum of hydrogen, but this model incorporated such a jumble of traditional concepts and radical ideas that it could not be generalized or refined" (antithesis).

Using this refined model, Rydberg atoms, particularly those of alkali metals, were investigated. "These elements are commonly chosen because they are easily turned into a gas, because their spectral absorption lines are at wavelengths conveniently generated by laser light and because they absorb light efficiently" (colon). Once produced, these atoms were studied in electric and magnetic fields.

In electric fields, the atoms' hydrogen-like qualities were evaluated, their degrees of degeneracy examined, and ultimately their resultant Stark effects analyzed (climax). This allowed successful definition of the relationship between experimental conditions and the specific shape assumed by the Rydberg atom in an electric field. Yet, attempts to define the electron's motion in a magnetic field were not as successful. Though significant progress was made, a complete explanation of our data is lacking. But, efforts continue. For, as we continue to excite these electrons, so these electrons continue to excite us (antemetaboly).

---

* Devices used are identified in parentheses following their use; quotation marks identify examples of devices taken verbatim from the original article.

Nonetheless, this view that technical writing must be boring to be good is not held by all authors of technical literature. Rather, one of the most eloquent statements about the need for true style in technical communications was offered over 30 years ago by Dr. J. Robert Oppenheimer, the renowned American physicist:

The problem of doing justice to the implicit, the imponderable, and the unknown is, of course, not unique to politics. It is always with us in science, it is with us in the most trivial of personal affairs, and it is one of the great problems of writing and of all forms of art. The means by which it is solved is sometimes called style. It is style which complements affirmation with limitation and with humility; it is style which makes it possible to act effectively, but not absolutely; it is style which, in the domain of foreign policy, enables us to find a harmony between the pursuit of ends essential to us, and the regard for the views, the sensibilities, the aspirations of those to whom the problem may appear in another light; it is style which is the deference that action pays to uncertainty; it is above all style through which power defers to reason.[4]

Toward better style. This same conclusion about the need for a broader appreciation and application of style in technical writing was also noted by other scientists. For example, in a recent book about language, V. V. Nalimov, a Russian mathematician and information scientist, had these thoughts about style and technical writing: "The transmission of thought is carried out on a logical level, but its perception is greatly influenced by some psychological factors which are not entirely understood. An idea is perceived more readily if it is shocking and requires an intellectual effort. A good scientific paper ought to (require this intellectual effort) . . . . Use of the metaphorical structure of language is only one of the techniques used to create intellectual strain."[5]

'Good' tech writing. We can infer from the representative selections more precisely what technical writing style should be: 1. It is writing that displays a literary quality, 2. It is writing that uses the best words, expressions, and phrases to communicate, and 3. It is writing that takes advantage of all devices or techniques that can enliven the prose without interfering with the communication of a precise, concise message. And we should be able to recognize that this is the definition

of writing Orwell is promoting when he advises us to choose the best terms and voice, and when he advises us to avoid the "barbarous." And, when trying to define more particularly what we are to "avoid" according to Orwell's injunction, we might consider what one philosopher noted: "Subject without style is barbarism."[6]

Creating style. Therefore, we need to know what devices or techniques we can use to add this element of style to our writing. Accordingly, I offer the following primer of ten stylistic devices. For each device I only supply a definition and an example or two of its use. Extensive detail is not warranted since the examples clearly suggest the strength and potential application of each device. Further, I have principally selected examples from political speeches; my reason for selecting political rather than scientific examples is simple: They will be more readily recognized and remembered than scientific quotations. Yet, to demonstrate the devices' use in a scientific text, I also include a summary of a recent article from *Scientific American* into which all ten devices are incorporated (Box, page 124).

Only when discussing metaphors do I give a more detailed analysis; this device warrants more coverage because the use of metaphor is as common in scientific writing as in any other form of expository prose—albeit its use may not be understood as thoroughly by authors of technical literature. The discussion of metaphors is therefore a reasonable place to begin our review of these stylistic devices: It illustrates the literary heritage technical writing shares with all other types of writing.

Metaphor. A metaphor is an implied comparison of dissimilar things; words of explicit comparison, such as "like" and "as," are omitted. As mentioned, metaphors are quite common in technical writing. For instance, consider the following metaphors, based on the shape of letters of the alphabet:

A frame

C clamp

D ring

F head engine

H beam (in structural engineering)

I beam (structural engineering)

J stroke (canoe paddling)

L head engine, pipe el (overlapping elbow)

N strut (interplane strut on biplanes)

O ring

P trap

S curve

T bolt

U bolt

V block, groove, brace

X brace

Y pipe

Z section, cut.[7]

In the book quoted previously, the use of metaphor in scientific discourse is lucidly explained by V. V. Nalimov:

If reading a scientific text, we stop for a moment and ponder the character of terms in our field of vision, we shall find that they are metaphorical. We have become so used to metaphors in our scientific language that we do not even notice it. We keep coming across such word combinations as "course of time," "the field of force," "temperature field," "the logic of experiment," "the memory of a computer," which allow us to express new notions with the help of rather unusual combinations of old, well-known, and familiar expressions. Recognizing the right of metaphors to existence in scientific language, scientists have permitted rather different senses for old terms with the emergence of these new theoretical conceptions. In science, theories are continuously changing, but the change does not cause a waterfall of new words. The new phenomena are interpreted through the old, familiar ones, through the old words for which the prior distribution function of meaning is slightly, but continuously, changed. Something remains unchanged but becomes of less importance, something new appears, entirely different from, and to a certain extent contradictory to, the former meaning of the word.[5]

Here in addition to the scientific metaphors already noted are two examples of how politicians used metaphors:

1. Adlai Stevenson: "The anatomy of patriotism is complex."

2. Lyndon Johnson: "This is what America is all about. It is the uncrossed desert and the unclaimed ridge. It is the star that is not reached and the harvest sleeping in the unplowed ground."

Simile. A simile is an explicit comparison of dissimilar things in which such words as "like" and "as" are used.

1. Thomas Paine: "Until an independence is declared, the Continent will feel itself like a man who continues putting off some unpleasant business from day to day, yet knows it must be done."

2. Abraham Lincoln: "Sending men to McClellan's army is like shoveling fleas across a barnyard—they don't get there."

Anaphora. Anaphora is the repetition of the same word, or group of words, at the beginning of successive clauses.

1. Winston Churchill: "We shall fight on the beaches, we shall fight on the landing grounds, we shall fight in the fields and in the street, we shall fight in the hills."

2. Martin Luther King: "Let freedom ring from the mighty mountains of New York. Let freedom ring from the heightening Alleghenies of Pennsylvania. Let freedom ring from the snow-capped Rockies of Colorado."

Epistrophe. Epistrophe is the repetition of the same word, or group of words, at the end of successive clauses.

1. Abraham Lincoln: ". . . and that government of the people, by the people, for the people, shall not perish from the earth."

2. Martin Luther King: "With this faith we will be able to work together, to pray together, to struggle together, to go to jail together, to stand up for freedom together, knowing that we will be free one day."

Alliteration. Alliteration is the repetition of the initial sounds of words.

1. Winston Churchill: "The Battle of France is over. I expect the Battle of Britain is about to begin."

2. Spiro T. Agnew: "Hysterical hypochondriacs of history," "nattering nabobs of negativism," "troubadours of trouble."

Colons. Colons are the division of an idea into equal grammatical parts, done in successive clauses, to impart a rhythm to the sequence.

1. Charles Dickens: "It was the best of times, it was the worst of times, it was the age of wisdom, it was the age of foolishness, it was the epoch of belief, ..."

2. Abraham Lincoln: ". . . that from these honored dead we take increased devotion to that cause for which they gave the last full measure of devotion; that we here highly resolve that these dead shall not have died in vain; that this nation, under God, shall have a new birth of freedom; and that government of the people, by the people, for the people, shall not perish from the earth." (In this quotation, there is a quadracolon—clauses beginning with the word "that"—and a tricolon—"of the people, by the people, for the people.")

Antithesis. Antithesis is the contrast of ideas by means of parallel arrangements of words or groups of words.

1. John F. Kennedy: "We observe today not a victory of party, but a celebration of freedom—symbolizing an end, as well as a beginning—signifying renewal, as well as change."

2. Abraham Lincoln: "The brave men, living and dead, who struggled here, have consecrated it far above our poor power to add or detract."

Climax. Climax is the arrangement of words, or groups of words, according to their increasing value or strength.

1. Julius Caesar: "I came, I saw, I conquered."

2. John F. Kennedy: "All this will not be finished in the first 100 days. Nor will it be finished in the first 1,000 days, nor in the life of this administration, nor even perhaps in our lifetime on this planet. But let us begin."

Antemetaboly. Antemetaboly is the

repetition of words in successive clauses, but in reverse order.

1. Thomas Paine: "For as in absolute governments the King is law, so in free countries the law ought to be King."

2. John F. Kennedy: "Mankind must put an end to war—or war will put an end to mankind."

"Let us never negotiate out of fear. But let us never fear to negotiate."

"And so, my fellow Americans, ask not what your country can do for you: Ask what you can do for your country."

Metonymy. Metonymy is when a word or image associated with a larger idea or concept is made to serve for the expression of that idea.

1. Press Release: "The White House (used here to serve as substitute for the President or the Executive Branch of government) said today that a formal statement would be issued later this week."

2. Richard Nixon: "In Europe, we gave the cold shoulder to DeGaulle, and now he gives the warm hand to Mao Tse-tung."

3. John F. Kennedy: "To those peoples in the huts and villages across the globe struggling to break the bonds of mass misery, we pledge our best efforts to help them help themselves, for whatever period is required."

Using Style

The first step in animating writing is developing an understanding and knowledge of these techniques. The second step, which is of equal importance, is their judicious use. This latter step can be divided into two seemingly contradictory components, caution and practice.

The caution is necessary to ensure their use is judicious, not whimsical or improper. Improper use will produce a turgid style and will detract from any professional communication.

Guidelines. A few commonsense guidelines are in order:

1. Make certain the device and its use are appropriate to the subject, purpose and audience.

2. Don't use greatly exaggerated devices that call attention to themselves; subtly interweave them into the fabric of your material. If in doubt about whether something is too exaggerated, leave it out.

3. Don't overuse the devices. Effectiveness is not measured by how many devices you use or how many times you use them. It is better to have only a few than to clutter your communication.

4. Although the poetic requirement of freshness is not essential, avoid using devices that are overworked, commonplace or cliche.

These simple cautions should allow you to make effective use of the devices while also focusing on your foremost responsibility: the presentation of an accurate, precise and concise message. You must remember that the literary merit must function as a support to—not a substitute for—the overall clarity, reasoning, organization, and straightforward presentation of your information.

Practice. Now, with these cautions in mind, let us briefly examine the other facet of this second step: practice. As all the great writers and speakers have known, literary ability must be developed; the art must be practiced. This is something the writers and speakers quoted in this essay knew well. Thomas Paine said: "Fit the powers of thinking and the turn of language to fit the subject, so as to bring out a clear conclusion that shall hit the point in question and nothing else." Similarly, Sir Winston Churchill stated: "There is no more important element in the technique of rhetoric than the continual employment of the best possible word."

This concern for language and the diligence with which these men practiced their art paid off. Thomas Paine's pamphlet *Common Sense* became the most discussed material in America prior to the Revolution. Winston Churchill was awarded the 1953 Nobel Prize in Literature for his "historical and biographical presentations and for his scintillating oratory."

The Kennedy speech. Yet, surely the best known quotations in this essay are those taken from John F. Kennedy's Inaugural Address. Kennedy is a prime example of the tangible results of diligent practice and study, as his Inaugural Address attests. Prior to drafting this speech, Kennedy reviewed all the previous Presidential inaugural addresses to uncover their stylistic strengths; he also requested his special counsel, Theodore Sorensen, "to study the secret of Lincoln's Gettysburg Address." That Kennedy learned the "secret" is evident from the many stylistic points the two speeches have in common. Kennedy also assiduously reworked his manuscript. For example, his famous sentences, "Ask not . . .," were revised and tested numerous times; they were reworked from speeches delivered on September 5 and September 20 and were again revised the morning of the Inaugural.

As a result of Kennedy's commitment to this writing, his Inaugural Address (whose length, coincidentally, was approximately that of the average conference paper, 14 minutes) was praised both for its substance and its language: "distinguished for its style and brevity as well as for its meaty content."

This compliment from the *New York Times* is the type to which all communications should aspire. It recognizes that the author has dutifully observed his primary mission to impart information; but it also credits the author's ability with language and his desire to communicate in a manner that elevates as well as enlightens.

LITERATURE CITED

[1] Plung, D. L., "Evaluate Your Technical Writing," *Hydrocarbon Processing*, July 1981.
[2] Orwell, G., "Politics and the English Language," *Shooting an Elephant and Other Stories*, London, Secker & Warburg, 1950.
[3] Angier, N., "Bell's Lettres," *Discover*, Vol. 2., no. 7, July 1981, pp. 78–79.
[4] Oppenheimer, J. R., "The Open Mind," *Bulletin of the Atomic Scientists*, Vol. 5, no.1, Jan. 1949, pp. 3–5.
[5] Nalimov, V. V., *In the Labyrinths of Language: A Mathematician's Journey*, R. G. Colodny, Ed., Philadelphia, ISI Press, 1981.
[6] Quoted in Asa Kasher, "Style! Why Bother?", *Scientific Information Transfer: The Editor's Role*, Miriam Balaban, Ed., Boston, D. Reidel Pub. Co., 1978, pp. 299–301.
[7] Harris, J. S., "Metaphor in Technical Writing," *Technical Writing Teacher*, Vol. 2, no. 2, Winter 1975, pp. 9–13.
[8] Kleppner, D., Littman, M. G., and Zimmerman, M. L., "Highly Excited Atoms," *Scientific American*, Vol. 244, no. 5, May 1981.

ROLPH E. ANDERSON & MARVIN A. JOLSON

It may be ill-advised for advertisers to avoid technical language in print media messages directed to household consumers. Results of an experiment reported here suggest that technical wording levels in ads combine with the audience's educational levels and product experience to generate a series of product perceptions, advertising evaluations, and purchase considerations.

TECHNICAL WORDING IN ADVERTISING: IMPLICATIONS FOR MARKET SEGMENTATION

A widespread apothegm regarding print advertising copy is "keep it simple." The assumed premise is that many readers have such limited vocabularies or low thresholds of boredom that the copywriter must use words readily understood and assimilated by the entire target audience. If the advertisement contains too many technical or unfamiliar words, it is feared that the message may be largely lost or ignored by some audience segments with an attendant waste of the advertising expenditure. At the very least, it is proposed that the more the wording of the ad approaches the language of the particular sector to which it is directed, the easier it becomes for the factors of comprehension and interest to retain the reader's attention (Abruzzini 1967).

The typical advertiser intuitively has presented the message in a manner highly compatible in both linguistic structure and semantic content with that commonly experienced and expected by the intended receiver. Accordingly, technical wordings are more predominant in trade or specialty publications than in mass print media such as general newspapers and magazines. Yet, many consumer durables such as electronic equipment, cameras, and household appliances have superior technical attributes which sponsors wish to promote as differentiating features. Lautman and Percy (1978) have speculated that these characteristics represent benefits to the prospective purchaser which can best be communicated by use of the advertiser's technical terminology. Other critics of semantic simplicity argue that a significant amount of advertising is talking down to people while insulting and irritating them (McNeal 1973).

Rolph E. Anderson is Professor and Chairman of the Department of Marketing, College of Business and Administration, Drexel University, Philadelphia, PA. Marvin A. Jolson is Professor of Marketing, College of Business and Management, University of Maryland, College Park, MD. The authors wish to acknowledge the valuable suggestions of Drexel University Professor Carl A. Silver, and the data-gathering contributions of University of Maryland Students Stuart Kahane and Steve Lazaras.

The Study

Purpose

The limited number of studies addressing advertiser-consumer language compatibility have looked at message comprehension level as the variable to be optimized. There has been no known empirical research that examines the impact of technical

Reprinted with permission from *J. Marketing,* vol. 44, pp. 57–66, Jan. 1980.
Published by the American Marketing Association.

language upon the household consumer's perceptions of the advertisement itself and of selected characteristics of the advertised product. Of ultimate importance is the question of the effect of technical wording upon the reader's overall product evaluation and propensity to consider a purchase. Finally, there are various audience characteristics which may act singly or in combination to make an individual more or less predisposed to be influenced by stimulus information.

This exploratory experiment was designed to test some authoritative, but unsubstantiated, predictions derived from practices of advertisers and to generate a number of hypotheses regarding the audience's responses to varying levels of technical content in print advertisements. These predictions, in concert with a number of previous research findings, suggest a number of questions to guide our research.

Related Findings

Examples of print advertisements were used in this study because of Berelson and Steiner's (1964) conclusion that when informational content is complex, print media are preferable to broadcast media from the standpoint of comprehension. This is because of the unique ability of print to permit the audience to control its own rate of exposure to the message. Berelson and Steiner found that when the audience has little or no prior knowledge of the communicator, it tends to decide a question on the basis of the message content itself—i.e., the conformity of the content to predispositions. Accordingly, a bogus advertiser was created for the purpose of the current experiment.

A number of studies suggest that message format and complexity contribute to the way consumers process information and evaluate product attributes (Sommers 1964; Bettman and Kakkar 1977). Specifically, it has been found that when major appliances are packaged with a highly technical operating manual, customers perceive these products to be difficult to operate and relatively durable and expensive (Luskin 1976).

Attribution theory, as introduced by Heider (1958) and extended by Kelley (1967), may offer some insights into the frequent correlation of the rating of some product features with the complexity of communications describing, promoting, or facilitating the use of these products. For example, if an appliance purchaser observes that products accompanied by technically written owner's manuals prove to be quite durable while appliances described by simplified manuals are short-lived, he/she may associate durability and technical content of de-

scriptive literature on the basis of covariance. In an experiment by Settle, Faricy, and Warren (1971), attribution theory is applied to the management of advertising message content and format.

Cox (1961) found that audience effects are caused by the combination of advertising and various mediating factors including audience predispositions. He offered two relevant generalizations:

(1) Some people are more predisposed than others to be influenced by advertising for a particular product or brand.
(2) Within that group which is more predisposed toward a particular product, some individuals or subgroups will be more predisposed to be influenced by certain kinds of appeals while others will be predisposed by different kinds of appeals.

Among the many prominent predisposing factors, certain demographic characteristics and a person's past experiences with a product or brand may be partial determinants of his future susceptibility to a given form of advertising. The findings of Berelson and Steiner (1964) support this contention. For example, it was found that the better educated are more likely to pay attention to serious communications and to acquire information from print media. The same researchers found the fuller the preexisting information, audience involvement, and interest, the more receptive the audience to congenial communications and the more resistant to uncongenial.

There is some reason to believe that an advertisement's technical content level affects the communication's power to generate believability, interest, attention, and the audience's overall belief in the product's merits. Maloney (1963), for example, suggests that selective perception can lead to the misunderstanding of a message because of misindexing—a form of message distortion. The reader's mind may be led astray or turned off by some "borrowed attention" device in the ad, e.g., words that are difficult to process, comprehend, and relate to perceived benefits of the advertised product.

Guideline Questions

In reflecting upon the findings of previous studies and following an examination of many advertising practices and myths, it seemed to us that the technical content of an advertising message merges with the audience's educational level and previous familiarity with the advertised product to determine the effectiveness of the communication. Of particular importance is the impact of the message upon the advertisement's believability and power to generate interest and attention and upon the audience's evaluation of cardinal product benefits and buying intentions. Accordingly, three broad questions were formulated to guide the research:

1. What is the impact of the technical level of a print advertisement upon:
   (a) the audience's evaluation of selected product characteristics such as durability, ease of operation, and price?
   (b) the audience's overall evaluation of the advertised product?
   (c) the audience's proneness to consider buying the advertised product?
   (d) the likelihood that the advertisement will gain and hold the interest and attention of readers?
   (e) the perceived believability of the advertisement?
2. What is the effect of the interaction of the technical level of an advertisement and the reader's degree of formal education upon:
   (a) the reader's overall evaluation of the advertised product?
   (b) the reader's proneness to consider buying the advertised product?
3. What is the effect of the interaction of the technical level of an advertisement and the reader's experience with the advertised or similar products upon:
   (a) the reader's overall evaluation of the advertised product?
   (b) the reader's proneness to consider buying the advertised product?

The Sample

Data were collected from 264 cooperating household consumers selected on a judgment basis in a large eastern city. Each subject completed a personally delivered product/advertisement evaluation questionnaire after reading one of three sequentially distributed mock advertisements that described a proposed new Japanese single lens reflex camera import. A fictitious brand, Taro D, was used to avoid any confounding effects due to brand predispositions and/or prior familiarity.

Advertisements

The camera advertisements used in the experiment (see Appendix) were carefully developed and pretested to represent three distinct levels of wording: (1) nontechnical, (2) partially technical, and (3) technical. The definition of technical language was in *Webster's Third New International Dictionary*: "pertaining to or confined chiefly to a particular

occupation or specified field of thought." Even such familiar words as "exposure" may be considered technical when applied to a specialized field such as camera advertisements.

Total words for each ad were determined by standard copycasting procedure, i.e., counting all words of three letters or more. The nontechnical ad contained seven technical words out of 101 total words, or 7% technical language. The partially technical and technical advertisements contained proportions of 17% and 30% technical wording, respectively. Pretesting the three advertisements within a sample of 60 shopping center consumers, selected on a convenience basis, substantiated the ranking of the advertisements according to the desired treatments, i.e., levels of technical language.

The Questionnaire

Responses were obtained to three questions pertaining to particular product characteristics (durability, ease of operation, and retail price),[1] two relating to summary evaluations (overall product evaluation and purchase consideration), two pertaining to attributes of the advertisement itself (interest/attention and believability), and two disclosing consumer background information (education level and camera experience). Seven-point semantic differential scales were utilized to record consumer perceptions of the product and advertisement, while respondents' education and camera experience were obtained on Likert-type scales.

Method of Analysis

The relative impact of the three treatment levels of technical wording used in the advertisements were analyzed by univariate analysis of variance. Covariance analysis was applied to determine the effects, if any, of the two consumer variables (education level and camera experience) on the results. Duncan's multiple range test was used to identify significant differences among pairings of the treatment groups.

Data for the study were submitted for computer analysis to the SAS GLM (General Linear Model) Procedure (Barr et al. 1976). This program performs both univariate and multivariate analyses of variance and covariance. Various other analyses, including Duncan's multiple-range test, can be obtained as part of the GLM output.

---

[1] Although numerous product characteristics are important to the consumer who contemplates the purchase of a camera, subjects participating in the pretest found these to be the three most determinant factors.

TABLE 1
Summary of Response Means and Significance Levels (ANOVA F-Tests)

Source of Variance	Durability V₁ (p)	Durability V₁ (X̄)	Ease of Operation V₂ (p)	Ease of Operation V₂ (X̄)	Retail Price V₃ (p)	Retail Price V₃ (X̄)	Overall Evaluation V₄ (p)	Overall Evaluation V₄ (X̄)	Purchase Consideration V₅ (p)	Purchase Consideration V₅ (X̄)	Interest & Attention V₆ (p)	Interest & Attention V₆ (X̄)	Believability V₇ (p)	Believability V₇ (X̄)	N
V₈ Technical Ad Level	.04		.0001		.0001		.05		.09		.02		NS		
Nontechnical		3.34		2.43		3.66		3.33		4.58		3.82		3.10	92
Partially technical		3.89		3.51		4.66		3.52		5.13		4.57		3.51	82
Technical		3.68		3.79		4.93		3.68		4.81		4.30		3.04	90
V₉ Camera Experience	.02		.0001		NS		.08		.001		.01		.04		
None		3.77		3.70		4.35		3.45		5.23		4.53		3.32	130
Some		3.31		2.98		4.32		3.69		4.38		3.84		2.93	90
Considerable		3.84		2.36		4.75		3.30		4.57		4.05		3.45	44
V₁₀ Educational Level	NS		.05		NS		NS		NS		NS		.07		
≤ High School		3.40		3.48		4.12		3.69		4.94		4.13		2.79	
Some College		3.71		3.41		4.45		3.41		4.91		4.27		3.16	116
College Degree		3.64		2.91		4.48		3.53		4.69		4.20		3.46	100
Interactions															
V₉ × V₁₀	NS		NS		NS		NS		NS		NS		NS		
V₈ × V₁₀	NS		NS		NS		.06		.01		NS		NS		
V₈ × V₉	.01		.01		NS		.08		.01		.03		NS		
V₈ × V₉ × V₁₀	.07		NS		NS		NS		NS		NS		NS		
Explained Variance	16%		27%		15%		23%		20%		15%		12%		

NOTE: Mean values are based on seven-point Likert-type scales. For variables 1, 2, 5, 6, and 7, lower scores indicate a more favorable response. For variable 4, a higher score is preferred. For variable 3 (perceived retail price), a higher score indicates a higher price.

Results

Technical Level of Advertisement

Response means for the seven criterion variables and the summary of significance levels for univariate analysis of variance are shown in Table 1. Examination of the table reveals that there are significant differences (.10 level) among the treatment levels of the advertisement for all the criterion variables except ad believability.

Readers of the nontechnical material attributed the highest level of durability to the advertised product. The level of technical content was found to be negatively correlated with the perceived ease of camera operation and positively related to higher perceived retail prices of the unit. It is likely that many readers associate a nontechnical product description with uncomplicated, time-tested component parts and assembly that are both "idiot-proof" and "fail safe," that is, impervious to continuous handling, careless treatment, and errors by the user.

On the other hand, a technical message may denote a complex design and engineering precision with an attendant high cost of production—e.g., "advanced technology is expensive."

Readers of the more technical ads tended to assign higher overall ratings to the camera. Even though readers of the nontechnical ad were more inclined to consider actual purchase than other readers, subjects who read the technical ad indicated stronger purchase interests than those exposed to the partially technical communication.

As expected, the nontechnical ad was more capable of gaining and holding the readers' interest and attention. However, these results are inconclusive since the technical ad outperformed the partially technical ad for variable 6 (see Table 1 for listing of variables). In terms of ad believability, the nontechnical and technical advertisements had almost identical ratings while the partially technical ad was least effective.

In addition to examining the global impact of

technical ad level on the seven criterion variables, we used Duncan's multiple-range test to explore significant differences among pairs of advertising treatments. All results were significant except in the cases of dependent variables V_5 and V_6 whereby no significant differences between the technical and partially technical ad treatments were disclosed.

Seemingly, respondents opted to take extreme positions in favor of either the technical or nontechnical advertisement. As shown in Table 1, the partially technical ad failed to receive the highest rating for any of the response variables while receiving the lowest rating for variables 5, 6, and 7. It was, therefore, worthwhile to investigate the relevance of camera experience and level of education as segmentation variables in the camera market.

The reader should be cautioned that the above findings are based on the questionable assumption that the distribution of sample respondents by educational level and camera experience is not statistically different from the distribution of those normally exposed to advertisements for similar products. Accordingly, the above results should be reevaluated in light of the following findings.

Camera Experience

Of the background covariates, camera experience (V_9) was helpful in explaining some of the differences in criterion variable scores. As expected, perceived ease of camera operation (V_2) was found to be an increasing function of camera experience. Subjects with "some camera experience" perceived the camera as most durable (V_1), assigned the highest overall rating (V_4), were most inclined to consider a purchase (V_5), and were most receptive to the advertisements (V_6 and V_7).

Clearly, the cognitive defenses of subjects with "some camera experience" were found to be less formidable than those respondents with "considerable" or "no experience." To the extent that a product is relevant to the person, an advertisement describing its features and uses can create indifference or even tension—if the information is incongruent with his existing attitudes toward that product. In keeping with Roger's (1962) classification schemes to account for differential diffusion rates, camera enthusiasts may attach no *relative advantage* to the Taro D in contrast to existing or their own cameras. Those without camera experience may not perceive the Taro D as compatible with their value systems and ways of life. Moreover, the more complex the item, the slower is the rate of diffusion within a market segment. A related issue is the perceived absence of divisibil-

ity, e.g., the new product's availability on a trial basis prior to a substantial financial obligation by an inexperienced prospective purchaser (Robertson 1971).

Level of Education

As shown in Table 1, educational level was significant only for consumer perceptions of ease of operation (V_2) and for ad believability (V_7). As expected, "ease of operation" was found to be an increasing function of the subject's educational level while ad "believability" was inversely related to education. The latter finding may reflect the educated consumer's underlying disillusionment with or cynicism toward advertising in general.

Interaction Effects

As disclosed in Table 1, the interaction of reader's education with technical ad level produced no significant effects for any dependent variables involving product or advertisement characteristics. When camera experience (V_9) and technical ad level (V_8) interacted, significant findings emerged for five of the seven criterion variables.

Consumers with little or no camera experience scored durability and ease of operation most favorably when exposed to the nontechnical ad while those with considerable camera experience perceived durability as lowest when exposed to the nontechnical ad and highest when viewing the technical ad. The latter group, as expected, felt that the camera would be easy to operate for all levels of ad treatment. Although not statistically significant, it is interesting to note in Table 1 that perceived retail price is an increasing function of the technical ad level for all experience and educational segments.

Consumers with little or no camera experience ranked the nontechnical ad highest for holding their interest and attention. In turn, the experienced group found the technical ad significantly more interesting.

The significant interaction effects involving the critical evaluation variables V_4 and V_5 (See Figures 1 through 4), are worthy of discussion since the goal of advertising is to influence people to favor the advertised product and consider purchase. These effects illustrate that different people tend to get different meanings from and respond differently to the same communication.

As indicated by Figure 1, subjects with no camera experience assigned almost identical overall evaluations to the product regardless of the ad treatment to which they were exposed. For respondents with some or considerable camera experience, the mean product evaluation was found to be an increasing function of the technical level of the advertisement. However, the technical and partially technical treatments generated inverted U-shaped curves with means maximized for consumers with "some" camera experience. The non-technical ad generated a concave downward curve with the minimum mean point at the maximum camera experience level.

Yet Figure 2 discloses that readers' overall evaluations are not directly translated into purchase considerations. In the cases of both technical and partially technical ad exposures, the respondents' propensity to consider a purchase was found to be an increasing function of camera experience. The concave function for the nontechnical ad audience suggests that consumers with little or no experience may be influenced to purchase when exposed to the simply worded ad while those with considerable experience are virtually turned off by the same communication.

As seen in Figure 3, the overall evaluation of the product by those with no college training or with college degrees is relatively constant when comparing the technical and partially technical ads. The nontechnical ad generated a maximum evaluation score by those with minimal education and a minimum score by college graduates. For readers with some college, overall product evaluation was found to be an increasing function of technical ad level.

In Figure 4, the consumer's purchase consideration was found to be an asymtotically decreasing function of education level in the case of the nontechnical ad treatment. Those with a high school education or less, strongly considered a purchase when exposed to a nontechnical ad while exposure to other advertisements appeared to have a strong demotivating effect. Both other ad versions showed that the subject's purchase consideration will rise almost linearly with increases in educational level. Clearly, the partially technical ad is not appealing to consumers without college degrees and only slightly more appealing than the nontechnical ad in the case of college graduates.

In Table 1, it is seen that only findings relating to V_1, durability, were significant for the three-way interaction of camera experience, education, and advertising treatment. Subjects with some camera experience and some college who saw the non-technical ad assigned the highest durability rating. In turn, the lowest rating emerged from respondents with college degrees and no camera experience who read the technical ad.

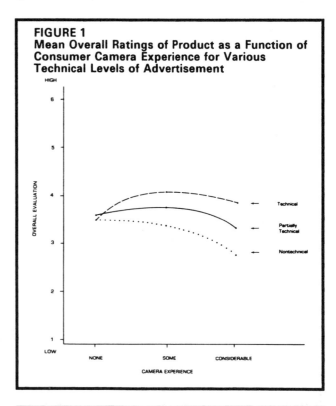

FIGURE 1
Mean Overall Ratings of Product as a Function of Consumer Camera Experience for Various Technical Levels of Advertisement

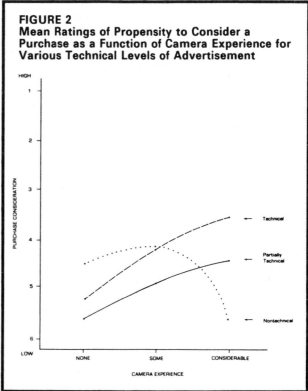

FIGURE 2
Mean Ratings of Propensity to Consider a Purchase as a Function of Camera Experience for Various Technical Levels of Advertisement

Summary and Conclusions

This study has investigated the role of advertiser-initiated appeals emanating from language as a means of coordinating the seller's message with

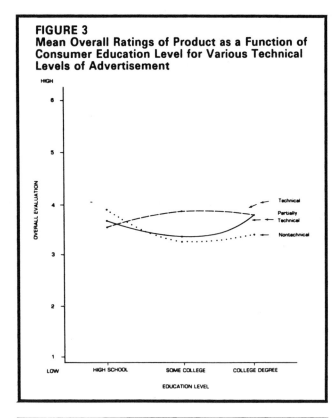

FIGURE 3
Mean Overall Ratings of Product as a Function of Consumer Education Level for Various Technical Levels of Advertisement

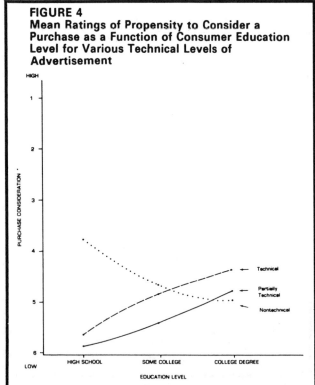

FIGURE 4
Mean Ratings of Propensity to Consider a Purchase as a Function of Consumer Education Level for Various Technical Levels of Advertisement

the needs of various segments within the overall market. Although the experimental product was a single lens reflex camera, marketers of other psychologically or economically important products or

services with obvious or hidden technical features may benefit from these findings. Examples are stereo systems, automobiles, golf clubs, health spa memberships, or burglar alarms. The market for each of these is comprised of people who seek differing product attributes and who vary in terms of educational level and familiarity or experience with the item promoted. As suggested by the explained variance percentages shown in Table 1, a number of additional independent variables contribute to audience responses.

Because of the use of a convenience sample and the limited external validity of a laboratory experiment, the findings should be viewed with some caution. However, it is hoped that the following responses to the guideline questions posed at the outset will suggest some useful advertising strategies and a number of tentative hypotheses for future researchers.

The salient findings are:

- As the technical level of an advertisement rises, readers perceive the advertised product to be:
  —less durable
  —more difficult to operate
  —higher priced.

- As the technical level of an advertisement rises, the ad is less likely to gain and hold the interest and attention of readers.

- The perceived believability of an advertisement is not significantly related to the technical content of the ad copy.

- People with no experience with the generic product assign an overall product rating which is independent of the level of technical content in the advertisement. However, novices are most inclined to purchase the product when exposed to the nontechnical and least inclined when exposed to the partially technical ad.

- When the audience consists of people with some or considerable experience with the generic product, the overall product rating is an increasing function of the technical content of the advertisement.

- The purchase intentions of those with considerable product experience are an increasing function of the technical content of the ad.

- A person's overall evaluation of the product is related to both his own educational level and the amount of technical content in the advertisement. For example, those with "some college" assign a product rating as an increasing function of technical content. Those without college training assign the highest ratings when exposed to nontechnical ads and approximately equivalent evaluations when exposed to other ads. The college graduate perceives the product's evaluation as highest when exposed to either a technical or partially technical ad and lowest when subjected to a nontechnical ad.

- In terms of purchase intentions, those with no schooling beyond high school are strongly motivated by nontechnical ads and almost completely demotivated by other ads. The effect is less pronounced for those with "some college" but nontechnical ads are somewhat preferred. College graduates will consider a purchase in direct proportion to the amount of technical content in an advertisement.

Readers respond to extremes in technical wording levels. Moreover, it was found that even though people with no experience prefer simplified ads, as one acquires even a limited amount of experience with a product, his responsiveness to technical content rises at an accelerating rate. Accordingly, for widely used products, it is probably better to provide too much technical language than too little.

Technical levels of advertising cannot be viewed as a universal dimension perceived identically by all audiences. Clearly, different submarkets exhibit different sensitivities to promotional strategies.

Advertisers face the stiff challenge of identifying the media reading habits of consumers with varying levels of familiarity with products containing technical dimensions. Copy in specialized publications such as *Modern Photography, Motor Trend, Security World, Golf Magazine*, or direct mail to established users should contain substantial amounts of technical content. In the case of more general media, surrogate measures of product familiarity/experience such as age, sex, income, life-styles may be required.

The results reject the traditional notion that technical terminology in mass media advertising should be avoided. Indeed, the study has uncovered a neglected dimension of advertising copy management that could assist market segmenters in communicating the differential advantages of their products. Future studies should measure the appropriate amount and type of technical words optimal for a spectrum of products aimed at various market segments.

Appendix: Advertisements Used in Experiment

Nontechnical Ad

Smile at the challenges of everyday life. All it takes is a sense of humor and a responsive camera to see the pictures that are everywhere.

If you have the insight, a Taro-D could be the camera. This is a 35mm reflex you'll be comfortable with from the moment you pick it up. It lets you concentrate on the picture because the viewfinder shows all the information needed for correct exposure and focusing. You never have to look away from the finder to adjust a Taro-D, so you're ready to catch the one photograph that could never be taken again.

The Taro-D does not care who is taking the pictures. Its numerous technical features make it fun to use and the results are something to behold. You can use the Taro-D in any type of light conditions, indoors or outdoors. Film is advanced automatically.

When subjects call for a different perspective, Taro-D cameras accept a complete system of interchangeable lenses.

Next time you see the funny side of life, be ready with a Taro-D.

Partially Technical Ad

Smile at the challenges of everyday life. All it takes is a sense of humor and a responsive camera to see the pictures that are everywhere.

You're comfortable with a Taro-D from the moment you pick it up. This is a 35mm reflex camera that lets you concentrate on mood and insight. The viewfinder gives you all the information you want for focusing and exposure. You never have to look away from the finder to adjust a Taro-D, so you're ready to catch the one photograph that could never be taken again.

The Taro-D gives you split-screen focusing with a microprism collar, and adds an aperture read-out to the shutter scale in the finder. It shows shutter speeds from 1 to 1/1000th second plus bulb, and the F-stop ranges from 1.2 to 32 with focus from 17 inches to infinity. The Taro-D makes it easy to get deliberate multiple exposures.

The metering system is the "CLC" through-the-lens type that protects you from underexposure by automatically compensating in the high contrast light.

When you see something that needs a different perspective, just snap in one of the complete systems of Exmore lenses from super-wide 16mm to super-long 1600mm.

Next time you see the funny side of life, be ready with a Taro-D.

Technical Ad

Smile at the challenges of everyday life. All it takes is a sense of humor and a responsive camera to see the pictures that are everywhere.

You're comfortable with a Taro-D from the moment you pick it up, until you've taken your last picture. The Taro-D is a 35mm SLR with a standard Exmore 58mm F/1.7 lens. The shutter ranges from 1 to 1/1000th and B.

Other features of the Taro-D are:

- *Viewfinder*—Eye-level pentaprism with microprism focusing spot and O-resnel screen. Distinctively sharp focusing capability.
- *Exposure Meter*—Through-the-lens, two-cell CdS that automatically compensates for high contrast light. ASA 6-6,400.
- *Flash Synchronization*—FP all speeds, X to 1/60. Synchronizes maximum light yield with shutter release.

The Taro-D lets you concentrate on the picture because the viewfinder shows all the information needed for correct exposure and focusing. Since you never have to look away from the finder to adjust for a picture, you're ready to catch the one photograph that could never be taken again.

The Taro-D uses a bayonet mount for its Exmore lenses. The Exmore lenses range from the super-wide 16mm to the super-long 1600mm, plus zoom and macro lenses. It takes just seconds, with no ASA or F/stop realignment, to snap in an Exmore lens.

Next time you see the funny side of life, be ready with a Taro-D.

REFERENCES

Abruzzini, Pompeo (1967), "Measuring Language Difficulty in Advertising Copy," *Journal of Marketing*, 31 (April), 22–26.

Barr, A. J. et al., editors (1976), *A User's Guide to SAS 76*, Raleigh, NC: Sparks Press, 57–65.

Berelson, Bernard and Gary A. Steiner (1964), *Human Behavior: An Inventory of Scientific Findings*, New York: Harcourt, Brace, and World, Inc., 527–547.

Bettman, James R. and Pradeep Kakkar (1977), "Effects of Information Presentation Format on Consumer Information Acquisition Strategies," *Journal of Consumer Research*, 3 (March), 233–240.

Cox, Donald F. (1961), "Clues for Advertising Strategists," *Harvard Business Review*, 39 (November-December), 165–166.

Heider, Fritz (1958), *The Psychology of Interpersonal Relations*, New York: John Wiley and Sons, 89–92, and 123.

Kelley, H. H. (1967), "Attribution Theory in Social Psychology," in *Nebraska Symposium on Motivation*, D. Levine, ed., Lincoln: University of Nebraska Press, 194–195.

Lautman, Martin R. and Larry Percy (1978), "Consumer-Oriented Versus Advertiser-Oriented Language: Comprehensibility and Salience of the Advertising Message," *Proceedings of the Association for Consumer Research*, 52–56.

Luskin, Jack (1976), "The Manufacturer's Contribution to Appliance Retailing," paper presented at the 1976 Discount Appliance Dealers' Conference, New York (November).

Maloney, John C. (1963), "Is Advertising Believability Really Important?" *Journal of Marketing*, 27 (October), 1–8.

McNeal, James U. (1973), *An Introduction to Consumer Behavior*, New York: John Wiley & Sons, 201.

Robertson, Thomas S. (1971), *Innovative Behavior and Communication*, New York: Holt, Rinehart, and Winston, Inc. 46.

Rogers, Everett M. (1962), *Diffusion of Innovations*, New York: The Free Press, 20–23.

Settle, Robert B., John H. Faricy, and Glenn T. Warren (1971), "Consumer Information Processing: Attributing Effects to Causes," in *Proceedings of the Association for Consumer Research*, David M. Gardner, ed., 278–288.

Sommers, Montrose S. (1964), "Product Symbolism and the Perception of Social Strata," in *Toward Scientific Marketing*, Stephen A. Greyser, ed., Chicago: American Marketing Association, 200–216.

THE NEWS RELEASE

A news release should and can be a beneficial communications tool. If it is incomplete, misleading or unprofessional, however, the release can raise more questions than it answers. In addition, the press release can be ignored by editors unless two elements are always remembered:

1. It must be interesting and informative to the media person involved. His or her job is easier if your press release is professionally prepared.

2. The release will not be interesting unless it relates to the community or audience involved or has overall significance and/or uniqueness.

Quality

The news release writer should know how to attract the immediate interest of the men and women who decide what goes into newspapers and magazines and over the airways. Each release competes with thousands of other news items going across their desks. And, in many instances, a time element is involved. Remember, editors do not like to print "yesterday's" news, and seldom do.

Here are some suggestions and ground rules in this area:

1. Do not try to peddle something old or boring. If the story is weak because of the time element, it is better to go on to the next release and resolve to plan more efficiently the next time.

2. In drafting a release, take a long, honest look at the news involved. Then get directly to that point. Do not clutter up lead sentences with long introductory phrasing designed to force commercials down the editor's throat. Too often, lead sentences are written which read like this:

> "John Smith, president and chief executive of XYZ Engineering, an
> international engineering consulting firm which has 31 offices
> with full engineering capabilities, announced today the appoint-
> ment of John Jones as chief operating officer."

Most editors would refuse to wade through those first 30 words of puff to find the news. Instead, it would land in the wastebasket.

Editors, at least most of them, are intelligent and busy, and they have more stories available than they need to fill a news "hole." They recognize trivia and self-serving releases. Therefore, get to the point quickly and professionally.

Company commercials can be included in subsequent paragraphs.

Referring back to the Jones news release, why not say:

> "John Jones has been appointed chief operating officer of
> XYZ Engineering, a Corvallis consulting firm."

Reprinted with permission from the Communications Department, *CH2M Hill.*

Timing

As noted earlier, timing is important. And this requires planning. Get the release to the media sources when it is convenient for their deadlines. Do not crowd them. There are times, of course, when a development must be reported immediately for legal and other reasons. However, most releases can be planned.

If you have a choice, it is unwise to release news which falls into the publication time frame of Saturday or holiday editions. Thought leaders and decisionmakers, like most people, relax then. Their reading is most intensive Mondays through Fridays. Besides, some papers do not publish on Saturdays and holidays.

If a weekly paper is published on Thursday, for example, copy should be in its office no later than Monday. You may wish to hand deliver a release, which should increase the chances that it will be reviewed. If you want the news break to occur in the morning papers first, then do not release it until after 2:00 p.m. on the day before, that is, after the evening paper for the day has gone to press. Likewise, if you want the evening paper to print the news in that day's paper, have your information at the paper well before 10:00 a.m.

Content

The content of a business/financial news release should differ from one directed to the local press and, certainly, to the trades. Too many releases intended for the general media carry a large number of technical details. Conversely, releases aimed at the trade press frequently include too few technical details. The effective news release writer knows the audience and provides information that is interesting and relevant. In a trade release, for example, get the technical angles high in the story and back them up quickly. If you are trying to interest a general audience, do not turn people off with technical jargon.

There is no "catch all" release. You cannot write a technical release and hope to satisfy the business/financial editor simply by adding general information after the first paragraph or two, nor can you satisfy the trade editors by including technical information after the general information. News releases must be structured for each audience.

CORPORATE NEWS RELEASES AND PROJECT NEWS RELEASES

Within XYZ Engineering, a distinction can be made between corporate news and project news. Of course, all project news must be cleared by the client. Here are some examples of the two types:

Corporate News

1. Opening a new office

2. Staff appointment or promotion

3. Incorporation of a new or unique concept in design

4. Submission of final design recommendations (This could fall in either category - corporate or project news - depending on how the release is handled. Release of the design may be up to the client, but someone from the firm should be prepared to communicate essential information to the public)

5. Corporate growth and financial statements

6. A corporate acquisition or merger

7. Presentation of important technical papers

8. Honors and awards

Project News

1. Signing of contracts

2. New design concepts under way

3. Reports on the functioning of designs after construction

4. Beginning construction

5. Progress of contruction at milestones

6. Project completion on dedication

7. Unusual project activity

Corporate news releases are localized in the first paragraph to give them local identity in each operating area of the company.

NEWS RELEASE FORMAT

A news release should be printed on news letterhead which includes the name, address and phone number of the firm. Type the release and print it onto the letterhead. Communications contacts in each office should have a supply of news letterhead.

There is a specific news release format to follow. Using it will increase the chances that the release will be used. Some of the basic rules are:

1. Press releases should be typed, double- or triple-spaced, on one side only of standard 8½" x 11" bond paper. Do not use odd sized, colored or otherwise nonstandard paper, and never single space or type on both sides of the paper.

2. Avoid typewriters with unusual typefaces, such as those designed to resemble handwriting or computer letters. Use a black ribbon.

3. Leave ample margins on both sides of the page.

4. At the top left of the first page type:

Name and title of contact person
Phone numbers (day and night) of contact person
Date of preparation
"Page 1 of X" (X equals total number of pages)
The release date (when the release may be printed)

5. About halfway down the page, begin typing the release itself. (The purpose of wide margins, of starting the release halfway down the page, and of double- or triple-spacing is to make it easy for an editor to use your release. If adequate space is provided—and if the release is well written—the editor can simply put editing markings on the story and send it to the composing room. Giving your phone numbers makes it easy for an editor to reach you with questions. If you are difficult to locate, the questions will not get answered and your release may not get printed. Following these mechanical suggestions adds to the impression that the release is professional and increases its chance of being used.)

6. Write in clear, straightforward, standard English. Avoid slang, jargon, governmentese and exaggeration. Simple sentences, following the subject-verb-object sequence, not only are adequate in most cases, but are preferable. Use the active voice ("he said," not "it was said") and strong verbs. Avoid adjectives and adverbs.

7. Write the release in news-reporting style. Do not slant the story so that it sounds like an editorial

8. Organize your release with the important facts first—who, what, when, where, and sometimes why and how. Then, in each succeeding paragraph, add details, from most to least important. Most straight news stories (as opposed to features) are written this way so the story can easily be shortened. Study your newspaper to see how it is done.

9. Write as much as you need to tell your story. Then stop.

10. Proofread your release with care. Correct typographical errors, spelling, punctuation mistakes, word omissions, inaccurate names, addresses, dates and any other mistakes. Errors will leap to the editor's eye and tend to discredit the rest of the release. If you have a name with an unusual spelling in the story, it is helpful to mark "ok" in pencil over the name.

11. If you wish, you may write a headline for your story. It should be short and it should capture the essence in the story in one or two lines. Your headline will almost certainly not be used (heads are written on stories at the last minute to conform to the layout of the paper), but it may serve to capture the editor's attention.

12. Mail your release or take it to the proper person at the newspaper. If you do not know who the proper person is, telephone and ask.

This mark, or this one: -30- goes at the end of your release to let the editor know you are through.

Use photos wherever possible. They bring more attention to the release and add an additional element, increasing chances that either the release or the photo, or both, will be used. Certain standards must be met, however:

1. Most newspapers prefer 8" x 10" glossy black-and-white pictures. Color pictures and Polaroid shots are almost never acceptable.

2. All pictures should be in sharp focus with good contrast: no fuzzy edges, clear sharp blacks and white and a good range of grays.

3. Information about the picture—a caption or "cutline"—should be as clear, complete and accurate as the release. Include your name and phone number in case the picture gets separated from the story.

   a. In writing captions, follow the style and format the newspaper uses. Identify each person in the picture from left to right by his full name and correct title. Summarize the information in your story briefly; that is, tell what the people are doing, and where and when.

b. The picture caption should be attached to the back with tape, not simply enclose in the same envelope. Do not write on the back of a picture or attach the caption with paper clips. Pencils, ballpoint pens and paper clips are likely to leave impressions on the picture surface.

4. Pose your pictures in an interesting way. Do not simply line people up looking at the camera, passing the gavel or shaking hands. With the newsprint shortage, more of these than ever are getting thrown out, and nothing inspires a bigger yawn from an editor anyway. Group people tightly and limit the number of people in the picture to two or three.

5. Pictures of buildings or projects have a better chance of being used if people are shown. This gives scale and adds human interest.

6. If you are submitting several pictures, include some vertical photos. These are very useful for newspaper layout and often difficult to come by in a newsroom.

7. "Head shots," or "mugs"—portrait-type or candid photographs of a single person— are always welcome at newspaper offices and often get used many times.

NOTE: News releases can be sent directly to clients and contacts as well as the media. Therefore, the release can be very beneficial in keeping your name in front of important publics, even if the release is not published or given the coverage you hoped it would get.

MEDIA RELATIONS

Good relations with local newspaper or trade magazine editors and radio and television staff are essential to the health and growth of any communications program. There is no substitute for a close, friendly relationship. That does not mean an occasional phone call concerning a release. It takes a consistent program including face-to-face contact.

Perhaps the best rule to remember is to treat the media the same way you would a client—with the same courtesy and care.

The bulk of media relations is to be handled by the communications staff in conjunction with any retained public relations counsel. However, the development and maintenance of good media relations is the task of everyone dealing with the media. The manager of communications should be advised of all media interviews scheduled in advance and should be advised immediately after any impromptu interviews.

When working with news reporters and photographers, do not try to tell them how to report. They know what their editors expect. However, there is nothing wrong in suggesting ideas for stories and photos.

Media people do not appreciate outsiders or their sources requesting to read their stories or edit them prior to printing them. Nothing can turn off a reporter quicker than someone saying, "I'd like to approve what you've written before you print it." It is a fact of life, whether we like it or not, that we have no right to ask to see copy prior to its being printed. A better way to ensure accuracy, at least in a technical sense, is to say, "Please feel free to call me if there is anything about this (technical subject) that you have questions about." Make sure the reporter understands that you are interested only in the technical accuracy, not his style of saying things or how he puts the story together. That is his business and he feels just as professionally capable in that area as you do in yours. Be available and willing to discuss the technical question as many times as it takes to get it right.

The reporter's information is only as good as his source.

It is important to give clear, complete information. It is also important to be straightforward and honest. But if there is something you do not wish reported, do not say it or show it. There is no such thing as "off the record"; if you give out classified or sensitive information, you may be compromising the news reporter who may feel it is her/his duty to report it to the public.

Maintaining good relations with the media enhances the potential for use of news and features developed by XYZ Engineering and establishes the firm as an "authority" in the

profession and as a source of reliable allied information. Ideally, local media should think of our firm first when they have a technical question, whether or not it relates to a firm project. Each local newspaper should have a corporate resume on XYZ Engineering describing the firm, its services and the key people who may be contacted for information.

Both project office managers and regional office managers should get to know the editor or reporter who handles business or technical stories at the local paper. This is also true for the local TV and radio stations as time permits—the news director or station manager is the proper person to contact. Always remember to have something specific of mutual interest to discuss with any editors or reporters. They are busy people and cannot be bothered with "small talk."

Interviews By The News Media

News media interviews of XYZ Engineering employees are likely to occur on the occasion of many newsworthy situations. A reporter might call on us to give general background material relating to pending legislation or more specific information regarding one of the firm's projects. The following are some basic dos and don'ts for dealing with the news media:

First the dos:

1. Be prepared. Know your subject throughly; anticipate the questions the reporter will ask. An excellent preparation device is a brainstorming session with colleagues and with your public relations consultant or manager of communications.

2. Be on time for the interview. Remember that the reporter may be working against a deadline. If the interview is in your office, assure there are no distractions (i.e., no phones ringing, etc.). Give the reporter your full attention.

3. Be yourself, be relaxed and, above all, be honest. Any degree of phoniness will be magnified many times over, especially on television. Be careful not to twist the facts even a little. More important than the substance of the interview is your general credibility.

4. Be brief. Answers that you have been able to formulate in advance will tend to make the interview go more smoothly, and more in your favor. Put the points important to you up front; otherwise, they may be edited out. Avoid technical jargon at all costs.

5. Ask the reporter at the outset—or at the time the appointment is made, if possible—what general areas he hopes to cover. Then be ready. If, in the course of the interview, you feel that you may be flubbing a response, do not try to cover up; stop, apologize and start from the beginning. If you don't know the answer, say so, but offer to find out and get back to them.

6. Offer to be available if they want to double-check their facts.

And here are some basic don'ts:

1. Don't try to be funny. Play it straight and be natural.

2. Never say "No comment." If you cannot answer, say so and go on to the next question.

3. Keep your composure no matter how trying the situation.

In addition to these points, the Allendale press guide, prepared by Paul Schofield of Allendale's Corporate Relations Department, provides us with additional items of importance. "Bear in mind that a reporter regularly faces two special demands. First, the result of his efforts is examined by great numbers of interested people, and every mistake is brought to his attention. Thus, the good reporter is always pursuing information that is precisely accurate. Secondly, a reporter is usually working against a deadline, sometimes only minutes away. Thus, his efforts are often characterized by considerable urgency. These two demands usually color how he does his job; remember this and you will understand why the interview may seem to take an aggressive tone, and why you may be pressed hard for details which are hard to come by on the spur of the moment. Yet, he wants his answers now."

Another point found in Schofield's manual is that it is generally unwise to refuse an interview, for two reasons. The reporter may piece together a story from other sources, which could turn out to be hostile. And a time might come when you will want to initiate a story with the same reporter. If you have turned him down on one occasion, he may have an understandably negative reaction in the future.

A few further recommendations taken from the Allendale press manual are worth remembering:

1. Assume that everything you say is for the record. If you are asked for information you cannot give, explain to the reporter that this is an area on which the client will have to comment or that the information is not available to you. If you do have to say that you are unable to answer for policy reasons, understand that a "no comment" response is often viewed as a hiding place.

2. Do not be afraid to admit mistakes. Everyone makes them; and if the information is bound to come out anyway, you might just as well take the heat and be appreciated for your candor.

3. If you can, make your story interesting. Do not hesitate to use examples and anecdotes if they are pertinent and really help make the point.

4. If you think there is a chance that you might be misunderstood, or if your answer is necessarily complex, repeat it. You might say, for example, "This subject tends to be confusing, or complicated. I'd like to be sure I've answered your questions clearly."

5. There is nothing wrong with volunteering information that has not been requested if you believe it relevant. It may help clarify some element of the interview and the reporter will usually appreciate it.

6. Do not ask that you be allowed to review the story before publication. If, of course, it has been written by you, or under your byline, you have every right to see it in advance; but the clearance of other kinds of articles, especially newspaper articles, is never offered and you should not expect it. In the case of technical or statistical material, it is perfectly in order to suggest that you will be glad to review and clarify any points which may develop in the course of writing.

7. Respect media deadlines. Provide promised information as quickly as possible. If you have made a commitment to get back to someone at the publication at a specific time, do so even if your information is incomplete.

Most of these suggestions seem like common sense. Unfortunately, common sense is not always at hand when professionals deal with the press. The bottom line is: Treat reporters as people with a job to do, and generally things will work out.

POLICIES AND PROCEDURES FOR NEWS RELEASES

When working with projects related to private industry, we will probably find that they employ their own public relations staff and would prefer to handle any releases internally. However, we could introduce ourselves to their public relations staff and offer any assistance in reviewing technical data related to the project, providing photographs, etc. This introduction and offer of assistance will hopefully remind them of our existence, and we will be given credit in all releases. When dealing with our small municipal and some private clients who may not have public relations services, we can offer to provide this assistance at appropriate times throughout the project.

Initiating a News Release

News releases can be initiated anywhere in the company as long as the approval process described in "Policies and Procedures" is followed.

Distributing the News Release

The communications staff keeps updated listings of all local and national media. The initiator of the news release will be given a form to check those media to which the release should go. The list will indicate only the city and the type of media; then the communications staff will provide names and addresses for distribution.

Example

Bellevue, Washington
   Daily Newspapers
   Weekly Newspapers
   Television Stations
   Radio Stations
   Business Press

Special Media
   Engineering News-Record
   American City
   Etc.
   Etc.

The news release will be sent only to those geographic media or special media indicated by the originator. Mail the relase to all media that feasibly would be interested. Watch timing. If a weekly paper is published on Thursday, for example, copy should be in its office no later than Monday. You may wish to hand deliver a release, which should increase the chances that it will be reviewed. If you want the news break to occur in the morning papers first, then do not release it until after 2:00 p.m. on the day before - that is, after the evening paper for the day before has gone to bed.

Another thing we need to keep in mind is that news releases are of interest not only to newspapers, but also to magazines, both special audience magazines and general news magazines.

THE ROLE OF TECHNICAL LITERATURE IN MARKETING COMMUNICATIONS AT STELCO: STANDARDS AND STYLE

Ernest Zucker
The Steel Company of Canada, Ltd.

Writers of advertising copy, tend to dramatize product performance even if it is fairly commonplace. Technical people often write in a dull manner about subjects that can be considered most interesting by selected audiences. The paper describes how the two styles can be reconciled. It also describes the great care taken by Stelco's editors to have visually attractive publications by judicious use of graphics, technical illustrations and photographs.

INTRODUCTION

"The shapes arise," said Walt Whitman writing in the 1860s "Shapes of Factories, arsenals, foundries, markets,
Shapes of the two-threaded tracks of railroads,
Shapes of the sleepers of bridges, vast frameworks, girders, arches."

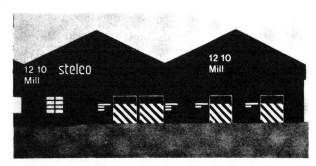

FIGURE 1

About Stelco: Established in 1910, The Steel Company of Canada, Limited, better known as Stelco, is Canada's leading steel producer and ranks ninth on the American continent. Steelmaking capacity approaches six million tons; this capacity will eventually be doubled when current expansion plans are completed. Stelco is building an entirely new steel plant at Nanticoke, Ontario, on Lake Erie. Advanced technology and plant layout combine to make this project one of the most efficient steelmaking operations anywhere. Facilities in Eastern, Central and Western Canada are also being expanded to provide significant increases in steel production.

At Stelco, the aim of its commercial and technical writing is not to write great prose but still maintain a very high standard. Only routine style guidelines are provided for staff writers – they are asked to write with clarity, conciseness and simplicity. New writers are given time to study existing Stelco publications, so that they become familiar with the type of writing expected from them. And they are instructed to adopt a routine method in describing products, projects or processes. Ideas are presented in a logical sequence with readability achieved by efficient use of words.

ERNEST ZUCKER
The Steel Company of Canada, Limited (Stelco)
Hamilton, Ontario, Canada L8N 3T1

Technical Writer, Marketing Communications and Promotion; Creative Services Department, The Steel Company of Canada, Ltd.
Responsible for Stelco brochures, technical bulletins, installation manuals

Education in Electrical Engineering
Member, Association of Professional Engineers of Ontario; officer, Engineering Institute of Canada

Reprinted with permission from *Proc. 23rd Int. Tech. Commun. Conf.*, 1976, pp. 157–162.

Writing, artwork and layout are the function of Stelco's Creative Services.*

This includes technical brochures, bulletins and manuals, press releases, newsletters, advertisements, several company magazines, audio-visual scripts, work on the Annual Report, etc. Marketing Communications at Stelco, like in other major corporations, can be classified as internal and external. Many have overlapping audiences (viz. the Annual Report). Company technical brochures, bulletins and regular publications, play a key role in market development of Stelco's multi-product operations. For those who produce these marketing communications, good product knowledge and recognition of customer needs, are a prerequisite. High quality communications help achieve management goals, particularly if each medium is carefully analyzed for each specific task. And, finally, everything that is done in a product's name affects the image not only of the product, but the company's image as well. For this reason, standards and style in Stelco's technical literature are believed to contribute significantly to its successful marketing communications.

THE 1970 CORPORATE IDENTITY PROGRAM

A corporate image can be defined as the company's reputation, hopefully good, that affects the degree of success it enjoys in the marketplace. Bad corporate images more often than not are self-created. A good image, no matter how spontaneous it seems, results from sound planning, good management and successful communications. Stelco's first comprehensive identity program was implemented in 1970. It covered not only items used in external and internal communications (advertising materials, stationary, packaging) but the company logo, buildings, signs and vehicles. See Figures 1 and 2.

Canadian English usage, in recent years, has been influenced by American style and spelling much more than in the past, when British influence predominated. Canadians trade with US business men, move in large numbers back and forth across the border, watch American TV and movies, read US publication ad books. As North Americans, both maintain their many relatively new words of the English language that were coined to denote many things indigenous to this continent. However, there still remain some differences in spelling (note some words in this paper - colour, centre, metre.)

*Creative Services are part of Marketing Communications and Promotion with J. K. Davy, Manager. They are headed by S. S. Dunmore, who has become a successful novelist in his spare time. The author extends his thanks to both these gentlemen for permission to write this paper.

FIGURE 2

FIGURE 3

The task for those designing the logo was set by asking for a symbol that looks good not only on paper, but on buildings, trucks and signs (see Figure 3 - Development of Stelco's logo). Since 1970, the new logo is included in all company communications so that, no matter where seen, the repeated use of the Stelco logo creates an unmistakable impact of common origin. Note that the logo is placed on the right-hand page of each spread in Stelco's literature, as well as on the front and back covers. As a key identifying mark, the new logo projects the company's progressive outlook forcefully and succinctly.

Colour coordination plays an important role in any successful corporate communications program. A strong, harmonizing colour scheme identifies various Stelco operations: primary steelmaking (green); rolling mills and finishing works (blue); service buildings (gray). Company vehicles are also colour-coordinated to correspond with the colour of the mill buildings in which they are located.(Bright stripes enhance their visibility.) Pictographs and non-verbal symbols are used for communications in the manufacturing areas - as shown in Figure 2. The program is described in some detail, because it also sets the standards for packaging and all printed matter.

Cover art, graphic layout of Stelco publications and colour schemes have become an integral part of this companywide program. In 1970, Stelco spent a lot of time and money in developing an organized approach to corporate looks, including all company printed materials. The corporate image, strengthened since then, is playing a major role in Stelco's continued growth.

STANDARDS AND STYLE

In 1975, Marketing Communications published thirty technical brochures and bulletins, eighteen periodicals, a dozen newsletters and over twenty new advertisements. From photographs of individual publications, the common look is apparent. (See Figures 4, 5, 6 and 7.) Technical literature is considered a real work-horse in comparison with consumer oriented printed matter. Under the heading brochures and bulletins, Stelco publishes design manuals and installation handbooks. Publication programs are established by the "Task" method, with each task corresponding to an industry. Each item within those tasks responds to a specific need expressed by the product, industry or sales engineering manager. Specific audiences are clearly defined.

Many of Stelco's brochures, bulletins and other publications communicate directly with architects, engineers, designers, home builders (developers) people Stelco's salesmen rarely see, for the simple reason they do not normally buy steel. They are, however, most important influences in selecting and specifying steels. Thus company technical literature acts as a surrogate sales force in an area where personal sales calls would be too costly. Stelco external communications, even those highly technical in content, carry certain image-building messages. Usually included are references to Stelco's:

☐ competence - experienced, skilled, qualified, authorative, research oriented, engineers and metallurgists at customer disposal.

☐ reliability - conservative, consistent in product quality, fully tested, integrated steel manufacturer.

☐ dynamism - progressive, modern, innovative pioneer, strong on research and development, expanding facilities.

☐ sociability - conscious of environment, ready to assist in design application of steel materials, backing steel service centres and steel fabricators.

FIGURE 4

FIGURE 5

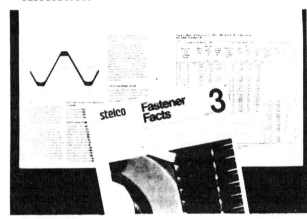

FIGURE 6

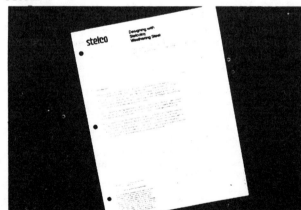

FIGURE 7

Stelco's three major audiences for technical literature are classified as heavy construction (builders of roads and bridges, buildings, pressure vessels); industrial* (manufacturers of automobiles, appliances, agricultural implements, general industry) and residential construction**(single and multi-family dwellings). A numerically limited audience, but important to the company's business performance, is the Service Centre industry*** essentially wholesaling steel products. In the past, Stelco used to issue a full catalogue that had obvious limitations. It rapidly became obsolete and with Stelco's large portfolio of products, was difficult to finalize for printing at a set date. Technical brochures that can be assembled into a catalogue but are issued individually, have become Stelco's key communicators since the comprehensive identity program was implemented in 1970. Relatively inexpensively, these technical brochures provide all information a customer needs. They allow him to determine quickly (and without obligation) whether or not he is interested in a particular Stelco product.

Three examples of Stelco's Technical Literature

Structural Steels: Selection and uses (Figure 4). This 106-page brochure serves as reference guide for structural engineers in specifying steels. Its twelve sections are separated by coloured dividers. Each section includes a colour spread of case histories that breaks the monotony caused by text and tables. An easily readable style is maintained, despite the highly technical content.

Stelcolour prefinished sheet steel (Figure 5). The graphic design on the cover is typical for many Stelco brochures. Colour illustrations are used throughout, because Stelcolour sheet steels are prefinished in a variety of colours. The contents: Introduction, how precoated steels are manufactured, specifications, how precoated steels are applied and a glossary of terms. This is a typical table of contents and many Stelco brochures follow an almost identical pattern.

*An important medium of communications with industrial designers is Stelco's periodical SCOPE. It concentrates on case histories representing unusual and interesting uses of steel by industry. New product ideas are highlighted. SCOPE is published quarterly.

**A regular Stelco publication STEEL IN HOMES is aimed at builders, urban developers and government housing officials. The magazine provides current news about steel in residential construction.

***Newsletters serve as Stelco's link with numerically limited audiences. The company publishes newsletters for SERVICE CENTRE, WIRE, STEEL IN TRANSPORTATION, PIPE AND TUBE customers. FARM REPORT covers the agricultural market, an important steel user. Because newsletters keep relatively small audiences well informed, at Stelco they have proved a useful tool for generating enquiries and have become "door-openers" for sales representatives. These newsletters carry valuable information which would be too specialized for other Stelco publications. Also, their format is not elaborate – they are typewritten and illustrations are in black and white.

Stelform spiral-weld pipe: Very often a new product or technical innovations (new process) becomes the victim of poor marketing communications. Stelco's approach in one particular case involved a departure from its own rigid graphic standards, to draw attention to the new Stelform pipe manufacturing method. The brochure is different and thus acts as special focus for this major technological achievement (the brochure is made oversize in comparison with Stelco's regular publications.) A flow diagram showing the novel process, forms the brochure's centre-fold. At a glance, readers can follow this relatively complex method of pipe manufacturing. Stelform pipe features are highlighted on the same page. Stelco publishes a series of Technical Bulletins.* These match the high calibre of papers published by learned societies but differ in two areas: the company image building message is included although kept low key and meticulous attention is paid to graphic layout.

Style recommendations

Experience shows that commercial readers (customers) tend to glance at introductory sentences, paragraphs (or abstracts) before deciding to proceed. Thus the best chance to be read is at the brochure's beginning – a good opening includes one or more image building messages, combined with a factual but easily readable summary of what follows. There is no need to be dramatic. Yet here is a place for departing from the dull prose of highly technical matter. The end is also most important, particularly in highly technical bulletins. Often technical writers forget to summarize their major points. So both the beginning and the end, should be used for stating (or restating) persuasive arguments.

Similarly, cutlines should receive as much care in writing (possibly more!) than body copy. Because far more people read cutlines than the brochure's text, they should contain some key points. They should interest the reader sufficiently to encourage him to read the text. Cutlines, for example, should be set up as follows:

"1: Wire strand suspension bridge supports. Each 3/4-inch designed to carry 4861lbs dead load. Note the 48-strand configurations." Waste-of-space phrases in cutlines such as"the photograph shows.." should be avoided. Here are other typical style notes recommended for Stelco writers:

*Stelco also publishes FASTENER FACTS, an informative series dealing with current fastener data. Fasteners have become indispensable since the beginning of civilization. Even today much of man's progress depends on his ability to fasten useful things together. Although highly technical in content, FASTENER FACTS' graphic design is considered unique for a business publication. Stelco green serves as illustration background, logos and issue numbers. Covers have a distinctive look, often using line art techniques (Figure 6).

Avoid pompous phrases. Use clear, familiar words. Never use a long word where a shorter one would do. A furnace is a furnace, not a thermal heating mechanism. Keep sentences short and simple. Language has been compared to a transportation system for words. It should be fast, direct and clear.

Include illustrative material (photos, drawings, charts) generously. Much as a Stelco sales representative is judged by appearance, so is good sales literature. Covers are particularly important to give the best possible first impression. The saying "A picture is worth a thousand words" may be a platitude but, when carefully chosen and executed, pictures support and augment the text. They also help keep up the reader's interest.

Abbreviations Avoid abbreviations as much as possible, so that sentences aren't peppered with periods throughout. Spell out words as Limited, Ontario, inch, etc. Accepted abbreviations are words as Mr., St., and frequently-used technical abbreviations such as: psi, ksi, OD, mph, HSS[*] - note the absence of periods between letters.

With metric measurements, always use symbols. Example: 16 m^2 (not 16 square metres). Exception: The symbol for litre is a script ℓ. If that presents difficulties it can be written out in full. (Canada is planning to convert to the metric system by 1980.)

Numerals In narrative passages, stick to words up to the number "nineteen", then use numerals. If, however, a series of numbers is involved, use numerals only. Exception: use numerals when stating dimensions of products, buildings, etc. Use spaces when writing numbers, tens of thousands and up, to isolate thousands. Example: 200 000. No space should be used for smaller numbers. Example: 2000.

Pay particular attention to the correct presentation of numerals pertaining to Stelco products. For example, gauge numbers are no longer used for sheet and plate products; the correct terminology is, say: 0.018-inch. In the case of HSS, always use the following form: 6 x 6 x 0.188 -inch. Note use use of zero before decimal point. Go to only three decimal places, even though your sources may provide more.

Use hyphens when numerals are used as adjectives. Example: 3-inch steel plate, otherwise no hyphens are necessary. Example: Steel plate 3 inches thick.

Clean copy saves time and money. It saves the typesetter's time because he can follow the manuscript quickly and easily. Later it saves proofreading time, if fewer errors need correcting in galley proofs. Remember the typesetter sets what is there, not what is supposed to be there.

*HSS - Hollow Structural Sections.

Headings: Use as few capital letters as possible; they slow down the proceedings. Sub-heads should be set into paragraphs as done in this paper.

Product Names: Remember: Stelco's propietary names must be used as adjectives not nouns. Examples: "Stelcolour prefinished steel", "Stelcoloy weathering steel". In the case of HSS, when the product name is first mentioned, state: "Hollow Structural Sections (HSS)", then use "HSS" thereafter. Some examples of Stelco products: "Monova barbed wire", "Ardox spiral nails", "Stelco siding", "Frost residential fence".

Complete copy saves time and money. When preparing copy for publications, prepare it all. Include all cutlines, credits and notes. Example from the outside back cover of TREND[*]:
"E. Jones   Editor
S. Smith   Consultant
E. R. Arthur   Professional consultant
B. Brown   Graphic design
Text in this publication may be reprinted editorially, provided the usual credits are given. Permission must, however, be obtained before any illustrations may be reproduced."

VISUALS Graphic layout and illustrations (sketches, photographs) play a vital part in Stelco's communications program. When a particular brochure is handed to the customer by the salesman, its looks can positively reinforce a given sales situation.

Stelco's technical literature and advertisements are designed to build a "multiple impression effect" by a common communications platform and, what is even more important, a common family appearance. The corporate identity guidelines at Stelco provide detailed instructions for the design of technical literature, advertisements and other company publications. Printed material formats are standardized (Figures 8 and 9). One advantage of this standardization: Illustrations often find a multiple use. For example, separated colour photographs are sized within the prescribed grid and readily fit into the standard layouts.

*In TREND Stelco commissions leading Canadian architects to solve modern building challenges and utilize steel. Their solutions include conceptual drawings, combined with structural details for readers who are engineers. TREND CONSTRUCTION REPORT is published as a companion piece to TREND for non-architectural structural applications. It focuses on case histories (current projects) and new applications for steel materials in construction. Examples from both publications: an engineering feature on how to design bridges in the Arctic with HSS; an in-depth analysis of structural characteristics on the CN Tower, Toronto, Ontario - currently the world's highest self-supporting structure. Architectural renderings and colour photos are used extensively throughout each issue. Published twice annually, TREND has met with considerable success since the program began in 1962.

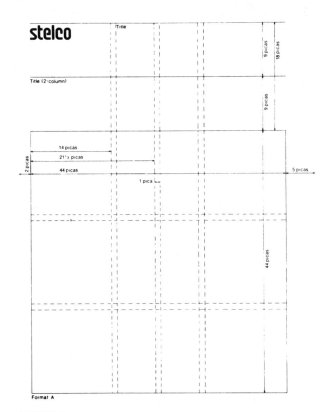

FIGURE 8

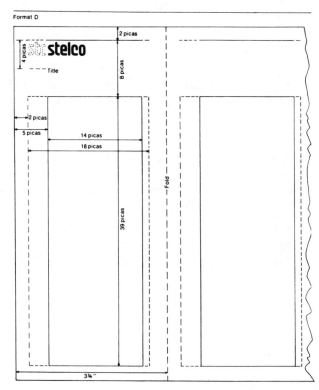

FIGURE 9

Now a word about Stelco brochure covers. They help form the first important impression in the reader's mind. Abstract designs, photograph (s) or drawing (s) usually are chosen, again maintaining as much graphic uniformity as possible. From this starting point, it is less difficult to attain the desired standards and style for each publication.

Someone once said that people engaged in written communications concentrate so much on the contents and style of their work that they neglect photographs and illustrations. For example, little attention is paid to photography, a form of communication which often takes up major space in advertisements and promotional brochures. A technical writer should use good photographs and illustrations to explain and bring alive even the most complicated text. While responsibility for layout and best use of visuals rightfully belongs to the art director at Stelco, each writer is asked to take responsibility for the message they should convey. The results confirm that this is the correct approach – throughout Stelco's publications, illustrations maintain a constant high standard whether in colour or black and white.

With regard to photographs, these are the criteria for technical excellence: sharpness, tone reproduction and lack of grain in the image. For colour shots, check colour and/ or tonal balance. (These need to be checked and rechecked during the colour separation process before printing.) Most of these criteria apply to other art, including good engineering drawings.

Often manufacturing and operating processes need to be explained in detail. One method uses an artist's concept of pipe manufacturing –handwritten cutlines are placed in strategic places on the drawing for maximum readability. This quick review highlights the importance of illustrations to technical writers. Only in combination, can good writing and good illustrations tell a story most efficiently.

CONCLUSION

The reasons for the differences between the writing of copywriters and technical writers, lie in the different purposes as well as working environments of these writers. Good commercial external and internal communications should strive to bridge the gap between these two different writing styles. Stelco's publications and technical literature in recent years have achieved the goal of explaining often complex processes in a relatively simple manner. (Samples of periodicals and brochures mentioned in this paper are available from the author.)

A skillful integration of photographs and illustrations into an article, the importance of graphic layout and visual appearance cannot be overemphasized.

THREE VITAL VIEWS FOR NEWS RELEASE WRITERS

Ernest Mazzatenta
General Motors Research Laboratories

This article tells how to increase the output of news releases within your organization without increasing your staff — and how to gain greater acceptance of these releases in outside publications. Achieving these objectives involves carrying out certain key activities well before the release takes shape.

Are some of your proposed news releases being rejected by the managerial approvers within your organization? By the outside publications in which you most want those releases to appear?

If your answer is "Never" to all of the above, you can skip this piece and go directly to the next one. Better yet, consider reporting your recipes for success in a future edition of the Proceedings. The sad fact is, most news release writers encounter some rejection of their efforts on both the inside and the outside. And rejection, of course, means wasted effort.

In some cases, whether he is willing to admit it or is even aware of it, the science writer himself is primarily to blame for the rebuffs; he is destined to fail because he doesn't plan for success.

Improving your rate of success — both inside your organization and on the outside — is the central concern of this paper. It has twin theses:

- assessing the news value of a particular science or engineering project requires more than introspection. Seeking out and weighing other, quite different perspectives is equally important.

- acquiring these perspectives should take place well before you invest time and energy into a first draft.

Even if you have heard these points before, the chances are you've found them easy to forget or difficult to implement. The pressures of deadlines . . . the demands of parallel writing assignments . . . your own, comfortable (lazy?) way of doing things . . . any of these factors can block implementation.

Yet time devoted to careful planning will result in time saved later. The plan I offer is not especially easy to implement, at least not at first. But follow it long enough and you almost certainly will wind up with more hits and fewer misses.

Before I deliver the specifics, let's look at the way in which you may be viewing a story idea at present. Undoubtedly you spend more than a little time thinking through and evaluating that idea. You gage it in terms of your own educational background ("Do I understand what is going on?"); preferred writing assignments ("Does this topic excite me?"); and personal reading habits ("Would I be inclined to stop and read this story if I spotted it in an outside journal?")

Notice those pronouns "I" and "me."

This personal view is useful but obviously limited in value. It limits results in terms of story development, acceptance by reviewers within your organization, and usage on the outside.

Enough about what often happens if one fails to recognize and apply other perspectives well before "Word One" is written. You have been waiting for

ERNEST MAZZATENTA
30611 Birchtree Drive, Warren, Mich.
(313) 575-7305

General Motors Research Laboratories, Warren, Mich.
Head, Science Writers' Group; Instructor, Science Writing.
Elected Associate Fellow of STC in 1979. Contributed papers to the ITCC *Proceedings* of 1972, 1973, 1975. B.A. cum laude, Kent State University, 1953; M.S.J., Medill School of Journalism, Northwestern University, 1954.

Reprinted with permission from *Proc. 27th Int. Tech. Commun. Conf.,* 1980, vol. II, pp. W169–W173.

me to get specific. The perspectives which I recommend to you are those of:

- —the scientist or engineer whose work you are interested in covering.
- —the executive whose signature of approval must be secured before the story can be issued.
- —the outside editor or other prospective user.

Identifying these people as keys to your success is not all that difficult. What is needed, of course, is a plan for acquiring their input. The observations and guidelines which follow constitute such a plan. They are the outgrowth of my experiences as both sender and receiver of news releases, and upon my investigation of recent research by others.

LOOK FIRST TO THE SCIENTIST

You may be working with research scientists and engineers as I do. Or you may be writing about the activities of other kinds of technical people. No matter. Regardless of their field or title, their opinion regarding possible news coverage of their projects must be carefully heeded.

Let's say you have skimmed through a scientist's detailed report on a project and think it has some news value. Before attempting an outline, tell that scientist of your interest. Then stand back and listen.

Does the scientist believe he has completed all the work on his project — or some sizeable portion thereof? Or does he think results are still preliminary? If the latter, postpone coverage and set a date for a second inquiry.

If the scientist has completed an appreciable amount of work, he probably has drawn some conclusions from the results. Does he believe the conclusions would be of interest to at least some groups of outside readers? Those in his specialty area? A broader segment of the scientific community? The public in general? If he is dubious about reader interest, proceed cautiously. Rethink your own reasons for wanting to pursue the story idea. But don't stop there; seek out the scientist's immediate supervisor for another opinion. Then make your decision.*

Finally, is the scientist enthusiastic about being written up or at least willing to cooperate in a friendly way? Or does he consider your visit an unnecessary intrusion into his life? An obstacle to getting

---

* *Do not ask anyone whether the project results are significant. This could lead to endless discussion, perhaps even debate, involving the scientist, his supervisor, the entire chain of command. If you wait for a unanimous vote on significance, you may never write about anything. Potential interest — not significance — is what should be gaged.*

other "more important" things done? If, for any reason, he is antagonistic or extremely hesitant about proceeding, you're probably better off moving on.

Persevere only if you think the story idea has unusual merit. That being the case, try to convince the scientist and his management of same. Even if you do manage to budge the scientist, recognize that it probably is going to be tough sledding from beginning to end.

Fortunately, at the General Motors Research Laboratories, science writers encounter very few "hostiles." In fact, more than a few scientists and engineers (or their managers) will call or write us and suggest possible news stories. Perhaps you enjoy the same treatment.

Whatever the case may be, you always should be ready when a subject balks; be ready to try a little selling if you sense it will help . . . or ready to retreat if he seems adamant.

THE EXECUTIVE SLANT

"Whether they are concerned with technical documentation, management information systems, or design, all service and support departments thrive best when they enjoy the understanding and support of their company's management."

— *Management Review, September, 1971*

No writer can gain such understanding and support unless he takes on the management perspective. What happens when you don't can be painful — and I have a personal story which attests to that. Up until just a few years ago, my fellow science writers and I sometimes found our proposed news releases being cancelled at the top management level at our facility — that is, just one step removed from actual distribution on the outside.

While management usually had good reason to withhold approval, such cancellations were always frustrating and sometimes traumatic. After all, cancellation meant hours of work invested in researching a topic, interviewing principals, writing and rewriting, had gone for naught.

What could be done to head off such "abortions"? How could we increase our chances of getting top management's support and understanding? Once we stopped to seriously ponder these questions, it became patently clear where we had gone wrong. Our own approval procedure was faulty.

Under this procedure, we sought the green light on a story idea only from the head of the department whose activities we were going to describe.

Later, once the story itself was approved by the department, we moved it up to the executive office at our facility for final approval. We followed this procedure for two main reasons:

1. We assumed that our executives would not want to be bothered with inquiries about story ideas.
2. We thought department management would always mirror executive management's feelings about the newsworthiness of a story.

We were, of course, wrong on both counts.

Now we have an approach which responds effectively to the problem:

First, we anticipate how our executives probably will react to a story idea, based on our knowledge of their past reactions to proposed coverage on specific subjects. Usually this means simply checking our memories and files; but it might also involve asking fellow writers for a reading.

Second, if this reflection leads us to believe the idea has a good chance, we call or send a note to the appropriate executive and request an O.K. on the idea. Then — and only then — do we proceed.

Once we have a draft which is acceptable to the cooperating engineer or scientist, we submit the draft to both the department head and the executive for parallel review. When we have all their comments together, we shape a final draft. This draft goes only to the appropriate executive for review.

Our new procedure has drastically reduced the number of releases being cancelled just "one step away" from dissemination. It also has reduced the blood pressures of all our writers. Because of these positive results, we strongly recommend the same or a similar procedure to those writers now suffering from this problem.

There is no doubt in our minds that the executive perspective is a "plus" as far as the news release business is concerned.

It's an advantage because top management at your location has a vastly different outlook than writers do — and at least a slightly different one than that of middle management. Your executives have an excellent understanding of what your corporate officers would like to see released publicly — and an equally sharp sense of what competitors, governmental bodies, and other outsiders should not see for various legitimate (e.g., proprietary) reasons.

THE NEWSMAN'S NEEDS

"Daily newspapers receive from 25 to 250 news releases a day. Approximately one of every 25 . . . is used."

— *IABC News, May, 1978*

Inside your organization, you have a ready, and perhaps waiting, audience for your technical articles, reports, and summaries. On the outside, you generally do not.

At best, outside editors will have only a fair amount of knowledge of the subject of your piece. These editors will start reading your story with a neutral, "wait-and-see" attitude. Among them are the editors of trade journals and professional society publications.

But other editors will have only meager or no understanding of the subject. They will start scanning with a skeptical "Show me" attitude. In this category are a good many editors of daily newspapers and magazines serving general interests. (Why expect otherwise?)

(Left unaddressed here are full-time science columnists and correspondents, a less numerous breed with special needs, all of which deserve detailed attention in some future ITCC paper.)

You must prepare for both types of editors well before you begin an outline. Such preparation demands that you gage the potential news value of your story from each editor's point of view.

Now that does *not* mean "putting yourself in the editor's shoes." Dr. H. J. Tichy, an STC Fellow, tells us that is not good enough. "A better admonition than 'Put yourself in the reader's place,'", she says, "is 'Forget yourself and become your reader.'"[1]

Sydney Harris makes the same important point when he observes: "The reason most of us fail when we try to put ourselves in someone else's place is that we insist on taking ourselves along."

To summarize, "becoming" an outside editor means assuming his education, his experience, his working environment, his grasp of reader interests. Next to impossible? Not for an industrious science writer intent upon gaining maximum coverage for his stories!

Here are two ways to work toward maximum impact:

1. Carefully examine those publications of most interest to you and your organization. What kinds of news generally receive the best play? What subjects appear time and again on the editorial page? Which get generous photo treatment? What kinds of industry people appear in interviews and feature stories? Answering these questions will help you to avoid mismatches of stories and editors.

2. Get to know as many of those outside editors as possible. You may not be able to visit very many but what about writing or calling them? Invite some to visit you for a tour and a discussion of their needs.

ASSESSING THE NEWS VALUE OF A SCIENTIFIC PROJECT

(A Check List for News Release Writers)

WHAT DOES THE SCIENTIST THINK?

1. Is the project far enough along to warrant a news release?

2. Are the results preliminary?

3. Can any interesting conclusions be drawn?

4. Specifically who — out there — would consider them interesting?

5. Would my cooperation with the writer mean falling far behind on other, urgent work?

6. Would publication of the story embarrass me?

WHAT DOES EXECUTIVE MANAGEMENT THINK?

1. Would the proposed story result in a give-away of new technical information before we want outside audiences to know about it?

2. Would public disclosure of this information impair the corporate decision-making process?

3. Would publication put us at a disadvantage in the marketplace?

4. Does this story lend itself to misinterpretation? Might it lead recipients to either overestimate or underestimate our rate of progress or the extent of our success?

WHAT DOES THE OUTSIDE EDITOR THINK?

1. Is this a legitimate news story, i.e., is it informative?

2. Is this an interesting story? In what way does it mesh with the interests of my readers?

3. Is this a well-written "translation" – or a jumble of jargon?

4. Is the story unnecessarily commercial in tone?

Author's Note: The executive management segment of this list is based in part upon material published in "How Much Privacy Does Business Need?", Russell B. Stevenson, Jr., *Business and Society Review*, Summer, 1979.

Because, early in my career, I served as a newspaper reporter and editor, I can assure you that personal contact means a lot. News releases coming from people we knew were the releases that most often got into the paper. Some actually made Page 1. Those stories did not get printed simply because we knew their authors but because they knew what we wanted — and provided it!

If recent research by others is any indication, things haven't changed since I left the newspaper world. For example, Group Attitudes Company, in the late '70's, asked outside science and trade editors what they would like to get from inside science communicators. One editor, voicing a commonly heard view, said: "More person-to-person contact is needed between the industry source and the reporter . . . I get too much printed material."(2)

A Canadian public relations counselor, writing in the IABC Journal, goes so far as to advocate calling in releases to "the news directors of radio and TV stations (and to newspaper reporters) in those parts of the country in which you want particularly full coverage. Indicate that a hard copy is . . . in the mail. Direct, personal contact pays off." (3)

Pick the particular approach to "getting acquainted" that best suits your situation — but do pick one. If you sustain the effort long enough, you will indeed develop a useful understanding of your markets, garner more space in more publications, and win at least a few, new friends to boot.

The writer who diligently works at this approach becomes expert at targeting his pieces. He will know, as the result of his contacts, whether a particular story idea will require:

> —a detailed treatment for limited release to a select group of special interest publications.

> —a somewhat shorter, less technical piece for broad-based trade journals and popular science publications.

> —an even shorter, human-interest feature for exclusive use in newspapers.

On those occasions when a story idea merits all three treatments, the resourceful science writer will be intelligent enough to perceive that and industrious enough to follow through.

He also will recognize the added impact gained by including an illustration of some kind. A survey we ran at GM Research revealed that releases complemented by a photograph of the scientist-in-action are four times as likely to get used as stories without a picture.

In summary, the writer of news releases who looks at his job as more than simply writing in terms of his own experiences is the one most likely to succeed. By collecting and carefully weighing the viewpoints and interests of other key people in the news release system — well before writing — he can increase the rate of acceptance for his material, both within his organization and in outside publications.

References:
1. Tichy, H. J., "Effective Writing for Engineers, Managers, Scientists," John Wiley & Sons, Inc., New York, N.Y., 1967.
2. Strasser, Joel A., "The Scientific Communications Gap," International Conference on Energy Use Management, Tucson, Ariz., Oct. 25, 1977.
3. Irvine, Robert, "Maximize Your PR Dollars. Do the News Release Right," IABC Journal, May, 1978.

YOU CAN OFTEN ENHANCE YOUR PRODUCT BY USING EXTERNAL RESOURCES
... *And Here's How*

Lois K. Moore

USING SUPPLEMENTAL EXTERNAL RESOURCES for editing and production has many advantages. The technique can be employed, in varying degrees, to meet both long- and short-term requirements, depending upon projected internal workloads. It requires sound planning and the cooperation of an enlightened management. This article details how to use vendors to supplement internal staff.

The most important final product of writing endeavors is the finished piece. Although the information it contains may take months or years to gather, the result should not take equal time to process through the publications cycle. To avert many common publication delays, the editor must establish realistic schedules and individual responsibilities, both of which can often be met more reliably by the use of outside publication resources. The result of using such help will be a leveling out of internal workloads, better quality control, and more finished material per month, without having to increase internal payroll.

ADVANTAGES OF USING MULTIPLE RESOURCES

To help you determine whether supplemental help from outside resources should be employed to meet your company's publication requirements, let's consider the principal advantages.

Time and Tact

The most obvious reason for considering external resources is to meet your publication delivery dates promptly. The use of vendors automatically eliminates the handicap of having to rely entirely on internal systems that may be backlogged with prior commitments, sometimes taking precedence over your work. And, just for the record, outside vendors can automatically remove your work from the internal political "pecking order," thus relieving otherwise friendly sources from the embarrassment of having to favor one job over another.

External vs. Internal Cost

It does not necessarily cost more, and in some cases can cost considerably less, to have certain aspects of publication work performed by one or more external suppliers. The lump-sum estimates of vendors may initally strike you or your budget office as expensive, but the picture will usually look quite different

Adapted from a paper presented at the 27th International Technical Communication Conference, Minneapolis, May 1980.

after you analyze an itemized breakdown of the total work and make an unbiased comparison with the *real* payroll, material and applied overhead costs of performing the same tasks internally. Even when the cost is slightly higher from the outside, the difference may be far more than offset by having on-time delivery guaranteed, with no "sorry-old-buddy" excuses for being late. The gratitude of satisfied sponsors who get top-quality results, exactly when promised, will undoubtedly result in greater long-range financial benefits to your company.

Quality and Efficiency

Although members of your own staff may be capable of producing work of the highest caliber in your field, you must still consider one elusive basic ingredient, *time,* and the fact that your regular staff may not have enough of it to do justice to all of the jobs being processed during a given period. Errors and oversights that originate internally, whether caused by rushing or some other reason, must also be detected and rectified internally, all at extra expense to your organization.

On the other hand, if such problems occur in work done externally, the suppliers are responsible for correcting them immediately--at their expense. Therefore, you are spared the disruption of other internal work flow, and the costs of revising, rescheduling, and rechecking are totally eliminated.

Another boost to your efficiency comes from dealing with a single vendor representative throughout each job; you can let the "rep" make the numerous, time-consuming, often frustrating internal contacts within the vendor company. You oversee the work being performed by an outside organization. The advantage here is that you spend your time managing projects instead of people.

You serve as a question-answering and problem-solving point of contact between the author and the vendor. All questions about the publication fall in your domain; you are the final authority on editorial matters and an intermediary with authors on content. This has major benefits for the author, who is buffered against frequent and sometimes unnecessary interruptions. And, perhaps most important, it is easier to ensure a top-quality finished product when you are dealing at each stage of review with clean, professionally prepared material.

SELECTING THE RIGHT RESOURCES

The process of selecting external publication resources can be divided into four logical phases.

Finding Qualified Candidates

1. *Previous Supplier.* If your company has published material for some time, it is possible that competent outside sources have supplied your organization with publication services in the past. Ask your purchasing or accounting departments. If they give you leads, be sure that the previous work was satisfactory and, by all means, use the same criteria to evaluate such references that you would apply to any other candidates.

2. *Peer Recommendation.* Good sources of candidates are your counterparts at other companies, particularly those writers or editors who are members of trade associations to

which you belong. The degree of seriousness with which you consider their suggestions should be largely governed by their *actual experience* with the firms and the *similarity of their work* to the work you plan to produce.

In preliminary candidate screening, you may assume that a company established for five or more years has an acceptable degree of stability and acumen; however, you should not avoid selecting a newer firm if it appears capable and financially sound, especially one headed by principals who personally have good business reputations and whose expertise is respected in the trade.

Criteria to Apply

1. *Security/Interest Conflicts.* In technical work, it is essential that your vendors have security clearances high enough to qualify for all of the work that you plan to delegate to them; also, it is prudent to have them verify, prior to the assignment of each job, that they are not engaged in a competitive endeavor or one that might risk any conflict of interest with your own organization or sponsor/client.

2. *Adequate Staff.* Ascertain in the preliminary interview that the proposed vendor has an adequate editorial staff, both in numbers and in expertise, to handle your work. Never hesitate to ask for specific data on the people who will be handling your assignments.

3. *Physical Equipment.* If typesetting, printing, and graphics are required, determine whether the vendors have the appropriate capabilities within their own plants or will have to subcontract parts of the work. The latter is much less desirable for reasons too numerous to list.

4. *Work Samples.* Request recent samples of finished work from the vendors that reflect their product quality, preferably on manuscripts somewhat similar to those you plan to submit. Assure the vendors that they may keep their client samples anonymous, but be sure you see enough to measure the finished product quality against your own company's standards.

5. *Method of Charging.* A reliable firm will gladly reveal to you exactly how its charges are determined. This usually involves, among other things, hourly rates for various types of services. (*Caution:* Hourly rates, though a good general cost indicator, should never be the overriding determinant in your final selection, since the efficiency and expertise of the personnel assigned to your work will undoubtedly vary from one company to another.)

6. *Written Estimates.* Have it understood with the vendors' representatives that advance written estimates may sometimes be requested before work is assigned. Assure them, however, that reasonable additional charges can be approved in their final billings for extra work resulting from changes or errors made by your own staff.

Candidate Validation

1. *Service Representative.* It is always best to establish at the outset one principal contact who is to be responsible for your work. The person you meet in the first interview may be in sales and not necessarily the individual who is going to service your account.

Insist that your actual service representative be present at all subsequent interviews. At those times, assure yourself, as best you can, that this person is knowledgeable about publications work and capable of understanding your organization's requirements.

2. *Facilities Inspection.* When a vendor meets with your general approval, according to the foregoing criteria, and you have narrowed the field of candidates to three or fewer, it is advisable to make an appointment to visit their establishments to meet other people who may be involved in your work, and to actually see the equipment the representatives have touted. Make notes, if necessary, for comparative use.

The Joy and the Agony

1. *Schedules and Deadlines.* In publications work, there is no universally accepted method of ensuring that even the most reliable vendors will always meet your deadlines. After all, their companies are made up, just like yours, of fallible human beings. However, when you have chosen a vendor, it is advisable, while announcing the good news of their selection, to underscore the seriousness with which you and your firm regard deadlines. Make it clear that a pleasant business atmosphere will depend heavily upon promptness, and a continuing relationship will require it.

2. *The Velvet Hammer.* After putting several candidates through the paces, especially if you have given them much encouragement, you should notify the losers tactfully that another firm has been selected "because they appear in a slightly better position to handle our immediate

needs." Assure them that the decision was difficult and that you will certainly prioritize them if circumstances change. This is more than mere business etiquette; it may form a pleasant foundation that you can build upon if you later discover you're not entirely happy with your initial choice.

Note: If you follow these suggested steps, you should immediately file relevant information on the "finalists" and rate them numerically, by preference. Then, if you need to change suppliers, or add new ones in a hurry, most of your homework will already be done.

VENDOR ORIENTATION

After selecting your vendor, you must establish and maintain an efficient and effective working relationship. This starts with--

a. defining more precisely what you expect and what can reasonably be expected from you;

b. meeting the editorial staff;

c. establishing in detail your preferred editorial styles and formats; and

d. specifying schedules for the initial assignments.

All of these matters must be handled as your individual requirements dictate; however, here are a few pointers that universally apply.

1. *Vendor Representative.* It is imperative that you keep this person apprised of any internal policy, procedure, or schedule changes that might affect the work the vendor is performing for you. Also, let the

"rep" know in advance if a publication is being planned that will have uncommon requirements, so the vendor can prepare to handle it efficiently. To avoid misunderstandings, all instructions (or a thorough summary) should be written, with copies distributed to all others involved in the project.

2. *Editorial Staff.* Be sure to retain a copy of each manuscript and all other materials submitted to the vendor. As sole contact, you will receive numerous questions from the vendor's editorial staff concerning work in progress. You can usually answer editorial questions immediately. Technical or factual inquiries may have to be answered by the author, with you acting as intermediary.

To protect the author from frequent interruptions, ask the vendor's staff to submit technical and factual questions in groups, when doing so doesn't jeopardize schedules or deadlines. *Note:* Make sure that you ask the same questions the vendor has posed and, even more important, that you accurately interpret and convey the answers.

3. *Style Guide.* Before releasing the first assignment, you should have or prepare an editorial style guide and typing format samples for the vendor. Each item should be reviewed, and any uncertainties thoroughly discussed, particularly specifications that may be peculiar to your company. Examples of items the guide should include are acceptable and unacceptable acronyms, approved common words and phrases, and methods of handling bibliography, references, and other components, so that all documents will appear consistent.

4. *Establishing Schedules.* Before an assignment is sent to the vendor, you should specify every step of its development and set specific target dates for each. This information is as vital to other "team" members as it is to the vendor, since it will establish individual responsibilities and underscore the importance of completing each part of the project on time.

Dates that should always be included:

- Manuscript submitted to vendor
- Typed copies delivered for review
- Marked-up review copy returned to vendor
- Final review copies delivered for approval
- Approved copy submitted to vendor for printing, and
- Final printed copies delivered for distribution.

If your scheduling requires other internal procedures, simply insert them where appropriate.

CONCLUSION

The properly balanced use of internal and external publication resources can produce better publications more consistently on schedule, with fewer crises and less overhead. The quality of the final product may be enhanced, too, while operational efficiency will certainly be improved.

What you have just read are *dictums,* not mere suggestions. If you follow these principles and are adequately informed, you will seldom, if ever, have irreconcilable problems with upper echelon.

Section IV-B
Design and Layout Techniques

"How to Get the Reader's Attention," by J.V. White, illustrates two attention-getting devices successfully used in the business.

"The Copy Chasers Rules: What Makes Good Business/Industrial Advertising," by the editors of *Industrial Marketing,* presents ten proven ways to improve advertising copy.

"AV Graphics: Talking with Type," by R.H. Davis, explains the importance of selecting the right type face to get your message across.

"Impact Without Impecunity—How to Boost Corporate Print Ad Effectiveness and Save Money," by P.A. Waring, examines results of studies made on print and TV advertising.

"How to Order Ads a La Carte," by I. Levison, provides information on how to locate independent copywriters and art directors when you can't afford the services of a full-service agency.

"The Most Important Difference Between Good and Bad Industrial Advertising," excerpted from *Industrial Marketing,* illustrates both good and bad examples of product advertising.

"What it Takes to Make Your Ad a Standout," excerpted from *Industrial Marketing,* describes proven ways to write and illustrate advertisements.

"Industrial Packaging Can Boost Sales," by H. Sharman, describes case histories of companies which have discovered marketing advantages in industrial packaging.

"Design is the Missing Link," by T. Faul, suggests taking full advantage of the design stage when developing new products for the marketplace.

HOW TO GET THE READER'S ATTENTION

The essential ingredient: a good editorial idea—one that is worth calling attention to. Without such value, no amount of graphic flamboyance makes sense. It may work that first time, and it may well yield some visual excitement for the issue. But that's cheating the reader who will grow suspicious of hype. And the magazine will suffer in the long run because of this inflation of presentation techniques.

BUT, if there is something worth trumpeting out loud, here is a collection of ways to do it (besides, of course, the fundamental way of making it big). Below: two useful attention-getting devices: 1) pinning the idea on someone the reader is likely to recognize and respect (Messrs. Napoleon, Beethoven and Shakespeare might fill the requirements?) and 2) elaborating the idea with symbols the reader recognizes as importance symbols (big exclamation points, out-of-scale quote marks, fat balloons). More on the pages that follow.

Smile -- tomorrow will be worse !

"Nothing is as easy as it looks"

Everything takes longer than you think

Reprinted with permission from *Graphic Idea Notebook,* by Jan V. White, pp. 12–18 and 34.
Published by Watson-Guptill Publications, New York, 1980. Division of Billboard Publications, Inc.
Originally published in *Folio,* vol. 9, no. 7, pp. 106–113, Dec. 1978.

Simplify: edit out the competition. Get rid of the distractions, so the viewer is forced to pay attention to the elements that are editorially essential (ie. the reason for publishing).

281

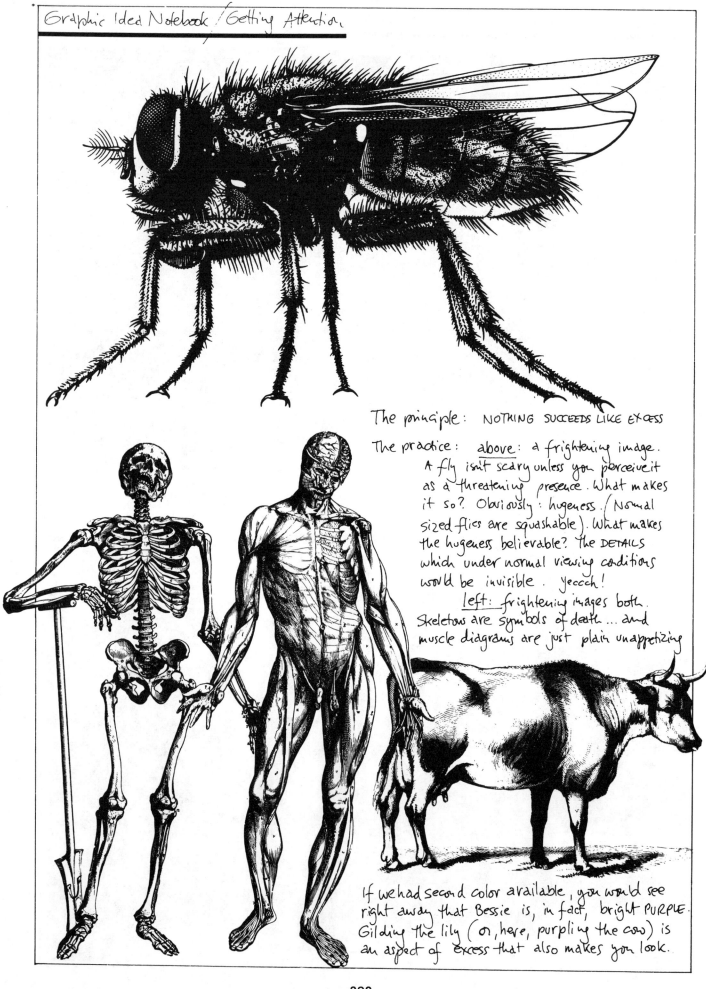

The principle: NOTHING SUCCEEDS LIKE EXCESS

The practice: above: a frightening image.
A fly isn't scary unless you perceive it
as a threatening presence. What makes
it so? Obviously: hugeness. (Normal
sized flies are squashable). What makes
the hugeness believable? The DETAILS
which under normal viewing conditions
would be invisible. Yecch!

left: frightening images both.
Skeletons are symbols of death... and
muscle diagrams are just plain unappetizing

If we had second color available, you would see
right away that Bessie is, in fact, bright PURPLE.
Gilding the lily (or, here, purpling the cow) is
an aspect of excess that also makes you look.

The principle: Unanticipated incongruity (whether it be playful and whimsical or irrational and thus surrealistic) will astonish, jar, shock, surprise, bewilder, amaze — and gain attention

The practice: above: combining images that are unexpected in subject as well as scale.

right: showing an ordinary image in an extraordinary technique or rendering

below: turning an image at an unexpected angle — like the USA map. (The skeleton just looks a bit more dead!)

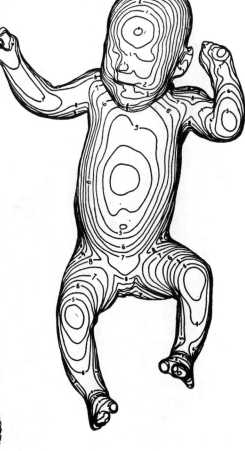

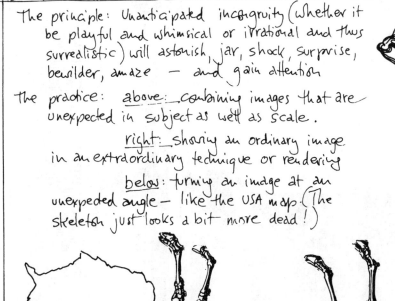

The principle: CONTRAST WORKS (as long as it is obvious enough — deliberately, strongly done).

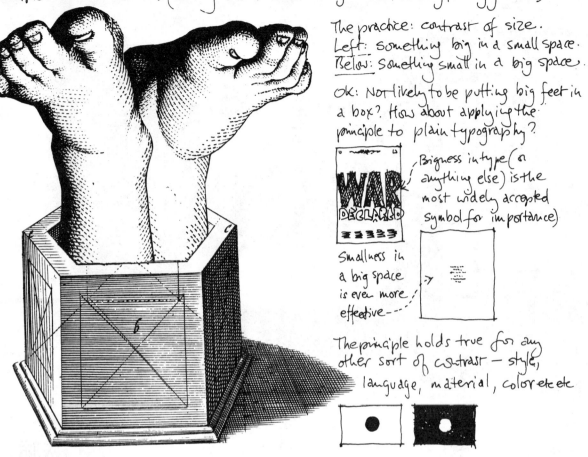

The practice: contrast of size.
Left: something big in a small space.
Below: something small in a big space.

OK: Not likely to be putting big feet in a box? How about applying the principle to plain typography?

WAR DECLARED

Bigness in type (or anything else) is the most widely accepted symbol for importance)

Smallness in a big space is even more effective——

The principle holds true for any other sort of contrast — style, language, material, color etc etc

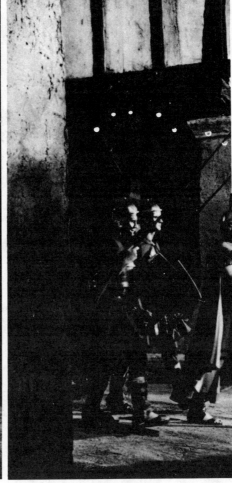

Capture the reader's eye by having an element in the picture poke out at him: the white space around the photo is the reader's space... the area inside the photo belongs to the people in the picture.

Break that subconscious barrier

<--Whenever possible, look at the subject from an unexpected unusual angle

If you can get away with it, crop that picture in some peculiar way (like chopping off the subject's head — made you look, didn't it?)

Don't just illustrate a scene with a picture, but increase its journalistic impact by physically manipulating it: e.g. emphasizing ACTIVITY here by cutting it into staggered strips

THE COPY CHASERS RULES:
What Makes Good Business/Industrial Advertising

Sometimes INDUSTRIAL MARKETING receives an irate letter or two from an advertising agency exec or a client complaining that his or her ad was unfairly skewered in the latest Copy Chasers' column. The complaints usually read the same and frequently end with the question, "Who are those Copy Chasers and what criteria do they use to make their criticisms?"

We're not going to identify the panel members except that they are experienced industrial advertising professionals. But we do think that the rules they follow in making their observations have held up well over time.

Initially we current editors thought that back in August 1936, when INDUSTRIAL MARKETING, ran the first Copy Chasers column (then called "Ok as Inserted") there would have been a long explanation introducing the new feature and explaining the basis for the evaluation. But when we checked back we found that the editors then didn't have as much gumption as we thought. The original column just appeared one month, with no explanation of the basic rules which the Copy Chasers, and all good business/industrial advertisers, consider gospel.

Not surprisingly, the same kind of irate letters as we receive today greeted that first column 46 years ago. It wasn't until eight months later that the Copy Chasers gave some brief, formal explanation of their evaluation criteria, then called "Mottoes for Industrial Advertising."

Nowadays, we get more requests for copies of the "Copy Chaser Rules" than we get irate letters. So here, we'll reprint those "mottoes," then print the current day "rules." You might want to clip them for future reference, for evaluating yours or your agency's work. We know some people who use the rules one-by-one to sell an ad to their clients or their bosses.

— IM editors

MOTTOES FOR INDUSTRIAL ADVERTISERS (INDUSTRIAL MARKETING, MARCH, 1937)

- Don't write essays—sell.
- Your years in business don't count much. There's a young fellow right behind you now.
- You are not as important to the fellow you're talking to, as he is.
- Unless you have a monopoly—make your ads work.
- The reader is reading because he expects to learn. Don't waste your space and his time boasting.
- Don't make a claim you don't back up.
- More verbs in your headlines—fewer nouns.
- Two men talking together isn't a new illustration.

1. THE SUCCESSFUL AD HAS A HIGH DEGREE OF VISUAL MAGNETISM

On average, only a small number of ads in an issue of a magazine will capture the attention of any one reader. Some ads will be passed by because the subject matter is of no concern. But others, even though they may have something to offer, fail the very first test of stopping the reader in his scanning of the pages.

Ads perish right at the start because, at one extreme, they just lie there on the page, flat and gray, and at the other extreme, they are cluttered and noisy and hard to read.

An ad should be constructed so that a single component dominates the area—a picture, the headline or the text—but not the company name or the logo.

Obviously, the more pertinent the picture, the more arresting the headline, the more informative the copy appears to be, the better.

2. THE SUCCESSFUL AD SELECTS THE RIGHT AUDIENCE

Often, an ad is the first meeting-place of two parties looking for each other.

So there should be something in the ad that at the reader's first glance will identify it as a source of information relating to *his* job interest—a problem he has or an opportunity he will welcome.

This is done by means either of a picture or a headline—preferably both—the ad should say to him, right away, "Hey, this is for you."

3. THE SUCCESSFUL AD INVITES THE READER INTO THE SCENE

Within the framework of the layout, the art director's job is to visualize, illuminate and dramatize the selling proposition.

And he must take into consideration the fact that the type of job a reader has dictates the selection of the illustrative material. Design engineers work with drawings. Construction engineers like to see products at work. Chemical engineers are comfortable with flow charts. Managers relate to pictures of people. And so on.

4. THE SUCCESSFUL AD PROMISES A REWARD

An ad will survive the qualifying round only if the reader is given reason to expect that if he continues on, he will learn something of value. A brag-and-boast headline, a generalization, an advertising platitude will turn him off before he gets into the message.

The reward that the ad offers can be explicit or implicit, and can even be stated negatively, in the form of a warning of a possible loss.

The promise should be specific. The headline "Less maintenance cost" is not as effective as "You can cut maintenance costs 25%."

5. THE SUCCESSFUL AD BACKS UP THE PROMISE

To make the promise believable, the ad must provide hard evidence that the claim is valid.

Sometimes, a description of the product's design or

operating characteristics will be enough to support the claim.

Comparisons with competition can be convincing. Case histories make the reward appear attainable. Best of all are testimonials; "They say" advertising carries more weight than "We say" advertising.

6. THE SUCCESSFUL AD PRESENTS THE SELLING PROPOSITION IN LOGICAL SEQUENCE

The job of the art director is to organize the parts of an ad so that there is an unmistakable entry point (the single dominant component referred to earlier) and the reader is guided through the material in a sequence consistent with the logical development of the selling proposition.

A layout should not call attention to itself. It should be only a frame within which the various components are arranged.

7. THE SUCCESSFUL AD TALKS "PERSON-TO-PERSON"

Much industrial advertising, unlike the advertising of consumer goods, is one company talking to another company—or even to an entire industry.

But copy is more persuasive when it speaks to the reader as an individual —as if it were one friend telling another friend about a good thing.

First, of course, the terms should be the terms of the reader's business, not the advertiser's business. But more than that, the writing style should be simple: short words, short sentences, short paragraphs, active rather than passive voice, no advertising cliches. Frequent use of the personal pronoun *you.*

A more friendly tone results when the copy refers to the advertiser in the first person: "we" rather than "the company name."

8. SUCCESSFUL ADVERTISING IS EASY TO READ

This is a principle that shouldn't need to be stated, but the fact is that typography is the least understood part of our business.

The business press is loaded with ads in which the most essential part of the advertiser's message—the copy —appears in type too small for easy reading or is squeezed into a corner or is printed over part of the illustration.

Text type should be no smaller than 9-point. It should appear black on white. It should stand clear of interference from any other part of the ad. Column width should not be more than half the width of the ad.

9. SUCCESSFUL ADVERTISING EMPHASIZES THE SERVICE, NOT THE SOURCE

Many industrial advertisers insist that the company name or logo be the biggest thing in the ad, that the company name appear in the headline, that it be set in bold-face wherever it appears in the copy.

Too much.

An ad should make the reader want to buy—or at least consider buying— before telling him *where* to buy it.

Incidentally, many industrial ads are cluttered with lists of other products, factories and sales offices, name of parent company, names of subsi-

diaries or divisions, association memberships and other items, most of which are never looked at and which, if essential, could be set inside the copy area at the very end.

10. SUCCESSFUL ADVERTISING REFLECTS THE COMPANY'S CHARACTER

A company's advertising represents the best opportunity it has—better than the sales force—to portray the company's personality—the things that will make the company liked, respected, admired.

A messy ad tends to indicate a messy company. A brag-and-boast ad suggests the company is *maker*-oriented, not *user*-oriented. A dull-looking ad raises the possibility that the company has nothing to get excited about, is behind the times, is slowing down.

What we are talking about is a matter of subtleties, but the fact remains: like sex appeal (which is not easy to define), some companies have it, some don't. And whatever it is, it should be consistent over time and across the spectrum of corporate structure and product lines.

Of course, there has to be substance behind the picture. You can't—at least for very long—promise a silk purse and deliver a sow's ear. But most successful companies have some sort of personality, and the advertising people should search for it and, finding it, transmit it to the people out there whom they want as friends.

As we said before, these criteria are just the application of common sense to the communications process. ■

AV Graphics:

Talking With Type

by Robert H. Davis, Ph.D.

"Learning to use type well is important in creating audio-visual programs that get your message across. A picture may be worth a thousand words, but titles make certain that your audience comes up with the thousand words you had in mind."

Figure 1

ABCDEFGHIJKLMNOPQR-STUVWXYZ. You have just skimmed through one of the major breakthroughs in human communication. Those 26 abstract shapes that make up the alphabet are easy to take for granted, yet they have the power to relate the entire spectrum of human experience.

The earliest forms of communication were no doubt confined to sounds and gestures. These tools form an important evolutionary step, but they are limited. Gestures are imprecise and depend upon line of sight. Utterances are restricted to hearing distances and, as words and phrases fall into disuse, their original meanings are often irretrievably lost. Man needed some method of communication that allowed transmission over distances and through time. The solution: written language.

Early attempts at written languages have probably been lost due to the impermanent nature of the materials used (hides, leaves, etc.). The examples that survived were done on more durable materials such as cave paintings (dating back to 35,000 BC), carvings in stone and clay tablets. These records reveal that written languages of ancient cultures were primarily ideographic. Ideographs are drawings of things observed. Egyptian hieroglyphics are one example of an ideographic written language. Although some ideographic written languages still exist, notably Chinese, most of them have died.

While ideographs passed the test of permanence, they failed still another important test of written languages—convenience. Ideographs are difficult to write and there are simply too many symbols for most communicators to handle. As communicators worked to simplify the written language, ideographs were modified and reshaped. Eventually they came to represent sounds rather than objects and the Latinate alphabet was formed. The process was a slow one extending through several civilizations.

Reprinted with permission from *Audio-Visual Commun.*, pp. 22, 23, 26–28, and 30, Sept. 1980.

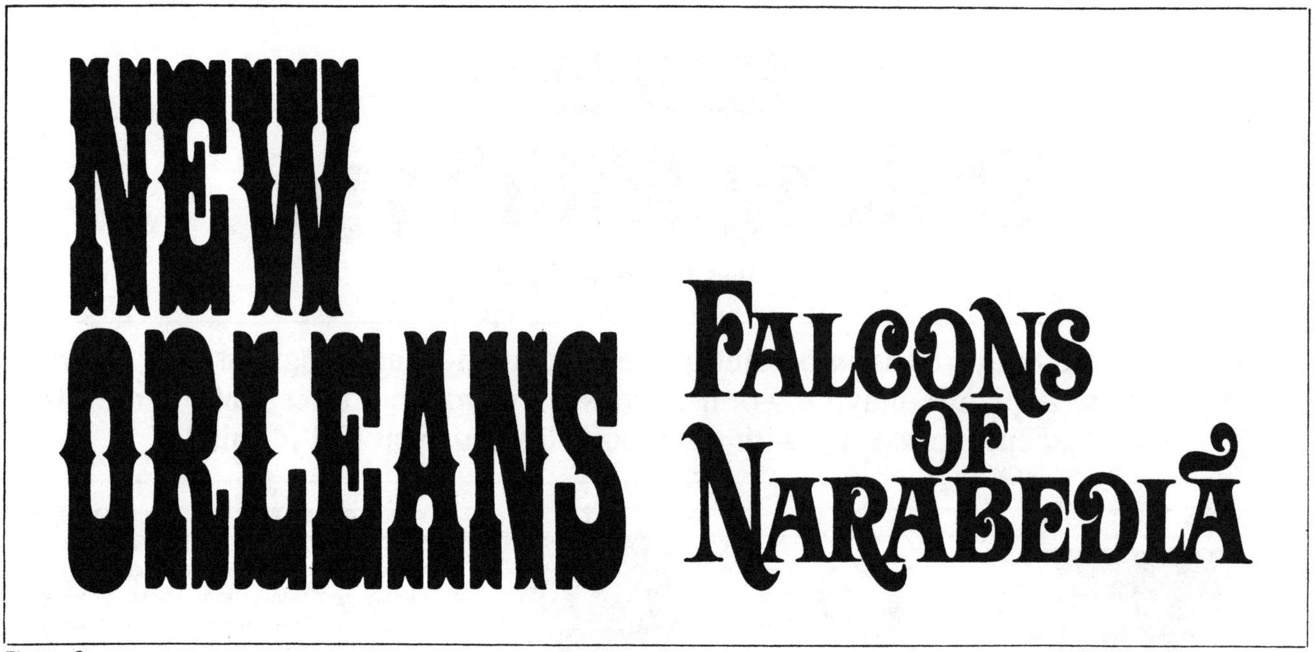

NEW ORLEANS

FALCONS OF NARABEDLA

Figure 2

The rise of the Roman Empire served to spread the Latinate alphabet and the version we use is the most common form for written language. Of course, numerous changes have been made since the Romans. For example, the letter "J" was added a mere 500 years ago. And technological changes in production of written language have changed the look of many letterforms.

Beyond minor changes in the alphabet is another major breakthrough in written language that took place in the fifteenth century. That technological leap forward was the invention of moveable type and the printing press. Gutenberg's innovation led to the art and science of typography and a whole new "language" for communicators to master.

Today, to use words in print effectively, you need to be able to talk with typography. And a working knowledge of typography is equally important in audiovisual communications to keep your messages on target.

Type selection. Type selection was a breeze in Gutenberg's time—you had one choice. Now there are something like 7,000 different typefaces that you can choose from. The question is: How do I decide which one to use?

First you need to understand why there are so many different typefaces. Like most photographs, type has two kinds of meanings: connotative and denotative. Denotative meanings are literal, i.e., the letter "E" is a letter "E." Connotative meanings are related to the feeling we get when we see a particular version of the letter "E." Figure 1 shows some examples which are all clearly "E's," yet some shout, some whisper, some are formal, some are informal, etc.

By selecting type based upon its conno-

RACES

1. ROMAN	Caslon
2. MODERN ROMAN	Exempla
3. BLACK LETTER	Gothique
4. SQUARE SERIFS	Hellenic wide
5. SAN SERIFS	Futura demi bold
6. SCRIPTS	Art Script
7. DECORATIVE	Melina

Figure 3

How Far Should Shelley Go?

Figure 4

Figure 5

THE HIGH ADVENTURE OF ERIC RYBACK

Figure 6

tative as well as its denotative meaning you can greatly increase the communicative power of typography. In **Figure 2**, notice how the feeling of the type relates to the denotative messages.

Type selection can be simplified by recognizing the seven basic categories, or races, of type: Roman, Modern Roman, Black Letter, Square Serifs, Sans Serifs, Scripts and Decorative. (It is possible to make finer distinctions; however, seven categories seem sufficient for most practical applications.) Figure 3 shows an example from each of the races.

Roman types are among the oldest in typography and trace their lineage back to the carved columns of the Roman Empire. These types are characterized by the thicks and thins within the strokes of letterforms. The design of the types reflects the drawing tools that marked the way for the sculptor's chisel. Note the serifs or thin perpendicular lines that end the major strokes of the letterforms. Originally intended as guidelines and to provide a clean, unchipped ending for carved letters, the serifs have been retained in many typefaces. Serifs provide decoration for type and also aid in the horizontal movement of the reading eye.

Roman typefaces are easy to read and project very well as long as the serifs remain legible. They connote tradition, stability and formality to your audience. If your visual messages call for the authority and weight of tradition, Roman types are an excellent choice.

Modern Roman typefaces have many of the same characteristics that we see in the Roman race. Modern Roman, however, shows some departures in design and improvements in the metallurgy used in creating type. The thin parts of the strokes are usually thinner and the serifs are very delicate. The "cup" or curve of the main stroke into the serif is often missing so that the serif becomes a straight line ending a straight main stroke. From a connotative standpoint, Modern Roman typefaces allow you to split the difference between tradition and a more contemporary flair in type design. In audio-visual productions, Modern Roman typefaces need to be fairly large so that delicate serifs and thin strokes are not lost in projection.

Black Letter typefaces have limited uses in typography. Based upon early handwritten scripts, the letterforms are unfamiliar to the modern reading eye. This race should be used sparingly in audio-visual communications, if at all. Black Letter typefaces are fine for certificates and diplomas where quick recognition and readability are not critical.

Square Serifs are typefaces with very heavy serifs, hence the name they bear. Many of the type designs found in this race trace their origins to early wood types used for posters and the like. Square Serifs have enjoyed a revival of sorts in recent years thanks to their popularity among advertising designers. This trend makes these typefaces a logical choice for a "with it" look in audio-visual productions. As long as there is not too much type on a slide, Square Serifs also have

Figure 7

Figure 8

sparingly for audio-visual productions.

Finally, we reach the catch-all category called Decorative types. The typefaces in this race are all intended for display purposes only. Many of them do not have a lowercase alphabet. Decorative typefaces also tend to be very complex. These qualities mean that Decorative typefaces need to be large to be legible. Many of them are too complex for audio-visual work where easy recognition and legibility are even more important than on the printed page. These types are often the result of fads and rely on gimmicks for their connotative meanings. If this is the case, Decorative typefaces will not stand the test of time in audio-visual presentations.

Type spacing. Choosing a typeface is only the beginning of the typographic decisions you need to make. Next you need to put the type into words and phrases. At this stage there are three important spaces to be considered: letterspace, word space and line spacing (or leading).

When type is set mechanically, in hot lead, there are not many choices. Letterspace is determined by the mechanical design of the type itself. Today, phototype and transfer or "press" type have opened up many design options.

Recent trends in advertising typography have been toward increasingly smaller spaces between letterforms. This trend allows larger type to be set in a smaller space—an obvious advantage if you are an advertiser and have to pay for the space. The design trend also recognizes that we read words and phrases, not letters. Stud-

the advantage of good legibility when projected.

The French word "sans" means without, thus the Sans Serifs race in typography refers to typefaces without serifs. This typographic race enjoyed a revival in the 1930's primarily because of the Bauhaus design school in Germany. Since many of the typefaces in this family are relatively new, they are the first choice for those desiring a modern feel from their typography. Sans Serifs were once considered less legible than serif types, but most contemporary type designers feel they are sufficiently readable for most applications, including audio-visual presentations.

Scripts are another typeface which pose some problems for the audio-visual specialist. Scripts are designed to look like cursive handwriting. Unfortunately, they are sometimes just as hard to read as handwriting. Scripts do convey a certain informal feel which makes them useful for some applications, but they should be used

Figure 9

ies have shown that, up to a point, tighter set type is more readable.

As letterspace gets tighter, word space also diminishes because all three categories of typographic spacing are interrelated. To tighten letterspace and leave word space unchanged would force the reader to read word by word. Reducing word space allows the reader to see words quickly, in groups and phrases.

Line space is also affected by the trend toward tighter typesetting. Contemporary designers work to "knit" type into typographic units or designs. This technique has become particularly popular in the case of logotypes, magazine mastheads, etc.

Compressing the three spaces used in typography is a good concept to follow in audio-visual productions. Since title slides, supers and the like are normally composed of only a few words or a short phrase, tight set units can be more easily read and help get a message across more quickly. Needless to say, it is not hard to overdo it, so tighten type with care. See Figures 5-9 for some successful examples.

Type design. The combination of good type selection and spacing can result in a successful typographic design. Designing with type is time consuming, but it is time well spent. Creating title slides, for example, allows you to produce "visual gestalts" instead of simply presenting information in type. According to gestalt theory, visual images may be considered or evaluated both in terms of their distinct components and also as a whole that becomes greater than the sum of its parts. That greater whole can add message impact and memorability.

One way to create visual gestalts is to look for ways to relate letterforms from line to line. Figure 4 shows how related letterforms (rounds and main strokes) can lead the eye through the phrase and at the same time unify it.

In Figure 5, the designer has incorporated the idea of a race into the typographic design by staggering the lines and using an italic to slant the letterforms forward in their own race.

"The High Adventure . . ." and "The Eiger Sanction" both have to do with

mountain climbing. The design of the titles serves to reinforce the concept of the works they represent. See Figures 6 and 7.

Finally, "The Summit" achieves the purpose of identifying an expensive high-rise condominium through the simple expedient of slanting the name and reversing the slant on the second "M". See Figure 8 on page 27.

Another way of achieving visual gestalts in type design is the incorporation of symbols into the type itself. Figures 9-12 illustrate how symbols can interact with type to form a unified whole which has a much greater impact than its component parts. This technique is widely used in logotypes and trademarks, and it is equally valid in audio-visual applications where quick recognition and memorability are desired.

Type contrast. In audio-visual productions where many title slides are required you need to place limits on your choice of typefaces. Generally, more than two typefaces in a single production where there are many typographic slides will water down the unity of the show and in some

Figure 10

Figure 11

considerable amount of use in graphic design often raise large "families." These type families contain many forms or designs, but all bear a family resemblance. It is a good idea to choose a type from a large family whenever you plan to have many typographic slides in your program. Helvetica, for example, is a type family with dozens of variations in form, including bold, extended, outline, shadow, condensed, etc. Choosing a typeface from a large family leaves room for variation and contrast while preserving the unity you will want in the finished audio-visual production.

The fourth method of obtaining contrast is changes in color. For audio-visual work this can be as simple as placing a color gel behind a type slide which has been reversed on lithographic film. One word of caution: whenever you use color for contrast be sure that there is sufficient contrast between the type and the background to insure readability.

Type tips. Unlike math and some of the other "hard" sciences, there is no single solution to any typographic problem. There are many solutions. However, there are some generally accepted practices worth mentioning at the end of this discussion on typography. Each of these suggestions must be evaluated before it is applied in a particular case, but they do provide a starting place for your typographic thinking.

☐ Using all capital letters retards reading speed by about 15 percent. If you have a lot of copy, use upper and lowercase letters.

☐ Italics and scripts are both hard to read when projected. Use them sparingly.

☐ Reverse type (light letters on a dark background) appear to be about ten percent larger than overprinted letters.

☐ The average outdoor advertisement (billboard) has about five words for the main message. That is a good planning figure for your slides unless they will be on the screen for a long time.

☐ Medium weight typefaces are usually easier to read than very heavy or very light types in audio-visual applications.

☐ Do not forget that the type you have been working with and know very well may have to be read and understood by an audience that has never seen it before.

☐ Break words and phrases for sense, not just for fit or appearance.

Typography is a fundamental element in mass communications. Learning to use type well is also important in creating audio-visual programs that get your message across. A picture may be worth a thousand words, but titles make certain that your audience comes up with the thousand words you had in mind. ☐

cases may even confuse the viewer. To obtain contrast without making a typographic grab-bag out of your production, use these four methods within a single typeface: change size, change weight, change form, change color.

The most obvious method for achieving contrast is to enlarge or reduce the size of type. Of course, the size of your slides will dictate the size variation you can achieve. As a rule of thumb, if you can read the type on the slide without magnification, your audience will be able to read it when it is projected.

Weight changes are accomplished by using the same typeface in bold, demibold, light, etc. One advantage of gaining contrast through a weight change is that it does not significantly affect the size of the type you are using. However, type designers will warn you not to overuse this technique for contrast. The old saw "all bold is equal to no bold" applies to audio-visual work as well as print.

Contrast can also be achieved by changing the form of type. Typefaces that see a

Dr. Robert H. Davis is an assistant professor of communication at the University of Central Florida, Orlando, FL.

Figure 12

Impact Without Impecunity

How to boost corporate print ad effectiveness and save money

by Priscilla Alex Waring

Common wisdom in advertising, particularly print, says that bigger is better, and the more colorful the better. So it would seem that size, color and other expensive embellishments are prerequisites for advertising with impact, especially corporate advertising which deals with ideas rather than hard product facts.

But common wisdom isn't enough to guide the growing volume of corporate advertising through today's tough economic environment. Campaign productivity and accountability are concepts of key importance.

How do you insure that your corporate advertising does it's job as effectively—and efficiently—as possible? And how can you measure the return on your corporate advertising investment?

Answering those questions forthrightly often finds the common wisdoms quite misleading. That is, research repeatedly suggests that some so-called impact-building ad executions aren't necessarily worth the money.

Creative impact comes from the viewpoint of *how* you present corporate advertising messages, rather than *what* you say, to *whom*. Whether you're talking to executives through business publications, or more general audiences such as activists or even the spinach salad set, communication is still a one-on-one operation. How you do it can make all the difference.

Gallup & Robinson has studied print and tv advertising

since the firm's founding in 1948, defining effectiveness as the ability of an ad or commercial to command attention, communicate a message and persuade its audience.

● We measure an ad's ability to command attention with a quantitative recall index called Proved Name Registration (PNR) for print, and Proved Commercial Registration (PCR) for tv. PNR, for example, measures the percentage of survey respondents who correctly describe the ad the day after exposure, adjusted for its size and color characteristics and to the score levels of other ads appearing in the same magazine.

● Message communication is measured qualitatively as "idea registration."

● Persuasion measures "favorable attitude," which, in the case of corporate advertising, reflects the degree to which

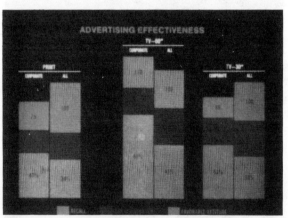

Above: Figure 1; Below: Figure 3

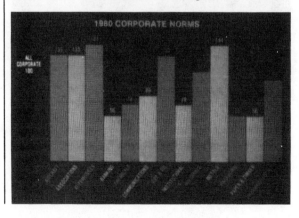

Reprinted with permission from *Industrial Marketing* (now *Business Marketing*), vol. 66, pp. 50–52, 56, 60, and 64, Mar. 1981.

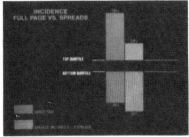

it builds a strong case for the advertiser's viewpoint.

Comparing corporate advertising to all advertising, as shown in Figure 1, we've found corporate advertising relatively weaker than all other ads in building recall, although it is stronger in communicating ideas and roughly equal in its ability to generate favorable attitudes.

Perhaps the recall boosting weakness of corporate advertising (which, interestingly, disappears in long, 60-second TV commercials) isn't surprising. Corporate advertising subjects are often less tangible and more complex than those in product advertising. But it's evident that impact, a corporate message's PNR, is a prime candidate for improvement especially in print, which carries the bulk of corporate ad expenditures yet has an impact norm 25% less than the "all advertising" norm.

CALCULATING ROI

Importantly, we adjust an ad's PNR by its relative size and color characteristics, allowing direct comparisons between different space and color combinations. Figure 2, for example, shows virtually identical PNRs for two Arco ads—one a single page, the other a spread—which are creatively identical. PNR thus reflects the relative impact of the execution itself.

The PNR Index discussed here also reflects the advertiser's industry norm, for as Figure 3 shows, ads for some industries such as metals or automobiles have more impact on average than ads for, say, packaging or banking.

In the case of the Arco ads in Figure 2, they only pro-

Figure 4

Figure 6

FOCUS

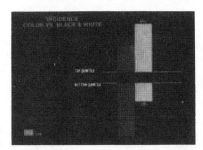

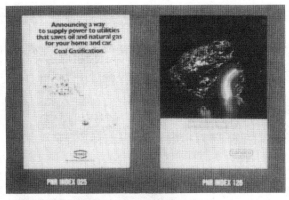

Right: Figure 7
Below: Figure 8

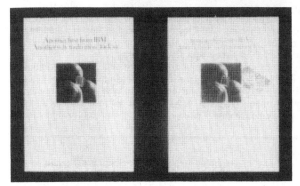

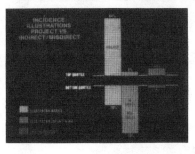

Above: Figure 9
Left: Figure 10

---

duced about 65% of the impact for oil and gas corporate ads with similar size and color. In effect, Arco achieved only 65% of the impact it paid for.

To be specific, the cost of running Arco's spread in *People*, at the one time, 4-color rate, is $57,620. But its dollar return, with a PNR Index of 063, is just $36,300. Therefore, Arco "lost" $21,320 of its advertising return on investment.

On the other hand, ads such as the St. Regis spread at the top of Figure 4, had an above average return on investment because, with St. Regis' PNR Index of 196, the spread increased recall twice as well as other ads in its category.

STRONG VS. WEAK

In our print advertising studies, we examined the highest and lowest scoring quintiles (the top 20% and the bottom 20%) of all corporate ad test scores from July 1978 through July 1980, to isolate executional factors most characteristic of the "winners" and "losers" in that group.

Let's study the creative elements that have the most direct bearing on investment: the space unit chosen and the use of color.

There is a theory prevalent that spreads provide extra clout and enhance the corporate image. We have evidence to the contrary. From a cost effectiveness standpoint, we already know that while the average single-page ad returns $1.00 for each $1.00 invested, the average spread returns only 86 cents.

Furthermore, a very recent survey we have done on the subject suggests that spreads do not enhance company image significantly over full-page ads, although use of color does. And sure enough, twice as many spreads were in the bottom quintile as were in the top quintile, as shown in Figure 5.

If spreads are used, *integration* is the key to improving impact. Is the spread treated as *one unit* or as two separate pages? Does the main illustration go across the fold? Does the headline cross the fold? Is the idea of product obvious on both pages? Is the identity of the advertiser prominent on both pages?

In Figure 4, the St. Regis spread has good integration and so does the Southern Railway half-spread. Both came close to doubling their ROI. But compare St. Regis and Southern to the Bendix spread in Figure 6, which has only one factor of integration, and the Bethlehem Steel spread beneath it, which has none at all. Both significantly fail to reach the norm.

COLOR?

As for the choice of color vs. black-and-white, the problem is to balance the undeniable aesthetic appeal of color against the economy of black-and-white. Two-thirds of the ads in the top quintile were in fact black and white (Figure 7), while three out of four of the bottom quintile were in color. But that does not necessarily imply that the magic formula is to use black and white; one-third of the top quintile ads were in color, for one thing. Nor do we deal in magic formulas. From a hard-nosed perspective, the data suggest you should ask the questions: Is color relevant to your message? Is it necessary? Is it worth the premium in cost?

For example, among several top-quintile ads run by IBM, those with black-and-white line art from the original drawing of Alice in Wonderland, a famous illustration, did not need color. It would have been superfluous. But the color photo of an electronic chip contrasted to the size of a fingertip, as in Figure 8 left, is enhanced by color. If produced in black-and-white (Figure 8 right), the identical photo becomes much more abstract and much less telegraphic. By contrast, both Texaco and Conoco are addressing exactly the same subject in Figure 9. Coal gasification presents a creative challenge if ever there was one. With

FOCUS

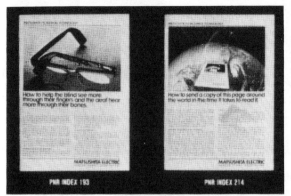

Figure 11

Figure 12

its stunning color photo, Conoco wins. This time the black-and-white execution loses. The point? Use color if it adds a communications dimension as well as an aesthetic one, but consider black-and-white otherwise.

MORE TACTICS

Now, to some of the factors which maximize communication and those which impede it, the strategy from which the tactics flow is simple: engage your audience, reward it for the attention paid and avoid elements that distract or create confusion. Help your audience, don't hinder it.

Remember, too, that you have to work fast. The world is not breathlessly awaiting your next ad, nor can you rely on most of your readers to find the point of your idea if it's buried in paragraph 10 of the copy.

Factors that engage your audience and increase communication include telegraphic illustrations, specific headlines, readable copy and an overall audience orientation, which means expressing your message in a way to which your audience can relate.

> '. . . engage your audience, reward it for the attention paid and avoid elements that distract or create confusion. Help your audience, don't hinder it. Remember, too, that you have to work fast.'

When it comes to illustrations, we found that 84% of the top quintile had illustrations which visually projected, or assisted in projecting, the subject of the ad (Figure 10). In the bottom quintile, 70% had illustrations which did the reverse by either distracting from the subject, or by failing to make a visual contribution to the ad's message.

The two Matsushita ads in Figure 11 present two different topics: its advanced medical technology for the blind and deaf, and the speed of its facsimile equipment. Product as hero and company as hero are elegantly expressed and reinforced with specific headlines. A winning treatment, returning 200% on the investment.

Compare the Itel ads in Figure 12 and ask, "What are those ads really about? Who is the advertiser?" Itel discusses capital equipment and how it keeps the company and its customers growing strong. But in the headline, Itel

Figure 13

Figure 14

298

FOCUS

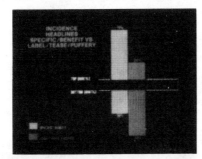

Right: Figure 15
Below: Figure: 16

Above: Figure 17
Left: Figure 18

mentions itself first, not its customers. The impact loss is 60%.

The Alcoa ads in Figures 13 and 14 make an interesting study in a less usual space format. While the illustrations may appear to be similar, the content of each one is in fact quite different, as is the impact. The Figure 13 ad is about insulating windows. All four panels actively communicate window/husky, window/Eskimo, window/technical demonstration and window/"It's cold outside" themes. Its impact is 84% above norm.

The second execution follows the same format, but does not focus on the product discussed which is siding. The first panel projects "porch," not siding; the second projects "woman," not siding, the third projects "window," not siding; and the last panel projects "house," not siding. At 68% below norm, that ad lost almost as much as the other gained.

HEADS UP

Of course, very few illustrations come without headlines. In the more intangible world of corporate advertising, good, strong headlines are even more important than in product/service ads.

We sorted the ads in our study into two groups: those whose headlines which were specific, direct or benefit-oriented, and those we categorized as labels, ego trips, teasers or word play.

Not unexpectedly, we found a heavy incidence of headlines that do *not* communicate effectively in the bottom quintile (Figure 15).

I suspect the reason lies in the theory that corporate communication audiences, having higher education and discerning wit, will appreciate how clever it all is. But, in fact, the target groups are the busiest as well as the brightest. They will appreciate a well-expressed idea more than a poorly-expressed one.

From among the many examples of weak headlines we found, a Budd Co. headline managed to include both a label and a brag: "The Budd Alternative. If it has wheels and moves products, we probably made part of it." That earned a PNR of 041.

Even worse, in Figure 16, NL Industries asks potential investors, "We help discover oil. Isn't it surprising so many investors have never discovered us?" With headlines like that, no, it isn't surprising. As for the MASCO ad, with its growth chart, say-nothing headline and almost invisible logo, no more needs to be said.

Which brings us to "benefit" again. Product advertisers have long known the strength of the customer-benefit of problem/solution approach. Corporate advertisers have used it as well for many years, of late realizing more clearly that the whole community is in fact their customer.

For comparison, consider the strength of the PPG campaign, in Figure 17.

The headlines are direct, clear, relevant and benefit-oriented, all in black and white. They more than doubled the impact of PPG's advertising dollar.

It's worth noting that using enough words in a headline to be specific and informative does not incur penalties in

299

FOCUS

Figure 19

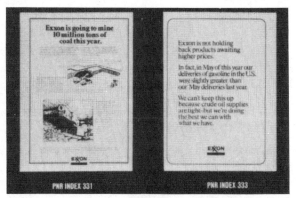

Figure 20

impact. We found that as few as one to five words, or as many as 15, can earn equivalent PNRs.

LOGOS

What about advertiser identification? Because much corporate advertising doesn't feature products *per se*, it is particularly important to adequately identify the advertiser. And if the company name isn't prominent in the

---

'Yet some corporate advertisers seem to have a distinct propensity to be shy these days, especially when spending stockholders' money on advocacy ads.'

---

illustration or headline, prominent use of the logo is vital.

Yet some corporate advertisers seem to have a distinct propensity to be shy these days, especially when spending stockholders' money on advocacy ads. The meek may inherit the Earth, but they don't inherit much impact.

On average, corporate ads with prominent logos earned a PNR of 112, while those with a small and buried logo earned just 45. Overall, the bottom quintile of our study contained five times more ads in which the advertiser was not obvious at first glance, than the top quintile.

The worst example of the shyness phenomenon we have ever seen, tested in 1976, found Hammermill Papers stating (Figure 18) "Shirley Rieger is alive today because you're such a careful painter."

Who is Shirley Rieger? Why should I care? And I don't paint unless I can possibly avoid it!

Hammermill intended to laud America's profit system by illustrating how it benefits real people. But every element of the ad worked against the idea. The illustration didn't even support the long, unfocused copy which describes how careful painters buying 3M masking tape enabled 3M to sponsor a Public Broadcasting program on breast cancer. Because of the program, Shirley Rieger self-diagnosed a malignancy, went to the hospital and had it removed before it became fatal. We only learn of Hammermill's admiration for the American Way in the next-to-last sentence, and we can barely discern the logo.

Whatever the subject, whatever the approach taken, all the elements of an ad offer opportunities to communicate, and the more they all work together to repeat and rein-

force the message, the better it is. Consider the two ads by GE in Figure 19.

The illustrations telegraph the subjects, the headlines are both specific and audience-oriented, the copy is explanatory and informative, and GE doesn't hesitate to highlight its role improving the state of modern medicine or developing an energy-saving car. The impact yield on the car ad is three times the norm.

ENERGY

It cannot have escaped your attention that energy is the hot topic in our current corporate advertising, as it is in all our lives. Four of five top quintile ads exploited energy's high-impact characteristics. It's news, it has a community benefit angle, it has a business benefit angle, and it has a direct line to any audience on a personal day-to-day basis. Energy is *relevant*. The combination of energy and news is so powerful that several advertisers have successfully let this approach carry itself, as Exxon has (Figure 20).

As we move into the 1980s, with more sophisticated and aware audiences, and more ways of reaching them efficiently, research suggests ways to improve your corporate advertising ROI. Without being dull, without over-reliance on magic numbers, without a futile search for safe formulas, you might ask yourself: Regardless of your message or your audience:

● Have you found a way to make your message *relevant* to your audience?

'Whatever the subject, whatever the approach, all the elements of an ad offer opportunities to communicate, and the more they work together . . . the better.'

● Whatever your execution, is the message *expressed clearly and directly?*
● Do all the elements and opportunities *reinforce* your message?
● Have you developed a stable of possible executions so that you can identify and *choose* the best ones? ∎

Priscilla Alex Waring is VP of Gallup & Robinson Inc., Princeton. This article excerpts her presentation to an Assn. of National Advertisers seminar last fall.

Selling & Marketing

HOW TO ORDER ADS A LA CARTE

By Ivan Levison

Jim Stevens walked into the offices of HyperCreative Advertising
feeling like one of the biggest frogs in the pond. He'd budgeted $100,000
for his new advertising campaign, and he

was sure that HyperCreative would welcome a chunk of business that big.

Jim Stevens got a rude awakening.

An agency account executive explained patiently to Jim that $100,000 really didn't mean much to HyperCreative. "Ordinarily an ad agency retains 15% of the money a client spends on magazine, newspaper, and broadcast advertising," the account executive explained. "With a budget of $100,000, that leaves only $15,000 for the agency to spend on creative and administrative work. To make your account profitable for us, HyperCreative would have to tack on a hefty monthly fee, plus production and other charges.

"And even at that," he added, "I have to admit you couldn't count on getting the services of any of our senior people."

"But I just need a few ads made up for our trade magazines," Jim stammered. "Nothing complicated, I promise. Why should that cost even $15,000?"

"Let me show you," the account executive said. He led Jim on a tour of the agency, past offices occupied by art directors and copywriters, media researchers, billing clerks, and public relations specialists. In one room, a computer hummed quietly; in another, market researchers were interviewing consumers about their reaction to a new detergent.

Back in the lobby—decorated with framed awards and an antique bubblegum machine—the agency man summed up Jim's problem. "It doesn't matter whether you use all of the services we have. They're part of the overhead, and we've got to charge you a fair price for that overhead."

Considerably disheartened, Jim Stevens walked out of the offices of HyperCreative Advertising. By the time he reached the sidewalk, he realized he had a new problem. If a full-service ad agency didn't want his business, who was going to produce the materials he needed for his $100,000 campaign?

In fact, Jim Stevens has an option that has worked successfully for lots of small company managers: He can buy his advertising services à la carte. Instead of working through an advertising agency, Stevens can work directly with independent copywriters and art directors—and get the same quality of services at a price that doesn't include computers, bubblegum machines, or other overhead he doesn't need.

There's a tradeoff, of course. To be successful at buying à la carte advertising services, a manager needs to invest some time in locating the people he wants, negotiating terms, and deciding whether the finished product does the job. That can be an intimidating job for the neophyte, but it's not impossible. You can sample various à la carte services until you find what you like.

Depending on your specific needs, here's what you can expect when you take the à la carte route:

□ ART DIRECTORS AND COPYWRITERS. The two professionals whose jobs are essential in advertising are the copywriter, who creates the language of an ad or brochure, and the art director, who translates the words into an effective visual presentation. Lots of talented copywriters and art directors—including many who hold down full-time jobs—are available on a freelance basis for small projects. Often, a copywriter or art director can also help you with many of the other arrangements you may need to make, such as placing ads, buying printing, or hiring other specialists.

It's worth spending a fair amount of time screening freelance copywriters and art directors, because skills in these fields—like any other creative work—vary widely, and you should feel comfortable that your advertising is in the hands of people whose competence and price are right. Referrals by other small company managers can be useful, but an even better way to build a list of candidates is to ask the creative director of a large local advertising agency for the names of a few freelancers whose work he respects (remember, though, that you're asking for a favor, and respect the fact that the creative director may not always have time to talk to someone who isn't an agency client).

Other sources for good names are regional and national advertising publications, such as *Adweek* and *Advertising Age*. Freelancers often advertise their services in these publications. You may also decide to run an ad of your own.

Once you've put together a list of names, the next step is to interview your candidates and review their portfolios. Look for a reasonably close match between the work you need done—say, a product brochure—and the

things the freelancer has done in the past. (When you look at an art director's work, though, you should realize that his or her job is primarily to provide concepts, create layouts, and select typefaces. The art director will probably bring in a photographer or artist to assist in executing the concept.)

You can expect to pay art directors and copywriters by the hour, at a rate that typically runs from $35 to $75, depending on the art director's skill and reputation, and on how difficult the project is. Some creative professionals prefer to price their work on a project basis, which helps prevent cost overruns. But creative work is notoriously difficult to price, so most professionals prefer to start by asking you to give them a budget range. Since an art director has to make decisions about how much to spend on photography, illustrations, typesetting, and other outside services, being candid about your budget is essential for good planning.

One area that's negotiable is whether the individual art director or copywriter will produce some rough concepts for you on a speculative basis. These roughs can be a great help in deciding whether you've found the right person, but many professionals don't believe in handing out free samples to sell their services. If you're serious enough about a candidate, it may be worthwhile to buy a couple of hours of creative time before proceeding with a major project.

□ GRAPHIC DESIGNERS. The distinction between art directors and graphic designers isn't always a sharp one, but designers are more likely to specialize in producing so-called collateral materials—brochures, catalogs, newsletters, and logos—which supplement the advertising materials that an art director creates. Graphic designers can be a big help in giving a company a consistent image; they also will provide expertise in working with printers, typesetters, and related kinds of suppliers.

Designers, unlike art directors, don't usually moonlight from full-service agencies. Instead, most operate their own studios, which are listed in the *Yellow Pages* and in various trade publications.

☐ PHOTOGRAPHERS AND ILLUS-TRATORS. You can turn over the task of selecting a photographer or illustrator to the art director you've put in charge of preparing your ads, but it can be handy to have a few specialists on call for an occasional public relations photo or new product sketch. Here, it is most important to look carefully at individual portfolios, because photographers and illustrators are definitely specialists. But you don't need to search blindly until you find someone whose style fits your needs perfectly: You can refer to the annual *Creative Black Book* ($40 prepaid, from Friendly Publications, 401 Park Avenue South, New York, NY 10016). This useful reference contains the names and addresses of hundreds of creative specialists, by region, as well as reproductions of the work of many of them. Even if you don't use a photographer or illustrator who appears in the *Black Book*, the book can be a handy source of examples and styles that will help you in conversations with an art director about the images you might want to use.

Photographers, and to a lesser extent illustrators, base their fees in part on the use to which you intend to put their work. Advertising in big-circulation magazines commands a higher rate than the same job executed for a small-circulation trade magazine; multiple uses (for example, a product photo) may earn a higher fee than work that will appear only once. Though this system may sound illogical, photographers do feel that pricing should partly reflect usage, so you need to establish clearly at the beginning of any assignment what rights you expect to purchase. A useful guide to rates and terms for photographers is contained in *The ASMP Professional Business Practices in Photography*, rev. ed. 1981 ($19, from American Society of Magazine Photographers, 205 Lexington Ave., New York, NY 10016). For illustrators, similar guidelines are found in *The Pricing and Ethical Guidelines*, 4th edition ($13.80 prepaid, from The Graphic Artists' Guild, 30 E. 20th St., New York, NY 10003).

☐ MEDIA-BUYING SERVICES. There's no great trick to qualifying as an "in-house" ad agency that can earn the standard 15% discount that most magazines, newspapers, radio, and television stations offer to independent ad agencies. You'll need to provide professionally produced materials, pay your bills on time, and perhaps create some stationery and insertion orders with your in-house agency name. It's that simple.

Operating an in-house agency is a reasonable choice, especially when you or your company managers have a clear idea of the publications in which you should spend your advertising dollars. But if your media decisions begin to be more complex, or if a lot of your money is going to be spent on consumer-oriented media, you may want to add another à la carte service—an independent media-buying firm.

Media-buying services offer a lot of specialized skills in building schedules, negotiating rates, and evaluating the ef-

---

Photographers base their fees in part on usage, so you need to establish clearly at the beginning of any assignment what rights you expect to buy.

---

fectiveness of various media. Full-service ad agencies, of course, also offer media-buying services, but only the larger agencies are likely to buy as much media research or have the kind of staff experts that you can expect from a specialized buying firm.

The cost? You may have to pay a percentage fee (15% is common) or a negotiated flat rate, depending on the difficulty of the schedule you and the media-buying firm come up with. But an independent media buyer should be able to demonstrate how this investment will pay off in a more sharply focused, efficient use of what is usually the largest part of any advertising budget.

☐ MARKET RESEARCH. Another service that you can buy independently of a full-service ad agency is market research. It's hard to create advertising with real impact if you don't know *why* your customers buy your product or services (or even who those customers are). Market research firms are specialists in getting feedback from the people your advertising is designed to reach and influence, and can tell you pretty accurately whether all that hard-earned cash in your ad budget is doing the job.

One of the most common tools that market research firms use is the focus group, a panel of 6 to 12 people who are representative of the market you need to reach. The group will be led by a trained, neutral leader who can keep the discussion on track without giving away the sponsor of the session. Most focus group facilities also offer two-way mirrors, so you can observe the proceedings

secretly. The total fee for arranging such a session is about $1,200.

Market research firms can also produce mail surveys, conduct telephone surveys ($15 to $20 per interview), or set up product demonstration interviews ($20 to $25 per demonstration). Once the data is collected, moreover, they'll help you interpret the results.

☐ PUBLIC RELATIONS. All kinds of promotional techniques come under the heading of "public relations," and many can be handled with the help of the à la carte services of photographers, copywriters, and occasionally art directors. If you're looking for a more elaborate campaign, though, you may want to draw on the services of an independent public relations consultant. For either an hourly fee or a flat charge per project, a public relations specialist can handle such assignments as a new product launch, a special event, or a broad effort to increase your company's visibility. Be realistic about your expectations (and the promises a publicist makes): You may pay for sending out news releases and for contacting editors, but you have no guarantees that editors will find the material worth publishing.

If you'd rather handle the work of sending out news releases yourself, your best bet is to get a copy of the current issue of *Bacon's Publicity Checker*, a mammoth two-volume summary of business, trade, consumer, and farm magazines, plus all daily and weekly newspapers. *Bacon's* ($112.80 prepaid, from Bacon's Publicity Checker, 14 E. Jackson Blvd., Chicago, IL 60604) gives you the names of editors to contact, and neatly organizes the types of publicity material each periodical accepts. Their computerized mailing service is also available to provide lists of editors by industry or business.

☐ PRODUCTION HOUSES. Television and radio commercials, as well as most audiovisual shows, are big budget items that small companies rarely tackle on their own. A slick TV commercial, for example, can easily cost upwards of $50,000 to produce, before a single dollar is spent on buying air time. Still, it's possible to deal directly with various kinds of production houses that can give you help on scripting, photography, sound recording, graphics, and even voice talent—at a modest price. But if you're really looking for economy in production, your best bet is often to ask for help from local radio or TV stations. Especially if you're planning to buy air time from the station, they can offer some of the best à la carte bargains around. ☐

Ivan Levison is president of Ivan Levison & Associates Inc., a San Francisco–based firm that creates advertising and marketing communications materials.

The Most Important Difference

Between Good and Bad Industrial Advertising

Presumably, when an ad goes to market, it represents the agency's best expression of the sales proposition and the well-considered judgment of the client.

Oh, now and then, the client will get carried away with some notion that doesn't make for good advertising and the agency will compromise in order to get an ad approved and running. But we believe, however, that such occasions are rare, that agency and client normally agree on the substance and the technique.

How, then, can it happen that so many ads—which both agency and client believe will accomplish the objectives—are so wrong.

To dramatize what makes the most difference between good and bad advertising, we have put together pairs of ads. One ad offers information or ideas readers will welcome while the other exemplifies reckless reader disregard. These shallow ads massage client self-esteem or showcase agency creative zeal reader expense.

Remember that the self-interest to be served by an ad is that of the reader, not the advertiser. But so often we hear industrial advertisers defend bragging, boastful copy with the justification, "That's what we wanted to say to prospects about our company and products."

Surely the advertiser must talk about himself and his products or services, but it must always be in terms of reader interest. That rule is as old as human speech itself.

Nonetheless, we continue to be amazed year after year by the volume of advertising that squanders already limited advertising budgets in the industrial marketplace. Therefore we feel there's no more important a message we can deliver in this INDUSTRIAL MARKETING's 65th anniversary issue.

Bethlehem and Monroe: Standing on the customer's side and just standing.

"**H**ow to shed pounds without giving up cold-rolled, low-carbon sheet steel" introduces **Bethlehem Steel's** new family of cold-rolled, stress relief annealed sheet steels having much higher strength levels than normally available.

The copy describes Bethlehem's process: combining special cold-rolling techniques with a controlled annealing cycle. "The low carbon content, combined with a lack of hardening elements, provides good spot weldability and formability, considering the high-strength levels of the steel."

The ad includes pictures of several automotive applications and a table of mechanical properties.

The layout is just right, and the typography is impeccable.

Where Monroe is standing is not made clear in "Monroe stands alone" so we must conclude the stance is most likely in the mind of the adver-

tiser. Nothing in the copy suggests any reason why "Excellence you can count on" is more available at wherever Monroe is standing than from any other source.

The orange background against which the reversed text struggles raises doubt that many readers will force themselves into the message. The few who do will probably give up upon encountering, in the second sentence, that "The name means it's made in Lexington, South Carolina."

We almost left the ad at that point. We didn't, but we still didn't learn what's so good about manufacturing in Lexington, S.C. We did find *one* fact: Monroe factory-trained service people operate out of 350 branch offices. But the ad continues with grandiloquences such as "state of the art design" and "performance that will increase productivity." Where Monroe stands in the reader's mind isn't the place the advertiser intended.

Reprinted with permission from *Industrial Marketing* (now *Business Marketing*), vol. 66, pp. 93–96, and 98, May 1981.

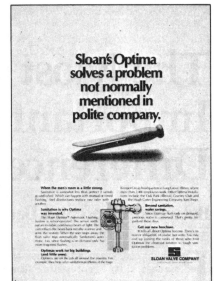

Insoport and Sloan: Irrelevant extinction vs. extinguishing relevancies.

Not many readers will come upon the Thermacore ad from **Insoport Industries** and fail to notice the green dinosaur. But even among those who are momentarily diverted by the headline—"Ah, the cold hard facts of failing to adapt to a changing world"—we feel there will be few whose curiosity will take them very far into copy beginning:

"For over 10 million years, the dinosaur faced little competition. Then the whole world changed. Suddenly, the environment which had served him so well became his biggest enemy. He could no longer turn a cold shoulder to the changes around him. And more flexible life forms took his place.

"Many of us have learned a lesson from the dinosaur and are succeeding where he failed."

All this, and still no clue (nor is there one in the illustration) as to what it's all about.

On the other hand, the headline in **Sloan's** ad is irresistable. "Sloan's Optima solves a problem not normally mentioned in polite company." And under the subhead, "When the men's room is a little strong," the opening paragraph keeps interest high:

"Sanitation is somewhat less than perfect in urinals that go unflushed. Which can happen with manual or timed flushing. And disinfectants replace one odor with another."

At this point, Sloan's product enters the scene, introduced by the subhead "Sanitation is why Optima was invented," and then described thusly:

"The Sloan Optima Automatic Flushing System is *sensor-operated.* The sensor sends out an invisible, continuous beam of light. The user reflects the beam back into the scanner and arms the system. When the user steps away, the flush valve trips automatically. Sanitation's automatic, too, since flushing is on *demand* only. No more forgotten flushes."

In addition to its excellent copy, the ad makes good use of white space and confines the color to the concentric circles around the scanner.

Bless you, Sloan. May you make millions of installations.

Posi-Seal and Calma: How to fire up an idea or bore readers silly.

NATCO's "Status symbol?" is one of the sappiest ads we've ever seen. Who cares anyway if you've got the snazziest status drilling machine on the block?

Considering the state of the economy, there must be something better to offer the metal-working industry than:

"A new NATCO multi-spindle drilling and tapping machine in your plant may not impress your friends and neighbors as much as, say, a new Rolls Royce in your driveway.

"But you can still feel pretty smug about having the world's most job-proven and versatile high production machine of its kind.

"And when other people talk about 'comparable' machines, just smile and hand them your Natco specs. Then watch their faces.

"So go ahead . . . feel a little superior.

"Because if you appreciate quality enough to choose a Natco machine, you're entitled.

"Write us for complete product information."

We say, you'd better, because you sure don't get any information in the ad.

In "The inverted bucket," **Armstrong** promises a savings of at least $1,000 per trap a year," and explains why its inverted bucket stream traps work better and last longer than disc traps.

The long copy has been written in the dispassionate style of a technical editor, in marked contrast to NATCO's pseudo status symbol.

Unfortunately, the illustration here wastes the chance to demonstrate the inverted bucket's energy and money-saving capabilities—facts which could have been more prominently mentioned in the headline rather than relying on the subhead to grab reader interest.

Nonetheless the copy delivers the kind of straightforward technical information the reader seeks when he picks up a business publication in the first place.

NATCO and Armstrong: Empty superlatives vs. superlative technology.

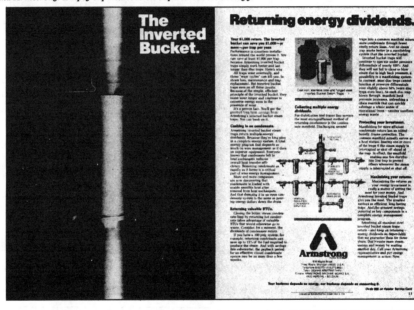

In "Don't get burned with an unsafe fire safe valve," **Posi-Seal International** starts out by warning the reader that "fire safe does not necessarily mean safe in a fire."

If we had the responsibility for fire protection where we work, we would jump into this copy:

"*All* fire safe valves must meet lab-based specs. Problem is: lab-based specs leave too much to chance.

"In the field, fires don't behave like they do in lab conditions. They don't always trigger the burn-away seats, complicated secondary mechanisms or other 'sure fire' systems most manufacturers rely on to give positive shut-off. No matter what they say . . . their valves aren't truly fire safe."

Then, "Posi-Seal Phoenix III meets all fire safe specs. In real fires." That subhead is followed by: "This new trunnion valve starts out with a solid, one-piece metal-to-metal seat with 100% positive shutoff before, during and after a fire. Its unique triple seal features twin-metal seats, protecting a recessed Teflon seal. Provides a positive, truly fire safe seal as soon as the valve is closed."

That's grabbing the reader and telling him facts he needs to know.

But the reader has no compulsion to stay very long with **Calma's** "The future belongs to those who reach for it fastest." Nor is the copy lead a grabber:

"To own the future, you must reach for it now.

"Your company must find better ways to do what you're doing today to

assure its survival. And you must find the best ways to do things tomorrow to assure its success."

We ask the writer: Do *you* like to be talked down to?

Calma is trying to promote its CAD/CAM systems. So-called computer-aided design/computer-aided manufacturing is one of the hottest new technologies going, with plenty of fascinating things to be said about it. Yet cliched admonitions like Calma's suggest that the copywriter really doesn't know much more about CAD/CAM than anyone else would learn in a grade B sci-fi flick. And Mr. Spock could write better copy avoiding such generalities in favor of specifics.

Cincinnati Milicron and Scott: Wheelhorse and wipeout.

Maybe **Cincinnati Milacron's** "Four years ago, we reinvented the wheel" would be more convincing if the ad included the names of the companies reporting savings when they changed to Super Cimform grinding wheels.

But it's a powerful ad even without the names, because the results are impressive.

The copy renews the original promise: "You can expect the super wheel to produce from two to four times as many parts per wheel . . . reduce dressing cycle time and wheel change downtime . . . and last up to four times longer than conventional wheels."

Scott Paper's ad presents testimony from satisfied users, too. But the statements are not attributed. It's our guess they were made up by a copywriter to go along with pictures of professional models. We've never seen such a clean looking bunch of industrial workers showing how the Scott product is 'America's #1 All-Purpose Wiper.'

If we're wrong, it's not our fault. The names of those satisfied users, even in tiny type, would have forestalled our suspicions.

And that type across the worker photos makes reading all the more difficult.

Besides, it's an awfully messy layout for a product that is supposed to keep things neat.

If **Standard Microsystems'** "When Sheik Ahmad heard we were famous for our custom work, he asked us to hand-tailor 100 suits" is a better heading than "How **Ronningen-Petter** liquid filters reduce equipment maintenance and downtime," then we're in big trouble.

The Standard Microsystems' ad points out what we have recently seen to be a troubling trend in the computer industry: the use of off-the-wall borrowed interest. Why do computer companies feel it is necessary to catch the reader's interest with sheiks and the like when they usually have cogent product stories to tell?

Standard Microsystems and Ronningen-Petter: Strained analogy vs. convincing filtration.

We sometimes think that advertising in the agricultural field is generally superior to that found in industrial publications.

Now we don't claim that these ads from **Stauffer Chemical** and **Precision Steel Warehouse** are typical. But judge for yourself.

Stauffer tells us "6 solid reasons why Sutan+ is the best incorporated corn herbicide." Then we get six reasons in subheads, explained by copy and illustrations.

Meanwhile Precision Steel Warehouse shows us a picture of the company president alongside the headline "You can depend on our quality." The alleged "reasons" backing that hackneyed promise include: "we carefully specify the finest materials . . . specially designed equipment manned by experienced people . . . we have worked hard to earn our reputation . . ." etc.

Where's the proof? Everybody else says the same thing. ■

Stauffer and Precision Steel: We'll depend on facts, thank you.

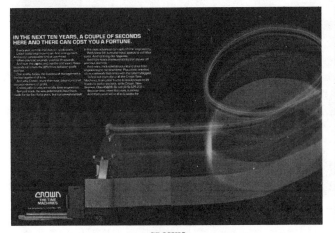

CROWN

PULLMAN

COPY CHASERS: WHAT IT TAKES TO MAKE YOUR AD A STANDOUT

Some years ago a one-page b&w ad was a very respectable unit of space. Then somebody got the idea of adding a second color—in order to stand out—and pretty soon there were so many two-color ads that by contrast a b&w page stood out.

So some advertisers went to spreads, which made good sense, because the spread not only stood out, it also allowed more room for a message. But as time went on, more of the space was devoted to bigger pictures because bigger pictures stood out.

The idea of pre-printed inserts was a brilliant advance in the art of standing out. The advertiser could print his ad in *four* colors—which would have been expensive for the publisher—and he gained the impact not only of the full color but also of the heavier paper stock (which stood out).

Then technology caught up, and full-color became available run-of-book. For a while, the few full-color ads dominated the magazines they were-in. But when prosperity turned the corner, it seemed that *everybody* rushed into full-color—which meant

that full-color no longer stood out.

So, many of them appropriated the additional money for four-color *spreads*. And now there are so many of *them* that advertisers are seeking ways to make *their* full-color spreads stand out from other full-color spreads.

This trend has culminated in a rash of what we call "the ad inside the picture"—that is, the picture

occupies the entire area, and the headline, text and signature have to be superimposed over the picture or reversed into it. Which does not make for easy reading of the message.

But what is worse: "standing out" is usually all that the ad does. Once attention has been gained, the ad often offers little in the way of message.

• The Crown ad offers: "In the next ten years, a couple of seconds here and there can cost you a fortune." That is mildly interesting, but if the reader cares to pursue the thought, all he finds in the copy is:

"Every year, as time marches on, so do costs.

"Labor costs keep moving up. And

HUNTINGTON

Reprinted with permission from *Industrial Marketing* (now *Business Marketing*), vol. 64, pp. 59, 62, 63, 66, and 69, May 1979.

PETERBILT

FAFNIR

COMBUSTION ENGINEERING

INTERNATIONAL HARVESTER

energy costs. And every conceivable kind of overhead.

"When you lose seconds, you lose thousands.

"And over the weeks and months and years, those seconds can mean the difference between profit and loss."

Isn't that a little elementary for the sophisticated businessman in a position to buy some pallet trucks?

• The headline in Pullman's ad declared its intention to tell "What U.S. business is wearing overseas today." But the letters in the text have filled in so badly that even if we really wanted to know what U.S. business is wearing overseas today, it would be too much of a chore to dig the words out of the background.

• A picture of a refinery commands the space in the Huntington Alloys ad. The headline states that "Sometimes INCOLOY alloys are all that stand between all-out production and a surprise shutdown." That is promising, but the copy, set over a

corner of the refinery photo (that has been air-brushed for the purpose), is, except for a reference to "dozens of case histories," just a warning that corrosion is a bad thing.

It seems to us that some of the space could have been devoted to one or more of the case histories (which presumably the readers would like to know about) and less to showing them what a refinery looks like (which they presumably know).

• In the Peterbilt spread, one of its trucks has been driven into a board room. The truck is called "The Money Machine." The copy (reversed) contains more enthusiasm than conviction:

"You know it. Your Board of Directors know it. When you go with the best right from the start it will pay off for you where it really counts—on the bottom line."

Near the end the ad suggests: "Don't take our word for it."

"Talk with drivers. Talk with

other fleet owners. Even talk with our customers' boards of directors. They'll tell you that The Money Machine is a truck of such quality in concept, design and performance that the alternatives seem hopelessly outdated."

We think the *advertiser* should have talked with drivers, other fleet owners and those boards of directors—then reported what he was told.

• The roller coaster makes a spectacular illustration for Fafnir's ad. But the copy doesn't say anything about the application—merely that "People in all industries depend on Fafnir bearings."

• Combustion Engineering's ad is more informative. The night view of Manhattan helps express the magnitude of the energy C-E helps save. Its Ljungstrom heat exchanger installed on a steam generator or process furnace, captures heat energy that would be lost through the smokestack and sends it back to work. "With the Ljungstrom, a utility, refinery or process plant uses up to 25% less fuel."

• International Harvester claims "the most widespread and complete truck dealer service system in the country" (including "the industry's largest parts network with a 24-hour computerized delivery system"), and the snow-swept scenery is an appropriate background for the headline, "The farther from home your trucks have to operate, the better you can feel about owning International."

• The picture in the Cross ad "Quantum jump," is a real *tour de force* in advertising art. But that's not all. Unlike the other ads we have shown you, this one tells what's happening in the picture:

"The Integrated Manufacturing System shown here is real. We cannot disclose the identity of the part it makes, but what we did for this customer, we can also do for you.

"The part was previously manufactured on a series of single-purpose machines. Between-machines handling was accomplished by people, tote pans, and a roller conveyor. Several machine operators were needed. And a bank of parts was stored at each machine.

"The system consists of . . ." etc. . . . up to a list of "Here's what all this meant to our customers."

This handsome and informative ad was produced by Robert Rogers, art director, and Ivan French, Copywriter, of French Sullivan Inc., Troy, Mich.

• Another good "ad inside the picture" is Borg-Warner's, "The elegant oil field." The picture makes the point that the copy also makes:

"Just off the coast of California there's a paradise where palm trees reflect against illuminated sculptures, and waterfalls rush past lush jungle foliage. . . . This lovely spot is an oil field."

And the copy goes on to tell the part played by Centrilift submersible pumps . . . "the natural answer since all the works are underground set deep in soundproof oil wells." They "lift greater volumes of oil, water and brine from greater depths than other pumps and get into places other pumps can't."

The credits for this attractive and

CROSS

BORG-WARNER

MILLENIUM

311

PENNSYLVANIA CRUSHER

AMERICAN PULVERIZER

selling ad go to David Stickles, art director, and Lynn Ahrens, Copywriter, McCaffrey & McCall, New York.

Jay Magoffin of Fluidyne, like many others before him, has suggested we devote more attention to small-space advertising. We have done this in the past and will continue to do so. But how about some contributions from companies who know their small-space advertising has been successful?

• Scott Foote says, he had a great deal of fun producing the Millenium ad, which is illustrated by the poker game analogy: "It's time to break up the old board float game." The subhead quotes one of the players: "Fifty percent of our ten million dollar board float is defective. Trouble is, we don't know which fifty percent."

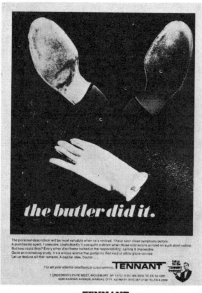

INTERNATIONAL PACKINGS

NASH ENGINEERING

TENNANT

Millenium offers a diagnostic "test lab in a suitcase," which we think probably deserves more space in this big ad than it got and better description than it got from such poker game phrases as "a royal flush in one unit. . . . We can get into the game. . . . For a whole new deal."

• Louis Flanagan sent two exhibits:

1. An ad his agency produced for Pennsylvania Crusher Corp. that appeared in coal mining publications in 1976 and in power publications in 1977.

2. An ad by American Pulverizer Co. that appeared in 1978. He asks: "Is it my imagination, or do I detect a strong resemblance?"

We think that question should be for American Pulverizer to answer.

• **Roger Patterson** of International Packings wrote a letter that makes a neat case history in advertising strategy. Wrote he:

"When 90% of a trade publication's readers, who make up one of our more important market audiences, were found to be unaware that our company manufactured homogeneous and fabric-reinforced diaphragms, management agreed that immediate and energetic response was called for. Though little advertised in the past, this product category had become a high priority activity and buying influences were supposed to know about all of our capabilities.

"Thoughts of two or four-color spreads were tempting, and probably would have been approved. But, we'd been using one format for almost four years, which has built scores, I believe, and an easily recognized family appearance. I felt we should position this unfamiliar product group with our better known products.

"I assembled plenty of background facts and started off with a strong headline. But, the results were too strong; even I was turned off by what I read back. How could we bombard readers with all this mass of information without becoming just another brag-and-boast advertiser?

"The final advertisement's subhead was originally a sarcastic scribble on an early draft to remind myself that a different approach was needed. When I got back to the typewriter, it suggested the idea of mildly spoofing the headline."

The subhead, in case you can't read it in the reproduction, is "(This is an advertisement about bragging and boasting)." And here is the opening copy:

"You already know that reliable performance of homogeneous or fabric-reinforced diaphragms can be critical for dependable functioning of fuel systems, brake systems, operating controls, accessories and other components.

"You also know that bragging and boasting had better be backed up with facts, so here they are."

There follows an avalanche of what he calls "brag and boast" but what we call good solid reasons for thinking about IPC design capabilities, such as "solved a transmission manufacturer's rubber-to-metal bonding problems with diaphragms exceeding their 1.5 million cycle bogey, never before achieved."

• Arthur Ward of Nash Engineering likes the work his "one-man agency," Sidney C. Lund, does for him. So do we.

We like the headline, "You're looking at a way to find more condenser efficiency," but we think the subhead would be even better: "If that sight glass isn't full, you may be losing condenser performance." The ad suggests:

"Just put a sight glass on your condenser discharge water box. If the glass isn't full, the top rows of tubes could be running dry. This cuts down on condenser efficiency —increases tube erosion—gives you the same symptoms as fouled tubes, reduced water flow or summer heat. . . . You correct this by removing air from a Nash priming system. Etc."

The layout and typography are perfect for the purpose.

• Bob Bolles nominates the Tennant ad as the "the most incomprehensible ad of the year." He asks: "Can you clear up the mystery of why any advertiser would spend good money to run such an ad?" No.

Copy Chasers

INDUSTRIAL PACKAGING CAN BOOST SALES

There is more to industrial packaging than boxes and brown paper. Some companies have realised that their packaging can help them to sell industrial goods just as it can help to sell consumer goods. Howard Sharman describes several case histories of companies who, in different ways, have discovered that there are marketing advantages in industrial packaging

Industrial packaging involves more than simply protecting the product. And it involves more than transporting the product from one place to another wrapped in brown paper or board. As with consumer goods packaging, there are positive marketing advantages to be gained from the packaging of industrial goods, and industrial marketers would be well advised to pay close attention to their packaging.

One point of view on industrial packaging is put by Alan Gledhill of Lucas Industries: 'All our products are packed in big brown boxes with the Lucas name on the side. The size of the box may vary, but the principle is the same. We are working on narrow margins, and can't cater for individual desires. Our packaging is done in the cheapest possible way, and cost-savings to the customer are irrelevant. I doubt it's an area that's paid much attention to.' Other manufacturers, however, have found that this is an area which is very well worth paying attention to; an area which can offer savings for both the manufacturer and his client, an area which can give one product a marketing advantage over other, similar, products.

Packaging helps to sell products

In some instances, the packaging itself can help a company to sell its products—a truism in the supermarket world, but not so obvious when selling highly complex radio-telephone equipment. Pye Telecommunications has to move a lot of its equipment around the world for exhibitions. Using conventional packaging materials, this used to be a highly expensive business at both the factory and the exhibition ends of the trip. Packing up the equipment used to take three men ten hours each, and assembling it on the exhibition stand took two engineers twelve hours. Now, using a suitcase-like pack made up from special extrusions and mouldings, together with standard panels of exterior grade plywood, melamine coated on both sides, and fitted out internally to the customer's exact requirements, these times can be cut right down. It now takes two men twenty minutes to pack up the equipment on leaving the factory, and one engineer can set the equipment up for use in one hour when it reaches the exhibition. What

Skypack helped Pye to sell   *Easy handling for Plysu bottles*

is more, in the past this fragile equipment had to be overhauled frequently because of the poor protection it was getting, and sometimes a piece of equipment had to be written off after one exhibition. Now the equipment does several exhibitions without coming back to the UK to be overhauled. It is also easy to satisfy the curiosity of customs men—who always want to see inside, but will never put things back together again.

The pack which has achieved these apparent miracles is Skypack, manufactured by Giltspur Packaging specifically for these sorts of problems. Each pack is unique to the customer and his product, and is not cheap; the cost savings listed above, however, more than justify the extra expenditure. Bill Wheel, Sales Promotion Manager of Pye Telecommunications, adds, 'Skypack is a positive marketing advantage since the equipment always works at exhibitions. Just showing it to the customers is also a marketing advantage—it is very impressive for them to see the ease of the assembly job.'

Transit packaging offers cost savings

A very different example comes from Rockware. The company is a bulk manufacturer of semi-finished goods—in this case, bottles—which have to be transported to another manufacturer.

Reprinted with permission from *Marketing* (UK), pp. 21, 22, and 43, Dec. 1976.

In the past, these bottles were transported in a number of ways—corrugated cartons, paper sacks, plastic crates, and cardboard trays. All these methods, however, involved a high degree of manual labour, and since the packs did not utilise space very well, the lorries were transporting a considerable amount of air, as well as bottles. This meant that the maximum carrying capacity of the lorries was not reached. Now the bottles are bulk palletised and shrinkwrapped. This can be done mechanically, thus saving labour, and the pallet itself gives a far better utilisation of space, enabling the lorries to carry more bottles—there can be up to a third more bottles on a lorry.

This is all excellent for Rockware, which benefits from the labour and transport savings, but the story does not end there. The shrinkwrap keeps the bottles extremely clean and dust-free (a customer advantage) and whilst palletisation makes for faster loading for Rockware, it also makes for faster unloading for the customer. The customer too can increase his savings if he, in turn, installs a de-palletising machine. This packaging development has coincided with vast increases of speeds on bottling lines, and without a mechanised form of bottle unloading, these speeds would have been unobtainable because the labour costs involved and the associated difficulties of handling would have been insurmountable. Rockware can thus offer a complete service to a potential customer, an integral part of which is the form of the transit pack used.

Ron Woodward, Packaging Consultant at Rockware, comments: 'It has been the glass industry's policy to sell bulk palletised glass at a reduced price, and this, combined with the customer's ability to make savings for himself, has meant that in the industry approximately half of the glass sold is now delivered in this new way. In marketing terms it is clearly a convenience pack for industry, and points the way in which many other industries may have to develop in order to cut the ever increasing cost of labour.' Who would you buy your glass from, a supplier who put it into paper sacks, or one who bulk palletised it straight onto your filling lines?

Plastic bottles give marketing advantages

Reckitt Industrial used to use one gallon metal containers for its range of industrial maintenance products. The marketing department wanted to go into plastic bottles because of the better image of plastic, and also because it gave Reckitt's customers an easier container to use. The plastic bottles made by Plysu offer easy pouring, and the set of four packs is particularly useful for customers who have changed from a bulk metal container to the 4×5 litre pack offered by Plysu.

Having made the decision to go into plastic bottles, Plysu and Reckitt worked out an efficient and cost saving method of delivering and filling the bottles. Plysu suggested packing the bottles straight into the Reckitt cartons, rather than delivering them in bulk, to be unpacked, filled, and then repacked. Reckitt, for its part, set aside a special loading bay for Plysu deliveries, automated the filling line, and developed a special filling machine which would fill the bottles in the cartons. Plysu also developed a new strapping machine which could secure the cartons onto the pallets on the lorries in such a way that it was easier for the Reckitt man to unload them. Thus at no time do the bottles leave the carton between the Plysu factory and the end-user.

The savings and advantages of this method of operation are immense. Reckitt gets savings in manpower in the handling of the containers, and on the filling line itself. Plysu gains from the quick turnround of vehicles offered by the special loading bay. The empty bottles are also conveyed more safely in the cartons, and perfect condition of the bottles is important for Reckitt, because leaks in the packs could be dangerous. This last advantage is passed on to the end-user, who also benefits from the original aims of the Reckitt marketing department. This operation has been a joint effort between Plysu and Reckitt, with ideas coming from both sides, and savings, as well as marketing advantages, also accruing to both.

One market which is highly competitive is the manufacture of

Bulk palletisation aids Rockware and its customers

cardboard boxes. In order to make any money in this field, box manufacturers have to have long runs of each box, and this, inevitably, leads to the cartons spending long periods in store. Problems arise when these long-stored cartons are put on automatic erecting lines, since the pressures of stacking either erase the creases in the board, or define them too clearly to allow the box to be erected easily. Taylors, a part of the British Printing Corporation, found that customers were complaining of poor performance of the cartons at the erecting machine, and, with the help of Sumapack, found an aswer to this problem which also helped them to sell more cartons.

Special pack protects cartons

To solve the stacking problem, Sumapack, manufacturers of industrial packaging, developed a 'flat-pack' to contain the cartons in relatively small quantities. This large pack can be stacked six high, with the minimum pressure being exerted on the bottom cartons. The pack also helped by doubling the stacking height in the warehouse. Taylors next had to make a decision on the size of a new fleet of lorries, and it decided to make the 'flat-pack' the modular base for the lorry sizes. The use of the pack as a module was then extended to control the minimum aisle widths in the factory, and the pack was used as the internal handling system for moving the cartons around from die-cutter to printer etc. The cartons are delivered to Taylor's customers in these packs, and they can slot them straight into the packaging line.

The 'flat-pack' can be used for an average of 74 return trips, so the original cost can easily be written off, and at the end of its life the pack can either be cannibalised, or used as a one-time export pack which has already been paid for. Danny O'Mahoney, Assistant Buyer at Taylors is sure that the 'flat-pack' helps to gain repeat orders for Taylors' product once customers have seen it in action. He makes sure that he gets these useful containers back by charging out for them at what he described as 'exorbitant rates'. Neville Labworth, Marketing Manager of Sumapack, comments, 'This all happened mainly by chance. The original idea was to develop the best possible box for the cartons to create customer satisfaction and product performance. The whole system occurred because one man saw the potential of the pack from its original use.' Chance, then, even in packaging does play a part, but both this case and the Plysu one quoted above show how important it is to think laterally about packaging. In the Plysu case, the use of the carton was extended back from the end of the filling line into Plysu's own factory, and the Sumapack 'flat-pack' has all but taken over at Taylors.

Special packs for the removal trade
One final case, also involving Sumapack, shows how industrial packaging can help to sell a service. A fast growing area in the removal trade is the storage of goods for people who are not moving directly into a new house. To cater for this, Sumapack designed a special container, four of which fit into a removal van. These containers are then filled with the customer's furniture in the van, sealed and stored until required. This, of course, led to much simpler warehousing, the only labour required being a fork lift truck. Whites is one of the firms to take up this idea, and Warehouse Director Gilbert Line says, 'It cost a lot to set up the system in the first place, but you have to go forwards, you can never stand still. We are making savings on labour and warehousing over the course of time, and the service can be advertised. It helps the customer by giving him perfect security for his goods, and it helps Whites.' White's vehicles are now multi-purpose, designed with this palletisation in mind. They have a side opening for the pallets, to make it easy for the fork-lift to operate, as well as a rear opening for the traditional removal operation. Other removal firms also use this method, but declined our offer of publicity (and free advertising) for their marketing shrewdness. Several firms refused to talk to us at all, for fear of their competitors learning what they were doing. This seems to us a very short-sighted view of the value of publicity.

Industrial packaging, then, offers many opportunities for taking a marketing advantage over competitors, whether it be a cost saving, the ability to offer an improved service, or a pack which will help a manufacturer to sell to his customers. It is a field which would repay the attention of many more industrial marketers. ☐

Design is the missing link

by Thomas Faul

When it comes to developing new products for the marketplace, Canadians are inveterate copycats.

Typical is the small or medium-sized manufacturer who, completely oblivious to the idea of good industrial design as a marketing tool, takes the existing product of another company and turns out his version of it.

He finds some wrinkle which he hopes will make his copy commercially viable—friends who will buy it, a source of cheap material, and some small design variation that will circumvent the patent.

Usually, however, the duration of his product in the marketplace is very

Otaco Limited had its vehicle seating line redesigned, and this highly successful "Innovator I" was the result.

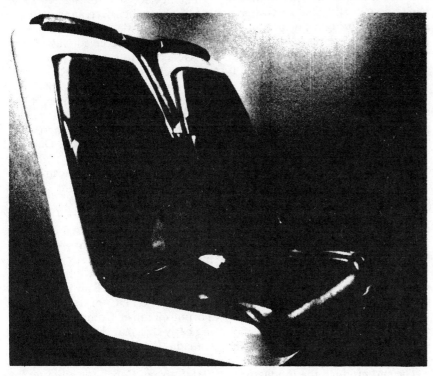

short. The minute he decides to copy, he is restricting the circle of his endeavor. He cannot market his product outside the country if it's an obvious copy of a foreign product. And, he cannot compete on his home ground with the already-successful original.

Only be cheaper

As long as the Canadian copier can hide behind an 18% tariff barrier, he has some chance to get by. But he can never be better that the guy he imitates—he can only be cheaper.

Technological development is advancing at such an incredible rate that what is commercially viable today will most certainly be obsolete tomorrow.

"Tomorrow" may be only a year away.

Most assuredly it is no more than 10 years away, as evidenced by the fact that about 80% of the sales of many companies are in products that weren't in existence 10 years ago. There is always multifaceted development going on world-wide, and the likelihood that such development will not affect your profit is absolutely zero.

You ask yourself: "Will my product be obsolete?"

The answer is: "Yes, without a doubt." The only unknown is when.

Many products obsolete

Many, many products on the market today are basically obsolete—not just because technology changes so quickly, but because human needs change, and buying habits, as a consequence, also change.

What do so many companies do when they find sales slipping? Instead of questioning the basic design of the product, either from a functional or an aesthetic point of view, they try to batter down the marketing door by spending large amounts of money on advertising and promotion—for what is basically an obsolete product.

Less competitive

All this money spent on advertising and promotion merely pushes the price of the product up to where it is even *less* competitive than before.

A relatively small sum (compared to the massive advertising budget) could be invested in a total redesign of the product which, after it is altered, updated, or whatever, will then command a good position in the

Reprinted with permission from *Canadian Business,* vol. 50, pp. 46–48, Jan. 1977.

marketplace because it now functions better, is more versatile, or may simply look better than anything else that's available.

Frankly, the cost of manufacturing an obsolete product is prohibitive. Instead of selling 100,000 widgets @ $6.95 at a profit of 13% (about $90,000), what if you could sell 300,000 @ $4.95 at a 30% profit—about $450,000?

Even if the design function needed to achieve the latter costs you $200,000, you would still be way ahead the first year. Surely this is the essence of good business.

Gillette knew what to do

To produce a TRAC II razor (say), as Gillette did, takes marketing. The tremendous success of such a product does not happen by accident: it takes superb manufacturing techniques, comprehensive marketing and some kind of technological breakthrough. Even after some fundamental development work has been carried out, it is highly likely that another manufacturer will come out with a competing item, the degree of patentability being what it is. Gillette had to come up with a new wrinkle (which it did) for the TRAC II—an adjustable head. And it would be astonishing if the same company doesn't have another development on the way.

That is marketing!

The interesting point about industrial design as a marketing tool (the way companies like GM, IBM and Westinghouse use it) is that it is self-perpetuating. The company that employs it can never run out of ideas, provided it doesn't stop its efforts in that direction.

Usually, when a company says "back to the drawing board" after a product has bombed in the marketplace, it's because that company did not go to the drawing board in the first place.

As it stands, an industrial designer in Canada is hired by a corporation only after some kind of emergency has arisen—sales are off drastically, a source of supply has dried up or a drastic reorganization is necessary.

The designers are not hired as a normal adjunct to the marketing process, but because something has gone terribly wrong. Maybe the problem is that the design function straddles both the marketing and manufacturing functions, and falls (as it were) between two stools. Perhaps what we

need is a new type of company officer who would be responsible for both—a vice president of "manufacturing."

Otaco Limited of Orillia, Ont., is one example of a Canadian company that achieved success through the use of good industrial design.

A manufacturer of transportation seating since 1926, Otaco's prime markets have always been in Canada. Every time you sit in a bus or subway car, you are probably sitting on an Otaco-built product.

But, in 1974, the company found itself in trouble on three counts:

1) the cost of materials was rising—the tubular steel for the seating frame, the plastic coating applied to it to prevent injuries to passengers who might hit the frame, the plywood that backed the seat cushions, the foam that cushioned the seats and the vinyl that covered it. Even the clips, bolts and welds used to hold the seats together were up in price.

2) labor costs were escalating—the labor used to build the seat components and to assemble them.

3) increasing freight charges meant it cost Otaco more to ship its products to customers. And those costs were particularly high because the seats were shipped in assembled form and most of the shipping space was filled with air.

At an impasse

Otaco was at an impasse. It knew it had to do more than reduce costs as a means of realizing a fair profit—its product was being made obsolete by the rising costs. A new bold redesign job was called for, but how could it be justified?

The small size of the Canadian market couldn't justify the R&D program that would be required for an original design. Well, Otaco became bold. With the help of an outside consultant, Otaco embarked on a design for a new generation of seating.

Out went the plywood, foam clips, plastic patches, steel tubing and fabric. A new kind of seat of formed stainless steel was designed in a shape that was strong enough for the job without the conventional tubing and supporting legs which add to a vehicle's daily maintenance costs. Otaco built the seats in standard modules adding molded vinyl-and-foam cushions in a variety of colors.

The end product, the Innovator I, is a simple system of seating which is mass-produced at a lower cost, easily

Thomas Faul, president of Thomas Faul Design Ltd, believes "We must abandon our linear thinking and look objectively at the product we are trying to sell. It's time to take full advantage of product design."

assembled and nested for inexpensive shipping. And, although it is a basic seat for all mass transit applications, it is readily modified to satisfy the individual design requirements of any customer without losing the cost-saving advantages of mass production.

The development of the new seating line brought Otaco an immediate and enthusiastic market response. The first order received was placed by General Motors Coach of Pontiac, Michigan for its new RTS-2 bus demonstrator unit. Innovator I demonstrator sets were later purchased for testing public acceptance by transit authorities in Chicago, Illinois, Portland, Oregon, Denver, Colorado, and Edmonton, Alberta. Then a larger order was placed by the Bi-State Transit Authority of St. Louis, Missouri. In 1976, Toronto's Urban Transportation Development Corporation ordered approximately 10,000 Otaco seats—low profile "Mini Back" versions of the Innovator I line. They will be installed in 200 LRVs (Light Rail Vehicles) to be built for UTDC for delivery to the Toronto Transit Commission starting early this year. Hawker Siddeley Canada Limited has also ordered some of the low profile units for 134 "H5 Subway Cars" it is building for the TTC. Delivery began in late 1976.

Otaco's transportation seating division which sells 85%-90% of the transit seats in Canada now reports that the introduction of the new-design Innovator I has increased their business 40% and enabled the company to gain wide acceptance in the United States.

Canadian Co-operative Implements, Winnipeg, is another company which turned to industrial design to solve serious problems that had arisen in the production and marketing of a line of swathers, an agricultural implement used in harvesting.

Years ago, the machines had evolved from the combined efforts of a group of handyman mechanics and inspired tinkerers among the farmers who had formed the co-op as a means of obtaining inexpensive equipment for their own needs.

"By guess and by God"

Although it was a machine built chiefly "by guess and by God," incorporating components from Germany, the United States and Scandinavia, the swather worked reasonably well.

Improvements were made as required. If the machine sagged too much, a piece of heavy steel was added as reinforcement. If the frame tended to become twisted, extra supports were wired in. If there was too much vibration, sheet steel panels were fitted to absorb it. By 1972, however, material and labor costs were pricing the complicated machine out of the market, while rising fuel and

When the original cast iron units were no longer available to the Canadian distributor of the U.S.-built Franklin stoves, the stoves were redesigned with substitute materials. Now Canadian made, the product's sales have quadrupled.

maintenance costs were making the cumbersome machine too expensive to operate.

At that point, the company turned to an outside design consultant for help, and they, in turn, enlisted the help of a computer to calculate stresses, determine where additional strength was needed and where parts could be eliminated.

The result was a new, lighter swather with fewer moving parts—a far more maneuverable machine that can service more fields in a day.

So successful is the new machine, that the annual sales of swathers, worth approximately $8,500 each, is projected to rise from 500 to 1,000 machines by 1977. Also, new markets for the swather opened in four U.S. states—North and South Dakota, Minnesota and Montana.

The company reports that with its existing facilities and personnel, it cannot keep up with new orders. But the success of the new swather is established, and the co-op has set up a full-fledged research and development facility that has placed it well on the road to more sophisticated product development.

Industrial designers keep well informed on new developments in materials technology—developments which occur very rapidly. Chances are, if you have not redesigned your product recently, you may not be aware that there may well be a new material that will do a better job for you than the one you're using now.

Such was the case with Selkirk Metalbestos Ltd of Brockville, Ont. who, until recently, marketed an 18th-century style cast iron Franklin stove built in the United States.

Early in 1974, the U.S. supplier advised Selkirk that, because of its burgeoning home market, it could no longer supply the Canadian firm with stoves.

The loss was a potential disaster for Selkirk since there was no alternate source of supply in Canada—there were simply not enough foundries north of the border to produce the cast iron stoves in quantity.

The problem was solved, by designing a stove in stamped steel with cast aluminum ornamentation finished to look, feel and smell like cast iron.

The new stove was tooled in Canada and was rolling off the production line in November of the same year—in time to meet Selkirk's market requirements before the inventory of imported products had been used up.

While tooling for the new stove was in the medium six figures range, the company was able to recover that cost in the first six months. Previously, it had sold 2,000 units, all imported. In those first six months with the new product, it sold 8,000 and opened markets in Denmark and Australia.

As these brief case histories demonstrate, a well-designed product is half way sold in the marketplace, and the costs of advertising are greatly reduced.

In difficult times like these, we must abandon our linear thinking and look objectively at the product we are attempting to sell.

Before you spend marketing money and effort on a product, apply the following checklist:
- Is the product making money?
- Would a price reduction through a redesign increase volume?
- Can it be improved aesthetically or functionally?
- Can it be redesigned to simplify manufacturing techniques, reduce labor and equipment or spare parts inventories?
- Can tool-and-die costs be reduced through redesign?
- Would a different material improve its performance or reduce costs?
- Can it be redesigned to simplify packaging and cut shipping costs?

Canada has some excellent industrial designers who will help you evaluate all these points. Don't hesitate to call one in to explore the possibilities and to see samples of his work.

Canadians, it's time to "de-rut" your thinking—time to take full advantage of product design.

Part V
Measuring Program Effectiveness

"Industrial Advertising Pays Off," by J.E. Morrill, presents a technique for measuring the dollar payoff of business-paper advertising.

"Ad Research: You Can't Protect Your Investment Without It," by C.P. Johnson, provides guidelines to follow when doing advertising research.

"New Product Strategy: How the Pros Do It," by J.R. Rockwell and M.C. Particelli, describes techniques for selecting, developing, and bringing new products into the marketplace in the 1980's.

"Ad Experiments for Management Decisions," by B.M. Enis and K.K. Cox, presents pros and cons of advertising experimentations.

"Pretesting the Effectiveness of Industrial Advertising," by P.V. Abeele and I. Butaye, explores pretesting of industrial advertising messages.

"Predicting Changes in Advertising Effectiveness," by C.A. Maile, describes a valuable communications model.

"How to Measure Your Advertising's Sales Productivity," by W. Parker, outlines a planning model business/industrial marketers can use to evaluate advertising's contribution to sales efficiency.

"The Effectiveness of Marketing's 'R&D' for Marketing Management: An Assessment," by J.G. Myers, S.A. Greyser, and W.F. Massy, contains highlights and recommendations of the Commission on the Effectiveness of Research and Development for Marketing Management.

Problems in Review

John E. Morrill

Industrial advertising pays off

Its value has often been questioned, but now a manager can assess its contribution to total selling effort

Foreword

Here the author gives the highlights of a novel and effective technique for measuring the dollar payoff of business-paper advertising. Mr. Morrill has been President of his own company, Sales & Advertising Controls Inc., for the past five years. Prior to that he was a Senior Partner of Sutherland Abbott Advertising Agency, and was associated with Ted Bates Advertising and Young & Rubicam. His clients have included some of the country's largest corporations, representing a broad variety of industries.

Over the years a great deal of research has been done on consumer advertising—in fact, compared with industrial advertising, it is now a well understood field. Industrial advertising, unfortunately, has been so badly neglected that it has been almost impossible for an executive to know just how effective his company's promotion of its industrial products has been, or whether it has had any real effect on sales at all.

The reasons why consumer advertising has been thoroughly researched and developed, and why industrial advertising has not, are obvious enough. In the consumer world, the person who does the buying does it for himself (or perhaps his family), and he distinguishes between brands for this purpose. Given the importance of his decision, industry has logically concentrated its advertising and promotional efforts on him to sway his choice, and allocated relatively generous budgets for this effort and for studies on how to do it best. Much talent has thus been absorbed by the consumer field. This drain has left relatively small resources to be applied to industrial-advertising efforts and research.

Furthermore, on the face of things, industrial advertising looks like a much less promising field for promotional efforts. The "buying locations"—by which I mean both the purchasers who buy from industrial suppliers and the various influences that bear on them and their decisions—are complex and sometimes mysterious. Sales tend to be competitively negotiated between salesman and buyer, and the relevance and influence of advertising is not as obvious as it is in the consumer context.

It is not surprising, then, that research techniques for assessing the sales payoff of industrial advertising have been neglected. The fact remains that they certainly are very much needed. Theodore Levitt's research demonstrates without question that advertising *does* play a definite role in industrial purchasing decisions.[1] The question is: How much? The businessman needs to know what he is getting for the money he devotes to industrial promotion and whether he should spend more or spend it differently. As a matter of fact, as techniques that my associates and I have recently developed show, he

1. *Industrial Purchasing Behavior* (Boston, Division of Research, Harvard Business School, 1965).

could usually spend his money more wisely, a point I shall develop later.

New technique

There are two serious difficulties in devising sound techniques for assessing the impact of industrial advertising.

First, it is impossible to assume the familiar principle that "what is recalled is effective" and then question buyers about what advertising they remember. There are a couple of reasons for this:

□ In the industrial sector, what a buyer recalls doesn't necessarily have anything to do with the decision to buy; there are too many other people and influences in on the act. Thus it is wiser to concentrate on "principal buying influences" rather than on the buyer who actually signs the purchase order. Throughout this article I shall use the simpler term "buyer"; but please remember that I mean this to include *all the men who exercise significant influence over a company's or a plant's choice of brand.*

□ It has been established that a company executive tends to continue to read the advertising of his company's suppliers rather than that of competing suppliers. He therefore tends to recall this advertising better, a fact that hopelessly biases his recall.

Second, it is difficult to isolate the creative qualities of an advertising campaign from all the other elements that go into it, such as frequency, market focus, and so forth, and compare it with a competitor's. In this article, however, I shall describe a method that allows one to avoid saying anything about the qualitative dimensions of advertising, except tangentially.

My associates and I have found it simpler and more efficient to concentrate attention on *the extent* of advertising in a particular advertising campaign and *the buyer's exposure* to it. If we can show that these correlate with levels of sales —if more advertising and more exposure mean more sales, and less of both mean fewer sales— then we can score a base hit. The new techniques *do* show this, roughly speaking. But before I get to results, let me explain the strategy we have used to measure exposure vis-à-vis market share.

Clearly enough, measuring the extent of a company's industrial advertising in the business papers is not subject to the special biases and distortions already mentioned. The fact that an executive reads a certain business magazine is *not* causally related to the fact that one or more of his company's particular suppliers happen to advertise in it—what he buys does not determine what magazines he reads. Also, his exposure to such media is relatively simple to determine accurately—simpler, certainly, than his exposure to brand advertising per se.

Once we decided to focus on the buyer's exposure to media, we had to find a way to pinpoint the relationship between this exposure and sales—share of customers and share of market dollars. To find how a buyer's exposure to a specific company's business-paper advertising affects that company's sales, we identified two large groups of buyers who purchased from this company, one that *had* been exposed to the advertising and another that had *not*.

Then, applying weighing techniques via EDP, we washed out all differences between the groups except this crucial one of exposure and non-exposure. Once this had been done, any behavioral difference between the two groups could be regarded as an effect of advertising. For a fuller description of this method, refer to the ruled insert on page 6.

Trade-off among selling costs

The effects of industrial advertising, we discovered, are profound—and profoundly useful to know about. Industrial management has long accepted business-paper advertising as an inexpensive way to communicate with the market; but the specific effect of this communication on sales and profits has remained something of a mystery. Now it is clear that the right kind of advertising in the right business papers, with appropriate frequency and for sufficient lengths of time, more than pays for itself by boosting sales and cutting selling costs. Thus, it can be an excellent investment.

I shall try to demonstrate and clarify these points about "appropriate frequency," "sufficient length of time," and similar parameters, working up to conclusions about how a company can trade off advertising expense, the cost of its own sales calling, and its wholesaler's sales-calling practice to maximize sales and minimize sales expense. My main point, once again, is that industrial advertising can significantly reduce selling costs as a percent of sales.

These are certainly not novel or radical ideas, but now, for the first time, hard data are available that back them fully and allow the execu-tive to make his trade-offs with precision—and with confidence.

Exposure, opinion & dollars

Over the four years in which this assessment method has matured, my company has studied, through nearly 100,000 interviews, some 1,000

Surveying exposed and unexposed groups

Once a manufacturer has decided to investigate the value of advertising its brand of a particular product or product line, the researcher first selects a random list of locations (usually about 1,000) at which it is purchased. These will include centralized purchasing facilities of giant corporations, or plants that are semi-independent parts of such a corporation, or small independent manufacturers, and so on.

Next, telephone interviewers call each location for a series of multiple interviews with the "buyers" there to determine, first of all, which individuals at the location exercise the main influence over the decision to buy Brand X rather than a competing brand. Two to seven interviews are usually necessary to establish this. The telephone interviews elicit other information, especially in the following areas:

○ What are the attitudes of the influential buyers toward various manufacturers of the product? These attitudes are specified over 15 or more different dimensions—competitiveness of pricing, quality, service, and so forth.

○ How much of this product was purchased at each location in the last year? (As explained in the article, a one-year period is often used. The particular time span depends on such considerations as the incidence of purchase.) Then, what proportions of this volume were purchased from the various manufacturers?

○ How many sales calls from the manufacturer did the influential buyer(s) receive in this period? How many from the distributors that represent him? And how many from competitors' salesmen?

○ What business papers (trade magazines and the like) does each influential buyer see? And how frequently does he see each one? These statistics on frequency are used to measure his exposure to the advertising these papers carry; exposure is one of the central variables studied.

The next step is to break the sample of buyers into two groups based on their exposure to business papers carrying the manufacturer's advertising.

The researcher does this by comparing the papers in which the manufacturer carries his advertising and the papers the buyers say they read when they respond to the final set of questions in the interviews. The basic procedure is this: if a buyer does not look at the magazines in which the manufacturer advertises, then he is put into an unexposed group, while if he does look at these magazines, then he goes into the exposed group.

In most of the studies mentioned in this article, we have considered a buyer to have been exposed to a supplier's advertising in a magazine if he says he has looked through 30% or more of the issues appearing in the period under investigation. If he says that he has looked through less than 30% of the issues, he has been categorized as unexposed. The exact criteria naturally vary, depending on the particular study involved.

Once the two groups have been identified, all other differences and bias factors—such as average order quantity, number of competitors, frequency with which sales calls are received, and the like—are balanced between the two groups by statistical weighting processes via computer programs. The computer thus "creates" two groups which can be compared with each other—two groups that are identical in every known way but one, the fact of exposure.

All the data belonging to the two groups are also balanced, and the computer prints out the corrected ratings each group gives the manufacturer on the attitude factors and the balanced market share each awards to the manufacturer, both in dollars and in number of customers. Since all known variables are acting on both processed groups in exactly the same way, any remaining differences between the two in attitudes and choice of manufacturer can be considered to be due to the power of the advertising the manufacturer ran.

Results have been cross-checked in many ways throughout the last four years, and the evidence confirms the soundness of the approach.

---

advertising schedules for 26 different product lines sold in 90 product markets at 30,000 different buying locations. In all these studies, the object has been to (a) examine two computer-matched samples of a product's buyers, one exposed to its advertising, the other unexposed; (b) estimate the attitudes of the two groups toward the product's competing manufacturers; (c) determine how much each group buys from competing suppliers advertising at different levels; and (d) correlate exposure and market share.

The general evidence is that exposure to a manufacturer's industrial advertising improves the buyer's opinion of the manufacturer, and that this improvement in opinion means a larger share of the market for the manufacturer.

Dollars follow opinions

One product studied is a basic chemical sold in quantity to a tight market of 500 processors. Sales prices are negotiated very competitively,

and a few large manufacturers cultivate the processors' buyers intensively through saturation sales calling. Under these circumstances, many manufacturers in this product market feel that business-paper advertising is a waste of time and money.

Significantly, of the three major manufacturers for this market, only the leader does any advertising. Company A (let us call it) placed some 17 pages of advertising in 3 business publications, while its two chief (but less successful) competitors, Companies B and C, ran only negligible advertising, as indicated in *Exhibit I*. As the exhibit shows, the study developed data on the opinions held about Company A and Companies B and C by two distinct groups of buyers, one exposed to A's advertising and the other unexposed. (The B and C figures have been combined.)

The columns titled "Differential" give the results of the study in succinct form. It appears, for example, that when the two groups rated Company A, the proportion of exposed

buyers naming A as preferred supplier was greater than the proportion of unexposed buyers who held this same opinion—in fact, it was some 23% greater.

When the two groups rated Companies B and C, complementarily, it appears that a relatively smaller proportion of the exposed group named either of these companies as preferred suppliers, while in the unexposed group relatively more did so. From Company A's point of view, it looks as though the company gained ground by advertising; from the opposite point of view, that of Companies B and C, it looks as though they lost ground to the competition.

Gains for A in the exposed group are evident elsewhere as one runs down its list of figures under "Differential." Although the differential in favor of Company A is not significant so far as second and third choice of suppliers is concerned, the differential in favor of considering A when purchasing the chemical in the future *is* fairly significant—some

Exhibit I. A chemical company: opinions of buyers about three competing suppliers when exposed and unexposed to their advertising

	About Company A, which ran 17 pages of advertising in one year			About Companies B & C, which did negligible advertising in one year		
Opinions	Exposed	Unexposed	Differential	Exposed	Unexposed	Differential
Preferred as supplier	.37†	.30	+ 23%	.09	.12	−25%
Second and third choice as supplier	.19	.19	*	.14	.14	*
Willing to consider	.56	.50	+ 6%	.24	.28	−14%
Leads in quality	.20	.18	+ 11%	.03	.03	*
Leads in price	.05	.07	− 29%	.03	.03	*
Leads in delivery	.18	.15	+ 20%	.04	.04	*
Best in your past experience	.22	.18	+ 22%	.05	.05	*
Best technical assistance	.20	.14	+ 43%	.04	.04	*
Salesmen lead in product knowledge	.13	.08	+ 63%	.05	.05	*
Salesmen lead in service	.11	.09	+ 22%	.02	.02	*
Most enthusiastic salesmen	.12	.06	+100%	.02	.02	*
Share of market						
In customers	.56	.47	+ 19%	.20	.23	−13%
In dollars	.38	.35	+ 9%	.13	.19	−32%

*No significant difference.   †Read: 37% of the buyers exposed to A's advertising preferred A as supplier.

6%. The advertiser also scored significant differentials in the ratings for best quality, delivery, best past experience, and technical assistance.

Ratings of A's salesmen, in particular, were much higher in the exposed group than in the unexposed, and this is evidence for an argument often advanced: that *advertising acts as a valuable introduction for the salesman to his prospective customer.*

The only dimension on which the advertiser scored a negative differential was its price image; 29% fewer of the exposed buyers felt Company A offered the best price. This opinion did not hurt sales, however, since the company scored gains in its share of customers and dollars via exposure. But the differentials in market share for Companies B and C are negative, as are their differentials on the preferred-supplier and future-consideration dimensions at the top of the right-hand column. It thus appears that the advertiser gained in these areas at the expense of its non-advertising competitor. Evidence in other cases I shall discuss reinforces this impression.

Next, how do Company A's gains affect total selling cost? This is hard to answer because the meaning of this phrase is unclear: the factors included under this head vary widely from one company to another. But interviewers obtained enough information on this category for each company to allow projection of a total expense figure *without advertising.* Once these figures were available, A's advertising expense was added into the total expense, and the cost of its sales to both the exposed and the unexposed group was calculated.

The result? The cost of selling to the first group was 5% *lower* than the cost of selling to the second.

Then, using the projected totals for B and C, we calculated *their* costs of sales to both groups. Their cost of selling to buyers exposed to A's advertising was 40% *higher* than their cost of selling to the unexposed buy-ers. Clearly, A's advertising created a real obstacle for B's and C's salesmen.

Contrary to the manufacturers' expectations, therefore, industrial advertising in this price-conscious, call-saturated market turned out to be an extremely profitable investment. The communicated message turned the buyers' thinking about Company A upward, and up went its market share of dollars and customers also.

Volume & change

Now let us look at three manufacturers who all make a low-priced electrical device used in quantity in all kinds of industrial plants. Plant-maintenance and purchasing staff are the principal buying influences. In the market competition is fierce, and suppliers believe that price, availability, and service primarily determine brand selection.

Exhibit II shows the number of pages of advertising each company ran in business papers over a 12-month period. Since the manufac-

Exhibit II. Companies purchasing a low-cost electrical device: opinions of buyers about three competing suppliers when exposed and unexposed to their advertising

									Proportion of buyers holding these opinions	
	About Company A, which ran 20 pages of advertising in one year			About Company B, which ran 16 pages of advertising in one year			About Company C, which ran 8 pages of advertising in one year		
Opinions	Exposed	Unexposed	Differential	Exposed	Unexposed	Differential	Exposed	Unexposed	Differential
Preferred as supplier	.144	.132	+ 9%	.363	.270	+34%	.091	.066	+ 38%
Second and third choice as supplier	.196	.177	+ 11%	.143	.148	*	.174	.140	+ 25%
Willing to consider	.341	.322	+ 6%	.499	.444	+12%	.265	.209	+ 27%
Leads in quality	.078	.044	+ 77%	.254	.196	+30%	.032	.025	+ 28%
Leads in price	.025	.001	+ 40%	.043	.023	+87%	.008	.008	*
Leads in availability	.078	.075	+ 4%	.172	.119	+45%	.054	.013	+315%
Leads in performance	.041	.019	+116%	.134	.104	+29%	.016	.016	*
Salesmen lead in product knowledge	.045	.042	+ 7%	.076	.063	+21%	.009	.011	*
Salesmen lead in service	.033	.033	*	.062	.051	+22%	.026	.008	+227%
Share of market									
In customers	.522	.495	+ 5%	.655	.615	+ 7%	.306	.250	+ 23%
In dollars	.194	.125	+ 55%	.238	.215	+11%	.102	.094	+ 9%

*No significant difference.

turers used the media in different combinations, it was necessary to identify different exposed and unexposed groups for each of the three. The total sample of buying locations was correspondingly large, totaling 1,000, with 2 to 7 interviews at each. The main results are these:

○ Company A, the largest advertiser, scored generally higher on attitudes and opinions all along the line. Although it achieved only a small positive differential in share of customers, it had a whopping 55% higher share of dollars in the exposed market. Apparently its ads helped attract a few very big customers.

○ Company B, the moderate advertiser, gained substantially in the second exposed group for all the attitudinal dimensions, with a comparative gain of 7% in customers and an 11% comparative gain in dollars.

○ Company C, the smallest advertiser, was not so well known to the general market as the other two to begin with. Still, it achieved substantial differentials in the exposed group's opinions, and gained some dollars and a lot of customers for its market share. This suggests that its advertising created primarily small- and medium-sized orders.

The differentials in each case are not strictly proportional to the number of pages run. Qualitative differences in the advertising doubtless account for this effect in part; differences in the audiences of the business papers used must also be responsible to some extent. While it is not possible to analyze such considerations in this article, I shall try to dramatize the importance of choosing the right vehicle for advertising in a later example.

Total selling expense without advertising was projected for these three companies, and these results emerged: A's costs were 28% lower in the first exposed group, B's costs were 6% lower in the second, and C's were 2% lower in the third. These again bear out the conclusions that advertising makes selling easier and cheaper. They also seem to show that the more advertising, the better. Within broad limits this is indeed true—but more on this point later.

Threshold of effectiveness

How *little* advertising can a company do and still get favorable responses from exposed buyers? To answer this question, we identified some companies which advertised at different levels in different, but closely comparable, business publications. *Exhibit III* shows a typical set of refined data. This particular company advertised in 3 magazines, but only got favorable differentials from buyers exposed to the first one, where it ran 6 pages in a one-year period. In the other magazines, 4 pages were ineffective against the competition. As a general rule, I have found that a frequency of 5 pages a year is needed to turn the scales in favor of a product or product line.

Period of sensitivity

How quickly can the executive expect results to show up in increased sales? So far I have simply assumed that one year is long enough for the executive to judge the effectiveness of his company's advertising. But, objectively speaking, if the differences between exposed and unexposed ratings result from advertising, then these must be cumulative effects that occur over a period which might be longer than a year.

We organized a large number of studies to confirm my impression that one year is long enough to allow the effects to develop. One typical study consisted of two investigations of the same market (an electrical product used in construction) spaced a year apart. The first study was made in 1966 and the second in

Exhibit III. The threshold of effectiveness in terms of frequency (differentials of exposed over unexposed)

Opinions	Magazine 1 (6 pages)	Magazine 2 (4 pages)	Magazine 3 (4 pages)
Preferred as supplier	3%	− 8%	3%
Second and third choice as supplier	8%	−12%	− 3%
Willing to consider	2%	− 9%	− 1%
Leads in quality	− 7%	− 4%	− 7%
Leads in price	17%	−16%	−22%
Leads in availability	1%	− 5%	10%
Share of market			
In customers	1%	− 6%	− 2%
In dollars	8%	−14%	− 7%

Exhibit IV. Effects of advertising on share of market in customers

Company	Year	Advertising pages	Exposed	Unexposed	Differential
A	1966	20	.57	.54	+ 6%
A	1968	10	.65	.62	+ 4%
B	1966	12	.47	.40	+18%
B	1968	9	.53	.50	+ 6%
C	1966	4	.45	.45	*
C	1968	4	.40	.40	*
D	1966	5	.34	.31	+11%
D	1968	8	.31	.25	+23%

*No significant difference.

1968. Notable effects that could be tied to changing advertising policies did indeed occur.

Exhibit IV lists customer shares for four major suppliers, along with the number of pages each ran in the two study years. The results reflected in the exposure differentials here are perhaps not as solid as they might seem, because the exposed and unexposed groups are different for the two studies as well as for each of the four advertisers. Still, a definite trend is evident:

O Companies A and B decreased the frequency of their advertising and showed a drop in differential as well, from 6% to 4% and from 18% to 6%, respectively.

O Company C ran 4 pages throughout, and its differential remained insignificant. Apparently this company was advertising below the threshold of effectiveness.

O Company D increased its frequency and was rated higher in 1968.

While these figures do not define the period of sensitivity absolutely, they do indicate that it is roughly a year. Other studies show the period varies from one month, for a product purchased frequently, to five years or more, for big-ticket purchases made in such industrial areas as utilities'

capital goods. But, usually, the executive can expect results in a number of months, or a year at most.

Too thin a spread

It is easy to underadvertise—in fact, I find this mistake is made as frequently or more frequently than any other. It rarely happens, on the other hand, that a company overadvertises any particular product line. When a company launches a strong campaign which seems to produce no results in a reasonable time, what has usually happened (the quality of the advertising content aside) is that it has spread its effort thinly over too many magazines and given space to too many different product lines. This can defeat the whole purpose of the campaign, as the *Exhibit V* example demonstrates.

Here Companies A and B have both manufactured power transmission equipment sold to a large OEM and replacement market. Differences in prices and in the products themselves are slight, but they are occasionally a significant factor with some of the larger buyers. The buyers consist mainly of maintenance, engineering, and purchasing staff.

Company A ran 26 pages a year in 6 magazines; and Company B, only 18 pages in 5 magazines. While

both advertisers show positive differentials in the opinions of the two exposed groups, only the smaller advertiser achieved the desired payoff in market share. Company B's smaller effort seems to have been more effective overall than Company A's. It achieved higher differentials overall on the opinion criteria than its competitor, and once again the dollars have followed opinions upward. Company A's advertising, on the other hand, seems to have decreased its market share among the buyers exposed to it. This loss certainly looks significant—a 7% drop in customers and a 10% drop in revenue.

Company B is obviously hitting on all cylinders. It is reaching the right audiences with messages at the right frequency—and it may well be that the content of its advertising is better than Company A's (although this issue is not a subject for discussion here). The correctness of B's approach contrasts strongly with what the interviewers learned about Company A's campaign—namely, that A's advertising was highly dispersed over the 6 magazines and it tried to convey information about several different product lines at once.

The effectiveness of B's campaign increased the effectiveness of its

Exhibit V. The importance of concentrating advertising

Opinions	About Company A, which ran 26 pages of advertising in one year			Proportion of buyers holding these opinions About Company B, which ran 18 pages of advertising in one year		
	Exposed	Unexposed	Differential	Exposed	Unexposed	Differential
Preferred as supplier	.114	.115	*	.072	.045	+60%
Second and third choice as supplier	.126	.038	+232%	.065	†	‡
Willing to consider	.291	.154	+ 89%	.158	.101	+57%
Leads in quality	.057	.058	*	.050	.034	+47%
Leads in price	.063	.058	+ 9%	.058	†	‡
Leads in availability	.057	.058	*	.050	.034	+47%
Best technical assistance	.025	†	‡	.036	.023	+56%
Salesmen lead in service	†	.058	−100%	.029	.045	−36%
Share of market						
In customers	.323	.346	− 7%	.180	.124	+45%
In dollars	.121	.135	− 10%	.085	.052	+63%

*No significant difference.

†Not available.

‡No useful figure (infinity).

salesmen and decreased the effectiveness of competing salesmen from Company A. Projections indicate that Company B's cost of selling to its exposed group dropped 25%, while Company A's cost of selling to its exposed group rose 6%. Company A was quite clearly defeating itself, and, just as obviously, Company B was not. The moral is that while a good campaign can be extremely profitable, a poor one can cost much more than the cost of the advertising itself.

Careful choice of magazines: The advertiser must not only avoid spreading a campaign too thin; he must also be careful to choose the right books to advertise in. For example, a manufacturer of electrical products used exactly the same advertising concurrently in 2 magazines, with the results shown in *Exhibit VI*. The

can measure them with some sensitivity. But an understanding of these techniques is fully useful to the executive only when he also understands how the gross effects interrelate with sales-calling practices—for sales calls are, after all, the most important of all communications media in industrial marketing operations.

I want to approach these interrelationships in two stages:

1. I will discuss the assistance that a manufacturer's product advertising gives to a distributor's sales force when the manufacturer himself does no sales calling.

2. I will pull together manufacturer advertising, distributor sales calling, and manufacturer sales calling in such a way as to map a method by which the manager can juggle all three to his company's best advantage.

sion. Calls on others have not been counted.

3. I define *probability of exposure* (*p*) as the product of the number of pages of advertising a manufacturer runs in a single magazine in one year and the proportion of issues of that magazine that the buyer has read. In other words, p = pages run × proportion of issues read. For example, if a manufacturer runs 18 pages in one magazine during the year and a buyer reads half the issues, then his probability of exposure is 9, since $p = 18 \times \frac{1}{2} = 9$.

Again, as with advertising, I am assuming that all differences between calls on principal buying influences have been washed out by the computer program. This simplifying assumption appears to be justified by the results I am now about to present.

Distributor sales calling

Exhibit VII shows how the distributor's market share varies with *p* at each of three different levels of sales calling. Here we must note that the manufacturer is making no sales calls whatever.

Looking at the lowest curve, we see that if the principal buyer sees no advertising and the distributor calls on him only once a year, then the distributor enjoys only about 22.5% of the market the buyer represents. As the principal buyer is exposed to more and more advertising, the distributor's market share goes up. When, for example, the buyer's exposure reaches 12, the distributor's dollar share shows an increase to one third of the total exposed market, an increment of about 37%.

The middle curve shows how things go when the distributor makes 10 calls a year on all the principal buyers. As the probability of exposure goes from zero to 12, his dollar share increases by 15%—a more modest, but still substantial, advance. The upper curve shows a 7% dollar increment for the same exposure where the distributor makes 20 calls a year—a rather small gain.

The fact that this increment declines as the distributor's calling frequency increases seems to imply that advertising provides its greatest sup-

---

Exhibit VI. Importance of the choice of magazine for one company
(differentials of exposed over unexposed)

Opinions	Magazine 1 (10 pages)	Magazine 2 (10 pages)	Magazine 3 (2 pages)
Preferred as supplier	12%	− 6%	−11%
Second and third choice as supplier	14%	− 7%	−11%
Willing to consider	10%	− 6%	− 9%
Leads in quality	2%	47%	− 7%
Leads in price	186%	26%	− 7%
Leads in availability	11%	− 8%	−12%
Share of market			
In customers	6%	− 3%	− 8%
In dollars	15%	20%	− 5%

---

advertising obviously had a positive effect on the attitude of those buyers who read Magazine 1. In this group its share of customers jumped 6%, and its share of dollars jumped 15%. Placing this advertising in Magazine 2 brought in fewer, but larger, orders. In a case such as this, additional research may be warranted to help this manufacturer determine the kinds of trade-offs he wants to achieve with his advertising.

Advertising & sales calling

Until now, I have concentrated on the gross effects of advertising and tried to prove that new techniques

I have chosen a single study of a manufacturer who makes a high-volume rubber commodity to illustrate my general conclusions. Before presenting results from this study, I should make three points clear:

1. The distributor of the commodity was responsible for 20% of all sales calls made on buyers in each situation discussed.

2. The sense in which I have used "sales call" is quite important. A sales call on a buyer has been counted into the calculations only if, at a given buying location, the salesman reached a man who exercised principal influence over the brand deci-

Exhibit VII. *Effect of advertising frequency on a distributor's share of market dollars*

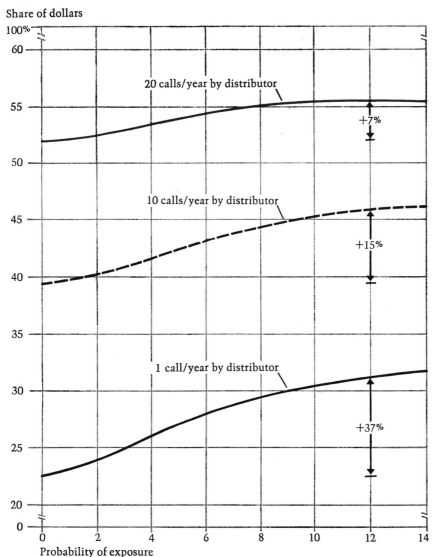

Share of dollars

20 calls/year by distributor   +7%

10 calls/year by distributor   +15%

1 call/year by distributor   +37%

Probability of exposure

port where his men are not getting through to the principal buyers. *Exhibit VIII* shows this effect more clearly.

The lower curve in *Exhibit VIII* charts the change in this distributor's dollar share of the market represented by unexposed buyers as he increases his calling frequency from once a year or less to once a week (50 calls per year). He can enlarge his market share by calling more and more frequently, up to about 35 calls per year, where his dollars peak out at 60% of the unexposed market. Calling at a higher frequency seems to be wasted effort, since the payoff curve declines toward the right there-

after. (It ought to be understood, however, that such high calling frequency is often due to product difficulties.)

The upper curve in this exhibit charts the distributor's market share when the principal buyers have been exposed to the advertising which is run by the manufacturer. This curve shows the results for the particular case where p, the probability of the buyers' exposure, has reached 12. It is clear that advertising strongly multiplies the distributor's dollars where the distributor calls on the principal influences infrequently, but this effect diminishes as his calling frequency increases, as reflected by the

narrowing gap between the two curves.

It is interesting to note that, in fact, in this particular market, the distributor is not usually able to get through to the principal buying influences with any regularity, particularly in the major buying locations. The manufacturer is therefore well repaid for his advertising here, since it functions as an essential part of the successful marketing mix.

I might note that the cost of this particular advertising program is only a fraction of 1% of the manufacturer's sales dollars. Its contribution to profits, relatively speaking, is extremely important.

Manufacturer reinforcement

Now let us look at what happens to the distributor when the manufacturer supports his efforts with both advertising and sales calls made by the manufacturer's own force—so-called *missionary* calls.

The lowest curve in *Exhibit IX* is exactly the same as the lower curve in *Exhibit VIII*. Once again, it shows how market share varies with distributor sales-calling frequency when these calls are entirely unsupported by the manufacturer.

The middle curve shows what happens to market share when the manufacturer, while still not doing any advertising, sends his own men into the field to make 2 calls per year on the principal buyers. The missionary obviously has a much stronger multiplying effect than advertising alone does (refer back to the upper curve in *Exhibit VIII*), particularly in the higher ranges of the distributor's sales-calling frequency. For example, if the distributor makes 20 calls per year, he can obtain a bit more than half the unexposed market. Exposing the principal buyers to 12 pages of advertising boosts the share by about 7%, as *Exhibit VIII* shows. But 2 missionary calls per year, with no advertising at all, increases the share by 27%.

Now, to see what power advertising has in this situation, look at the top curve in *Exhibit IX*. This curve shows how the distributor's market share changes when the manufacturer not only supports him with 2

Exhibit VIII. Distributor's sales calls supported by advertising only

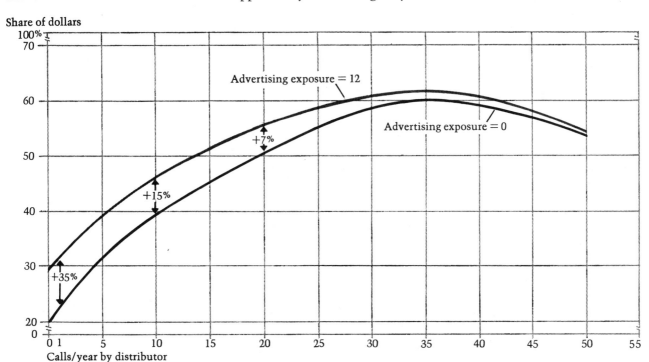

Share of dollars

Advertising exposure = 12

Advertising exposure = 0

+7%

+15%

+35%

Calls/year by distributor

Exhibit IX. Distributor's sales calls supported by both manufacturer's sales calls and advertising

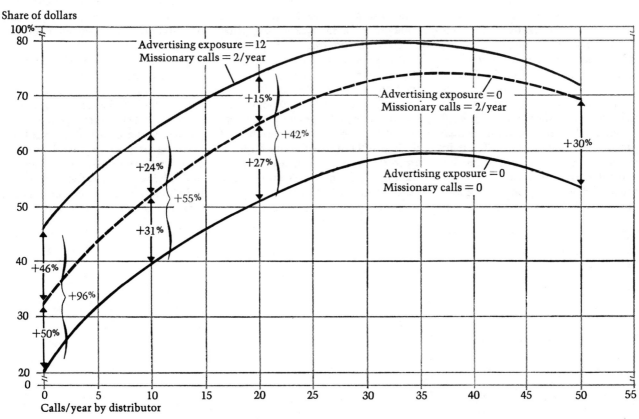

Share of dollars

*Advertising exposure = 12
Missionary calls = 2/year*

*Advertising exposure = 0
Missionary calls = 2/year*

+15%

+42%

+30%

+24%

+27%

+55%

*Advertising exposure = 0
Missionary calls = 0*

+31%

+46%

+96%

+50%

Calls/year by distributor

missionary calls a year on each buyer, but supports him with enough advertising so that the buyers' exposure reaches 12. Where the distributor calls 20 times a year, this additional support is worth 15% more of the market than the distributor could have obtained without the advertising. And the total manufacturer support, in missionary calling and advertising, causes an increment of 42% in the distributor's market. (All figures in gray in the exhibit are simple, uncompounded sums of the two investments.)

Where the distributor calls with less frequency, this advertising and missionary support is worth even more. For example, note the difference it makes where the distributor calls only half as often, at the rate of 10 calls per year: the total increment in market share then is 55%, of which 31% is due to the missionaries' efforts and 24% is due to the missionaries' efforts plus the advertising program.

As the distributor's calls drop to zero, the value of this missionary schedule and the value of this advertising program not only *increase*, but become *more nearly equal*.

One cannot draw any general conclusions about the relative importance of advertising frequency, missionary-calling frequency, and distributor-calling frequency from this highly specialized example. But experience shows that effects as dramatic as these are common rather than rare, and that it is well worth a company's time to investigate them precisely so that it can trade off between them efficiently. Perhaps one company could increase its advertising and save money on missionaries; perhaps another should pressure its

distributors to call more frequently; and so on. The possible situations and alternatives are endless—but until a company studies them systematically and learns to control them, these trade-offs will remain mysterious, and many opportunities for increasing profits will never be recognized. The tools are now at hand.

Other factors: There are of course a host of other factors that affect the success of an advertising program— product quality, the quality of the salesmen, the quality of the advertising itself and the media in which it is placed, publicity measures, promotional and marketing aids, and so on. These lie beyond the scope of this article, however. The point I set out to prove is, quite simply, that if other things are more or less equal, the contribution of business-paper advertising in the industrial sector can be assessed exactly; and, when properly used, it can be a source of increased profitability for the manufacturer.

Conclusions

Finally, let me summarize the conclusions I have derived from many studies like the ones illustrated here:

□ Advertising does change opinions and attitudes. These changes build up to a maximum level that depends on the frequency (and the content) of the advertising.

□ In most cases, share of customers and share of dollars follow a curve similar to that of the opinions.

□ An adequate program can significantly improve the number of closings of both distributor and manufacturer salesmen. It is usually most helpful where the distributor's salesmen are not able to reach the principal buyers with any regularity.

□ Although qualitative features are doubtless of great importance to a program's success, *lack of frequency* of advertising is the single most common cause of program failure. Out of several hundred failures I have studied, more than 90% ran fewer than 5 pages of advertising in 1 magazine in a 12-month period.

□ Given adequate frequency, most industrial advertising appears extremely profitable. Total cost of selling to groups exposed to the advertising often drops by 10% to 30%.

□ The nonadvertiser stands at a serious disadvantage in a well-advertised market. His cost of selling to groups exposed to his competitors' advertising may actually increase 20% to 40%.

□ There are very few industrial markets in which advertising is not profitable. Some executives feel that advertising won't work for their company because sales are all negotiated, because brands seem interchangeable to the purchasers, because the ticket size is so large that upper management must approve choices between brands, and so forth. I have a file of cases in which sound advertising programs have paid off handsomely under such conditions.

There is no question that a company can sell without advertising—but advertising certainly increases profitability. Aside from increasing a company's market share, perhaps the greatest value of a well-planned advertising program is that it can reduce the overall costs of selling by multiplying the effectiveness of the individual salesman far more than it increases direct selling costs.

Basic research is guaranteed to boost management's respect for advertising, according to Mr. Johnson.

AD RESEARCH: YOU CAN'T PROTECT YOUR INVESTMENT WITHOUT IT

By Curtis P. Johnson, advertising manager, plastics, Rohm & Haas Co., Philadelphia

Doing advertising research will not solve all your problems. Doing some basic research will not convince management to replace your personal selling force (sales force) with more non-personal selling (commonly referred to as industrial advertising). Nor will doing research automatically double your budget because management will suddenly realize the importance of industrial advertising.

But, the research will do something very basic and important—protect your company's investment in non-personal communication.

Forget your old excuses about not having enough time or money. Would you spend $75,000 for a house

and then never paint the house? Would you spend $6,000 for a new car and refuse to change the oil?

You are probably in this business because you're intelligent . . . and, oh yes, creative. Or maybe you're so creative you're a little afraid of what the research will show. We know that isn't true, so let's forget the old excuses and make a real effort.

There is one good excuse—a lack of market research knowledge. There are many ways of overcoming this problem and by following the guidelines listed below we will learn about advertising research as we go along.

The guidelines are:

1. Always do brand awareness or company awareness studies for every product and market. The existing awareness is a critical starting point when establishing initial strategy. Also, knowing your present situation is a necessity for establishing measurable future objectives.

The money required for this initial research is very little—never more than $2,000. The studies are illustrated on Page 40 and in most cases they were performed by the market research departments of publishing companies. Take advantage of the available professional market researchers. Also, if you choose a publishing company where you are presently advertising, the research cost is often reduced and sometimes free because of their existing merchandising programs.

Reprinted with permission from *Industrial Marketing* (now *Business Marketing*), vol. 64, pp. 36, 40, and 44, Feb. 1979.
Copyright © 1979 Crain Communications, Inc.

Top photo shows an array of Rohm & Haas' ad research studies, which always include a benchmark brand awareness study, and pre- and post-studies on all major campaigns.

Center photo: the most recent inquiry follow-up study netted a 25% return; for the past three years, returns have ranged between 20% and 40%.

Photo left: A simple letter and postcard are used for inquiry follow-up studies.

The publishing companies provide the best possible research at the cheapest cost—sounds like a creative solution to me.

2. In any major campaign, (either space or direct mail) do pre- and post research, which measures awareness and preference for your company or brand.

Not only will this prove useful in evaluating and justifying programs, but pre- and post research establishes current guidelines to help you establish future budgets.

For example, if a $100,000 program increases awareness from 10% to 20% and if your three year plan is 40% awareness, you know you're going to need to spend at least $100,000 for the next two years in order to achieve your 40% objective.

One potential problem to be aware of concerns doing pre- and post research on short campaigns or campaigns with limited funding. Don't bother to do the post research—without proper frequency your campaign will not be measurable. Generally you need a minimum of a high frequency six month campaign in order to create a measurable effect.

3. Always do cost-per-inquiry calculations on any non-personal communication program. Whether you are comparing postcard mailings, magazine inquiry results, or direct mail programs, the short-term and long-term comparisons provide valuable information.

Cost-per-inquiry figures are especially important when evaluating trade magazines. Inquiries are not the most important factor in industrial advertising, but they are real and measurable. There are other important actions created by advertising, but phone calls, meetings, letters, and readership figures are difficult to measure and compare. Inquiries are easy to measure and compare. And remember, inquiries are an excellent indication of readership.

4. Another measurement tool we have found very useful is inquiry follow-up studies (center left).

By doing our own inquiry follow-up studies we provide a check and balance for our cost per inquiry figures. We avoid becoming too dependent on cost-per-inquiry guidelines, and beside we often are able to make definite judgments concerning the quality of readership. For example, we have often compared two magazines whose cost per inquiry figures are comparable, but our conversion to sales was as much as 10 times greater for magazine A than for magazine B.

Incidentally, the reason for doing your own studies (Bottom photo, Page 40 illustrates how easy the letter and postcard are to produce) is to better control the variables. If publications do the research, the timing will be different, the questions may be different, and the results are not 100% comparable.

5. Insist on ad readership studies from all magazines you advertise in. The basic purpose of the ad readership study is not to see how you fare with competitive ads, but to help you do a better job of producing ads which achieve their objective—readership.

It is simply unprofessional to spend the time and money needed to produce an ad and then never find out what percentage of the audience noted and read most of the ad. Without a study you have no idea if your ad strategy worked and no idea where to go in the future.

What do you do if the magazine refuses to offer the ad readership study? Insist on meeting with the publisher. Insist on your right to

decent service, which includes a few studies per year so your ad schedule will result in at least one study.

Following the above guidelines does not require much money, but your initial efforts will require some time. The effort will result in management's gaining new respect for the non-personal communications function, but more importantly you will feel 100% better about your investment and your company's investment in your function.

In industrial selling, management's respect for non-personal communication will never equal their respect and dependence on personal communication, but a commitment to basic research will guarantee more respect in the future than has been evident in the past.　■

The mythical Sisyphus was condemned to push a large boulder up a mountain, only to find himself at the bottom again after almost reaching the summit. New products managers have faced a similar frustration over the past 25 years.

Although the sophistication and effectiveness of bringing new products to market successfully has improved during the past 25 years, the benefits derived from them have been diluted by a variety of changes in the new products environment: new, global competition; slow-growth markets; sophisticated segmentation; escalating costs; constrained resources.

Improvement in the new products management process has only helped us stay even in performance. On average we have seen no appreciable change in new product success rates during the past 25 years. Like Sisyphus, new product managers are still at the bottom of the mountain striving for the summit. Only the boulder seems to be getting larger and the mountain steeper.

Responding to that concern, Booz-Allen & Hamilton conducted a year-long survey of more than 700 U.S. manufacturers in new product management, covering more than 13,000 new product introductions. Figure 1 illustrates the types of products introduced.

Sixty percent of respondents represented industrial goods companies in the information processing, instruments and controls, industrial machinery, chemicals, power-generating equipment, OEM components, and textile industries; 40% represented consumer goods companies, divided equally between durables and nondurables.

Our 1981 survey indicates that, on average, our improvement just kept our performance on par. The success rate remains at two out of three commercialized products. However:
● It now takes only seven concepts to yield one successful product.
● Improvement in mortality has come from changes in new products management and organization.
● Those changes have altered how we spend money on new products. More is directed toward homework and less toward testing and commercialization.
● That shift in spending has resulted in less of the new products dollar being spent on failures.

WINNERS AND LOSERS

Clearly, averages are misleading. And beating the average is the name of the game. In the 1960s there were a lot of average players in the new product game. Few companies were above average—not many were below. The vast majority of companies performed adequately and achieved adequate results.

But by the 1970s, the new product game started to polarize. A growing number of "best practices" companies emerged. The number of "average" companies decreased and the number of companies performing below average increased.

As we enter the decade of the 1980s, it is becoming clear that, even with increasing sophistication, success in new products management will be increasingly difficult. In the future, if the trend continues—and we believe it will—the new products game will have only winners and losers.

New products management will only get more difficult as shifts in the external environment continue to change the requirements for success. But those pressures also create additional product development opportunities.

Our study suggests that those opportunities will bear fruit only in proficient new products organizations. Even those companies with the effective approaches of today are not assured of success tomorrow.

Companies without "best practices" and improvement will not even be in the game.

The losers of tomorrow will have characteristics common to many companies performing well today. They will:
● Know market characteristics;
● Define new products strategy as a planning focus;

John R. Rockwell and Marc C. Particelli are senior VP and VP, respectively, at Booz-Allen & Hamilton, New York. This article is adapted from their presentation to the Assn. of National Advertisers' new product workshop last fall.

NEW PRODUCT STRATEGY:
How the Pros Do It

by John R. Rockwell and Marc C. Particelli

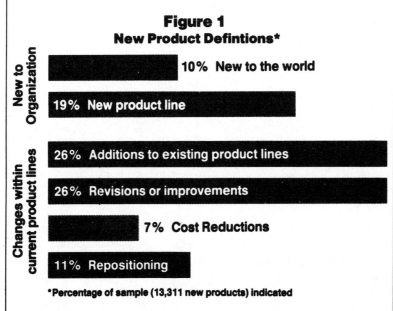

Figure 1
New Product Definitions*

New to Organization

10% New to the world

19% New product line

Changes within current product lines

26% Additions to existing product lines

26% Revisions or improvements

7% Cost Reductions

11% Repositioning

*Percentage of sample (13,311 new products) indicated

- Set flexible performance criteria;
- Refine their investments in the new products process;
- Experiment with organizational structures
- Identify opportunistic advantages;
- Accumulate experience;
- Manage innovation;
- Measure success by volume improvements.

The winners of tomorrow will be

time. They are also more likely to have a strategic plan, and be committed to growing through internally developed new products.

The new product strategy links corporate objectives to the new product effort, and provides direction for the new product process. The step identifies the strategic roles to be played by new products—roles that depend on the type of product itself and the industry. It also helps set the formal financial criteria to be used in measuring new product performance and in screening and evaluating new product ideas.

Change has altered the mortality curve for new product ideas dramatically.

Our 1968 survey of new product practices found that it took 58 new product ideas or

need five; industrial goods companies need seven.

More management attention and more financial resources are devoted to the early steps in the new product process than was the case a decade ago.

In 1968, roughly one-half of all new product expenditures were made during the commercialization stage (Figure 4). Today, commercialization accounts for only one-fourth of all new product expenditures. Conversely, the portion of expenditures in the early steps—idea/concept generation, screening and evaluation, and business analysis—more than doubled during the same period, from 10% in 1968 to 21% in 1981.

We are not suggesting, however, that the fundamentals of success in new products management have changed. The factors contributing to success remain much the same as in the past. Products must meet

Figure 2
Seven Stages of the New Product Process

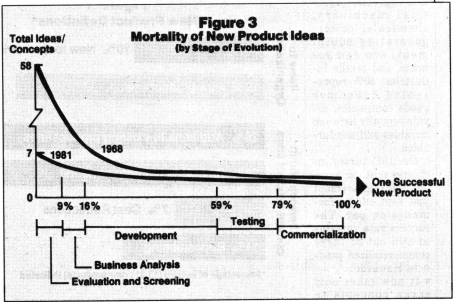

companies that realize success is a journey, not a moment in time. They will continue to improve. Committed to change, they will:
- Address the specific needs of market segments;
- Use strategy as a management prerequisite;
- Manage with stringent criteria;
- Reorder investments, focusing more on homework;
- Customize structures based on strategic roles of new products:
- Build sustainable advantages in economics and marketplace value;
- Exploit cumulative experience from each new product introduction;
- Institutionalize entrepreneurship through incentives for risk taking;
- Reward the new products manager for return rather than volume.

THE PROCESS

How well-prepared U.S. companies are to select, develop and successfully bring new products to the marketplace in the 1980s is suggested by the major survey findings:

Most companies use a formal new product process, usually beginning with identifying the new product strategy (Figure 2).

Companies that have successfully launched new products—a success being a product which met or exceeded its objectives—are more likely to have had a formal new product process in place for a longer period of

concepts to generate one successful new product. Today, greater understanding of the importance of the marketplace has reduced concept mortality to an average of seven ideas per successful new product, as indicated in Figure 3. The change has affected all industries. Packaged goods companies need 16 concepts per one success; consumer durable companies

Figure 3
Mortality of New Product Ideas
(by Stage of Evolution)

337

market needs. True innovation often requires identification of as yet unarticulated market needs. Products must be based on technological superiority, and they need support from top management.

Interestingly, comparing product development in the United States and Japan, a major difference is the extent to which the Japanese invest in up-front analysis—defining new products prior to extensive investment. While Americans have improved in that area of new products management, the Japanese are still ahead.

The percentage of total new product expenditures allocated to products that are ultimately successful has increased.

As Figure 4 illustrates, that percentage grew from 30% in 1968 to 54% today. The probable causes are the reduction in the number of ideas considered and the increase in resource allocations to early process steps.

New products managers define specific new product roles.

Some roles are clearly market driven. Others are internally driven. In many cases, those roles fill multiple needs, as indicated in Figure 5 where the percentages based on responses to our survey add up to far more than 100%.

Today, companies have some kind of financial measurement system for detailed new product analysis.

Of all the firms sampled, 65% formally measure new product performance, most using multiple performance criteria.

Their measurement "kits" include such approaches as calculating internal rates of return and present value in addition to the criteria of sales volume, contribution to profit and length of payback period.

Companies often vary their measurement approach based on the roles expected of their new products efforts. For example, entering a new market with a new-to-the-world product presents high risks and requires a higher expected performance to compensate for those risks. But companies recognize the probable inaccuracy of forecasts. They apply financial criteria as disciplines to thinking rather than impediments to risk taking.

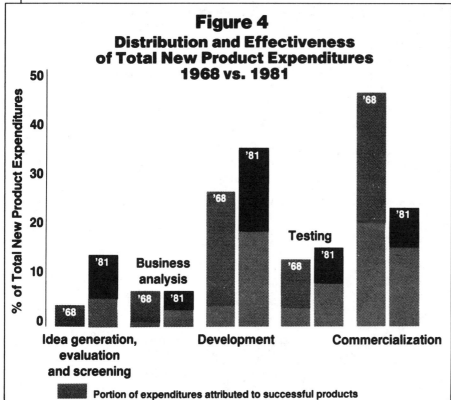

Figure 4
Distribution and Effectiveness of Total New Product Expenditures 1968 vs. 1981

Portion of expenditures attributed to successful products

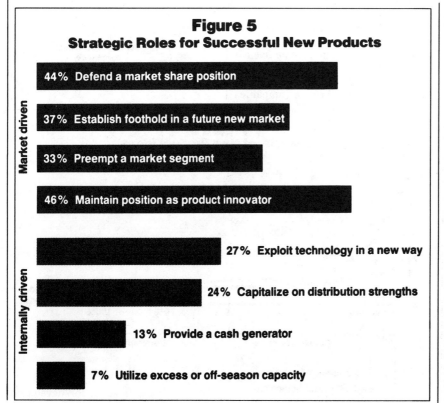

Figure 5
Strategic Roles for Successful New Products

Market driven
- 44% Defend a market share position
- 37% Establish foothold in a future new market
- 33% Preempt a market segment
- 46% Maintain position as product innovator

Internally driven
- 27% Exploit technology in a new way
- 24% Capitalize on distribution strengths
- 13% Provide a cash generator
- 7% Utilize excess or off-season capacity

The more successful companies have pursued a consistent, disciplined new products effort for an extended period of time.

Another focus of our 1981 study was the value of experience and consistency. We found that experience yields a 71% cost curve. That is, after a company has introduced one new product, the cost of introducing the second new product will be 71% of the first.

A doubling of the number to four introductions reduces the cost again by 29%. At each doubling of the number of new products introduced, the cost of the most recent introduction declines at a 71% rate (See Figure 6. On a logarithmic scale, the cost curve is a straight line).

An organization can achieve a competitive advantage from experience. For example, if Company A and Company B both introduce two new products and are equally effective in managing them, both will experience the same cost-per-introduction. If, however, Company B continues to devote resources and attention to new products, moving ahead of Company A in experience, Company B will achieve a sizable and sustainable new product introduction cost advantage.

Experience also improves effectiveness and increases the rate of success. We believe that cost decline and the benefits of experience require continuity in the new products process. Fits and starts diminish an organization's ability to achieve cost declines and effectiveness improvements.

Almost half the companies surveyed use more than one type of organization structure to guide new product programs.

More than three-fourths of those companies tie their choice of structure to specific requirements of the products introduced. Some organization schemes can be described as freestanding: a separate team reports to a general manager. Others can be described as functionally based: a team housed within a functional department and relies on part-time support from other departments if required. Figure 7 indicates our findings on the distribution of the different types of organizations.

Successful companies tend to use more than one organizational concept, mixing and matching not only the approach but the types of skills and the leadership elements of the team.

THREE APPROACHES

Companies use three basic organizational approaches and relate them and their organizational elements to the requirements for differing new product types (Figure 8).

The first is the *entrepreneurial* approach, typically used for developing

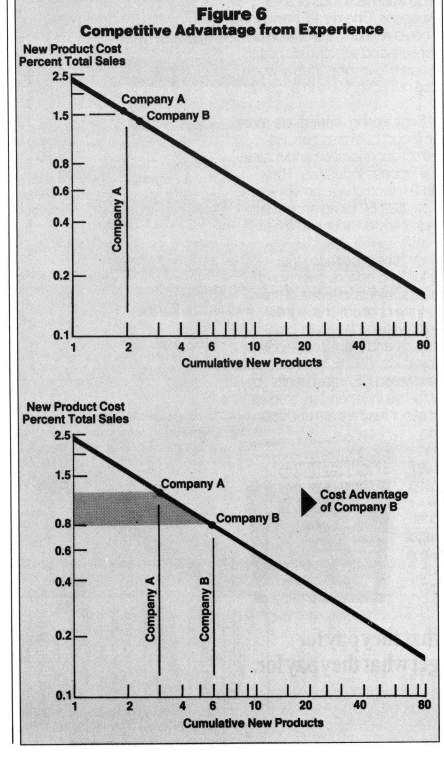

Figure 6
Competitive Advantage from Experience

new-to-the-world products. The structure requires an interdisciplinary venture team and a manager with the ability to integrate diverse functional skills. It operates as an autonomous new products group, usually reporting to a general manager. Success requires the involvement of, and a strong commitment from top management.

Typically, the process, the measurement structure, and the requirements for formal business planning are less rigid than in other approaches. Usually, an incentive system promotes risk taking by rewarding handsomely for success.

The second is the *collegial* approach, typically used to enter new businesses or add substantially different products to existing lines.

It requires strong senior-management support and participation in decision making, a commitment to risk taking, and a formal new products process to guide the effort and ensure discipline.

It also requires a clear commitment to provide whatever is necessary for success and for expediting decisions.

The third is the *managerial* approach. This is the standard process used for existing business management. It involves strong planning and heavy emphasis on functional leadership to drive new products in manufacturing, distribution, marketing or the like.

It tends to be a rigid new products process involving many levels of management, quick promotion of successful new product managers, limited risk incentives, and rigorous application of financial criteria.

The more successful companies match all those elements to specific new products opportunities. The organizational approach and extent of top-management support vary, based on the specific needs of each new products opportunity. As the newness of the product increases, the entrepreneurial, integrative focus of the team increases, along with the involvement and support of top management, as illustrated in Figure 8.

> **The success rate of commercialized new products has not improved, on average during the last two decades.**

In the period from 1963 to 1968, 67% of all new products introduced were successful; they met company-specific financial and strategic criteria. From 1976 to 1981, a 65% rate of success was achieved.

More companies are using a more sophisticated new product process, thereby reducing the number of new ideas needed to generate a successful product and increasing the portion of total resources spent on market "win-

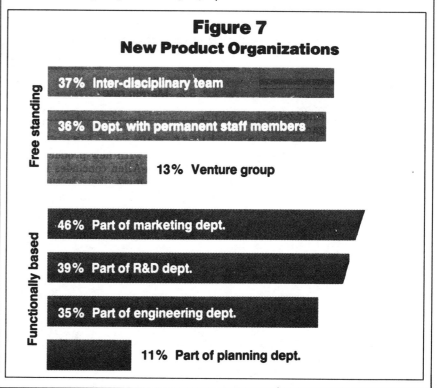

Figure 7
New Product Organizations

Free standing
- 37% Inter-disciplinary team
- 36% Dept. with permanent staff members
- 13% Venture group

Functionally based
- 46% Part of marketing dept.
- 39% Part of R&D dept.
- 35% Part of engineering dept.
- 11% Part of planning dept.

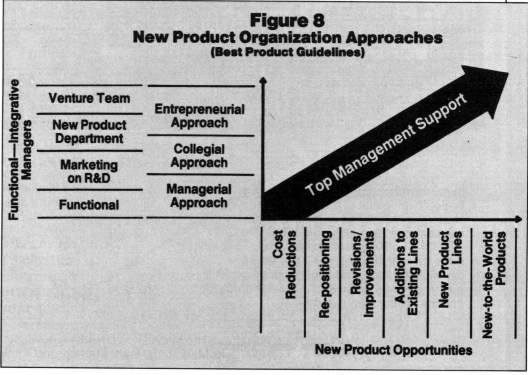

Figure 8
New Product Organization Approaches
(Best Product Guidelines)

Functional—Integrative Managers:
- Venture Team
- New Product Department
- Marketing on R&D
- Functional

Approaches:
- Entrepreneurial Approach
- Collegial Approach
- Managerial Approach

Top Management Support

New Product Opportunities:
- Cost Reductions
- Re-positioning
- Revisions/Improvements
- Additions to Existing Lines
- New Product Lines
- New-to-the-World Products

Figure 9
Top Management Expectations
for Coming Five Years
(Improvement over past five years)

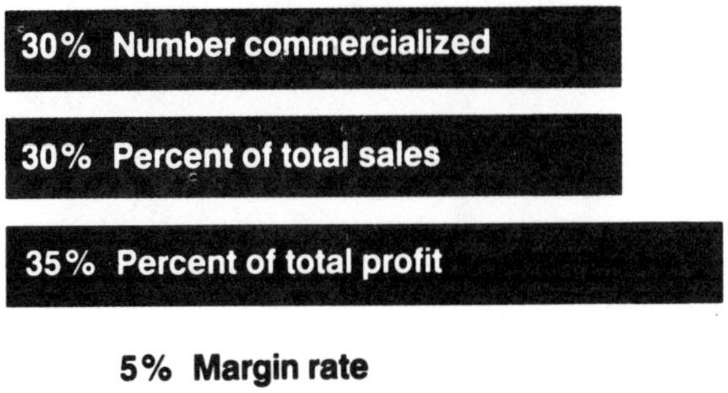

30% Number commercialized

30% Percent of total sales

35% Percent of total profit

5% Margin rate

ners." And more companies are fitting the organization structures used to their product-specific requirements.

Yet, there has been virtually no change in the rate of successful introductions.

New product managers therefore face the challenge of improving new product performance to meet their greater new product objectives (Figure 9).

To that end, and based on our findings from the survey and our in-depth interviews with new product executives, Booz-Allen concludes that the companies most likely to succeed in the development and introduction of new products in the 1980s will be those which:

● Make the long-term commitment needed to support innovation and new product development;

● Implement an approach tailored to the company and driven by corporate objectives and strategies, with a well-defined new product strategy at its core;

● Capitalize on accumulated experience to achieve and maintain competitive advantage;

● Establish an environment—a management style, organizational structure, and degree of top management support—conductive to achieving company-specific new product and corporate objectives. ■

From a review of several studies,

the authors show the pros and

cons of . . .

Ad Experiments for Management Decisions

Ben M. Enis and Keith K. Cox

That old shibboleth "you cannot measure the effectiveness of advertising decisions" is under attack. A potent weapon in this attack is experimentation. Consider these examples:

A well-known manufacturer measured the effectiveness of advertising for one of its customer products by budgeting an amount equal to last year's advertising appropriation in three territories, one-and-one-half times last year's appropriation in three other territories, and four times last year's appropriation in three additional territories. For each appropriation, one territory had a low market share, one a medium market share, and one a high market share. (Buzzell, 1964)

Housewives about to enter a supermarket were asked to detour through a large van equipped as a movie studio. The housewives viewed a set of television commercials, including two different versions of a commercial for the product of interest. Then their

purchases of that product in the supermarket were measured. (Jennsen, 1966)

A trade association wanted to know the effect of promoting apples with a general health theme versus an apple-use theme. The sales of apples using both promotions in a group of supermarkets were then measured. (Henderson, Hind, and Brown, 1961)

A manufacturer of felt pens wanted to measure the effect of a new point-of-purchase display in retail stores. The sales of pens using both new and existing displays were measured in drug and stationery stores. (McClure and West, 1972)

College students evaluated the effects of corrective advertising upon an actual advertisement for a gasoline additive. The attitudes of the students were measured given different attack and inoculation levels. (Hunt, 1973)

Each of these five examples is an experiment in advertising effectiveness,

although they may appear at first glance to be very different. While the potential value of experimentally generated information for advertising decision-making has often been expounded in the literature, much of the actual value of such information is often lost upon those who actually make the decisions. Many marketing managers do not (i.e., cannot or will not) interpret and use experimental data effectively in decision-making, particularly in the advertising area.

The purpose of this article is to present three areas that should aid those who must make decisions about advertising in understanding and using experimental data. First, the nature of experimentation is developed by defining and explaining each element in an experimental model. Next, the evaluation of experimental results, involving questions of internal and external validity, is explained. Third, a framework for managerial interpretation of an experiment is presented.

Nature of Experimentation

The first step in understanding the nature of experimentation is to define the term. Our definition is:

> an experiment is performed when explanatory variables are manipulated, and the effects of this manipulation upon a dependent variable are measured.

Note that the distinguishing characteristic of an experiment is that the ex-

Ben M. Enis (Ph.D., Louisiana State University) is professor of marketing at the University of Houston. He has written in such scholarly publications as *The Journal of Marketing, Journal of Advertising Research, California Management Review, Business and Society Review/Innovation, Business Horizons, Decision Sciences* and *Journal of Retailing*. Dr. Enis's teaching ability has been recognized in separate awards by the University of Houston's College of Business Administration Alumni Association and its Faculty Senate. He is the author of *Marketing Principles: The Management Process*, and coauthor of *The Marketing Research Process, Marketing Decisions: A Bayesian Approach*, and *Experimentation for Marketing Decisions*. He is also coeditor of the anthology *Marketing Classics*, now in its second edition.

planatory variable is manipulated—before measuring the effect upon the dependent variable. Unfortunately, the process of measuring the effects of this manipulation is often confounded by other extraneous variables. Managerial interpretation of marketing experiments therefore can be a complex task.

One way of simplifying this task is to view the experiment from a systems perspective: inputs processed to produce outputs. As shown in Figure 1, the inputs are two types of independent variables: the explanatory variable (variable being manipulated) and the extraneous variables. Processing is accomplished by test units, and the output is the effects of the independent variables upon the dependent variable.

Applying the model to marketing situations, one begins by precisely defining each of the four elements of the experimental model:

1. **Explanatory Variable.** The independent variable or variables which the experimenter will manipulate. In marketing, explanatory variables are generally some aspect of the marketing mix; advertising strategies are often tested.

2. **Test Units.** These are the entities affected by the manipulation of the explanatory variables and the influences of extraneous variables. In marketing, the two broad classes of test units are people (customers or potential customers) and physical entities (stores, sales territories, product lines, etc.).

3. **Dependent Variable.** This is the criterion or standard for measuring attainment of the experimental objective. In marketing, the ideal dependent variable is sales or profit, but the effect of various extraneous variables upon sales is often difficult to determine. Consequently, other variables such as adver-

tising recall scores, brand preference ratings, and customers' attitudes are also used.

4. **Extraneous Variables.** These are factors other than the explanatory variable that affect the dependent variable. In marketing, there are so many such influences that it is useful to categorize them. Broadly speaking, the categories are internal (organizational) and external (environmental). The internal extraneous variables are those aspects of the marketing mix—product, price, promotion, distribution—that are not manipulated in a given experiment. The external category can be subdivided into customer variables (individual attitudes

Keith K. Cox is professor of marketing at the University of Houston. He is presently vice president of the marketing education division of the American Marketing Association. Dr. Cox has previously published articles in such diverse journals as the *Journal of Marketing, Journal of Marketing Research, Journal of Advertising Research, Public Opinion Quarterly, Social Science Quarterly*, and *Journal of Retailing*. He is a member of the editorial board of the *Journal of Marketing* and *Journal of Business Research*.

and actions, and group influences), competitors (marketers of similar products, and other products that satisfy the same generic need), and other influences — e.g., economic trends and conditions, actions of governmental bodies, technological advances, seasonal variations, etc.

Using these definitions, the experimental model shown in Figure 1 can be applied to any marketing experiment. Table 1 illustrates such an application to the five experiments presented in the introduction.

For example, the advertising effectiveness study attempted to explain various levels of profitability of a certain product (the dependent variable) in terms of differences in the level of advertising expenditures (independent variable) in certain sales territories (test units). There were, however, a number of other (extraneous) influences upon product profitability, including different market shares in the territories, competitors' actions, advertising copy, climate, and so on. Application of the model to the other situations is similarly interpreted. The point is that if experimentation is viewed from a systems perspective, the nature of the various elements of marketing experiments can be comprehended rather closely.

Validity of an Experiment

Comprehension is an important first step, but the manager's interest focuses on information that is useful for decision-making. The function of information is to reduce uncertainty as to the best course of action in a given situation. The marketing manager, therefore, needs not only to comprehend, but also to know how to evaluate an experiment. Evaluation of experiments involve basically two considerations; internal validity and external validity.

Internal Validity. An experiment is said to have internal validity if the experimentor has confidence that the ex-

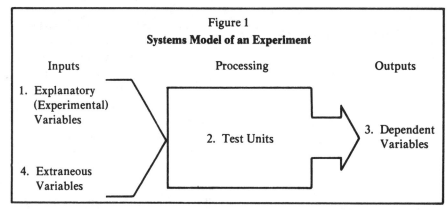

Figure 1
Systems Model of an Experiment

Inputs
1. Explanatory (Experimental) Variables

4. Extraneous Variables

Processing

2. Test Units

Outputs

3. Dependent Variables

planatory variable caused the result observed in the dependent variable. That is, an ideal experiment occurs when the effect upon the dependent variable is caused only by the explanatory variable. Three conditions are necessary to show causation. First, there must be a correlation between the explanatory (independent) variable and the dependent variable. Second, the manipulation of the independent variable must have occurred before the effect is observed in the dependent variable. And third, alternative plausible explanations for the observed effect of the dependent variable must be eliminated.

The first two conditions are relatively straightforward. If some degree of correlation is not observed, and if the independent variable did not occur first in time, then there is no basis for an argument that the independent variable caused the dependent variable to occur. The elimination of alternative plausible explanations for correlations, however, is a more complex condition to meet. In general, there are four possible explanations for an observed correlation; these are summarized in Table 2.

As the table illustrates, the researcher is attempting to show that X causes Y: for example, an increase in advertising causes an increase in sales. But there are three alternative possibilities: It may be that Y caused X, or at least occurred before X occurred (the time sequence condition); or it may be that a third variable Z caused the change in both X and Y; or for some undetermined

reason, the dependent variable Y is correlated with some other variable. If there is correlation between X and Y and the time sequence is correct (i.e., X occurred before Y did), then determination of causation rests upon control of the effect of other extraneous variables and the effects of chance. In the literature, these two effects are referred to as bias and random error, respectively.

In general there are five types of biases, termed "threats to internal validity" by Campbell and Stanley (1963). These are:

1. **History**—refers to the occurrence of specific events during the period of the experiment; e.g., changes in competitive strategies, seasonal variation, changes in customer tastes, new governmental regulations. The longer the time period of an experiment, the more likely it is that historical development may have biased the experiment.

2. **Maturation**—occurs when the test units themselves mature (change) over the period of the experiment. Customers grow older, for example, and supermarkets become physically obsolescent over time.

3. **Testing Effects**—arise when the test units are measured before the explanatory variable is manipulated, and then remeasured after manipulation; knowledge that the measurement is to occur can cause changes in the test unit. Testing effects are prominent when people are used as test units.

4. **Instrumentation**—measurement error;

i.e., changes in the recording instrument over the period of the experiment; illegible entries, counting mistakes, programming errors, etc.

5. **Equivalency**—the result of unequal influence of the test units in the experiment. For example, if total sales in one supermarket are larger than total sales in another, sales of the product of interest are also likely to be larger in the first store, regardless of the effect of the explanatory variable.

In general, bias is controlled physically. For example, if advertising copy is the explanatory variable, the effects of history can be controlled by holding constant the price of the product, its distribution channels, packaging, etc. Instrumentation can be controlled by carefully training and supervising interviewers, and by double checking calculations. Testing effects can be handled by omitting or disguising

the before measurement, and equivalency is achieved by selecting stores or territories of the same size or sales level.

Bias can also be controlled statistically. In the DuPont advertising effectiveness study, each of the three experimental treatments was assigned to three different territories to account for different levels of market share. The effects of different market shares was then statistically removed (the usual terminology is "blocked") from the effects of the explanatory variable.

Statistical control is more often used to account for the effects of chance. Test units are assigned randomly to different groups, and explanatory variables (treatments) are randomly assigned to test units, to allow the application of mathematical probability techniques to the measurement of the effects of chance. Such measurements are useful in experiments, and have been refined to a high degree of precision. (Banks, 1965;

Cox and Enis, 1969). This precision, however, sometimes results in overemphasis upon controlling the effects of chance—at the expense of controlling the effects of bias.

Most advertising experiments use some type of test of statistical significance. A statistically significant result means, roughly speaking, that chance is unlikely to have played a major role in this particular observed result. Before statistical significance can be translated into causation, however, the effect of bias must also be accounted for.

In his search for internal validity, the experimenter has a number of alternative experimental designs at his disposal. That is, there are various standard models for constructing an experiment. From a managerial viewpoint, the names and mechanics of constructing a specific design are not essential to an understanding of their purpose, which is to increase the internal

Table 1

The Experimental Model Applied to Five Advertising Situations

Model Elements

Situation Description	1. Explanatory Variable	2. Test Units	3. Dependent Variable	4. Extraneous Variables (Examples)
Advertising Effectiveness (Buzzell)	Levels of advertising expenditure	Sales territories	Product profitability	Market share, competitors' actions, quality of advertisements, climate, product quality, price
Types of Television Commercial (Jennsen)	Different TV commercials	Shopping center patrons	Sales redemption of product coupons	Customers' attitudes, competing ads, product quality, availability, price
Apple Promotion (Henderson, et al)	Different promotion themes (use vs. health)	Supermarkets	Sales of apples	Customer preferences, total store sales, seasonal variations, competing promotion, price
Point-of-Purchase Promotion (McClure, et al)	Different POP displays	Drug and stationery stores	Sales of felt markers	Competitors' actions, out-of-stock conditions, weather
Product Attitude Measurement (Hunt)	Corrective and inoculation advertising themes	University students	Attitude toward product	Students' product knowledge, laboratory setting, Use of students

validity of an experiment. The manager can evaluate the internal validity of an experiment by checking physical and statistical controls upon bias and random error.

External Validity

In addition to internal validity, the second dimension of an experiment is external validity—generalizing the experimental results to situations other than the one in which the experiment was conducted. Note that we stress in addition to, not instead of: an experiment must possess internal validity to be of any value at all. If it does have internal validity, the managerial usefulness of an experiment increases to the degree that its results can be generalized to other situations. Basically, generalization can occur in two ways: from sample to population and from the particular elements employed in an experiment to other elements.

The first type of external validity is generalization of the specific sample of elements employed to the population of those elements. In the types of television commercial experiments, the results would be more useful if they applied to all customers in the city, not just to the shopping center patrons who actually participated in the experiment. A second type of generalization occurs where the results from the population in the experiment can be generalized to other types of population. Could the apple promotion results, for instance, be applied to promotions for pears, potatoes, or other fruits and vegetables?

From the perspective of the researcher performing the experiment, the basic procedure for increasing external validity is to replicate the experiment, using different elements from the same population or even elements from different populations. In terms of managerial evaluation, there are two bases for judging external validity: internal validity and relevance to reality.

Table 2
Four Explanations of Correlation

Symbolic Relationship	Explanation	Marketing Example
$X \rightarrow Y$	The independent variable X causes a change in dependent variable Y.	An increase in advertising (X) causes an increase in sales (Y).
$X \leftarrow Y$	The dependent variable Y causes a change in independent variable X.	An increase in sales (Y) causes advertising (X) to increase — many advertising budgets are set on a percentage of sales basis.
$X \nwarrow^{Z}\nearrow Y$	Another independent variable Z causes a change in X and Y.	An increase in GNP (Z) causes sales (Y) and advertising (X) to increase.
Chance $U \leftrightarrow Y$	For no plausible reason, U and Y happen to be correlated.	Over time, sales (Y) are highly correlated with salaries of ministers (U)

First, as noted above, it should be obvious that if an experiment is not internally valid, then it is of little value. Invalid data cannot legitimately support generalization.

Even an internally valid experiment, however, may not be relevant to the particular decision which a manager faces. The situation in which the experiment was actually performed must be sufficiently representative of the one in which the manager is interested so that applying the results provides useful information for the situation of interest. Relevance is, of course, determined by the manager.

Manager's Guide to Interpretation

The systems model of experimentation and the discussion of experimental validity provide the bases for a framework for the managerial interpretation of any experiment. This framework is presented in Table 3.

The first step in interpreting an experiment is to understand the problem as defined by the experimenter. This

step makes use of the systems model to first define the elements of the experiment: the explanatory variable, ex-

Table 3
Framework for the Managerial Interpretation of an Experiment

1. **Problem Definition**— What is the purpose of the experiment?
   a. elements: explanatory variables, test units, dependent variable
   b. hypotheses of the study

2. **Evaluation**—How good are the experimental results?
   a. internal validity
   b. external validity

3. **Results**—What do the data show?
   a. the numbers
   b. managerial assessment of the numbers

4. **Decision Implications**—How do the results contribute to decision-making?
   a. action suggested by results
   b. possible consequence of this action

traneous variables, test units, and dependent variable. Once these are identified, the purpose of the experiment should be easy to determine. That is, the hypotheses should be readily apparent once the elements have been identified. Evaluating the experiment is simply a matter of applying the discussion of internal and external validity to the situation at hand. With respect to internal validity, the manager should check for physical or statistical controls on history, maturation, instrumentation, testing effects, and equivalency of test units. External validity, as previously noted, is a matter of internal validity plus relevance to the problem at hand.

Once the problem definition is understood and the experiment evaluated, the next step is to determine the results of the experiment. This step has two phases: identifying the pertinent numbers and assessing the managerial significance of the numbers. The apple promotion experiment, for example, is reported in terms of percentage change of the health and apple-use themes from no promotion, and an F-ratio significant at the one per cent level. The manager must first identify these numbers, and then ask himself what they mean in managerial terms. In this case, it turned out that the apple-use theme produced the largest percentage change in sales of apples, and it would be highly unlikely that a change of this magnitude could be the result of random fluctuation in sales levels of apples.

Finally, the manager should assess the decision implications of these results. The apple promotion results suggest that the apple growers should concentrate on an apple-use theme in their advertising and point-of-purchase displays. Before deciding to implement this action, however, the manager should give some thought to possible consequences to this action—e.g., the cost of such a theme and possible reaction by competitors.

To illustrate the application of this framework in a systematic fashion, it is applied to the Hunt (1973) study on product attitude measurement. This is not a scholarly critique of Hunt's work to be studied by other experts. Rather, the purpose is to present his experiment via a procedure that a manager not particularly well-versed in experimental methodology can understand and use in decision-making.

Problem Definition. Hunt carefully defined the problem he investigated. The explanatory variables were (1) three levels of attack (none, general, and explicit); and (2) three levels of inoculation (none, supportive, and reputational). Technically, this is a three-by-three factorial design, which permits measurement of the interactions among independent variables. The test units were junior and senior students in a major university. The dependent variable was an attitude scale: degree of liking for the product. Extraneous variables that could influence liking for the product might include the artificiality of the test situation (students as subjects, a pencil-and-paper test), the nature of measuring scale (ordinal or internal, 29-point scale), general social attitudes toward pollution, and competitors' advertisements.

Two major hypotheses were clearly labeled in the article. First, attack statements about the product reduce the favorable attitude toward the product. Secondly, inoculation against possible attacks inhibits the reduction of favorable attitudes due to the attack. The experimental design also implies a belief that different levels of attack and inoculation interact.

Evaluation. This experiment has a fairly high degree of internal validity. History and maturation bias were minimized by conducting the experiment in one sitting, and not requiring repeat measures over time. However, the equivalency bias might be high, since the group of students assigned to each treatment may not have similar attitudes toward the product before the experiment.

Testing effects might also be significant here. The students knew that they were participating in an experiment involving a socially significant topic — pollution. It may be that this knowledge biased their responses. Evaluation of the instrument used becomes a bit technical. A statistician, for example, might question Hunt's assumption that the attitude scale used can measure in interval rather than ordinal terms. And a psychologist might wonder whether a subject can effectively discriminate even in ordinal fashion, among 29 degrees of liking for a product. However, these issues are common in behavioral research. Most researchers would agree that the internal validity of Hunt's experiment is adequate.

More serious questions can be raised about the external validity of the experiment. Students' attitudes may not represent those of most users of gasoline. And since they apparently were not randomly selected, it would be theoretically incorrect to project sample results even to the population of students.

Also, generalizing the results to other products or to other types of attitude scales is probably not justified without replicating the experiment. This study alone does not prove the efficacy of the corrective ad concept.

Results. The analysis of variance shows that attack ads do generally result in less favorable levels of attitudes. In addition, there is a statistically significant interaction between the inoculation and attack variables. This means that inoculation against possible attacks did inhibit attack effects in this study. Differences of this magnitude are unlikely to be the result of chance. Since other possible causes of observed differences were adequately controlled, one can comfortably accept Hunt's findings.

This study showed that in at least one instance, corrective attack ads do reduce favorable attitudes toward the advertised product. In addition, a refutational inoculation appeal before an explicit attack argument tended to inhibit the attack effects. The study demonstrates potential broad applications of inoculation theory. Specifically, Hunt's rule of inoculation explicitness appears possible.

It must be emphasized, however, that these conclusions are derived from one experiment, and one of rather limited external validity at that. Decision-makers —both public-makers and advertising strategists—should regard these results as tentative and subject to further research. Hunt's work is generally sound methodologically; it is provocative, and is potentially very significant. But it is not conclusive. Additional work in this area is required to support sound decision-making.

Conclusions

Experimentation can be a very useful data-generating procedure for advertising decision-making. One of the limitations has been a lack of skill in interpreting experiments on the part of marketing decision-makers. Organizing the interpretation procedure into a framework provides a foundation for improving decision-making expertise in this area. Knowledgeable decision makers would then be in a position to evaluate the costs and benefits of experimentation relative to other data generating procedures.

We believe that marketing managers should place a high priority on attaining such knowledge, because we expect the use of experimentation in advertising to increase in the future. The costs of making incorrect decisions are rising, concepts and techniques of experimentation in marketing are improving, and public policy-makers are increasingly requiring documented evidence of advertising effectiveness. For these reasons, we believe that the framework offered here for interpreting advertising experiments can be useful in decision-making.

References

Banks, Seymour. *Experimentation in Marketing.* New York: McGraw-Hill, 1965.

Buzzell, Robert D. E.I. DuPont de Nemours & Co., Inc. *Mathematical Models and Marketing Management.* Boston: Harvard Business School Division of Research, 1964.

Campbell, Donald T. and Julian C. Stanley. *Experimental and Quasi-Experimental Designs for Research.* Chicago: Rand McNally Co., Inc., 1963.

Cox, Keith K. and Ben M. Enis. *Experimentation for Marketing Decisions.* Scranton, Pa.: International Textbook Co., Inc., 1969.

Hunt, H. Keith. Effects of Corrective Advertising. *Journal of Advertising Research,* Vol. 13, No. 5, pp. 15-22.

Henderson, Peter L., James F. Hind, and Sidney E. Brown. Sales Effects of Two Campaign Themes, *Journal of Advertising Research,* Vol. 1, No. 4, pp. 15-20.

Jennsen, Ward J. Sales Effects of TV, Radio, and Print Advertising. *Journal of Advertising Research,* Vol. 6, No. 2, pp. 2-7.

McClure, Peter J. and E. James West. Sales Effect of a New Counter Display. *Journal of Advertising Research,* Vol. 9, No. 1, pp. 29-34.

Pretesting the Effectiveness of Industrial Advertising

P. Vanden Abeele

I. Butaye

This article addresses the pretesting of industrial advertising messages diffused through (mass) communications media such as professional and trade journals. It is based on case-study experience and presents a normative framework for pretesting industrial advertising.

FRAMEWORK FOR PRETESTING INDUSTRIAL PRINT ADVERTISING

Industrial advertising is characterized by wide variety of communication tasks, situations, and targets. It is well documented that the communication affects the predispositions and decisions of the audience in several ways, depending on the situation and the prospect [1-3]. A distinction is made between three decision hierarchies: the high-involvement–learning hierarchy, the high-involvement–dissonance hierarchy, and the low-involvement–self-perception hierarchy. The high-involvement hierarchy assumes a rationally disposed individual facing a potential decision situation. His acts are largely guided by his evaluation of the decision alternatives based

Address correspondence to: Dr. Vanden Abeele, D.T.E.W. Katholieke Universiteit Leuven, Dekenstraat 2, B-3000 Leuven, Belgium.

on available and acquired information. Promotion and advertising fulfill the multiple tasks of informing the prospect, of shaping his evaluative assessments, and facilitating the decision making. The high-involvement-dissonance hierarchy assumes a rationalizing individual. Promotion and communication serves the purpose of bolstering the audience's confidence in the adequacy of a choice already made. This "maintenance" function is realized by providing additional supporting information in order to strengthen the evaluation of the selected alternative, in order to foster loyalty. The low-involvement–self-perception hierarchy assumes an individual who is not motivated to search or acquire information nor to rationalize. Advertising mainly serves the purpose of making the prospect aware of the offer and of providing him with a concise symbol or meaning in order to facilitate his potential interaction with the advertised product or service.

These three decision hierarchies usually apply to industrial advertising. Compared to consumer convenience goods promotion, the rational mode is expected to occur more frequently because of the involvement inherent in the choice or important decision. The rationalizing mode may occur in instances where the choice decision did not reveal a clearly superior alternative or where the customer is bound to face some disappointment following

Reprinted with permission from *Industrial Marketing Management*, vol. 9, pp. 75–83, Feb. 1980.
Copyright © 1980 by Elsevier Science Publishing Co., Inc.

purchase. The low-involvement mode applies where advertising is not concerned with a particular product or service, but rather with the identity of a unknown or complex supplier.

These decision hierarchies tend to assign a different role to advertising and require a rather different communication process.

1. In the high-involvement, rational mode the emphasis lies first on communication of information, next on creating favorable evaluation, and finally on helping to elicit behavior. Therefore advertising messages should be designed less to attract initial attention. They should allow easy self-selection by the interested target segment (illustration, headline). They should facilitate the transmission of factual information and lead to favorable evaluations. Behavior elicitation may be less relevant unless the message can elicit a proxy for the ultimately desired response (send for more information, request trial, etc.). Repetition is less likely to be useful in this context.

2. In the high-involvement–rationalizing mode, positive evaluation is likely to spontaneously follow behavioral commitment. Information consistent with these evaluations and with experience is likely to be sought out. As in the previous high-involvement hierarchy, gaining initial attention is a function less of the message than of the respondent. The advertisement should allow the prospect to self-select himself as a member of the target audience. The message must convey information (communication) which is consistent with the evaluation. Repetition with variation is more likely to pay.

3. In the low involvement mode, positive evaluation

should follow behavioral commitment due mainly to nonadvertising stimuli. The task of advertising is to make the audience aware of the offer or of the advertiser and to establish a concise set of symbols or referents; eventually the purpose may also be to strengthen this set of symbols and their meaning or to alter them. In order to fulfill his task, the message must be able to capture initial attention and to convey "meaning-in-a-nutshell" to the uninvolved reader. It is important to ascertain that the desired "image" is communicated. Repetition is likely to be an important means for realizing these objectives.

Table 1 details the role of particular communication effects for influencing the audience's decision process.

Audience

Careful targetting of industrial advertising is very important since the market potential and the need for information differs from individual to individual. Different communication approaches are to be used depending on whether the audience is a purchaser, an initiator, a decision influencer, decision orientator, or decision approver. The characteristics of these types are shown in Table 2.

In addition, it is important to consider the impact of previous commitments to a supplier on the effectiveness of industrial advertising. Research on consumer convenience goods advertising shows that the test results of commercial messages are influenced by the respondent's loyalty to the brand or supplier [4]. Such effects could be even stronger in the case of industrial advertising, where the commitment tends to be stronger and the exposure context more involving.

The main characteristics of the audience, insofar as they affect pretesting can be summarized as follows:

- It is important to test the communication with the (carefully specified) target group.
- The communications task to be fulfilled will differ according to the decision role of the target.
- The target will generally be receptive to the information, if the information search or information reception mode prevails. This will be less the case for corporate image advertising.
- Previous supplier commitments and attitutdes are likely to be potent determinants of advertising effectiveness.

P. VANDEN ABEELE is a faculty member at the Department of Applied Economic Sciences at the Katholieke Universiteit Leuven in Belgium. He teaches courses in Marketing and directs the MBA Program of his University. He is a graduate in Applied Economics from Leuven and holder of a MS statistics and Ph.D. in Marketing from Stanford University. He is researching the communication process of advertising and consulting in advertising research.

I. BUTAYE holds a degree in Applied Economics from Leuven University and an MBA from Cornell University. He was formerly a research assistant in Marketing and Advertising. He presently heads the Market Research and Consultancy Agency IMARA.

TABLE 1
Decision–Communication Matrix

Communication Process Elements	Decision Hierarchy Type		
	High-Involvement Rational	High-Involvement Rationalizing	Low Involvement
Initial attention	Less important	Less important	Important
Continued attention	Important, respondent should be able to self-select	Important, respondent should be able to self-select	Hard to gain
Symbolic communication	Less important	Less important	Important; message should be able to communicate meaning concisely
Communication of factual information	Factual information important and sought for	Less important; information should be consonant	Less important
Yielding facilitators	Important; should be mobilized	Less important; yielding already occurred	Less important
Yielding inhibitors	Important, should be neutralized	Less important; yielding already occurred	Less important, critical reactions, e.g., source derogation to be prevented
Repetition/retention	Less important, except to increase reach	Moderately important; maintenance and variety required	Important; cognitive learning to be attained

Pretesting Context

Before proceeding to the discussion of case study experience, a comment should be made concerning the research context. Pretesting consumer convenience goods messages is made difficult by several factors which are less prevalent in industrial promotion. The consumer tends to be less involved with the message and its object while the industrial buyer tends to be more involved. Consumer image advertising aims at cognitive shifts which are the outcome of a campaign rather than of a single ad; industrial advertising aims rather at the communication of factual information [5]. The industrial audience is involved with the message in an organizational and nonpersonal way. It is familiar with advertising and promotion in its own firm. It brings a role of expert to the situation which is not out of line with its role in the firm and with its rational approach in being exposed to commercial communication. Therefore, industrial advertising pretests need not be disguised and allow valid investigation of single-exposure effects. The target population may be hard to find for pretesting purposes. The targets may be limited in number or hard to gain access to [6].

TABLE 2
Audience–Communication Needs

Audience Type	Communication Needs
Purchaser	Build up store of factual information on available suppliers and their offer.
Initiator	Suggest use of new products/services; evaluate alternative suppliers.
Influencer	Obtain factual information concerning offer of suppliers. Create favorable attitude towards supplier.
Orientator	Create awareness of and positive attitude towards supplier (image).
Approver	Create awareness of and positive attitude towards supplier.

CASE EXPERIENCE IN PRETESTING ADVERTISEMENTS FOR INDUSTRIAL SERVICES

This case experience deals with an advertisement for industrial services, namely computer services offered by financial institutions as a substitute for or complement to administrative work performed by companies. The advertiser is a leading financial institution having a large share of the corporate customers. The service is not new in concept, but is new in the range of services offered by financial institutions. The prime targets are decision influencers and initiators in administration, finance, EDP, or management.

The message was a full-page advertisement with a four-color illustration, headline, informative copy, sub-illustration, and subheadline. It was inserted in general information journals or professional journals directed at general and functional management. The respondents for the pretest were selected from the target group according to a convenience sample.

Pretesting Methodology

Three types of pretesting were carried out, each on a sample of 25 respondents. The *portfolio-method* [7] exposes the respondent to a folder of potentially relevant industrial advertisements. Normal exposure and reading conditions are simulated. The respondent is probed for message recall and for evaluative comments after a short diversionary conversation intended to blunt immediate memory.

1. *Portfolio Method*. This method has the advantage of its rather natural exposure context. Only responses strong enough to overcome the forgetting process are elicited. The procedure may be lo√ in reactivity, especially if the responses are made in writing. In our case study responses were made verbally to the interviewer. The Portfolio method is hypothesized to be more adequate for assessing responses lower on the communication and decision hierarchies. It allows comparative assessment of messages. On the negative side, the method yields only limited information. Some messages are not recalled, the extent of further responding per recalled message is low and is less adequate for probing a range of responses which are potentially relevant. It should be more appropriate for messages in the rationalizing or low-involvement mode. Finally, the method does not easily allow quantification of responses. This may hinder further analysis of the results.

2. *Jury Method*. This method forces unnatural exposure on the respondent, who is to act as an expert. This role may be appropriate only when the message fits in a rational mode of communication. The

industrial advertising pretest need not be disguised

The *jury method* [7] requires the respondent to comparatively assess a number of potentially relevant industrial advertisements on a set of evaluative scales. In contrast to the foregoing methods, the *Target-Plan method* [8] uses only the pretested message as stimulus. The message is shown successively for a very brief interval, a moderately short interval, and for unlimited time. Appropriate questions follow each of these exposures in order to test what has been noticed, what interpretation is given, and what evaluative comments are elicited. The advertiser supplies the researcher with his "communication targets" to be checked in the test. The presumed properties of the pretesting method w.r.t. the communication and decision process are outlined in Table 3. Table 3 rates the extent to which a method is able to gauge particular responses by means of a +(good), −(bad) or ±(advantages and disadvantages).

We have observed the following:

method is suited to delve deeper into the communication and decision process. It lends itself to quantification and is the least reactive of the three systems. It is well suited to comparative assessment of messages. On the negative side, it is less adequate to gauge the reactions lower in the communication or decision hierarchy and it does not allow for the flexibility needed to investigate responses of interest to one particular message (e.g., targets, image components).

3. *The Target Plan Method*. This is easily the most reactive of the three systems, due to the direct interaction between respondent and interviewer. From Table 3 it is seen to be adequate or reasonably adequate for gauging a wide spectrum of responses, as long as those do not require natural exposure. It is especially adequate for testing decision-process effects either 'n reality or as perceived by the re-

TABLE 3
Measurement Characteristics for Three Pretest Models

Communication Process Effects	Portfolio	Jury	Target Plan
Gain Initial Attention	+ Recall of advertisement	− Direct evaluation of impact	± Short-exposure degree of communication
Gain Continued Attention	± Recall of advertisement, extent of recall	± Direct evaluation of interest, relevance	± Interest in further exposure, direct probing for relevance
Communicate Concise Symbolic Meaning	± Recall of main argument	± Direct evaluation of image-building potential	± Short-exposure interpretation of stimulus
Communicate Factual Information	± Recall of arguments	± Direct evaluation of information transmission	+ Medium-exposure recall of arguments
Facilitate Yielding/ Neutralize Yielding Inhibitors	− Spontaneous or elicited comments	+ Direct questioning of facilitating reactions	± Unlimited-exposure comments
Yielding	− Elicited comments	+ Direct questioning of yielding reactions	± Unlimited-exposure probing
Facilitate Behavioral Intention	± Spontaneous or elicited comments	+ Direct questioning of facilitation	± Unlimited-exposure probing
Retention	+ Recall of message	− Direct questioning of memorability	± Short- and medium-exposure extent of recall
Decision Process Effects Awareness	+ Recall of message, source, object	− Direct questioning of awareness change	± Direct probing of awareness change
Factual Knowledge	− Recall of message components	− Concise check on communicated information	+ Check on communication targets
Image	− Recall of main arguments	− Concise check on communicated symbol	+ Check on image, perception
Attitude/Attitude Change	− Spontaneous or elicited evaluation	± Direct questioning on attitude/attitude change	± Probing of attitude/ attitude change
Behavioral Intention/ Intention Change	− Spontaneous or elicited intention	± Direct questioning on intention/ intention change	± Probing of intention/intention change

spondent. Such is mainly due to the flexibility of the semistructured interview, allowing extensive probing tailored to a specific message. This advantage trades off with the limited opportunity for comparative assessment and for quantification. A major drawback lies in the necessity for synthesizing and interpreting the responses. The method is suited for several communication modes (high involvement, low involvement).

Pretesting Results

We will first deal with the results from each method separately, and then attempt to derive conclusions. Be-

cause of the nature of the data, the jury method results will account for a large part of the discussion.

PORTFOLIO METHOD. The test message was best in spontaneous recall (Table 4) when compared with other messages in the portfolio (the position of ads in the portfolio was rotated systematically). On the other hand, correct recall of advertiser and his service jointly occurred less frequently. Familiarity with the advertiser and novelty of the service for the advertiser may explain these results to some extent. Problems in communication of information resulting in lower awareness and knowledge may also account for the results.

The concise interpretation of the message given by the

TABLE 4
Extent of Unaided Recall (N=25)

Advertisements	Advertiser and/or Service	Advertiser Only	Advertiser and Service/Product
Test ad	21	17	4
A	17	11	6
B	13	7	6
C	13	13	0
D	10	1	9
E	6	2	4
F	2	1	1
G	1	1	0

respondents concerns the pictorial and verbal components of the message. While the format elements are judged as eye catching and evaluated positively by about half the interviewees, it appears that the respondent has difficulties in meaningfully structuring the pictorial elements. This may lead to the negative evaluations by an important minority of respondents. Total absence of recall is noted for the headline. While the message does attract initial attention, it tends to show some weaknesses in the identification of its potential relevance to prospects. Of the 25 respondents, 4 are able to summarize the gist of the message, 8 respondents give only an approximation and the remainder fail to give an adequate summary. These data confirm the likelihood of limited "communication-in-a-nutshell" or of difficulties in respondent self-selection.

Spontaneous recall of factual information results only in limited information. Only 12 of the 25 respondents are able to recall some arguments, while the other interviewees play back only one or a few striking elements, or even vague or erroneous content arguments. The target reactions, specified by the advertiser in view of the Target Plan system, account for a very small share of the already restricted amount of content recall. A further check on the target reactions with aided recall shows somewhat better results for factual information transfer. Copy elements have an average correct recall of 45%, an average faulty recall of 17% and a "don't know" percentage of 38%. Some specific copy elements have low correct recall with a high proportion of "don't know" answers. The content of the message, the copy, is evaluated positively by a majority of respondents.

Concluding for the portfolio test, one observes that the respondents are positively disposed towards the message, even though a large minority is not interested in the service as such. The message performs well in terms of catching initial attention, which may be due to the incongruous illustration. The headline does not play a constructive role in the communication process. The communication of factual information is not unqualifiedly positive, but this aspect of the results is affected by the varying degree of readership and interest in the sample of respondents.

JURY METHOD. The test advertisement was assessed comparatively with five industrial product or service messages selected from the same journal in which the test message occurred. Six-point semantic differential scales were given to the respondent with the request to rate messages within scales (rating scales within adverts enhances halo effects). The concepts or traits hypothetically measured by the scales as well as the average score obtained for each message are shown in Table 5. The test ad is seen to be rated most favorably in comparison to other advertisements, except in terms of its informative character (2nd rank) and of its credibility (4th rank).

Table 6 shows the variance between means, the average ("within") variance of the mean scores and the ratio of the later to the former, which may serve as a crude reliability, or discriminatory power index, for the scale (or rather as the complement of reliability of discriminatory power, the maximal reliability being 1.00).

Scales which discriminate less reliably between messages are those measuring new learning, expression of interest, supplier preference, positive product evaluation and message familiarity. Scales discriminating rather re-

TABLE 5
Mean Evaluation Scores for Five Industrial Advertisements (N=25)

	Test ad	Ad A	Ad B	Ad C	Ad D
1. Eye catching message	1.6	2.9	3.3	3.9	3.4
2. Visually pleasing message	1.9	3.6	3.6	4.1	3.2
3. New learning through message	3.5	3.9	4.2	4.2	4.5
4. Interesting message	2.7	3.2	4.2	3.7	4.0
5. Informative message	2.7	2.2	3.3	3.0	3.7
6. Credibility	3.5	2.6	3.2	3.1	4.1
7. Source derogation-continued attention	2.3	3.4	4.2	3.8	3.9
8. Retention of message	2.0	3.3	4.0	4.3	3.8
9. Personal relevance	1.8	3.3	3.2	2.7	4.0
10. Curiosity	2.5	4.2	4.5	3.9	4.2
11. Favorable attitude to service	2.5	3.0	3.3	3.2	3.6
12. Clarity-comprehensibility	2.5	2.7	3.4	2.9	3.8
13. Favorable attitude to advertiser	2.8	2.8	3.4	3.6	3.5
14. Recognition	1.9	2.9	3.3	3.8	3.4
15. Positive evaluation of service	2.0	2.1	2.5	2.4	3.0
16. Message familiarity	2.8	3.4	4.0	4.2	3.5
17. Image building impact	1.9	2.6	3.7	3.5	3.0
18. Support/counter-arguing	2.2	2.8	3.3	3.2	3.6

Note: in reading this table, lower ratings are considered more favorable.

354

Variance Between Means, Average Variance of the Mean and Discriminatory Power for 18 Ratings on 5 Stimuli (N = 25)

Scale #	Variance of Means	Average Variance of Mean	Discriminatory Power
1	0.606	0.073	0.12
2	0.549	0.065	0.12
3	0.277	0.096	0.35
4	0.169	0.061	0.36
5	0.241	0.071	0.29
6	0.240	0.063	0.26
7	0.430	0.064	0.15
8	0.670	0.087	0.13
9	0.520	0.079	0.15
10	0.488	0.082	0.17
11	0.150	0.041	0.27
12	0.227	0.066	0.29
13	0.128	0.059	0.46
14	0.419	0.072	0.17
15	0.110	0.050	0.45
16	0.244	0.107	0.44
17	0.288	0.060	0.21
18	0.213	0.046	0.22

liably are those measuring initial and visual impact, continued attention, memorability, personal relevance, curiosity thoughts, and supplier recognition. Other scales are intermediate in reliability. While the evidence is tenuous, as it depends on the sample of messages and of respondents, it is not at all conflicting with what was mentioned above concerning the measurement properties of the Jury Method. More information on the structure of the reaction process is gained by an analysis of the pattern of associations between responses for each advertisement.[1] Table 7 shows the most pronounced loadings and other statistics for a principal components factor analysis (Kaiser extraction, varimax rotation) of the test advertisement. The factors represent separate response dimensions which summarize the most important part of the structure underlying the respondents' reactions. The number of factors necessary to account for most of the underlying structure given an idea of the complexity (dimensionality) of the response pattern.

The test advertisement needs six factors for identification of the underlying structure. It has the highest complexity of all messages tested by the jury method. An analysis of the loadings leads to the tentative interpreta-

tion of the response dimensions as (1) interest/personal relevance, (2) impact, (3) informativity/positive evaluation, (4) recall (recognition/familiarity), (5) clarity/credibility, and (6) image building effect. The first factor accounts for a large share of the explained variance, stressing the importance of interest and message relevance both for communication and for pretest respondent selection.

Advertisements A, B, and C have five factors in their factor solution. Message A advertises a well-known visual presentation aid and includes substantial copy as well as a picture and return coupon. Its headline is short and powerful, its copy is informative. The factors can be labeled as (1) continued attention/relevance, (2) impact and recognition, coupled with positive product evaluation, (3) informative, clear, (4) credibility/familiarity, and (5) new learning.

Message B is by a supplier of office equipment. It consists of a headline stressing the availability of equipment for small and large buyers. This is elaborated on by a short text. Two office machines are presented visually and in text. The remaining half of the message space is used for the company logo and identification. The five factors can be described as (1) continued attention/relevance, (2) positive product evaluation, (3) communication of new information, (4) visual impact, and (5) credibility/familiarity.

Message C advertises office suppliers. The upper half shows a typewriter and headline. The lower half is devoted to "reason-why" copy and contains the names of the advertiser and his products as well as a return coupon. The first factor contains information transfer, curiosity thoughts, and creation of favorable attitude. The second factor combines positive evaluation with credibility. Factor three is the visual impact. Factor four contains credibility and personal relevance. Factor five, finally, lists recall, recognition, and supplier preference as components.

The final advertisement, D, is one in which a financial institution offers its services to businessmen when abroad. Two-thirds are devoted to a picture, one third to a text which is oriented less to information transfer than to persuasion. The factorial pattern is simple, as it is limited to three factors; the first factor accounts for half the variance to be explained. The interpretation of the factors is rendered difficult, since a large number of concepts now amalgamate into a factor. Factor 3 is relatively simple, as it loads on supplier preference and recognition. Factor 2 contains the ideas of informativity, credibility and of continued retention. Factor 1 points to

---

[1]Further research of consumer goods advertisements has shown that factor-analyzing the average ratings across advertisements cannot inform us about the structure of response to advertisements. Rather, a correlation matrix for each message should be analyzed separately.

TABLE 7
Factor Loadings for the Test Advertisement

	Factor 1	Factor 2	Factor 3	Factor 4	Factor 5	Factor 6	Communality
1. Eye catching message		0.72					0.68
2. Visually pleasing message		0.74			0.42		0.90
3. New learning through message		0.50					0.36
4. Interesting message	0.41	0.79					0.96
5. Informative message	0.41		0.73				0.91
6. Credibility					0.47		0.44
7. Source derogation-continued attention	0.82						0.80
8. Retention	0.48			0.60			0.78
9. Personal relevance	0.75						0.77
10. Curiosity	0.80						0.72
11. Favorable attitude to service	0.70		0.60				0.92
12. Clarity-comprehensibility			0.73		0.47		0.90
13. Favorable attitude to advertiser			0.62				0.71
14. Recognition				0.84			0.74
15. Positive evaluation of service			0.81				0.76
16. Message familiarity				0.48			0.27
17. Image building impact						0.91	0.86
18. Support/counter-arguing		0.42	0.68				0.78
% explained variance	39.6	14.6	8.7	8.2	5.7	5.6	

persuasive effects and to positive evaluation along with image-building effects.

The factor analysis of the responses to industrial advertisements is quite instructive and goes a long way towards supporting our confidence in several hypotheses advanced in this text. Except for message D, which is less informative and more image-building than the other advertisements, the structure underlying the responses is rather differentiated. The test message and ads A and B list interest and personal relevance, a respondent self-selection response, as most important. That this is not the case for Message C is possibly due to the universal relevance of the message and to the relative lack of familiarity with the supplier. Visual or short-term impact is listed as a separate reaction in most instances, as would be expected for industrial ads. Information transfer occurs as a separate factor combining communication and persuasion processes. Finally, credibility (often coupled with familiarity) is obtained as a process in its own right, moderating the yielding processes.

The general impression about the test ad derived from the consumer jury method is that it compares favorably with a sample of four messages belonging to the same category of advertisements. Potential weaknesses are indicated by the lesser performance on the dimensions of informativity and credibility. Problems in unsatisfactory communication have already been alluded to in the discussion of the portfolio results. The credibility problem is

caused by skepticism as to the ease of introducing any computerized service. The analysis shows that quite a number of evaluative scales have adequate discriminatory power, and that these are mainly concepts expected to be measured best by means of the jury method. The factor analysis reveals a structure of expected complexity and identifiability. With respect to the test ad, the factors reveal the response dimensions of relevance, impact, information-persuasion, recall, credibility, and image. This is in line with previous test evidence of (1) problems with identification of relevance, (2) repeated comments on impact, (3) positive evaluation of information, and (4) good message recall. The credibility factor identifies a new potential weakness of the message. The image-effect, finally is not unexpected for a widely known advertiser in an oligopoly situation.

TARGET PLAN METHOD. The test advertisement was presented individually to a group of 25 respondents. A very brief and a limited exposure (each followed by adequate questioning) were subsequently extended into a discussion with the message in full view.

Short-exposure results confirm the absence of "instant communication" for industrial advertising. The test ad seems to suffer from poor identification of the service offered and of its relevance when briefly exposed. Problems with the interpretation of visual components and with headline (content) playback, discovered in the folio test, are confirmed. Limited exposure results also confirm the portfolio findings; the message content is generally recalled by means of a few isolated copy components. Evaluative responses to the format and copy elements are positive. The target reactions are generally well reproduced. Spontaneous comments skeptical of the ease of introducing computerized services are not infrequent.

The Target-Plan method has, in general, confirmed the findings in the previous two test procedures. To some extent this is a welcome replication; we should also acknowledge that the Target Plan method could be used more extensively to borrow on its strengths as discussed in Table 3. Its use in a target-response testing mode and especially in the verification of target-response patterns can be useful. For this purpose trained and experienced researchers and interviewers are a prerequisite.

CONCLUSIONS

This study was a case investigation of the properties of advertisements and of advertising pretesting methods in the framework of industrial marketing. A conceptual and normative perspective was established, based on our knowledge of consumer goods advertising research and of industrial marketing. The evidence presented in the article is based on a case study and used to explore, rather than test, broad hypotheses. The results concerning both messages and pretest methods are encouraging and show that clear hypotheses can be developed for conclusive statistical testing.

The important conclusions are

1. The communication process in industrial marketing is of a specific and variable nature.
2. The identity, role and needs of the audience should be kept in mind when creating a message and when testing it.
3. The pretest methods applied in consumer advertising research are suited for industrial advertising, if a mix of methods is used with emphasis put on

specific components of the mix, depending on the communication situation.

4. There is some confirmation of the role to be assigned to each method of pretest research in the investigation of particular elements of the communication and decision process.

REFERENCES

1. Derbaix, Christian, Les Réactions des Consommateurs á la Communication Publicitaire et la Hiérarchie des Effects, *Revue Française du arketing*, Sept.-Oct., 7-25 (1975).
2. Ray, Michael L., Marketing Communication and the Hierarchy of Effects, *Marketing Science Institute, Working paper*, November 1973.
3. Krugman, Herbert E., The Measurement of Advertising Involvement, *Public Opinion Quarterly* 30, 583-596 (1967).
4. Stapel, J., *Reclameresultaten meten voor Marketing*, Alphen a/d Rijn, 1972.
5. Brown, Herbert E. and Brucker, Roger W. The BuyerProblem Foundation of Industrial Advertising, *Industrial Marketing Management* 5, 163-167 (1976).
7. Lucas, Daniel B. and Henderson Britt, Steuaert *Measuring Advertising Effectiveness*, McGraw-Hill, New York, 1963.
8. Holzhauer, F.F.O. *Briefing*, Stenfert Kroese b.v., Leiden 1976.

ADDITIONAL BIBLIOGRAPHY

Alexander, Ralph S., Cross, James S., and Cummingham, Ross M., *Industrial Marketing*. R. D. Irwin, Homewood, IL, 1956.
Bucklin, Louis P., "Retail Strategy and the Classification of Consumer Goods," *Journal of Marketing*, pp. 50-55 (1963).
Holton, Richard H., "The Distinction Between Convenience Goods, Shopping Goods, and Specialty Goods," *Journal of Marketing*, pp. 53-56 (July 1958).
Katona, G., *Psychological Analysis of Economic Behavior*. American Elsevier, New York, 1975.
Levitt, Theodore, Industrial Purchasing Behavior: A Study in Communications Effects. Division of Research, Harvard Business School, Boston, 1965.
Morrill, John E., "Industrial Advertising Pays Off," *Harvard Business Review* (March-April, 1970).
Webster, Frederick E., and Wind, Yorem, *Organizational Buying Behavior*, Prentice Hall, Englewood Cliffs, NJ, 1972.
Wind, Yoram, "Industrial Source Loyalty," *Journal of Marketing Research*, VII, 450-457 (November, 1970).

Predicting Changes In Advertising Effectiveness

Carlton A. Maile

CARLTON A. MAILE is associate professor of marketing at Northern Illinois University. He holds a Ph.D. in marketing from the University of Georgia. His academic background and previous executive experience are both utilized in frequent consulting assignments with companies in the United States, Canada and Latin America. He is author of recent articles about marketing theory, advertising, corporate social audits and executive development.

More accurate predictions of advertising effectiveness may be possible with the help of a communications model which portrays changing relationships between a buyer's persuasibility, his self-esteem, the credibility of an advertiser, and the nature of a promotional message. A recently published marketing communications model may constitute a partial framework for predicting advertising effectiveness.[1] However, because the original model was proposed to assist in a broad variety of marketing decisions, its applicability to advertising was not fully developed. Also, the usefulness of the original model in predicting advertising effectiveness would be limited to a brief time period after transmittal of a promotional message. However, as shown in this paper, the initial model can be extended by modifying its form to reflect possible changes in advertising effectiveness which may be associated with a communications phenomenon called the "sleeper effect."

Initial Relationships

The basic communication model shows how a buyer's persuasibility is initially affected by his self-esteem, the credibility of a message source, and the nature of a persuasive message or advertisement. Persuasibility refers to situations in which a communicator presents his position on an issue, accompanied by emotional or rational argumentation.[2] The degree of persuasibility is then equated to the degree of attitude change occurring between pre- and post-communication measurements. A receiver's persuasibility is in turn affected by his self-esteem or his customary sense of worthiness as expressed in terms of this attitude toward his actual self. Resulting self-esteem/persuasibility relationships are negative linear, inverted U-shaped, and positive linear. These relationships are influenced by the credibility of a message source. Credibility of a source (source credibility) is defined as "the image held of a communicator at a given time by a receiver. . . ."[3]

In Figure 1, low, medium, and high source credibility levels are respectively associated with the negative linear, inverted U-shaped, and positive linear forms. Continually decreasing persuasibility associated with increasing self-esteem results in a negative linear relationship, ABC. An inverted U-shaped relationship, DEF, is produced by a respective rise and fall in persuasibility associated with increasing self-esteem. A positive linear form, GHI, is produced by continuously rising persuasibility in association with increasing self-esteem.[4]

Similar relationships between communication discrepancy and persuasibility are also proposed in the model. Communication discrepancy can be defined as the difference between an individual's pre-communication attitude and that advocated by a communication source.[5]

After a period of several weeks, the factors of self-esteem, source credibility, and com-

Reprinted with permission from *University of Michigan Business Review*, vol. 31, pp. 18–22, July 1979.

munication discrepancy may have different effects on an advertising audience. Preliminary research indicates that the initial model may be useful in predicting advertising effectiveness immediately after a message has been communicated.[6] However, other studies suggest that relationships between advertising effectiveness and other variables may change over time as the result of a phenomenon known as the sleeper effect.[7]

Emergent Relationships

The sleeper effect results from changes in the perceived credibility of a message source over a period of time. For example, if the source associated with a persuasive message is initially perceived to have low credibility, this source will be associated with a higher credibility level after a time lapse of about four weeks. Similarly, if the source associated with a persuasive message is initially perceived to have high credibility, this source will be remembered as having a lower credibility level after a four week period. Both high and low credibility levels will, in effect, merge into the same moderate level of credibility. This phenomenon can be called the sleeper effect because it is latent in an initial communication situation and appears after a time lag of about four weeks.

The sleeper effect, and the merging of extreme source credibility levels would be associated with all levels of self-esteem. Therefore, persuasibility values associated with each level of self-esteem should also merge, causing the three initial relationships to coalesce into a single inverted U-shape as shown in Figure 2. The inverted U-shape, D′E′F′, should be con-

Proposed Communications Model*
(Initial Form)

a. Three Dimensional Form

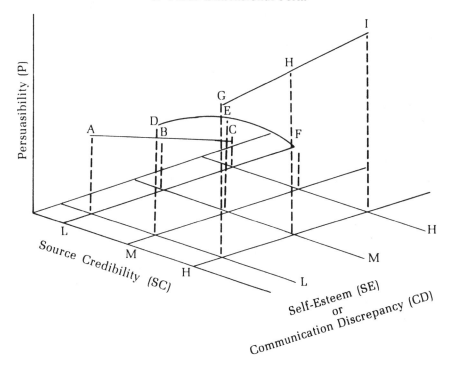

*The proposed model can be viewed as consisting of two parts, one superimposed over the other. The source credibility, communication discrepancy, persuasibility (SC-CD-P) portion is superimposed over a source credibility, self-esteem, persuasibility (SC-SE-P) counterpart.

b. Two Dimensional Form

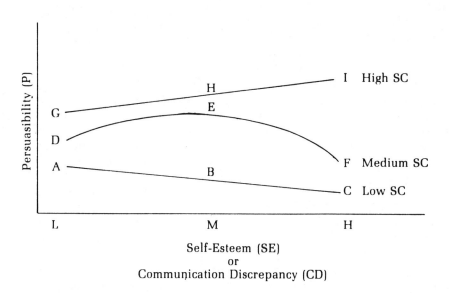

Self-Esteem (SE)
or
Communication Discrepancy (CD)

Figure 1

gruent with curve DEF in Figure 1. Similarly, the three communication discrepancy/persuasibility relationships proposed in Figure 1 should also merge into the form of curve D′E′F′; within about four weeks after the transmittal of an advertising message. Therefore, Figure 2 is considered to represent an extension, or an "emergent form," of the proposed model.

Matching the Model with Advertising Variables

As a basis for developing specific applications, it is useful to show how the proposed model accommodates major components of an advertising situation.[8] Advertising is considered to be, in part, the process of changing buyer attitudes. Buyers and suppliers are, respectively, communication receivers with various levels of self-esteem, and communication sources with various degrees of credibility. Comparatively unknown and long-established suppliers or advertisers are associated respectively with low and high credibility levels. Suppliers' attempts to influence buyers' attitudes are persuasive communications or advertisements with various degrees of communication discrepancy. Changes in buyers' attitudes are indicated by corresponding changes in sales volume.[9] These changes in sales volume may also be considered as indirect measures of advertising effectiveness.

Applications to Advertising Decisions

The initial and emergent forms of the proposed model have many potential applications to advertising decisions. The initial form should be used to deter-

Proposed Communications Model
(Emergent Form)

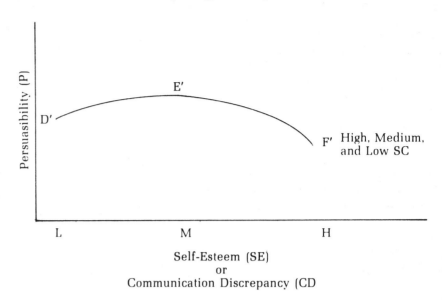

Figure 2

mine the effects of persuasive messages up to four weeks after they reach an audience. However, the emergent model should be used to determine the effects of messages after a time lapse of four weeks or more.

Both forms of the proposed model should be most useful in suggesting general approaches to marketing problems, rather than as a formula for yielding precise results. In this context, many practical applications can be devised. SC-SE-P and SC-CD-P parts as shown in Figure 1 can be applied separately or together.

Identifying the Audience

As indicated in the SC-SE-P portion of the initial model, different suppliers or advertisers should emphasize different target markets in order to maximize sales. Low and high credibility suppliers will be at their least disadvantage and greatest advantage respectively in reaching low and high self-esteem markets because these are the market segments which

they can persuade most effectively. However, after a four week time lapse, the emergent form of the model indicates that buyers with medium self-esteem levels should constitute the most profitable markets for suppliers at all credibility levels. In both situations, before and after the sleeper effect, maximum persuasibility should be reflected in maximum sales per unit of marketing effort.

Selecting the Media

The SC-SE-P portion of the initial model can also be used for selecting advertising media. Little-known media and well-recognized message channels would be associated respectively with low and high credibility levels. Correspondingly, according to the initial model, these communications channels can best be used for reaching low and high self-esteem markets. For example, the *Wall Street Journal* may be considered as a better recognized and more credible medium for the sale of Florida vacation properties than a tabloid such as *The National Enquirer*. Therefore the *Wall Street Journal* could be most effective in reaching high self-esteem markets, while *The Enquirer* could have its greatest influence on low self-esteem people. However, after the emergence of the sleeper effect, as shown in the emergent model, buyers would view both of these advertising media as having equal credibility. Therefore, the medium self-esteem people will be most persuaded by either source after the advertising messages are more than four weeks old.

Analyzing Content and Format Requirements

The products, channel members, prices, and product comparisons mentioned in an advertisement can have a predictable influence on its effectiveness. Suppliers could use the SC-CD-P portion of the model in determining which products may be advertised most effectively. Little known items and those easily associated with need satisfaction would be the objects of communications with respectively high and low discrepancy levels.[10] According to the initial model, an established high-credibility supplier would realize his greatest advantage in selling new and therefore highly discrepant products. However, after the sleeper effect occurs, both types of suppliers will be viewed as having medium credibility. Therefore, messages with extremely high or low discrepancy levels will both be less effective than moderately discrepant messages after a four-week time lapse. This also means that a product associated with a medium discrepancy level will have maximum acceptability after the initial advertisements are more than four weeks old.

The nature of distribution channel members should also be considered in predicting advertising effectiveness. Manufacturers may use advertising to convince prospective consumers to make their purchases from certain retailers. The SC-CD-P part of the initial model would indicate that traditional and unique retailers would be the objects of communications associated respectively with low and high discrepancy levels. Little known or low credibility manufacturers could best sell through traditional middlemen, whereas established high credibility manufacturers could realize their greatest advantage in selling through new or novel types of channel members. For instance, a new or little known manufacturer of shotguns could best sell his products through conventional outlets, such as sporting goods stores. However, a well-known and long-established manufacturer of shotguns may be able to sell more of his products by employing non-conventional outlets, e.g. grocery stores. However, the sleeper effect could also cause manufacturers to modify this decision process. After four weeks, and after the convergence of source credibility perceptions, both extremely new and traditional retailers will be viewed as less acceptable than moderately conventional ones. Therefore, the moderately conventional outlets, such as hardware stores or discount houses may be most acceptable to customers over an extended period of time.

The SC-CE-P part of the initial model can also be used to determine which suppliers can best introduce new price levels. Because new (usually higher than normal) price levels are associated with higher communication discrepancy levels, they can be introduced most profitably by established high credibility suppliers. For in-

stance, if higher price levels are to be introduced at retail service stations, the long established and higher credibility suppliers, such as Exxon, would be in the most advantageous position for initiating price increases. Concurrently, little known low credibility suppliers would be at their greatest initial advantage when adhering to conventional price levels. In this example, the sleeper effect would again cause both suppliers to have a pricing effectiveness which is ultimately suboptimal. After about four weeks, moderate price changes would seem most persuasive to consumers.

Suppliers can use similar reasoning in choosing the best types of advertising formats. Newly established or low credibility suppliers should use traditional formats, whereas well-respected high credibility sellers may be most effective with non-traditional or highly discrepant layouts (e.g. formats involving clever comparisons and derogations of competitive offerings). However, as a result of the sleeper effect in this decision situation, both types of suppliers may want to choose moderately conventional formats for advertisements which will ultimately have the maximum effect on consumer attitudes.

Determining Message Frequency

The initial and emergent forms of the proposed model can also serve as guidelines for determining how frequently a given advertisement should appear in the media. In order to be most effective in persuading high self-esteem audiences, advertisements should be placed at intervals of less than four weeks. However, if low or medium self-esteem audiences are the primary targets, advertisements should be placed at intervals of four weeks or more. Low credibility suppliers can be most effective in reaching buyers with medium self-esteem by advertising at intervals of greater than four weeks. High credibility suppliers can advertise most effectively to all markets at intervals of less than four weeks. However, advertisements from medium credibility suppliers may be equally effective when placed without regard to the four week time period and the sleeper effect. These guidelines should be applicable regardless of whether the products, price levels, or ad formats are new or traditional.

Summary and Conclusions

The proposed model suggests an approach to advertising decisions which includes considerations of relationships between selected characteristics of the audience, message, media, and supplier. Some applications are presented here to show how initial decisions may be modified after the onset of the sleeper effect. It is important for decision makers to recognize the implications of the sleeper effect in order to minimize long range errors which could result from us-

ing only the initial form of the model. If promotional messages are scheduled at intervals of four weeks or less, one set of decisions would be desired from the initial model. However, if persuasive communications are scheduled at intervals of more than four weeks, a second set of decisions derived from the emergent model may be more appropriate. The model indicates that high credibility suppliers will usually realize their greatest advantage in placing advertisements at intervals of less than four weeks. However, because of the sleeper effect, low credibility suppliers may be able to communicate with markets less frequently, cut media costs, and yet achieve greater advertising effectiveness. Because the proposed model is, in its present form, intended to be a general framework for marketing decisions, it cannot be used for developing answers with computer precision. However, it is hoped that the model could be applied with greater precision after further refinements and additional empirical testing.

[1]C. A. Maile and A. H. Kizilbash, "A Marketing Communications Model," *Business Horizons* (20 December 1977), pp. 77-84.

[2]W. J. McGuire, "Personality and Susceptibility to Social Influence," in *Handbook of Personality Theory and Research*, ed. by Edgar F. Borgatta and William W. Lambert (Chicago: Rand McNally and Company, 1968), p. 1133.

[3]K. A. Anderson and T. Clevenger, Jr., "A Summary of Experimental Research in Ethos," *Speech Monographs* (30 June 1963), p. 59.

[4]For empirical evidence supporting the validity of these proposed relationships, see C. A. Maile, "The Apparent Lack of Self-Esteem and Persuasibility Relationships," *Journal of Psychology* (96 June 1977), pp. 123-129.

[5]Maile, *op. cit.*

[6]Maile, *op. cit.*

[7]For the results of previous studies and a further explanation of the sleeper effect, see C. I. Hovland and W. Weiss, "The Influence of Source Credibility on Communication Effectiveness," *Public Opinion Quarterly* (15 Winter 1951), pp. 636-646.

[8]There is no attempt to include all elements of the advertising situation in the proposed model, nor is there any claim that it should be used alone as the advertising manager's only decision making tool. Throughout this discussion, it is anticipated that, in addition to the proposed model, other decision tools and surrounding circumstances will be considered in shaping the final advertising decisions.

[9]The relationship between attitude change and sales volume is oversimplified here for the sake of brevity.

[10]New or unfamiliar products are considered to be the objects of highly discrepant communications because their potential capacity for need satisfaction differs from the known capacity for need satisfaction associated with traditional products.

HOW TO MEASURE YOUR ADVERTISING'S SALES PRODUCTIVITY

by William Parker

Reprinted with permission from *Industrial Marketing* (now *Business Marketing*), vol. 68, pp. 54, 55, 58, and 60, Feb. 1983.

This article will outline a planning model business/industrial marketers can use to evaluate their advertising's contribution to sales efficiency. We'll show an example, adapted from one firm's actual experience, to illustrate how advertising increased a company's sales efficiency by 800%, raising profitability from £32,000 to £112,000 on an investment of £50,000.

One cannot help but feel, however, that the discussion should be preceeded by answering a fundamental question: Can business/industrial advertising make a profit?

Despite the millions of pounds industry spends on advertising every year, few companies really consider it an integral part of their marketing and selling effort. If they define a role for it at all, it's likely to be of the vague "corporate" variety—expressed as "getting the name across" or "maintaining a presence in the market." It's likely that the advertising will have a purely ritualistic quality in which subjective pictorial taste and literary pretension vie with each other in futile efforts to reconcile a nagging awareness of waste with cliches such as "it pays to advertise."

Of course it pays to advertise. It also pays to eat. But both advertising and eating can also make you feel pretty sick.

The problem confronting the serious industrial advertiser is knowing when a certain advertising diet can improve the company's health. The answer to a severe dose of advertising poisoning is not to give up advertising altogether.

Those vague corporate objectives do have a role to play in industrial marketing and advertising. But nine times out of ten it should be a secondary role, as we shall see.

Knowing how much advertising is enough starts with examining key principles, such as the difference between consumer and business/industrial advertising. Many of the industrial advertiser's problems can be traced to confusion between the two.

The primary objective of industrial advertising, fundamentally different from that of consumer advertising, is to support the salesman by providing him with qualified leads and increas-

William Parker is a copywriter and a director of the London office of Stockholm-based Anderson & Lembke. That agency has adapted the planning model discussed in this story to computer programs named Procal.

'The problem confronting the serious industrial advertiser is knowing when a certain advertising diet can improve the company's health. The answer to a severe dose of advertising poisoning is not to give up advertising altogether.'

ing his lead conversion rate. In other words, the job of industrial advertising is to locate prospects for the salesman to increase his productivity.

FUNDAMENTALS

Many companies have a national sales force with a fixed and predictable cost. Based on its particular experience, a company will probably be able to predict the call rate for each of its salesman and the closing rate each will ultimately achieve. Hence the company can predict the salesman's profitability.

If the company wants to increase that profitability, it's often thought there are only three ways to do it:
• Have the sales force devote more time to the most profitable products —although that often quickly reaches a point of diminishing returns.
• "Incentivise" the sales force so that sheer effort achieves greater sales. Yet last year's privilege tends to become this year's right, so incentivising is seldom short-term in anything but its effect.
• If the company isn't already national it can hire more salesmen. But their productivity and their profitability will be low to begin with.

All of that can lead to the mistaken conclusion that the company's sales operate at or near a finite value and that nothing can be done about it. That is seldom true, however. Advertising can usually do something about it, and in a way that is almost as predictable as the results of the sales-

men's efforts.

A second big difference between industrial and consumer advertising is that consumer advertising is all about influencing awareness and attitudes prior to behavior, while industrial advertising influences behavior which will subsequently affect more behavior.

In other words, consumer marketing assumes that advertising works in steps of exposure-awareness-interest-attitude-action. Advertisements take consumers from unawareness through knowing, becoming interested, actively liking the product and finally buying it.

With industrial marketing it is generally more productive to assume that advertising works like this: exposure-action-attitude-interest-action. Exposure to an advertising message leads directly to some form of action, which in turn leads to a decision, an attitude, for or against the advertiser and the product. If the decision is favorable, the recipient will actively acquire more knowledge of the product. That in turn leads to further action—buying.

That tells us that advertising should be out there creating action. And that means a response—coupons, reply-paid cards, phone calls, telexes, letters, carrier pigeons—almost any response. For if we succeed in persuading somebody to take action in relation to our product, we have created a special relationship with that person. We'll have broken the ice. From then on he will not only be predisposed to listen to us, but will also be more ready to seek information and pass it on to colleagues within his company. That last point is especially important because most industrial buying decisions (unlike consumer buying decisions) involve many different people.

BASIC MATHEMATICS

Actually, the typical salesman spends most of his time doing tasks other than selling. A recent British study found, for example, that 39% of his time is devoted to traveling, 13% to waiting, 11% to breaks and 6% to administration. Data from other industrialized countries are comparable.

The interesting thing is how little time the average salesman spends with customers in the course of the day—about 30%, say 2½ hours. Only half of that is effective selling time— about 1¼ hours. And we know from other studies that salesmen spend at

'The most surefire way of learning a lesson the hard way is to take an existing sales performance and merely extrapolate it to a greater sales volume. One cannot say that if 40 sales take 360 hours selling time, 140 sales will require 1,260 hours.'

least 80% of all effective selling time with existing customers.

In other words only 20% of average daily selling time—about 15 minutes —is spent with new prospects. That's how much time the salesman has to get the new orders that will keep his business growing. Obviously the shortest route to better profitability is enabling salesmen to make more efficient use of their time.

How much more efficient will the salesman be if traveling and waiting time is cut? We know that much of that time is wasted chasing poor quality leads and blind calls. Yet before we can measure the effect of improving the quality of leads or reducing the number of blind calls we need to find a suitable measure of sales efficiency.

We calculate sales efficiency as *contribution per salesman-hour*. We take the total value of the salesman's sales, deduct all manufacturing and sales costs (including his own) and divide the result by the number of hours the salesman has worked. The higher the contribution per salesman-hour, the higher the sales profitability.

Now we must assess how much influence the advertising campaign will exert on profitability. That, together with the cost of the advertising and

the contribution per sale, allows us to predict the actual profitability of a campaign.

Let's examine a simplified case based on an actual Anderson & Lembke client experience to see how the method works in actual practice. The company in question sells, among other things, measuring systems.
- The systems cost £2,600 each.
- The company expects the product to contribute about 30% of that as profit, or £800 per system.
- Sales amount to 40 systems per year —all to existing customers.
- So the total annual contribution from this product comes to around £32,000.
- Those existing customers need reminders to buy from time to time, so the average salesman makes three calls per sale to keep business ticking over.
- The economic climate being what it is, the company has an urgent need to generate revenue; measuring systems with their good profit margins look like an attractive expansion. After a close look at the market, management believes that a unit sales target of 180 systems is feasible.
- Management also reckons that the 40-unit sales level achieved the previous year can be sustained with existing customers.

The problem: finding new buyers for the remaining 140 systems. If they could be found those sales would represent a contribution to profit of £112,000.

OPTIONS

The company and the agency asked four key questions: could those buyers be found if the sales force spent more time on that product, would the resulting sales be satisfactorily profitable, how much advertising would be needed to reach the target, and would resulting sales, considering the cost of advertising, still be profitable?

Obviously none of those questions could be answered without a basis for comparison. So in the next step, the company examined how it is achieving current profitability. What is the current contribution per salesman-hour?

To calculate that, the company needed only one additional figure— the amount of time needed for the average sales call. In practice that is not an easy figure to calculate. Call duration can vary widely. But with perseverance it is almost always possible to come up with an acceptable average.
- The company set the figure at three

hours.
- If it takes three calls of three hours each to make a sale, each sale takes nine salesman-hours.
- The 40 current sales therefore require 360 salesman-hours.
- The contribution of 40 sales (£32,000) divided by 360 salesman-hours provides a contribution per salesman-hour of £88.

In our experience, and by anyone's measure, that is a fair return for an hour of a salesman's time. Right away one can see that advertising will be unlikely to achieve quantum leaps in profitability because the number of calls per sale is comparatively low and all business is coming from existing customers. Already the figures suggest that backing the product with additional sales force time or advertising demands careful study. The figures tell us that the product is doing quite well as it is.

UNAIDED SELLING EFFORT

The most surefire way of learning a lesson the hard way is to take an existing sales performance and merely extrapolate it to a greater sales volume. One cannot say, for example, that if 40 sales take 360 hours selling time, 140 sales will require 1,260 hours.

To estimate the likely time required to find new customers, look back to when the product was introduced to the market for the first time. (That assumes that the records were kept!)

The prudent company in this example had the records and, along with asking salesmen, determined that:
- It took six blind calls to find one interesting prospect.
- Those interesting prospects could be closed at a rate of 25%.
- The average new buyer purchased two systems in the first year.
- Therefore, it took an average of 24 calls to find one new buyer.
- To sell 140 additional systems, the company needs to find 70 new buyers.
- The average call duration is 3 hours.
- Selling 70 buyers requires 24 calls at 3 hours each, equaling 5,040 salesman-hours.
- The contribution of 140 additional sales is £112,000, or about £22 per salesman-hour.

So a 14-fold increase in selling time produces a 3.5% increase in unit sales, but with a 75% decrease in sales efficiency (£22 compared to £88). That clearly calls into question the wisdom of relying on the salesforce alone. It produces diminishing returns.

'The conclusions to draw? First, advertising can help achieve the given sales target without jeopardizing sales productivity. And second, advertising cut the amount of required selling time dramatically — in our example by sevenfold.'

WITH ADVERTISING HELP

How much advertising is needed to help the sales effort? To estimate how advertising might influence the various sales ratios, we start with the required result, and work backwards through the various possibilities.

• The company expects that an effective campaign will boost the closing rate to 35% from 25%. In most cases the salesman is able to immediately see the person who responds to an advertisement. That person is more likely to be a buying influence than the person a salesman first reaches on a blind call to a new prospect. And effective advertising presells the prospect to some extent before the salesman's call.

• With a 35% closing rate, a 1-in-3 chance of closing vs. a 1-in-4 chance, advertising needs to produce inquiries from 210 genuinely interested prospects (3×70).

Of course, more people inquire than those who are interesting to the selling company. Yet experience has shown that the number of worthless inquiries is predictable and depends on the medium used. If space advertising is the only medium, usually about half of all replies are worthless in the short term. If direct mail is the only medium and the mailing list is reasonably accurate, the number of worthless replies usually goes down to about 20%. And if a combination of both media are used the number lies somewhere in between.

A company determines its inquiry waste factor for itself. In the case of our measuring system campaign, the company estimates worthless replies as 30% of the total. In other words 70% of all inquiries should be worth following up.

So the campaign should produce 300 inquiries. But what proportion of those exposed to the ads will respond at all? That figure can vary tremendously between the "customary" expected response of 0.1% to 9.5% to which most companies resign themselves, to responses of 70% or greater produced by very high interest product campaigns.

The factors to keep in mind about response rates are: how attractive is the offer, will the offer really be interesting enough for prospects to want to talk business, how easy will it be for prospects to respond, and how easy will it be to reach target groups with available media?

In our example, the measuring system company decided that a 4% response to direct mail would be realistic, requiring reaching 7,500 companies to get the 300 inquiries needed.

MULTIPLE BUYING INFLUENCES

But companies don't buy products; people do. In measuring systems, for example, three key people are involved in the purchase decision: the production manager, the design manager and the purchasing officer. So to reach three people in each of 7,500 companies, we need to put the message before at least 22,500 individuals. Yet, the company determines that the most efficient media selection could provide 65% coverage of the target market.

Media analysis discloses that, to allow for inefficiency, the message must reach 34,000 people in about 11,500 companies.

In the end, the cost of mounting a direct mail campaign to an audience of that size, backed by trade press advertising, came in at around £50,000 —far more than the company had anticipated spending (it had considered plowing back 50% of the previous year's profit contribution, £16,000, which wouldn't be enough).

But in cash outlay terms, it's already possible to see that the company might make £62,000 profit on the 140 units sold to new customers (the gross contribution of £112,000 less the £50,000 advertising cost).

Worthwhile? That was for the company to decide, but not before it considered the effect of the investment on sales efficiency. To predict that, it estimates the sales force time needed to follow up the response.

• The target is 300 responses, 30% of which are expected to end up in the dustbin.

• The best way to sort out the wheat from the chaff is with telephone calls (which can also be used for making appointments with good prospects). We assumed that an average phone call takes 15 minutes, so that 300 calls could be completed in 75 salesman-hours.

• Each worthwhile response must be followed up with a personal visit. If each of those 210 calls takes 3 hours, personal call follow up will take 630 hours. That makes a total of 705 hours.

• To calculate sales efficiency, the £62,000 contribution (net of advertising costs) divided by the hours (705) equals £88 per salesman-hour.

The conclusions to draw? First, advertising can help achieve the given sales target without jeopardizing sales productivity. And second, advertising cut the amount of required selling time dramatically—in our example by sevenfold.

In this article, we've simplified figures for presentation, but the figures themselves are not the most important point of the exercise. The important part is the probabilities those figures represent. This is a typical marketing/advertising/sales model, containing the values relevant to a particular set of selling circumstances. Those values might change from case to case; various criteria may be added or deleted in practice. But in the end a model such as this is the only way in which the profitability of advertising can be predicted.

We have been asked if it is "unrealistic" to expect the contribution per hour to remain the same before and after a campaign. In our experience, well-planned and executed advertising almost invariably *increases* the contribution per salesman-hour; sometimes as much as 300% to 400%. That seems to demonstrate not so much the efficiency of advertising as it indicts the inefficiency of trying to sell without it. ∎

JOHN G. MYERS, STEPHEN A. GREYSER & WILLIAM F. MASSY

This article presents some of the highlights and recommendations of the Commission on the Effectiveness of Research and Development for Marketing Management. Based on a review of the field of marketing over the past 25 years, the article provides an overall assessment and some specific recommendations.

THE EFFECTIVENESS OF MARKETING'S "R&D" FOR MARKETING MANAGEMENT: AN ASSESSMENT

In 1976-1977, William F. Massy, then vice president of the American Marketing Association's Education Division, initiated a "blue ribbon" Commission to study the effectiveness of research and development for marketing management (Massy, Greyser, and Myers 1979). He enlisted Stephen A. Greyser to join the effort as co-chairman of the Commission. John G. Myers served as a Commission member along with many others[1] and became more deeply involved as the Education Vice President following Massy. This article draws heavily on the work of the Commission and presents some of our own reflections on the state of research utilization in marketing and its "effectiveness" over

John G. Myers is Professor of Business Administration at the School of Business Administration, University of California, Berkeley. Stephen A. Greyser is Professor of Business Administration, Harvard Business School and Executive Director, Marketing Science Institute, Cambridge, MA. William F. Massy is Professor of Business Administration and Vice President for Business Finance, Stanford University.
The authors are indebted to the American Marketing Association and the Marketing Science Institute for financial and other support for the work of the Commission on the Effectiveness of Research and Development for Marketing Management.

the 25-period from the early 1950s to the present.[2] It represents a summary of and observations on those elements of the Commission's work that we believe to be of broadest interest.

BACKGROUND AND MISSION

The Commission considered a retrospective look at marketing—where we are and how we got there—to be of potential value in enhancing the process of creating new marketing knowledge and disseminating/utilizing it. By understanding the process of knowledge-creation and diffusion and the barriers and blocks to the process, marketers should be able to learn something about how to make it work more effectively. The Commission was charged with both an *evaluation* function—to assess the effectiveness of research and development in marketing[3] for marketing management over the past quarter century—and a *prescriptive* function—to make recommendations of ways in which the generation and diffusion process could be improved.

The Commission accepted as a given the goal of the long-run relevance of knowledge created to practice in marketing. In this setting, knowledge implies all forms of academic and professional marketing re-

Reprinted with permission from *J. Marketing,* vol. 43, pp. 17–29, Jan. 1979.
Published by the American Marketing Association.

367

search, and practice incorporates individuals and organizations such as line and staff marketing managers, senior corporation executives, and decision makers in government and nonprofit organizations. Its focus was thus on attempting to understand and evaluate the knowledge-creation and diffusion process in marketing. Where and how do changes originate? Where and with whom do ideas incubate and concepts become articulated? Where are the new methods tested and the techniques refined?

The concern for the study of these kinds of questions in marketing lies in the continuing serious debate as to the *relevance* of much of the knowledge-generating sector's activities to marketing management practice. It is obvious that a knowledge-creating sector does exist within marketing. Contrary to the views of many academics, the knowledge-creating sector is not solely, nor even largely, the province of academic researchers. Rather, it encompasses basic research mostly done in universities; applied and problem-oriented research in universities, research institutes, and government or nonprofit organizations; as well as problem-solving research in corporations, advertising agencies, marketing research firms, and consulting organizations. Attesting to a growth in quantity, albeit not necessarily in quality, of what is intended to be useful marketing knowledge over the past quarter-century was the creation of the AMA-sponsored *Journal of Marketing Research,* in addition to the *Journal of Marketing;* the advent of the multidisciplinary *Journal of Consumer Research* with its large proportion of marketing-based content; and an expansion of marketing-related articles in journals such as *Management Science* and *Operations Research.* But a fundamental question is whether all or most of these segments do create *useful* knowledge. Although terms like "useful," "effective," and "relevant" are hard to define tightly, there is little question that a hard-headed demand for demonstrations of relevance to practical marketing problems has, to a considerable degree, replaced a post World War II faith that knowledge is

useful "in its own right." This is not to deny that much research—particularly basic research—is difficult to manage and inherently "wasteful" by post-hoc judgment. However, the Commission believed that it should be possible to trace *some* degree of impact of basic and other research on improvements in marketing management practice over a 25-year period.

Another way of expressing the driving force behind the Commission's work is to say that it was fundamentally interested in research accountability. Is the investment in knowledge-generation in the field of marketing worthwhile? Is the process self-generating (like a breeder reactor), or does it require explicit and continuing investments of time, talent, and money? If the process is not now as effective as it should be, what are the barriers and blocks that prevent new knowledge and research from being utilized?

More specifically, the objectives of the Commission were:
- To identify changes in the marketing profession and practice over the past 25 years.
- To examine the nature and objectives of knowledge generation and R&D in marketing and provide examples of new knowledge developed during the period.
- To explain the process of knowledge-creation and the diffusion of knowledge in the field of marketing.
- To assess the contributions, or lack thereof, of marketing knowledge to marketing practice, and develop a list of recommendations directed to specific constituencies within the field.

The balance of this article is structured along these lines. Definitive conclusions in any of these areas are not easy, and not immediately amenable to the usual kinds of empirical research operations. The Commission employed a variety of methods and procedures to address each topic and illuminate the issues involved.

Methods

The work of the Commission involved five different operating methods and data generation procedures.

---

[1]The Commission consisted of 18 people, eight from universities, including the two co-chairmen, four from independent research, consulting, and advertising firms, and six from operating companies. The four from independent firms were professional researchers while the six from operating companies were evenly split between management and research functions. Other members were: Seymour Banks (Leo Burnett Co.), Frank Bass (Purdue University), Robert Burnett (Meredith Corporation), Robert D. Buzzell (Harvard University), Henry J. Claycamp (International Harvester), Robert Ferber (University of Illinois), Ronald E. Frank (University of Pennsylvania), John G. Keane (Managing Change, Inc., President, AMA, 1976-77), Philip Kotler (Northwestern University), Lawrence Light (BBD&O, Inc.), Elmer Lotshaw (Owens-Illinois), William T. Moran (Ad Mar Research), Bart R. Panettiere (General Foods), W.R. Reiss (American Telephone & Telegraph), and Dudley M. Ruch (The Quaker Oats Company). Christopher Lovelock (Harvard University) served as staff director, and John Bateson, an HBS doctoral candidate and Marketing Science Institute research assistant, served as project assistant.

---

[2]The 25-year reference period was chosen as a useful time span for several reasons. It was considered long enough to provide evidence for a thoughtful review of changes in marketing practice and knowledge without being too long to be inaccessible to memory. It also encompassed several important events in the development of marketing. The computer was beginning to emerge onto the business scene at the beginning of the period. The Gordon and Howell (1959) and Pierson (1959) reports were completed during the early part of the period, significantly affecting curricula in business schools. An acceleration of change in the practice of marketing management and marketing research also took place during this period.

[3]By "research in marketing," we mean research addressed to any and all zones of the marketing field, rather than "marketing research" or "market research" alone, which typically imply research on consumers and/or on characteristics of markets.

First, commissioners and selected "friends" of the Commission[4] were polled for their opinions on four challenging questions: What were the major changes in the practice of marketing over the past 25 years? What major, new, useful approaches and techniques had been introduced over the period? What major problem areas remain? What major research approaches and techniques (in the commissioner's judgment) had failed to fulfill their promises?

Second, several face-to-face meetings of the commissioners were held during 1976 and 1977. Much attention, particularly in the later meetings, was given to the discussion and development of perspectives and viewpoints on the idea-generation and diffusion process in marketing.

Third, a study of changes in marketing journals and textbooks over the 25-year period was undertaken by the Commission's staff. The journal study involved content analysis at five-year intervals of the *Journal of Marketing, Journal of Marketing Research, Harvard Business Review,* and *Journal of Consumer Research.* Examined were "hot topics" at the beginning and end of the period, topics that appeared to be an ongoing source of interest as well as topics that seemed to fade and others that were introduced, and the business/academic affiliation of authors. Details of this study, as well as all other studies undertaken by the Commission, are given in its final report (Massy, Greyser, and Myers 1979). One self-evident watershed, however, was the 1964 founding of the *Journal of Marketing Research* with its emphasis on reports of empirical research and multivariate data analysis.

The textbook study involved content analysis of 15 marketing textbooks (mostly those in multiple editions) ranging from Maynard and Beckman to Kotler, Enis, and Heskett. The period was characterized by a move from principles texts "about marketing" to managerial and decision-oriented texts "for marketing managers." Early texts covering institutional views and topics such as commodities and agricultural marketing were replaced by managerially-oriented texts emphasizing components of the marketing mix. Kotler's first edition (1967) extended this focus by incorporating much more behavioral science and quantitative material and was, in some sense, a precursor to a decade of quantitatively rigorous management science and marketing books. Consumerism, environmental issues, multinational marketing, and marketing for nonprofit organizations are characteristic new topics introduced in textbooks towards the end of the period.

A fourth type of effort involved a survey of AMA members on various aspects of idea generation and diffusion. The focus was on determining the amount of awareness and usage of 13 different types of analytical techniques, models, or research approaches. Here again, the details of this study are given in the main report (Massy, Greyser, and Myers, 1979).

Finally, attempts were made to elaborate on specific aspects of the overall project. Special interviews were conducted by the Commission staff to "track" the intellectual and applications evolution of new developments, in particular what many considered to be a highly successful example—that of conjoint analysis. Also, the Commission staff developed alternative skeletal views of the idea generation and diffusion process for use in Commission discussions of various conceptions of this process. Finally, the co-chairmen developed several "think pieces" on the types, nature, and functions of marketing research and the role of the marketing academic community.

How Marketing Practice has Changed

Readers who are old enough to remember marketing in the 1950s will appreciate the diversity of changes that have taken place both in the marketing manager's environment and in the nature of the marketing operations themselves. They also might appreciate the difficulty of attempting to capture the nature and type of these changes in a few paragraphs! From the viewpoint of managerial practice, much that has changed is traceable to a change in managerial perspective contained in the familiar "marketing concept" with its emphasis on the identification and satisfaction of consumer wants and needs rather than on the "selling" of products. The implications of this externally focused attitude on how to run a business, and the basic idea that various components of marketing such as product, pricing, promotion, and distribution should be integrated into an overall comprehensive marketing plan, had far-reaching consequences for marketing practice and knowledge development over the period.

An external focus, for example, leads logically to a heightened awareness and stronger motivation for information-gathering and marketing research. This undoubtedly contributed to academic and professional concentration on understanding and predicting consumer behavior and was a major impetus in the creation of the consumer behavior field, the Association for Consumer Research, and numerous new consumer behavior textbooks and journals. The new focus gave increased stature and significance to marketing as a vital business function. Many of the aspects of a "profession" such as the scientific and explicit use of information in decision-making, the educational and uni-

---

[4]Particularly useful communications were obtained from Charles R. Adler of the Eastman Kodak Company, Paul N. Reis of the Procter and Gamble Company, C.R. Smith of Nabisco, Inc., and William D. Wells of Needham, Harper & Steers Inc.

versity role in training managerial talent for marketing positions, and the numerous other trappings, are traceable to this change in overall managerial focus. The evolution of marketing research in some corporations from a purely data-gathering function to include complex decision models and multivariate analysis which characterize modern-day "marketing information systems" seems, in retrospect, a natural evolution of this fundamental idea. Another type of evolution is the application of marketing principles to nonprofit organization management, a trend particularly apparent in recent years.

An equally persuasive explanation for changes in marketing management practice and knowledge development can be found in technological innovations and in social, economic, and environmental changes that have occurred over the past 25 years. Perhaps the most significant innovations from the viewpoint of their effect on marketing management practice were the development of the computer and television. The 25-year period spans the time in which each of these inventions came into being on a commercial scale and had far-reaching impact on marketing (as well as on other aspects of the nation as a whole). Computers made possible the management of very large amounts of data both in terms of accessibility and analysis. This, in turn, stimulated the need for models, theories, and perspectives to guide the data collection and analysis process. Highly complex multivariate methods became feasible analysis alternatives, and a whole generation of model-builders, statisticians, and computer specialists began to look at marketing as an applications area in which to pursue their interests. Progress in adapting the computer to basic discipline studies on which marketing researchers continued to draw their inspiration and insight—economics, psychology, sociology, and others—further emphasized and expanded the important role of the computer.

Parallel reasoning could be applied to assessing the impact of television (as well as many other types of period-specific innovations or product-line extensions such as jet air freight and travel, the space program, etc.). Television created entire industries of market-related specialists in advertising, research, production, and so on. Methodologies developed in basic social science ranging from econometrics to pupilometrics and psychometrics were quickly adopted, refined, and in some cases rejected by marketing academics and commercial research firms doing television and advertising research. The marketing manager, for the first time, could direct messages to a mass market of millions of households via a total communications package (both audio and visual channels) at a comparatively low cost-per-thousand viewers reached. The absolute costs of television usage involving hundreds of thousands or

millions of advertiser dollars increased marketing budgets accordingly. Many commissioners identified an overall increase in the scale of marketing operations as a characteristic change over the period. Obviously, when a marketing manager's budget has increased significantly, the requirements and opportunities for the use of marketing research data differ greatly.

Many other environmental factors affected marketing management over the period. Commissioners noted the increased role of government in marketing decision-making. Consumerism was a movement of the 1960s which impacted greatly on marketing. Energy and other shortages characterized manager concern towards the end of the period. Along with an overall increase in the scale of marketing operations, decisions became much more consequential or "risky" in terms of the stakes involved.

These are some of the major changes in marketing management practice and the forces that affected changes in practice over the period. The next question examined by the Commission concerned the nature and objectives of knowledge-generation and R&D in marketing and types of new knowledge that had been generated. The R&D on which the Commission focused does not refer to new technical inventions, chemical discoveries, and so on flowing from the nation's laboratories or what might be called the research and development associated with production. Rather, it refers to marketing research developments and new knowledge pertaining to advancement of marketing management practices.

Marketing's R&D

Throughout the balance of the article, the terms marketing R&D and marketing knowledge are used interchangeably. The R&D term is introduced to emphasize the fact that much of what a marketing manager considers "state-of-the-art" knowledge is *not* limited to the literature. Professionals in an applied field, such as marketing, do not rely solely (or even primarily) on journal materials as their source of knowledge—a fact often overlooked by academics for whom journals represent the major storehouse of new and accumulated knowledge. For marketing professionals, the proprietary research information resident in their companies (from both the company's own research and outside commercial sources) as well as the folklore and accumulated experience of managerial colleagues are important components of the "state-of-the-art." As will be seen, it is possible to document changes in marketing knowledge by examining journal materials, but extremely difficult or impossible to document important aspects of the total storehouse of knowledge generated over the period.

An equally difficult question concerns the effectiveness measure. What are, or should be, the objectives of knowledge-generation in marketing? We examine this controversial question next.

Objectives of Knowledge-Generation in Marketing

Although a viable argument can be made that knowledge development should be pursued for "its own sake" and much basic research in marketing is generated in this way, the Commission took the position that the objectives of knowledge-generation in our field should be to improve marketing management practice. Thus, even basic research if it is to be considered "effective" should, over the long run, contribute something to improved decision-making or other aspects of management practice. But how should "good" practice and management be defined? What is an effective marketing manager? More generally, what is an effective marketing organization? In either case, the usual criteria of sales and profits are often suspect because of the dynamics of markets and marketing operations. Good sales and good profits can result from "good luck!" The Commission's position was that management should be evaluated also on the basis of "good judgment" and the specific ways in which budgets and people are managed, plans developed, actions implemented, and operations controlled. As one CEO is reported to have said: "Don't tell me about sales and profits, tell me whether or not I have a good marketing operation."

Entire books have been written on the qualities of a good manager or, more generally, the "functions of the executive" (Barnard 1968). A marketing manager needs to possess a whole bundle of qualities captured in the notion of "leader"—the capacity to motivate people working under him or her, the capacity to efficiently manage large amounts of funds and expenditures, and the capacity to make difficult and risky decisions in an environment of great uncertainty. Increasingly, however, marketing managers must be capable of managing large amounts of complex data which can be used to reduce the uncertainty in decision-making. To do so, they need to be able to recognize and conceptualize important problems, and to distinguish the important from the trivial. In the Commission's view, they need a capacity to develop good "theories" or "models" of their operations, to be able to distinguish cause and effect, and understand the implications of their decisions.

The modern manager, in other terms, must be a good planner. The development of a good marketing plan where realistic and worthwhile objectives are carefully specified, the resources marshalled to carry them out, and control mechanisms introduced to evaluate them, is an important characteristic of good management. To this, we believe, should be added the capacity to guide research efforts, to marshall facts and data relevant to stated objectives, and the capacity to analyze and interpret complex information. The ideal manager must be able to bridge the gaps between an original theory/model specification, the research design actually used to generate data, and the interpretation of the final data results. The overriding point is that modern managers should display at least some of the characteristics of the scientist—a willingness to use theories, models, and concepts, a capacity to identify important problems, and a healthy respect for the value of objective information and research in seeking answers to problems. Managers need to know the "why" of their operations in the sense of a theory or model, the "what" in the sense of relevant facts and data that pertain to them, and the "how" in terms of the implications of implementation and control.

The difficulty of documenting that marketing managers were "better" at the end of the period than at the beginning should be obvious. The Commission did not attempt to test this proposition and we, frankly, don't know. We do know that more managers held the MBA degree, that there was much more marketing research information available, that the demands for in-company information systems and information to support decisions were higher, and that there was a marked rise in the size and scale of the marketing research industry generally. The criterion of "better practice" was thus left implicit rather than explicit in the Commission's deliberations, and the focus directed to better understanding the nature of marketing knowledge.

The Nature of Marketing Knowledge

Marketing "R&D" as referred to in this study encompasses a broad range of types of "knowledge" and ways in which it can be generated. Types of knowledge are in effect the "ends" to be achieved—the *objects* of research in marketing. The ways to generate knowledge represent the "means."

The Commission recognized two broad types of knowledge "objects" in this sense: (1) context-specific knowledge, and (2) context-free knowledge. Context-specific knowledge is specific to a particular firm or industry or specific to a particular managerial problem or situation: Does potato chip advertisement A generate more recall than advertisement B? Two subclasses of context-specific knowledge can be identified as (1a) product industry-specific, and (1b) situation-specific. Context-specific marketing knowledge is usually proprietary, particularly if it is current. It also is probably the most useful base of empirical evidence on which general facts and laws could eventually evolve. That is, by looking for regularities across product, industry, or situation-specific cases, we might come closer to more useful, relevant generalizations in the field of marketing. There are examples of this type of work (Clarke 1976; Haley 1970), but it is comparatively rare.

Context-free knowledge encompasses three subclasses referred to as: (2a) general facts and laws, (2b) theories or conceptual structures, and (2c) techniques. Examples are the advertising-to-sales ratios of Fortune 500 companies, theories of buyer behavior, and factor analysis, respectively. What we know about the duration effects of advertising, and patterns of brand loyalty and switching from stochastic brand choice research fit the 2a category, and contrasting theories of advertising effects (hierarchy, low-involvement, conflict, and so on) fit 2b. Conjoint analysis, to be discussed later, is an example of what is considered 2c, a technique, although there is certainly a model or theory which motivates this approach to data collection. These latter types of knowledge-generation are largely, but not exclusively, the domain of academics and university research and make up the content of much of our journal materials.

The means of knowledge-generation can be broadly classified as different kinds of marketing research. We note that many recent marketing research textbooks make a distinction between "Basic" research and "Decisional" research (Churchill 1976; Green and Tull 1978; Tull and Hawkins 1976). Basic research usually involves *hypothesis-testing* of some kind, a prediction based on the hypothesis, devising a test of the prediction, conducting the test, and developing an analysis plan to determine whether the results are statistically significant at some researcher-specified confidence level. Decisional research, on the other hand, begins with a specification of alternative *solutions* to a marketing problem, the possible outcomes of each alternative, the design of a method to predict actual outcomes, and data analysis which relies more on Bayesian-type reasoning than on that of classical statistics. The decision-maker is often mostly interested in how the information changes his/her prior probabilities of likely outcomes than in statistical significance.

Although many "classic" data collection and analysis techniques are included in most marketing research textbooks, the decision-theory viewpoint, or "decisional" research, is becoming much more widely adopted, particularly where the emphasis is placed on the building of a model for which very specific demands are made on the data-collection process. Decisional research also differs in other fundamental ways. There is much more attention to considering trade-offs between the cost and value of the information which, in turn, implies less attention to replication and questions such as reliability and validity. The decision-maker is more interested in knowing the probability level of the results rather than whether they are statistically significant. Finally, the fact that the user of the research and researcher are in direct association with one another, distinguishes decisional from the basic or classical research. What seems evident is that marketing research textbooks are becoming more "decisional" than "basic" in these terms, and this appears to us to be a healthy trend.

A further delineation within the "decisional" category can provide a better understanding of a research taxonomy in marketing, namely distinguishing *problem-solving* research from *problem-oriented* research.

- Problem-*solving* research addresses a very specific applied issue or problem, and is usually proprietary in character; that is, it is usually done within a company or under contract by a commercial firm/consultant for a company. Advertising testing research is one example.

- Problem-*oriented* research addresses a *class* of issues or problems, and typically has at least limited generalizability across firms or situations. The topics examined are usually of a conceptual character, but oriented to applied problems—for example an effort to classify the kinds of products and consumer purchase situations in which the hierarchy of advertising effects might operate in different ways.

The major criterion for assessing problem-solving research in marketing is whether it helps improve a specific business decision. For problem-oriented research, the criteria are whether it improves our understanding of particular kinds of phenomena in marketing (as an applied social science) and whether it contributes to advancements of theory and method in a basic discipline. The narrowness of the problem, the time frame for utility, and the context of the application all are factors differentiating problem-solving from problem-oriented research.

Two important conclusions flow from these views on the means and ends of marketing's R&D. First, there has been a progressively stronger *leveraged role* for research in marketing practice. With larger markets, more dollars are riding on marketing decisions. With more complex, highly segmented and fragmented markets, there is a higher premium on developing and reaching one's distinctive part in the market. And those companies which know how to harness the array of research tools, help develop and apply them ahead of others, and employ them swiftly and effectively in marketing decisions have an advantage over competition. Second, the huge growth of marketing research information and techniques has resulted in a multifaceted role for the marketing research manager. At least three separate missions can be discerned—facilitator, gatekeeper, and translator. *Facilitator* basically relates to planning and conducting studies and projects and bringing together managers and research specialists. *Gatekeeper* involves monitoring new research techniques and ideas, exploring, "filtering," and trying to apply some of them within the organization. The *translator* puts management issues and problems into researchable propositions and converts research findings into managerial terms.

Knowledge Development Over the Period

As noted earlier, it is impossible to document the full scope of new knowledge developed over the 25-year period for much resides in the mind and mores of practicing managers. The overview in this section is largely confined to published materials. Suffice it to say, that marketing as a field is still characterized both by a management philosophy that emphasizes intuition, executive experience, and the "art" of marketing, and an emerging philosophy that emphasizes research, information-gathering, and what some call the "science" of marketing.

From this perspective, the Commission concluded that much had taken place during the 25 years in the direction of increased use and dependency on scientific marketing research information. The increased size and sophistication of commercial marketing research services as well as a general expansion in the industry was noted. A marked shift from trade to consumer research and from secondary to primary research took place. Much more use was made of test marketing before new product introductions. By the end of the period, most of the large consumer packaged goods corporations had some form of marketing information system, and were making increasing use of models and methods to simulate consumer and competitive reactions.

The development of the computer and television noted earlier as impacting on management practice also impacted heavily on knowledge-generation. *Marketing and the Computer* (Alderson and Shapiro 1963) contained papers by a new generation of eager, young students such as Al Kuehn, Ralph Day, Paul Green, Hans Thorelli, Purnell Benson, Bill Massy, and Arnie Amstutz and was, in retrospect, a major precursor of things to come. The largest commercial marketing research service, A.C. Nielsen, Inc., is currently also one of the largest worldwide users of computers. Television required the development of new theories of consumer behavior and communication, new methods to study its effects (e.g., dozens of new commercial services such as Burke's DAR, AD-TEL, ASI In-Theater Testing, etc), and significant new models of advertising decision-making such as MEDIAC (Little and Lodish

1969). ADBUG (Little 1970), POMSIS (Aaker 1968) and AD-ME-SIM (Gensch 1973) which utilized computer capacity to assist decision-making in television and mass media generally (for a recent review of related models, see Larreche and Montgomery 1977).

New knowledge in marketing, particularly that which has heavily impacted on changes in marketing practice, is very difficult to document. In medicine, the discovery of penicillen, X-rays, control of diseases like polio, tuberculosis, and syphilis are clearly definable events. In marketing, no "drug" has yet been invented that will "cure" the problem of new product failures. But it is, nevertheless, possible to trace some of the new ideas, theories, tools, and decision-aids introduced during the period.

Exhibit 1 shows a listing of 64 examples of knowledge development in marketing from 1952 to 1977 organized into four categories; (1) Discipline-Based Theories, (2) Managerial Frameworks and Approaches, (3) Models and Measurement, and (4) Research Methods and Statistical Techniques. This listing is illustrative only and is intended to provide a sampling of the variety of identifiable new theories, concepts, methods, and techniques. It is interesting to note the degree to which much that is "new" in marketing is closely related to new developments in the basic disciplines, particularly economics and psychology. Much new marketing knowledge is by definition an application and refinement of basic theories and methods in these social sciences and, in some instances, has had major impacts on the development of their theory and method. An interesting characteristic is the comparative speed by which marketing academics and professional researchers have adopted or "tried out" those ideas. In general, marketing knowledge generated over the period 1952 to 1977 changed principally in the degree to which it increased in quantitative and behavioral science sophistication. The introduction of a management science/engineering perspective to the field moved us closer to considerations of marketing as an applied science, and in general a "social engineering" view of the profession.

The next section deals with the third type of charge to the Commission: what is the nature of the knowledge-creation and diffusion process in marketing?

The Knowledge-Creation and Diffusion Process

The Commission recognized two major patterns by which new knowledge is created and diffused to line managers: knowledge that is essentially idea, concept, or methods-driven and problem-driven knowledge.

EXHIBIT 1
Examples of Knowledge Development in Marketing, 1952-1977

DISCIPLINE-BASED THEORIES	MANAGERIAL FRAMEWORKS AND APPROACHES	MODELS AND MEASUREMENT	RESEARCH METHODS AND STATISTICAL TECHNIQUES
Demand and Utility Theory	Marketing Concept	Stochastic Models of Brand Choice	Motivation Research and Projective Techniques
Market Segmentation	Marketing Mix - 4Ps	Market Share Models	Survey Research
General and Middle-Range Theories of Consumer Behavior	Development of Marketing Cases	Marginal Analysis and Linear Programming	Focus Groups and Depth Interviewing
Image and Attitude Theory	DAGMAR	Bayesian Analysis	Experimental and Panel Designs—ANOVA
Theories of Motivation, Personality, Social Class, Life Style, and Culture	Product Life Cycle	Advertising Models, eg., Mediac, Pomsis, Admesim, Brandaid, Adbug	Advances in Probability Sampling
Expectancy-Value Theory	Marketing Plan	Causal Models	Hypothesis Formulation, Inference, Significance Test
Theories of Advertising Processes and Effects	State Approaches to Strategy Development	Sensitivity Analysis and Validity Tests	Multivariate Dependence Methods—Multiple Regression and Multiple Discriminant Analysis, Canonical Correlation
Information Processing Theory	Product Portfolio Analysis	Response Functions	
Attitude Change Theories (consistency and complexity theories)	Physical Distribution Management	Weighted Belief Models, Determinant Attributes	
Attribution Theory	Marketing Information Systems	Simulation and Marketing Games	Multivariate Interdependence Methods—Cluster and Factor Analysis, Latent Structure Analysis
Perceptual Processes	Product Positioning and Perceptual Mapping	Multidimensional Scaling and Attitude Measurement	
Advertising Repetition	Segmentation Strategies	Sales Management Models, eg., Detailer, Callplan	Advances in Forecasting Econometrics, and Time Series Analysis
Distribution Theory	New Marketing Organization Concepts, eg., Brand Management	New Product Models, eg., Demon, Sprinter, Steam, Hendry	
Refutation and Distraction Hypotheses	Territory Design and Salesman Compensation	Bid Pricing Models	Trade-Off Analysis and Conjoint Analysis
Theories of Diffusion, New Product Adoption and Personal Influence	Marketing Audit	Computer-Assisted Marketing Cases	Psychographics and AIO Studies
Prospect Theory	Demand State Strategies	Product Planning Models, Perceptor, Accessor	Physiological Techniques— Eye Camera, GSR, CONPAAD
	Creative Approaches and Styles		Unobtrusive Measures, Response Latency, Nonverbal Behavior.
	New Search and Screening Approaches		
	Refinements in Test Marketing Approaches		

The first can arise in the academic *or* professional sphere when someone has a good idea and the energy and persistence to pursue the research, testing, and publication required to disseminate it.[5] Examples of this in marketing are the idea of a "hierarchy of effects" and the subsequent expectancy-value models to explain consumer decision-making and information processing. Consumer information processing, in particular, is now a very popular marketing academic subject which, some might say, is being driven mostly by the inherent interest of researchers in attempting to understand this phenomenon.

The second type of new knowledge might arise when a manager needs to predict his brand share for a new product. This leads logically into sales forecasting techniques (and new developments in this area, Bass

and Wittink 1975), which in turn leads to the concept and use of panel data and, for example, stochastic models of brand choice (Morrison 1965), basic concepts such as market segmentation (Frank, Massy, and Wind 1972; Myers and Nicosia 1968; Wind 1978b) and to a variety of other new models and methods developments (e.g., Silk and Urban 1978; Srinivasan and Shocker 1973). Much segmentation research during the early part of the period appeared to be basically "idea-driven" (researchers were more interested in testing new types of multivariate methods factor analysis, cluster analysis, latent structure analysis, Sheth 1977), whereas during the latter part, particularly with the publication of *Market Segmentation* (Frank, Massy, and Wind 1972), research appeared more problem-driven and efforts were concentrated on situation-specific-type variables.

To better understand the process, the Commission chose conjoint analysis as a means of studying one

---

[5]An academic administrator once correctly observed that even the most brilliant ideas contain no social value if they remain lodged in the heads of their proponents!

pattern of adoption and diffusion. It is an example of an idea or methods-driven pattern, even though the problem (deriving a preference function and/or determining the utilities, "part-worths," of attribute levels) has been a part of marketing since the days when marketers were told to "sell the sizzle and not the steak!" The example illustrates several important ideas such as the role of nonmarketing academics, the importance of consulting arrangements in the diffusion process, and the contributions of academic and professional researchers in getting a complex idea widely disseminated and used.

It is generally held that a breakthrough article on conjoint analysis was published in 1964 in the *Journal of Mathematical Psychology* (Luce and Tukey 1964). It was a breakthrough in the sense of a long tradition of psychological and attitude measurement perspectives going back to Thurstone and others (nonmarketing academics) who make up the field of psychometrics and mathematical psychology. The first major publication in marketing literature on the subject was a 1971 *Journal of Marketing Research* article (Green and Rao 1971).[6] Green and his colleagues focused on developing a "full-profile" approach to the fundamental task of generating part-worth utilities on sets of decision criteria or salient brand/product attributes. A professional researcher, Richard Johnson of Market Facts, Inc., Chicago, working independently from the Wharton group, developed a parallel procedure based on a "two-factor-at-a-time" approach which he called "trade-off analysis" and published the new procedure in *JMR* (Johnson 1974). What is important for our purposes is to note the location of each individual, one in a university environment and one in a commercial or "external" marketing research firm. Also of significance is the pattern, particularly of the marketing academic in this case, of essentially using real-world marketing applications as the laboratory for further testing and refining the methods reflected in numerous studies involving actual situation-specific decisions and data.[7] A similar pattern from the professional researcher viewpoint was going on through the normal process of a marketing research firm (Market Facts) dealing with numerous clients, many of whom were being introduced to the technique over the period via this channel. Both individuals also were appearing at conferences and presenting papers on the subject further enhancing the diffusion process. Robinson and

---

[6]This was preceded by several working papers and a paper published as early as 1968 by Green and his colleagues at Wharton.

[7]This process of refinement has continued to the present and involves different types of data collection procedures, different types of scale assumptions (nominal, ordinal, interval, ratio), and basic extensions such as categorical conjoint measurement and second generation models such as componential segmentation. (See Wind 1978a).

Associates (Philadelphia), another "external" marketing research firm, was also an early adopter of conjoint analysis and introduced the technique to many of its clients. Wharton students, particularly graduating Ph.D.s who accepted positions at other universities across the country, were significant forces in the general refinement and diffusion of conjoint analysis. One estimate is that there have been, to date, over 300 commercial applications (separate and distinct studies) of conjoint analysis, and interest is still high and spreading to applications in the nonprofit and government sectors.

In sum, this is an example of one of the most successful types of new knowledge introduced over the period in terms of making a complex idea developed in a basic discipline of direct use and benefit to line marketing managers and marketing decision-making. The basic ingredients of the process are a methodological breakthrough in basic research, the adaptation and refinement of the ideas by a small "innovator group" of marketing academics and professionals, and subsequent diffusion to line managers involving external marketing research companies, internal marketing research departments, students, journals, consultants, meetings, and conferences.

What can be said generally about the efficiency and effectiveness of this system over the 25 years? First, the Commission concluded that much innovation, particularly as perceived by academics, never reaches line managers, and in retrospect, has contributed little to improvements in marketing management practice. Second, and discussed in the next section, there is a great deal of "promising" development which is used little by managers. Third, important new developments have come from *both* academics *and* professionals. In marketing there is a relatively small "*innovator group*" made up of both professionals and academics from which a significant number of the major new, useful ideas flow. Finally, the Commission concluded that neither the idea nor the problem necessarily comes first at the initiation stage, and problems and ideas find themselves in different ways. There is no single, dominant pattern. In some cases, particularly among academics, a technique is developed and then applied to a real-world problem. In others, a problem is posed, and a search for new solution techniques is initiated. In either event, much effort is needed to test and hone the development before it becomes widely adopted or commercially useful. Unfortunately, problems often reside with management people who are not well trained to articulate them to research people unfamiliar with management life. The Commission was struck by the discrepancies between the volume of new knowledge generated over the period and the comparatively low rate of adoption at the line manager level. Is this type of "failure rate" endemic to the field? What causes it? What can be done about it?

Barriers to Innovation and Diffusion

The Commission recognized two types of barriers to the diffusion and adoption process broadly classified as Structural and Organizational (S/O) barriers and Substantive and Communication (S/C) barriers. On reflection, we have become impressed with the seeming rediscovery of C.P. Snow's "two cultures" within the field marketing, not characterized so much as that of academic/business as that of researcher/manager. We are reminded of the "those who think and never act" and "those who act and never think" distinction. Into this mix must be poured the numerous types of research specialists that have arisen in marketing over the 25 years, many of whom communicate in a language inherently foreign to one another.

More specifically, the Commission recognized as S/O barriers the inherent differences in occupational roles and incentives among managers, researchers, and academics. In particular, the impact of the reward system and the drive to do research and publish for academics is a significant cause of the volume and type of research and new-knowledge generation in marketing. In some universities, only contributions to basic research carry any weight, and it is often nonmarketing academics (economists, psychologists, sociologists) who are doing the evaluating. Built-in barriers between line and staff people within an organization, the proprietary and confidential nature of much marketing research information in corporations, the lack of exposure to and formal quantitative training of line managers,[8] and other characteristics of line managers and their positions (too busy, conservative, inherent inertia, etc.) were seen as S/O barriers to the process.

Numerous Substantive and Communication (S/C) barriers were identified. A common theme was the inappropriateness of many quantitative models and techniques to marketing problems as perceived by marketing managers. The length of time needed to test, adapt, and make a new idea useful was mentioned. Some commissioners recognized current marketing journals as a barrier—our journals represent mostly academics talking to one another, and reflect the *supply* of new knowledge rather than the *demand* for it. The

credibility of much academic work comes into question when trivial problems are given treatment equal to that given important problems. The annual AMA conference structure was singled out as a barrier in the sense that two, separate conferences, one for educators and one for professionals, are held. The lack of line manager membership in the AMA, and/or the lack of time to participate actively in such organizations by line managers, was another type of S/C barrier. Particularly for managers, there are few incentives or rewards for contributing to new knowledge *per se,* and attention is often focused on short-run sales and profit generation.

Many of these barriers and blocks reduce to attitudinal factors residing in the make-up of each of the participants. Managers, often uncomfortable with complex quantitative and abstract materials, or with no time to learn about them, are prone to dismiss much that could be valuable as academic nonsense. Patterns such as the "not invented here" syndrome, anti-intellectualism, and other defenses develop to rationalize the basic position. Researchers, particularly those who are scholarly-inclined, often write-off practical marketing problems as irrelevant to what they do, or as an interference with their scholarly progress. Patterns of "let them learn what I am doing" develop with little or no commitment to translating ideas into the practical world of the marketing decision-maker.

Assessment and Some Recommendations

Three broad observations appear germane to the overall charge to the Commission of assessing the effectiveness of marketing research and development for marketing management:

- Knowledge-generation in marketing, like in any other professional or academic field, is to some degree "inefficient." There will always be waste in the system in terms of false starts, blind alleys, and so forth. Throughout its work, the Commission held to an initial view that the most meaningful criterion—perhaps the only criterion—for assessing and making new investments in developing marketing knowledge was its ultimate contribution to marketing practice. At the same time, there was broad recognition that *basic* research both warranted and demanded support, even though many who engage in it do so with the principal (and sometimes sole) motivation of enriching knowledge rather than improving practice. The often indirect impacts on practice—despite the aforementioned inherent inefficiencies in and unpredictability of basic research to be "useful"—remain important enough to sustain and encourage it.

---

[8]We note that the "average" brand or product manager in a major corporation may now be much more comfortable with quantitative techniques given the likely exposure to them in classroom situations over at least the past 10 years. One estimate is that there are about 25,000 marketing majors produced annually in the United States. If only 1000 per year are MBAs exposed to quantitative methods in our better business schools, there should be 10,000 managers out there for whom models and techniques are a familiar part of marketing knowledge.

- All forms and types of marketing research increased in both quality and quantity over the 25-year period. In quality terms, the direction has been toward greater quantitative and behavioral science sophistication. This has been manifested in the professional marketing and marketing research community and particularly in the ways marketing is taught in business schools. The latter, in turn, feeds the world of practice at the entry level.

- A significant amount of marketing research effort, new knowledge development, model-building, and theorizing has had relatively little impact on improving marketing management practice over the period. Although controversial, this observation represents our interpretation of a widely-held belief among Commission members after many months of deliberation on events of the past 25 years. As one Commissioner noted, "There isn't a single problem area with regard to the practice of marketing management that marketing research or the world of technology and concepts has mastered." Another said, "The tendency (is) for many marketing decisions to be made either without any research or on the basis of extremely sloppy research. The fact that the vast majority of new products put on the market turn out to be failures may be a manifestation of the phenomenon."

In reflecting on these assessments, we recognize that marketing is still in a rather primitive state of development. Unlike our impression of some other business fields such as accounting and finance, there is still no unifying marketing theory or model which holds together the diversity of perspectives and viewpoints. Materials which are widely taught in the classroom such as Bayesian analysis do not appear to be widely used by practicing managers. Although there are numerous examples of what might be considered "successful" knowledge development, measured in terms of managerial adoption, we are struck by the degree to which much that has been developed and *could be* useful is *not* being used.

What the Commission in effect rediscovered in the management science/model-building area was a reaffirmation of what many model-builders themselves have long believed—comparatively few firms or practicing management people seem to be using their models. This is particularly true for early, complex model formulations that often went through a cycle of trial and rejection. The most recent model-building trend—to begin with relatively simple concepts and functions, to involve the manager in the model-building effort, and to establish long-run relationships with the client firm—appears to us to be a very healthy one. Many behavioral researchers might well go through a similar

type of introspective process with respect to how their work impacts on marketing practice, and the degree of its adoption or nonadoption by marketing decision-makers.

On a more optimistic note, we see marketing at somewhat of a turning-point with respect to the effectiveness of its R&D efforts. A major barrier to the diffusion process, particularly in terms of utilizing formal models, is largely one of scale of operations, the sizeable investments of funds required to develop and maintain on-going data bases, and the teams of specialists needed to achieve an effective utilization of research and knowledge-generation resources. The basic combination of scale and a willingness to invest now appears to us to exist in many corporations, and there are numerous examples of the fully-integrated information system model which this implies.

In retrospect, then, the quarter-century contained a significant amount of "ineffectiveness" regarding marketing's R&D. *The contributions of research and knowledge-development at best can be characterized as mixed.* The impacts have been significant, but far less than "what might have been." The reasons lie primarily in the numerous types of barriers and blocks to the diffusion process. We think concerned people in the field should examine their own organizations with respect to both the S/O and S/C barriers. Many of the Commission's recommendations pertain to various ways to reduce these barriers.

Recommendations

There are numerous recommendations given in the Commission's full report. Many relate to the fundamental needs for open lines of communication between researchers and managers, the needs to find ways to break down the barriers and blocks to the idea-generation and diffusion process, and the needs for conscious effort, investment, and continuing funding to make the process work. In our view, the process is not like a breeder reactor, it is *not* self-generating; rather it requires conscious effort to sustain it. More sources need to be found for supporting research, particularly of the "problem-oriented" kind, and better ways need to be developed to bridge the gaps between knowledge-generation and knowledge-utilization.

Among the many recommendations, we view the following as particularly important and provide some of our own reflections on the implications and impact of each:

1. *More support should be provided for basic and "problem-oriented" research in marketing.* Both the professional and the academic marketing communities need to give "problem-oriented" research much more attention. The company role here goes beyond provid-

ing financial support, to contributing data and information on company experiences. In this way, more progress can be made to develop experience-based "conditional generalizations," i.e., knowledge and concepts that apply under specified kinds of product, market, or consumer conditions. On the academic side, more appreciation is needed of the "respectability" of such research for academic knowledge-building. (See item 5, below.)

On the whole, relatively few institutions—notably the Marketing Science Institute, the now phased-down National Science Foundation's Research Applied to National Needs program, the American Association of Advertising Agencies' Educational Foundation—exist with "problem-oriented" research as their major focus. Such marketing research typically is not "basic" enough to gain support from institutions principally geared to "harder" sciences; this appears to have been the experience at NSF. Yet problem-oriented research is usually not immediately practical enough to warrant support from company operating budgets. In short, "problem-oriented" research is a stepchild. So far, the limited success in gaining support for such research has been rooted in institutional systems, such as MSI's, that catalytically bring together conceptually-oriented professionals with practically-oriented academics (Greyser 1978).

This focus on "problem-oriented" research does not reduce the importance, in our view, of basic research. It *is* important over the long-run. We think, however, that business and academe alike have given too little recognition and value to problem-oriented research.

2. *Nontechnical reviews of new concepts, findings, and techniques in marketing should be published far more frequently. At the same time, publications that permit researchers to write to other researchers need to be preserved and encouraged.* This recommendation basically addresses both ends of the knowledge development/knowledge utilization spectrum. For the former, we underscore the importance of having an "archival resource" that not only provides a medium where new research results can be published, but also permits such work to be accessed readily by other researchers over time. "Relevance" is not the appropriate criterion on which to assess such journals. The *Journal of Marketing Research* is obviously a specific example.

At the other end, nontechnical reviews represent one way of attempting to break the technical jargon block which many Commissioners thought was a major impediment to good communication. Complex ideas must often be expressed in formal, mathematical terms, but they should be capable of being communicated in terms that a broader audience can understand. The "annual reviews" in fields such as psychology were cited as illustrations, as were some of the "state-of-the-art" articles in current journals, and the concept of the *Review of Marketing*.

3. *Senior executives of major companies in the consumer, industrial, and services sector should be encouraged to develop a climate within their organizations which is amenable to exploration of and experimentation with new research ideas and techniques. Further, practicing managers must become more appreciative of the value of "good theory," and develop more capacity to conceptualize, supervise, and interpret information relevant to decision-making.* Unless the right climate of receptivity is developed within the organization, there is little chance of significant adoption of new knowledge. People simply won't want to take the necessary risks of introducing new ideas. Moreover, an attitude which assumes that new ideas and techniques are automatically of low or no relevance to one's operations needs to be guarded against. Anti-intellectualism, in whatever forms it may take and for whatever motivations it may arise, appears to us not to be in the best interests of either the firm or the manager. This recommendation may have a "motherhood" (maybe even a "Pollyanna") character, but we think it needs restatement here.

4. *A "clearinghouse mechanism" should be established in which company data files can be made available to academic and professional researchers.* This is not a new idea, but one which the Commission recommends receive attention and effort. It would do much to meet the needs of academic researchers for empirical data, and consequently increase the usefulness (real and perceived) of their work.

The difficulties of implementing such an activity are widely recognized. Major difficulties include the concerns of companies regarding proprietary information, and the lack of congruence of categories and questions from study to study (even ones done by the same company). Although much time and careful effort is necessary, we think these problems can be mitigated.

One commissioner suggested that what is needed to facilitate a clearinghouse mechanism is some motivation for contributing companies. Conscious as we are that many company studies are underanalyzed (even in terms of their own objectives), we think one possible avenue would be for companies contributing data to suggest particular perspectives/approaches for consideration by researchers working with the data through the clearinghouse.

5. *Marketing educators and university administrators must be made aware of the crucial need to*

maintain open lines of communication with professional researchers and practicing managers. They should be persuaded to support teaching, consulting, and research activities which foster this communication and involve real-world marketing problems. This recommendation relates in large part to our earlier comments on "two cultures." In our view, too many academics think that "being practical" is not desirable (and may even be explicitly undesirable). For marketing academics, this tendency can become exacerbated when people from nonbusiness fields are involved, as in universitywide promotion reviews. Understanding practice, and contributing to it, can lead to major contributions to knowledge-development itself.

Conclusion

What do we hope will emerge from the Commission's work? First and foremost, our hope is for greater sensitivity to and concern for the state of research in marketing today—whether that research be basic, problem-oriented, or problem-solving. From such sensitivity and concern we think will emerge an improved climate for all research, both in universities and in the business community. In turn, professionalism in marketing decision-making will be enhanced—a goal that we believe should be shared by all in the field.

REFERENCES

Aaker, David A. (1968), "A Probabilistic Approach to Industrial Media Selection," *Journal of Advertising Research*, 8 (September), 46-54.

Alderson, Wroe and Stanley J. Shapiro, eds. (1963), *Marketing and the Computer*, Englewood Cliffs, NJ: Prentice-Hall, Inc.

Barnard, Chester I. (1968), *Functions of the Executive*, Cambridge, MA: Harvard University Press.

Bass, Frank M. and Dick R. Wittink (1975), "Pooling Issues and Methods in Regression Analysis with Examples in Marketing Research," *Journal of Marketing Research*, 12 (November), 414-425.

Churchill, Gilbert A. Jr. (1976), *Marketing Research: Methodological Foundations*, Hinsdale, IL: The Dryden Press.

Clarke, Darral G. (1976), "Econometric Measurement of the Duration of Advertising Effect on Sales," *Journal of Marketing Research*, 13 (November), 345-357.

Frank, Ronald E., William F. Massy, and Yoram Wind (1972), *Market Segmentation*, Englewood Cliffs, NJ: Prentice-Hall, Inc.

Gensch, Dennis H. (1973), *Advertising Planning: Mathematical Models in Advertising Media*, Amsterdam: Elsevier Publishing Co.

Gordon, Robert A. and James E. Howell (1959), *Higher Education for Business*, New York: Columbia University Press.

Green, Paul E. and Vithala R. Rao (1971), "Conjoint Measurement for Quantifying Judgmental Data," *Journal of Marketing Research*, 8 (August), 355-363.

———————— and Donald S. Tull (1978), *Research for Marketing Decisions*, Englewood Cliffs, NJ: Prentice-Hall, Inc.

Greyser, Stephen A. (1978), "Academic Research Marketing Managers Can Use," *Journal of Advertising Research*, 18 (April), 9-14.

Haley, Russell I. (1970), "We Shot an Arrowhead (#9) Into the Air," *Proceedings*, 16th Annual Conference, Advertising Research Foundation, New York, 25-30.

Johnson, Richard M. (1974), "Trade-Off Analysis of Consumer Values," *Journal of Marketing Research*, 11 (May), 121-127.

Kotler, Philip (1967), *Marketing Management: Analysis, Planning & Control*, Englewood Cliffs, NJ: Prentice-Hall, Inc.

Larreche, Jean-Claude and David B. Montgomery (1977), "A Framework for the Comparison of Marketing Models: A Delphi Study," *Journal of Marketing Research*, 14 (November), 487-498.

Little, John D. C. (1970), "Models and Managers: the Concept of a Decision Calculus," *Management Science*, 16 (April), B466-485.

———————— and Leonard M. Lodish (1969), "A Media Planning Calculus," *Operations Research*, 17 (January-February), 135.

Luce, Duncan R. and John W. Tukey (1964), "Simultaneous Conjoint Measurement: A New Type of Fundamental Measurement," *Journal of Mathematical Psychology*, 1 (February), 1-27.

Massy, William F., Stephen A. Greyser, and John G. Myers (1978), *Report of the Commission on the Effectiveness of Research and Development for Marketing Management*, Chicago, IL: American Marketing Association.

Morrison, Donald G. (1965), "Stochastic Models for Time Series with Applications in Marketing," *Program in Operations Research*, Stanford University, Technical Report No. 8.

Myers, John G. and Francesco M. Nicosia (1968), "On the Study of Consumer Typologies," *Journal of Marketing Research*, 5 (May), 182-193.

Pierson, Frank C. et al. (1959), *Education of American Businessmen: The Study of University-College Programs in Business Administration*, New York: McGraw-Hill (Carnegie Series in American Education).

Sheth, Jagdish N., ed. (1977), *Multivariate Methods for Market and Survey Research*, Chicago, IL: American Marketing Association.

Silk, Alvin J. and Glen L. Urban (1978), "Pre-Test Market Evaluation of New Packaged Goods: A Model and Measurement Methodology," *Journal of Marketing Research*, 15 (May), 171-191.

Srinivasan, V. and Allan D. Shocker (1973), "Linear Programming Techniques for Multidimensional Analysis of Preferences," *Psychometrika*, 38 (September), 337-369.

Tull, Donald S. and Del I. Hawkins (1976), *"Marketing Research: Meaning, Measurement, and Method*, New York: MacMillan Publishing Co.

Wind, Yoram (1978a), "Marketing Research and Management: A Retrospective View of the Contributions of Paul E. Green," in *Proceedings of the Tenth Paul D. Converse Awards Symposium*, Alan Andreasen, ed., Urbana, IL: University of Illinois Press.

———————— (1978b), "Issues and Advances in Segmentation Research," *Journal of Marketing Research*, 15 (August), 317-337.

A Selected Bibliography of Industrial Marketing Literature

This selected bibliography was prepared as a supplement to the articles found in this reprint volume. It provides an annotated list of articles which are readily available, reasonably current, and broadly applicable to a variety of industrial marketing circumstances.

This book contains some writing from unpublished sources, from foreign journals, and from other sources that would be difficult to obtain for most readers. Collecting such materials into a single reference work is one of the benefits of this anthology. For the anthology user who desires further information, however, this bibliography concentrates on those articles contained in magazines and journals that are available in many libraries.

Also, there was a necessary time lag between the time the selection of articles for the anthology was finalized and the actual printing of the book; this bibliography was prepared to help bridge that gap by adding references for additional timely articles. Accordingly, many of the references contained in this bibliography were published during those interim months; others were published in recent years and represent current theory and application in industrial marketing.

It was also felt that it would be helpful for those with little formal training in marketing if some references were provided to articles containing basic principles that have broad application. While some of these articles may appear to deal with special, apparently unrelated circumstances, the principles detailed are directly applicable to industrial marketing also.

Therefore, this bibliography both complements and supplements this anthology. It is hoped that this bibliography will add to this book's currency and will make it an even more valuable addition to your marketing library.

Lynn J. Whiting

"A tip for ad practitioners: People always interest other people," *Industrial Marketing*, pp. 74, 76–82, June 1978. Useful ideas about using real people in advertising are examined.

M. Banks, "Industrial advertising media—The agency stepchild," *Industrial Marketing*, pp. 64–66, Sept. 1977. Advertising agencies generally do not have the necessary expertise specifically for dealing with industrial products or services. Problems and possible solutions are discussed.

I. Belth, "Lists are not just lists," *Industrial Marketing*, pp. 90–92, Sept. 1980. The article describes how to coordinate direct mail and list marketing into a sales strategy. Types of lists and their applications are discussed.

"Billboards: A twist in want ads," *Business Week*, p. 42k, Dec. 25, 1978. The use of billboards in industrial advertising is somewhat unusual, but can provide a significant marketing avenue in certain circumstances.

J.S. Bindra, "Product development: Your most important activity," *J. Appl. Management*, pp. 24–29, 32, May/June 1979. The very survival of an organization in a high technology field depends on its new product/process development program. Companies can improve their success at turning innovative ideas into useful end products.

R.W. Bly, "What business/industrial copywriters can learn from the mail order folks," *Business Marketing*, pp. 70–74, Feb. 1984. By using the "three E's" of mail order copywriting—enthusiasm, empathy, and economy—a company can breathe new life and excitement into flat, lackluster business literature.

T.V. Bonoma, "Get more out of your trade shows," *Harvard Business Rev.*, pp. 75–83, Jan.-Feb. 1983. Various aspects of how to select trade shows and how to make participation in them more effective are examined.

——, "Market success can breed 'marketing inertia,'" *Harvard Business Rev.*, pp. 115–212, Sept.-Oct. 1981. Marketers must avoid the temptation to rely on old strategies that ignore changes that disrupt the marketplace. The author recommends a number of practices to monitor markets and customers' attitudes.

R.W. Bucker, "How to estimate your advertising profit payoff," *Business Marketing*, pp. 60–66, Jan. 1984. The author develops a method for estimating the profit return on business/industrial advertising. It's based upon the viewpoint that advertising's prime contribution is acquiring new customers.

J.B. Bushman, "Inquiry handling—On the double," *Industrial Marketing*, pp. 36–37, 40, Dec. 1978. A problem with advertising- and publicity-inspired inquiries is that their effectiveness is directly related to the speed with which they are processed. A method to handle all inquiries within 24 hours is discussed.

"Business-to-business direct response promotion," *Industrial Marketing*, pp. 51, 56, 60–61, Sept. 1980. A recent survey indicates that direct response promotion and advertising must be balanced in the marketing program. The author examines various aspects of direct response promotion.

R.C. Christian, "1978: Year of changes for the marketing communicator," *Industrial Marketing*, pp. 50–52, June 1978. The changing environments of advertising, selling, and buying are discussed, as are the needs for new strategies and new tactics.

——, "Corporate advertising: Its role in the software revolution," *Industrial Marketing*, p. 96, July 1980. Five basic guidelines are presented for ensuring that corporate advertising makes a positive contribution to the company's marketing effort.

"Conception to resurrection better than womb to tomb," *Marketing News*, p. 9, July 13, 1979. In marketing high technology products, it is important to consider the product in proper perspective. Four steps in market planning are discussed.

"Copy chasers: More letters to 'Dear Addy,'" *Industrial Marketing*, pp. 109–114, June 1981. Some basic advertising layout assumptions are challenged. A number of industrial ads sent in by various readers are critiqued.

E.R. Corey, "Key options in market selection and product planning," *Harvard Business Rev.*, pp. 119–128, Sept.–Oct. 1975. Key choices that affect the success of industrial marketing are examined. The strategic choices of which markets to serve and when to enter them are developed.

J. Couretas, "Counting smokestacks: Census help for marketers," *Business Marketing*, pp. 86–88, Jan. 1984. The 1982 Economic Census (and subsequent issues of the Census) by the U.S. Department of Commerce can be used to forecast sales, evaluate performance, determine territories, and allocate advertising budgets. Helpful ideas and applications are examined.

H.B. Crandall, "Ten ways to move more industrial products with direct mail," *Industrial Marketing*, pp. 86–89, Sept. 1980. The article examines five things direct mail does well and ten methods of making direct mail more effective.

D.W. Cravens, "Strategic marketing's new challenge," *Business Horizons*, pp. 18–23, Mar.–Apr. 1983. A rapidly changing business environment dictates closer attention to strategic planning in marketing.

J.L. DeFazio, "An inquiry-based MIS: How your management information system should sort hot leads from cold lemons," *Business Marketing*, pp. 54–68, Aug. 1983. Sales leads can be a powerful marketing intelligence source. A proven, inquiry-based management information system is discussed; this system uses data from sales leads to provide a strong competitive advantage.

E. Dichter, "Emotion, the third ear and industrial sales," *Industrial Marketing*, pp. 80–81, July 1980. Emotion often plays a role in a person's perception of a product. By learning to watch for this emotional response, marketers can improve communications with customers.

B. Donath, "Direct response marketing," *Industrial Marketing*, pp. 42–46, Sept. 1980. Much potential for improvement exists in the way most firms handle their direct mail and other direct response marketing.

——, Ad Copy Clinic: "They (should have) laughed when I sat down to write an ad," *Industrial Marketing*, pp. 102–105, June 1982. Copy and art pretesting can be a useful tool to an industrial advertiser. A pretesting system that predicts readership scores is discussed.

G.R. Dundas and K.A. Krentler, "Critical path method for introducing an industrial product," *Industrial Marketing Management*, vol. 11, pp. 125–131, 1982. Introducing a new industrial product is extremely risky. This paper outlines a method for monitoring the critical path in the product's life cycle.

P. De Vasconcellos Filho, "Strategic planning: A new approach," *Managerial Planning*, pp. 12–20, Mar.–Apr. 1982. The author outlines a new approach to strategic planning. As organizations consider their missions, their interfaces, their competition, and their strengths and weaknesses, they can lay a foundation for their survival and prosperity.

S. Fraker, "High-speed management for the high-tech age," *Fortune*, pp. 62–66, Mar. 5, 1984. Rapidly changing technology is making it necessary to adopt new management and marketing techniques. Several approaches are examined.

A. L. Frank, "Software authors should define market," *Computerworld*, pp. 31–33, May 5, 1980. A number of important areas that must be included in the marketing plan for software offer insight into the basic considerations for marketing most industrial products or services.

N. Frothingham, "Keeping print advertising costs under control," *INC*, pp. 95–96, Sept. 1979. Rising advertising costs make it important to examine old premises. Ideas for reducing advertising costs and increasing effectiveness are presented.

M.E. Goretsky, "Frameworks of strategic marketing information needs," *Industrial Marketing Management*, vol. 13, pp. 7–11, 1983. In developing a framework for a management information system, several areas need careful consideration. Key questions a company should consider are provided.

E. Greif, "On-site support: Cost effective trade show traffic builder," *Industrial Marketing*, pp. 78, 82, 84–85, Apr. 1979. Trade shows and exhibits are an essential part of many industrial marketing programs. Methods are discussed to increase their effectiveness in attracting customers.

P.A. Hopkinson, "How to promote industrial business in less developed countries," *Industrial Marketing*, pp. 68–75, Oct. 1978. A basic plan for determining a company's likelihood of successfully marketing products in developing countries is defined.

F. Houghton, "How ads can sell more than products," *Nation's Business*, pp. 61–62, Mar. 1984. Corporate image building can pay off with the public and with employees too.

"Industrial marketing: Designers take to selling," *Business Week*, pp. 150E, 150F, Nov. 6, 1978. Firms in fields which traditionally have relied on informal approaches to marketing are beginning to rely on newly formed marketing groups to ensure their success.

"Industrial marketing survey: Business/industrial direct response promotion," *Industrial Marketing*, pp. 75–76, Aug. 1982. Survey results yield useful insights into the use of direct mail in marketing industrial products.

"Industrial publicity: One of the best promotional tools," *Industrial Marketing Management*, vol. 12, pp. 207–211, July 1983. Publicity, a frequently forgotten and misunderstood promotional tool, is discussed. Surveys in trade journals rank it as one of the most effective methods, having high credibility and low cost.

P. Kotler, "From sales obsession to marketing effectiveness," *Harvard Business Rev.*, pp. 67–75, Nov.–Dec. 1977. An approach to basic marketing is supplied. Also, a rating form is introduced to let a company determine if it understands its marketing responsibilities.

R.P. Kotz, "Developing products people don't understand, aren't sure they need," *Advertising Age*, p. 64, Oct. 29, 1979. High technology products using microprocessors face new and unique marketing challenges. The problems with marketing high technology products and the emerging trends are examined.

"Lear Siegler teases computer market with project X campaign," *Industrial Marketing*, pp. 44–45, Dec. 1978. Lear Siegler used an unusual "tongue-in-cheek" approach to introduce five new computer products to the normally conservative computer industry.

M.M. Lele and U.S. Karmarkar, "Good product support is smart marketing," *Harvard Business Rev.*, pp. 124–132, Nov.–Dec. 1983. The identification of customer expectations regarding product support and the development of cost-effective strategies for meeting those expectations are a major facet of successful marketing today.

T. Levitt, "After the sale is over . . ." *Harvard Business Rev.*, pp. 87–93, Sept.–Oct. 1983. A number of changing aspects in the sales process are examined and numerous fresh insights are provided.

G.L. Lilien, "Keeping up with the marketing Joneses," *Industrial Marketing*, pp. 76–84, Mar. 1980. Practical tools are presented to help analyze and plan marketing budgets. The "ADVISOR" studies for M.I.T. are discussed and analyzed.

L.M. Lodish, "Don't leave well enough alone," *Wharton Magazine*, pp. 27–32, Summer 1982. Advertising decisions are filled with uncertainty. Methods to better understand and reduce that uncertainty are examined.

P. Maher, "IM's complete guide to market research sources," *Industrial Marketing*, pp. 75–82, Mar. 1982. A survey of marketing personnel identifies the sources useful for gathering secondary information. The use of these sources is examined.

J.A. Mahoney, "A 'how to' for industrial distributor advertising," *Industrial Marketing*, pp. 54–56, 58, Jan. 1979. Elements of preparing and implementing an effective industrial distribution advertising program are examined.

R. Manville, "Why industrial companies must advertise their products . . . and consumer companies should advertise theirs," *Industrial Marketing*, pp. 46, 47, 50, Oct. 1978. Underlying factors that affect the successful advertising of industrial products are explored.

"Marketing: The new priority," *Business Week*, pp. 96–106, Nov. 1983. Changes in the makeup of America's traditional mass market are forcing companies to rethink their strategies and to target specific segments.

C.R. Milsap, "Consumer-tech: The key to software marketing," *Business Marketing*, pp. 86–88, July 1983. A different slant is explored for marketing a technical product through consumer rather than technical media.

T. Mulligan, "A Brit reflects on stateside sell," *Business Marketing*, pp. 124, 126, Oct. 1983. A British manufacturer explains how American marketing techniques can also be adapted to marketing in the U.K.

H. Novik, "The case for 'reps' vs. direct selling: Can reps do it better?" *Industrial Marketing*, pp. 90–98, Mar. 1982. Guidelines are presented to help an organization develop a rep system and avoid some common pitfalls.

D. Ogilvy and J. Raphaelson, "Research on advertising techniques that work—and don't work," *Harvard Business Rev.*, pp. 14–18, July–Aug. 1982. Specific insights into increasing advertising effectiveness are explained.

"100 leading U.S. business advertisers," *Industrial Marketing*, pp. 79–127, Apr. 1982. Concise summaries of the advertising strategies and activites of each of the top 100 business advertisers are offered.

M. Paskowski, "Industrial advertising—It ain't what it used to be (thank goodness)," *Industrial Marketing*, pp. 76, 78, May 1981. The progress of industrial advertising is reviewed and future techniques elaborated.

P.D. Petre, "Mass-marketing the computer," *Fortune*, pp. 61–67, Oct. 31, 1983. Mass marketing the computer illustrates problems and challenges of marketing a technological product today.

J.A. Quelch, "It's time to make trade promotion more productive," *Harvard Business Rev.*, pp. 130–136, May–June 1983. Lessons learned about the application and misapplication of trade promotions are discussed.

"Rebirth of a salesman: Willy Loman goes electronic," *Business Week*, pp. 103–104, Feb. 27, 1984. Changes in the costs of selling force firms to increase productivity without increasing personnel. New affordable techniques and innovative technology are making it possible.

M.A. Richfield, "Pros and cons of using stylized line drawing in industrial advertising," *Industrial Marketing*, p. 56, Feb. 1978. The advantages and use of line drawings in advertising are examined.

A. Ries and J. Trout, "Positioning cuts through chaos in the marketplace," *Advertising Age*, pp. 51–54, May 1, 1972. A classic article on how to use advertising to position a product in the customer's mind.

O. Riso, "Industrial marketing communicators—What are they made of?" *Industrial Marketing*, pp. 92–96, June 1977. The different roles of sales and advertising persons are explained. Insights for improved effectiveness are suggested.

J.A. Roberts, "Industrial marketing roundtable—Reindustrialization: What does it mean to marketers?" *Industrial Marketing*, pp. 86–90, May 1982. Five marketing executives discuss reindustrialization as it relates to marketing.

——, "Marketing research," *Industrial Marketing*, pp. 44–46, 50–53, Jan. 1981. Marketing research investigates why purchasing decisions are made and what kinds of products industrial customers want to buy. The value of market research techniques is noted.

M. Roman and B. Donath, "Exclusive, first-ever survey: What's really happening in business/industrial telemarketing," *Business Marketing*, pp. 82–90, Apr. 1983. A survey of 700 companies gives insights into their application of telemarketing. Selling, lead generation, control procedures, and standards are discussed.

H.G. Sawyer, "Faddy words of business and help for the overdog," *Industrial Marketing*, pp. 86, 87, Sept. 1977. The use of fad words in advertising and marketing techniques is explored.

——, "Illogical to change ad campaigns every year," *Industrial Marketing*, p. 100, Sept. 1978. The traditional thinking about advertising strategies and budgets is challenged. Fresh insights are offered.

——, "Progress in a primitive art—Advertising . . . and so much must be done," *Industrial Marketing*, pp. 81–82, 85, May 1981. Areas of industrial advertising warranting further professional evaluation are identified. Insights for improvement are given.

B. Schellerbach, "Back to basics—Tie in your ads with your business aims," *Industrial Marketing*, pp. 86, 88, Sept. 1975. Different kinds of businesses require different kinds of marketing strategies. Several categories of industrial goods and their respective strategies are discussed.

D.E. Schultz and R.D. Dewar, "Technology's challenge to marketing management," *Business Marketing*, pp. 31–41, Mar. 1984. Willy Loman's "smile and a shoeshine" are no longer enough in today's world. The choice for today's marketing manager is adapt, change—or disappear.

B.P. Shapiro, "Industrial pricing to meet customer needs," *Harvard Business Rev.*, pp. 119–127, Nov.–Dec. 1978. Pricing of industrial products defines the type of market and can dictate demand for the product. Several pricing systems approaches are discussed.

K.T. Stephens, "Industrial marketing planning for increased profit growth," *Industrial Marketing*, pp. 38, 40, 44, Aug. 1977. The need for a marketer to make better and more specific plans for marketing effectiveness is explored. Ten areas to consider are discussed.

N. Sweet, "Let the salesmen do the talking," *Advertising Age*, pp. M18–M21, June 20, 1983. How to reduce costs and increase effectiveness with business-to-business telemarketing are discussed.

"Telephone marketing commanding increased attention," *Industrial Marketing,* pp. 83, 86, Aug. 1977. Telephone marketing can help make marketing expenditures more cost-effective and cost-accountable.

G.B. Thayer, Jr., "Industrial high tech positioning: How to choose the competitive battlefield," *Industrial Marketing,* pp. 60-62, 66-68, June 1982. Lessons learned from consumer product marketing can be applied to industrial markets. Ten concepts to include in a product positioning strategy are explored.

D.B. Tinsley and J.H. Lewis. "Industrial services: Choosing the best media mix to reach the market place," *Industrial Marketing,* pp. 52-54, Dec. 1977. Services require unique marketing approaches. Effective techniques are examined.

"The new TV ads trying to wake up viewers," *Business Week,* pp. 46-47, March 19, 1984. As the TV viewing audience becomes bored with commercials and successfully tunes them out, advertisers are turning to new ways to make viewers sit up and take notice.

"The top business/industrial ad agencies," *Industrial Marketing,* pp. 126-173, Sept. 1983. A guide to business/industrial advertising agencies is provided.

R.K. Van Leer, "Industrial marketing with a flair," *Harvard Business Rev.,* pp. 117-124, Nov.-Dec. 1976. The author develops a novel approach for best determining when one product is becoming too much like the competing products . . . and for solving this problem.

"What ad agencies' billings mean—or do not mean—to a client," *Industrial Marketing,* pp. 54-55, Nov. 1975. The relationship of an advertising agency to its client is examined. Considerations to assure a proper fit are discussed.

W.G. Young, "How to buy radio for industrial selling," *Industrial Marketing,* pp. 74, 76, 80, Mar. 1978. Radio is primarily a consumer medium, but with a few guidelines, efficient radio buys can be made for industrial advertising. Guidelines to reach the greatest number of appropriate listeners are given.

Author Index

Subject Index

Lois K. Moore (M'79–SM'83) is a Technical Writer and Editor of *McClure Center Magazine,* a publication of the Johns Hopkins University Applied Physics Laboratory (JHU/APL), Laurel, MD. She has over a quarter century in the communications field, with extensive experience through previous employment at Trans-Sonics, Inc., Technical Operations, Inc., RCA, and IBM, the last ten years having been at JHU/APL.

Ms. Moore, a Senior Member of the Society for Technical Communication, chaired the Writing and Editing Stem of the 1981 International Technical Communication Conference, Pittsburgh. An active Senior Member of the IEEE, she is a member of the Advisory Committee of the Professional Communication Society and its current Vice President. She chaired both the 1982 (Boston) and 1983 (Atlanta) conferences. Two of her most recent responsibilities include serving as a member of the Communications Committee of the IEEE United States Activities Board and as Associate Editor of IMPACT MAGAZINE, which covers the activities of the Governmental Affairs Committee. She has published numerous articles on communications and computer-related topics.

Daniel L. Plung (M'83) received the B.A. in English from the City College of New York, and the M.A. and Doctor of Arts degrees from Idaho State University.

He is Publications Manager for Westinghouse Idaho Nuclear Company, Idaho Falls, a contractor at the Department of Energy's Idaho National Engineering Laboratory. Prior to serving in this position, he was an Assistant Professor of English and also a supervisor at a marketing research corporation.

Dr. Plung coedited the IEEE PRESS book, *A Guide for Writing Better Technical Papers,* and has published or presented numerous papers on various aspects of technical communication. He has been active in the IEEE Professional Communication Society for the past three years, serving one year as the organization's National Secretary.